PENGUIN BOOKS

SHOPPING MANHATTAN

Corky Pollan is the "Best Bets" columnist for *New York* magazine, a position she has held for the past nine years. She is the co-author of *The Best on Martha's Vineyard*, a 1974 guide to restaurants and shops on the island, and has contributed to scholarly journals. Ms. Pollan graduated from Bennington College and has a master's degree in English literature from Long Island University. The mother of four children, she lives with her husband, Stephen, in Manhattan and summers on Martha's Vineyard.

SHOPPING
MANHATTAN
CORKY POLLAN

THE DISCRIMINATING

BUYER'S GUIDE

TO FINDING

ALMOST ANYTHING

PENGUIN BOOKS

PENGUIN BOOKS
Published by the Penguin Group
Viking Penguin, a division of
Penguin Books USA Inc.,
40 West 23rd Street,
New York, New York 10010, U.S.A.
Penguin Books Ltd, 27 Wrights Lane,
London W8 5TZ, England
Penguin Books Australia Ltd,
Ringwood, Victoria, Australia
Penguin Books Canada Ltd, 2801 John Street,
Markham, Ontario, Canada L3R 1B4
Penguin Books (N.Z.) Ltd,
182–190 Wairau Road, Auckland 10, New Zealand

Penguin Books Ltd, Registered Offices:
Harmondsworth, Middlesex, England

First published in Penguin Books 1989

10 9 8 7 6 5 4 3 2 1

LIBRARY OF CONGRESS CATALOGING IN PUBLICATION DATA
Pollan, Corky.
    Shopping Manhattan : the discriminating buyer's
guide to finding almost anything / Corky Pollan.
        p. cm.
    ISBN 0 14 01.2401 2 : $12.95
    1. Shopping—New York (N.Y.)—Guide-books. 2. Manhattan
(New York, N.Y.)—Description—Guide-books. I. Title.
TX336.5.N482N476   1989
380.1'45'000257471—dc20   89-33651

Printed in the United States of America
Set in Memphis
Designed by Michael Ian Kaye
Maps by Mark Stein Studios.
Copyright © Viking Penguin,
a division of Penguin Books USA Inc., 1989

To Stephen,
without whose prodding
this book would never have
been written, and to my children
—Michael, Lori, Tracy, and Dana—
for their patience when
I couldn't come
out to play.

I wish to thank
Lisa Schneiderman,
Judith Belzer, and Beth Burstein
for their help in checking the accuracy
of the information herein, and my editor,
Lori Lipsky, for her fine suggestions.

Contents

CONTENTS

MAPS OF MANHATTAN 511

INDEX 519

Introduction

At least a dozen times each week my office phone rings and the voice on the other end plaintively asks, "Where can I find a terrific ———?" What follows is a request for shopping information on a myriad of things. Calls come from stylists, editors of other magazines, art directors, reporters, TV prop people, presidents of corporations, readers, friends, and friends of friends. They know that as *New York* magazine's "Best Bets" columnist (a position I've held for the past nine years), I scout the city each week, trekking through unlikely neighborhoods in search of the best, the newest, and the most original. When they call and ask where they can find such esoteric items as fencing gloves, vintage toasters, deep-sea-diving gauges, Victorian stuffing spoons, Renaissance tiles, or a Spiro Agnew watch, I know just where to send them. And if they're looking for less-exotic items—a cutting-edge gown, a lamp with a Retro look, custom-made shirts, or a silk bustier—I know where they can find the best of those, too. I came to realize that it isn't only tourists or visitors who need assistance in locating what they want among the riches this city—perhaps the world's greatest shopping capital—has to offer. Savvy New Yorkers often need help, too.

This guidebook, then, is designed to fill that need. I will tell you where to shop for just about everything, from a medieval tapestry to a vintage couture suit to a regulation dartboard to a tony dress, and at prices that range from inexpensive to costly. Although broad in its range, *Shopping Manhattan* is also highly specific. I've suggested exactly what a reader is likely to find in each store, and since shops are exhaustively cross-indexed, readers can quickly locate just what they're looking for. There are forty-nine main categories, from adult games to umbrellas, and I've covered approximately 000 stores.

Things change very rapidly in this city, and a store's stock varies each season. Yet what remains constant is the character, quality, and style of merchandise a shop handles. Therefore the specific items that I mention are not intended as a definitive shopping list, but as a guidepost to what a reader may expect. And since there is inevitably a lag between reporting and publication, it is likely that a few of the stores I have listed may have closed. Telephone numbers are included in each store listing so that you can call ahead to check.

HOW TO USE THIS BOOK

Stores are indexed by name, type of merchandise they carry (men's shoes, antique silver, maps, chocolates, etc.). Shops with a significant stock in more than one category are cross-indexed. Thus Polo/Ralph Lauren will be fully listed in the Men's Contemporary Clothing section with address, phone number, hours, and credit-card information. But since the shop also offers Ralph Lauren's designs for women, you'll find it cross-indexed under Women's Designer Clothing. Polo has an excellent boys' department and a fine bed linen one, too, so it will be cross-indexed under each of these sections. A sentence or two will indicate what the store offers under these headings, followed by a page number so a reader can quickly flip to the full listing for complete information on the store.

Where a shop accepts credit cards, the following abbreviations are used:

AE	American Express
CB	Carte Blanche
DC	Diner's Club
MC	MasterCard
V	Visa
All Major	All of the above

Many stores accept personal checks with proper identification—a driver's license and two major credit cards—and most stores have a two-week return policy for credit, with presentation of a receipt. Almost all stores, whether large or small, will mail purchases.

HOURS

Hours for midtown emporiums and those on the Upper East Side are usually from 10 a.m. to 6 p.m., Monday through Saturday, with late hours (until 8 or 9 p.m.) on Thursdays. While Upper West Side shops don't open until 11 a.m., they remain open until 7 or 8 p.m., and they are generally open on Sundays. Don't go to SoHo or lower Broadway before noon and don't go on a Monday, since many of the stores are closed that day. The East Village doesn't come alive until early evening; shops often keep erratic hours and don't even open until 1 or 2 p.m., and many of the boutiques are closed on Mondays and Tuesdays. In Greenwich Village and Chelsea, store hours begin at around noontime, but they're open late and on Sundays.

Midweek is generally the quietest time to shop anywhere in Manhattan, and you can be confident that all the shops will be open on Wednesdays and Thursdays. Avoid SoHo, lower Broadway, and the East Village on weekends unless you love crowds and people-watching.

Most establishments have extended Christmas hours during November and December. There may be seasonal variations as well—in summer, South Street Seaport and Columbus Avenue are open later each day to accommodate tourists and evening strollers. Antiques establishments, on the other hand, often keep shorter hours and are often closed on Saturdays and Sundays in summer.

NEIGHBORHOODS

Although Manhattan is a sprawl filled with an incredible diversity of shops, there are neighborhood patterns. Browse through the East Village, SoHo, and lower Broadway for hip clothing and vintage finds; lower Madison Avenue and Wall Street for conservative men's things; upper Madison Avenue for women's designer creations. There's a concentration of antiques emporiums on upper Madison and Lexington Avenues, on 57th Street, and on Broadway in the teens. You'll find camping gear and sports clothing for the serious athlete in lower Manhattan; fashionable shoes for men and women midtown. And except for Barneys New York, the city's department stores are also midtown—from 34th to 59th Streets—and the majority are on Fifth Avenue.

I believe this book may prove to be the next-best thing to having an expert along on your buying trips. It's dedicated to taking the hassle out of shopping in a city packed with merchandise.

Adult Games

ANTIQUE

JAMES II GALLERIES
A splendid assortment of nineteenth-century board games, including ivory chess sets, cribbage, checkers, dominoes, and playing cards. (See **China and Glassware**, p. 64.)

CONTEMPORARY

Macy's has a very complete game department with adult board games of all kinds. See **Museum Gift Shops** (p. 403) as fine sources for beautiful jigsaw puzzles, many of which are reproductions of paintings in the museums' collections.

ABERCROMBIE & FITCH
The vast stock of games includes everything from croquet to darts, cribbage to horseshoes, board games to shuffleboard. (See **Sporting Goods**, p. 446.)

ACE SPORTSWORKS
315 West 39th Street
Sixteenth floor
868-9155
Mon.–Fri.: 8 a.m.–5:15 p.m.
No credit cards

Since 1900 card players have been coming to Eddie Fliegelman's well-stocked shop, since he carries cards in every color and in sizes that range from miniature to poster. In addition to his vast assortment of

1

cards, Fliegelman offers chess pieces, backgammon sets, dominoes, casino chips, gaming tables, casino equipment, and dice.

BLATT BILLARDS

The largest selection of antique and contemporary pool tables in the city, along with custom cues, balls, cloths, and other accessories. (See **Sporting Goods,** p. 452.)

THE COMPLEAT STRATEGIST

320 West 57th Street
582-1272
Mon.–Sat.: 11 a.m.–8 p.m.; Sun.: 12 noon–5 p.m.

11 East 33rd Street
685-3880
Mon.–Wed., Fri., Sat.: 10:30 a.m.–6 p.m.; Thurs.: 10:30 a.m.–9 p.m.

630 Fifth Avenue, near 50th Street
265-7449
Mon.–Fri.: 10:30 a.m.–5:30 p.m.
AE, DC, MC, V

When it first opened on 33rd Street, the Compleat Strategist specialized in military games, and its stock covered just about every battle and every period in history. Recently the company has broadened its scope to include science fiction, murder mysteries, adventure, and fantasy, so now you'll find strategists of the French Revolution shopping alongside those addicted to Dungeons and Dragons. Although the stores carry chess and backgammon sets, Risk and Monopoly, many of the games are exclusive and these emporiums are fascinating and friendly places to while away the hours.

DARTS UNLIMITED

English darts and darting equipment. (See **Sporting Goods,** p. 454.)

GAME SHOW

474 Avenue of the Americas, near 12th Street
633-6328
Mon.–Sat.: 12 noon–8 p.m.; Sun.: 12 noon–6 p.m.
AE, MC, V

Joel Schneider and Ed Martinedes's toy store for adults wins points for its superior organization. Games are arranged by category—from real estate to politics to sports to TV to religion—and all the treats are tidily displayed. Under "politics" you'll find Hail to the Chief and Russian Roulette; sports offers Pari-Mutual and the Rodeo Game; the strategy section, Mastermind, Zomax, and Input. In addition to the classics—chess, Go, checkers, and dominoes—there's a large selection of esoteric games and those made by small companies. The shop's design is as well thought out as its inventory and features an old-fashioned bank teller's booth as a checkout counter, a checker-board floor, and tables with game-board markers for legs.

V. LORIA & SONS
A complete line of billiard equipment and bowling gear, as well as Ping-Pong tables and supplies, poker tables, and pinball machines. (See **Sporting Goods,** p. 452.)

VILLAGE CHESS SHOP
230 Thompson Street
475-9580
Daily: 12 noon–12 midnight
MC, V

The Village Chess Shop is an appealingly relaxed place where chess lovers can play a game for $1.50 an hour or pick up an unusual chess set. There are dozens to choose from, including very classic versions in ivory, ebony, onyx, pewter, wood, marble, and brass, along with high-tech ones in the shape of nuts and bolts. The shop also carries an equally large inventory of backgammon and cribbage sets, the game Go, and chess books.

Art
Supplies

ARTHUR BROWN & BROTHER, INC.
2 West 46th Street
575-5555
Mon.–Fri.: 9 a.m.–6:30 p.m.; Sat.: 11 a.m.–5 p.m.
AE, D, MC, V

New York's largest art supply store is an excellent source for the student artist. The range of materials is extensive, and the staff is informed and helpful to beginners. In the International Pen Shop you'll find just about every brand of pen from around the world. There's a fine selection of technical pens along with others designed for musicians, artists, calligraphers, and cartographers, as well as all the popular brands—Mont Blanc, Waterman, Dunhill, and Cartier.

CHARRETTE
215 Lexington Avenue, near 33rd Street
683-8822
Mon.–Fri.: 8:30 a.m.–7 p.m.; Sat.: 10 a.m.–4:30 p.m.;
Sun.: 12 noon–5 p.m. (except summer)
AE, MC, V

Charrette caters to professional architects, draftsmen, graphic designers, and engineers and the stock includes more than 36,000 items so it's wise to know exactly what you're looking for when you shop here. Everything from the drafting tables to the desk lights to the drafting paper is top quality, and the staff knows the field and is very helpful to novices.

DAVID DAVIS
346 Lafayette Street
982-7100
Mon.–Fri.: 9:30 a.m.–6 p.m.; Sat.: 11 a.m.–6 p.m.
AE, MC, V

David Davis is the shop where established artists go for their art supplies. The selection of oils and dry pigments is unusually broad and the quality of brushes outstanding. There's an impressive array of handmade papers, along with excellent French pastels and drawing books. Davis primes and sells the finest Belgium linens, stretchers made from top-quality woods, and superior easels of the shop's own design, and Davis will make stretchers and easels to any size.

EASTERN ARTISTS
5 West 22nd Street
645-5555
Mon.–Fri.: 8:30 a.m.–7 p.m.; Sat.: 11 a.m.–6 p.m.; summer:
Mon.–Fri.: 9 a.m.–6:30 p.m.
AE, MC, V

Eastern Artists caters to ad agencies and graphic artists. The stock is enormous and includes everything a commercial artist might need and since the shop's customers are professionals, the quality at Eastern is superior.

80 PAPERS
510 Broome Street
431-7720
Mon.–Wed.: 12 noon–7 p.m.; Thurs.–Sat.: 12 noon–8 p.m.;
Sun.: 1 p.m.–7 p.m.
AE, D, MC, V

80 Papers is known for its stock of beautiful handmade papers that are suitable for photography, calligraphy, and bookbinding. Owner Wendy Stewart has put together a colorful assortment of marbleized papers from Sweden, England, and the United States; papers embedded with flowers and leaves from France; lace and rice papers from Japan; and 100 percent linen papers by a local artisan. Although most of the art papers come in large sheets, Stewart also carries Japanese, American, and European handmades in letter size, along with hand-bound photo albums, journals, and guest books.

LEE'S ART SHOP
220 West 57th Street
247-0110
Mon.–Fri.: 9 a.m.–7 p.m.; Sat.: 9:30 a.m.–6 p.m.
All major

Lee's Art Shop calls itself "a department store for the artist." It's located directly across the street from the Art Students League, and it's crammed full of all the necessities the professional or amateur artist might need. There's a Fine Arts Department for the painter, sculptor, and printmaker; an Air Brush Department, and a Graphics Department stocked with such names as K & E, Leroy, Chromatec, Kohinoor, Kroy, and Letraset. Lee's carries drafting furniture, a large supply of popular brand-name pens, and it offers same-day framing.

NEW YORK CENTRAL ART SUPPLY
62 Third Avenue, near 11th Street
473-7705
Mon.–Sat.: 8:30 a.m.–6:15 p.m.
All major

All the major international brand names, along with a number of obscure ones, can be found in this friendly store. In addition to paints, brushes, canvas, easels, and stretchers, New York Central stocks drawing and drafting tools, printmaking supplies, pens and inks, along with drawing tables and lamps. It also offers a superior selection of handmade papers and parchments, including Egyptian papyrus, marbleized papers by a New Jersey artisan, and cotton papers embedded with dried algae from India.

PEARL PAINT
308 Canal Street
431-7932
Mon.–Sat.: 9 a.m.–5:30 p.m.; Thurs.: 9 a.m.–7 p.m.;
Sun.: 11 a.m.–4:45 p.m. (except summer)
MC, V

Pearl Paint is a good source for supplies for both the art student and the professional. It carries every major brand and the prices are excellent, and the salespeople helpful. On its six floors, all jam-packed with merchandise divided into specialty sections, you'll find fine art supplies (including imported French brushes and quality papers), along with silk-screening, drafting, carving, etching, casting, graphic arts, and craft materials. Its huge pen department features such top names as Mont Blanc, Waterman, Cross, Parker, and Lamy.

SAM FLAX
233 Spring Street
620-3000
Mon.–Fri.: 8:30 a.m.–5:30 p.m.; Sat.: 10 a.m.–5 p.m.;
Sun.: 10 a.m.–3 p.m.

25 East 28th Street
620-3040
Mon.–Fri.: 9 a.m.–6 p.m.

747 Third Avenue, at 46th Street
620-3050
Mon.–Fri.: 9 a.m.–6 p.m.; Sat.: 10 a.m.–5 p.m.

425 Park Avenue, at 55th Street
620-3060
Mon.–Fri.: 9 a.m.–6 p.m.; Sat.: 10 a.m.–5 p.m.

12 West 20th Street
620-3038
Mon.–Fri.: 8:30 a.m.–6 p.m.; Sat.: 10 a.m.–5 p.m.; Sun.: 12 noon–
5 p.m.
AE, MC, V

The Sam Flax stores are known for their enormous stock of fine art and drafting supplies, photographic equipment, drafting and drawing tables, and storage units. Each of the stores offers attractive canvas totes in every size and many colors for carrying drawings, architectural renderings, and large-size paintings. The 20th Street store is primarily devoted to furniture, and it's filled with functional pieces that work for home or office. The 55th Street store houses the Writing Shop with its wide assortment of pens that range from antique fountain pens, to S.T. Dupont's lacquered beauties, to sleek Parkers, to everyday Flairs.

UTRECHT ART & DRAFTING SUPPLIES
111 Fourth Avenue, at 11th Street
777-5353
Mon.–Sat.: 9:30 a.m.–6 p.m.
MC, V

Utrecht is a manufacturer of art and drafting materials, and in this retail shop it sells the supplies it manufactures. Popular with professional artists and architects, it's also a good source for the student painter or hobbyist, since prices are excellent.

Bath Accessories

ANTIQUE
AND VINTAGE

COBWEB
Antique wrought-iron washstands and wood commodes, many with marble tops and porcelain basins. (See **Furniture,** p. 273.)

GREAT AMERICAN SALVAGE COMPANY
The stock is ever-changing, but there are always a few claw-footed bathtubs, porcelain pedestal sinks, and an assortment of old glass, chrome, and brass towel bars, soap dishes, and sponge racks. (See **Furniture,** p. 231.)

IRREPLACEABLE ARTIFACTS
Antique porcelain bathtubs, some with claw feet, also reproductions of an early-twentieth-century tub that's made of marble dust and polyester resin. (See **Furniture,** p. 231.)

T & K FRENCH ANTIQUES LTD
Old European copper tubs, brass soap dishes and towel racks. (See **Furniture,** p. 272.)

URBAN ARCHAEOLOGY
Sinks on fluted porcelain pedestals, nineteenth-century toilets, claw-footed tubs, and scores of brass towel bars, hooks, soap dishes, and sponge racks, some old, some reproductions that have been made from old molds. (See **Furniture,** p. 232.)

CONTEMPORARY

The department stores stock a wide variety of shower curtains, bath towels, mats, and accessories. On Bergdorf Goodman's seventh floor you'll find elegant towels, as well as handsome brass towel bars, hooks, and soap baskets. See **Linens and Quilts,** for bath towels, p. 381.

AD HOC SOFTWARES
A selection of good-looking shower curtains; also thirsty oversized cotton bath sheets; thick cotton bath mats; simple laundry hampers; along with soaps and bath brushes, towel racks, and soap dishes. (See **Linens and Quilts,** p. 388.)

THE BATH HOUSE
215 Thompson Street
533-0690
Tues.–Sat.: 11 a.m.–11 p.m.
All major

Cindy Annchild's sweet-smelling store is crowded with natural and chemical-free soaps, bath salts, scrubs, lotions, and bubble baths, along with dozens of oils to add to the bath for relaxation, to alleviate aches, or to elevate one's mood. Customers can create their own special scents from a mix of blends, and they can custom-order gift baskets filled with bath goodies. There are towels inspired by Japanese engravings and lovely soap dishes made of colored glass or cloisonné.

CASWELL-MASSEY CO. LTD.
518 Lexington Avenue, at 48th Street
755-2254
Mon.–Fri.: 9 a.m.–7 p.m.; Sat.: 10 a.m.–6 p.m.

South Street Seaport
21 Fulton Street
608-5401
Mon.–Sat.: 10 a.m.–7 p.m.; Sun.: 12 noon–5 p.m.

Herald Center
244-0411
Mon.–Sat.: 10 a.m.–7 p.m.

2 World Financial Center
945-2630
Mon.–Fri.: 10 a.m.–6 p.m.; Sat. & Sun.: 12 noon–5 p.m.
All major

Caswell-Massey Co. has the distinction of being the country's oldest apothecary. It's been around since 1752, and since it still sells the same soaps, colognes, lotions, and potions that it did when it first opened, you can still buy George Washington's favorite eau de cologne, Sarah Bernhardt's night cream, and Jenny Lind's lozenges. In addition to these oddities it carries the largest selection of soaps in the world. There are herbal, glycerine, Castile, coconut oil, oatmeal, buttermilk, fruit, and special treatment bars, and they come in all the classic shapes and in dozens of pastel or intense colors. In fact, you'll find everything to do with the rituals of soaking, cleansing, and anointing in these irresistibly Old World shops.

CONRAN'S HABITAT

Thick terry-cloth towels, cotton bath mats, and shower curtains, along with wooden soap dishes, bath brushes, towel racks, hampers, and vanities. (See **Furniture,** p. 267.)

CRABTREE AND EVELYN

30 East 67th Street
734-1108
Mon.–Sat.: 10 a.m.–6 p.m.

1310 Madison Avenue, near 93rd Street
289–3923
Mon.–Fri.: 10 a.m.–7 p.m.; Sat.: 11 a.m.–6 p.m.; Sun.: 12 noon–5 p.m.

322 Columbus Avenue, near 75th Street
595-0159
Mon.–Wed.: 11 a.m.–7 p.m.; Thurs.–Sat.: 11 a.m.–9 p.m.;
Sun.: 12 noon–7 p.m.

2768 Broadway, near 106th Street
663-4717
Mon.–Sat.: 10 a.m.–7 p.m.; Sun.: 1 p.m.–7 p.m.

620 Fifth Avenue, near 50th Street
581-5022
Mon.–Sat.: 10 a.m.–6 p.m.

153 East 53rd Street
308-6164
Mon.–Fri.: 10:30 a.m.–7:30 p.m.; Sat.: 10:30 a.m.–6 p.m.;
Sun.: noon–6 p.m.
AE, MC, V

Delights for the bath and table are charmingly packaged in the Crabtree and Evelyn shops that are an American invention, yet manage to re-create the look of Old England in New York. Shampoos and bath oils are scented with almond, corn, or oatmeal fragrances, bath and hair brushes are first-rate, and soaps come in a variety of enchanting shapes—everything from seashells to angels to sheep to Alice in Wonderland. There are sweet-smelling potpourri, fragrant teas, crunchy cookies, and luscious jams.

D. F. SANDERS

Thirsty cotton-shag bath mats, high-quality plastic soap dishes and towel bars, and metal laundry hampers. (See **Housewares and Hardware,** p. 337.)

ELEGANT JOHN

812 Lexington Avenue, near 62nd Street
935-5800
Mon.–Wed., Fri., Sat.: 10 a.m.–6 p.m.; Thurs.: 10 a.m.–7 p.m.
All major

Large and brightly lit, the Elegant John is brimful of glitzy bathroom accessories. There's a full stock of large-scale things—vanities, mirrors, medicine cabinets, lighting, and wallpaper—as well as small items that range from shower curtains to towels to faucets to decorated toilet tissue to towel bars to toilet seats. Chrome, brass, and Lucite are the favored materials.

FLORIS

703 Madison Avenue, near 62nd Street
935-9100
Mon.–Sat.: 10 a.m.–6 p.m.
AE, MC, V

Investment banker James Niven, the late David Niven's son, was instrumental in bringing Floris and its sweet-smelling wares to New York. This venerable company's Madison Avenue shop with its curved glass display cases and rich wood cabinetry is a faithful re-creation of the Jermyn Street emporiums. It's a tranquil haven filled with floral-scented perfumes, colognes, and toilet waters; delicate bath essences and soaps; and fresh-smelling room sprays, sachets, candles, and potpourri. Ceramic soap dishes come complete with Edwardian Bouquet soaps, and there are mouthwashes, dusting powders, and pure badger shaving brushes.

GRACIOUS HOME

The shiny array of brass hardware for the bath includes towel bars, soap holders, and hooks; and there are plastic shower heads in primary colors; as well as shower curtains, towels, bath mats, hampers, and all the other bath paraphernalia. (See **Housewares and Hardware,** p. 338.)

HASTINGS

230 Park Avenue South, at 19th Street
674-9700
Mon.–Wed., Fri.: 9:30 a.m.–6 p.m.; Thurs.: 10:30 a.m.–7:30 p.m.;
Sat.: 10 a.m.–5 p.m.
MC, V

It's located in the city's hottest restaurant district and it has an interior by the high-style design firm Studio Morsa so it's no wonder people keep mistaking Hastings for a fashionable dining spot. But Hastings provides other of life's necessities: kitchens, bathrooms, and fittings for both. The sleek loft space with its gargantuan columns and enormous plate-glass windows sets off the cutting-edge designs for which Hastings is known: bold ceramic tiles by Gabbianelli, Bardelli, and Vogue; state-of-the-art Miele kitchen appliances, dramatic Poggenpohl and Downsview cabinets. And if the lacquered bird's-eye-maple cabinets don't tempt you, the towel bars of metal tubing in zingy colors or the futuristic "washmobil" will.

M. WOLCHONOK & SON
Authentically reproduced Victorian plumbing fixtures, brass towel racks, and soap baskets, along with sleekly modern ones in chrome and Lucite. (See **Housewares and Hardware,** p. 339.)

NEMO TILE
Bathroom vanities and medicine cabinets, along with attractive towel bars and soap dishes in brass and bright colors. (See **Tiles,** p. 478.)

SCENTSITIVITY
870½ Lexington Avenue, at 65th Street
988-2822
Mon.–Fri.: 10 a.m.–6 p.m.
AE, MC, V

Ann Pellegrino's fragrant little shop is no bigger than a closet, yet it's crammed with a surprisingly first-rate selection of bath oils, shower gels, bubble baths, soaps, room sprays, loofahs, bath brushes, aromatic oils, and potpourri. Pellegrino believes that each room should have a different aroma, and to this end she'll make up personalized perfumes and special blended potpourri. Made-to-order gift baskets are another of her specialties.

SHERLE WAGNER INTERNATIONAL
60 East 57th Street
758-3300
Mon–Fri: 9:15 a.m.–5 p.m.
No credit cards

Sherle Wagner has the distinction of stocking the most luxurious—and the most expensive—bathroom fixtures in New York. The smashing basement showroom displays sinks, tubs, and toilets embellished with every costly material, including lapis and other semiprecious stones. Crystal, marble, gold-plate, and hand-painted porcelain are among the costly choices, and the accessories match the fixtures in opulence and price.

SIMON'S HARDWARE
Faucet sets, towel bars, soap holders, and sponge baskets in brass, chrome, gold-plate, and Lucite. (See **Housewares and Hardware**, p. 340.)

SOAP OPERA
51 Grove Street
929-7756
Mon.–Fri.: 1 p.m.–7:30 p.m.; Sat.: 12 noon–7 p.m.; Sun.: 1 p.m.–6 p.m.

The Concourse
30 Rockefeller Center
245-5090
Mon.–Fri.: 10 a.m.–6 p.m.
AE, MC, V

More than 400 natural and herbal soaps are available in these tiny soap supermarkets that retain the same name but are now under different ownership. Bath oils, bubble baths, soap powders, and creams fill the shelves, along with many products for scenting the home. These include carpet fresheners; drawer liners scented with lily of the valley, honeysuckle, or wild orchid; and pots of Simmering Scents to which only boiling water has to be added to fill an entire room with the fragrance of bayberry, balsam, or cranberry. Since many of the products are manufactured by Crabtree and Evelyn, they're beautifully packaged, and, in addition to the fragrant offerings, the shops also stock teas, cookies, and jams.

TIGER'S EYE BED & BATH
157 West 72nd Street
496-8488
Mon.–Fri.: 11 a.m.–7 p.m.; Sat. & Sun.: 1 p.m.–6 p.m.
AE, MC, V

The depth of selection in bath and bed accessories in this friendly neighborhood emporium is a pleasant surprise—it rivals that of the major department stores. On two spacious floors you'll find vanities, hampers, and standing towel racks; dozens of shower curtains in plastic, satin, moiré, and cotton; bath mats in every size and shade; towel bars and soap holders in brass and Lucite; and towels and bath sheets in scores of prints and colors. The inventory of brand-name and designer bed linens, bedspreads, duvet covers, and comforters is equally broad, and the shop also handles custom-made curtains and draperies.

WILLIAM HUNRATH CO.
The decorative bathroom fixtures in Lucite, brass, and chrome include faucet sets, towel bars, soap holders, and mirrors. (See **Housewares and Hardware**, p. 341.)

Books

AMERICAN INDIAN

BOB FEIN BOOKS
150 Fifth Avenue, at 20th Street
Sixth floor
807-0489
Mon.–Fri.: 12 noon–6 p.m.; or by appointment
No credit cards

Bob Fein's unusual shop is the city's only bookstore devoted to the literature of native Americans. Fein has collected more than 3,000 volumes, including out-of-print books. He also has a broad selection of titles on pre-Columbian art, along with works on Mexican artists of the twentieth century and he stocks facsimile pre-Columbian codices and Smithsonian publications and reports.

MUSEUM OF THE AMERICAN INDIAN
A large stock of books on the Indians of North and South America that includes historical works, as well as titles on Indian lore and Indian arts and crafts; also a collection of histories, fables, and stories for children. (See **Museum Gift Shops,** p. 403.)

ANTIQUARIAN

ANTIQUARIAN BOOKSELLERS INTERNATIONAL
Place des Antiquaires

125 East 57th Street

751-5450
Mon.–Sat.: 11 a.m.–6 p.m.
AE, MC, V

Antiquarian Booksellers International is a new cooperative with roots in the prestigious forty-year-old Antiquarian Booksellers Association of America, and in its spartan gallery sixty book experts offer the finest examples of rare and antique titles. You'll find incunabula (works printed before the sixteenth century) along with those of the twentieth century. The European and American volumes cover just about every subject and are in all languages. The gallery also carries an enchanting array of early editions of children's classics. And in addition to selling books, the cooperative mounts changing exhibitions of autographs, manuscripts, historical documents, letters, and celebrity photographs.

APPELFELD GALLERY
1372 York Avenue, near 73rd Street
988-7835
Mon.–Fri.: 10 a.m.–5:30 p.m.; Sat.: 11 a.m.–3 p.m.
No credit cards

Appelfeld's is old-fashioned in the best sense, filled with rare books and staffed by knowledgeable and amiable people. Its walls are lined with bookcases that hold first editions, sets of rare volumes by English and American writers, and privately printed works. Many of the books are illustrated and have fine leather bindings.

ARGOSY BOOK STORE
116 East 59th Street
753-4455
Mon.–Fri.: 9 a.m.–6 p.m.; Sat.: 10:30 a.m.–5:30 p.m.; closed Sat. May–Sept.
MC, V

Dark-paneled walls, polished brass railings, and shelves crammed with miles of leather-bound volumes gives Argosy the look of a comfortable and well-used library. Although its six floors are cluttered with first editions and scholarly works on all subjects, Argosy is best known as a source for out-of-print histories, biographies, rare medical works, and assorted Americana. Yet Argosy appeals to more than bibliophiles. Interior designers and those in the know come here for early Currier and Ives prints, equestrian engravings, vintage botanicals, and the city's most comprehensive collection of antique and vintage maps. Among the vast selection are maps of the ancient world, early city maps, as well as vintage ones of the Northeastern states and counties.

BOOKS 'N THINGS
64 East 7th Street
533-2320

Mon.–Sat.: 1 p.m.–6 p.m.
No credit cards

Gertrude Briggs's cluttered little shop is dense with antiquarian, used, rare, and out-of-print volumes that are piled on the floor and packed on groaning shelves. Although the chief attractions are art and poetry titles, Briggs offers works on all the performing arts—music, dance, film, and theater—and in addition to books this tiny shop is brimful of antiquarian post cards.

GOTHAM BOOK MART & GALLERY
41 West 47th Street
719-4448
Mon.–Fri.: 9:30 a.m.–6:30 p.m.; Sat.: 9:30–6 p.m.
AE, MC, V

In the midst of New York's teeming diamond district stands the city's most revered bookstore. Founded by the late Frances Steloff in 1920, it's been at the same location for more than fifty years and is looked upon as something of a literary shrine. Among its more then 300,000 titles—half old, half new—are hard-to-find, out-of-print, and rare volumes on twentieth-century literature and poetry, literary criticism, and the dramatic arts. Indeed, Gotham's selection of books on film is one of the best in the city. Lining the walls from floor to ceiling are contemporary first editions, and filling the aisles are 150 literary and underground magazines, including little-press poetry editions and back issues of many of the literary magazines of the twenties and thirties. Gotham stocks all the classics, as well as a full range of contemporary titles, yet in addition to the thousands of books there's an impressive collection of literary manuscripts, letters, and archives. The staff is exceptionally knowledgeable and can magically produce, out of the clutter, exactly what you're looking for.

GRYPHON BOOKSHOP
2246 Broadway, near 80th Street
362-0706
Daily: 10 a.m.–12 midnight
MC, V

Former opera director Marc Lewis and Henry Holman, a former teacher, have managed to crowd their tiny shop with more than 40,000 rare, hard-to-find, and out-of-print volumes. First editions of contemporary authors, books on the performing arts, poetry, and painting are among its chief attractions, but Lewis and Holman also carry a large array of early children's titles, including Oz and Baumiana, along with handsome illustrated works. There's an annex around the corner with mainly new volumes, and both stores are open every day until midnight.

H. P. KRAUS
16 East 46th Street
687-4808
Mon.–Fri.: 9:30 a.m.–5 p.m.
MC, V

H. P. Kraus occupies five floors of a handsome town house, and this unique bookstore is filled with medieval manuscripts, illustrated works, and early printed volumes. Although incunabula (books printed before 1500) is one of the gallery's specialties, there are later works—those printed before 1700—as well. Internationally known for handling only the rarest and most sought-after works, Kraus stocks bibliographies, books on natural science, geography, and Americana, along with exceptionally fine ancient maps.

J. N. BARTFIELD BOOKS
30 West 57th Street
Third floor
245-8890
Mon.–Fri.: 10 a.m.–5 p.m.; Sat.: 10 a.m.–2:30 p.m.
No credit cards

Since 1937 J. N. Bartfield has been selling beautiful books, and its shelves are filled with single volumes and complete sets of leather-bound, illustrated editions of old and rare titles, as well as a large selection of first editions and color-plate books. Literary classics and works on art, history, biography, philosophy, and natural history are generously mixed with such subjects as flowers, birds, travel, and the American West. Sporting books are a specialty, but if you're searching for an Aububon folio or a seventeenth-century atlas or a complete set of Sir Walter Scott works, you'll find them here.

LEONARD S. GRANBY
1168 Lexington Avenue, near 80th Street
249-2651
Mon.–Fri.: 11 a.m.–5 p.m.; Sat.: 11 a.m.–4 p.m.
No credit cards

Rare volumes and limited editions fill every inch of this attractive little shop. The store's specialties include English, American, and French literature from the seventeenth through the nineteenth centuries, with a sprinkling of twentieth-century works, but you'll also find an admirable collection of signed art books.

PAGEANT BOOK & PRINT SHOP
109 East 9th Street
674-5296
Mon.–Thurs: 10 a.m.–6:30 p.m.; Fri.: 10 a.m.–8 p.m.; Sat.: 11 a.m.–7:30 p.m.
No credit cards

The grandchildren of the original owners of Pageant Book & Print Shop now staff the counters of this beguilingly old-fashioned store that's crammed with thousands of old books and prints. It's a relic of the time when Fourth Avenue between Eighth Street and Fourteenth Street was known as Book Row with dozens of shops selling used volumes. Climb Pageant's creaky stairs to the second floor and if you're a book lover you'll think you've died and gone to heaven. It's filled with an esoteric mix of first editions, art works, early American fiction, and Americana of all kinds. Some books are rare, some hard-to-find, and some are just used and old. Downstairs, neatly organized by subject amidst the seeming hodgepodge, are literally hundreds of thousands of antique prints and engravings from the fourteenth through the twentieth centuries. Heraldry, architecture, views, fashion, birds, beasts, flowers, music, sports, science, and mathematics are all generously represented, and the stock of vintage maps is outstanding. There are maps of the ancient world along with an extensive collection of county maps of the Northeastern states. Pageant offers some real finds, and prices are excellent.

RICHARD B. ARKWAY, INC.
538 Madison Avenue, near 54th Street
Third floor
751-8135
Mon.–Fri.: 9 a.m.–5:30 p.m.; or weekends by appointment
No credit cards

Voyages and explorations are Richard B. Arkway's passion, and his unusual shop is filled with rare sixteenth- to nineteenth-century books on these subjects, along with exceptionally fine sixteenth- and seventeenth-century maps and atlases. Early scientific and medical works and illustrated volumes are among Arkway's other specialties.

THE STRAND
828 Broadway, at 12th Street
473-1452
Mon.–Fri.: 9:30 a.m.–9:30 p.m.; Sat.: 9:30 a.m.–6:25 p.m.; Sun.: 11 a.m.–6 p.m.

South Street Seaport
159 John Street
809-0875
Mon.–Sat.: 10 a.m.–8 p.m.; Sun.: 12 noon–8 p.m.
All major

The Strand is the nation's largest used bookstore, and it stocks more than two and a half million volumes. Opened in 1929 and now run by the son of the original owner, it's crammed inside and out with bargain tables that are a browser's delight, and its creaky old shelves hold best-sellers at half price, along with titles that range from current fiction, to the social sciences, to history, to Americana. Downstairs, in a dusty warren, you'll find the Strand's collection of art books, and it's one of the city's largest and most varied. On the second floor is the store's Rare Book department, filled with a vast collection of first editions and handsome leather-bound volumes in just about every field, although twentieth-century signed and limited editions are a chief attraction. In fair weather the Strand mans a kiosk on Fifth Avenue at 61st Street.

URSUS BOOKS & PRINTS
981 Madison Avenue, near 76th Street
Mezzanine
772-8787
Mon.–Fri.: 10 a.m.–6 p.m.; Sat.: 11 a.m.–5 p.m.
AE, MC, V

Don't come to this rather elegant bookstore, located on the mezzanine of the Carlyle Hotel, for the latest glossy coffee-table book on Fragonard. Ursus specializes in scholarly out-of-print and hard-to-find art reference works and books on architecture and design for the serious collector. Among owner Peter Kraus's stock of more than 19,000 titles are rare illustrated manuscripts and volumes that date back to the sixteenth century, as well as early twentieth-century works. He carries exhibition catalogues, monographs, *catalogues raisonnés*, original artist's books of all periods—from Dürer to Fishl—and more than 1,000 titles covering science and literature. The print department is run by Evelyn Kraus, and here, neatly arranged by subject, are drawer upon drawer crowded with seventeenth- through nineteenth-century decorative prints, engravings, and watercolors of architectural details, gardens, Victorian follies, fashion, flora and fauna, even vintage crate labels.

XIMENES RARE BOOKS, INC.
19 East 69th Street
744-0226
Mon.–Fri.: 9 a.m.–5 p.m.
No credit cards

Ximenes is one of New York's few antiquarian bookstores that carry a large general stock rather than a few specialties. Among the highly eclectic mix are sixteenth- to nineteenth-century literary works, Americana, history, and rare and first-edition English and American books on travel, science, and medicine. Owner Stephen Weissman is knowledgeable and helpful, and his prices are good.

ARCHITECTURE

The Cooper-Hewitt Museum Bookstore (p. 404) has a wide range of books on architecture. See also the Metropolitan Museum of Art Bookstore (p. 405) and **Art Books.**

HACKER ART BOOKS
A vast selection of old and rare books on architecture, also reprints of important works. (See **Art Books,** p. 22.)

JAAP RIETMAN
A first-rate selection of books on modern architecture, as well as periodicals. (See **Art Books,** p. 23.)

PERIMETER
144 Sullivan Street
529-2275
Tues.–Sat.: 1 p.m.–8 p.m.; Sun.: 1 p.m.–6 p.m.
AE, MC, V

Small and spare, Perimeter is owned by Kazumi Futagawa, who has filled her tiny 500 square feet of space with hard-to-find titles on architecture, furniture, and design. She carries the city's most complete selection of current Japanese publications (including Japanese-English editions), along with folios published by the Architectural Association of London, books by small Italian houses like Mazzotta and Centro Di, and inexpensive soft-cover monographs on well-known architects. The unusual architectural posters and postcards that Futagawa collects from around the world add visual interest to the shop.

RIZZOLI
Current architectural titles. (See **Art Books,** p. 24.)

STUBBS BOOKS & PRINTS, INC.
28 East 18th Street
Third floor
982-8368
Tues.–Sat.: 11 a.m.–6 p.m.

835 Madison Avenue, near 69th Street
Second floor
772-3120
Mon.–Sat.: 11 a.m.–6 p.m.
AE Madison Avenue store only

John and Jane Stubbs's Old World bookshops offer a lavish stock of seventeenth- through twentieth-century rare and out-of-print books on architecture, archaeology, and allied arts; old trade catalogues; and early prints and drawings. Works on Mediterranean archaeology, rare architectural titles, along with architectural and decorative prints and drawings, dominate the downtown gallery; uptown the focus is on more recent architectural works, but there are also vintage titles on the decorative arts and landscape gardening as well as cookbooks from the turn of the century through the fifties. If you need Asher Benjamin's *The Practical Carpenter*, written in 1830; or Candace Wheeler's *Content in a Garden*, you'll find it at Stubbs.

URBAN CENTER BOOKS
457 Madison Avenue, at 51st Street
935-3595
Mon.–Wed., Fri, Sat.: 10 a.m.–6 p.m.; Thurs: 10 a.m.–8 p.m.;
Sun.: 12 noon–5 p.m.
No credit cards

Urban Center Books is located in the north wing of the former Villard houses (now the Helmsley Palace) in an elegant Georgian room, and it's operated by the Municipal Art Society, so it's somehow fitting that this well-stocked bookstore specializes in architecture and design. Among the 4,000 neatly arranged works are the latest domestic and international titles on architectural history, theory, and design technology, as well as books on the decorative arts, landscape architecture, and historic preservation. The inventory of international architectural and design magazines, periodicals, and exhibition catalogues is impressive, as is the myriad materials on the city that includes guides and maps.

URSUS BOOKS & PRINTS
Out-of-print and hard-to-find architectural titles. (See **Antiquarian Books,** p. 19.)

V. L. GREEN
Rare, out-of-print, and new architectural works. (See **Gardening Books,** p. 34.)

WITTENBORN ART BOOKS
A large inventory of out-of-print and new books on architecture. (See **Art Books,** p. 25.)

ART

The museum stores offer a wide range of art books in their respective specialties. The Metropolitan Museum of Art Bookstore is stocked with thousands of titles that reflect the Museum's wide-ranging art collections; the Museum of Modern Art Bookstore carries twentieth-century books and art-related magazines on painting and sculpture; and the National Academy of Design Bookshop has a fine stock of art catalogues covering nineteenth- and twentieth-century art exhibitions. See **Museum Gift Shops,** p. 403.

E. WEYHE
794 Lexington Avenue, near 62nd Street
838-5466
Mon.–Sat.: 9:30 a.m.–4:45 p.m.
No credit cards

Step into E. Weyhe and you step into another era. Narrow and dusty and dense with books, it's been at the same location since 1926, and on its creaky old shelves you'll find a serendipitous mix of rare, out-of-print, old, used, and recent works. Although E. Weyhe carries a wide range of titles on art and architecture of all periods, the strength of the collection is twentieth-century art. Upstairs is a small gallery cluttered with hundreds of prints and engravings. Twentieth-century art is the strength here too, but Gertrude Denis, the original owner's daughter, does offer earlier examples, as well as architectural and decorative prints. E. Weyhe is an old-fashioned bookstore in the very best sense, and it's run by knowledgeable, obliging, and friendly people.

EX LIBRIS
160A East 70th Street
249-2618
Tues–Fri.: 10 a.m.–5 p.m.; Sat.: 12 noon–5 p.m.
No credit cards

Ex Libris is located on the ground floor of a handsome brownstone, and this well-stocked bookstore specializes in rare and out-of-print books on twentieth-century avant-garde art movements. Thousands of volumes on Dada, Surrealism, Russian Constructivism, the Bauhaus, German Expressionism, and Futurism crowd the shelves. The shop also offers a brilliant array of avant-garde graphics—posters, illustrations, and original maquettes.

HACKER ART BOOKS
54 West 57th Street
Second floor
757-1450
Mon.–Sat.: 9:30 a.m.–6 p.m.
No credit cards

Cluttered and dusty and cavernous, Hacker Art Books is crammed floor to ceiling with a mix of old, rare, and new books on art and architecture. Seymour Hacker carries from 50,000 to 60,000 volumes on the visual arts, books on both well-known and esoteric artists, as well as an outstanding collection of titles on such things as costume design and crafts. Hacker also publishes reprints of important scholarly art works.

HARMER JOHNSON LTD.
38 East 64th Street
Second floor
752-1189
By appointment
No credit cards

Harmer Johnson, former head of Sotheby's Ancient and Primitive Art Department, and Peter Sharrer, an art historian, have transformed a tiny second-floor apartment into a snug little gallery and filled it with scholarly works on ancient art and archaeology. Among their rare, out-of-print, and current titles are books on the tribal arts of Africa, the Pacific, and the Americas. They also offer a wide range of vintage and recent museum catalogues of exhibits of ancient and primitive art.

JAAP RIETMAN INC., ART BOOKS
134 Spring Street
Second floor
966-7044
Mon.–Fri.: 9:30 a.m.–6 p.m.; Sat.: 9:30 a.m.–6 p.m.
AE, MC, V

A spartan SoHo loft is home to Jaap Rietman's enormous and very fine collection of books on the contemporary art scene that's especially strong on European art. Besides the vast inventory of art titles, Rietman carries a first-rate selection of books on modern architecture and photography. On his neatly organized shelves you'll find art exhibition catalogues and international periodicals, too, along with small press publications on art, architecture, photography, and design.

KOLWYCK-JONES
588 Broadway, near Houston Street
Ninth floor
966-8698
Tues.–Fri.: 11 a.m.–6 p.m.; Sat.: 11 a.m.–5 p.m.
No credit cards

Rare and out-of-print reference books on twentieth-century art are the specialty at Kolwyck-Jones, the newest of the art bookstores. Opened just over a year ago and located in New York's nascent art district, it's small but has more than 2,500 titles. In addition to volumes on painting and sculpture, you'll find works on architecture and applied arts, along with *catalogues raisonnés*, monographs, and museum catalogues.

OCEANIC PRIMITIVE ART
9 East 38th Street

Fourth floor
779-0486
By appointment only
No credit cards

Along with its impressive collection of primitive art, this beguiling gallery stocks an outstanding selection of rare, out-of-print, and current books on the subject. There are anthropological titles and museum exhibition catalogues, old and new.

PRINTED MATTER
77 Wooster Street
925-0325
Tues.–Sat.: 10 a.m.–6 p.m.
MC, V

You won't find books about artists or art movements in this comfortably cluttered shop. What you will find are artworks in book form. Printed Matter offers more than 2,500 titles by 1,500 mostly contemporary artists, and many of the books are signed and printed in very limited editions. The results—from serious to hilarious—are extraordinary, so keep this small shop in mind when you're hunting for an unusual gift for a special friend. Prices range from under ten dollars to hundreds.

RIZZOLI
31 West 57th Street
759-2424
Mon.–Sat.: 9:30 a.m.–10 p.m.; Sun.: 12 noon–8 p.m.

454 West Broadway
674-1616
Mon.–Thurs.: 11 a.m.–11 p.m.; Fri. & Sat.: 11 a.m.–12 midnight;
Sun.: 12 noon–8 p.m.

3 World Financial Center
385-1400
Mon.–Fri.: 10:30 a.m.–7 p.m.; Sat.: 12 noon–6 p.m.
AE, D, MC, V

Rizzoli offers a first-rate selection of current art books at each of its handsome locations. At the elegant uptown branch the spacious second floor is devoted to painting and sculpture, architecture, design, fashion, and photography. Although many of the works are of the glossy coffee-table variety, and many are Rizzoli's own imprint, there are scholarly works as well, along with a fine stock of monographs. Rizzoli's other locations are smaller, yet here, too, you'll discover an in-depth inventory of the current art, architecture, and applied art titles.

THE STRAND
One of the city's largest and most varied collections of art books. (See **Antiquarian Books,** p. 18.)

WITTENBORN ART BOOKS, INC.
1018 Madison Avenue, near 78th Street
Second floor
288-1558
Mon.–Sat.: 10 a.m.–5 p.m.
MC, V

Known for its selection of scholarly works—Renaissance art is a specialty—Wittenborn carries out-of-print, rare, and antiquarian volumes along with foreign printings. The bookstore was founded in 1937 and is now a favorite with serious art students who come for its vast inventory of old and new art titles. Wittenborn also offers an outstanding collection of works on architecture, archaeology, fashion, and the decorative arts, covering every period from medieval times to the present.

BIOGRAPHY

BIOGRAPHY BOOKSHOP
400 Bleecker Street, at 11th Street
807-8655
Tues.–Fri.: 1 p.m.–9 p.m.; Sat.: 12 noon–10 p.m.; Sun.: 12 noon–5:30 p.m.
AE, MC, V

Biographies, autobiographies, journals, diaries, and books of letters are all you'll find in this sunny, well-organized little shop. Although the selection might at first seem limited, the range of subject matter is incredibly broad. You'll find sections devoted to every important field—from science to fashion, anthropology to architecture, films to mathematics—and every famous name covered. There are biographies for children, too.

CARS

ALBION SCOTT-MOTOBOOKS LIMITED
48 East 50th Street
Third floor
980-1928

Mon.–Fri.: 10 a.m.–7 p.m.; Sat.: 10 a.m.–6 p.m.
AE, MC, V

Albion Scott is unique in that all the books in this no-frills shop deal with cars and racing. If you want a book on the history, performance, and workings of a Porsche or Maserati or Rolls-Royce, or if you need a repair manual for any one of a dozen cars, or if you're looking for a coffee-table tome filled with auto photographs, you'll find them all here. *Formula I* and *Indie* are among the current popular titles. In addition to books, there's a delightful collection of matchbox cars.

CHILDREN'S BOOKS

ANTIQUARIAN BOOKSELLERS INTERNATIONAL
Children's books for the collector that include first and early editions of the classics, along with rare picture books. (See **Antiquarian Books,** p. 14.)

BOOKS OF WONDER
464 Hudson Street
645-8006
Mon.–Sat.: 11 a.m.–7 p.m.; Sun.: 12 noon–6 p.m.

132 Seventh Avenue, at 18th Street
989-3270
Mon.–Sat.: 11 a.m.–7 p.m.; Sun.: 12 noon–6 p.m.
AE, MC, V

Books of Wonder has the largest collection of Oz and Baumiana in the world, and it's known as a prime source for rare, out-of-print, and vintage children's books. Less well known is the fact that owners Peter Glassman and James Carey offer the very best of the new titles for children. Most of the books are hardcover, since Glassman believes children should be encouraged to build a library of their favorites, so in addition to rare books and handsomely illustrated reprints of the classics, Books of Wonder is stocked with the finest in current children's literature.

EEYORE'S BOOKS FOR CHILDREN
2212 Broadway, near 78th Street
362-0634

Mon.–Sat.: 10 a.m.–6 p.m.; Sun.: 10:30 a.m.–5 p.m.

25 East 83rd Street
988-3404
Mon.–Sat.: 10 a.m.–6 p.m.; Sun.: 12 noon–5 p.m.
AE, MC, V

Eeyore's stocks more than 20,000 volumes, and they're all exclusively for children, so at these well-organized stores you'll discover just about every children's book in print and titles for every age, from infant to teenager. Holidays (including the important Jewish ones) and each new season are marked by window displays and shelves filled with appropriate literature. There's a quiet corner where youngsters can sit and read, a weekly story hour, and a knowledgeable and helpful staff eager to offer guidance.

GRYPHON BOOKSHOP
A large selection of rare, out-of-print, and hard-to-find children's books, including Oz and Baumiana. (See **Antiquarian Books**, p. 16.)

STORYLAND
1369 Third Avenue, near 78th Street
517-6951
Mon.–Sat.: 10 a.m.–6 p.m.; Sun.: 11 a.m.–6 p.m.
AE, MC, V

Storyland is sunny and spacious and offers a full range of all the currently popular children's titles. There are fiction and nonfiction books for youngsters of all ages, from infant to teenager, along with audio and video cassettes.

COMIC BOOKS

ACTION COMICS
318 East 84th Street
249-7344
Mon.: 11 a.m.–7 p.m.; Tues.–Sat.: 11 a.m.–7:30 p.m.; Sun.: 12 noon–
6 p.m.
MC, V

Action Comics is a favorite with serious comic book lovers, since owner Stephen Passarelli knows the field and has crammed his small shop with a very complete stock. *Superman* and *Captain Marvel* from the fifties, early Walt Disneys, along with the best of the new crop, cover every inch of space. Passarelli also offers a fine collection of robots, baseball cards, and assorted memorabilia.

FORBIDDEN PLANET
A vast selection of sci-fi comic books. (See **Science Fiction Books,** p. 46).

FUNNY BUSINESS COMICS
666 Amsterdam Avenue, at 92nd Street
799-9477
Mon.–Fri.: 1 p.m.–6 p.m.; Sat., Sun.: 12 noon–5 p.m.
AE

Comic books are simply stacked in cardboard boxes on metal tables in this tiny shop (display is not one of Funny Business Comics' strengths), but there are some treasures to be found among the enormous stock of current favorites and early issues.

ST. MARKS COMICS
11 St. Marks Place
598-9439
Sun.–Wed.: 10 a.m.–11 p.m.; Thurs.–Sat.: 10 a.m.–1 p.m.
AE, MC, V

A friendly neighborhood shop, St. Marks receives new comics every day, but comic book fanatics come here for the vast selection of back issues. Early Silver and Golden Age comics are a specialty.

VILLAGE COMICS
227 Sullivan Street
777-2770
Mon.–Wed.: 11 a.m.–8 p.m.; Thurs.: 10 a.m.–9:30 p.m.; Fri., Sat.: 10 a.m.–10:15 p.m.; Sun.: 12 noon–6 p.m.
MC, V

One of the city's most comprehensive comic book stores, Village Comics specializes in Marvel, DC, and Epic comics, yet it features Spiderman, the Teen Titans, and DNA Agents, too. You'll find rare collector's items, back issues, and European comics, along with underground ones and those put out by the small independent publishers. It's a friendly shop run by knowledgeable people.

COOKING

KITCHEN ARTS & LETTERS
1435 Lexington Avenue, near 93rd Street

876-5550
Mon.: 1 p.m.–6 p.m.; Tues., Fri.: 10 a.m.–6:30 p.m.; Sat.: 11 a.m.–
6 p.m. Closed Sat. in summer.
MC, V

Even if you're not in the market for a cookbook, Kitchen Arts & Letters is worth visiting just for the opportunity to chat with Nach Waxman about food. A former editor and steadfast food lover, Waxman carries more than 5,000 volumes on food, wine, and cooking. In addition to hundreds of cookbooks, he has books on kitchen antiques and design, restaurant reviews, along with wonderful volumes on culinary history, the anthropology of food, even food-related fiction. He takes delight in carrying esoteric titles not available anywhere else in New York, so if you're looking for a copy of the traditional recipes of Laos come here. Waxman was the first in the city to offer John Thorne's slim treatises on food, and he always has a delightful stock of regional cookbooks that he gathers from around the country. He carries vintage food advertisements, old crate labels, and antique menus, too.

M. M. EINHORN MAXWELL, BOOKS
80 East 11th Street
228-6767
By appointment only
No credit cards

The Maxwells call themselves specialists in gastronomy, dance, and the theater arts, and they have two separate rooms for their diverse collections. One is crammed floor to ceiling with books on food and wine, the other is devoted to dance and the performing arts. Most of the cookbooks are rare or out-of-print editions, so you're likely to find a copy of Apacius's *Cookery and Dining in Imperial Rome* or an 1883 edition of *Bordeaux and Its Wines*, or a volume on the art of bread-making in 1895. But you'll also discover such standard in-print classics as Waverley Root's *Food of Italy* or Paula Wolfert's *Mediterranean Cooking*. The performing arts room offers rare, out-of-print, and hard-to-find works by all the important dance writers—including the Russians—biographies of the world's famous dancers, along with old dance magazines and vintage ballet programs. The Maxwells have also put together the city's most complete library on puppetry, and this husband-and-wife team are delightful to deal with and exceptionally knowledgeable.

STUBBS BOOKS & PRINTS, INC.
Out-of-print cookbooks, many from the twenties and thirties. (See **Architecture Books,** p. 20.)

DANCE

THE BALLET SHOP
1887 Broadway, near 62nd Street
581-7990
Mon.–Sat.: 11 a.m.–7:45 p.m.; Sun.: 12 noon–6 p.m.
All major

Don't come to the Ballet Shop for leotards or tutus. This is a bookstore, and it specializes in both in- and out-of-print books on dance. You'll find Gelsey Kirkland's recent best-seller *Dancing on My Grave*, along with Felicity Gray's *Ballet for Beginners*. The shop carries biographies of all the ballet greats, a very complete selection of dance periodicals, as well as records, videos, and ballet memorabilia.

M. M. EINHORN MAXWELL, BOOKS
A vast array of rare, out-of-print, and hard-to-find books on dance. (See **Cooking Books,** p. 29.)

RICHARD STODDARD–PERFORMING ARTS BOOKS
Out-of-print books on dance. (See **Theater Books,** p. 48.)

FILM

APPLAUSE CINEMA BOOKS
100 West 67th Street
787-8858
Mon.–Sat.: 10:30 a.m.–7 p.m.; Sun.: 12 noon–6 p.m.
AE, MC, V

Applause Cinema Books is the city's largest film bookstore, and it's a shop for serious film buffs. Owner Glenn Young has more than 7,000 titles lining the walls, and he prides himself on carrying every critique, biography, and book in print on the subject of film, including such intellectual works of criticism as those of Roland Barthes and Jan M. Peters. In addition to his vast array of books, Young stocks screenplays and shooting scripts for just about every American and British motion picture, manuals on film and video camera techniques, dictionaries of media terms, even directories of acting coaches.

GOTHAM BOOK MART & GALLERY

One of the best collections of old, rare, and new books on film in the city. (See **Antiquarian Books,** p. 16.)

RICHARD STODDARD–PERFORMING ARTS BOOKS

An in-depth selection of books on film. (See **Theater Books,** p. 48.)

FOREIGN

ASIA SOCIETY BOOKSTORE

An impressive inventory of books that cover all aspects of Asian culture, history, art, and religion. (See **Museum Gift Shops,** p. 403.)

CHINA BOOKS & PERIODICALS

136 West 18th Street
627-4044
Mon.–Sat.: 10 a.m.–6 p.m.
MC, V

China Books is a publisher, importer, and distributor of books about China, so it's not surprising that the bookstore offers the city's largest assortment of such books—many of them in Chinese. Oriental medicine is a specialty, but there are volumes on Chinese history, literature, and all facets of the country. Periodicals and magazines of all kinds, beautifully illustrated art works, and unique imported handcrafts are all appealingly displayed.

IRISH BOOKS AND GRAPHICS

90 West Broadway
962-4237
Mon.–Fri.: 11 a.m.–5 p.m.; Sat.: 12 noon–5 p.m.
MC, V

Angela Carter, owner of Irish Books and Graphics, claims to carry the largest selection of books on Ireland outside of the Emerald Isle. Her inventory is vast and includes out-of-print, hard-to-find, and current titles that cover Irish literature and a broad range of Irish subjects. But if she doesn't happen to have what you're searching for, she'll order it for you. Carter also offers some wonderful Irish engravings and prints. It's a delightfully friendly little shop stocked with some unusual finds.

KINOKUNIYA BOOKSTORE

10 West 49th Street
765-1461

Daily: 10 a.m.–7 p.m.
AE, MC, V

A New York branch of Japan's famous bookstore, Kinokuniya is located in Rockefeller Center and boasts the city's largest and most complete selection of books from and about Japan. Its walls and shelves are neatly stacked with more than 20,000 English and Japanese titles covering all aspects of Japanese culture—from cooking, to economics, to literature, to martial arts.

LIBRAIRIE DE FRANCE/LIBRERIA HISPANICA

610 Fifth Avenue, near 49th Street
581-8810
Mon.–Sat.: 9:30 a.m.–6:15 p.m.

115 Fifth Avenue, at 19th Street
673-7400
Mon.–Sat.: 9:30 a.m.–6 p.m.
AE, MC, V

The owners allege that there is not another bookstore like it in the world, and it's difficult to imagine one that even comes close. At both locations, under one roof, you'll find a French and Spanish bookstore along with a dictionary store and a learn-a-language center. Bestsellers from France, Spain, Puerto Rico, and Latin and Central America share the space with 10,000 dictionaries in languages from Afrikaans to Yoruba, and tapes to help you learn any language from Assimil to Serbo-Croatian. There are children's books, cookbooks, technical works, medical volumes, textbooks, Michelin travel guides and maps, along with business, finance, legal, and science titles. To round out the already impressive inventory, these stores also offer all the French and Spanish daily papers, not to mention comic books, periodicals, and calendars.

PARAGON BOOK GALLERY LTD.

2130 Broadway, at 75th Street
Mezzanine
496-2378
Mon.–Fri.: 10 a.m.–6 p.m.; Sat.: 11 a.m.–5 p.m.
MC, V

From an unlikely location on the mezzanine of the Beacon Hotel, Linda Kramer and Roberta Huber offer more than 50,000 new, used, rare, and out-of-print books on Asia, the Middle East, and the Orient. Just about any book even remotely connected with the Orient is carefully catalogued and inventoried here. There's a vast stock of art books, and catalogues covering everything from painting and sculpture to snuff bottles and Oriental rugs, along with current titles from Mainland China, Hong Kong, Japan, and Taiwan.

UNIVERSITY PLACE BOOK SHOP
821 Broadway, near 12th Street
Ninth floor
254-5998
Mon.–Fri.: 10 a.m.–5 p.m.
No credit cards

Rare, out-of-print, and hard-to-find books on Africa, the West Indies, and Afro-Americans are randomly piled all over this cavernous and dusty loft. There are hundreds of books on African dialects, volumes on black America, communism, socialism, and other radical movements, along with an enormous assortment of contemporary titles. Owner William French is knowledgeable and friendly and can magically retrieve from the untidy stacks any book you're looking for.

VICTOR KAMKIN, INC.
149 Fifth Avenue, at 21st Street
673-0776
Mon.–Fri.: 9:30 a.m.–5:30 p.m.; Sat.: 10 a.m.–5 p.m.
AE, MC, V

The old wooden bookshelves at Victor Kamkin's Russian bookstore are crowded with books printed in Cyrillic. They encompass modern titles, classics, children's books, dictionaries, histories, reference works, and political treatises. If you're looking for a copy of the Soviet edition of Mikhail S. Gorbachev's *Perestroika: New Thinking for Our Country and the World*, volumes on Khrushchev or Chernenko, copies of *Pravda*, *Izvestia*, the *Moscow News* or the magazine *Ogonyok* (at the forefront of *glasnost*), come to this family-run bookstore. About 10 percent of the stock is in English, and in addition to the hundreds of books there are Soviet-made souvenirs, lacquer boxes, painted wooden dolls, and records.

GARDENING

MORTON, THE INTERIOR DESIGN BOOKSHOP
All the latest gardening books. (See **Interior Design Books**, p. 35.)

STUBBS BOOKS & PRINTS, INC.
Rare and out-of-print books on landscape architecture, including such practical works as a treatise on pruning and a book on water gardening, along with beautifully illustrated volumes. (See **Architecture Books** p. 20.)

URBAN CENTER BOOKS

A fine selection of books on landscape gardening. (See **Architecture Books** p. 21.)

V. L. GREEN BOOKSELLERS

19 East 76th Street
439-9194
Mon.–Fri.: 9:30 a.m.–6 p.m.; Sat.: 10 a.m.–5 p.m.
AE, MC, V

V. L. Green Booksellers is a cozy little shop outfitted with Oriental rugs and well-used bookcases. And owners Virginia Green and Joan Gers have stocked it with a mix of rare, out-of-print, European, and new titles on landscape gardening, architecture, and the decorative arts. Gertrude Jekyll's works are here, along with limited editions of Humphrey Repton's *Observations on the Theory and Practice of Landscape Gardening*, and volumes filled with exquisite reproductions of Basilius Besler's seventeenth-century botanicals. There are books on English water gardens and German private gardens, as well as practical works on creating topiaries. Interior designers frequent this shop for its superior inventory of English, American, and French furniture, design, and textiles, as well as esoteric works on fireplaces and painted finishes. Among the architectural titles you'll find *Grand Oriental Hotels from Cairo to Tokyo, 1800–1939*, along with monographs and books of sketches.

GAY LIBERATION

A DIFFERENT LIGHT

548 Hudson Street, near Perry Street
989-4850
Sun.–Thurs.: 11 a.m.–9 p.m.; Fri., Sat.: 11 a.m.–11 p.m.
AE, MC, V

Gay and lesbian literature is the specialty at A Different Light and this store stocks more than 7,000 titles. Tidy and well organized by subject, the shelves hold volumes on everything from poetry to health, from religion to psychology, and from coming out to parenting. *The Selected Letters of T. E. Lawrence*, E. M. Forster's *The Hill of Devi*, Victoria Glendinning's *Vita*, and *The Victorians and Ancient Greece* are among the mix of titles. The magazine selection is broad and includes more than 100 gay publications, including foreign-language ones from countries as diverse as Japan, Scotland, Norway, and France. There are cards and videos and the owners publish a periodic newsletter and hold readings throughout the year.

JUDITH'S ROOM
A large selection of books on lesbianism, including both fiction and nonfiction works. (See **Women's Books,** p. 49.)

OSCAR WILDE MEMORIAL BOOKSHOP
15 Christopher Street
255-8097
Mon.–Fri.: 12 noon–7:30 p.m.; Sat.: 12 noon–8:30 p.m.
AE, MC, V

The Oscar Wilde Memorial Bookshop caters to both men and women, and although it's a tiny shop, it offers a good selection of books dealing with the educational, spiritual, sexual, and medical interests of homosexuals. The fiction section has such gay classics as James Baldwin's *Giovanni's Room* and Radclyffe Hall's *The Well of Loneliness.* Among the nonfiction titles are such practical works as *Mobilizing Against AIDS* and *A Legal Guide for Lesbian and Gay Couples.* The bookshop carries travel guides and gay and feminist periodicals as well.

HISTORY

See also **Military Books,** p. 36.

ARGOSY BOOK STORE
An entire floor is filled with out-of-print and rare books on American history, and Argosy has thousands of volumes on European history, too, along with a fine selection of biographies of historic figures. (See **Antiquarian Books,** p. 15.)

INTERIOR DESIGN

MORTON, THE INTERIOR DESIGN BOOKSHOP
989 Third Avenue, near 59th Street
421-9025

Mon.–Thurs., Sat.: 11 a.m.–8 p.m.; Fri.: 11 a.m.–6 p.m.
AE, MC, V

Sleek and high-tech and located on the same block as the D & D Building—New York's shrine to interior design—it's fitting that Morton's specializes in design, decoration, architecture, and gardening. You'll find all the current titles, the newest coffee-table extravagances, plus practical works on woodworking and *faux* finishes, as well as price guides to buying antiques.

PERIMETER
Hard-to-find titles on furniture and design. (See **Architecture Books,** p. 20.)

RIZZOLI
A lavish stock of books on interior design, furniture, and the decorative arts. (See **Art Books,** p. 24.)

V. L. GREEN BOOKSELLERS
A superior collection of books on English, American, and French furniture, design, textiles, and such esoteric subjects as fireplaces and painted finishes. (See **Gardening Books,** p. 34.)

MILITARY

THE MILITARY BOOKMAN
29 East 93rd Street
348-1280
Tues.–Sat.: 10:30 a.m.–5:30 p.m.
No credit cards

Harris and Margaretta Colt offer rare, out-of-print, and used military, naval, and aviation histories in their cozy shop that's located in a turn-of-the-century town house. The Colts are obliging and knowledgeable booksellers, and their unusual collection ranges from works on the use of stones to space satellites in military encounters. If you're looking for a book on the Boer War, an obscure general, the history of armored vehicles, or the French Foreign Legion, you'll find it among their 8,000 titles. In addition to books the Colts carry a well-edited selection of military prints.

SKY BOOKS INTERNATIONAL
48 East 50th Street
688-5086

Mon.–Sat.: 10 a.m.–7 p.m.; summer: Mon.–Sat.: 10 a.m.–6 p.m.
No credit cards

Sky Books was started in 1975 by Bill Dean, a former RAF flight instructor, as a mail-order book club. It now boasts the world's largest selection of books on military and naval history and aviation, with special emphasis on twentieth-century military aviation. Here's where you'll find a flight manual for a B-17, a detailed analysis of the German Luftwaffe, books on tactical bombing, and *Soldier of Fortune*. There's an impressive periodical selection, too, stocked with the latest issues of *After the Battle* and *Airpower*.

THE SOLDIER SHOP

1013 Madison Avenue, near 78th Street
535-6788
Mon.–Fri.: 10 a.m.–5:30 p.m.; Sat.: 10 a.m.–4:30 p.m.
AE, MC, V

The Soldier Shop has been a fixture on Madison Avenue for more than twenty-three years and this shop is for the serious collector. Since owner Peter Blum specializes in things military, he stocks books, tin soldiers, prints and engravings of important heroes and battles, games, even plates decorated with soldiers. There are old and rare books on military history, battles, and theory, as well as biographies of famous figures. Blum also has a first-rate inventory of current titles and his tin-soldier collection ranges from one-of-a-kind, pricey antiques to finely made contemporary examples.

MYSTERY

FOUL PLAY BOOKS OF MYSTERY AND SUSPENSE
10 Eighth Avenue, at 12th Street
675-5115
Mon.–Fri.: 11 a.m.–9:45 p.m.; Sat.: 11 a.m.–9:45 p.m.;
Sun.: 11 a.m.–7 p.m.

Foul Play Mystery Books
1465B Second Avenue, near 76th Street
517-3222
Mon.–Fri.: 12 noon–10 p.m.; Sat.: 11 a.m.–11 p.m.;
Sun.: 12 noon–7 p.m.
MC, V

Bold black and red interiors, lacquered shelves, and a well-organized inventory distinguishes these bookstores that are devoted exclusively to murder mysteries, espionage, thrillers, and whodunits. Although the stores carry only in-print works, you'll find all the important writers in these genres—from Agatha Christie to Lawrence Sanders—well represented.

MURDER INK
271 West 87th Street
362-8905
Mon.–Wed., Fri., Sat.: 1 a.m.–7 p.m.; Thurs.: 1 p.m.–10 p.m.
No credit cards

Carol Brener's cozy shop is inhabited by two well-fed cats—Humbleby and Clouseau—a friendly staff, and the city's best selection of current detective writers. Rare and used books can be found here too, as well as all the Dashiell Hammett, Raymond Chandler, and Agatha Christie classics. In fact it's difficult to name an in- or out-of-print mystery or book about mystery writers that's not on Murder Ink's shelves. Brener also stocks back issues of mystery periodicals.

THE MYSTERIOUS BOOK SHOP
129 West 56th Street
765-0900
Mon.–Sat.: 11 a.m.–7 p.m.
AE, MC, V

The Mysterious Book Shop, ensconced on the first and second floors of a crumbly old graystone with creaky wood floors and well-worn wooden bookcases, looks like it belongs in an old-fashioned novel. But mild-mannered Otto Penzler sells mystery, crime, suspense, espionage, and detective books, and he's assembled more than 15,000 titles. On the bottom floor are the hardcover and paperback books, but climb the circular staircase and you'll find a trove of rare, out-of-print, and hard-to-find volumes. There's a cabinet filled with first and early editions of Sherlock Holmes, stacks of used books, worn red-leather chairs, and certainly enough titles to keep any mystery lover happy.

NAUTICAL

BOOK & CHART STORE
Vintage copies of Conrad and Melville; navigational guides; how-tos of boat building, sailing, knotting, and the like; along with national geodetic charts and maritime periodicals. (See **Museum Gift Shops,** p. 409.)

NEW YORK NAUTICAL INSTRUMENT & SERVICE CORP.
Books on navigation and sailing for the serious and advanced sailor.
(See **Sporting Goods,** p. 461.)

NEW YORK

CITYBOOKS
2223 Municipal Building
1 Center Street
669-8245
Mon.–Fri.: 8:30 a.m.–5 p.m.

61 Chambers Street
669-8245
Mon.–Fri.: 9:30 a.m.–5 p.m.
No credit cards

Just about everyone is familiar with the *Green Book,* the pocket-size
directory that lists governmental and New York city and state agencies and courts, but few realize that Citybooks, a government agency,
offers more than 120 other official publications to help New Yorkers
cope with the complexities of living in the city. There are paperback
volumes on each of the boroughs, books on black history, tenant hand-
books, *The Big-Apple Fix-Up Book,* historic district reports, studies on
housing and city budgets, along with directories of mental health and
senior citizen services. In addition Citybooks carries all manner of
New York memorabilia—from liberty buttons to cast-iron seals rescued
from the West Side Highway, to Sanitation Department sweatshirts.

THE MUSEUM OF THE CITY OF NEW YORK GIFT SHOP
Books, guides, and maps about the city, along with novels set in New
York. (See **Museum Gift Shops,** p. 407.)

NEW YORK BOUND BOOKSHOP
50 Rockefeller Plaza
245-8503
Mon.–Fri.: 10 a.m.–6 p.m.; Sat.: 11 a.m.–5 p.m.
AE, MC, V

Barbara Cohen has recently moved her New York Bound Bookshop to
spacious new quarters in Rockefeller Center. It's the city's only bookstore that specializes in New York itself, and the city's diversity is
celebrated in the shop's eclectic mix of old, rare, out-of-print, and
current volumes about New York. Books on the city's architecture, and
transportation, early-nineteenth-century guidebooks, vintage advertis-

ing directories, old city reports, early atlases and maps, handwritten wills, and ancient deeds are among Cohen's stock, along with E. B. White's classic *Here Is New York* and Ward McAllister's 1890 social tome *Society as I Have Found It*. Ephemera includes memorabilia from the 1939 World's Fair, early photographs, vintage city bonds, song sheets about the city, and nineteenth-century newspapers.

URBAN CENTER BOOKS

A large selection of books on New York architecture, along with city guides and maps. (See **Architecture Books,** p. 21.)

OCCULT

ESOTERICA BOOKSHOP

61 Fourth Avenue, near 9th Street
529-9808
Mon.–Thurs.: 11 a.m.–9 p.m.; Fri., Sat.: 11 a.m.–11 p.m.; Sun.: 12 noon–9 p.m.
AE, MC, V

You won't find Tom Wolfe's latest epic here. As its name suggests, this bookstore prides itself on its stock of esoteric titles. Somewhat spartan, quiet, and serene with Indian music in the background, Esoterica's neatly organized blond-wood shelves are filled with books on astrology, palmistry, numerology, and the healing arts, along with works that deal with magic. There are also numerous volumes on philosophy and Eastern religions.

NEW YORK ASTROLOGY CENTER

545 Eighth Avenue, near 37th Street
Tenth floor
719-2919
Mon.–Fri.: 10 a.m.–6:30 p.m.; Sat.: 11 a.m.–5 p.m.
AE, MC, V

The New York Astrology Center runs a three-year course and gives lectures on astrology, but it also stocks hundreds of books on the subject and such related topics as numerology, palmistry, acupuncture, tarot cards, and the healing arts. You'll find Edgar Cayce's books and remedies, Hindu astrological chart services, video tapes, and matrix software, too.

SAMUEL WEISER

132 East 24th Street
777-6363

Mon.–Wed., Fri.: 9 a.m.–6 p.m.; Thurs.: 10 a.m.–7 p.m.;
Sat.: 9:30 a.m.–5 p.m.; Sun.: 11 a.m.–5:30 p.m.
MC, V

Samuel Weiser's well-ogranized shelves hold the city's best selection
of current and out-of-print books on the occult and Eastern philosophy.
Weiser carries books on just about any subject that is otherworldly—
from witchcraft to flying saucers to E.S.P. to crystal balls—and such
rare works as a seventeenth-century volume on demonology. There's
also a first-rate stock of periodicals and foreign publications, along
with tarot cards, videos, and crystal balls.

PHILOSOPHY

EAST WEST BOOKS
Books on Chinese, Indian, and Western philosophies. (See **Religion
Books,** p. 44.)

ESOTERICA BOOKSHOP
A good selection of philosophic works. (See **Occult Books,** p. 41.)

PHOTOGRAPHY

INTERNATIONAL CENTER OF PHOTOGRAPHY
1130 Fifth Avenue, at 94th Street
860-1777
Tues.: 12 noon–8 p.m.; Wed.–Fri.: 12 noon–5 p.m.;
Sat.–Sun.: 11 a.m.–6 p.m..

1133 Avenue of the Americas, at 43rd Street
Tues., Wed.: 11 a.m.–6 p.m.; Thurs.: 11 a.m.–8 p.m.;
Fri.–Sun.: 11 a.m.–6 p.m.
AE, MC, V

The gift shop at I.C.P. is small, yet it manages to stock more than 1,000
in-print photography titles that range from monographs to technical
manuals. There's an in-depth coverage of the esthetics and theory of
photography, as well as biographies of famous photographers past and
present, books of their photographs, volumes on photojournalism, and
catalogues of old and current shows. The somewhat larger midtown

41

bookstore offers documentary and fine art titles along with photographic works and photo albums.

A PHOTOGRAPHER'S PLACE
133 Mercer Street
431-9358
Mon.–Sat.: 11 a.m.–6 p.m.; Sun.: 12 noon–5 p.m.
MC, V

The city's only bookstore exclusively devoted to photography is crammed with more than 4,500 titles by and about photographers past and present. Owner Harvey Zucker carries rare, out-of-print, hard-to-find, and current volumes on photographic history, criticism, and technique; books of photographs by all the leading artists; and price guides to collectible cameras, as well as old prints and a fine group of vintage cameras.

POETRY

BOOKS 'N THINGS
Rare, used, and out-of-print poetry books. (See **Antiquarian Books,** p. 15.)

GOTHAM BOOK MART & GALLERY
A large and fine assortment of poetry books with a heavy emphasis on twentieth-century poets. (See **Antiquarian Books,** p. 16.)

POLITICAL SCIENCE

LAISSEZ FAIRE BOOKS
532 Broadway, near Spring Street
Seventh floor
925-8992
Mon.–Fri.: 10 a.m.–6 p.m.; Sat.: 11 a.m.–6 p.m.
MC, V

In this out-of-the-way bookstore, tucked away on the seventh floor of a no-elevator building, you'll find works by all the important free-market authors. Books are carefully organized under such categories as Anarchism, Social Disharmony, Revisionist History, Free Market Economics, Libertarian Political Theory, and Taxes. Laissez Faire stocks free-market periodicals as well, and handles a large mail-order business.

UNIVERSITY PLACE BOOK SHOP
A large inventory of works on communism, socialism, and other radical movements. (See **Foreign Books**, p. 33.)

VICTOR KAMKIN, INC.
Books on all the important Communist leaders, along with Soviet political treatises, newspapers, and periodicals. (See **Foreign Books**, p. 33.)

PSYCHOLOGY

BRUNNER/MAZEL BOOKSTORE
19 Union Square West, near 15th Street
Eighth floor
924-3344
Mon.–Fri.: 9 a.m.–4:45 p.m.; Sat.: 10:30 a.m.–3:30 p.m.
AE, MC, V

Don't expect to find any "pop" psychology books at Brunner/Mazel. What you will find on the miles of metal bookcases lining a long, spare room are the complete works of Freud, Jung, Klein, Erikson, and other leading therapists. Among the more than 3,000 volumes are works on psychiatry, psychology, child development, psychosocial stress disorders, family therapy, hypnotherapy, and Kurenberg manuals of disorders. Yet hidden among the serious titles are such surprises as the slim satirical work *Oral Sadism and the Vegetarian Personality*.

RELIGION

CALVARY BOOKSTORE
139 West 57th Street
315-0230
Mon.–Tues., Thurs., Fri.: 10 a.m.–6 p.m.; Wed.: 10 a.m.–8 p.m.;

Sat.: 11 a.m.–4 p.m.
AE, MC, V

The Calvary Bookstore is located near the Calvary Baptist Church, and it calls itself "New York City's Bible Center" and offers the Bible in scores of translations and styles. The shop stocks a variety of nondenominational religious books and reference works as well.

CHRISTIAN PUBLICATIONS BOOK AND SUPPLY CENTER
315 West 43rd Street
582-4311
Mon.–Fri.: 9:30 a.m.–5:30 p.m.; Sat.: 9:30 a.m.–4:30 p.m.
MC, V

The largest Christian bookstore in New York is stocked with more than 10,000 titles. Bibles in many styles and dozens of languages, along with religious works, fill its shelves to overflowing. The center sells religious records, tapes, and videos, too, and much of its stock is available in Spanish translation.

EAST WEST BOOKS
78 Fifth Avenue, near 13th Street
243-5994
Mon.–Thurs.: 11 a.m.–7:30 p.m.; Fri.–Sun.: 11 a.m.–6 p.m.

568 Columbus Avenue, near 87th Street
787-7555
Mon.–Sat.: 12 noon–7:30 p.m.; Sun.: 11 a.m.–6 p.m.
AE, MC, V

East West Books is more than just a bookstore. It's a holistic health shop that claims to "provide an oasis of tranquillity for those in search of a deeper self," and the staff does seem pleasantly relaxed and serene. There's new age music in the background and shelves stocked with books on Eastern religions, health and healing, metaphysics, yoga, Sufism, self-help Gurdjieff, psychology, astrology, and Chinese, Indian, and Western philosophies. East West sells the new age music that it plays, and there's a video section with tapes on Jesus and spiritual teachings.

ESOTERICA BOOKSHOP
A large selection of books on Zen, Buddhism, and other Eastern religions. (See Occult Books, p. 41.)

THE JEWISH MUSEUM
The book section is well stocked with a broad range of titles on religion, history, and the observance of Jewish holidays and the Sabbath. (See Museum Gift Shops, p. 405.)

J. LEVINE COMPANY BOOKS & JUDAICA
5 West 30th Street
Second floor
695-6888
Mon.–Wed.: 9 a.m.–6 p.m.; Thurs.: 9 a.m.–7 p.m.; Fri.: 9 a.m.–2 p.m.;
closed Sat.; Sun.: 10 a.m.–5 p.m.; closed Sun. in July
AE, MC, V

A delightful jumble of gifts, religious paraphernalia, and books on Judaism greets you when you open the door at J. Levine. The company has been around since 1820 and piled everywhere are traditional Jewish texts, the city's largest selection of recently published works on Jewish subjects, reference books and dictionaries, not to mention such beautiful tabletop volumes as *The Ashkenazi Haggadah* and such erudite titles as *A History and Guide to Judaic Encyclopedias and Lexicons*. There are scores of Bibles, along with books in English and Hebrew on Jewish history, liturgy, kabbalah, philosophy, Israel, and the Holocaust. But there are lighter things too: *The Passover Gourmet* and *The Complete Jewish Wedding Planner* as well as Kosherland, a board game for children, and *What Happened to Crazy Yosel,* a children's book. Seder plates, menorahs, Torah covers, yarmulkes, and tallithim are among the store's stock of items for observation of the Sabbath and the Jewish holidays. But customers come here for more than the merchandise—they come for the staff's knowledge of Hebrew law and tradition and for the general friendliness.

PARACLETE BOOK CENTER
146 East 74th Street
535-4050
Tues.–Fri.: 10 a.m.–6 p.m.; Sat.: 10 a.m.–5 p.m.
No credit cards

Paraclete Book Center was named for a sermon delivered by the Jesuit poet Gerard Manley Hopkins, and this bookstore is for those who are serious about theology. All the important Christian theologians fill its shelves, there's a strong philosophy section, and an obliging, well-informed staff.

UNION THEOLOGICAL SEMINARY BOOKSTORE
3041 Broadway, at 120th Street
662-7100
Mon.–Fri.: 9 a.m.–5 p.m.
No credit cards

Union Theological Seminary's bookstore is located just inside the seminary itself, and it caters to theology students. It's an unusual store, recognized worldwide for its progressive titles, and displayed on its well-organized shelves are books on history, psychology, black studies, women's studies, economics, politics, comparative literature, sociology, even children's books. But its theology section is vast and covers just about every in-print work even remotely connected with the subject.

SCIENCE

ARGOSY BOOK STORE.
An extensive selection of early and rare medical and scientific titles. (See **Antiquarian Books,** p. 15.)

GENERAL MEDICAL BOOK COMPANY
310 East 26th Street
532-0756
Mon.–Fri.: 10:30 a.m.–6 p.m.; Sat.: 10:30 a.m.–5 p.m.
MC, V

For more than seventy years the General Medical Book Company has bought and sold medical, dental, nursing, and veterinary books. It has a vast inventory of titles, mostly geared to students and practitioners.

SCIENCE FICTION

FORBIDDEN PLANET
821 Broadway, at 12th Street
473-1576
Mon.–Thurs., Sat.: 10 a.m.–7 p.m.; Fri.: 10 a.m.–8 p.m.;
Sun.: 12 noon–6 p.m.

227 East 59th Street
751-4386
Mon.–Fri.: 11:30 a.m.–8:30 p.m.; Sat.: 10 a.m.–9 p.m.;
Sun.: 12 noon– 7 p.m.
AE, MC, V

Forbidden Planet is certainly much more than just a bookstore, but in both these branches of Mike Luckman's London store you'll find just about every science-fiction book ever written. The stock of vintage sci-fi comic books is mind-boggling, and there's an impressive selection of robotic toys and, at Halloween, all manner of masks, both scary and comical.

SCIENCE FICTION SHOP
56 Eighth Avenue, at Horatio Street
741-0270
Mon.–Fri.: 11:30 a.m.–6:45 p.m.; Sat.: 11 a.m.–6 p.m.; Sun.: 12 noon–
6 p.m.
AE, MC, V

Appropriately jet black, the Science Fiction Shop's walls are lined with
books, and this tiny store offers perhaps the most complete stock in the
world of science fiction and fantasy titles. Some are new, more are
used, out-of-print, rare, or first editions. The shop carries many of the
British authors, hard and soft covers, the complete *Star Trek* series, as
well as periodicals.

THEATER

APPLAUSE THEATER BOOKS
211 West 71st Street
496-7511
Mon.–Sat.: 10 a.m.–8 p.m.; Sun.: 12 noon–6 p.m.
AE, MC, V

At Applause they claim to have the script for just about every British
drama, and among the bookstore's more than 4,000 titles there is an
amazing selection of British plays. Everything from the complete Shake-
speare, to Ford's gory classics, to the latest from London's West End
cram the tidy shelves. But there are scores of scripts for contemporary
American and Australian works, too, along with directories for actors,
children's dramas, audition scenes, and books on acting, directing,
voice, and movement. Applause also offers historical and critical titles
and biographies.

DRAMA BOOKSHOP
723 Seventh Avenue, near 48th Street
Second floor
944-0595
Mon.–Tues., Thurs., Fri.: 9:30 a.m.–7 p.m.; Wed.: 9:30 a.m.–8 p.m.;
Sat.: 10:30 a.m.–5:30 p.m.; Sun.: 12 noon–5 p.m.
AE, MC, V

The Drama Bookshop is well-known for carrying the city's most complete selection of plays, scripts, scores, and librettos. Yet this actors'
hangout, always crowded and bustling with people, is equally strong
in its array of critical works and biographies. All aspects of the theater

are covered—from props to lighting to makeup—and the store is stocked with an equally in-depth collection of books on dance, film, and all the performing arts.

RICHARD STODDARD–PERFORMING ARTS BOOKS
18 East 16th Street
Second floor
645-9576
Mon., Tues., Thurs.–Sat.: 11 a.m.–6 p.m.
No credit cards

There are enough old Broadway playbills (more than 5,000) to delight theater buffs, and enough scholarly volumes to interest the serious student of drama in Richard Stoddard's delightful bookstore. Stoddard specializes in rare and out-of-print plays, biographies, and works of criticism dealing with the theater, yet he also offers a broad selection of technical titles, as well as books on film, movies, dance, even the circus. His collection of scenic and costume designs is rare and outstanding.

THEATREBOOKS
1600 Broadway, near 48th Street
Tenth floor
757-2834
Mon.–Fri.: 10:30 a.m.–6 p.m.; Sat.: 12 noon–5 p.m.
AE, MC, V

Robert Emerson's bookstore is popular with professional actors who come here for the acting editions of current plays and actor's monologues, but Emerson also carries a good selection of new, used, and out-of-print books on all aspects of the theater. The mix is eclectic, and the store specializes in esoteric titles.

TRAVEL

THE COMPLETE TRAVELLER BOOKSTORE
199 Madison Avenue, at 35th Street
679-4339
Mon.–Fri.: 9 a.m.–6:30 p.m.; Sat.: 10 a.m.–6 p.m.; Sun.: 12 noon–
5 p.m.
AE, MC, V

The Complete Traveller is New York's oldest bookstore devoted to travel, and it's a spacious shop filled with all the current and most popular travel guides, including Nagel's encyclopedic work, maps for every known country, as well as foreign language dictionaries and cassette tapes in all languages. Bookcases lining the back of the store hold authentic Baedekers and other used and out-of-print travel titles.

TRAVELLER'S BOOKSTORE
22 West 52nd Street
664-0995
Mon.–Fri.: 9 a.m.–6 p.m.
AE, MC, V

Although this small jewel of a bookstore may not house the city's most complete collection of travel books, it offers the most intelligently or-dered and edited shelves. Candy Olmsted, Jane Grossman, and Martin Rapp have arranged their shop geographically, and each area is repre-sented by the very best in guidebooks for each country, plus maps, nonfiction musings, picture books, and fiction. In the Italian section there's John Kent's *Venice*, Kate Simon's *Italy the Places in Between*, and Waverley Root's *The Food of Italy*, along with the Michelin guides, books on walks, and photography books of Italian hill towns. The United States is represented by regional guides, books on country inns and bed-and-breakfasts, antiques guides, plus Calvin Trillin on ribs and chicken. Since the owners import many of their titles directly from England, France, Italy, Ecuador, Australia, and New Zealand, you'll find books and guides here that are not available anywhere else in New York.

WOMEN'S BOOKS

JUDITH'S ROOM
681 Washington Street, near Charles Street
727-7330
Tues.–Thurs.: 12 noon–8 p.m.; Fri., Sat.: 12 noon–10 p.m.
AE, MC, V

New York's only women's bookstore is stocked with over 3,500 hard-cover and paperback volumes that are by or about women. All of the fiction, mystery, and science fiction works are written by women and there are both classic and current titles. Feminism, history, biography, literary criticism, poetry, spirituality, lesbianism, health, travel, psy-chology, women of color, parenting, and cooking are among the sub-jects tackled in this neat and well-organized store. There are books for children, too, along with magazines and travel guides.

Buttons

GORDON BUTTON COMPANY
142 West 38th Street
921-1684
Mon.–Fri.: 9 a.m.–5:30 p.m.
No credit cards

The Gordon Button Company carries more than 5,000 varieties of buttons in wood, metal, pearl, rhinestone, and plastic, in styles that range from classic to novelty to bizarre. Since this family-run business, now operated by Peter Gordon, has been around for more than fifty years, it has an enormous stock of antique and vintage buttons, too, and all the various examples are neatly arranged in boxes. There's a large inventory of belt buckles as well.

RELIABLE BUTTON WORKS
65 West 37th Street
Second floor
869-0560
Mon.–Fri.: 8 a.m.–5 p.m.
No credit cards

Climb the stairs to Reliable Button Works and it's like being back in the nineteenth century. For more than fifty-five years this dusty, old-fashioned workshop has been manufacturing and supplying New Yorkers with buttons. Handmade covered ones, made from a customer's own fabric, is the store's chief attraction, and bridal buttons are a specialty. But Reliable also stocks hundreds of ready-made examples, and the company makes covered belts, too, as well as studding and rhinestoning clothing.

TENDER BUTTONS
143 East 62nd Street
758-7004

Mon.–Fri.: 11 a.m.–6 p.m.; Sat.: 11 a.m.–5 p.m.;
closed Sat. in summer
No credit cards

As much cozy museum as store, Diane Epstein and Millicent Safro's long and narrow shop, brightly lit by nineteenth-century fixtures, is filled with more than 1,000 cardboard boxes, each marked with a button corresponding with those inside. The boxes are organized into sections and arranged by color and style. In addition to European fashion buttons for coats and suits and more than 500 styles of blazer buttons new and old, there are exceptionally fine ones of horn, bone, mother-of-pearl, wood, ivory, marcasite, semiprecious stones, brass, and cut steel. Victorian, Edwardian, Art Deco, and Art Nouveau examples are here as well, along with the most endearing collection of little wooden mice, Mickey Mouse characters, tiny fruit and vegetables, baseball bats, and fairytale characters for children. There are antique eighteenth- and nineteenth-century buckles, and Victorian and Edwardian cuff links and stud sets too. Prices range from 25 cents for a simple shirt button to hundreds for a rare eighteenth-century hand-painted ivory one.

Candles

B. Altman & Co., Bloomingdale's, Lord & Taylor, and Macy's offer a variety of candles in all sizes, shapes, and colors. Azuma and the large greeting-card stores also stock a wide array. See **Handcraft Galleries** (p. 323) for hand-dipped candles. See also **Housewares and Hardware,** p. 336.

THE CANDLE SHOP
118 Christopher Street
989-0148
Tues.–Sat.: 12 noon–7 p.m.; Sun.: 1 p.m.–6 p.m.
AE, MC, V

Hundreds of candles, some as big as a bottle of wine, others as slim as a reed, fill Rob Kilgallen's colorful shop. He has candles that look like antique paperweights, others like Santa Claus, along with conventional dinner tapers, natural beeswax ones, hand-dipped varieties, scented versions, votives, and candles in every size, color, and shape—including animals. There are candle holders of crystal, brass, and glass; bobeches to catch the overflow of wax; even brass followers with miniature lamp shades attached.

CONRAN'S HABITAT
A large assortment of candles in a multitude of colors as well as beeswax ones in a range of sizes. (See **Furniture,** p. 267.)

D. F. SANDERS
Classic candles in white and ecru along with beeswax varieties. (See **Housewares and Hardware,** p. 337.)

PERFORMER'S OUTLET
Hand-dipped candles in jewel tones are a specialty, and there are tapers in all sizes, along with others that are squat and chunky. (See **Handcraft Galleries,** p. 327.)

POTTERY BARN
Tall spirals of natural beeswax and other candles in a range of sizes and colors. (See **China and Glassware,** p. 76.)

WEST TOWN HOUSE
A first-rate supply of candles in dozens of colors and a range of sizes. (See **Gifts,** p. 313.)

WILLIAMS-SONOMA, INC.
Well-stocked with candles in a full range of colors and sizes. (See **Kitchenware,** p. 369.)

ZONA
Beeswax candles in sizes from long and tapered to short and stout. (See **Handcraft Galleries,** p. 328.)

Carpets and Tapestries

ANTIQUE AND VINTAGE

ABC CARPET CO., INC

Semi-antique Serapi carpets in pale and subtle colors, along with a sizable group of semi-antique tribal rugs, vintage Navaho weavings, and hand-knotted Persians. (See **Contemporary Carpets and Tapestries,** p. 60.)

A. BESHAR & COMPANY

611 Broadway, near Houston Street
Fourth floor
529-7300
Mon.–Fri.: 9 a.m.–5 p.m.; Sat.: 9 a.m.–4 p.m.; closed Sat. in summer
No credit cards

A. Beshar & Company, a family-owned and -run operation, has been buying and selling old Oriental and European rugs since 1898, so it's unfortunate that most people know the company only because of its famous Besharizing Cleaning Process. Yet Beshar is an excellent source for small- and large-size carpets from Iran and Turkey, as well as Aubussons, Savonneries, antique Melez, and antique and semi-antique kilims. Beshar has a first-rate stock of vintage European tapestries as well.

AMERICA HURRAH

A fine group of early hooked rugs. (See **Linens and Quilts,** p. 384.)

A. R. BROOMER LTD.

Richly figured tapestries from the seventeenth through the nineteenth centuries. (See **China and Glassware,** p. 64.)

BERDJ ABADJIAN
201 East 57th Street
Second floor
688-2229
Mon.–Fri.: 9 a.m.–5 p.m.
No credit cards

For four generations discerning New Yorkers have come to the Berdj Abadjian gallery for fine-quality antique European, Persian, and Turkish rugs. An exemplary selection of such coveted European rugs as Aubussons and Savonneries, along with English and French needlepoints, are among its offerings. There are Tabriz, Oushak, and Sultanabad carpets from the Near and Far East, flatweaves and Agra rugs from India, and fine Chinese examples. The owners are knowledgeable, and they handle restoration and cleaning as well.

CENTRAL CARPET
426 Columbus Avenue, near 80th Street
787-8813
Mon.–Wed., Fri., Sat.: 9 a.m.–6 p.m.; Thurs.: 10 a.m.–7:30 p.m.;
Sun.: 11 a.m.–5 p.m.
MC, V

One of a handful of Columbus Avenue survivors, Central Carpet has been at the same location for thirty-seven years, and although it originally sold Oriental rugs to its middle-class, middle-aged neighbors, it now sells them to affluent, young Upper West Siders. The city's largest selection of handmade Chinese Art Deco rugs from the twenties shares space in this multilevel shop with an impressive assortment of rare Caucasian ones that are as early as 1890, as recent as the twenties. But among the eclectic mix of more than 10,000 carpets are scores of antique Persian, Rumanian, Chinese, and Turkish kilims, as well as a mind-boggling assortment of contemporary floor coverings that include dhurries, kilims, Berbers, Chinese, and handmade Indian Bokharas. Prices are good.

CHEVALIER INC.
157 East 64th Street
249-3922
Mon.–Fri.: 9:30 a.m.–6 p.m.
No credit cards

The grand French house of tapestries, Galerie Chevalier, opened a New York branch four years ago, and this illustrious company has filled its elegant space with rare and important weavings. There are late-seventeenth-century Flemish tapestries, unusual eighteenth-century German ones, along with many other museum-quality examples from France and Belgium. The gallery is run by Dominique and Pierre Chevalier, who are experts in the field, and in addition to tapestries they offer fine European carpets.

THE CHINESE PORCELAIN COMPANY.

Museum-quality Chinese carpets that might include a rare antique Khotan and a fine Pao Tou. (See **Furniture,** p. 283.)

COBWEB

A fine stock of vintage kilim rugs. (See **Furniture,** p. 273.)

THE COMMON GROUND

A beguiling collection of vintage Navaho and other American Indian rugs. (See **Ethnic Items,** p. 210.)

DILDARIAN

595 Madison Avenue, at 57th Street
Third floor
288-4948
Mon.–Fri.: 10 a.m.–5 p.m.
No credit cards

Dildarian is one of New York's oldest and largest rug dealers—it's also one of the city's most reliable. The company began business in 1916, and it operates in association with the prestigious Vigo-Sternberg Galleries of London. A sober and subdued shop, this is where you'll find fine nineteenth-century Savonneries, rare Chinese carpets, along with antique Orientals, Bessarabians, and Aubussons. The showroom also offers a fine collection of antique tapestries. Very expensive.

DORIS LESLIE BLAU GALLERY

15 East 57th Street
Fifth floor
759-3715
By appointment only
No credit cards

If you're looking for a fine but *typical* Oriental carpet look elsewhere. Come to Doris Leslie Blau's discreetly understated gallery only if you're a serious collector interested in very rare and unique specimens. Blau's stock dates from about 1875 to 1925—although there are a few seventeenth-century Isfahans—and most of her rugs are room-size. You might find a Persian Bijar carpet with an intriguingly beautiful abstracted pattern, an early-nineteenth-century Bessarabian of extraordinary subtlety, a somewhat whimsical Northwest Persian Tabriz, or an Amritsar with geometric floral motifs. But Blau also has Aubussons, Savonneries, decorative Orientals, and needlepoints—each of incomparable beauty. There are exquisite antique tapestries, too, along with woven fragments of merit. Very expensive.

FIFTY/50

A selection of fifties area rugs in that era's favorite colors and designs. (See **Furniture,** p. 256.)

F. J. HAKIMIAN
136 East 57th Street
Second floor
371-6900
Mon.–Fri.: 9:30 a.m.–5:30 p.m.; appointment suggested
No credit cards

A favorite with the city's interior designers—Hakimian rugs have graced the rooms in the Kips Bay Decorator Show House for the past four years—this gallery's inventory includes the most extensive collection of French Aubusson and Savonnerie carpets in New York, as well as all the important Persian names (Kerman, Tabriz, and Ziegler). Hakimian carries French and English needlepoints and Art Deco rugs, along with seventeenth-century French and Belgian tapestries.

FRENCH & COMPANY
A small but very special group of French tapestries. (See **Furniture**, p. 249.)

THE GAZEBO
A large inventory of antique and vintage rag, hooked and braided rugs. (See **Linens and Quilts**, p. 385.)

KAMDIN DESIGNS
Antique and semi-antique European and Oriental rugs that include Aubussons, Savonneries, Serapis, Kermans, and Agras. (See **Contemporary Carpets and Tapestries**, p. 62.)

KELTER-MALCE
An appealing group of vintage rag and hooked rugs. (See **Linens and Quilts**, p. 385.)

KILIM GALLERY
150 Thompson Street
Second floor
533-1677
By appointment only
AE

Linda Miller has collected kilims for the past twenty years, and her spacious loft is filled with scores of unusual and beautiful examples. She has flatweaves from Turkey, Russia, and Persia—both tribal and village rugs—and a collection of rare antique Sehna kilims that rival fine old European needlepoints and petit points in their sophistication, coloring, and intricacy of weave. There's a small group of new flatweaves and Turkish pile rugs, too, but most of her stock is old and includes fine prayer kilims, saddle and grain bags, pillows, and runners in all sizes.

LA CHAMBRE PERSE
347 Bleecker Street
243-4287
Mon.–Sat.: 12 noon–8 p.m.; Sun.: 2:30 p.m.–5 p.m.
All major

Hundreds of antique and semi-antique flatweave rugs from Afghanistan, Persia, Turkey, Rumania, Yugoslavia, and the Middle East—neatly stacked according to size—occupy every inch of space in this small but orderly store. Owners Fred and Mary Parvin opened the shop in 1973, and they were among the first to import flatweave rugs into the country. Today they offer Sumacks, Orientals, and kilims in a full range of sizes, along with pillows and small, exquisitely worked rugs appropriate for hanging. In addition to old carpets, the Parvins periodically bring in a large shipment of new kilims from around the world.

L'ANTIQUAIRE & THE CONNOISSEUR
Tapestries from the Middle Ages and the Renaissance. (See **Furniture,** p. 254.)

LAURA FISHER/ANTIQUE QUILTS AND AMERICANA
A small but tempting inventory of Early American hooked and American Indian rugs. (See **Linens and Quilts,** p. 386.)

MARIAN MILLER
148 East 28th Street
Third floor
685-7746
Mon.–Sat.: 10 a.m.–6 p.m. Appointments suggested
No credit cards

Marian Miller began selling kilims from her third-floor walk-up apartment in 1968. At that time few knew about these flat-woven tribal rugs, and Miller was one of the city's first rug dealers to feature them. She's still selling kilims, but now many of her rugs are fine antique examples from Turkey, Iran, and the Caucasus woven of vegetable-dyed yarns. Miller offers prayer rugs, runners, and saddle bags, along with a very special group of old cotton dhurries. She has new kilims, too, and American rag rugs.

MARVIN KAGAN, INC.
625 Madison Avenue, at 58th Street
Second floor
535-9000
Mon.–Fri.: 9:30 a.m.–5:30 p.m.; Sat.: 10 a.m.–5:30 p.m.
AE

The Marvin Kagan gallery is known for its stock of unusual and exceptionally fine antique Oriental carpets, so you'll find all the most sought-after examples here—Ziegler, Serapi, Tabriz, and Kemin. Kagan carries semi-antique Persian and Turkish rugs, and kilims, too, along with antique tapestries. In addition to its carpets, the gallery offers an outstanding collection of rare coins and Greek and Roman antiquities.

MATTHEW SCHUTZ LTD.
A select but beautiful group of antique European carpets that includes Aubussons, Bessarabians, and Savonneries. (See **Furniture,** p. 251.)

NUSRATY AFGHAN IMPORTS
A rich stock of antique and vintage kilims. (See **Ethnic Items,** p. 212.)

THE RUG TOWER
A small selection of antique and semi-antique Oriental rugs. (See **Contemporary Carpets and Tapestries,** p. 63.)

THE RUG WAREHOUSE
2222 Broadway, at 79th Street
Second floor
787-6665
Mon.–Wed., Fri., Sat.: 10 a.m.–6 p.m.; Thurs.: 10 a.m.–8 p.m.;
Sun.: 11 a.m.–5 p.m.
MC, V

A cavernous no-frills warehouse, this carpet emporium is crammed with thousands of rugs of all ages and types that come from every rug-weaving country. There are antique and semi-antique examples from Persia and the Caucasus, a large group of Chinese Art Deco carpets from the twenties, along with vintage flatweaves. The stock of contemporary rugs is vast and includes kilims, dhurries, and Oriental rugs from Persia, India, and Pakistan. There are fine Chinese needlepoint rugs that look like antique English ones, and a full range of modern area rugs. Prices are good.

THOS. K. WOODARD AMERICAN ANTIQUES AND QUILTS
A vast selection of rag carpets and runners—some old, some new—woven in traditional patterns, along with a charming group of early hooked rugs. (See **Linens and Quilts,** p. 387.)

TURKANA GALLERY
125 Cedar Street
732-0273
By appointment only
No credit cards

Peter Davies has one of the largest collections of antique tribal Turkish, Persian, Caucasian, Balkan, Afghan, and Moroccan Berber kilims on the East Coast. Every spring Davies goes on a buying trip abroad, and he personally selects the rugs he sells. He chooses them for quality, rarity, and beauty, and his gallery is filled with unusual examples. In addition to rugs you'll find wall hangings, pillows, saddle bags, and old textiles from Japan, Central Asia, China, the Ottoman Empire, and Africa.

VOJTECH BLAU INC.
800 B Fifth Avenue, near 61st Street
249-4525
Mon.–Fri.: 8:30 a.m.–4:30 p.m.
No credit cards

In Vojtech Blau's spacious and beautiful gallery tapestries grace the walls and rugs adorn the floor, and the colorful stacks of carpets are carefully organized so that all the Persian and Tabriz weavings are in one area, Chinese and Turkish rugs in another, European carpets in still another. Blau's specialty is European and Oriental rugs from the sixteenth through the nineteenth centuries, and these are represented by only the finest examples. Since most of the stock was purchased from estates, there are many oversized carpets to choose from, along with exquisite tapestries, that date from Gothic times to the nineteenth century. Very expensive.

CONTEMPORARY

Bloomingdale's and Macy's carry a large selection of rugs in a full range of styles.

ABC CARPET CO., INC.
881 Broadway, near 19th Street
473-3000
Mon., Thurs.: 10 a.m.–8 p.m.; Tues., Wed., Fri.: 10 a.m.–7 p.m.;
Sat.: 10 a.m.–6 p.m.; Sun.: 11 a.m.–6 p.m.
MC, V

ABC Carpet has been around for more than 100 years, and what began as a pushcart business now occupies a block-long stores and on two cavernous floors you'll find more than 35,000 rugs. Among the vast assortment are Virginia patchwork, Portuguese needlepoint, Carolina flower, and Victoriana, and these co-exist with Aspen flatweaves, American hooked, Irish cottage, Mexican hand-weaves, Indian hand-knotted, rag rugs, and zebra-patterned examples. But there are also all the standards: Rumanian, Turkish, and Bessarabian kilims; dhurries; and more than 6,000 antique and semi-antique Orientals. Prices are excellent.

ASIA MINOR BASDOGAN
801 Lexington Avenue, near 62nd Street
Second floor

223-2288
Mon.–Fri.: 10 a.m.–6 p.m.; Sat.: 11 a.m.–6 p.m.
AE, MC, V

The main attraction at Asia Minor Basdogan is Turkish flatweaves, and although the gallery occupies a small second-story space, it carries more than 2,000 semi-antique and new carpets. The appealing selection ranges from boldly patterned kilims in bright colors that would complement a modern interior, to paler versions with a Sante Fe look, to the more traditional antique Turkish and Persian varieties. Basdogan also has a large supply of pillows made from new kilims.

BEYOND THE BOSPHORUS
79 Sullivan Street
219-8257
Tues.–Sun.: 12 noon–6 p.m.
AE, MC, V

Ismail Basbag has stocked his tiny sliver of a SoHo shop with a colorful array of Turkish kilims. Most of his rugs are 35 years old, although some are over 100 and made with traditional vegetable dyes, and designs range from bold to subtle, yet all have the rich earth tones characteristic of Turkish carpets. Basbag makes pillows from fragments of damaged carpets and also sells handbags made of kilims.

CENTRAL CARPET
The vast selection of contemporary rugs includes dhurries, kilims, Berbers, Chinese, and handmade Indian Bokharas. (See **Antique and Vintage Carpets and Tapestries,** p. 55.)

CONRAN'S HABITAT
An excellent source for handsome, yet inexpensive rugs of all kinds that include graphic modern designs, along with flokati, wool shag, rag, dhurrie, chenille, cotton samalka, and even grass carpets. (See **Furniture,** p. 267.)

ELIZABETH EAKINS
1053 Lexington Avenue, near 74th Street
Second floor
628-1950
Mon.–Fri.: 11 a.m.–6 p.m.; Sat. by appointment
All major

In Elizabeth Eakins's sunny shop handmade wool, silk, and linen area rugs and runners can be ordered in just about any size and shape. There are unlimited colors to choose from and scores of patterns and designs. Most have a country look, but there are others that are formal and sophisticated. All the rugs are dyed and handwoven in Eakins's New Hampshire mill, and she offers coordinated upholstery fabrics and bed throws, as well as hand-painted ceramic tiles, platters, and bowls.

FURNITURE OF THE TWENTIETH CENTURY

Reissues of thirties classics along with a group of carpets designed by contemporary architects who were inspired by the Art Deco, Art Nouveau, and Russian Constructivist movements; also rugs created by such artists and architects as Roy Lichtenstein, David Hockney, and Matteo Thun. (See **Furniture**, p. 279.)

KAMDIN DESIGNS

791 Lexington Avenue, near 61st Street
Second floor
371-8833
Mon.–Wed., Fri.: 10 a.m.–6 p.m.; Thurs.: 10 a.m.–8 p.m.;
Sat.: noon–5 p.m.
All major

Owner Manjit Kamdin takes pride in her stunning collection of Gobelin-stitch Portuguese petit-point rugs from Madeira, and her Arraiolos carpets in traditional European and contemporary designs. Kamdin also offers chain-stitch rugs and dhurries that can be custom-made to match any color scheme. Recently Kamdin expanded her shop and added a room filled with rare antique and semi-antique European and Oriental rugs. Among her temptations are Aubussons, Savonneries, Serapis, Chinese petit point, Kermans, and Agras.

LA CHAMBRE PERSE

The owners periodically bring in a large shipment of new kilims from around the world. (See **Antique and Vintage Carpets and Tapestries**, p. 58.)

LOVELIA ENTERPRISES

356 East 41st Street
490-0930
By appointment only
No credit cards

Lovelia Albright imports machine-woven cotton Gobelin and wool Aubusson tapestries from Belgium, France, and Italy. Most are reproductions of masterpieces from the fifteenth to the nineteenth centuries and depict classic medieval scenes. Albright also carries a few contemporary tapestries, as well as artists' limited editions and tapestries in upholstery weights.

MABEL'S

A winning array of Preston McAdoo's hand-hooked rugs that are patterned with holsteins, ducks, Canada geese, and dozens of other animals. (See **Gifts**, p. 307.)

MARIAN MILLER

A selection of new Turkish kilims and American rag rugs. (See **Antique and Vintage Carpets and Tapestries**, p. 58.)

THE MUSEUM OF MODERN ART
A group of bold area rugs created by artists Sam Francis, Sol Lewitt, Roy Lichtenstein, and Arata Isozaki. (See **Museum Gift Shops**, p. 406.)

THE RUG TOWER
399 Lafayette Street
677-2525
Mon.–Fri.: 10:30 a.m.–8 p.m.; Sat.: 10 a.m.–6:30 p.m.;
Sun.: 11 a.m.–6 p.m.
AE, MC, V

Veteran Oriental rug purveyors Mike Sheaber and John Memelok opened The Rug Tower in the landmark DeVinne Press building, and they turned their cavernous 11,000-square-foot space into a veritable rug bazaar. Exquisite antique carpets decorate the brick walls, and thousands of handmade Oriental rugs, kilims, and dhurries are neatly stacked by size. Rugs come from every rug-producing country in every possible style, size, and color. There are Art Deco Chinese, pale florals from Tibet, Persian rugs with tribal designs, Turkish kilims, and one of the largest selections of Oriental rugs in the city. The selection of decorative pillows is equally eclectic.

THE RUG WAREHOUSE
Among the huge inventory of contemporary rugs are kilims, dhurries, and Orientals, as well as modern area rugs. (See **Antique and Vintage Carpets and Tapestries**, p. 59.)

SAINT RÉMY
Machine-woven reproductions of medieval tapestries are available as wall hangings, place mats, pillows, and by the yard. (See **Gifts**, p. 309.)

S. CHAPELL
1019 Lexington Avenue, at 73rd Street
744-7872
Mon.–Sat.: 10 a.m.–6 p.m.
AE, MC, V

Sonia Chapell's bright and sunny shop is filled with an exuberant mix of handmade needlepoint rugs from Madeira, along with carpets created by Casa Caiada of Brazil, needlepoint pillows, chair coverings, and exquisite hand-embroidered linens. Her rugs are intricately designed treasures, and come in a range of soft and subtle pastels or deep jewel tones. Chapell also carries hard-to-find Trame kits from Madeira, and a selection of yarns.

China
and Glassware

ANTIQUE

Bergdorf Goodman carries a varied array of antique china and porcelains, along with fine crystal decanters, candlesticks, and bowls. Barneys New York has one of the city's largest collections of Clarice Cliff, Shelley, and Susie Cooper pottery from the twenties and thirties, as well as antique majolica. See also **Furniture, Orientalia,** p. 282.

AGES PAST ANTIQUES
1030 Lexington Avenue, near 73rd Street
628-0725
Mon.–Sat.: 11 a.m.–6 p.m.
AE

Richard Duchano's cozy little shop is packed floor to ceiling with nineteenth-century English pottery and porcelain. Row upon row of Staffordshire jugs, platters, figurines, figures, and commemorative items peer down from his neatly arranged shelves. Blue and white transferware along with lusterware in pink, copper, canary, and silver resist are among Duchano's specialties.

A. R. BROOMER LTD.
Place des Antiquaires
125 East 57th Street
421-9530
Mon.–Sat.: 11 a.m.–6 p.m.
No credit cards

Amanda Broomer and Norman Weiss specialize in ceramics from the seventeenth through the nineteenth centuries, and their attractive gallery is filled with early Chinese pottery, export mandarin bowls, blue and white Oriental porcelain, as well as Dutch delftware. Rounding out the collection is a selection of seventeenth-century European furniture and works of art, along with richly figured tapestries and paintings.

BARDITH LTD.
901 Madison Avenue, near 72nd Street
737-3775
Mon.–Sat.: 11 a.m.–5:30 p.m.; closed Sat. in summer

Bardith
31 East 72nd Street
737-8660
Mon.–Sat.: 11 a.m.–5:30 p.m.; closed Sat. in summer
No credit cards

Even if you're tiny and graceful you'll feel like a bull at Bardith—it's so crammed full of china. Platters, plates, cups and saucers, and jugs in all sizes are stacked on open shelves that reach from the floor to the ceiling. Most of the porcelain and pottery is English and dates from the mid-eighteenth to the nineteenth century. Coalport, creamware, Staffordshire, Minton, Derby, and every other leading porcelain maker is well represented. But there's English glass, hanging glassbell lanterns, and an exquisite collection of papier-mâché trays. The newer and spacious 72nd Street store offers complete china services—many with a country look—by all the legendary old companies, dozens of platters, lots of majolica, along with antique Welsh cupboards, servers, and dining tables.

THE CHINESE PORCELAIN COMPANY
Pedigreed export porcelains from the seventeenth and eighteenth centuries. (See **Furniture**, p. 283.)

EARLE D. VANDEKAR OF KNIGHTSBRIDGE
15 East 57th Street
Second floor
308-2022
Mon.–Fri.: 10 a.m.–5:30 p.m.; Sat.: 10 a.m.–4:30 p.m.
AE

Earle D. Vandekar of Knightsbridge is a well-respected English company with branches in Europe, and it's known as a fine source for seventeenth-century faience and pottery, yet its selection of Chinese exportware and decorative nineteenth-century English porcelain and pottery is equally impressive. On a recent visit, there was a 1755 Chelsea botanical charger, along with early and rare famille rose soup tureens and cornucopia-shaped wall pockets. And the gallery glistens with eighteenth- and nineteenth-century crystal chandeliers. The shop is staffed by experts and this company offers only the best, whether it's a bowl for a hundred dollars or one for many thousands.

FIFTY/50

An ever-changing but fine stock of art glass and ceramics from the fifties and sixties that usually includes a few Venini vases and bowls. (See **Furniture**, p. 256.)

FISHS EDDY

551 Hudson Street
627-3956
Daily: 10 a.m.–11 p.m.
No credit cards

A vest-pocket-size shop, Fishs Eddy (named for a Catskill town) is brimming with some of the most whimsical china in town. New and old dishes from diners in Mississippi share the cluttered space with plates, creamers, bouillon cups, mugs, and monkey dishes from country clubs and country day schools, colleges and academic societies. It's possible to put together a complete set of china embossed with governmental emblems, or take home plates from the Downtown Athletic Club or Washington Irving High. Prices are a delight.

GEM ANTIQUES

1088 Madison Avenue, near 81st Street
535-7399
Mon.–Sat.: 10:30 a.m.–5:30 p.m.
AE, DC, MC, V

Although Gem Antiques is tiny, it's well stocked with European and American ceramics, and houses the city's largest collection of paperweights by Clichy, Saint Louis, Banford, Ayotte, and Baccarat. Art Pottery is a specialty, and there are always at least a dozen one-of-a-kind Rookwood pieces to choose from, along with the works of Grueby, Ohr, Newcomb, Moorcroft, Gouda, and Pilkington. Porcelains by Royal Doulton, Wedgwood, Worcester, and Belleek complete the array.

GUILD ANTIQUES

1095 Madison Avenue, near 82nd Street
472-0830
Mon.–Sat.: 10 a.m.–5 p.m.
V

In this tiny warren of a gallery the china is set out on tables or displayed in antique polished mahogany cabinets just as it might be in an elegant formal home. Chinese export porcelains and English china from the eighteenth and nineteenth centuries are the chief attractions, and Crown Derby, Minton, and Coalport are among the illustrious names. The mostly English furniture is from the eighteenth and early nineteenth centuries.

HUBERT DES FORGES

The colorful array of antique majolica includes asparagus plates, platters, bowls, and tureens. (See **Gifts,** p. 294.)

JAMES ROBINSON

Complete dinner and tea services, from the eighteenth and nineteenth centuries, including the finest from such lofty English companies as Derby, Minton, Spode, Coalport, and Worcester; also a select group of Georgian cut-glass stemware, bowls, and centerpieces. (See **Silver,** p. 440.)

JAMES II GALLERIES

15 East 57th Street
Sixth Floor
355-7040
Mon.–Fri.: 10 a.m.–5:30 p.m.; Sat.: 10:30 a.m.–4:30 p.m.;
closed Sat. in summer
AE, MC, V

James II Galleries is an engagingly eclectic shop and one of my personal favorites. Barbara Munves and her daughter, Julie Seymour (both warm, friendly, and knowledgeable), select each piece they sell, and this accounts for the quality and uniqueness of their treasures. Everything is neatly organized, cleaned, and polished till it shines, and the range and depth of their collection is staggering. Among the china and porcelain treats you'll find Wedgwood drabware, Ridgeway and Mason ironstone, Staffordshire, Spode, and Worcester. There are full dinner services, mostly florals, along with covered vegetable dishes and compotes, dessert sets, even enchanting children's tea sets. Bristol claret jugs, hyacinth vases in jewel tones, cut and clear decanters and jugs, cranberry glass bowls and goblets, rinsing bowls of all kinds, and crystal candlesticks only suggest the myriad glassware you'll find here. And the assortment of Victorian silver-plate is equally as boggling: trays in all sizes (including footed waiters), pitchers, candlesticks, sweetmeat bowls, spoon warmers, glass-lined jam pots, vegetable dishes, and domed meat servers. Especially appealing is the selection of stuffing spoons, soup ladles, berry spoons, and mother-of-pearl-handled fish forks and knives that are pleasantly affordable and make welcome wedding or Christmas gifts. The antique jewelry selection is first-rate and includes cut-steel bracelets and brooches, Scottish agate turks, and Victorian gold pieces. And everywhere you look there are humidors, walking sticks, brass fireplace tools, nutcrackers, and umbrella stands, as well as footstools, painted wood armchairs, screens, mirrors, and Anglo-Indian tables.

KENTSHIRE GALLERIES

Blue-and-white Chinese exportware, Staffordshire and Coalport platters, and majolica plates and asparagus dishes fill the well-stocked shelves, along with a fine assortment of crystal decanters, jugs, and stemware. (See **Furniture,** p. 243.)

67

LEO KAPLAN LTD.

967 Madison Avenue, near 75th Street
249-6766
Mon.–Sat.: 10 a.m.–5:30 p.m.; closed Sat. in summer
AE, MC, V

Leo Kaplan offers four quite different specialties in his spacious gallery, and each is well-organized and attractively displayed. Among the impressive list of eighteenth-century English pottery and porcelain is Staffordshire (including tortoiseshell and glazed and unglazed redware), Wedgwood creamware, first period Worcester, and Prattware in Toby jugs, teapots, and pitchers of all sizes. Paperweights—both antique and contemporary—bear the names of Baccarat, Saint Louis, and Clichy, and the shop carries Art Nouveau glass by Gallé, Daum, and Webb. Finally, there are Russian enamels and porcelains of the Pan-Slavic period, and these include rare Fabergé examples.

LINDA HORN

Dramatic and elaborate majolica centerpieces, bowls, and plates along with crystal pitchers, jugs, and decanters, many with sterling-silver stoppers. (See **Furniture**, p. 251.)

MAISON JEAN-FRANÇOIS

The most complete collection of Quimper in New York. (See **Furniture**, p. 276.)

MALVINA L. SOLOMON

1122 Madison Avenue, near 83rd Street
535-5200
Mon.–Fri.: 11 a.m.–5:30 p.m.; Sat.: 11 a.m.–5 p.m.
AE, MC, V

Although Malvina L. Solomon's windows are cluttered with hundreds of vintage Bakelite brooches, rhinestone earrings, paste and marcasite pins, and Mexican sterling-silver bracelets, once inside this tiny shop you'll discover that American Art Pottery is a specialty here as well. All the important names—Rookwood, Roseville, Fulper, Grueby, Ohr, Newcomb, and Gouda—are represented. An additional surprise is the shop's beguiling collection of antique European hand-painted floral and figurative tiles from the turn of the century through the thirties.

MARVIN KAGAN, INC.

Roman, Byzantine, and Islamic glasses and jugs from the third century B.C. to the eleventh century A.D. (See **Carpets and Tapestries**, p. 58.)

MEISEL-PRIMAVERA

133 Prince Street
254-0137

Tues.–Sat.: 10 a.m.–6 p.m.; closed in August
AE, MC, V

Clarice Cliff's exuberant Art Deco pottery from the thirties and forties lights up this sunny gallery. Dozens of this English artist's biscuit boxes, jugs, teapots, sugar shakers, and bowls crowd the shelves, but Meisel-Primavera also stocks streamlined chrome toasters and irons from the thirties, along with fifties furniture by George Nelson and Italian designers Gio Ponti and Carlo Molino. Castillo's Mexican silver jewelry, and sterling-silver pieces by Georg Jensen, Sam Kramer, and Ed Weiner that date back to the forties and fifties are here as well.

MICHAEL B. WEISBROD, INC.
Porcelains from the neolithic, Ming, and Ch'ing dynasties, along with rare and early Chinese pottery. (See **Furniture,** p. 285.)

MINNA ROSENBLATT
Art Nouveau vases by Daum, Loetz, and Gallé; Steuben perfume bottles; Tiffany opalescent goblets. (See **Furniture,** p. 236.)

MOOD INDIGO
The city's largest supply of FiestaWare, along with Hall china, Russel Wright dinnerware, Depression glass plates and bowls, chrome-topped glass martini shakers, and kitchen glasses from the thirties and forties. (See **Furniture,** p. 256.)

MURRAY HILL ANTIQUE CENTER
The china and glassware is as early as Victorian, as recent as the forties, and there are complete china sets in delicate florals or Art Deco geometrics, along with glassware that ranges from long-stemmed crystal goblets, to cranberry-glass cordials, to kitschy glasses with flamingos. (See **Furniture,** p. 289.)

NIELS BAMBERGER
1070 Madison Avenue, near 80th Street
737-7118
Mon.–Fri.: 9 a.m.–5:30 p.m.
AE, DC, MC, V

Niels Bamberger's old-fashioned shop looks as though it has been around since the turn of the century. It's tiny, dusty, and crammed from floor to ceiling with vintage and new Scandinavian china, sterling-silver animals, and antique Royal Copenhagen porcelains and figurines. Early Flora Danica tureens, bowls, teapots, and dishes share the space with Weinblot's boldly decorative Christmas plates. Bamberger is friendly and knowledgeable, and his prices are good.

NURI FARHADI, INC.

The largest selection of Chinese porcelains in the city. (See **Furniture**, p. 286.)

OLDIES, GOLDIES & MOLDIES

The china and porcelain, stemware and crystal, dates from the 1800s through the 1950s, and you'll find complete china services, cobalt and cranberry-glass goblets, serving pieces, cups and saucers, and old-fashioned sets of kitchen glasses in metal trays. (See **Furniture**, p. 236.)

PRICE GLOVER

An exemplary collection of seventeenth- and eighteenth-century pottery, Delftware, and Chinese export porcelain. (See **Lighting Fixtures**, p. 374.)

QUORUM ANTIQUES

Place des Antiquaires
125 East 57th Street
752-3354
Mon.–Sat.: 11 a.m.–6 p.m.
MC, V

Gary Stradling is a leading authority on American porcelain and pottery, Edward Sheppard is an expert on ceramics and glass, and James Labaugh II and Irving Slavid not only know all about eighteenth-century glass and enamels, they're also well informed on the subject of English Continental and Chinese porcelain. These partners have combined their knowledge, and their gallery is filled with eighteenth- and nineteenth-century blown and molded glass, colorful enamels, as well as American, Continental, and Chinese export porcelains and pottery.

RALPH M. CHAIT GALLERIES

12 East 56th Street
758-0937
Mon.–Sat.: 10 a.m.–5:30 p.m.; closed Sat. in summer
AE, DC, MC, V

A small jewel of a shop, Ralph M. Chait Galleries is the country's oldest source for Chinese treasures, and it offers the finest selection of Chinese porcelains and pottery one is likely to see outside of museums. Neolithic through Tang pottery and Sung through Ch'ing porcelains, famille noire and famille verte pieces from the K'ang Hsi period, blue-and-white porcelains from the Ming dynasty, and the finest examples of Chinese exportware (including plates and bowls with armorial patterns) are among the amazing array. The gallery also has a most unusual collection of China-trade silver from the nineteenth century that are skillful copies of Western styles. These include tea sets, trays, tankards, and tureens. Costly.

R. BROOKE
A colorful stock of antique majolica, along with crystal decanters and jugs. (See **Gifts,** p. 297.)

RUTH BIGEL ANTIQUES
Canton porcelains are a specialty, and there's a fine group of important pieces. (See **Furniture,** p. 230.)

S. J. SHRUBSOLE
A notable selection of Irish and English Georgian glass stemware, decanters, and jugs. (See **Silver,** p. 442.)

SYLVIA TEARSTON ANTIQUES
1053 Third Avenue, near 62nd Street
838-0415
By appointment
No credit cards

Sylvia Tearston, the doyenne of antiques dealers, has crammed her small shop with English, American, and French period furniture, paintings, and prints from the eighteenth and nineteenth centuries. Particularly noteworthy is her selection of porcelain and glass made before 1840—English pottery and porcelains and rare eighteenth-century Chinese exportware. Her shelves offer a colorful profusion of platters, pitchers, dinner plates, teapots, sauce boats, tureens, and figurines.

S. WYLER, INC.
Pedigreed porcelains from the eighteenth and nineteenth centuries by Royal Crown Derby, Minton, Worcester, Coalport, and Spode. (See **Silver,** p. 443.)

CONTEMPORARY

The major department stores have very complete china and glassware departments: Barneys New York, Bergdorf Goodman, and Henri Bendel offer exclusive designs not found elsewhere.

AVVENTURA
463 Amsterdam Avenue, near 82nd Street
769-2510
Mon.–Thurs.: 10:30 a.m.–7 p.m.; Fri.: 10:30 a.m.–4 p.m.;
Sun.: 11 a.m.–6 p.m.; closed Sat.
AE, MC, V

Avventura supplies savvy West Siders with their trendy tablewares. They come to this spacious and sparkling shop for Carlo Moretti barware, stemware, and decanters; Venini bottles; Morano crystal; Alessi cruet sets; and Ricci and Georg Jensen flatware. China, vases, bowls, candlesticks, serving pieces, and coffeepots by all the leading European designers are here as well.

BACCARAT, INC.
625 Madison Avenue, near 58th Street
826-4100
Mon.–Sat.: 10 a.m.–6 p.m.
AE, MC, V

Legendary names in china, silver, and crystal are ensconced in this elegant little jewel of a shop. Baccarat has been recognized as the king of crystal for more than two centuries, and this illustrious house is still richly deserving of its title. Stemware—plain or richly cut, classic or modern—is here in glistening profusion along with barware, vases, decanters, pitchers, and re-creations of the Baccarat Museum Collection. There's Limoges china by Bernardaud, Ceralene, Puiforcat, and A. Raynaud, along with fine silver flatware and hollowware—mostly with an Art Deco look—from Puiforcat and Christofle. Pricey.

CARDEL
621 Madison Avenue, near 58th Street
753-8690
Mon.–Sat.: 9:30 a.m.–6 p.m.
AE, MC, V

Cardel is a favorite with Park Avenue matrons who come to this narrow shop with its sparkling china and crystal displays for their own table-top needs or to select a bridal registry for their daughters. Meissen, Herend, Minton, and Limoges are a few of the grand European houses represented by Cardel, but there's bone china by all the illustrious English companies as well. The gleaming stemware boasts the names of Lalique, Rosenthal, Saint Louis, Stuart, and Val St. Lambert, and the sterling silver flatware is from Old Newbury Crafters. The shop also carries Lalique crystal sculptures.

CERAMICA
182 Hester Street
966-3170
Mon., Tues.: 11 a.m.–6 p.m.; Wed.–Sun.: 11 a.m.–10 p.m.
AE, MC, V

Ceramica is a clone of all the whitewashed pottery stores in Assisi, Italy, and it's filled with an exuberant array of all the plates, pitchers, espresso sets, compotes, platters, and bowls you fell in love with there but just couldn't figure out a way to cart home. Hand-painted ceramics, many decorated with traditional fifteenth-century motifs or centuries-old designs, and reproduction majolica cover every bit of wall space, and they're piled high on shelves, and spill over onto the floor. Since the owners import their wares directly from Italy, prices are excellent.

CONRAN'S HABITAT

The impressive inventory of china and glassware includes everything from reproductions of Victorian favorites to bistro ware; delicate crystal stemware to chunky green glass goblets. (See **Furniture,** p. 267.)

CONTEMPORARY PORCELAIN

105 Sullivan Street
219-2172
Tues.–Sun.: 12 noon–7 p.m.
AE, MC, V

Marek and Lanie Cecula's dark and minimalistic gallery is a showcase for cutting-edge porcelain designs. A number of Marek's creations—his obelisk vases, black-and-white creamer and sugar sets, and inventive rice bowls with chopstick indents—are by now considered classics and are a part of the Museum of Modern Art's permanent collection. In addition to their own innovative work, the Ceculas mount exhibits of porcelains and ceramics done by the leading avant-garde European and American artists, so this tiny shop is a must for those interested in au courant directions in pottery.

DAUM CRISTAL FRANCE

694 Madison Avenue, near 62nd Street
355-2060
Mon.–Sat.: 10 a.m.–6 p.m.
AE, MC, V

Daum Cristal was founded more than a century ago in Nancy, France, and the company's stark steel-gray Madison Avenue boutique offers the entire Daum crystal collection of stemware, barware, and decorative pieces. The shop is accented with cactus plants, and among the displays are Hilton McConnico's seductive crystal pieces adorned with *pâte de verre* cacti. A crystal dish is held by two cacti and these spiky green succulents are used as stoppers for a set of decanters. French furniture designer Philippe Starck has created innovative pieces for Daum, including a table with four glass legs, one of which can be used as a vase. The shop also carries vintage cars in solid crystal, as well as crystal clocks in a variety of geometric forms.

D. F. SANDERS

Cutting-edge Swid-Powell china and glassware, art glass vases, as well as simple restaurant china. (See **Housewares and Hardware,** p. 337.)

ELIZABETH EAKINS

Hand-painted pottery with a country look in the same pastel palette as

73

Eakins rugs includes oversized plates, candlesticks, bowls, and mugs. (See **Carpets and Tapestries,** p. 61.)

FISHS EDDY
New and old dishes from diners, country clubs, colleges, the U.S. Navy, and New York landmarks. (See **Antique and Vintage China and Glassware,** p. 66.)

HOWARD KAPLAN'S FRENCH COUNTRY STORE
China with a French country look. (See **Furniture,** p. 274.)

THE HOYA CRYSTAL GALLERY
450 Park Avenue, near 57th Street
223-6335
Mon.–Sat.: 10 a.m.–6 p.m.; closed Sat. in summer
All major

Hoya is world renowned for its crystal of exceptional purity, brilliance, and clarity, and in the company's tranquil and serenely beautiful Park Avenue gallery it offers both starkly simple and elaborately etched designs. Ten in-house artists (along with Fumio Sasa, Hoya's design leader) have created magnificent crystal art sculptures as well as distinctive functional pieces. Stemware, saki glasses, barware, vases, bowls, clocks, candlesticks, ashtrays, and decanters are among the tempting mix.

LALIQUE
680 Madison Avenue, at 61st Street
355-6550
Mon.–Fri.: 10 a.m.–6 p.m.; Sat.: 10 a.m.–5:30 p.m.
AE, MC, V

Lalique's small and glistening freestanding store showcases this illustrious house's opulent crystal designs. All the important pieces are on display (including "Tosca," a reinterpretation of a twenties Art Deco pattern) and the company's lesser-known works are shown here on a rotating basis. There's stemware and barware, the complete perfume bottle collection, magnificent clocks, and chunky glass rings in regal colors, as well as the company's popular crystal sculptures.

LA TERRINE
1024 Lexington Avenue, at 73rd Street
988-3366
Mon.–Sat.: 10:30 a.m.–6 p.m.
AE, MC, V

Hand-painted Portuguese, Italian, and French faience in appealing patterns with a rustic look fills this sunny shop to overflowing. Pitchers, covered butter dishes, platters in all sizes, espresso cups, vegetable dishes, bowls, and coffeepots are stacked everywhere, and in addition to the clutter of china you see, complete dinner services can be special-ordered.

LE FANION
Pottery from the south of France includes terra-cotta water jugs and vivid green- and red-glazed ceramic café au lait cups, cereal bowls, and chocolate pots. (See **Furniture,** p. 275.)

LS COLLECTION
Hand-blown stemware, white glass decanters from Japan, Murano glass vases, along with ceramic tableware from Italy. (See **Gifts,** p. 306.)

MAYHEW
507 Park Avenue, near 59th Street
759-8120
Mon.–Fri.: 9 a.m.–5 p.m.
No credit cards

Stroll past the oversized porcelain animals that guard the entrance to Mayhew and you'll find the largest assemblage of china in the city. Every important name is ensconced in this large two-level shop that's a virtual china department store. There's Limoges, Haviland, Crown Derby, Royal Doulton, Wedgwood, Ginori, Spode, Royal Worcester, and dozens more. Upstairs are the formal styles, many with gold borders, but downstairs you'll see faience from Italy, Quimper and Longchamp from France, and scores of other patterns with a country look. Mayhew carries silver-plate and stainless flatware, along with stemware by all the most lofty names. And it also stocks an enormous selection of patio and garden furniture in styles that range from Victorian-inspired wicker pieces to wooden porch sets, and from French steel bistro tables to reproduction cast-iron garden chairs.

THE MEDITERRANEAN SHOP
876 Madison Avenue, near 71st Street
879-3120
Mon.–Fri.: 10 a.m.–5:30 p.m.; Sat.: 10 a.m.–5 p.m.; summer, Mon.–Fri.: 10 a.m.–5 p.m.
No credit cards

Delightfully cluttered, this tiny jewel box of a shop is crammed with reproduction eighteenth-century faience hand-painted in France and Italy. There's open stock dinnerware, along with an enticing array of platters, pitchers, *pots-au-crème*, teapots, espresso cups, and sugars and creamers. Hand-embroidered Italian linens are equally tempting, as are the frames and desk accessories covered in Italian papers.

NEW GLASS
345 West Broadway

431-0050
Tues.–Sun.: 12 noon–6 p.m.
AE, MC, V

Art glass is transformed into functional pieces for the home in this handsome gallery. Some are unique one-of-a-kind signed designs by top Scandinavian and European glass artists, others are from a numbered series, still others have been produced in quantity. The shop offers a vivid assortment of brightly colored glass bowls, vases, decanters, stemware, and perfume bottles at a wide range of prices, so this is a fine shop to keep in mind if you're searching for a distinctive gift for family or friends.

ORREFORS CRYSTAL GALLERY
58 East 57th Street
753-3442
Mon.–Fri.: 10 a.m.–6 p.m.; Sat.: 11:30 a.m.–5 p.m.
AE, MC, V

A limited number of Orrefors crystal and stemware designs have been available in New York for many years, but it's only this Swedish firm's sparkling green-marble gallery that stocks the entire collection. One-of-a-kind and limited-edition ornamental pieces co-exist with a superb selection of stemware, bowls, candlesticks, decanters, and vases.

PAVILLON CHRISTOFLE
Limoges china from A. Raynaud, Ceralene, and Haviland, along with crystal stemware from Baccarat and Saint Louis. (See **Silver,** p. 444.)

PLATYPUS
126 Spring Street
219-3919
Mon.–Sat.: 11 a.m.–6 p.m.; Sun.: 12 noon–6 p.m.
AE, MC, V

An eclectic mix of china, glassware, and kitchenware—along with chocolates that can be purchased by the pound—fills Platypus's sunny bi-level shop. Although the interior is high-tech, with stainless-steel shelving, black rubber floors, and white walls, the china has a country look and is hand-painted and colorful. There's earthenware from Italy, China, and France; chunky stemware and glassware; selective kitchenware that includes pasta machines, espresso pots, cutlery, and teapots; small-size rugs; cuddly stuffed platypus toys; vintage pine furniture, and whatever else catches the owners' fancy.

POTTERY BARN
250 West 57th Street
315-1855
Mon.–Fri.: 10 a.m.–8 p.m.; Sat.: 10 a.m.–7 p.m.;
Sun.: 12 noon–6 p.m.

117 East 59th Street
753-5424
Mon.–Wed., Fri., Sat.: 10 a.m.–6:30 p.m.; Thurs.: 10 a.m.–8 p.m.;
Sun.: 12 noon–5 p.m.

231 Tenth Avenue, near 23rd Street
206-8118
Mon.–Fri.: 11 a.m.–7 p.m.; Sat.: 10 a.m.–6:30 p.m.;
Sun.: 12 noon–5 p.m.

51 Greenwich Avenue, near 6th Avenue
807-6321
Mon.–Sat.: 11 a.m.–8 p.m.; Sun.: 12 noon–6 p.m.

700 Broadway, at 4th Street
505-6377
Mon.–Sat.: 11 a.m.–9 p.m.; Sun.: 12 noon–7 p.m.

Pier 17
89 South Street
233-2141
Mon.–Sat.: 10 a.m.–7 p.m.; Sun.: 12 noon–8 p.m.

1451 Second Avenue, at 76th Street
988-4228
Mon.–Fri.: 10 a.m.–7:30 p.m.; Sat.: 10:30 a.m.–6:30 p.m.;
Sun.: 12 noon–6 p.m.

2109 Broadway, near 73rd Street
595-5573
Mon.–Fri.: 10 a.m.–8 p.m.; Sat.: 10 a.m.–7 p.m.; Sun.: 12 noon–6 p.m.

1292 Lexington Avenue, near 87th Street
289-2477
Mon.–Sat.: 10 a.m.–7 p.m.; Sun.: 10 a.m.–5 p.m.
AE, MC, V

Popular and ubiquitous, the Pottery Barn stores offer great value in china and glassware, so they're ideal spots for stocking up on all the essential accessories, and utensils needed for outfitting a new kitchen or sprucing up an old one. They carry everything from formal porcelain dinnerware, to casual earthenware, to sturdy stoneware, not to mention an enormous inventory of stemware and barware both elegant and rustic. Various and sundry kitchen gadgets, candles in a range of colors, cutlery and pots, garbage pails, plastic picture frames, beach chairs, and all manner of cut-to-order shelving complete the inventory.

PRO KITCHEN WARE
4 Bleecker Street, at the Bowery
529-7711
Mon.–Fri.: 9:30 a.m.–5 p.m.
No credit cards

Although Pro Kitchen Ware is a restaurant-supply store, it sells some single items—pots, pans, ladles, cutlery, and flatware—along with multiples of china and glassware. It's an excellent source for durable and moderately priced everyday china, and a good place to stock up on quantities of china and glassware for large-scale entertaining. You'll find such names as Hall and Buffalo, Libby glass, along with stainless steel flatware in classically simple designs. Service is at a minimum, but the range of china and serving pieces available here, and the prices, make it worth a stop.

ROYAL COPENHAGEN PORCELAIN/GEORG JENSEN SILVERSMITHS
683 Madison Avenue, near 61st Street
759-6457
Mon.–Sat.: 9:30 a.m.–5:30 p.m.
AE, MC, V

Designs from these legendary Scandinavian companies are simply displayed in their spacious and spartan gallery. Royal Copenhagen's richly ornate and hand-painted Flora Danica porcelain dinnerware, along with the company's starker patterns, share half the space with the simple elegance of Nissen's beech-wood cheese boards, fondue sets, and salad bowls; Orrefors and Kosta Boda crystal; and Dansk's spare wood pieces. The other half of the store is devoted to Georg Jensen's compelling creations—flatware and hollowware, along with his sterling-silver jewelry and his elegant watches.

SCULLY & SCULLY
All the most wanted names and china patterns are represented in this well-stocked store—Ceraline, Crown Derby, Wedgwood, Staffordshire, and Herend. (See **Gifts,** p. 310.)

SIMON PEARCE
385 Bleecker Street
924-1142
Mon.–Sat.: 11 a.m.–6 p.m.; Sun.: 12 noon–6 p.m.
AE, MC, V

Glass and pottery handmade by the Pearce clan (if an Irish family can be called a clan) is the attraction in this friendly store. All of Simon's glass designs are available here, from his popular chunky goblets to his handsome, one-of-a-kind signed vases and bowls. And there's handmade pottery from the Irish workshops of Simon's father, Philip, and his brother, Stephen. Philip works in red clay dug from the Blackwater River and makes traditional black-and-white tableware. Stephen's classic ceramics are paler—terra-cotta embellished with a white glaze.

SOLANÉE, INC.
138 East 74th Street

Second floor
439-6109
Tues.–Fri.: 10:30 a.m.–5:30 p.m.; Sat.: 11 a.m.–6 p.m.
MC, V

Atelier de Ségriès Moustiers, the world's largest faience producer, has made hand-painted pottery since the seventeenth century, and Solanée is both the company's American wholesale distributor and a retail outlet. In its small and spare second-story shop it offers all of Moustiers's designs: the original ones from the seventeenth and eighteenth centuries, along with the company's more recent patterns that are based on historical roots. Complete dinner sets can be special-ordered, but the shop stocks compote dishes, chocolate pots, sugar shakers, cachepots, and bowls, all with the charm of Provence. There's also bubble glassware from Brittany and linens edged with Battenberg lace.

STEUBEN GLASS
715 Fifth Avenue, at 56th Street
752-1441
Mon.–Sat.: 10 a.m.–6 p.m.
AE, MC, V

For the past forty years every American President has chosen Steuben crystal as a gift of state, and although America's premier glass company is especially known for the remarkable design and craftsmanship of its glass sculptures, its functional pieces are equally extraordinary. And in the company's hushed and tranquil showroom, both are beautifully displayed. Olive and nut dishes, vases, bowls, candlesticks, stemware, and barware are among the elegantly simple designs. Pricey.

STUPELL LTD.
29 East 22nd Street
260-3100
Mon.–Sat.: 10 a.m.–6 p.m.
AE, DC, MC, V

For years the Carole Stupell china shop was a fixture on 57th Street, known for carrying all the famous names in china and crystal, along with the owner's highly idiosyncratic designs—plates in the shape of lobsters and leaves, bowls that looked like acorns. The shop is now run by Carole's son Keith, who recently moved it to roomier quarters downtown, and here he continues to offer fine-quality china, glassware, and silver along with his mother's quirky designs.

THAXTON & COMPANY
780 Madison Avenue, near 66th Street
988-4001

Mon.–Sat.: 10 a.m.–6 p.m.
AE, MC, V

In its tiny, sparkling shop Thaxton & Company offers all the necessary elements for setting a masterful table. Many of the china patterns are designed exclusively for the store, and the wonderful selection of dinnerware ranges from Limoges, to earthy hand-painted ceramics, to lacquered wooden plates in a rainbow of colors. There is gold-etched French crystal stemware, chunky goblets, sterling and vermeil flatware, along with table linens in hand-loomed Irish weaves, hand-painted silks, or sheer linens embossed with embroidery or trapunto. And Thaxton & Company stocks an enticing array of antique tabletop accessories as well.

TIFFANY & COMPANY
On the third floor is the company's extraordinary selection of china by all the top names, along with Tiffany's Private Stock (a line hand-painted in Paris exclusively for the store), and bone, porcelain, and earthenware patterns not available anywhere else. The impressive stock of crystal and glass comes from such famous manufacturers as Brierley, Riedel, and Baccarat and includes barware, stemware, and a mind-boggling inventory of vases, pitchers, bowls, and candlesticks in just about every price range. (See **Jewelry**, p. 358.)

THE VILLAGE CUPBOARD
China with a country look from France, Portugal, Italy, and England, along with chunky hand-blown glassware. (See **Kitchenware**, p. 369.)

VILLEROY & BOCH
974 Madison Avenue, at 76th Street
535-2500
Mon.–Sat.: 10 a.m.–6 p.m.
AE, MC, V

Villeroy & Boch, a family-owned 240-year-old grand china house, has installed every one of its dinnerware patterns in its sunny Madison Avenue duplex. The ubiquitous vitro porcelain Basket Weave pattern (loved by the nouvelle cuisine crowd) is here, along with the Old World bone-china Empress, and Paloma Picasso's seductive designs, but you'll find country florals, Deco-inspired place settings, and stark all-white ones, too. There is crystal stemware in stark modern or gold-etched versions, and Wilkens stainless-steel, silver-plate, and sterling-silver flatware.

WILLIAMS-SONOMA, INC
A colorful stock of pottery and china dishes, bowls, platters, pitchers, and teapots. (See **Kitchenware**, p. 369.)

WOLFMAN GOLD & GOOD COMPANY
116 Greene Street

431-1888
Mon.–Sat.: 11 a.m.–5:45 p.m.; Sun.: 12 noon–5 p.m.
AE, MC, V

Pine shelves, bleached-wood floors, and whitewashed walls give Peri Wolfman's appealing shop a decidedly country look, but the tablewares she carries look just as right in a Park Avenue apartment as in a beach house in the Hamptons. Almost everything here is white, most of it is oversized, and everything in the shop reflects Wolfman's impeccable taste. Many of the platters, dishes, bowls, and pitchers are imported from France and England, but a lot of it is simply American restaurant china. Glassware, too, ranges from sturdy restaurant barware to more elegant crystal. There's a fine selection of antique silver, along with crystal decanters, lace-edged napkins, and lacy paper doilies in all sizes that can double as place mats or place cards. And there are always serendipitous finds, the work of craftspeople Wolfman has discovered, or quirky treasures she's unearthed—architectural birdhouses, vine-covered chandeliers, brushed metal chairs, doll-sized twig furniture, papier-mâché angels, skinny plate stands. Wolfman also stocks fabrics by the yard, and she has lots of lacy whites suitable for curtains, stripes in a range of colors, and luscious prints. This shop is a joy to be in, and a personal favorite.

Chocolates and Candies

B. Altman & Co., Barneys New York, Bergdorf Goodman, Bloomingdale's, Macy's, and Saks Fifth Avenue all have candy departments that offer a wide variety of truffles and chocolates by the pound.

CHOCOLATES BY M
254-2636
AE, MC, V

Maimie Lee and Jane Hsueh use the finest-quality chocolate for their butter crunch and truffles and for hand-dipping caramels, glazed oranges, and fresh strawberries. Although they have closed their retail store their goodies are still available mail order by phone.

ELK CANDY CO., INC.
240 East 86th Street
650-1177
Mon.–Sat.: 9 a.m.–6:30 p.m.; Sun.: 10 a.m.–5:30 p.m.
No credit cards

A disarming marzipan array of tiny pink pigs, yellow ducks, white rabbits, and fruits and vegetables of all kinds fills Elk's eye-catching windows, and for more than forty years Elk has been supplying Yorkville with moist, luscious marzipan that is handmade by European candy makers right in the store. Yet this closet-size shop offers other delights—crackling brittles, turtles, nougats, Florentines, and, at Easter, the best jelly beans around. At Christmastime, in true Old World fashion, Elk is crammed with gingerbread houses and Elisen Lebkuchen.

FIFTH AVENUE CHOCOLATIERE
120 Park Avenue, at 42nd Street
370-5355
Mon.–Fri.: 9:30 a.m.–5 p.m.

575 Fifth Avenue, at 47th Street
867-7320
Mon.–Wed.: 9 a.m.–6 p.m.; Thurs.–Sat.: 9 a.m.–8 p.m.;
Sun.: 10 a.m.–7 p.m.
AE, MC, V

Krön has closed its retail shops, but Krön addicts can take heart; all the Krön favorites are available at the Fifth Avenue Chocolatiere. Fresh and dried fruits dipped in semisweet chocolate; fresh and intense truffles; and, for those who like that sort of thing, telephones, champagne bottles, records, tennis racquets, golf balls, even lady's legs, molded of bittersweet or milk chocolate. The stores also stock a wide selection of imported chocolates by all the top names.

GODIVA CHOCOLATIER
793 Madison Avenue, at 67th Street
249-9444
Mon., Tues., Wed.: 10 a.m.–6 p.m.; Thurs., Fri., Sat.: 10 a.m.–7 p.m.;
Sun.: 12 noon–5 p.m.

701 Fifth Avenue, near 55th Street
593-2845
Mon.–Wed.: 10 a.m.–6 p.m.; Thurs.–Fri.: 10 a.m.–7 p.m.;
Sat.: 12 noon–6 p.m.; Sun.: 12 noon–5 p.m.

560 Lexington Avenue, at 50th Street
980-9810
Mon.–Fri.: 10 a.m.–6 p.m.; Sat.: 11 a.m.–6 p.m.

33 Maiden Lane
809-8990
Mon.–Fri.: 9 a.m.–6 p.m.

85 Broad Street
514-6240
Mon.–Fri.: 9 a.m.–6 p.m.

2 World Financial Center
945-2174
Mon.–Fri.: 10 a.m.–6 p.m.; Sat., Sun.: 12 noon–5 p.m.
AE, MC, V

Godiva's legendary sweets are available in their signature gold box all over the city, but they can be purchased loose (and often fresher) in Godiva's retail stores. These chocolates are velvety, creamy, and beautifully made. The Madison Avenue shop has a small café where weary shoppers can sample Godiva ice cream sundaes or European pastries. Hot chocolate, cappuccino and espresso are also served.

J. WOLSK & COMPANY
81 Ludlow Street

475-7946
Sun.–Thurs.: 8 a.m.–4:30 p.m.; Fri.: 8 a.m.–2 p.m.
No credit cards

J. Wolsk is an old-fashioned company that has been roasting nuts and selling candies since 1938, and the freshness and the quality of the nuts, and Wolsk's prices, are exceptional. Tidy and well-organized, its shelves are filled with a vast and colorful assortment of penny candies, dried fruits of all kinds, boxed and loose chocolates, halvah, and such old-fashioned favorites as jujubes, chocolate babies, Fizzers, and jaw-breakers that are sold by the pound. Although Wolsk is off the beaten track, serious bakers and candy lovers will find a trip here worthwhile.

LE CHOCOLATIER MANON
872 Madison Avenue, near 71st Street
288-8088
Mon.–Sat.: 10 a.m.–6 p.m.
AE, MC, V

A tiny jewel of a shop, Le Chocolatier Manon is filled with exquisite chocolates that are displayed and packaged like gems. Handmade in Belgium from turn-of-the-century molds are bittersweet bouchons filled with *crème fraîche*, gold and silver dragées, tiny gianduja sea horses, sinful truffles, luscious caramels, velvety marzipan, and memorable chocolate pralines.

LI-LAC CHOCOLATES
120 Christopher Street
242-7374
Tues.–Sat.: 10 a.m.–7:45 p.m.; Sun., Mon.: 12 noon–7:45 p.m.
AE, MC

Li-Lac is a Greenwich Village institution that has been turning out chocolates for more than sixty years, and the owners still make them the old-fashioned way—by hand, in small batches, from only the fresh-est ingredients, and with no preservatives. Fabulous fudge, chewy tur-tles, sinful peanut-butter bark, crunchy brittles, and incredible mint patties are among the assorted irresistibles. Even the molds—Empire State buildings, spacemen, and vintage cars—taste good.

MONDEL CHOCOLATES
2913 Broadway, at 114th Street
864-2111
Daily: 11:30 a.m.–6:30 p.m.; hours vary in summer
No credit cards

A warm and friendly neighborhood store, Mondel has supplied Upper West Siders and Columbia University students with homemade choco-lates since 1943. Standouts are the turtles, hand-dipped apricots, and tiny solid chocolate cups flavored with espresso, mint, or kirsch. The fanciful molds of dark chocolate are a delight. Pigs, mice, alligators, cowboys, guitars, skis, tennis rackets, Volkswagens, and Rolls-Royces were among the recent sightings.

NEUCHÂTEL CHOCOLATES
Plaza Hotel
2 West 59th Street
751-7742
Mon.–Sat.: 9 a.m.–9 p.m.; Sun.: 10 a.m.–6 p.m.

1369 Avenue of the Americas, near 55th Street
489-9320
Mon.–Fri.: 9:30 a.m.–7:30 p.m.; Sat.: 10 a.m.–6 p.m.;
Sun.: 11 a.m.–4 p.m.

55 East 52nd Street
759-1388
Mon.–Fri.: 10 a.m.–7 p.m.; Sat.: 12 noon–5 p.m.;
closed Sat. in summer

66 Trinity Place
227-1712
Mon.–Fri.: 10 a.m.–6 p.m.
AE, MC, V

Neuchâtel, named for a town in Switzerland, sells sweets that are prepared in Long Island by a Swiss chocolatier who uses old family recipes and only Swiss chocolates. The resulting product is deliciously fresh, and the rich orange creams, pralines with fruits and nuts, and handmade truffles are true treasures.

PERUGINA
636 Lexington Avenue, at 54th Street
688-2490
Mon.–Sat.: 10 a.m.–6 p.m.
All major

Perugina is available all over the city, but you'll find the largest assortment in the company's own attractive freestanding store. Chocolate Baci, butter creams, pralines, and gianduja come packaged in an array of exciting gift boxes and lovely porcelain bowls.

PLUMBRIDGE
30 East 67th Street
744-6640
Mon.–Fri.: 10:30 a.m.–5 p.m.; in Dec., Sat.: 10:30 a.m.–5 p.m.
All major

The city's oldest confectionary has been around since 1883, and it's still run by the original family, and it still sells its treats to New York's wealthiest families. French mocha nuts, pecans coated with brown sugar and cinnamon, glazed apricots, dragées, and mint chocolates are among the shop's specialties. These can be tucked into Plumbridge's tiny gift boxes that might be topped with a colorful crepepaper parrot, a flower bouquet, or a clown.

ST. MORITZ CHOCOLATIER
506 Madison Avenue, near 52nd Street
486-0265
Mon.–Sat.: 10 a.m.–6 p.m.

200 Liberty Street
945-0445
Mon.–Fri.: 10 a.m.–6 p.m.; Sat., Sun.: 12 noon–5 p.m.

1 World Financial Center
945-0445
Mon.–Fri.: 10 a.m.–6 p.m.; Sat., Sun.: 12 noon–5 p.m.
AE, MC, V

A good measure of St. Moritz's popularity is due to the wide assortment of bittersweet and milk-chocolate corporate logos and molds (tennis rackets, records, baseball bats, and the like) that come boxed in wooden crates. The stores also offer fresh fruits dipped in bittersweet chocolate, double-dipped Oreo cookies, truffles, and a whole range of other sinful delights.

TEUSCHER CHOCOLATES
25 East 61st Street
751-8482
Mon.–Sat.: 10 a.m.–6 p.m.

620 Fifth Avenue, at 50th Street
246-4416
Mon.–Wed., Fri., Sat.: 10 a.m.–6 p.m.; Thurs.: 10 a.m.–7:30 p.m.
AE, MC, V

Teuscher's champagne truffle has been judged by the experts the best truffle in town, but the others (orange, nougat, butter crunch, and cocoa) are prize winners, too. And the rich and creamy filled chocolates—bittersweet-chocolate ganache, luscious orange creams, pralines, and marzipan—are not to be overlooked. The goodies in these jewel-box-size stores are made from natural ingredients and flown in weekly from Switzerland, to ensure freshness, and the packaging (dolls, bunnies, flowers, Santa Clauses, teddy bears) is as enticing as the chocolates.

Clothing

CHILDREN'S CLOTHING
VINTAGE

JEAN HOFFMAN–JANA STARR ANTIQUES
Hidden among all the clutter are frothy christening gowns, lacy bonnets, sweet little cotton dresses for girls, and linen and cotton rompers for boys. (See **Women's Clothing**, p. 87.)

REMINISCENCE
A small group of vintage children's clothing from the forties and fifties—dresses for little girls and shirts, slacks, and jackets for boys. (See **Women's Clothing**, p. 170.)

TROUVAILLE FRANÇAISE
Gossamer christening gowns, fleecy flannel pinafores, darling dotted Swiss dresses, turn-of-the-century buntings, lacy infant caps, and cozy flannel-lined dresses for girls; for boys there are little rompers and vintage French-farmer's shirts. (See **Linens and Quilts**, p. 383.)

CLASSIC

Barneys New York, and Saks Fifth Avenue's children's departments offer very classic, European-styled children's clothing. Barneys Boys Town has very traditionally cut suits, slacks, and shirts for boys.

AU CHAT BOTTÉ

903 Madison Avenue, near 72nd Street
772-7402
Mon.–Sat.: 10 a.m.–6 p.m.
AE

Au Chat Botté's very classic (and very expensive) children's clothing is made of the finest fabrics imported from England and France. Among the assorted irresistibles are delicately smocked dresses, pristine sailor suits, silk party frocks with a Victorian air, frothy christening gowns in silk or cotton, and Christopher Robin spring coats. Clothing sizes range from newborn to size 8 for boys, to size 14 for girls and in addition to clothing, the shop carries a beguiling selection of hand-painted children's furniture from France.

BONPOINT

1269 Madison Avenue, at 91st Street
722-7720
Mon.–Sat.: 10 a.m.–6 p.m.
AE, MC, V

Bonpoint is the New York outpost of a famous French children's clothing store known for its splendid fabrics, matchless workmanship, and enchanting styling. Total outfitters for boys and girls (from newborn to sixteen), Bonpoint carries everything from underwear to shorts, school blazers to suits, party dresses to matching shoes, and it's all made in the company's own ateliers. Dresses are hand-smocked, and only superior cottons, wools, and linens are used to create the very expensive, very classic children's things. Bonpoint also stocks a collection of children's furniture that includes shiny-white cribs, high chairs, and changing tables, along with child-size replicas of antique chairs and settees.

BROOKS BROTHERS

Scaled-down versions of the Brooks Brothers look is available in the Boys' Department where you'll find three-button blazers and suits in glen plaids or solids; wool, poplin, chino, and cotton slacks; button-down oxford-cloth shirts; Fair Isle sweaters; and polo shirts all with a decidedly preppy look. (See **Men's Clothing**, p. 116.)

E. BRAUN & CO.

A charming array of hand-embroidered and smocked baby things that includes dresses, rompers, blouses, and beautiful hand-knit sweaters, all at surprisingly gentle prices. (See **Linens and Quilts**, p. 389.)

THE ELDER CRAFTSMAN

Hand-smocked floral print dresses, adorable hand-knit sweaters (many with animals or country scenes), handmade rompers, robes appliquéd with storybook characters—for children newborn to 10 years old. (See **Handcraft Galleries**, p. 324.)

F. A. O. SCHWARZ

Tucked away in "The Grandma Shop" on the second floor are delicate little cotton suits and dresses in soft pastels, lacy christening dresses and bonnets, cable-knit coveralls, and buttoned rompers for children, newborn to one-year-olds. (See **Toys,** p. 496.)

LA LAYETTE . . . ET PLUS

170 East 61st Street
688-7072
Mon.–Sat: 10:30 a.m.–6 p.m.
AE

The hassle of putting together a layette for her pregnant daughter convinced Vivian Pachter that New Yorkers needed an inviting and soothing spot where mothers—and grandmothers—could select both practical and elegant infant clothing. So Pachter and partner Marion Tarnofsky traveled to Europe and assembled an exquisite collection of stretchies, onezies, day dresses, and receiving blankets, and opened an enticing little shop outfitted with cozy chairs. In addition to their handpicked European finds they carry exclusive American designs for newborns and babies up to one year old, along with custom-made linens for crib or cradle, and silver mugs and rattles. And Pachter and Tarnofsky stock frothy christening gowns, hand-knit sweaters, terry bath towels, embroidered quilts, buntings, and tiny shoes as well. All the infant finery is soft and comforting and made from natural fabrics.

LAURA ASHLEY

Among the children's clothing—as enchanting as an English country garden—are party dresses in tiny florals, chambray pinafores, matching brother and sister sailor outfits, cotton-batiste petticoats with eyelet flounces, and airy sun dresses; for boys and girls six months to twelve years. (See **Women's Clothing,** p. 155.)

MAGIC WINDOWS

1046 Lexington Avenue, near 74th Street
517-7271
Mon.–Fri.: 10 a.m.–6 p.m.; Sat.: 10:30 a.m.–5 p.m.

1186 Madison Avenue, near 86th Street
289-0028
Mon.–Fri.: 10 a.m.–6 p.m. Sat.: 10:30 a.m.–5 p.m.
AE, MC, V

Magic Windows are well-stocked and friendly stores that are known for personalized and monogrammed children's things—everything from "name" sweaters to hooded rain slickers to lace-trimmed cotton panties—but the pleasant surprise is the lovely assortment of traditional children's clothing in sizes newborn to preteen. Brother and sister hand-smocked and -embroidered sailor suits, hand-smocked dresses, button-on romper suits, hand-knit sweaters, and infants' receiving blankets and gowns are all beautifully executed. For older

89

youngsters there are gray flannel blazers and English coats and snow-suits.

MARIMEKKO
Tiny dresses, overalls, and shirts in the same bold prints as the women's clothing. (See **Fabrics and Trimmings,** p. 218.)

NEW YORK EXCHANGE FOR WOMEN'S WORK
Among the handmade baby things that look as if Grandmother had made them are irresistible little sweaters, smocked dresses, bibs, and cotton rompers. (See **Handcraft Galleries,** p. 326.)

POLO/RALPH LAUREN
Clothing for boys ages four through twenty, with the Lauren old-moneyed look: traditional blazers; well-cut sports jackets in wools, linens, and cotton madras; handsome slacks and walking shorts; preppy T-shirts; and classic wool and cotton sweaters. (See **Men's Clothing,** p. 124.)

D. PORTHAULT & CO.
The finest-quality cotton is used for the beautifully smocked dresses and for the tiny rompers, shirts, and hooded terry-cloth robes that come in sizes newborn to 18 months old. (See **Linens and Quilts,** p. 389.)

PRATESI
Winning lace-trimmed wool-challis dresses, hand-smocked dresses, tiny cotton shirts, and darling stretch wool-knit leggings with matching sweaters come in infant sizes; for girls up to six years old, Pratesi carries adorable cotton dresses and blouses. (See **Linens and Quilts,** p. 382.)

SPRING FLOWERS
1710 First Avenue, near 88th Street
876-0469
Mon.–Sat.: 10 a.m.–6 p.m.

410 Columbus Avenue, near 79th Street
721-2337
Daily: 11 a.m.–6 p.m.
AE, MC, V

Spacious and comfortable with an Old World feeling, Spring Flowers is filled with lacy confirmation and romantic party dresses, beautifully made French and Italian creations, classic English coats, and sportswear by HangTen, Marèse, Tartine et Chocolat. The more fashion-forward youngster will find sporty European separates, and the private school crowd complete school uniforms. But these shops also stock everything else the well-dressed infant or preteen may need—hats, scarfs, shoes, and all the accessories.

CONTEMPORARY

All the department stores have very complete, well-stocked children's clothing departments; Kidz at Bendels offers a collection that manages to look trendy and classic at the same time.

AGNÈS B.
Leggings, snap-front cardigans, and classic striped T-shirts in infant and kiddie sizes. (See **Women's Clothing,** p. 159.)

BÉBÉ THOMPSON
98 Thompson Street
925-1122
Daily: 12 noon–7 p.m.
AE, MC, V

Bébé Thompson is owned by Yasmine, a successful model, and she has filled her attractive, vest-pocket-size shop with an eclectic mix of clothing to fit infants to seven-year-olds. She offers black jogging pants, splashy cotton jumpsuits, skinny leggings, and leopard-print shoes for the cutting-edge set; Balinese batik tops and pants for lovers of the ethnic look; and for classic tots, hand-embroidered shifts, French rompers, hand-knit sweaters, and lacy, hand-embroidered christening gowns. Yasmine also stocks the complete Petit Faune and Claude Vell lines. From moderate to expensive.

BENETTON 012
1162 Madison Avenue, near 85th Street
879-7690
Mon.–Sat.: 10 a.m.–5:45 p.m.; Sun.: 12 noon–5 p.m.

996 Lexington Avenue, near 72nd Street
879-3735
Mon.–Sat.: 10 a.m.–6 p.m.

601 Fifth Avenue, near 48th Street
879-3735
Mon.–Sat.: 10 a.m.–6 p.m.
AE, MC, V

The 012 Benetton stores carry only children's things, and all the shelves and displays are at child level so the bright candy-colored separates are completely accessible to the young shopper. Innovative stripes and an occasional cartoon motif decorate T-shirts, sweatshirts, shorts, slacks, sweaters, and miniskirts, and everything in these stores is designed to be mixed and matched and layered. Fabrics are natural, the look is spare and casual, and it's all for children ages two to teenage. Pleasantly affordable.

BEN'S FOR KIDS

Casual separates for infants and tots; layettes for newborns, stretchy one-piece outfits, cotton playsuits in sizes 0 to toddler 4. (See **Furniture**, p. 264.)

BEN'S UP AND UP

1335 Third Avenue, near 76th Street
744-2520
Mon.–Fri.: 10 a.m.–6 p.m.; Sat.: 11 a.m.–6 p.m.
AE, MC, V

Bright and colorful, Ben's Up and Up carries a broader range of children's clothing than Ben's for Kids, the parent store, can manage to cram into its cluttered space. This shop is brimful of casual separates by all the most wanted names, along with an appealing array of pretty party dresses, blazers, and wool pants (for youngsters newborn to eight years old).

BOY OH BOY

18 East 17th Street
463-8250
Mon.–Fri.: 11 a.m.–6:30 p.m.; Sat.: 11 a.m.–5 p.m.
AE, MC, V

It was her personal life that led Anne Merkin to open Boy Oh Boy. When her son turned ten, Merkin suddenly found it difficult to find attractive clothing for him. So she and her sister, Mary Johnston, opened a store devoted to boys. Although there are things here for toddlers, the store shines in its selection of jackets, pants, shirts, and sweaters for pre-teeners. Among the designs from America, France, England, and Austria are those of Kid Boxer, Christian Dior, Petit Boy, Kite Strings, Basic Elements, Maser, and Gotcha. Even the toys—snakes, alligators, dinosaurs, and magic tricks—have boy appeal.

THE CAMP SHOP

41 West 54th Street
505-0980
Mon.–Fri.: 9 a.m.–5 p.m.; March–June: Sat.: 9 a.m.–4 p.m.; closed in February
No credit cards

Three generations of Kamers have outfitted New York youngsters for private schools and camps. This is the Kamers's only business, and they stock a full selection of school uniforms, riding outfits, and footwear, and they offer everything a child or camp counselor needs for camp, including blankets and name-taping.

CELANDRA

1226 Madison Avenue, near 88th Street
410-3340

Mon.–Sat.: 10 a.m.–6 p.m.; Sun.: 12 noon–5 p.m.
AE, MC, V

Preteens and junior misses come to Celandra for party or Communion dresses, and in addition to an attractive stock of silk, moiré, cotton, and knit imports from Italy, France, and Israel, the owners will design and custom-make special party frocks. For those important occasions for young men, the store carries Italian suits in a variety of fabrics. But Celandra also offers sporty separates and swimsuits for infants through teenagers, and although the dressy things are costly, the sportswear is moderately priced.

CERUTTI

807 Madison Avenue, near 67th Street
737-7540
Mon.–Sat.: 9 a.m.–5:30 p.m.
AE, MC, V

Cerutti is a popular shop with Upper East Side mothers, who love it for its wide range of styles. They know they'll find traditional and classic European looks as well as sporty American ones. There are always dozens of party dresses—everything from delicately smocked, Empire-waist floral-printed cottons, to royal-looking velvets with lacy collars—and Cerutti will handle custom-made designs. Casual separates and swimwear along with jeweled jean jackets and miniskirts also fill the racks. The choice for boys is just as eclectic and includes hand-embroidered button-on rompers, traditional suits, and jazzy leather bomber jackets. And the store carries a full stock of petticoats and crinolines, tights and socks, and underwear. Prices are as varied as the styles, and though party dresses can go into the hundreds, much of the clothing (for newborns to teenagers) is reasonably priced.

THE CHOCOLATE SOUP

946 Madison Avenue, near 75th Street
861-2210
Mon.–Sat.: 10 a.m.–6 p.m.; Sun.: 1 p.m.–6 p.m.
AE, MC, V

A warm and friendly shop, the Chocolate Soup is stuffed from floor to ceiling with whimsical delights. Cotton T-shirts and leggings come in every conceivable color, OshKosh overalls sport hand-painted scenes, tiny vests are a patchwork of fabrics, animals adorn hand-knit sweaters, and there are flowers, hearts, and cartoon characters printed, embroidered, or hand-painted on just about everything else. Hand-smocked Liberty of London dresses are surprisingly affordable, and the shop carries tiny and colorful Hawaiian shirts, funky jewelry, and lots of small and inexpensive toys that are perfect as stocking stuffers or party favors. And, of course, the store still stocks the classic Danish school bag that was once exclusively sold here. (For newborns to twelve-year-olds; prices range from inexpensive to costly.)

CHOU-CHOU
1351 Third Avenue, at 77th Street
249-8899
Mon.–Sat.: 10:30 a.m.–6:30 p.m.
AE, MC, V

Joyce Letterman was charmed by the funky look and gentle prices of
California designer Malina's children's clothing, so she opened a shop
devoted to Malina's things. Patterns are Malina's forte and she does
pinstripes, squares, polka dots, checks, and tiny flowers in the softest
cottons and rayons. Her slacks, shirts, skirts, dresses, and jumper suits
are meant to be mixed and matched and layered. There are suspenders
and velvet or canvas shoes, too, and everything fits youngsters newborn to six years old.

CHRISTIAN DE CASTELNAU
Playful cotton knit separates for children, infant through preteens. (See
Women's Clothing, p. 166.)

CITYKIDS
130 Seventh Avenue, near 18th Street
620-0906
Mon.–Sat.: 10 a.m.–6 p.m.
AE, MC, V

The colors are upbeat, the styling adventuresome, and everything in
this attractive store is neatly organized. Domestic and imported clothing geared more to play than to partying includes such popular names
as Petit Boy, Jean Bourget, and Creation Stummer, along with City-
kids's own line and the fashions of neighborhood designers. T-shirts
(many hand-printed), overalls, rompers, pants, swimsuits, skirts, and
jackets (in sizes newborn to 10) are among the tempting mix. There's an
irresistible group of children's sneakers and casual shoes, as well as a
nicely edited selection of books, stuffed animals, toys, and small and
inexpensive party favors and stocking stuffers.

THE COCKPIT
Authentic-looking but newly manufactured military garb—bomber jackets, parachute pants, R. A. F. sweaters, and Flying Tiger khakis—in
children's sizes. (See **Men's Clothing,** p. 132.)

DINOSAUR HILL
302 East 9th Street
473-5850
Daily: 12 noon–7 p.m.
AE, MC, V

Dinosaur Hill offers offbeat finds for youngsters six months to six years
old. Much of the stock is gathered from around the world or created by
neighborhood designers. Embroidered angel pinafores and colorful

straw hats are imported from Mexico; bright appliquéd vests come from China; vivid striped-cotton shirts, overalls, and skirts from Guatemala; and hand-knit sweaters from Ecuador. Local artists supply the hand-painted T-shirts, lovable hats, and boldly printed separates. In addition to the clothing, Dinosaur Hill is crammed with an enticing assortment of old-fashioned toys, such as clay whistles and glass marbles, wind-up animals, and tiny wooden cars and trucks. Prices are excellent.

FIORUCCI

The children's clothing manages to look trendy and retro at the same time; dresses, rompers, pants, and shirts are made from the same zany prints as the grown-up fashions. (See **Men's Clothing**, p. 133.)

FUSEN USAGI

138 East 74th Street
772-6180
Mon.–Sat.: 10 a.m.–6 p.m.
All major

The wonderfully wearable cotton clothing at Fusen Usagi is from Japan and it's both ultrasimple and terribly chic. Much of it comes in sophisti-cated prints in such nontraditional children's colors as black and gray. Layettes for newborns are a specialty, but there's a delightful line of stretchy sleepwear, as well as overalls and T-shirts for youngsters up to age seven. Accessories—high-fashion canvas shoes, belts, and suspenders—are irresistible and prices are moderate. Ensconced on the second floor of this duplex shop is infant furniture from France and Italy: canopied cribs, chests of drawers, changing tables, child-size chairs and tables, strollers, and carriages.

GAP KIDS

1164 Madison Avenue, at 86th Street
517–5202
Mon.–Sat.: 10 a.m.–7 p.m.; Sun.: 12 noon–6 p.m.

215 Columbus Avenue, at 70th Street
874-3740
Mon.–Thurs.: 10 a.m.–8 p.m.; Fri.–Sat.: 10 a.m.–9 p.m.; Sun.: 10 a.m.–8 p.m.

250 West 57th Street
956-3142
Mon.–Fri.: 10 a.m.–8 p.m.; Sat.: 10 a.m.–7 p.m.; Sun.: 12 noon–5 p.m.

133 Second Avenue, at St. Marks Place
473-8835
Mon.–Sat.: 10 a.m.–9 p.m.; Sun.: 10 a.m.–8 p.m.

354 Sixth Avenue, at Washington Place
777-2420
Mon.–Sat.: 10 a.m.–9 p.m.; Sun.: 12 noon–7 p.m.
AE, MC, V

Everything about Gap Kids is clean, tidy, and appealing. You'll find all the Gap favorites—jean jackets, cotton camp shorts, three-button polo shirts, cotton sweaters, buffalo-plaid flannel shirts, miniskirts, high-top sneakers, leather hiking boots, and chinos—scaled-down to kiddie size. It's a great all-American look for the sandbox and preteen set (sizes 2 to 14), and prices are excellent.

GRANNY MADE

The classic Granny Made cable-knit sweaters come in children's sizes, and there are tiny ski caps hand-knit by Granny herself, cotton playsuits from Sweden, hand-loomed animal hats from Vermont, and cotton-knit overalls and shirts from Brazil. (See **Sweaters,** p. 144.)

GREENSTONE & CIE

442 Columbus Avenue, near 81st Street
580-4322
Mon.–Sat.: 11 a.m.–7 p.m.
AE, MC, V

Greenstone & Cie imports more than seventy high-fashioned children's labels from Italy, England, and France, as well as carrying most of the popular domestic lines. Pint-sized leather bomber jackets, separates in fluorescent colors, hand-knit sweaters, Liberty of London pinafores, party dresses, the latest swimwear looks, along with lots of khaki and denim will please toddlers and preteens whose passion is fashion. Sneakers, canvas shoes, and boots, and in winter a fine skiwear selection complete the stock.

THE HIRED HAND

1324 Lexington Avenue, near 88th Street
722-1355
Mon.–Fri.: 10 a.m.–6:30 p.m.; Sat.: 10 a.m.–6 p.m.; Sun.: 11:30 a.m.–5 p.m.
AE, MC, V

The Hired Hand is bright and cheery, and filled with unusual American-made clothing and toys for children, newborn to age seven. Hand-smocked, provincial-print dresses come from South Carolina; boldly patterned acrylic sweaters are from Maine; striped overalls from Osh-Kosh in Wisconsin; and comfortable baggy rompers from California. There are soft cuddly animals, lots of personalized things, handmade wooden trucks and cars, and charming handmade patchwork crib quilts. Prices are moderate.

JUDY CORMAN

198 Columbus Avenue, near 68th Street
496-9315
Mon.–Sat.: 11 a.m.–7 p.m.; Sun.: 12 noon–6 p.m.
AE, MC, V

Judy Corman opened a shop in the Hamptons a few years ago, and she quickly became known for her lovable hand-painted sundresses and T-shirts. She now has a tiny New York branch, and it's crammed with her hand-painted things, along with a full range of children's wear for youngsters newborn to eight years old. There are casual separates for boys and girls, as well as school and party clothes. Prices are moderate.

KIDO
208 Columbus Avenue, near 69th Street
787-6564
Mon.–Sat.: 11 a.m.–8 p.m.; Sun.: 12 noon–6 p.m.
AE, DC, MC, V

Kido's high-fashion children's sportswear is made in Japan for the American market, and almost everything comes in vivid colors splashed with geometrics, letters, or numbers, and in natural fabrics—cotton, flannel, and wool. The store carries bright patent-leather belts, suspenders, hats, sunglasses, and wildly patterned socks, too. For boys and girls six months to seven years old.

KIDS, KIDS, KIDS
436 Sixth Avenue, near 9th Street
533-3523
Mon.–Fri.: 11 a.m.–6:30 p.m.: Sat.: 11 a.m.–6 p.m.
AE, MC, V

La Petite Fleur's crossword-puzzle shorts and matching pullover, and Cynthia Finch's cropped tops and shorts dotted with colorful buttons are some of the playful styles you're likely to find in this friendly shop. The fashions and accessories (for infants to seven-year-olds) are casual and fun, the colors vivid or sophisticated with lots of black, and prices are not outrageous for such high-fashion looks.

KINDERSPORT OF ASPEN
1260 Madison Avenue, near 90th Street
534-5600
Mon.–Sat.: 10 a.m.–6 p.m.
AE, MC, V

Budding downhill racers will find serious skiwear at Kindersport. A New York branch of an Aspen store, it carries down jackets, ski pants, jumpsuits, sweaters, hats, and gloves from the top European and American manufacturers for children two to fourteen years old. Summertime there's an appealing selection of swimwear, along with cotton shorts, dresses, shirts, and overalls. The staff is obliging and very knowledgeable.

MIMI LOVERDE

Loverde's cotton-dyed separates—T-shirts, skinny leggings, pinafores, miniskirts—come in kiddie sizes and in a rainbow of colors. (See **Women's Clothing**, p. 169.)

MONKEY BUSINESS

506 Amsterdam Avenue, near 84th Street
873-2673
Mon.–Sat.: 11 a.m.–7 p.m.; Sun. 12 noon–6 p.m.;
closed Sun. in summer
AE, MC, V

Alyssa Bell carefully hand picks everything she sells, and she offers an enticing mix of classic and funky children's wear in her tidy and well-organized store. The open design makes sizes easy to find and there's a separate area for infant wear and baby gifts. Mousefeathers, Malina, Monkey Wear, and No Kidding are some of the designers Bell carries in sizes newborn to seven. Handpainted crib quilts, books, and a well-chosen assortment of playthings complete the stock.

OLÉ ÈLO

122 West 72nd Street
877-4672
Mon.–Sat.: 10:30 a.m.–7 p.m.; Sun.: 12 noon–6 p.m.
AE, MC, V

Olé Èlo carries fashions for children of all ages and their moms from Oilily, a Dutch company, and the splashy interior is the perfect setting for the bouncy clothing. There's a windmill (the Dutch connection), a neon-yellow tube for kids to crawl through, and a tiny pedal car for them to drive. Shapes are loose and comfortable, the colors bold, and the combinations endearing. Although the line is pricey, everything has been designed to be worn for years: Pants are meant to be rolled, tops are oversize, dresses are long, and coats are lined to span the season.

PEANUT BUTTER & JANE

617 Hudson Street
620-7952
Mon.–Sat.: 10:30 a.m.–7:30 p.m.; Sun.: 12 noon–5 p.m.

138 Duane Street
619-2324
Mon.–Sat.: 10:30 a.m.–6:30 p.m.
AE, MC, V

Although Carolyn Capstick's original store on Hudson Street is small and unbelievably cluttered, her newer location on Duane is tidy and spacious, and in both shops she stocks one-of-a-kind cotton clothing for children newborn to preteen that runs the gamut from the traditional to the practical, to the fashionable, to the downright wacky. Sweet hand-smocked dresses share the space with the high-fashion looks of Petite Bateaux and Petit Boy and the funky ones of neighborhood artists. Capstick carries sporty separates ideal for school or play, practical coveralls, along with an array of casual shoes that might include tiny cowboy boots, leopard sandals, brightly patterned high-top sneakers, and candy-colored plastic jellies. There are educational toys and books, too, and prices are moderate.

PUSHBOTTOM FOR KIDS
252 East 62nd Street
888-3336
Mon.–Sat.: 11:30 a.m.–6:30 p.m.
AE, MC, V

Pushbottom for Kids offers the same hand-loomed cotton sweaters that are staples in the wardrobes of the well-put-together, scaled down to fit newborns to seven-year-olds. The sweaters come in crewneck or cardigan styles and in bouncy colors, but this tiny store also stocks matching slacks, skirts, and shorts, as well as bright cotton shirts and jumpers.

ROBIN'S NEST
1397 Second Avenue, near 73rd Street
737-2004
Mon.–Sat.: 10 a.m.–6 p.m.
AE, MC, V

Tiny and unbelievably cluttered, Robin's Nest is crammed from floor to ceiling with stylish children's things. All the fashionable European and domestic names—Naf Naf, Trotinette, Mousefeathers, Clayeaux—are represented, and there's a complete stock of party, school, and casual clothing for children, newborn to eight years old, in a wide range of prices.

SPACE KIDDETS
46 East 21st Street
420-9878
Mon., Tues., Thurs., Fri.: 10:30 a.m.–6 p.m.;
Wed.: 10:30 a.m.–7 p.m.; Sat.: 11:30 a.m.–5:30 p.m.
No credit cards

Cynthia Radocy and Judith McCabe were considered pioneers when they first opened their children's shop on 21st Street in what was then an unlikely retail neighborhood in the shadow of the Flatiron Building. But eight years later the neighborhood is now hot and they're still going strong. Originally they were known for clothing with a retro look: little boy's cardigans and pants inspired by Fred Astaire movies, girls' dresses in the fabrics of the forties. Although some of their clothing for youngsters newborn to ten years old is still vintage or recalls old movies, much of it is now funky (polka dot shoes, neon suspenders, jazzy ties) or a

99

bit more mainstream. It's a pleasant, spacious shop with ample room for strollers, and a staff who actually seems to enjoy the company of children.

SWANTJE-ELKE LTD.
1031 Lexington Avenue, near 73rd Street
570-1075
Mon.–Fri.: 10 a.m.–6 p.m.; Sat.: 10 a.m.–5 p.m.
AE, DC, MC, V

Swantje-Elke is a vest-pocket-size shop stocked with what well may be the city's most costly girls' clothing. Christening gowns are frothy confections, and couture party dresses, handmade of exquisite fabrics, are small fantasies, and just about everything is European one-of-a-kind and exclusive to the store. There are precious day gowns and hand-knit sweaters for infants, as well as a smattering of more practical, and less costly, sports separates for girls as old as twelve.

TIM'S
878 Madison Avenue, near 71st Street
535-2262
Mon.–Sat.: 10 a.m.–6 p.m.
AE, DC, MC, V

Sophisticated young blades ages two to twenty will find styles to their liking in this two-level shop that carries everything from Spencer tuxedos and wing-collared shirts, to traditional double-breasted suits, to prep-school blazers, gray flannel shorts, and club ties. For the less fashion-minded there are cotton and wool sweaters in pales and brights, leather outerwear, plaid shirts, raincoats, baseball jackets, Loden coats, and some wonderful bathing trunks. From moderate to pricey.

TYKE-OONS
858 Lexington Avenue, near 64th Street
517-2011
Mon.–Fri.: 10:30 a.m.–6:30 p.m.; Sat.: 11 a.m.–5 p.m.
AE, MC, V

The imaginative stock of European, Canadian, and American children's wear is cleverly organized in cubbyholes by sizes (0 to 8), and this well-laid-out shop has tiny tables where little ones can sit and color while Mommy shops. Dresses are hand-smocked or lacy and romantic; separates (by such top names as Babymine, Creation Stummer, and Patchagogo) lean toward the funky and trendy; and the hand-knit sweaters are top-notch. Educational wall hangings, books, and soft and cuddly stuffed animals, too. Moderate to pricey.

WICKER GARDEN'S CHILDREN
1327 Madison Avenue, near 93rd Street

410-7001
Mon.–Sat.: 10 a.m.–5:30 p.m.
AE, MC, V

Green-and-white trellised, Wicker Garden's Children is an amazingly well-stocked store filled with everything from layettes, to frilly ballet-length silk dresses, to practical school clothes, to sturdy play clothes, and there's a surprisingly in-depth selection of each. Styles range from classic sailor suits and hand-smocked dresses to trendy separates and come in sizes to fit infants to ten-year-olds. This large two-level empo-rium has a complete underwear and accessories department and a shoe section staffed by experts and filled with classic school shoes, updated Mary Janes, funky sneakers, and practical rain and snow boots. From moderate to very expensive.

YOUNG AMERICANS FOR KIDS
1503 First Avenue, near 78th Street
517-4554
Mon., Fri.: 11 a.m.–6 p.m.; Tues., Wed., Thurs.: 10:30 a.m.–7:30 p.m.;
Sat.: 11 a.m.–6 p.m.
AE, MC, V

Although Young Americans for Kids is not much bigger than a closet, it offers a well-chosen selection of attractive clothing, toys, and accesso-ries for youngsters newborn to preteen. The shop's own line of boldly patterned European sweaters is a specialty, but there are lovely chris-tening gowns, lacy caps, classic button-up romper suits, and colorful sports separates. Don't miss the appealing selection of infant gifts that includes silver mugs, spoons, brushes, frames, and rattles; the delight-ful children's clocks; and the cuddly-soft stuffed animals.

COSTUMES
VINTAGE

See **Men's** and **Women's Clothing, Antique and Vintage.**

GENE LONDON'S STUDIO
106 East 19th Street
Ninth floor
533-4105
By appointment
No credit cards

Costumers for movies and the theater have come to Gene London's Studio for years, but London also rents his magnificent collection of antique and vintage clothing to private individuals. He has exquisite wedding gowns (Victorian whites and others from the thirties and forties) and opulent ball gowns, along with elegant Edwardian finery, as well as Fred Astaire type classics from the twenties and thirties for men. Once a year, in December, London has a month-long sale.

CONTEMPORARY

ABRACADABRA
10 Christopher Street
627-5745
Mon.–Sat.: 11 a.m.–9 p.m.
AE, MC, V

Abracadabra stocks the largest selection of costumes for adults in the city. Magnificent American Indians in full feather, English bobbies, Dracula, Santa Claus, animals of every species, and cartoon characters are among the fantasy dress-ups that can be purchased or rented. The collection of hats includes everything from Lord Nelson's admiral's hat to World War I helmets, and Abracadabra carries masks, wigs, and makeup, along with knives and magic tricks.

ANIMAL OUTFITS FOR PEOPLE COMPANY
2255 Broadway, at 81st Street
Third floor
877-5085
Mon.–Fri.: 12 noon–6 p.m.; Sat., Sun.: by appointment
No credit cards

Animal Outfits for People is affiliated with the famed Doherty Costume Studios, and it will custom-make an incredible range of imaginative costumes for adults. If you wish to appear as an eggplant, carrot, green pepper, kiwi, or pear, any animal real or imaginary, any personality, famous or infamous, the talented crew can create a costume for you. Expect to pay a lot, there's little here for under $100, but the company does rentals, too.

FORBIDDEN PLANET
At Halloween the stores carry an amusing assortment of Latex masks, everything from fright ones (Dracula, vampires, and hairy apes), to silly ones (pink pigs and fat ladies in hair curlers), to space age varieties (robots and creatures from outer space). (See **Books, Science Fiction,** p. 46.)

GORDON NOVELTY COMPANY
933 Broadway, at 22nd Street
254-8616
Mon.–Fri.: 9 a.m.–4:30 p.m.
No credit cards

Robert Gordon, the present owner of this 65-year-old company, claims to have the largest selection of costumes and masks in the city and, indeed, he offers everything from werewolves and political figures to barnyard animals and English bobbies. Gordon stocks over 500 hats, including space helmets and Napoleonic bicornes; and wigs that range from dreadlocks to a Lady Pompadour do. And the range of accessories is as eclectic. He has tomahawks, tiaras, fangs, Roman shields, hula skirts, swords, and funny noses.

I. BUSS UNIFORM COMPANY/ALLAN UNIFORM RENTAL SERVICE
112 East 23rd Street
529-4655
Mon.–Fri.: 9 a.m.–5 p.m.; Sat.: 11 a.m.–3 p.m.
AE, MC, V

I. Buss Uniform Company no longer sells the military surplus that made it a favorite with the East Village crowd. It now offers only uniforms— police, fireman, and doorman—and a large selection of costumes that can be rented at Halloween or year round. You'll find the standards— Santa Claus, animals of all kinds, police, and theatrical characters—in a full range of adult sizes.

LOVE SAVES THE DAY
At Halloween there are costumes, masks, and witches' hats, but the twenties gowns and fifties tulle prom dresses are ideal for costume parties year round. (See **Women's Clothing**, p. 149.)

YOUTH AT PLAY
A pleasing assortment of traditional children's costumes: bridal gowns, good fairies, ballerinas, witches, and black cats. (See **Toys**, p. 500.)

FURS

All the major department stores have well-stocked fur departments; Bergdorf Goodman carries the designs of Galanos, Gianfranco Ferré, Giuliana Teso, and Geoffrey Beene; Fendi Furs are at Henri Bendel; and

Revillon, with its sumptuous fur fashions by Karl Lagerfeld, Massimo Tabak, Isaac Misrahi, and other top designers, is at Saks Fifth Avenue.

ANTONOVICH

333 Seventh Avenue, at 29th Street
Second floor
244-3161
Mon.–Fri.: 9 a.m.–7 p.m.; Sat., Sun.: 9 a.m.–6 p.m.

1345 Sixth Avenue, at 54th Street
956-4400
Mon.–Sat.: 10 a.m.–9 p.m.; Sun.: 10 a.m.–6 p.m.
All major

Antonovich has been around for twenty years, and this company is a favorite with career women who are buying a fur coat as a luxurious gift for themselves. It's the world's largest manufacturer and seller of Blackglama mink, and in its huge showrooms that famed fur is made up into coats and jackets in all the popular styles, but there's a vast selection of other furs as well. You'll find blue, red, silver, and crystal fox; beaver and raccoon; Canadian lynx; and lots more. Prices are good, but skins may be of only ordinary quality.

BEN KAHN SALON

150 West 30th Street
Eighteenth floor
279-0633
Mon.–Fri.: 9 a.m.–5 p.m.; Sat.: 9 a.m.–2 p.m.
AE

Ben Kahn is America's oldest fur manufacturer, and it's known for its top-quality skins and for minks and sables worked into very classic and elegant styles. Yet in its sedate and sober showroom that caters to traditionalists, you'll find younger looks, too—a baum marten trench-coat with big patch pockets and notched lapels, and Koos van den Akker's casual ways with fur. Everything at Ben Kahn's is first-rate and expensive.

BEN THYLAN FUR DESIGNERS GROUP

150 West 30th Street
Eighteenth floor
753-7700
Mon.–Fri.: 9 a.m.–5 p.m.; Sat. 9 a.m.–2 p.m.
AE, MC, V

The furs at this couture furrier reflect the designs of Ben and Bernice Thylan and their associates Ritter Brothers, Alfred Rainer, Georges Kaplan, Irene Spierer, and J. Diamond, all honored names in American fur fashion. Classic and uncluttered styles in a wide variety of furs are the main attraction, but they're tempered by young and sporty looks, too, as well as fur coats for men, and fur-lined raincoats for both men and women in a choice of furs.

BIRGER CHRISTENSEN
150 West 30th Street
947-7910
By appointment only
No credit cards

Considered the prince of furriers—by appointment to both the Danish and Swedish courts, and to Her Majesty the Queen of Greece—Birger Christensen has collected some of the world's top designers under its prestigious wings. This famed Scandinavian company offers Claude Montana's dramatic looks, Donna Karan's showstoppers, Marc Jacobs's classics, and Vicky Tiel's formal furs. Since the look at Birger Christensen is young and trendy, you'll find parkas with drawstring waists, sheared furs in forest colors, lean mink duffel coats, caramel-colored sheared mink, kolinsky, and squirrel. But Birger Christensen also has a full complement of mink, Russian sable, Persian lamb, and silver fox worked in traditional ways.

CHRISTIE BROS.
333 Seventh Avenue, near 28th Street
736-6944
By appointment only
AE, MC, V

Five generations of the Christie family have helped make this company one of the country's finest. Christie is known as a traditional furrier devoted to top-quality skins, high standards of design, and fine workmanship, and it turns out rich mink and sable coats and chinchilla jackets with jewel necks and dolman sleeves. But recently the company has leavened sable, broadtail, and chinchilla with lively colors (green and topaz) and offbeat shapes (capes, ponchos, and parkas).

ELENA BENARROCH
733 Madison Avenue, at 64th Street
517-4557
Tues.–Fri.: 10 a.m.–6 p.m.
AE, MC, V

Ermine polo coats, argyle-patterned mink vests, squirrel jackets in feathery patterns, and high-style sheared beaver are just a few of the unique designs in Elena Benarroch's snappy store. Everything comes from Spain, and skins range from squirrel to lamb to sable. Benarroch works fur as if it were fabric so jackets are cut small and fitted like suits, and coats are long and slim or short and swingy. Expensive.

THE FUR VAULT
581 Fifth Avenue, near 48th Street

765-3877
Mon.–Thurs.: 10 a.m.–8 p.m.; Tues., Wed., Fri.: 10 a.m.–7 p.m.; Sat.:
10 a.m.–6 p.m.; Sun.: 12 noon–5 p.m.
AE, MC, V

Once known as Fred the Furrier and located in Alexander's Department
Store, Fred has moved on to his own freestanding shop. Fred furrier has
revolutionized the city's fur industry by appealing to the single career
woman, and he has made it easy and affordable for her to indulge in a
fur coat. Fred's selection is incredible, and his prices are excellent, and
he carries all the popular skins, as well as the designs of Chlöe, Christian Dior, Alfred Sung, Giancarlo Ripa, and John Puntar. Styles, however, tend to be staid or utterly flamboyant, and skins at times may be
of only ordinary quality.

GOLDEN-FELDMAN
345 Seventh Avenue, near 29th Street
Twelfth floor
594-4415
Mon.–Fri.: 9 a.m.–5 p.m.; Sat.: 9 a.m.–1 p.m.
AE, MC, V

Golden-Feldman has been a family-run business since 1909, and this
furrier is famed for fine furs and a high standard of workmanship. Au
courant silhouettes from Basile, Mauro, Geoffrey Beene, Pigozzi, Chlöe,
and Peter O'Brien are featured in this handsome and friendly fur salon,
along with elegantly classic designs. There are styles for traditionalists
who like their furs long and flowing in natural Russian lynx, golden
Russian sable, stone marten, Canadian fisher, tanuki, coyote, opossum,
and nutria. But there's a wide choice of casual shapes, too—silver fox
wraps, simple but stunning mink greatcoats, fox-trimmed nutria jackets, swing toppers, and fur pea jackets.

JINDO FURS
41 West 57th Street
754-1177
Mon. & Thurs.: 10 a.m.–9 p.m.; Tues., Wed., Fri., Sat.: 10 a.m.–
7 p.m.; Sun.: 12 noon–6 p.m.

575 Fifth Avenue, at 47th Street
Third floor
867-0710
Mon.–Sat.: 10 a.m.–6 p.m.; Sun.: 12 noon–5 p.m.

1010 Third Avenue, at 60th Street
754-1166
Mon. & Thurs.: 10 a.m.–9 p.m.; Tues., Wed., Fri., Sat.: 10 a.m.–
7 p.m.; Sun.: 12 noon–6 p.m.
AE, MC, V

Jindo is a Seoul-based corporation that claims to be the world's largest furrier. It buys pelts worldwide, manufactures fur coats, and manages its own fur salons. The company works with leading Italian, French, and American designers to create a variety of styles, and although mink accounts for most of the company's sales, it also offers tanuki, beaver, coyote, raccoon, and fox. Designs range from classic to all the popular fur looks, and Jindo has a large selection of fur-lined raincoats and jackets, along with fur coats for men. Prices are good, but skins may be of only ordinary quality.

MAXIMILIAN
20 West 57th Street
Third floor
765-6290
Mon.–Sat.: 9 a.m.–5:30 p.m.
AE, MC, V

Society's favorite furrier and a legendary name in fur, Maximilian is known for high-fashion looks, fabric-like treatment of skins, exquisite workmanship, classic detailing, and the very finest-quality skins. Although sumptuous evening furs and sables are Maximilian's specialty, there's always an outstanding selection of sporty designs as well. Casual jackets, swing coats in fisher or fox, floor-length cardigans, pea jackets, and duffel coats were among recent sightings. Very expensive.

MICHAEL FORREST
333 Seventh Avenue, near 28th Street
Nineteenth floor
564-4726
Mon.–Fri.: 9 a.m.–5 p.m.
AE, MC, V

Michael Forrest furs are often pictured in the top fashion magazines, and Louis dell'Olio for Anne Klein is one of the company's featured designers. Dell'Olio does silver-fox cardigans, bathrobe wraps in golden sable, and glamorous coats in fisher and mink. But Michael Forrest carries a full range of furs in all the most wanted styles, and all the skins—from fox to sable—are first-rate and prices are good.

MOHL FURS
345 Seventh Avenue, near 29th Street
Fifth floor
736-7676
Mon.–Fri.: 9 a.m.–5 p.m.
No credit cards

Mohl is famous for its fine selection of mink and for Arnold Scaasi's exciting fur designs. Scaasi turns out white mink coats and jackets, sporty chinchillas, and hooded floor-length coats and blue mink capes.

But Mohl also offers top quality fox, raccoon, fisher, beaver, and Persian lamb. Expensive.

STEVEN CORN FURS
141 West 28th Street
695-3914
Mon.–Sun.: 10 a.m.–6 p.m.
All major

Steven Corn Furs has been selling furs for more than ninety years, and this family-run furrier offers a vast selection of furs of all kinds. Black Mist mink is a Corn exclusive, but there are fox, raccoon, coyote, beaver, and all the other popular furs here as well. The company manufactures its own furs and stocks a full range of sizes, from petite to large. Prices are good, but skins may be of only ordinary quality.

LEATHER CLOTHING
VINTAGE

See **Men's Clothing, Vintage,** for vintage leather military jackets and coats: Antique Boutique, Chameleon, and Weiss & Mahoney have large selections.

CONTEMPORARY

AGNÈS B.
A small but very special high-style collection of glove-soft leather coats and jackets for men and women, along with skirts and slacks for women. (See **Women's Clothing,** p. 159.)

ANDREW MARC
404 Columbus Avenue, near 79th Street
769-2400
Mon.–Thurs.: 11 a.m.–8 p.m.; Fri.: 11 a.m.–9 p.m.; Sat.: 11 a.m.–7 p.m.; Sun.: 12 noon–7 p.m.
AE, MC, V

Andrew Marc's glitzy glass-and-steel emporium is stocked with high-fashion leather and suede sports separates and fur-trimmed leather jackets and coats. Each season the hottest new Euro-American looks are transformed into leather shirts, blazers, pants, and skirts that can be teamed with the store's wool sweaters for a coordinated fashion look. In addition to styles for men and women, Marc offers a small group of children's leather outerwear that are pared-down versions of the adult line. Prices range from moderate to costly.

BILLY MARTIN'S WESTERN WEAR

Western-inspired leather clothing, including fringed suede and leather jackets. (See **Shoes,** p. 421.)

CHARIVARI

Cutting-edge leather separates for men and women. (See **Men's Clothing,** p. 126.)

THE COCKPIT

Re-creations of vintage leather flight jackets, sheepskin-lined Air Force jackets, and military leather coats; in sizes to fit men, women, and children. (See **Men's Clothing,** p. 132.)

LOEWE

711 Madison Avenue, at 63rd Street
308-7700
Mon.–Fri.: 10 a.m.–6 p.m.; Sat.: 10 a.m.–5:30 p.m.
AE, DC, MC, V

Loewe has been fashioning leather goods for the Spanish nobility and the best families of Madrid since 1846. This venerable company uses only the most supple nappa leathers and the softest suedes to create beautifully crafted clothing for men and women. Suits, dresses, slacks, skirts, jackets, and coats—many trimmed with beaver or mink—are simple in design but come in lush colors created from natural dyes that are applied by hand. Handbags and luggage in this attractive duplex store reflect the same simplicity and attention to detail. Expensive.

MACDOUGLAS

645 Madison Avenue, near 59th Street
935-1177
Mon.–Sat.: 10 a.m.–6 p.m.
All major

A French company with a distinctly unGallic name, MacDouglas was created more than forty years ago by Pancho Paubert, who put together a leather collection inspired by the U.S. Air Force's bomber jacket. It soon became a hot fashion look in Paris. Today MacDouglas has stores throughout Europe and manufactures leather sportswear for famous designers. In the Madison Avenue branch classically styled jackets and coats in shearling, leather, and suede share the space with body-hugging bustier dresses, safari shorts, and neoclassic suits that break with tradition. Expensive, but only the finest leathers are used, and the craftsmanship is excellent.

MADE IN THE U.S.A.
130 East 59th Street
838-5076
Mon.–Sat.: 10:30 a.m.–7:30 p.m.; Sun.: 12:30 p.m.–6 p.m.
AE, MC, V

True to its name the stylish leather and suede clothing in this pleasant shop is made in the U.S.A., but it's made from glove-soft English leathers. Jackets and shirts come in short and long lengths, coats are crisp and tailored or romantic with luxurious fox collars, dresses are sexy and body-hugging. Colors range from black and brown, to luggage and cinnamon, to olive green and blue.

NORTH BEACH LEATHER
772 Madison Avenue, at 66th Street
772-0707
Mon.–Fri.: 10 a.m.–7 p.m.; Sat.: 10 a.m.–6 p.m.; Sun.: 1 p.m.–6 p.m.
AE, DC, MC, V

The New York branch of the popular Los Angeles store offers the same kind of adventurously styled, boldly colored, glove-soft leather and suede clothing as its California counterpart, so you're likely to bump into visiting movie stars in for their leather fix. The hides in the body-hugging dresses are as beautifully worked as silk, and the store carries designer Michael Hoban's bustier dresses, high-waisted pants, suits with bolero jackets, and tempting skirts, along with coats, fringed Western jackets, jeans, and blazers for both men and women. Prices are high but not outrageous, and the staff is attentive and friendly.

TANNERY WEST
191 Front Street
South Street Seaport
509-6095
Mon.–Sat.: 10 a.m.–7 p.m.; Sun.: 12 noon–6 p.m.

Trump Plaza
1040 Third Avenue, near 61st Street
319-5112
Mon.–Fri.: 11 a.m.–8 p.m.; Sat.: 10:30 a.m.–7 p.m.;
Sun.: 12 noon–6 p.m.

586 Columbus Avenue, near 88th Street
874-2130
Mon.–Sat.: 11 a.m.–8 p.m.; Sun.: 12 noon–6 p.m.
AE, MC, V

Tannery West sells only leather, and it's stocked with imported apparel by such leading European designers as Vakko, Maxima, and Marc Buchanan, along with the company's own label. Colors tend to be hot and styling high-fashion and dramatic. There are jackets with quilted plackets and trapunto stitching, lambskin cocktail dresses, double-breasted lambskin blazers, and classic flight jackets in distressed lambskin.

MEN'S CLOTHING
VINTAGE

ACADEMY CLOTHES
1703 Broadway, at 54th Street
765-1440
Mon.–Sat.: 9:30 a.m.–6:30 p.m.
AE, DC, MC, V

Academy is cluttered with never-worn vintage clothing that it rents to movie companies and the theater, but it also sells to individuals. Although it carries things for both men and women, it's the menswear that's the chief attraction, and its selection of formal wear, sports jackets, dress shirts, slacks, and accessories (top hats, canes, spats, ascots, and cummerbunds) is abundant and outstanding. Women will find a limited selection of day dresses, suits, blouses, and sweaters. Inexpensive.

ANDY'S CHEE-PEE'S
A good stock of all the vintage standards from seersucker jackets to forties suits, to tuxedos. (See **Women's Clothing,** p. 147.)

THE ANTIQUE BOUTIQUE
712 Broadway, at Washington Place
460-8830
Mon.–Thurs.: 10:30 a.m.–9 p.m.; Fri.,
Sat.: 10:30 a.m.–11 p.m.; Sun.: 12 noon–8 p.m.

227 East 59th Street
752-1680
Mon.–Thurs.: 11 a.m.–8 p.m.; Fri.,
Sat.: 11 a.m.–10 p.m.; Sun.: 12 noon–6 p.m.
AE, MC, V

The Antique Boutique calls itself New York's largest vintage clothing store, and indeed, both sprawling and well-organized outlets are filled with an enormous selection of nostalgic fashions. Rack upon rack are crammed with formal wear (including brocades and cutaways), white dinner jackets, tuxedo shirts, tweed overcoats, not to mention seersucker suits, leather coats and jackets, wool cardigans, and Bermuda shorts. And there are hundreds of Hawaiian, baseball, and bowling shirts and scores of skinny ties. Tulle prom and satin cocktail dresses, capris and clamdiggers, sixties miniskirts, beaded blouses and sweaters are among the stock for women. Most of the clothing is from the forties through the sixties, and everything is clean and in fine condition, and prices are good.

CANAL JEAN COMPANY
504 Broadway, near Spring Street
226-1130
Sun.–Thurs.: 10 a.m.–8 p.m.; Fri., Sat.: 10 a.m.–9 p.m.
AE, MC, V

Canal Jean Company began life as an Army and Navy store on Canal Street. Cluttered with sailors' pants and middy blouses, army fatigues, and other assorted military surplus, it now occupies a cavernous space on Broadway, where in addition to the military surplus, it offers vintage clothing from the forties through the sixties, along with new jeans, cotton tanks, painters' pants dyed dozens of shades, T-shirts, and cotton sweaters in a rainbow of colors. Although the vintage stock includes few surprises (military trenchcoats, old jeans, gabardine shirts, sports jackets in tweeds, seersuckers, and madras, Hawaiian and bowling shirts, cardigan sweaters), prices are excellent.

CHAMELEON VINTAGE CLOTHING
270 Bleecker Street
924-8574
Mon.–Thurs.: 12 noon–9 p.m.; Fri., Sat.: 12 noon–11 p.m.;
Sun.: 12 noon–9 p.m.
MC, V

Military and aviator leather jackets are Chameleon's chief attraction, though this smallish shop, disregardful of its name, *always* has a fine selection of pea jackets, army pants, authentic Hawaiian shirts, tweed overcoats, wool sweaters, and silk ties. Women will find appealing cotton nightshirts, an array of navy and printed dresses and tailored suits from the forties through the sixties, along with skirts, lovely silk kimonos, and hats. Prices are good.

CHEAP JACK'S VINTAGE CLOTHING
841 Broadway, near 14th Street
777-9564
Mon.–Sat.: 11 a.m.–8 p.m.; Sun.: 1 p.m.–7 p.m.

AE, MC, V

Spacious, clean, and tidy, Cheap Jack's is filled with all the vintage staples—tweed jackets and coats, suits from the forties, gabardine shirts, tuxedos, and slacks of all kinds. Although 60 percent of the stock is geared to men, there's an attractive group of print dresses from the thirties and forties for women, as well as beaded sweaters and wool skirts.

DUKE'S

57 Grand Street
966-2946
Daily: 12 noon–7 p.m.
AE

Clothing that has been lightly worn by upper-crust Brits is the attraction Duke's, a spacious shop housed in a centuries-old building. Owner Leonard Dukeman is an antiques dealer who scours English country estates for his wares and in the process he's collected vintage gentlemen's fashions from Savile Row, Bond Street, and King's Road. Among the treasures are tuxedos, morning coats, cutaways, dress trousers, and military uniforms. But there are business suits, hunt jackets, and plus fours, along with authentic cricket sweaters and Royal Yachting Association ties. Old bench-made riding boots, antique walking sticks, vests, hatboxes, and vintage leather suitcases complete the tempting stock.

SCREAMING MIMI'S

495 Columbus Avenue, at 84th Street
362-3158
Mon.–Fri.: 11 a.m.–8 p.m.; Sat.: 11 a.m.–7 p.m.; Sun.: 1 p.m.–7 p.m.
All major

Biff Chandler and Laura Wills's ever-changing assortment of vintage clothing is always trendy and au courant. Their large and orderly shop is filled with classic formal wear from the forties through the seventies, along with swim trunks, jackets, Bermudas, shirts, ties, worn jeans, and slacks in outrageous fabrics. Printed rayon dresses, capri pants, prom dresses, and bathing suits for women are from the thirties, forties, and fifties and Chandler and Wills carry jewelry, handbags, and shoes from the same period, along with new fashions by young designers. Prices are good and the owners a delight.

WEISS & MAHONEY

142 Fifth Avenue, at 19th Street
675-1915
Mon.–Fri.: 9 a.m.–6 p.m.; Sat.: 9 a.m.–5 p.m.
No credit cards

Weiss & Mahoney has been around since 1924, and this popular army and navy surplus store sold military surplus clothing years before cheap chic became a fad. It's still a fine source for leather flight jackets, jumpsuits, navy pea coats, trenchcoats, fatigues, army and navy sweaters, along with all the other most wanted surplus accessories.

FORMAL WEAR

Barneys New York, Bergdorf Goodman, Bloomingdale's, and Saks Fifth Avenue offer a fine selection of men's formal wear. See also **Men's Clothing, Vintage.**

THE ANTIQUE BOUTIQUE
The formal clothing includes brocades and cutaways, white dinner jackets, tuxedo shirts and accessories. (See **Vintage Men's Clothing,** p. 111.)

A. T. HARRIS
47 East 44th Street
Second floor
682-6325
Mon.–Wed., Fri.: 8:30 a.m.–6 p.m.; Thurs.: 8:30 a.m.–7 p.m.; Sat.:
10 a.m.–4 p.m.; or by appointment
AE, DC, MC, V

Since 1892 A. T. Harris has sold natural shoulder tuxedos, shawl-lapel white-wool dinner jackets, strollers, and cutaways to the diplomatic corps and wedding parties. The quality of its fabrics is first-rate, and the cut of its formal wear is decidedly English. It carries all the traditional accessories as well: collapsible silk top hats, walking sticks, Chesterfield topcoats, ascots, spats, waistcoats, and gloves of buttery white kidskin or mocha suede. Tuxes can be purchased, rented, or custom-made, and the staff is knowledgeable and can advise customers on the proper outfit for any formal occasion.

BEAU BRUMMEL
A fine stock of tuxedos, many cut loose and very relaxed. (See **Contemporary Men's Clothing,** p. 120.)

BRIONI
Impeccably tailored tuxedos, frockcoats, and formal accessories that are classic yet ultrafashionable. (See **Contemporary Men's Clothing,** p. 120.)

F. R. TRIPLER & COMPANY
114   Traditionally cut tuxedos and dinner jackets of fine-quality fabrics,

along with dress shoes and all the accessories. (See **Traditional Men's Clothing,** p. 117.)

GIANPIETRO BOUTIQUE
Sophisticated and beautifully tailored tuxedos, vests, and formal shirts. (See **Contemporary Men's Clothing,** p. 122.)

JACK AND COMPANY FORMAL WEAR
128 East 86th Street
722-4609
Mon.–Fri.: 10 a.m.–7 p.m.; Sat.: 10 a.m.–4 p.m.; July and August: Mon., Wed., Fri.: 10 a.m.–6 p.m.; Tues., Thurs.: 10 a.m.–7 p.m.
AE, MC, V

Jack and Company rents or sells head-to-toe formal wear, and it stocks a full range of sizes (including extra-small and extra-large). Although the tuxes are not top-of-the-line and fabrics are often blends, they're serviceable and inexpensive. You'll find After Six, Lord West, and Palm Beach, and the shop has a reputation for offering good service.

TRADITIONAL

ALFRED DUNHILL OF LONDON
620 Fifth Avenue, at 50th Street
489-5580
Mon.–Sat.: 9:30 a.m.–6 p.m.

65 East 57th Street
355-0050
Mon.–Sat.: 9:30 a.m.–6 p.m.
AE, MC, V

In 1907 Alfred Dunhill opened a tiny tobacconist shop in London's West End, but when the shop introduced the Dunhill pipe, followed by the famous Dunhill lighter, it became known as a source for fine luxury goods. The company soon spread worldwide, and in 1977 it introduced a line of menswear, and in 1985 acquired Dunhill Tailors, an independent New York company. The menswear continues the Dunhill tradition of high quality and attention to detail, and in its comfortable cherrywood paneled stores Dunhill offers three types of suits—off-the-peg, special order, and custom hand-tailored. Each of these suits is cut from the finest cashmere, camel hair, alpaca, or mohair and impeccably tailored, and Dunhill's custom suit is sewn completely by hand. Shirts and shoes can also be purchased off-the-peg, special order, or custom made, and the workmanship is top-of-the-line. There are hand-sewn

115

silk ties, handsome calfskin attaché cases, mat-finish crocodile belts, and of course, the Dunhill lighter. Expensive.

BROOKS BROTHERS
346 Madison Avenue, at 44th Street
682-8800
Mon.–Wed., Fri., Sat.: 8:30 a.m.–6 p.m.; Thurs.: 8:30 a.m.–7 p.m.

1 Liberty Plaza
267-2420
Mon.–Fri.: 8:30 a.m.–5:30 p.m.
AE, MC, V

Today's customers come to Brooks Brothers, the country's oldest menswear shop, for the same well-tailored classic clothing that their great-great-grandfathers came for in 1818. Suits are still three-button with natural shoulders, lapel widths barely change, and the same colors and fabrics appear year after year, so the suit you buy this year will look just like the one you bought ten years ago and the one you'll buy ten years from now. On the always crowded main floor counters are piled high with Shetland and cashmere sweaters in V- and crew-neck styles, the famous button-down Oxford-cloth shirts (in solids and stripes), Rep and paisley ties, socks, amply cut pajamas in cozy flannels and soft cottons, and bathrobes in wools, terry cloth, and handsome paisleys. The shoe department, also on the ground floor, carries all the classics—wing tips, saddles, tassels, and white-and-tan bucks—at prices that range from reasonable for most, to costly for the benchmade versions. The Brooksgate Department, on the fifth floor, is popular with young lawyers and professionals who prefer a slimmer preppy look. And the boys' department, on four, offers pint-size versions of the Brooks look. There are nicely tailored suits in tweeds and linen for the executive or preppy woman, very proper silk or challis blouses, shirt dresses in tweeds and linens, along with Shetland sweaters and well-made coats. Once considered a very costly clothier, Brooks prices are now surprisingly affordable.

BURBERRY LIMITED
9 East 57th Street
371-5010
Mon.–Wed., Fri., Sat.: 9:30 a.m.–6 p.m.; Thurs.: 9:30 a.m.–7 p.m.
AE, DC, MC, V

Just a few years back no well-dressed New Yorker would be seen without a Burberry trenchcoat with its signature plaid scarf flapping in the wind. Although no longer ubiquitous, Burberry rainwear is still popular, and this New York outpost of the London store carries the city's largest selection. It's also a fine source for very classic British clothing for men, women, and children. Men will find traditional topcoats, overcoats, slacks, sweaters, and ties. Women can find tartan and Scotch-plaid jackets and skirts, as well as simply styled shirts, blouses, suits, and overcoats. And there are nicely done scaled-down versions of the adult styles for children.

BURTON LTD.
14 East 41 Street
685-3760
Mon.–Wed., Fri.: 9 a.m.–7 p.m.; Thurs.: 9 a.m.–7 p.m.;
Sat.: 10 a.m.–6 p.m.
AE, MC, V

Burton's offers nicely tailored classics for men who like their suits understated. Handsome tweed jackets, well-cut suits, pleated pants, and shirts are stitched from good-quality natural fabrics, and there's a vast selection of silk ties, a good choice in rainwear, and a fine group of overcoats from Canada. The atmosphere is comfortably clubby and the salesmen are attentive.

F. R. TRIPLER & CO.
366 Madison Avenue, at 46th Street
922-1090
Mon.–Wed., Fri.: 9 a.m.–5:45 p.m.; Thurs.: 9 a.m.–6:30 p.m.;
Sat.: 9 a.m.–5:30 p.m.
AE, MC, V

Dark-wood paneling, leather sofas, and an obliging staff give this store an air of a private men's club, but F. R. Tripler has been selling fine-quality conservative clothing since 1886. Prestigious labels include the world's largest selection of hand-tailored Hickey-Freeman, as well as Oxxford, Graham & Gunn, and the store's own Downing Street line. Tuxedos and dinner jackets, dress shoes, and all the necessary formal accessories are all handsomely done, and same-day alterations are part of the extraordinary Tripler service. Scottish cashmere sweaters, cotton knitwear, custom- and ready-made shirts, elegant robes and pajamas, and made-to-measure suits appeal to the most discriminating gentlemen. And for the executive woman, there are suits, jackets, dresses, and skirts with the same fine tailoring but with a softer, more feminine look.

J. PRESS
16 East 44th Street
687-7642
Mon.–Sat.: 9:15 a.m.–5:30 p.m.
AE, MC, V

A bastion of preppyness, J. Press has turned out quintessential Ivy League clothing since 1902. Blazers are blue, suits come in two- or three-button natural shoulder styles, shirts are cut straight and button-down, and everything (except for Burberry raincoats) carries the J. Press label. Fabrics include classic flannels in clerical gray, herringbones, sharkskins, and glen plaids. Ties range from traditional Rep stripes to

117

English silks flecked with unlikely animals such as whales, hippos, and lobsters, and the company is known for exuberant calico patchwork shorts and slacks. Sports jackets, trousers, overcoats, dinner clothes, even custom-tailored suits are very fairly priced.

PAUL STUART
Madison Avenue at 45th Street
682-0320
Mon.–Wed., Fri.: 8 a.m.–6 p.m.; Thurs.: 8 a.m.–7 p.m.;
Sat.: 9 a.m.–6 p.m.
AE, DC, MC, V

Luxurious fabrics and sophisticated tailoring transform Paul Stuart's conservative clothing into high-fashion. Everything here is private label and exclusive to the store. The handsome inventory of jackets and suits in tweeds, Shetlands, herringbones, glen plaids, and cavalry twills, and the classic benchmade shoes, are sure to delight any resident Brit. Hand-knit sweaters in alpaca, cashmere, and Shetland wool, and the rugged jackets and outerwear will please the country gentleman. And the selection of custom-designed and fitted shirts, mostly of Sea Island cotton, will satisfy the most fastidious male. The women's clothing, attractively displayed on the mezzanine, offers meticulously tailored suits, beautifully cut silk or wool challis shirts, and handsome pleated skirts in ancient madders, wools, and gabardines. Slacks are neatly tailored, sweaters artfully worked, and there are sturdy benchmade shoes to complete the English-gentry look.

SULKA & CO.
430 Park Avenue, at 55th Street
980-5200
Mon.–Fri.: 9 a.m.–6 p.m.; Sat.: 10 a.m.–5 p.m.

Waldorf-Astoria lobby
301 Park Avenue, at 49th Street
872-4592
Mon.–Fri.: 9 a.m.–6:30 p.m.; Sat.: 10 a.m.–5 p.m.
AE, MC, V

Sulka has been known for fine-quality, English-style clothing since 1895 and it stocks suits tailored of fine imported fabrics, along with handsome blazers, slacks, and sports jackets. Shirts are cut from Sulka's own patterns, and single needle stitching is used throughout, and, in addition to ready-mades, Sulka handles made-to-measure and custom orders. Silk pajamas, robes, and smoking jackets are understated and outstanding, and even the boxer shorts come in beautiful shirting fabrics. Expensive.

WALLACH'S
555 Fifth Avenue, near 46th Street

687-0106
Mon.–Wed., Fri., Sat.: 9 a.m.–6 p.m.; Thurs.: 9 a.m.–7:30 p.m.

150 Broadway, at Liberty Street
513-7660
Mon.–Wed., Fri.: 8:30 a.m.–6 p.m.; Thurs.: 8:30 a.m.–7 p.m.
AE, DC, MC, V

Wallach's is a favorite with businessmen who want attentive service, an unhurried atmosphere, and famous label suits with a respectable look. They come for Hickey Freeman, Hart Schaffner & Marx, Pierre Cardin, Bannister, and Bill Blass suits that are traditional and safe—if a bit bland and a trifle dated. But the salespeople are extremely helpful, measurements are kept on file for phone-in ordering, and shopping at Wallach's is comfortable and comforting.

CONTEMPORARY

All the major departments stores offer a good selection of contemporary menswear.

ALAN FLUSSER
16 East 52nd Street
Penthouse
888-7100
By appointment only: Mon.–Fri.: 10 a.m.–7 p.m.; Sat.: 10 a.m.–5 p.m.
AE, DC

Alan Flusser's tiny showroom is tucked away in a penthouse overlooking St. Patrick's Cathedral. Here, in a comfortable clubby setting complete with a mahogany bar and Regency armchairs, Flusser offers the kind of menswear that the Duke of Windsor and Fred Astaire made famous. Suits have natural shoulders and a drape cut; slacks have a thirties slouch; sweaters are classic cardigans or V-necks or the old-fashioned tennis kind; polo shirts are discreetly patterned; pajamas and smoking jackets are lush but understated; and even swim trunks recall an earlier era. Flusser's fabrics are some of the best around and include English and Scottish woolens and tweeds, and his styling, though classic, is on today's cutting edge. Flusser gained added recognition for the slick suit he designed for Michael Douglas in *Wall Street*, and although these suits are more conventional than his thirties drape styles, they are also available in the shop. In addition to the full stock of ready-mades, suits and shirts can be custom-ordered, and service is refreshingly Old World.

BEAU BRUMMEL

421 West Broadway
219-2666
Mon.–Sat.: 11 a.m.–7 p.m.; Sun.: 12 noon–7 p.m.

410 Columbus Avenue, near 79th Street
874-6262
Mon.–Sat.: 11 a.m.–7 p.m.; Sun.: 12 noon–7 p.m.

1113 Madison Avenue, near 83rd Street
737-4200
Mon.–Fri.: 11 a.m.–7 p.m.; Sat.: 10 a.m.–6 p.m.: Sun.: 12 noon–5 p.m.
All major

Beau Brummel offers slightly different silhouettes, fabrics, and cuts in each of its emporiums. The largest branch, on West Broadway, and the one on Columbus Avenue attract a young, trendy customer, so here the suits, trousers, jackets, and shirts are more cutting edge. Since the Madison Avenue customer tends to be a tad more conservative, this shop carries the more tailored things. In addition to Beau Brummel's own line, there's Hugo Boss, Bill Kaiserman, and Gruppo Storrico. Many of the suits are double-breasted and even classic gray suits might come with a rust pinstripe. Each of the stores has a good stock of tuxedos, many cut loose and very relaxed, and there are dress and sports shirts, often inspired by the Japanese designers, along with scores of handsome ties.

BRIONI

55 East 52nd Street
355-1940
Mon.–Sat.: 9:30 a.m.–6 p.m.
AE

Although Brioni was established in Rome as recently as the forties, this famous company has brought an Old World elegance to men's fashion, and its luxurious New York boutique is filled with the city's most costly menswear. Suits, jackets, and coats are hand-cut and hand-stitched from lush silks, wools, cashmeres, and alpaca, the cut and styling are European, and business suits come single- or double-breasted. Brioni's tuxedos and frockcoats are impeccably tailored, and the formal shirts, ties, and cummerbunds have the proper moneyed look. Brioni offers made-to-measure suits, too, and each of these are made from a personal pattern that is kept on file. There's an extensive selection of cotton and silk shirts, leather belts, shoes, even luggage—all at astronomical prices.

CAMOUFLAGE

141 Eighth Avenue, at 17th Street
691-1750
Mon.–Fri.: 12 noon–7 p.m.; Sat.: 11 a.m.–6 p.m.; Sun.: 12 noon–5 p.m.

Camouflage Downtown
139 Eighth Avenue, near 17th Street
691-1750
Mon.–Fri.: 12 noon–7 p.m.; Sat.: 11 a.m.–6 p.m.; Sun: 12 noon–5 p.m.
AE, MC, V

Magazine stylists and the modishly dressed come to Camouflage. They know that in this small storefront shop in Chelsea they'll find the best looks in menswear. Over the years owners Gene Chase and Norman Usiak have carried all the important American names—Garrick Anderson, Bill Robinson, Willi Smith, Perry Ellis, Ralph Lauren, Jeffrey Banks, Alexander Julian—and their stock represents a carefully edited selection of updates on the classics. Ties, scarfs, and sweaters are often the work of neighborhood designers and are exclusive to the store, but in addition to the Americans you might find blazers from Shamask and shirts from Paul Smith. Camouflage Downtown carries such indispensable additions to any wardrobe as cotton chinos and Russell Athletic football jerseys, witty T-shirts, along with funky separates that appeal to a younger crowd. These stores are low-key, high-fashion, warm and friendly places to shop, and personal favorites.

DAVIDE CENCI
801 Madison Avenue, near 67th Street
628-5910
Mon.–Wed., Fri., Sat.: 10:30 a.m.–6:30 p.m.;
Thurs.: 10:30 a.m.–7:30 p.m.
AE, DC, MC, V

Housed in a handsome granite and glass duplex Davide Cenci offers classic and impeccably tailored suits and jackets, sportswear, formal wear, and accessories, all updated with a dash of flair. Fabrics are luxurious, the styling understated yet elegant, and the outstanding selection of topcoats, sweaters, and pleated trousers makes this store well worth a visit. Come, too, for the buttery-soft driving shoes and handsome versions of classic tassel loafers and wing tips. Expensive.

EMPORIO ARMANI
110 Fifth Avenue, at 16th Street
727-3240
Mon.–Sat.: 10 a.m.–7 p.m.
AE, MC, V

Giorgio Armani created Emporio in 1981 for the kids who couldn't afford Armani. At first the small Emporio store in Milan sold only jeans and bomber jackets, but by 1985 Emporio had expanded to a complete line of sportswear, and by 1988 it had evolved to include less-pricey versions of the designer's costlier fashions. Now Emporio is ensconced in an imposing Stanford White building on lower Fifth Avenue, whose stark interior is an adaption of Shaker style, and here the entire collection is on view. So in addition to the casual sweaters, jeans, and slacks there are

Armani's classic separates for men and women, along with his softly tailored dresses and his outstanding Emporio shoes. Here, too, the designer offers winning accessories for the home: soaps, potpourris, luggage and small leather goods, shagreen frames, Shaker boxes, and stationery, as well as underwear and lingerie, jewelry, and vintage watches.

FDR DRIVE MEN
80 Thompson Street
334-0170
Tues.–Sun.: 1 p.m.–7 p.m.
AE, MC, V

FDR Drive Men, pocket-sized and comfortably cluttered, is stocked with a seductive array of jackets, slacks, and shirts that are cut from vintage patterns with the full and slouchy look of the thirties, and they come in the favored fabrics of the era—gabardines, linens, and tropical wools. They're old-fashioned and classic, yet they're on today's cutting edge. Coats and jackets have wide shoulders, slacks are pleated and pegged or bell-shaped, and although FDR doesn't carry suits as such, jackets and trousers can be custom-ordered in the same fabric to serve as suits. To complement the Retro look, there are vests and such appropriate accessories as walking sticks, silver cigarette cases, bowties, and suspenders. Moderate to expensive.

GIANPIETRO BOUTIQUE
207 East 60th Street
759-2322
Mon. & Thurs.: 11 a.m.–8 p.m.; Tues, Wed., Fri., Sat.: 11 a.m.–7 p.m.
AE, MC, V

Sophisticated, slightly jazzy Italian menswear, along with the high-fashion designs of Bill Kaiserman and Canali, are what you'll find in Gianpietro's airy and attractive shop. Formal wear is a specialty, and tuxedos and vests are beautifully tailored, and there's an appealing selection of formal shirts as well as handsome dress shoes. But then everything at Gianpietro is neatly done—from the suits, to the luxurious silk shirts, to the handwoven sweaters, to the suede and leather jackets. Costly.

GIVENCHY GENTLEMAN
1020 Madison Avenue, near 78th Street
517-8900
Mon.–Sat.: 11 a.m.–7 p.m.
All major

Givenchy's classically simple designs for men are ensconced in an appropriately clubby setting—comfortable leather chairs, polished wood appointments, a sweeping staircase, and antique linen presses filled with shirts and sweaters. Suits are double-breasted or single

three-button styles, fabrics are luxurious silks and woolens, and everything is beautifully understated. Shirts in fine cottons or silks, sports
jackets, slacks, shoes, and accessories are equally well-executed and
subdued. Pricey.

GUCCI

Handsome alpaca coats, covert-wool trousers, argyle polo sweaters,
and hounds-tooth-checked jackets. (See **Women's Clothing**, p. 154.)

LANVIN

872 Madison Avenue, at 71st Street
288-9210
Mon.–Sat.: 10 a.m.–6 p.m.
AE, MC, V

In the Lanvin men's store with its signature black-and-gold interior
everything has been made in the company's own factory and imported
from France. The look in suits, jackets, shirts, and slacks is classically
Parisian. The fabrics are first-rate and the detailing excellent. The
store has a custom shirt department so that customers can have their
measurements taken here and have shirts made for them in Paris.

LOUIS, BOSTON

131 East 57th Street
308-6100
Mon.–Fri.: 10 a.m.–7 p.m.; Sat.: 9:30 a.m.–5:30 p.m.
AE, MC, V

Thirties style dominates this 20,000-square-foot, triplex store in the
Place des Antiquaires building. The Deco-influenced interior has a spiral staircase, mahogany-paneled walls, and Biedermeier furnishings.
And although the clothes, too, take their cue from the thirties, they've
been updated for the nineties. Owner Murray Pearlstein offers double-
breasted suits with a relaxed look. They have wider lapels and broader
shoulders than the "Ivy League" cut, and he shows them with fuller ties,
along with shirts with higher collars. Pearlstein selects only the finest
fabrics and the detailing in his menswear collection is excellent. Louis,
Boston stocks a complete line of casual clothing, too, that includes
slacks, shirts, sweaters, and jackets. Among the elegant designs for
women—also influenced by a thirties sensibility—are shawl-collared
suits, mid-calf-length accordion-pleated challis skirts, softly tailored
blouses, silk-chiffon tea dresses, and cashmere sweater dresses.

NEW REPUBLIC CLOTHIERS

93 Spring Street
219-3005
Mon.–Sat.: 12 noon–7 p.m.; Sun.: 1 p.m.–6 p.m.
AE, MC, V

New Republic has the feeling of an old-fashioned haberdashery, and it's no wonder. The wood fixtures and the doors come from a thirties department store, and owner Thomas Oatman has filled his shop with classic Retro-Modern clothing. Originally New Republic offered vintage English menswear, but as sources for quality old things dried up, Oatman began designing new clothing that looked old. Slouchy pleated trousers, forties-style gabardine shirts, square-cut jackets, comfortable cardigans, and pointy-toed takes on classic oxford and saddle shoes are attractively displayed in this beguiling store.

PAUL SMITH
108 Fifth Avenue, at 16th Street
627-9770
Mon.–Sat.: 11 a.m.–7 p.m.
AE, MC, V

Paul Smith is an English fashion designer whose clothing is hip enough for rock stars, yet restrained enough for Wall Street, and his handsomely appointed New York store, with its old English apothecary fixtures and firmly masculine interior, showcases both aspects of this popular designer's work. Fine tailoring and handsome fabrics characterize his English- and Italian-made traditional and pricey line of suits, sports jackets, and slacks, but his more reasonably priced sportswear is young, innovative, and somewhat quirky. Classic button-down shirts might be flecked with espresso beans or apples; cotton handkerchiefs dotted with cows, pigs, or daffodils; long-sleeved polo shirts have far too many buttons; and socks look like Aztec art. Smith's shoes are nicely done versions of classic saddles and wing tips, and he offers winning canvas bags and belts. Given that Smith calls himself a typical English eccentric, there are toys, old workman's tools, vintage first editions, and Tom Dixon's slightly mad furniture crafted from salvaged scrap metal.

POLO/RALPH LAUREN
Madison Avenue, at 72nd Street
606-2100
Mon.–Wed., Fri., Sat.: 10 a.m.–6 p.m.; Thurs.: 10 a.m.–8 p.m.
AE, DC, MC, V

The restored Rhinelander mansion with its baronial staircase, Oriental rugs, framed family portraits, and frayed leather chairs is a fitting setting for Ralph Lauren's menswear with its scrupulous look of old money. Neatly displayed on the main floor are myriad shirts, ties, scarfs, and handkerchiefs. Here, too, in glass-and-mahogany cases you'll find antique jewelry, gentlemanly flasks, hairbrush sets, and desk accessories. And in the shoe department are crocodile tassel loafers, white bucks, handsome suede saddles, brogues, and wing tips that are fashionable takes on the classics. The second floor is comfortably masculine and stocked with suits and sports jackets tailored from such old-fashioned fabrics as glen plaids, Prince of Wales and houndstooth checks, herringbones, flannels, and camel's hair. The Young Gentlemen's Club, also on two, offers scaled-down versions of Lauren's preppy sportswear, along with nicely cut sports jackets and trousers. Romantic women's clothing fills most of the third floor with seductive silks and cashmeres, cottons in country prints, along with beautifully tailored suits and slouchy slacks in menswear fabrics. Accessories, such as Lauren's winning crocodile bags and benchmade shoes, are here as well. And, on the fourth floor are all the linens, quilts, blankets, pillow shams, and furniture needed to transform our homes into Lauren's vision of subdued Old World splendor.

SAINT LAURIE LTD.
897 Broadway, at 20th Street
473-0100
Mon.–Wed., Fri., Sat.: 9:30 a.m.–6 p.m.; Thurs.: 9:30 a.m.–7:30 p.m.;
Sun.: 12 noon–5 p.m.
AE, DC, MC, V

In a century-old landmark building in the Flatiron district, amid a "living" museum devoted to the art of tailoring and a huge hand-painted mural that traces the history of men's fashion since the company's birth in 1913, Saint Laurie manufactures and sells hand-tailored men's and women's suits. Conservative in styling, they're made of good-quality fabrics, and they're extremely well-constructed, and, since Saint Laurie doesn't deal with a middleman, prices are excellent. The company also offers well-made, very traditional custom-made suits at prices that are half what you would have to pay uptown.

VERRI UOMO
802 Madison Avenue, near 67th Street
737-9200
Mon.–Wed., Fri., Sat.: 10:30 a.m.–6:30 p.m.; Thurs.: 10:30 a.m.–
7:30 p.m.
AE, DC, MC, V

Distinctive and sophisticated Italian menswear is appealingly displayed in this stylish store. Suits and sports jackets have a European cut and are fashioned from wool, alpaca, camel's hair, and silk; tuxedos and formal wear neatly update the traditional; and there's an enticing selection of sweaters in mohair, silk, cashmere, and cotton.

CUTTING EDGE

CHARIVARI 57
18 West 57th Street
333-4040
Mon.–Wed., Fri.: 10 a.m.–7 p.m.; Thurs.: 10 a.m.–8 p.m.;
Sat.: 10 a.m.–6:30 p.m.; Sun.: 12:30 p.m.–6 p.m.

Charivari for Women
2315 Broadway, near 84th Street
873-1424
Mon.–Wed.: 10:30 a.m.–7 p.m.; Thurs.: 10:30 a.m.–8 p.m.;
Sat.: 10:30–6:30 p.m.; Sun.: 12:30–6 p.m.

Charivari for Men
2339 Broadway, near 84th Street
873-7242
Mon.–Wed., Fri.: 10:30 a.m.–7 p.m.; Thurs.: 10:30 a.m.–8 p.m.;
Sat.: 10:30 a.m.–6:30 p.m.; Sun.: 12:30 p.m.–6 p.m.

Charivari Workshop
441 Columbus Avenue, at 81st Street
496-8700
Mon.–Wed., Fri.: 11 a.m.–8 p.m.; Thurs.: 11 a.m.–9 p.m.;
Sat.: 11 a.m.–7 p.m.; Sun.: 1 p.m.–6 p.m.

Charivari Sport
201 West 79th Street
799-8650
Mon.–Wed., Fri.: 11 a.m.–8 p.m.; Thurs.: 11 a.m.–9 p.m.;
Sat.: 11 a.m.–7 p.m.; Sun.: 12 noon–6 p.m.

Charivari 72
257 Columbus Avenue, at 72nd Street
787-7272
Mon.–Wed., Fri.: 11 a.m.–8 p.m.; Thurs.: 11 a.m.–9 p.m.;
Sat.: 11 a.m.–7 p.m.; Sun.: 12:30 p.m.–6 p.m.
AE, MC, V

Selma Weiser opened her first Charivari store over twenty years ago and today her high-tech-looking, family-operated boutiques dot the Upper West Side landscape. **Charivari 57** (the largest, starkest, and the only midtown Charivari branch) offers radical looks in everything from formal wear to bathing trunks. High-style menswear is designed by such leading lights as Jean-Paul Gaultier, Giorgio Armani, Byblos, and Yohji Yamamoto; the trendy women's wear by Max Mara, Gaultier, and Matsuda. **Charivari for Women** is stocked with eminently wearable fashions by Tahari, Max Mara, Finity, Anvers, and Nicole Miller and among

126

the mix are career-oriented suits, sport separates, and dresses. **Chari-vari for Men** carries the latest in suits and sports jackets by Armani, Cerutti, and Versace as well as hip sports shirts in unlikely patterns and colors, boldly patterned sweaters, and pleated slacks in wools, linens, and cottons. The **Workshop** is the Weisers' avant-garde shop, so the look and the designers are in a constant state of flux—whatever is hottest and most outrageous is here. English and Japanese designers are favorites, so you'll find Workers for Freedom, Comme des Garçons, Matsuda, Katharine Hamnett, Yamamoto, Paul Smith, and Jean-Paul Gaultier among the regulars, and they're spiced with the Weisers' most recent finds. Breezy and colorful sportswear is at **Charivari Sport,** and prices here are well below those of the other stores. Jazzy jackets and shirts, underwear looks from Tous les Caleçons, cycling pants, Carnaby Street shirts, and Body Map sweaters are featured. Although **Charivari 72** carries many of the same designers as the 57th Street emporium and the men's store, the look is less avant-garde, more classic in cut and fabric.

COMME DES GARÇONS
116 Wooster Street
219-0660
Mon.–Sat.: 11 a.m.–7 p.m.; Sun.: 12 noon–6:30 p.m.
AE, DC, MC, V

Hard-edged, cavernous, and intimidating with gray stone walls and floors, Comme des Garçons' minimalist interior is a fitting showcase for Japanese designer Rei Kawakubo's stark creations. The clothing is simply displayed on the wooden dowels, and the menswear runs to loosely constructed suits and oversized trenchcoats, baggy or peg-legged slacks in somber tones, and winning shirts. Dresses have a purity of line and hang loose or just graze the body, and recently Kawakubo has added some shocking color news by showing piercing brights among her dark shapes. Cropped tails and jackets with draped asymmetric lapels, pedal-pushers, chemises, and tiny yokelike boleros are among the current fashion shapes. Expensive.

FORZA
269 Columbus Avenue, near 72nd Street
877-2070
Mon.–Sat.: 11 a.m.–7:30 p.m.; Sun.: 1 p.m.–6 p.m.

288 Columbus Avenue, near 73rd Street
496-5900
Mon.–Sat.: 11 a.m.–7:30 p.m.; Sun.: 1 p.m.–6 p.m.
AE

The Forza emporiums are crammed with the most au courant looks from Milan. Fabrics, styles, and colors reflect the hottest European trends (whatever attracts owner Selin Aykan's practiced eye on his shopping forays to Italy) and are in a constant state of flux. But jeans are a staple, and you'll always find jackets, slacks, shirts, sweaters, ties, and belts in the trendiest fabrics and styles. In the tiny original store near 72nd street you'll find Aykan's casual clothing, while the larger duplex store carries the dressier looks, along with cutting-edge fashions for women.

GIANNI VERSACE
816 Madison Avenue, at 68th Street
744-5572
Mon.–Sat.: 10:30 a.m.–6 p.m.
AE, DC, MC, V

The setting may be austere—marble floors, gray walls, and steel appointments—but Gianni Versace's clothing is lush and inviting. Relaxed, textured suits and unusual shirtings are signature Versace looks that fall somewhere between the trendy and the conservative. His shapely three-button suit with its expanded chest and lowered button placements is a tribute to American tailoring, and Versace's fabrics are sedately luxurious. Sweaters are winners, and loose alpaca greatcoats first-rate. His women's collection highlights the figure with dresses of sensuous draping, and body-hugging lines, and his coats, many big and collarless, come in sizzling-hot colors. Very expensive.

GIORGIO ARMANI
815 Madison Avenue, near 68th Street
988-9191
Mon.–Wed., Fri., Sat.: 10 a.m.–6 p.m.; Thurs.: 10 a.m.–7 p.m.
AE, MC, V

An elegant but spartan Madison Avenue town house houses Giorgio Armani's finely tuned designs. Using wide lapels, broad shoulders, an unconstructed cut, and a built-in slouch, Armani is responsible for transforming the look of menswear. His fabrics are sumptuous without being showy, seams are finished by hand, and his suits, sports jackets, and topcoats have a restrained look of luxury. The cut of his women's wear is just as sure. Suits, blouses, and dresses have a proper insouciance, and Armani's slacks are the best around. Evening wear is simple but beguiling, and his silk lingerie manages to look both chaste and sexy at the same time.

ISSEY MIYAKE
Jackets, shirts, slacks, coats with Miyake's signature detailing. (See **Women's Clothing,** p. 173.)

JEKYLL AND HYDE, LTD.
93 Greene Street
966-8503
Mon.–Wed.: 11 a.m.–6:30 p.m.; Thurs., Fri., Sat.: 12 noon–7 p.m.;
Sun.: 12 noon–6:30 p.m.
AE, MC, V

Jekyll and Hyde, the store—unlike the story—lets men happily indulge their dual personalities. Here they can mix serious classics (double-breasted navy flannel jackets) with casual wear (slouchy pleated cotton-chino slacks) or cutting-edge clothes (wedge-shaped jackets and over-sized dropped-shoulder unconstructed coats). There's an enthusiastic attention to detail: Chinos come with suspender buttons and a V-shaped back vent; the coats are designed to fit neatly over broad-shouldered jackets; and shirts come in a range of subtle white-on-white cottons. There are shoes, too (made in Italy but designed by an Englishman), sweaters from Italy and Scotland, and belts, ties, socks and leather goods, all displayed in a setting reminiscent of an elegant spacious dressing room.

MATSUDA
461 Park Avenue, at 57th Street
935-6969
Mon.–Fri.: 11 a.m.–7 p.m.; Sat.: 11 a.m.–6 p.m.

156 Fifth Avenue
979-5100
Mon.–Sat.: 11 a.m.–7 p.m.
AE, DC, MC, V

Everything Matsuda designs is *outré*, but in a quiet, understated way, and the stores' stark high-tech interiors reflect the subdued quality of the clothing. Gently oversized jackets come in unusual textured fabrics, slacks are pleated and full, and shirts are intricately detailed. Matsuda's designs for women include dresses, skirts, and jackets, and they're unconstructed, flowing, and eminently wearable. Accessories—suspenders, ties, jewelry, and socks—have a Retro look, like things you'd find in your grandfather's closet. The new store on lower Fifth is the world's largest Matsuda outlet and here devotees will find his complete collection of men's and women's wear along with Matsuda's grooming aids and linens for bed and bath. Expensive.

PARACHUTE
121 Wooster Street
925-8630
Mon.–Fri.: 12 noon–8 p.m.; Sat.: 12 noon–7 p.m.; Sun.: 1 p.m.–7 p.m.

309 Columbus Avenue, near 74th Street
799-1444
Mon.–Fri.: 12 noon–9 p.m.; Sat.: 12 noon–8 p.m.; Sun.: 1 p.m.–8 p.m.

1061 Madison Avenue, near 80th Street
744-9040
Mon.–Sat.: 10 a.m.–7 p.m.; Sun.: 12 noon–6 p.m.
AE, MC

Parachute's stark, cavernous, and minimalist interiors are perfect foils for the hard-edged fashions. Jackets tend to be either broad-shouldered and oversized or short and skimpy, skirts skinny; shirts snap up to stand-up collars, trenchcoats sport rows of buckles and buttons, and colors are monochromatic except for the occasional zap of turquoise or white. There are nicely done pleated slacks and hip leather jackets, along with clunky takes on classic oxford lace-up and brogue shoes. The assertive accessories include hats, ties, or belts, sunglasses, briefcases, and handbags. The newer Madison Avenue shop has the higher end of the line and softer looks in silks and gabardines. From moderate to expensive.

CASUAL

ACA JOE
313 Columbus Avenue, near 74th Street
362-4370
Mon.–Thurs.: 11 a.m.–9 p.m.; Fri., Sat.: 11 a.m.–9 p.m.; Sun.:
11 a.m.–7 p.m.

Pier 17
South Street Seaport
406-0770
Mon.–Sat.: 11 a.m.–7 p.m.; Sun.: 11 a.m.–6 p.m.

744 Broadway, near Astor Place
529-8775
Mon.–Sat.: 10 a.m.–9 p.m.; Sun.: 12 noon–6 p.m.

2345 Broadway, near 85th Street
874-9181
Mon.–Sat.: 11 a.m.–7 p.m.; Sun.: 12 noon–6 p.m.
AE, MC, V

ACA Joe is the bright idea of designer Joseph Rank who began selling knit shirts with the ACA JOE logo in Acapulco a few years ago. An immediate hit with the vacation crowd, the shirts soon spawned franchised stateside stores, where seasonless all-cotton separates, along with the original T-shirts, are displayed in spare, high-tech interiors. Among the easygoing sports basics that are piled floor-to-ceiling in metal crates, you'll find sweaters, shorts, rugby shirts, sweat pants, and chambray shirts, and everything is color-coordinated for easy shopping. The shapes and styling are simple and practical, and the prices a delight.

BANANA REPUBLIC
205 Bleecker Street

473-9570
Mon.–Sat.: 10 a.m.–9 p.m.; Sun.: 12 noon–6 p.m.

2376 Broadway, at 87th Street
874-3500
Mon.–Sat.: 10 a.m.–8 p.m.; Sun.: 12 noon–6 p.m.

130 East 59th Street
751-5570
Mon.–Sat.: 9:30 a.m.–9 p.m.; Sun.: 12 noon–6 p.m.

215 Columbus Avenue, near 70th Street
873-9048
Mon.–Sat.: 11 a.m.–8 p.m.; Sun.: 12 noon–6 p.m.

Pier 17
South Street Seaport
732-3090
Mon.–Sat.: 10 a.m.–7 p.m.; Sun.: 12 noon–6 p.m.
AE, MC, V

No-nonsense, sturdy, and comfortable sportswear inspired by safari garb (or the kind worn on safaris by the movie stars of the fifties) is the chief attraction in these palm-tree-laden shops that are guaranteed to inspire the traveling urge. Styles are traditional, and the fabrics (in such low-key colors as khaki, gray, brown, and olive) all natural. Bush jackets, Oxford-cloth shirts, comfortable shirtwaist dresses, Gurkha shorts, khaki pants, fleece-lined flight suits, and trenchcoats abound. The accessories—canvas and woven leather belts, canvas duffels and shoulder bags, and stylish yet practical hats—are especially winning. Prices are reasonable.

BEAU BRUMMEL SPORT
410B Columbus Street, near 79th Street
595-9600
Mon.–Sat.: 11 a.m.–7 p.m.; Sun.: 12 noon–7 p.m.
All major

This tiny vest-pocket-size shop carries the sporty Beau Brummel fashions for men. You won't find a suit or a sport jacket or a tie, only slacks, sweaters, and sport shirts. The look is casual and relaxed, perfect for country weekends or summer vacations.

BENETTON
Simple, yet stylish, Italian-knit separates and a fine selection of sweaters. (See **Sweaters,** p. 143.)

BEN'S VILLAGE
7 Greenwich Avenue
924-3360
Mon.–Wed.: 11 a.m.–7 p.m.; Thurs., Fri., Sat.: 11 a.m.–8 p.m.

Sun.: 12 noon–6 p.m.
MC, V

Fancy display is not one of Ben's strengths. Comfortable yet fashionable casual wear is simply piled everywhere in this pleasingly old-fashioned store. T-shirts, sweats, and sweaters are basics, but you'll find more fashion-forward jackets, pleated pants with a thirties cut, as well as big blousy shirts in rayon. Prices are excellent.

CAMOUFLAGE DOWNTOWN

Witty T-shirts, casual slacks and shorts, and cutting-edge separates that appeal to a younger crowd. (See **Contemporary Men's Clothing,** p. 121.)

THE COCKPIT

595 Broadway, near Prince Street
925–5455
Mon.–Sat.: 11:30 a.m.–7 p.m.; Sun.: 12:30 p.m.–6 p.m.
AE, MC, V

The Cockpit, a bustling, loft-size store, is filled floor to ceiling with old and authentic-looking, but newly manufactured, military garb. It's a favorite with those who like their vintage wear to fit, and bomber jackets, flight suits, parachute trousers, R.A.F. sweaters, and Flying Tiger khakis come in a full range of sizes, including women's and children's. There are shorts, shirts, shoes, even watches, all with a military look.

DOWN HOME AMERICA

1367 Third Avenue, at 78th Street
861-4200
Mon.–Fri.: 11 a.m.–8 p.m.; Sat.: 11 a.m.–7 p.m.; Sun.: 1 p.m.–5 p.m.;
closed Sun. in July and Aug., Jan. and Feb.
MC, V

As the name suggests, Down Home America is filled with sportswear garnered from all over the United States. Just about everything in this bright and sunny shop is playful and amusing, and you'll find T-shirts with vivid graphics, pants from L.A., hats and gloves from Michigan, enormous tote bags from California, colorful skirts from Georgia, exuberant sweaters from all over. But Down Home also stocks more subdued and classic denim and khaki shirts, shorts, and skirts.

THE EXPRESS

Casual, comfortable, and colorful sportswear that's a mix of T-shirts, classic sweaters, slouchy slacks, and soft rayon skirts. (See **Casual Women's Clothing,** p. 167.)

59TH STREET ARMY & NAVY STORE

221 East 59th Street
755-1855

Mon., Thurs.: 10 a.m.–8 p.m.; Tues., Wed., Fri.: 10 a.m.–7 p.m.;
Sat.: 10 a.m.–6 p.m.; Sun.: 1 p.m.–6 p.m.
AE, MC, V

For years this Army and Navy store has been a favorite with the town's top models and high-schoolers from the city's poshest private schools. They've come for the enormous selection of Levi's—the classic 501 button-fly, the boot-leg, the 505 zippered straight-leg, the 550 baggy— and they've stocked up on tank tops and shorts dyed a rainbow of colors, jean jackets, fatigues and painter's pants, flannel shirts, chinos, sweats, fringed leather jackets, Keds, hiking boots, and Topsiders. And they keep coming back because of the friendly and efficient service in this neat and well-organized store.

FIORUCCI
125 East 59th Street
751-5638
Mon.–Wed., Fri., Sat.: 10 a.m.–6:30 p.m.; Thurs.: 10 a.m.–8:30 p.m.;
Sun.: 2 p.m.–5:30 p.m.
AE, MC, V

Young and knowing New Yorkers flock to Fiorucci's warehouse-like high-tech space for witty and offbeat Italian sportswear. They know that whatever is hottest—Retro, cowboy, or just plain funky—is sure to be here. The signature jeans and the playful dresses are the mildest of the attention-grabbing clothes, all of which have Elio Fiorucci's special flair and most of which have his amusing graphics. Shirts, jackets, and slacks sport silly prints; ties and swimtrunks are outlandish; totes and handbags come in outrageous colors; and the children's department offers the same cutting-edge Fiorucci style for tiny tykes.

FORZA
Jeans and a full stock of casual clothing. (See **Cutting-Edge Men's Clothing,** p. 127.)

THE GAP
2109 Broadway, at 73rd Street
787-6698
Mon.–Sat.: 10 a.m.–9 p.m.; Sun.: 12 noon–7 p.m.

2551 Broadway, at 96th Street
864-3600
Mon.–Sat.: 10 a.m.–9 p.m.; Sun.: 12 noon–7 p.m.

1164 Madison, at 86th Street
517-5763
Mon.–Sat.: 10 a.m.–7 p.m.; Sun.: 12 noon–5 p.m.

757 Third Avenue, at 47th Street
223-5140
Mon.–Fri.: 9 a.m.–8 p.m.; Sat.: 9 a.m.–7 p.m.

445 Fifth Avenue, near 39th Street
532-8633
Mon.–Fri.: 10 a.m.–8 p.m.; Sat.: 10 a.m.–7 p.m.; Sun.: 12 noon–5 p.m.

22 West 34th Street
695-2521
Mon.: 9:30 a.m.–8:30 p.m.; Tues.: 9:30 a.m.–7 p.m.;
Wed.: 9:30 a.m.–8 p.m.; Thurs., Fri.: 9:30 a.m.–8:30 p.m.;
Sat.: 10 a.m.–8 p.m.; Sun.: 12 noon–5 p.m.

113 East 23rd Street
533-6670
Mon.–Fri.: 9:30 a.m.–8 p.m.; Sat.: 10 a.m.–7 p.m.;
Sun.: 12 noon–6 p.m.
Additional branches all over town
AE, MC, V

The Gap began in the sixties as a store devoted to jeans. It grew like Topsy and in the eighties has spawned a flock of well-organized blond-wood shops that are a fine source for inexpensive but stylish sports clothing. Although you will still find denim jeans and jackets, The Gap is now the place to come for attractively styled sportswear in natural fabrics geared to city or country living. Pleated chino and khaki slacks, striped T-shirts in a range of styles, classic shorts, skinny cotton-knit leggings, slouchy cotton dresses, micro-miniskirts, copious canvas-and-leather tote bags, oversized cotton sweaters are just a few of the temptations. And many of the branches have children's sections in which the popular jean jackets, cotton sweaters, ten-button T-shirts, cotton-knit dresses, and khaki pants are cut to kiddie size.

J. CREW
South Street Seaport
203 Front Street
385-3500
Mon.–Sat.: 10 a.m.–9 p.m.; Sun: 11 a.m.–7 p.m.
AE, MC, V

J. Crew has brought its popular catalogue to life in a historic building in the South Street Seaport. The retail store (the company's first) occupies a 4,150-square-foot duplex and the cherry walls and white-washed-oak flooring provide a pleasing setting for J. Crew's classic American sportswear. The clothing is timeless and has a scrubbed-clean, healthy look and the mix includes socks and hats, swimsuits and shorts, jeans and sneakers, shirts and skirts, slacks and sports jackets. Everything comes in natural fabrics in a rainbow of bright colors, and J. Crew's prices are excellent.

J. MCLAUGHLIN
1343 Third Avenue, at 77th Street

879-9565
Mon.–Fri.: 11 a.m.–9 p.m.; Sat.: 11 a.m.–6 p.m.; Sun.: 12 noon–6 p.m.

1311 Madison Avenue, near 92nd Street
369-4830
Mon.–Wed., Fri.: 10 a.m.–6 p.m.; Thurs.: 10 a.m.–7 p.m.;
Sat.: 11 a.m.–6 p.m.; Sun.: 12 noon–5 p.m.

976 Second Avenue near 51st Street
308-4100
Mon.–Sat.: 11 a.m.–9 p.m.; Sun.: 12 noon–5 p.m.
AE, MC, V

Well-tailored, understated sportswear that manages to look both preppy and fashionable is the attraction in these comfortably clubby stores. Traditionally cut slacks in linen, khaki, and flannel; hand-knit English bulky-knit sweaters; and button-down shirts in unlikely color combinations are among the highlights for men, along with an outstanding selection of outerwear, and ties and braces. For women there are softly pleated skirts in lush ancient madders, paisley silks, and flannels; nicely tailored slacks; and beautifully detailed hand-knit sweaters.

LOUIS, BOSTON
A complete line of casual clothing that includes slacks, shirts, sweaters, and jackets. (See **Contemporary Men's Clothing**, p. 123.)

THE LOFT
89 Christopher Street
691-2334
Mon.–Sun.: 11 a.m.–midnight
All major

Guys who've rented shares in summer houses on Fire Island or the Hamptons stop here first to stock up on workout and beachwear. Sweatshirts, T-shirts, and tanks dyed dozens of breezy colors, printed camp shirts, drawstring cotton pants, shorts, a huge selection of socks, cotton sweaters, swim trunks, along with Lycra biking garb, fill the tidy shelves. Winter choices are less tempting. Inexpensive.

REMINISCENCE
Pleated linen pants, wool blazers, gabardine baseball jackets, peg-legged jeans with a fifties look. (See **Women's Clothing**, p. 170.)

STREET LIFE
470 Broadway, near Broome Street
219-3764
Mon.–Sat.: 11 a.m.–7 p.m.; Sun.: 12 noon–6 p.m.

422 Columbus Avenue, near 80th Street
769-8858
Mon.–Sat.: 12 noon–7 p.m.; Sun.: 12 noon–6 p.m.
AE, MC, V

The decor is certainly not a strong point at Street Life, but these spartan shops offer casual clothing that's ultrasimple, yet stylish and always interesting, and almost everything is manufactured and distributed by the company whose name they bear. The styles change radically each season, but cotton knits are often quilted, jackets are generally oversized, pants are pleated, shorts are baggy and Bermuda length, and skirts mini. Jumpers and shifts are favored shapes in women's dresses, and checks and plaids are popular in pants. Inexpensive.

SHIRTS

All the major department stores offer large selections of shirts. Barneys New York has a made-to-measure shirt department; Bergdorf Goodman and Saks carry shirts from London's legendary Turnbull & Asser.

ADDISON ON MADISON
698 Madison Avenue, near 62nd Street
308-2660
Mon.–Sat.: 10:30 a.m.–6:30 p.m.
AE, MC, V

All that Addison on Madison sells in its long and narrow shop with its appropriate pinstripe wallpaper is shirts and the stuff that goes along with them—silk ties, cuff links, and pocket squares. Although the shirts are made in France, they're cut long and full for the American frame. Tattersall plaids, stripes and solids in poplins and Oxford-cloth come with regular or white collars in button-down or spread or wing-tip styles, and with regular or French cuffs. There's a nice group of silk ties in unusual Reps, along with handsome silk pocket squares. Prices are excellent for such fine quality.

ARTHUR GLUCK
37 West 57th Street
Fourth floor
758-0610/755-8165
Mon.–Wed., Thurs., Sat., Sun.: 9 a.m.–4:30 p.m.; Fri.: 9 a.m.–2 p.m.
No credit cards

Arthur Gluck has been making custom shirts for his well-dressed customers for more than thirty years, and in his comfortable but spare fourth-floor workroom-shop he offers dozens of colors, patterns, and fine fabrics to choose from. Gluck requires two months and a minimum order of six shirts, but given his exemplary workmanship, it's well worth the wait. Expensive.

ASCOT CHANG
7 West 57th Street
759-3333
Mon.–Sat.: 9:30 a.m.–6 p.m.
AE, MC, V

For years Hong Kong shirtmaker Ascot Chang has dressed presidents and celebrities, and now he offers ready-made and custom shirts to New Yorkers from his headquarters located in a beautiful landmark building. Chang's fabrics are some of the best around—Sea Island cotton, Oxford cloth, cotton broadcloth, voile, crepe de chine—and there are more than 2,000 to choose from, along with twelve different collar styles. Italian made-to-measure suits, silk pajamas and dressing gowns, silk handkerchiefs and handcrafted umbrellas are a few of the other temptations. Prices are excellent for such fine quality.

CHRIS-ARTO CUSTOM SHIRT COMPANY
39 West 32nd Street
Sixth floor
563-4455
Mon.–Fri.: 8 a.m.–5:30 p.m.
No credit cards

Tucked away on the sixth floor of an old building are Chris-Arto Shirt Company's shop and workroom, where shirts are made the old-fashioned way and require a number of fittings—but they're well worth the trouble. There's a large selection of luxurious fabrics to choose from, and the workmanship is first-rate. In addition to shirts, Chris-Arto offers custom-made pajamas. There's a minimum order of six shirts; allow one month for delivery.

COMME DES GARÇONS SHIRT
454 West Broadway
979-1995
Mon–Sat.: 11 a.m.–7 p.m.; Sun.: 12 noon–6:30 p.m.
All major

Japanese designer Rei Kawakubo conceived the notion of a tiny shop devoted to shirts and in this spare, 1,000-square-foot shop that's all you'll find. Like her fashions, the shop's interior is stark and minimalistic. Shirts for men and women hang from a sculptural curved rack or are neatly folded on a long, low shelf. Most of Kawakubo's shirts are multicolored, but there are a group of white shirts, and all have the designer's genius for detailing.

CUSTOM SHOP
555 Lexington Avenue, at 50th Street
759-7480
Mon.–Sat.: 9 a.m.–6 p.m.

1400 Broadway, near 38th Street
244-2748
Mon.–Fri.: 9 a.m.–6 p.m.

1364 Avenue of the Americas, at 55th Street
582-4950
Mon.–Sat.: 9 a.m.–6 p.m.

115 Broadway, near Pine Street
267-8535
Mon.–Fri.: 8:30 a.m.–5:30 p.m.

618 Fifth Avenue, near 49th Street
245-2499
Mon.–Sat.: 9 a.m.–6 p.m.

338 Madison Avenue, near 43rd Street
867-3650
Mon.–Sat.: 9 a.m.–6 p.m.
AE, DC, MC, V

Custom-made shirts at the Custom Shop cost about the same as ready-to-wear ones in most other stores, yet in these attractive little boutiques you have the choice of more than 300 cotton and cotton-blended fabrics, along with the comfort that comes from a shirt tailored to your own proportions. They make a full range of dress shirts, too, along with classic shirts for women. Allow six weeks for delivery; and there's a minimum order of four.

DUHAMELL
944 Madison Avenue, near 74th Street
737-1525
Mon.–Sat.: 10 a.m.–6:30 p.m.
AE, MC, V

Duhamell is not only known for the fine quality of its custom-made shirts; it's known for the elegant shirting fabrics it uses in making them. Egyptian and Sea Island cottons, silks, Swiss voiles, and broadcloths are among the hundreds of fabric possibilities. In addition to shirts, Duhamell offers equally fine custom suits and leather jackets. Allow three weeks for delivery on shirts; there's a minimum order of six.

FIL À FIL
610 Fifth Avenue, near 49th Street
247-4291
Mon.–Sat.: 10 a.m.–6:30 p.m.
AE, D, MC, V

The name Fil à Fil refers to a common French shirting weave, but it is also the name of a French manufacturer and retailer with shops all over Europe and one pocket-size outpost in New York. Full-cut shirts for men come in dozens of solids and stripes and in collar styles that range from button-down to classic, and from spread to tuxedo. There's a selection for women, too, in classic men's shirting fabrics and styles, along with many others that are more feminine and fashion oriented.

PAUL STUART
Made-to-measure men's shirts can be selected from an extensive array of patterns, colors, and fabrics in a wide range of collar, cuff, and pocket choices. (See **Traditional Men's Clothing,** p. 118.)

SEEWALDT & BAUMAN
17 East 45th Street
Seventh floor
682-3958
Mon.–Fri.: 8 a.m.–5 p.m.
No credit cards

Seewaldt & Bauman have been in the business of making custom shirts since 1921, and this company still makes shirts the old-fashioned way, using paper patterns that are individually cut for each customer. It's a small showroom cluttered with fabrics, patterns, and shirts in various stages of completion since the shirts are made in workrooms right on the premises. Only the very finest imported cottons are used, the styling is Old World classic, and the quality of the workmanship is superior. Allow four to six weeks for delivery. Expensive.

SULKA & CO.
Custom shirting fabric can be chosen from more than 1,000 fine examples, and the quality and workmanship of the finished product are superb. (See **Traditional Men's Clothing,** p. 118.)

CUSTOM SUITS

ALAN FLUSSER
Made-to-measure suits cut from fine Scottish and English woolens with a thirties' styling. (See **Contemporary Men's Clothing**, p. 119.)

ALFRED DUNHILL OF LONDON
Exquisitely tailored custom suits that offer fine workmanship, lush fabrics, and traditional boardroom styling. (See **Traditional Men's Clothing**, p. 115.)

BRIONI
Beautifully styled and worked custom-made suits. (See **Contemporary Men's Clothing**, p. 120.)

CHIPP OF NEW YORK
342 Madison Avenue, at 43rd Street
Second floor
687-0850
Mon.–Sat.: 9 a.m.–5:30 p.m.; closed Sat. in summer
AE, DC, MC, V

In a comfortable library-like setting the Winston brothers present an incredible range of made-to-measure and custom-made suits. Conservative, classic, two or three-button American suits are the chief attraction, but it's possible to order a suit in just about any cut and style. Custom-riding garb is a specialty, along with Chipp's custom ties emblazoned with any sport, animal, or logo of one's choice. Ready-to-wear suits, jackets, and slacks, too.

DIMITRI COUTURE
110 Greene Street
431-1090
Sixth floor
Mon.–Fri.: 9 a.m.–5 p.m.; by appointment

Dimitri Salon
382 West Broadway
431-7336
Tues.–Sun.: 11:30 a.m.–6:30 p.m.
AE, MC, V

Known as the tailor to the stars, Piero Dimitri produces custom-made suits that look both classically conservative and trendy. His suits are precisely made and stitched by hand in his cavernous SoHo loft. There's a large selection of luxurious Italian and English fabrics to

140

choose from, and the styling tends toward a natural-shoulder English-American look with a hint of Armani. Allow six weeks; expensive. Dimitri's salon on West Broadway carries ready-made clothing for both men and women.

F. R. TRIPLER & CO.
Traditionally styled, well-tailored made-to-measure suits cut from lush fabrics; allow six weeks. (See **Traditional Men's Clothing,** p. 117.)

JOHN REYLE
20 East 46th Street
753-1663
By appointment only
No credit cards

John Reyle is considered by many experts the most knowledgeable tailor this side of the Atlantic, and his customers include the top media and business names. In his unpretentious workshop he offers suits in a full range of styles, from conservative, to fashion-forward, to any combination of styles a customer wishes. His fabrics are top quality and his workmanship exquisite. Allow four weeks.

SAINT LAURIE LTD.
Nicely priced, conservatively styled made-to-measure and custom-made suits (in both standard and luxury fabrics) are offered in a clublike setting. (See **Contemporary Men's Clothing,** p. 125.)

UNDERWEAR

All the major department stores carry a complete selection of men's underwear. See also **Men's Clothing, Vintage,** for vintage boxer shorts, smoking jackets, pajamas, and robes.

ASCOT CHANG
Made-to-measure silk pajamas and dressing gowns. (See **Men's Shirts,** p. 137.)

BROOKS BROTHERS
Boxer shorts and undershirts, cotton and cotton-flannel classic-cut pajamas, and a fine selection of terry cloth, wool, and paisley bathrobes. (See **Traditional Men's Clothing,** p. 116.)

CHRIS-ARTO CUSTOM SHIRT COMPANY
Custom-made pajamas that are made the old-fashioned way. (See **Men's Shirts,** p. 137.)

PAUL STUART
Sea Island cotton pajamas and classic robes in a range of fabrics. (See **Traditional Men's Clothing**, p. 118.)

SULKA & CO.
Classic button-front boxer shorts made from fine cotton shirting fabrics, luxurious silk pajamas, silk and brocade smoking jackets, and bathrobes in cottons, wools, silks, and paisleys. (See **Traditional Men's Clothing** p. 118.)

UNDER WARES
1098 Third Avenue, near 64th Street
535-6006
Mon.–Fri.: 10 a.m.–7 p.m.; Sat.: 10 a.m.–6 p.m.; Sun.: noon–5 p.m.
AE, MC, V

Under Wares was the city's first shop devoted exclusively to men's underwear, and owner Ron Lee stocks more than forty styles of briefs and boxer shorts, along with pajamas and robes, in styles that range from conservative to funky. He carries skintight briefs along with pleated boxers and these come in dozens of fabrics and in a wide range of solids and prints. Hard-to-find European briefs and T-shirts; nightshirts and kimonos, socks, and an extensive collection of swimwear year round—everything from kinky G-string bikinis to baggy jams in wild prints—account for the shop's popularity.

VICTORIA'S SECRET
A handsome selection of robes, boxer shorts, briefs, pajamas, and undershirts in a range of colors, prints, and fabrics. (See **Women's Clothing**, p. 179.)

SWEATERS
MEN'S AND WOMEN'S

The department stores offer a large selection of sweaters in a range of styles and prices. See **Men's Clothing** and **Women's Clothing, Vintage,** for vintage sweaters. See also **Men's Clothing** and **Women's Clothing, Casual and Traditional.**

A. PETER PUSHBOTTOM
1157 Second Avenue, near 61st Street

879-2600

Mon.–Sat.: 11 a.m.–6:30 p.m.
AE, MC, V

A. Peter Pushbottom is a spare and neatly ordered shop that's lined with shelves stacked with hand-loomed cotton sweaters in very classic styles—crew-neck or V-neck cardigans and pullovers that come either plain, cable, or stockinette stitched. What makes them special is the quality of the yarns and the incredible choice of solid colors. They're simple and basic, yet wonderful additions to anyone's wardrobe and pleasantly priced. Around the corner, at Pushbottom for Kids, is a selection of cotton sweaters for children.

BENETTON
601 Madison Avenue, near 57th Street
751-3155
Mon.–Sat.: 10 a.m.–6 p.m.; Sun.: 12 noon–5 p.m.

805 Lexington Avenue, at 62nd Street
752-5283
Mon.–Wed, Fri., Sat.: 10:30 a.m.–6:30 p.m.; Thurs.: 10:30 a.m.–8 p.m.

475 Fifth Avenue, near 41st Street
685-2727
Mon.–Wed., Fri.: 10 a.m.–7 p.m.; Thurs.: 10 a.m.–8 p.m.; Sat.:
10 a.m.–6 p.m.

Additional branches all over town
AE, MC, V

Benetton, the inventor of "fast fashion," has more than 4,000 franchises in more than fifty countries, and now is almost as ubiquitous in New York as it is in Italy. In the outlets that dot just about every city street, you'll find a complete range of simple yet stylish Italian knit separates for men, women, and children that are meant to be mixed and matched and layered, yet Benetton excels in its selection of sweaters. There are classic V-neck vests, boldly patterned ski sweaters, bulky ribbed cottons, traditional cardigans, all in an endless range of colors and at very affordable prices

BOMBA DE CLERCQ
100 Thompson Street
226-2484
Mon.: 1 p.m.–6 p.m.; Tues.–Sun.: 1 p.m.–7 p.m.
All major

Doll-size sweaters line the walls of this enchanting shop, the New York branch of Cristina Bomba's Via dell'Oca store in Rome. The miniatures serve as samples of the adult-sized versions stored in boxes just behind, and the sweaters themselves are as irresistible as the display. Most are hand-knits in old-fashioned, classic shapes with arresting details and beguiling color combinations. You might find patchwork stripes, chevron patterns, rows of tiny pearl buttons, and intricately detailed collars. Bomba offers cardigans, pullovers, dresses, and jackets in cotton, wool, silk, cashmere, alpaca, and linen. Pricey, but think of these knits as timeless investments.

BROOKS BROTHERS
An extensive selection of well-priced cotton, Shetland wool, and cashmere sweaters in solids, collegiate stripes, and argyles. (See **Men's Clothing,** p. 116.)

CASHMERE-CASHMERE
Classic and high-fashion sweaters made of cashmere, including some that are 10-ply, in solids, argyles, and bold prints. (See **Women's Clothing,** p. 153.)

CHARIVARI
An outstanding selection of sweaters by cutting-edge designers. (See **Men's Clothing,** p. 126.)

FINE DESIGN
11 West 18th Street
741-7498
Mon.–Thurs., Sat.: 10 a.m.–7 p.m.; Fri.: 10 a.m.–8 p.m.;
Sun.: 12 noon–6 p.m.

Pier 17
South Street Seaport
406-3661
Mon.–Sat.: 10 a.m.–7 p.m.; Sun.: 12 noon–6 p.m.
AE, MC, V

Ellen Fine's cozy stores, with their scrubbed English pine armoires and baskets of potpourri, are filled with nicely done, traditionally styled sweaters. Classic Shetlands and cotton crew- and V-neck pullovers and cardigans in pales and brights fill the tidy shelves, along with polo shirts, skirts, shorts, and slacks. Fine offers tempting bed and table linens and things for the home, too, that might include comforters in tartan-plaid flannel, boldly colored blankets, pillows, place mats, towels, fabric-covered frames, and baskets. Prices are amazingly good.

GRANNY MADE
381 Amsterdam Avenue, near 78th Street
496-1222
Mon.–Fri.: 11 a.m.–7 p.m.; Sat.: 10 a.m.–6 p.m.; Sun.: 12 noon–5 p.m.
All major

Michael Rosenberg's grandmother is the inspiration behind his friendly and appealing store. For seventy years Granny designed and knit classic cable sweaters for his family, and now Rosenberg has adapted her original designs and has found a contractor to produce them on knitting machines. In addition to his grandmother's cables, Rosenberg offers a myriad of boldly patterned hand-loomed sweaters by Basco, Bill Ditford, and Prima Maglia, as well as knit skirts, leggings, dresses, scarves, hats, and gloves. Granny's classics come in children's sizes, too, along with tiny ski caps hand-knit by Granny herself, cotton playsuits from Sweden, hand-loomed animal hats from Vermont, and cotton-knit overalls and shirts from Brazil.

J. MCLAUGHLIN
Classic crew- and V-neck sweaters in a range of shades along with bulky hand-knits from England for men; beautifully detailed hand-knits for women. (See **Men's Clothing**, p. 134.)

MATTIE HASKINS SHAMROCK IMPORTS
205 East 75th Street
288-3918
Mon.–Sat.: 11 a.m.–6 p.m.
AE, MC, V

Mattie Haskins stocks everything from Irish candy, to hometown newspapers, to Celtic crosses, to Waterford crystal in her friendly and unbelievably cluttered store. But come for the classic hand-knit Irish fishermen's sweaters. They're thick and handsome and come in off-whites and flecked browns, the color of Irish sheep. The tweed hats, as well as the rugged tweedy men's sports jackets, are also worth a visit.

MISSONI
Subtly blended colors and complex and imaginative patterns distinguish the Missoni sweaters for men and women. (See **Women's Clothing**, p. 163.)

PAUL STUART
The array of stylish sweaters ranges from classic cotton crewnecks in a dozen shades, to subdued alpaca cable knits, to thick cashmeres in hard-to-find pastels. (See **Men's Clothing**, p. 118.)

SPORTWORKS
1046 Madison Avenue, at 80th Street
879-4594
Mon.–Sat.: 10 a.m.–6 p.m.; Sun.: 12 noon–5 p.m.
All major

Tiny mother-of-pearl buttons and pastoral scenes are likely to appear in the handmade sweaters at Sportworks. Don't come here for the classics, although you might find a few plain versions in solid colors, but come for the myriad sweaters with distinctive detailing and such unusual designs as multicolored pastel windows, arrowheads, and pockets knit with squares of bold colors. Expensive.

STELLA FLAME

Hand-knit, boldly patterned sweaters are a Stella Flame specialty, so there's always a tempting assortment for men and women. Some are emblazoned with yellow taxicabs, some with silly animals; others sport overall geometric patterns. (See **Women's Clothing**, p. 157.)

STEWART ROSS

754 Madison Avenue, near 65th Street
744-3870
Mon.–Sat.: 11 a.m.–6 p.m.

105 West 72nd Street
362-9620
Mon.–Fri.: 12 noon–7 p.m.; Sat., Sun.: 12 noon–6 p.m.

150 Spring Street
966-1024
Mon.–Wed., Fri., Sat.: 12 noon–7 p.m.; Thurs.: 11 a.m.–7 p.m.;
Sun.: 12 noon–6 p.m.
AE, DC, MC, V

Stewart and his brother Steven design boldly patterned sweaters that are hand-made for them in England, and they carry English designer Susan Duckworth's intricate geometric knits. Although these sweaters are made in England, they're decidedly not classic. Patterns might include a map of Florida dotted with orange groves, alligators, and water-skiers; multicolored pepperoni slices; faded flowers, or whatever else suits the brothers' fancy. Relaxed and pleated slacks, graceful skirts and dresses, great T-shirts, along with a small but very special selection of stylishly rugged shoes and work boots, are among the other attractions.

WOMEN'S CLOTHING
ANTIQUE AND VINTAGE

See also **Men's Clothing**, **Vintage**.

ACADEMY CLOTHES

Never-worn day dresses, suits, blouses, and sweaters. (See **Men's Clothing**, p. 111.)

ALICE UNDERGROUND

380 Columbus Avenue, at 78th Street
724-6682
Daily: 11 a.m.–8 p.m.

481 Broadway, near Broome Street
431-9067
Daily: 10 a.m.–7 p.m.
No credit cards

Alice Underground has been a fixture on Columbus Avenue for years. Its cavernous basement space is filled with old armoires and vanities neatly stacked with vintage treasures: bed and table linens; teddies, slips, nightgowns, and robes; gloves and handbags. Racks are crammed with clothing that's as early as the thirties, as recent as the seventies. Both the original shop and the newer outpost on Broadway are strong on fifties cotton dresses and printed rayon frocks from the forties; prom dresses in tulles, laces, and failles; vintage jeans; assorted jewelry and old suede and leather jackets. Prices here are some of the best in town.

ANDY'S CHEE-PEE'S

14 St. Marks Place
674-9248
Daily: 12 noon–9 p.m.

16 West 8th Street
460-8488
Daily: 11 a.m.–8 p.m.
AE, MC, V

Not for the faint of heart, these stores require stamina and perseverance since they're bulging with vintage clothing unceremoniously heaped in piles on the floor and hung from the rafters. All the vintage standards—from cotton day dresses, to twenties laces, to wedding gowns—are here in multiples. Among the formal wear and prom dresses are styles as early as Victorian, as recent as the sixties. Men will find seersucker jackets, forties suits, and tuxedos along with shirts of all kinds. Much of the merchandise is in need of cleaning and repair, but prices, as the name says, are cheap.

ANN LAWRENCE

Victorian whites, turn-of-the-century tea dresses, twenties batiste afternoon dresses, and beaded gowns. (See **Linens and Quilts,** p. 381.)

THE ANTIQUE BOUTIQUE

Vintage tulle prom and satin cocktail dresses, Capri pants and clam diggers, beaded blouses and sweaters, and sixties miniskirts. (See **Men's Clothing,** p. 111.)

BOGIES ANTIQUE CLOTHING AND FURS
201 East 10th Street
260-1199
Mon.–Thurs.: 12:30 p.m.–5:30 p.m.; Fri., Sat.: 12:30 p.m.–6 p.m.
No credit cards

Clothes are piled from floor to ceiling in this astonishingly cluttered store, yet there are some real treasures to be unearthed from the clothing heaps. Although the strengths are fifties day dresses, beaded sweaters, blouses, and scarves, you'll find delicate silk and satin nightgowns and slips well worth searching for. There are fur coats and leather jackets, too, and although things are *cheap*, be prepared to clean and mend.

CHAMELEON VINTAGE CLOTHING
Cotton nightshirts, tailored suits, navy and print dresses from the forties through the sixties, along with lovely silk kimonos and shoes. (See **Men's Clothing**, p. 112.)

CHEAP JACK'S VINTAGE CLOTHING
Rayon dresses from the thirties and forties as well as beaded sweaters and wool skirts. (See **Men's Clothing**, p. 112.)

DOROTHY'S CLOSET
335 Bleecker Street
206-6414
Mon.–Fri.: 2 p.m.–8 p.m.; Sat., Sun.: 1 p.m.–9 p.m.
AE, MC, V

This aptly named store, not much bigger than a closet, is a charming place to shop for clothing from the twenties through the sixties. Sexy black or navy dresses with unusual detailing, exquisite lingerie, hats, blouses, and silk-print skirts are the main attractions. For men there are classic rayon shirts, ties, and jackets from the forties, fifties, and sixties. Although the selection is limited, everything has been carefully chosen, cleaned, and mended by owner Dorothy Tyler.

HARRIET LOVE
412 West Broadway
966-2280
Mon.–Sat.: 12 noon–7 p.m.; Sun.: 12 noon–6 p.m.
AE, MC, V

Harriet Love was one of the first to sell top quality and high-fashion vintage clothing, and in her tidy, well-organized shop she still offers some of the finest examples around. It's a carefully edited collection, and everything is in pristine condition and geared to the latest fashion trends. You'll find designer originals from the thirties and forties—Adrian, Chanel, and Norell—along with cocktail dresses, beaded sweaters, jewel-neck blouses, alligator and crocodile handbags, and an attractive selection of pewter and sterling-silver jewelry that includes Mexican baubles from the forties; also Zelda Vintage (dresses and suits made from thirties and forties patterns). Men will be tempted by the vivid assortment of Hawaiian shirts and evening scarves. Pricey.

JOIA
1151 Second Avenue, near 60th Street
754-9017
Mon.–Fri.: 11 a.m.–7 p.m.; Sat.: 11 a.m.–6:30 p.m.
AE, DC, MC, V

Everything from Victorian whites to forties day dresses is temptingly displayed in this immaculate shop. Silk nightgowns and robes, evening gowns cut from such sensuous fabrics as silk, crepe, and satin, and fringed-and-embroidered silk shawls are among the other finds offered by owner Carol Caver. Her collection of vintage Western and Hawaiian shirts is outstanding, and there are some exceptional pieces of forties costume jewelry, Bakelite bracelets from the thirties, and Mexican silver. Clarice Cliff's hand-painted pottery from the twenties and thirties—cookie jars, sugar shakers, jam jars, and bowls—provides a bright backdrop to the clothing. Prices at Joia are reasonable, considering the quality, condition, and location of the store.

LOVE SAVES THE DAY
119 Second Avenue, at 7th Street
228-3802
Mon.–Fri.: 12 noon–10 p.m.; Fri., Sat.: 12 noon–11 p.m.; Sun.: 1 p.m.–9 p.m.
AE, MC, V

Known as the spot to pick up funky vintage clothing, Love Saves the Day gained additional fame from its brief appearance in the movie *Desperately Seeking Susan*. Although the Jimi Hendrix jacket is of course long gone, there are lots of other treats for those in search of the East Village look, since the shop is crammed with Army coats, inexpensive fifties and sixties skirts, dresses, beaded sweaters, and men's tweed jackets, along with more costly twenties and thirties evening gowns. At Halloween there's a beguiling array of costumes (including authentic-looking American Indians), masks, and hats.

PANACHE
Broad-shouldered forties silk and faille dresses, a tempting selection of designer jackets, and beautifully worked beaded sweaters and blouses. (See **Wedding Gowns and Evening Wear,** p. 182.)

SCREAMING MIMI'S
Capri pants and clam diggers, rayon dresses, prom gowns and fifties bathing suits. (See **Men's Clothing,** p. 113.)

THE SECOND COMING

Printed rayon day dresses and black and navy silks and failles from the forties and fifties, along with beaded sweaters and vintage shoes (including saddles with pointed toes and patent-leather flats). Prices are plainly marked and dresses are arranged by size. (See **Furniture,** p. 257.)

CONSERVATIVE

The department stores offer a large assortment of conservative business suits.

ALCOTT & ANDREWS

335 Madison Avenue, at 44th Street
818-0606
Mon.–Wed., Fri.: 10 a.m.–8 p.m.; Thurs.: 10 a.m.–9 p.m.;
Sat.: 10 a.m.–6 p.m.; Sun.: 12 noon–5 p.m.

1301 Avenue of the Americas, at 52nd Street
315-2796
Mon.–Wed., Fri.: 10 a.m.–8 p.m.; Thurs.: 10 a.m.–9 p.m.;
Sat.: 10 a.m.–6 p.m.; Sun.: 12 noon–5 p.m.
AE, MC, V

Alcott & Andrews specializes in clothing for the executive woman, so everything in these handsome stores with their bleached-wood floors, comfortable sofas, and classical music is carefully arranged to make shopping speedy and painless. Organization is the key: Jackets, skirts, suits, blouses, and dresses are sorted by color (either matching or co-ordinated), and navy, burgundy, beige, gray, and soft pastels abound. For the more confident executive woman there's an appealing selection of sensuous silk blouses, flowing skirts, shirtwaist dresses, and sleeve-less sheaths. The lower level offers casual separates for the busy execu-tive's weekend life.

BROOKS BROTHERS

Well-made and well-priced suits, coats, shirtwaist dresses, and softly feminine blouses, along with classic Brooks Brothers button-down shirts cut for women. (See **Men's Clothing,** p. 116.)

F. R. TRIPLER & CO.

Classic women's wear on the third floor offers the same top-quality fabrics and fine workmanship as the men's clothing, but the silhouette is softer and feminine. (See **Men's Clothing,** p. 117.)

JAEGER INTERNATIONAL
818 Madison Avenue, near 68th Street
628-3350
Mon.–Wed., Fri., Sat.: 10 a.m.–6 p.m.; Thurs.: 10 a.m.–7 p.m.

19 East 57th Street
753-0370
Mon.–Wed., Fri., Sat.: 10 a.m.–6 pm; Thurs.: 10 a.m.–7 p.m.

620 Fifth Avenue, near 50th Street
247-4020
Mon.–Wed., Fri., Sat.: 10 a.m.–6 p.m.; Thurs.: 10 a.m.–7 p.m.
AE, MC

Jaeger offers few surprises, but the quality of its classic British clothing is outstanding. There are kilts, Shetland and cashmere sweaters, nicely tailored skirts, jackets, and slacks. Colors are subdued, befitting clothing that is meant to be worn for years. Suits and sportswear for men are equally traditional and well executed.

JONAL
Well-tailored and sophisticated suits—both off-the-rack and made-to-measure—for the executive woman. (See **Contemporary Women's Clothing,** p. 154.)

PAUL STUART
On the mezzanine you'll find the women's private-label clothing that's finely tailored, yet soft and feminine, and cut from the same high-quality fabrics as the men's line. (See **Men's Clothing,** p. 118.)

POLO/RALPH LAUREN
For the well-heeled executive woman there are beautifully tailored suits, jackets, skirts, and shirts cut from the finest fabrics. (See **Men's Clothing,** p. 124.)

TAHARI
The beautifully tailored suits are designed to take the busy female executive from the office to an evening out. (See **Contemporary Women's Clothing,** p. 158.)

CONTEMPORARY

The department stores offer a full range of contemporary women's clothing.

ANN TAYLOR

3 East 57th Street
832-2010
Mon.–Wed., Fri., Sat.: 10 a.m.–6 p.m.; Thurs.: 10 a.m.–8 p.m.

575 Fifth Avenue, at 47th Street
818-0720
Mon.–Wed., Fri., Sat.: 10 a.m.–6 p.m.; Thurs: 10 a.m.–8 p.m.

Herald Center
1 Herald Square
695-4474
Mon.–Sat.: 10 a.m.–7 p.m.

South Street Seaport
25 Fulton Street
608-5612
Mon.–Sat.: 10 a.m.–7 p.m.; Sun.: 12 noon–6 p.m.

805 Third Avenue, at 50th Street
308-5333
Mon.–Wed., Fri.: 10 a.m.–7 p.m.; Thurs.: 10 a.m.–8 p.m.; Sat.:
10 a.m.–6 p.m.

2017 Broadway, at 69th Street
873-7344
Mon.–Fri.: 10 a.m.–8 p.m.; Sat.: 11 a.m.–7 p.m.; Sun.: 12 noon–5 p.m.

1293 Broadway, at 34th Street
695-4474
Mon.–Sat.: 10 a.m.–7 p.m.

2 World Financial Center
245-1991
Mon.–Fri.: 10 a.m.–7 p.m.; Sat.: 10 a.m.–6 p.m.; Sun.: 12 noon–5 p.m.
AE, MC, V

Ann Taylor offers stylish yet comfortable clothing that appeals equally
to the college student, working woman, young mother, and matron of a
certain age. Although the fashions aren't on the cutting edge, they're
always au courant. Wearable knit separates; hand-sewn leather jackets and skirts; wool and linen skirts, slacks, and blazers; and rayon and
silk dresses come in the most-wanted colors and styles. Shoes by Joan
and David, attractive leather bags and belts, and a wonderful array of
socks and tights make these stores irresistible.

BETSEY BUNKY NINI

746 Madison Avenue, near 64th Street
744-6716
Mon.–Fri.: 10:30 a.m.–6 p.m.; Sat.: 11 a.m.–6 p.m.
AE, MC, V

The look is too subdued to be considered cutting edge but hip customers come here for casually chic clothes that are offbeat yet feminine and pretty. You'll find Byblos and Montana and Patricia Clyne, along with emerging young designers and Zelda Vintage (new clothing made from vintage patterns) represented in the shop's stock of quietly fashionable dresses, suits, and separates. Delightful handmade sweaters from England and T-shirts occupy the front of the store. Pricey.

CASHMERE-CASHMERE
840 Madison Avenue, near 69th Street
988-5252
Mon.–Fri.: 10 a.m.–6 p.m.; Sat.: 10 a.m.–5:15 p.m.;
Sun.: 12 noon–5 p.m.

595 Madison Avenue, near 57th Street
935-2522
Mon.–Sat.: 10 a.m.–6 p.m.
AE, MC, V

Everything at Cashmere-Cashmere is made of that classy stuff except for the occasional appearance of leather or suede in slacks or skirts. Styles range from simply fashioned, but luxurious, crew-neck dresses to argyle sweaters to sweat suits to cashmere and suede blankets. Men will find thick robes, eight-ply cardigans, ribbed pullovers, socks, and slippers. Expensive.

FDR DRIVE
109 Thompson Street
966-4827
Tues.–Sun.: 1 p.m.–7 p.m.
AE, MC, V

FDR Drive was once known for its collection of vintage clothing and linens, but owners Rita Brookoff and Wayne Mahler now turn out new designs inspired by the old styles. Jewel-neck blouses encrusted with beads and sequins, oversize rayon shirts made from vintage fabrics, slouchy slacks, forties-inspired suits, and drop-waist dresses are some of the things you're likely to find in this pocket-size store. But there's still a well-edited selection of antique linens (including Marseilles spreads), Victorian white dresses and organdy blouses, along with a tempting assortment of vintage jewelry, and, tacked on the walls, an enchanting array of antique beaded evening bags.

FONDA BOUTIQUE
209 East 60th Street
759-3260
Mon.–Fri.: 11 a.m.–8 p.m.; Sat.: 11 a.m.–7 p.m.; Sun.: 11:30 a.m.–
6 p.m.
AE, MC, V

Fonda has been producing unusual, one-of-a-kind clothing for over a dozen years and everything in her colorful shop is unique without being ultratrendy. She makes skirts from a patchwork of antique scarves, suits from Battenberg lace, dresses and jackets from vintage kimonos, and lively evening wear from Italian and French silks. Fonda carries an eclectic mix of antique and contemporary beaded bags, vintage hand-embroidered piano throws, and Egyptian shawls of silk and hammered-silver, too. Prices are fairly reasonable for one-of-a-kind creations.

GUCCI
683 Fifth Avenue, near 54th Street
826-2600
Mon.–Wed., Fri., Sat.: 9:30 a.m.–6 p.m.; Thurs.: 9:30 a.m.–7 p.m.
AE, DC, MC, V

Saddler Guccio Gucci (whose interlocked initials account for the company's signature) opened a small leather workshop in Florence in 1904, where he produced fine saddles and harnesses for the local aristocracy. But when Gucci began making sturdy walking shoes, decorated with a horse's bit, an empire was born. Today, over 6,000 items fill the company's catalogue, and its glitzy Fifth Avenue outpost is a small-scale department store stocked with Gucci products. It offers suits and dresses for city living, taffeta circle skirts and cashmere spencer jackets for evening wear, and suede quilted jackets and flannel slacks for the country. For men there are handsome alpaca coats, covert-wool trousers, argyle polo sweaters, and houndstooth-checked jackets. Shoes lean toward the classic—suede kilty loafers and wingtips for men, flats with suede bows, crepe-soled lace-ups, and conservative pumps for women. And fine leather luggage, silks scarves, traditional handbags, umbrellas, and scores of wallets and key cases fill the well-stocked shelves.

HONEYBEE
7 East 53rd Street
688-3660
Mon.–Wed., Fri.: 10 a.m.–6:30 p.m.; Thurs.: 10 a.m.–8 p.m.;
Sat.: 10 a.m.–6 p.m.
All major

Honeybee is the spacious flagship store of a well-known catalogue company and it offers a range of fashion looks for a range of women. There's a designer collection of fashionable, stylish, and well-priced separates for the college bound, tempting sportswear geared to young mothers, and conservative outfits appropriate for the boardroom. It's staffed by amiable people who keep records of previous purchases and can help customers choose the right wardrobe for business trips to any city in the country.

JONAL
1281 Madison Avenue, near 91st Street

860-8101
Mon.–Fri.: 10 a.m.–6 p.m.; Sat. by appointment
AE, MC, V

Although Jonal is known for its trendy, high-fashion clothing, its spirit
has always been closer to the thirties frock salon pictured in old movies, the kind that excels in attentive service. Two years ago the shop
moved to a Victorian townhouse and it now has the proper setting for
its old-fashioned charms: elegant fireplaces, polished wood moldings,
converted gaslight fixtures, and a baronial staircase. Here you can buy
off the rack—or from a *prêt-à-couture* line—beautifully tailored suits
and dresses for the boardroom, wonderfully versatile day ensembles to
see you through a White House luncheon or a tête-à-tête at Le Cirque,
terribly chic maternity dresses, elegant evening creations, and made-
to-measure debutante fantasies and bridal gowns. The wedding gowns
are traditional, yet sophisticated, and fabrics include such Old World
delights as silk eyelet, cotton piqué, and delicate organza, and the
shop can supply veils, hats, shoes, and dresses for the entire bridal
party. Expensive.

LAURA ASHLEY
21 East 57th Street
752-7300
Mon.–Fri.: 10 a.m.–7 p.m.; Sat.: 10 a.m.–6 p.m.

4 Fulton Street
South Street Seaport
809-3555
Mon.–Sat.: 10 a.m.–7 p.m.; Sun.: 11 a.m.–6 p.m.

398 Columbus Avenue, at 79th Street
496-5110
Mon.–Wed., Fri., Sat.: 11 a.m.–7 p.m.; Thurs.: 11 a.m.–8 p.m.;
Sun.: 11 a.m.–6 p.m.
AE, MC, V

The name Laura Ashley is synonymous with romantic English-country
looks, and the company offers clothing that captures the charm of another era. Everything is sweetly feminine and adorned with a profusion
of tiny floral prints; virginal-looking sundresses, prim blouses, pretty
cotton petticoats, and winning nightgowns abound. Demure, high-
necked, lace-edged, Victorian and Edwardian bridal and bridesmaid
gowns are ideal for a pastoral wedding. The 57th Street store carries the
complete Laura Ashley collection while the Columbus Avenue store has
a nicely edited selection.

MICHELLE NICOLE WESLEY
126 Prince Street, near Wooster Street
334-1313
Mon.–Sat.: 11:30 a.m.–7 p.m.; Sun.: 11:30 a.m.–6 p.m.
AE, MC, V

Idiosyncratic designs reminiscent of ballerina gowns and old-fashioned lingerie are Michelle Nicole Wesley's specialty. She does mostly cotton knits such as drop-waist dresses, camisole tops, skinny leggings, dusters, and oversize T-shirts in black and white with the occasional blush of lavender, mint, peach, or celadon. And Wesley always has a stock of serendipitous finds—marbleized pencils and journals, soaps and scents, lacy drawer liners, delicate bed linens, and bath towels.

MONSOON

842 Lexington Avenue, at 64th Street
888-0810
Mon.–Sat.: 10 a.m.–6:30 p.m.; Sun.: 12 noon–5 p.m.
AE, MC, V

In its comfortable blond-wood and batik American flagship store, Monsoon, a ubiquitous English clothing chain, offers timeless designs: unstructured smocked-cotton dresses, intricately tucked voile blouses and skirts, body-hugging Dupioni-silk suits, wrap skirts, slouchy slacks, and the outrageous prints that only the British can do. The selection of evening wear is appealing, especially the romantic strapless floral-chintz gowns. Prices are surprisingly gentle.

OUTRE MER

91 Spring Street
966-1046
Mon.–Sat.: 11 a.m.–7 p.m.; Sun.: 12 noon–6 p.m.
AE, MC, V

Outre Mer's French fashions appeal to New Yorkers searching for au courant clothing. The spartan, but winning, shop is filled with the creations of seven young French designers, along with those of our own Robespierre. Among the stylish mix are high-waisted slacks, princess dresses, beautifully cut coats and jackets, intriguing sweaters, and hats made from ties.

PUTUMAYO

339 Columbus Avenue, at 76th Street
595-3441
Mon.–Sat.: 11 a.m.–8 p.m.; Sun.: 12 noon–6 p.m.

857 Lexington Avenue, near 64th Street
734-3111
Mon.–Sat.: 11 a.m.–7 p.m.

147 Spring Street
966-4458
Mon.–Sat.: 11 a.m.–7 p.m.; Sun.: 12 noon–6 p.m.
AE, MC, V

Delightfully comfortable designs and simple styling account for Putumayo's popularity. In summertime look for cool and practical sundresses and wrap skirts, in wintertime rayon separates, light wool slacks, and warm alpaca and wool jackets. Year-round you'll find cotton dresses, madras separates, and bulky-cotton sweaters from South America and India. Woven sashes, straw hats, eye-catching South American jewelry, and appealing handbags round out the temptations, and prices are excellent.

SERMONETA
740 Madison Avenue, near 64th Street
744-6551
Mon.–Fri.: 10 a.m.–6 p.m.; Sat.: 11 a.m.–5 p.m.
AE, MC, V

Teenagers and their moms come to this colorful and sunny store for romantic cotton dresses and nightgowns that are not cloyingly sweet. Handsome hand-knit sweaters imported from South America and Europe are a year-round attraction, as are the hand-woven sisal bags and belts from Africa and Ecuador. In summer there's a stock of vivid one-of-a-kind Panama straw hats, hand-knit wool ones in winter. Sermoneta is a warm and friendly place to shop where prices are as attractive as the clothing.

THE SMITHS
454 Broome Street
431-0038
Mon.–Sat.: 11 a.m.–7 p.m.; Sun.: 1 p.m.–6 p.m.
AE, MC, V

At The Smiths you'll find a small, well-edited collection of timeless clothing with the attention to detail paramount. There's a respect for stitching, buttons, and the press and drape of a garment. Owners Elizabeth and Tony Smith and Lisa Friscia offer their own creations as well as those of Margaret Howell and Marina Spadafora. There are beautifully cut jackets, pleated skirts, and Irish jacquard-linen dresses and dusters for women. Slacks with a relaxed forties fit, Sea Island cotton shirts, and nicely executed sport jackets for men.

STELLA FLAME
476 Columbus Avenue, near 82nd Street
874-5262
Tues.–Sat.: 12 noon–7 p.m.; Sun.: 12 noon–6 p.m.
AE, MC, V

You can buy a tea gown or a tea pot at Stella Flame. Tucked in among the clothing are antiques that are as distinctive as the selection of dresses, skirts, and blouses. Owner Stella Flame (her real name) has an eye for the unusual and carries turn-of-the-century frames, Clarice Cliff china, and vintage watches in addition to the appealingly fashioned ready-to-wear suitable for the office or the opera. Hand-knit, boldly patterned sweaters are a Flame specialty so there's always a tempting assortment for both men and women. Some are emblazoned with yellow taxi cabs, some with silly animals, others sport overall geometric patterns. Men will find jackets and slacks cut from beautiful fabrics and finished by hand. Flame and her partner, Ricardo Mercado, also offer custom-made clothing for men and women.

TAHARI
802 Madison Avenue, near 67th Street
535-1515
Mon.–Wed., Fri., Sat.: 10:30 a.m.–6:30 p.m.; Thurs.: 10:30 a.m.–
7:30 p.m.

2 World Financial Center
945-2450
Mon.–Wed.: 10 a.m.–6:30 p.m.; Thurs.: 10 a.m.–8 p.m.;
Sat. & Sun.: 12 noon–5 p.m.
AE, DC, MC, V

Beautifully tailored suits that are designed to take the busy female executive from the office to an evening out are offered under the Tahari label. The name belongs to Elie Tahari, a former electrician in the garment district who built a multimillion-dollar business from a single tube top. Graceful silk, rayon, and gabardine dresses; nicely cut slacks; and ultra-feminine silk blouses are offered in Tahari's attractively appointed shops.

VICTORIA FALLS
451 West Broadway
254-2433
Mon.–Sat.: 11 a.m.–7 p.m.; Sun.: 12:30 p.m.–6:30 p.m.
AE, DC, MC, V

Originally, Victoria Falls was a vintage clothing store that specialized in Victoriana, but when owner Rena Gill realized that the supply of high-necked blouses wouldn't last forever, she began making her own. Now more than half the stock is made up of Gill's romantic designs that are evocative of earlier eras. Among the mix are linen or crepe drop-waist dresses; middy blouses with sailor collars; hand-knit "skimp" sweaters; wool crepe suits; starched white nightshirts; bias-cut silk skirts; and beautifully styled jackets. Yet, in the back of the store, the racks are still filled with the exquisite antique wedding dresses and fine old lingerie that first brought the rich and famous to Victoria Falls.

DESIGNER

AGNÈS B.
116 Prince Street
925-4649
Mon.–Sat.: 11 a.m.–7 p.m.; Sun.: 12 noon–6 p.m.

1063 Madison Avenue, near 81st Street
570-9330
Mon.–Sat.: 11 a.m.–6 p.m.; Sun.: 12 noon–6 p.m.
AE, MC, V

French designer Agnes de Fleurieu (the B. stands for Bourgois, the name of her first husband) does idiosyncratic takes on the most current fashion trends and comes up with understated and wonderfully wearable clothing that's *branche* without being show-offy. Her things have a distinctly French schoolgirl look that somehow manages to work as well for teenagers as for their moms. Striped cotton T-shirts, along with cropped snap-front cardigans and skinny pants, are classics; once a customer has one she always comes back for more, and Agnes B.'s buttery-soft leather jackets are additional must-haves. Stock disappears quickly in these spare shops, so if there's something you like, buy it; it's not likely to be around when you return. Well-cut pleated slacks, nicely done jackets, lush cashmere sweaters, oversized shirts in traditional shirting stripes, as well as colorful paisleys, brocades, and linens, are among the temptations for men. And there are snap-front cardigans, classic striped T-shirts, and tiny leggings in children's sizes.

ALAÏA
131 Mercer Street
941-1166
Tues.–Sat.: 12 noon–7 p.m.; Sun.: 12 noon–6 p.m.
AE, MC, V

People come to Azzedine Alaïa's store as much to stare at the dramatic interior as to admire the clothing. Designed by Jacqueline Schnabel (with furniture, sculptures, and display racks by her husband, artist Julian), the shop has the look of a ravaged theatrical set. Huge bronze Etruscan-vase columns, cast-bronze rolling racks, massive dressing tents hung with heavy velvet draperies, immense gilt mirrors, and two huge plaster-cast and glass-topped casket-like display cases dominate the space. Underfoot is an uneven flooring of rough-hewn wood. The sexy, modern, beautifully made (and shockingly expensive) Alaïa clothing is barely noticeable in the enormous high-ceilinged space.

BETSEY JOHNSON
248 Columbus Avenue, near 71st Street

362-3364
Mon.–Sat.: 12 noon–7 p.m.; Sun.: 1 p.m.–6 p.m.

130 Thompson Street
420-0169
Mon.–Sat.: 12 noon– 7 p.m.; Sun.: 1 p.m.–6 p.m.

251 East 60th Street
319-7699
Mon.–Sat.: 12 noon–7 p.m.; Sun.: 1 p.m.–6 p.m.
AE, MC, V

Hot-pink walls, black-and-white checkerboard floors, earsplitting rock music, and a partying mood—it's not the newest club, it's Betsey Johnson. For twenty years Johnson's body-hugging fashions have guaranteed entrance to the hottest clubs around, and they still do the trick. Entertaining evening looks in Lycra and Spandex, frilly crinolines, skintight skirts and tops, micro-minis, floral-printed sexy knits, silly gloves and hats are all Johnson trademarks geared to her philosophy that dressing up should be an adventure. Prices are excellent for such high-fashion fun.

CHANEL BOUTIQUE
5 East 57th Street
355-5050
Mon.–Wed., Fri., Sat.: 10 a.m.–6 p.m.; Thurs.: 10 a.m.–7 p.m.
AE, MC, V

It's fitting that the Chanel Boutique is at 5 East 57th Street since "5" has been the magic number for this illustrious house of fashion. Indeed, Chanel No. 5, as well as all the ready-to-wear and the full line of accessories and cosmetics, is available in this mirrored black-and-white jewel of a shop. Timeless white silk shirts with CC-monogrammed pockets, cashmere cardigans with brass buttons, divine evening gowns, along with signature little black dresses and braid-trimmed brass-buttoned collarless suits are among the irresistible items. And there's the classic Chanel pump, sautoia necklaces with pearls and crystals, and quilted-leather chain-handled bags to lust after, too. Expect to pay hundreds for a bag or blouse, thousands for a suit or evening dress.

COMME DES GARÇONS
Dresses have a purity of line and hang loose or just graze the body and fluid, high-waist chemise styles, and floaty drop-waist ones coexist with long jackets with cutout armholes, roomy cropped pants, and straight and narrow skirts. (See **Men's Clothing,** p. 127.)

EMANUEL UNGARO
803 Madison Avenue, near 67th Street
249-4090
Mon.–Wed., Fri., Sat.: 9:30 a.m.–6:30 p.m.; Thurs.: 9:30 a.m.–7:30 p.m.

AE, DC, MC, V

Emanuel Ungaro uses outrageously lush fabrics in unlikely combinations to create body-hugging, elegantly sexy clothes. His mix of colors and silhouettes is legendary. Party dresses of brilliant silk prints, long jackets to wear over skinny skirts, vampy suits, sensuous high-waisted slacks, and delicious scarves are some of the treats you're likely to find in his abundantly mirrored store. Expect to spend more than five hundred dollars for a blouse and at least a thousand or two for a dress.

EMPORIO ARMANI
Younger-looking fashions by the master at about half the price of his couture clothing. He does beautifully cut jackets, soft silk blouses, draped skirts, jaunty shorts, even fun shoes. (See **Men's Clothing**, p. 121.)

GIANNI VERSACE
Dresses highlight the figure with their sensuous draping and body-hugging lines, and coats, many big and collarless, come in sizzling-hot colors. Pencil-thin or cropped jackets are paired with pants or short skirts. (See **Men's Clothing**, p. 128.)

GIORGIO ARMANI
His fabrics are sumptuous without being showy, and suits, blouses, and dresses have a proper insouciance. Evening wear is simple yet beguiling, his silk lingerie manages to look both chaste and sexy at the same time, and Armani's slacks are the best around. (See **Men's Clothing**, p. 128.)

GIVENCHY BOUTIQUE
954 Madison Avenue, at 75th Street
772-1040
Mon.–Sat.: 10 a.m.–6 p.m.
AE, MC, V

The high-fashion ready-to-wear of Givenchy, the master designer, is elegantly displayed in his spacious Madison Avenue duplex. Evening gowns are Givenchy's forte, and there are stunning examples here, as well as suits and dresses and exquisite blouses, all, alas, at stunning prices. Scarves, handbags, hats, and costume jewelry, although pricey, are more in the realm of possibility.

JANET RUSSO
1270 Madison Avenue, near 90th Street
427-8770
Mon.–Wed., Fri., Sat.: 10 a.m.–6 p.m.; Thurs.: 10 a.m.–7 p.m.
AE, MC, V

Wasp-waisted dresses and gowns perfect for proms or society balls are Nantucket designer Janet Russo's specialty, and her Madison Avenue duplex with its soft pink walls and pale blue ceiling provides an appropriate setting for the ultra-feminine fashions. Many of Russo's styles are strapless and come in silks, velvets, and taffetas, but there are lacy dresses with spaghetti straps and enchanting cottons in intense or dreamy colors. Sweet hand-knit sweaters and ballet slippers complete the virginal look. Prices are moderate.

JOSEPH TRICOT
804 Madison Avenue, near 67th Street
570-0077
Mon.–Wed., Fri., Sat., Sun.: 10 a.m.–6 p.m.;
Thurs.: 10:30 a.m.–6:30 p.m.
AE, MC, V

Joseph Ettedgui's shop on London's South Molton Street is known as the place to spot some of the hippest new trends, and although his outpost on Madison Avenue is somewhat more restrained, it still offers the latest from London. Spare knits come in simple shapes—skinny leggings, and narrow tubular skirts, oversized or cropped sweaters—and are designed to mix and match and layer. Colors, except for the occasional wildly patterned sweaters, are subdued. In addition to sportswear there are handbags in up-to-the-minute shapes, and backpacks in luscious suedes or tapestries. Although the cotton-knit jersey separates are pleasantly affordable, the rest of the line is pricey.

KENI VALENTI
120 Thompson Street
966-7519
Tues.–Sun.: 12 noon–7 p.m.
AE, MC, V

Gray-stucco and spare, this tiny store is the perfect foil for Keni Valenti's minimalist clothing. One of the first to offer couture clothing on Avenue B, Valenti recently moved to SoHo, where he offers stretchy T-shirts and pants, cotton-Lycra minis, wool-jersey dresses whose shape was inspired by a bottle of Joy, along with a couture collection for habitués of the club scene.

KENZO
824 Madison Avenue, at 69th Street
737-8640
Mon.–Wed., Fri., Sat.: 10 a.m.–6 p.m.; Thurs.: 10:30 a.m.–7 p.m.
AE, MC, V

Kenzo, a Japanese designer who settled in Paris in the sixties, mixes Eastern restraint with French flair and produces clothing in exuberant colors and unlikely patterns. Conservatively cut men's and women's suits come in wild fabrics, shirts in unique prints, and dresses often combine bold cabbage-rose prints with vivid stripes. Kenzo's canvas shoes for men and women in houndstooth checks, awning stripes, and oversized prints are inexpensive and totally addictive.

KRIZIA
805 Madison Avenue, near 67th Street
628-8180
Mon.–Wed., Fri., Sat.: 9:30 a.m.–6:30 p.m.; Thurs.: 9:30 a.m.–9:30 p.m.
All major

In addition to Krizia's signature feline sweaters, this glistening flagship store offers Mariucci Mandelli's complete collection, along with Krizia Uomo for men. Sensuous evening gowns cut along ultra-simple lines, easy tweed suits, pale wool vests, minis, and gentle, unconstructed slacks with cropped jackets were among the recent sightings. Very expensive.

LANVIN
831 Madison Avenue, near 69th Street
472-9436
Mon.–Fri.: 10 a.m.–6 p.m.; Sat.: 11 a.m.–6 p.m.
AE, MC, V

At Lanvin the classically elegant clothing is displayed in a properly reserved setting. Evening gowns of silk, satin, and chiffon share the space with seductive suits and blouses. It's all very wearable, and prices are not quite as shocking as at other French designer houses.

LOUIS, BOSTON
Elegant designs for women influenced by a thirties sensibility: shawl-collared suits, mid-calf-length challis skirts, softly tailored blouses, silk-chiffon tea dresses, and cashmere sweater dresses. (See **Men's Clothing**, p. 123.)

MATSUDA
Dresses, skirts, and jackets are beautifully detailed, unconstructed, flowing, and eminently wearable. (See **Men's Clothing**, p. 129.)

MISSONI
836 Madison Avenue, at 69th Street
517-9339
Daily: 10 a.m.–6 p.m.
AE, MC, V

Subtly blended colors and complex and imaginative patterns are the signature of Rosita and Tai Missoni's designs and you'll find a full complement of their famous knits in this sleek, mirrored, all-black emporium. In addition to sweaters for men and women, there are coats, jackets, dresses, ties, scarves, and socks, all with the special Missoni flair, along with nicely done but far less unique silk, wool, and cotton shirts and dresses.

NICOLE MILLER
780 Madison Avenue, near 66th Street
288-9779
Mon.–Fri.: 11 a.m.–7 p.m.; Sat.: 10 a.m.–6 p.m.
AE, MC, V

Nicole Miller's designs were a favorite with young career women who sought out her very wearable silk and rayon dresses at Barneys and Charivari. But in 1981 Miller opened a comfortable, understated shop of her own so she could showcase her complete line of evening gowns, sportswear, and day dresses. The look is feminine with distinctive silhouettes, often in splashy prints, and prices are affordable.

OMO NORMA KAMALI
11 West 56th Street
957-9797
Mon.–Sat.: 10 a.m.–6 p.m.
AE, MC, V

Norma Kamali's dramatic, multileveled shop sports Corinthian columns and rococo gilt mirrors, and it's an appropriate backdrop for her deliciously feminine fashions that have plenty of pizzazz. Her designs run the gamut from jewelry, to swimwear, to shoes, to lingerie, to suits, to wedding gowns. Dresses and suits with a forties look have broad shoulders and curved waists; jackets sport embroidery reminiscent of Spanish shawls; skirts are fringed with curtain draping; crepe pantsuits recall the young Katharine Hepburn, and there are fake furs in everything from brief boleros to sweeping greatcoats. Kamali makes crushable taffeta evening dresses in acidy colors, velvets with nipped-in waists, slithery sweater dresses, and bathing suits that are the most imaginative and well-designed around. Brides in search of a sophisticated wedding dress, one that won't make them look like Scarlett O'Hara, should check Kamali's bridal department with its filmy silk-chiffons and ultra-simple satins.

POLO/RALPH LAUREN
The romantic women's clothing fills most of the third floor with seductive silks and cashmeres, smashing evening gowns, cottons in country prints, along with beautifully tailored suits and slouchy slacks in menswear fabrics. (See **Men's Clothing,** p. 124.)

SAINT LAURENT RIVE GAUCHE
855 Madison Avenue, near 70th Street
988-3821
Mon.–Sat.: 10 a.m.–6 p.m.
AE, MC, V

One of the first French designers to open a boutique on Madison Avenue, Saint Laurent's maroon and mirrored store is stocked with the fanciful prêt-à-porter this master is famous for. Exquisite gowns, classic skirts, well-cut jackets, softly draped pantsuits, and luxurious silk blouses that are a staple of those on the best-dressed lists are here for those who can afford the high tariff.

SONIA RYKIEL
792 Madison Avenue, at 66th Street
744-0880
Mon.–Wed., Fri., Sat.: 9:30 a.m.–6:30 p.m.; Thurs.: 9:30 a.m.–7:30 p.m.
All major

Skinny, soft, and sexy knits that are a delight to wear are offered in Sonia Rykiel's appropriately understated boutique. Narrow skirts, full-cut trousers, updates on the sailor look, and beautiful sweaters are her signature, but you'll find wonderful silk and crepe dresses, fur and wool coats, and pleasantly affordable cotton velour and jersey-knit separates. Although most of the Rykiel line is pricey, these are classics you'll wear for years.

VALENTINO
825 Madison Avenue, near 68th Street
744-0200
Mon.–Sat.: 10 a.m.–6 p.m.
AE, MC, V

In his gray marble and black lacquer palazzo, Valentino offers lavish high fashion in daywear, suits, and evening clothes. For more than twenty-five years the Valentino look has been embraced by such celebrities as Audrey Hepburn, Jacqueline Kennedy, and Sophia Loren. His skirts are short and sexy, jackets broad-shouldered and slim-hipped, and Valentino uses opulent silks and luscious wools in his sophisticated prêt-à-porter fashions. His suits for men, although classically cut, are no less luxurious. Very expensive.

WILLIWEAR
119 Fifth Avenue, at 19th Street
353-3980
Mon.–Wed., Fri.: 11 a.m.–7 p.m.; Thurs.: 11 a.m.–7 p.m.;
Sat.: 11 a.m.–6 p.m.; Sun.: 12 noon–5 p.m.
AE, MC, V

Willi Smith's comfortable casual clothing tends to get lost in his whimsical, jungle-like shop. Leaves and vines crawl up the walls, across the ceiling, and cover the huge Corinthian columns, and everything is spray-painted dove-gray. But if you search you'll find short-cropped jackets, slacks, and sheath dresses in cottons, linens, and stretchy twill for women; slouchy pleated pants and oversized jackets for men. There are scarves, hats, and umbrellas, too.

YOHJI YAMAMOTO
103 Grand Street

966-9066
Mon.–Sat.: 11 a.m.–7 p.m.; Sun.: 12 noon–6 p.m.
AE

Fluted columns, frosted glass walls, richly dark walnut flooring, steel fixtures by English artist Antony Donaldson, and James Horrobin's unique sculptural display racks warm up and add dramatic visual interest to the otherwise spectacularly spare, cavernous, and minimalist 3,000-square-foot space that houses Yohji Yamamoto's entire fashion collection. Long considered the most tailored and least esoteric of the Japanese designers, Yamamoto does Edwardian styles, asymmetrical jackets, loose cropped pants, high-rise buttoned stoles over long column dresses, redingotes with stand-out hips, trapeze dresses, and whimsical takes on French couture designers. His men's line includes double-breasted jackets, shirred waistcoats, and sweaters with intarsia designs. Colors tend to be deep and dark with the occasional white or forest green, fabrics soft jerseys and crepes or wool coverts and felts. Expect to spend more than five hundred dollars for a rayon shirt, at least nine hundred dollars for a jacket.

ZORAN
214 Sullivan Street
Third floor
674-6087
By appointment only
No credit cards

Less is more is Yugoslavian designer Zoran's credo. His delightfully minimalist creations—T-shirts, slouchy trousers, slinky skirts, sparse jackets—in luscious cashmere, silky knits, and other equally sensual fabrics attest to the effectiveness of his ideal.

CASUAL

ACA JOE
Seasonless, all-cotton separates: sweaters, shorts, rugby shirts, sweat pants, and chambray shirts. (See **Men's Clothing,** p. 130.)

BANANA REPUBLIC
No-nonsense, sturdy, and comfortable sportswear inspired by safari garb; traditional styling and natural fibers in such low-key colors as khaki, gray, brown, and olive. (See **Men's Clothing,** p. 130.)

CHRISTIAN DE CASTELNAU
775 Madison Avenue, near 66th Street

535-7511
Mon.–Sat.: 10 a.m.–6 p.m.
AE, MC, V

A French company with a California sensibility, Christian de Castelnau offers easy cotton-knit separates for women and girls in its pale ash-wood and eggshell-white flagship store. Spare cotton-knit tank dresses; appealing skirts, slacks, and tops for women; and playful knit separates for *jeunes filles* two through fourteen years old fill Castelnau's small but well-organized emporium.

C. P. SHADES
341 West Broadway
966-6500
Mon.–Fri.: 11 a.m.–7 p.m.; Sat.: 11 a.m.–6 p.m.; Sun.: 12 noon–6 p.m.
AE, MC, V

In a spare, understated setting this New York branch of the San Francisco–based company offers high-style casual clothing made of high-quality cotton T-shirting fabrics. Among the wonderfully comfortable shapes for women are short-cropped shirts, slouchy skirts, baggy trousers, and soft jackets. Men will find shirts, shorts, and pants. Colors lean toward pastels or sophisticated shades of olive, brown, and purple.

DOWN HOME AMERICA
T-shirts with vivid graphics, enormous tote bags from California, colorful skirts from Georgia, exuberant sweaters. (See **Men's Clothing**, p. 132.)

THE EXPRESS
667 Madison Avenue, near 60th Street
754-2721
Mon.–Wed., Fri.: 10 a.m.–7 p.m.; Thurs.: 10 a.m.–8 p.m.;
Sat.: 10 a.m.–6 p.m.; Sun. 12 noon–6 p.m.

321 Columbus Avenue, near 75th Street
Mon.–Thurs.: 11 a.m.–8 p.m.; Fri., Sat.: 11 a.m.–10 p.m.;
Sun. 12 noon–7 p.m.
AE, MC, V

The Express stores, now numbering 430 and still counting, were inspired by owner Leslie Wexner's visits to Paris, and the murals and art trappings that grace the multilevel interior reflect that inspiration. Walls are hung with send-offs of Fragonard, Magritte, and Man Ray, and the men's shop on the lower level is outfitted with French military campaign furnishings. The clothing, however, is pure American and reflects the American way with sportswear. It's casual, comfortable, and colorful, and incorporates everything from gauzy skirts to high-waisted denim shorts to handsome brocade vests to bold African-print dresses. The mix for men is equally appealing—T-shirts in every color, classic shorts, slouchy slacks, and cozy rayon shirts.

FIORUCCI
Witty and off-beat Italian sportswear with Elio Fiorucci's special flair. (See **Men's Clothing**, p. 133.)

THE GAP
Attractively styled sportswear in natural fabrics geared to city or country living: classic shorts, skinny cotton-knit leggings, slouchy cotton dresses, micro-mini skirts. (See **Men's Clothing**, p. 133.)

HENRY LEHR
1079 Third Avenue, near 63rd Street
753-2720
Mon.–Fri.: 10:30 a.m.–7 p.m.; Sat.: 10 a.m.–6 p.m.;
Sun.: 12 noon–5 p.m.

772 Madison Avenue, near 66th Street
535-1021
Mon.–Fri.: 10 a.m.–7 p.m.; Sat.: 10 a.m.–6 p.m.

464 West Broadway, near Prince Street
460-5500
Mon.–Sat.: 11 a.m.–7 p.m.; Sun.: 12 noon–6 p.m.
AE, MC, V

In the sixties Henry Lehr was known as London's "King of Jeans," but it wasn't until the seventies that Lehr brought his special brand of casual dressing to New York. Pre-washed, pre-wrinkled, incredibly comfortable, and *très outré* is his signature look. Crumpled silk jackets, jumpsuits, dresses, and pants come in baby pales, jeans are stone-washed or dyed unlikely colors, and there are Go Linen, Go Leather, and Go Knit separates of Lehr's own design. It's all *très* chic, casually luxurious, and costly.

J. CREW
Classic American sportswear that is timeless: swimsuits and shorts, jeans and sweaters, shirts and skirts, socks and hats. (See **Men's Clothing**, p. 134.)

J. MCLAUGHLIN
Among the mix of understated separates for women are softly pleated skirts in lush ancient madders, paisleys, silks, and flannels; nicely tailored slacks; and beautifully detailed hand-knit sweaters. (See **Men's Clothing**, p. 134.)

THE LIMITED
691 Madison Avenue, at 62nd Street
838-8787

Mon.–Fri.: 10 a.m.–7 p.m.; Sat.: 10 a.m.–6 p.m.; Sun.: 12 noon–5 p.m.

Pier 17
South Street Seaport
619-2922
Mon.–Sat.: 10 a.m.–7 p.m.; Sun.: 11 a.m.–6 p.m.
AE, MC, V

With the opening of the Limited's glitzy, multilevel store in November 1985, Middle America arrived on Madison Avenue. The store is filled with racks of separates that are often a season behind au courant fashions. But the styles are comfortable and very wearable, and it's a fine source for casual clothing. You'll find Krizia's lower-priced designs; Forenza, the Limited's own label; along with Limited Express for juniors. Leather handbags are particularly well done, and there are attractive accessories as well. The store's Victoria's Secret Boutique offers appealing lingerie both sweet and sexy: teddies, tap pants, gowns, slips, and robes in cottons and silks. Prices are moderate.

MARIMEKKO
Dresses and sports separates cut along easy and comfortable lines. (See **Fabrics and Trimmings,** p. 218.)

MIMI LOVERDE
158 Franklin Street
431-3971
Mon.–Fri.: 10 a.m.–6 p.m.
AE, MC, V

In 1974 Mimi Loverde, the doyenne of dye, began over-dying cotton work shirts and jeans in scores of colors, and she soon sparked a cotton revolution. Originally Loverde wholesaled her things to specialty stores around the country, and although she still does, Loverde now has a tidy little shop in TriBeCa filled with her cheerful cottons. Shapes are simple, yet classic and often sophisticated, and include everything from one-size-fits-all T-shirts to skinny leggings to oversized jackets to linen suits. And everything is inexpensive and available in dozens of bright or muted shades.

NAF-NAF BOUTIQUE INC.
1188 Madison Avenue, at 87th Street
289-6333
Mon.–Wed., Fri.: 10 a.m.–6 p.m.; Thurs.: 10 a.m.–7 p.m.; Sat.:
10 a.m.–7 p.m.; Sun.: 12 noon–5 p.m.

452A West Broadway, near Prince Street
353-3667
Mon.–Fri.: 12 noon–7 p.m.; Sat.: 11 a.m.–7 p.m.;
Sun.: 12 noon–6 p.m.
AE, MC, V

Naf-Naf's sophisticated, trendy sportswear had been a hot seller at Macy's and Bloomingdale's for a number of years before this French-based company opened its own freestanding store. These spare and mirrored stainless-steel interiors are filled with the company's complete line of ultra-casual separates. There are pants, shirts, shorts, and skirts in dyed and washed-out cotton, corduroy, and denim; sweaters and assorted tops; suede jackets; and unisex rompers for children.

REMINISCENCE
74 Fifth Avenue, near 13th Street
243-2292
Mon.–Sat.: 11:30 a.m.–8 p.m.; Sun.: 1 p.m.–6 p.m.

Reminiscence Garage
175 MacDougal Street
979-9440
Mon.–Sat.: 12 noon–8 p.m.; Sun.: 1 p.m.–6 p.m.
AE, MC, V

Stewart Richer opened Reminiscence on MacDougal Street in the seventies and stocked it with vintage clothing, army overalls, and painter's pants that he dyed unlikely colors. It quickly became a favorite with the young and the hip, and Richer soon developed a line of nationally distributed sportswear with a Retro look and moved to larger quarters on lower Fifth Avenue as Retro as the clothing. His slouchy rayon and linen slacks, linen shirts in a rainbow of colors, skinny ribbed tube skirts, and oversized baseball jackets are some of the best around. You'll find a nicely edited selection of children's clothing, vintage day dresses and frilly prom gowns from the thirties through the sixties, madras Bermuda shorts, Hawaiian shirts, and, of course, the cotton pants dyed outlandish colors that Richer pioneered. Don't overlook the jewelry. Glass-topped cases hold everything from silly brooches, to one-of-a-kind pieces done by local artists, to designer creations, to a sprinkling of antiques. The shoe department offers cutting-edge styles from England, Italy, and France that might include clunky crepe-soled oxfords and gingham-checked sandals—whatever is up-to-the-minute. And this mini-department store carries fifties housewares, pottery, Lava lamps, clocks, even soaps. Prices at Reminiscence are as unbeatable as the styles. The original MacDougal Street store is now called the Garage, and it's stocked with the overflow from the Fifth Avenue shop at even cheaper prices.

STREET LIFE
Tight-curvy knits, high-waisted skirts, body-hugging sheaths with scooped necks, jumpers and shifts. (See **Men's Clothing**, p. 135.)

UNIQUE CLOTHING WAREHOUSE
726 Broadway, near Waverly Place
674-1863
Mon.–Thurs.: 11 a.m.–8 p.m.; Fri., Sat.: 10 a.m.–9 p.m.;

Sun.: 12 noon–8 p.m.
All major

Harvey Russack was one of the first to sell military surplus and vintage clothing (he opened the Unique Clothing Warehouse in 1969), but as sources dried up for old clothes, Russack began stocking his store with new things inspired by the vintage styles, along with punk and new wave designs. Now the stock, in his snappy glass-fronted store created by the SITE architectural team, has become more mainstream and includes such labels as Reminiscence, French Connection, and Pandemonium, along with do-it-yourself hand-painted and hand-splashed clothing, and fashions from young East Village designers. Yet Russack still offers a sprinkling of vintage clothing and leather jackets, as well as lots of T-shirts and accessories of all kinds.

URBAN OUTFITTERS
374 Sixth Avenue, at Waverly Place
677-9350
Mon.–Sat.: 10 a.m.–10 p.m.; Sun.: 12 noon–8 p.m.

628 Broadway, near Bleecker Street
475-0009
Mon.–Sat.: 10 a.m.–10 p.m.; Sun.: 12 noon–8 p.m.
AE, MC, V

Urban Outfitters is a Philadelphia company that began its existence in 1970 as a small store located near the University of Pennsylvania. It soon become a hangout for the college crowd, and the company now has shops in Boston, Georgetown, and New York. Bi-level mini-department stores with exposed cement walls and piping, they're filled with Esprit, Brats, Guess, Girbaud, the French Connection, Kiko, and WilliWear, along with the company's own sportswear label. But in addition to clothing, Urban Outfitters' cavernous spaces are crammed with handbags, shoes, and accessories, toys and household items, and dishes and glassware.

CUTTING EDGE

Barneys New York, Bergdorf Goodman, Bloomingdale's, Henri Bendel, and Macy's offer clothing from some of the hottest new designers.

ALAÏA

Sexy, modern, and beautifully made clothing. (See **Designer Women's Clothing;** p. 159.)

BETSEY JOHNSON

Body-hugging fashions guaranteed to provide entrance to the hottest clubs in town. (See **Designer Women's Clothing,** p. 159.)

CAROL ROLLO/RIDING HIGH

1147 First Avenue, near 62nd Street
832-7927
Mon.–Wed., Fri., Sat.: 11 a.m.–7 p.m.; Thurs.: 11 a.m.–8 p.m.; Sun.:
12 noon–6 p.m.
AE, MC, V

Carol Rollo fills her austere bi-level store with aggressively styled new wave designs, and among her wild things are Thierry Mugler's opulent and revealing gowns, the bold creations of Moschino, Jean-Paul Gaultier's assertive styles, Romeo Gigli's waif-like fashions, and the latest from Chlöe and Sitbon, as well as spirited looks from the next wave of young designers. Rollo carries striking shoes and boots, along with jewelry, scarves, hats, and gloves that complement the clothing, and she offers custom-made gowns and maternity dresses that are stitched-up by European seamstresses.

CHARIVARI

Up-to-the-minute fashions by advanced designers are available at each of the Charivari stores, but the Workshop and Charivari 57 offer the most radical and experimental designs. (See **Men's Clothing,** p. 126.)

COMME DES GARÇONS

Japanese designer Rei Kawakubo's dresses have a purity of line and hang loose or just graze the body, and there are fluid, high-waist chemise styles, as well as floaty drop-waist ones, along with long jackets with cutout armholes, roomy cropped pants, and narrow skirts. (See **Men's Clothing,** p. 127.)

EINSTEIN'S

96 East 7th Street
598-9748
Wed.–Mon.: 1 p.m.–7 p.m.; in summer, Wed.–Sat.: 1 p.m.–7 p.m..
AE, MC, V

Julia Morton and Paul Monroe dub their shop "a pearl in a sea of tuna," and certainly their clothing and jewelry are funky gems. Just about everything here tends toward the outrageous, yet there are such surprises as the shop's great collection of vintage Chanel. Morton was one of the first to make dresses for men and jackets that look as if they were stitched out of Astro-turf. Monroe is responsible for jewelry encrusted with stones or whatever objects he finds, and together this duo offer the very latest in downtown counter-couture looks. On a recent visit, there were the old Chanels (along with a fine group of contemporary Chanel belts and jewelry), Teri Toye T-shirts, surreal fabric-and-wire dolls.

ENZ'S
5 St. Marks Place
420-1857
Mon.–Sat.: 11:30 a.m.–8 p.m.; Sun.: 12 noon–7 p.m.
AE, MC, V

Decadent dress-up is designer Mariann Marlowe's trademark, and her small, narrow shop is crowded with body-hugging prom dresses, slinky evening gowns, stretchy separates, bustiers with studs and rhinestones, frilly skirts, and cropped tux jackets. Marlowe carries outrageous accessories and jewelry, too, along with fishnet stockings, a variety of wigs, and patent-leather thigh highs and boots from England. Prices are moderate.

IF BOUTIQUE
474 West Broadway
533-8660
Mon.–Sat.: 12 noon–7:30 p.m.; Sun.: 12 noon–7 p.m.
All major

Jeanette Bird has filled her spacious shop with advanced designs by such leading lights as Thierry Mugler, Jean-Paul Gaultier, Romeo Gigli, Moschino, Marc Jacobs, Martine Sitbon, and Angelo Tarlazzi, along with her own private-label fashions. Up-to-the-minute jackets, body-hugging dresses, long and narrow or short and skinny skirts—whatever is most trendy—share the space with an equally assertive selection for men. Bird carries nicely executed belts and bags, some jewelry, as well as Robert Clergerie's shoes that are avant-garde without being funky.

ISSEY MIYAKE
992 Madison Avenue, at 77th Street
439-7822
Mon.–Fri.: 10 a.m.–6 p.m.; Sat.: 11 a.m.–7 p.m.
AE, MC, V

This stark yet austerely elegant men's and women's clothing store is Issey Miyake's first free-standing New York boutique. The modern decor designed by Shiro Kuramata and Toshiko Mori features corrugated-metal walls and wire-cable clotheslines for displaying the apparel. Opulently draped iridescent silk-chambray evening coats, one-of-a-kind silk evening suits, knit-mohair sweaters, and bell-bottom pants coexist with the men's designs. These include full-length leather coats, and jackets, shirts, and slacks with Miyake's signature detailing.

173

109

115 St. Marks Place
260-2622
Mon.–Sun.: 12 noon–8 p.m.
AE, MC, V

No longer located at 109 St. Marks Place, this popular boutique has moved to roomier quarters down the block. Once known for its East Village look, 109 has gone somewhat mainstream and now carries more widely available clothing designs. Yet it's still possible to find the wild styles of young American, French, and Italian designers—Thea Anema, York and Cole, and Phizoa—in the eminently wearable selection of suits, dresses, shirts, slacks, and shoes.

PATRICIA FIELD

10 East 8th Street
254-1699
Mon.–Sat.: 12 noon–8 p.m.; Sun.: 12 noon–6 p.m.
AE, MC, V

Whimsical, unpredictable, and ever-changing, Patricia Field mixes the old and the new with detritus from the city's street cultures. Bikers', skateboarders'—even surfers'—gear and apparel in Day-Glo colors share the all-black space with gem-studded bras, Mark Wong Nark's Spandex "Barbarella" dresses, tiny "cheerleader" skirts, body-hugging jackets, Retro halter tops, and hats of all kinds. Most of Field's stock is downright funky, but Patricia Field is a trend setter, so you'll see things in her shop years before they migrate uptown.

SAN FRANCISCO CLOTHING

975 Lexington Avenue, near 70th Street
472-8740
Mon.–Fri.: 10 a.m.–7 p.m.; Sat.: 11 a.m.–6 p.m.
All major

When San Francisco opened more than twenty years ago, it was filled with the kind of Old World, rich-looking clothing that has since become Ralph Lauren's trademark. But owner Howard Partman has moved on to other styles, and San Francisco now looks like an East Village shop transplanted to the Upper East Side. Skintight dresses, bicycle pants, psychedelic leggings, miniskirted peplum suits, cropped flannel shirts in buffalo plaids and oversized checks, and fish-shaped ties are among the mix of whimsical, exuberant, and funky fashions. Traces of the shop's classic roots can still be seen in Partman's group of gabardine suits with velvet collars, gingham separates, and his Macintosh raincoats.

SHRIMPTON & GILLIGAN

70 East 1st Street
254-1249

Mon., Wed.–Sun.: 11 a.m.–7 p.m.
AE, MC, V

Angel Zimick and Chris Isles design very wearable clothing with a Retro look, and their appealingly understated shop is filled with easy fashions: high-waisted, relaxed slacks and skirts, dresses with keyhole tops, daisy-strewn sweaters, gently shaped knit-jersey separates. There are seersucker, linen, and embroidered cottons for summer; double-knit Lycra, lace, rayons, and woven jacquards for winter. The stress is on fabric and shape—milk-bottle skirts, high-waisted pants, shift dresses. Zimick and Isles carry unusual jewelry, bold socks, and silly kiddie-size handbags for grown-up party girls, too.

TRASH AND VAUDEVILLE
4 St. Marks Place
982-3590
Mon.–Thurs.: 12 noon–8 p.m.; Fri.: 11:30 a.m.–8 p.m.;
Sat.: 11 a.m.–8 p.m.; Sun.: 1 p.m.–7 p.m.
AE, MC, V

"Rock n Roll" to wear is the store's logo, and you'll find everything from chains and leather to blue jeans at Trash and Vaudeville, one of the original boutiques devoted to punk. In addition to the store's own line of clothing and the house line, Tripp, there are over-the-top imports from England, reasonably priced leather jackets, rubberwear, cowboy styles, fun swimsuits, kinky lingerie, studded belts, three-piece suits, and evening wear for men and women. In the back of the store is the shoe section filled with the very latest in funky English styles.

LINGERIE
VINTAGE

See also **Antique and Vintage Women's Clothing.**

ALICE UNDERGROUND
Delightfully affordable silk lingerie from the thirties and forties, chenille robes, plus a sprinkling of Victorian white nightgowns. (See **Antique and Vintage Women's Clothing,** p. 147.)

DOROTHY'S CLOSET
Vintage silk slips and nightgowns from the thirties and forties. (See **Antique and Vintage Women's Clothing,** p. 148.)

GENE LONDON'S STUDIO
Exquisite silk chemises, slips, gowns, and robes from the twenties through the forties. (See **Costumes**, p. 101.)

LORRAINE WOHL COLLECTION
Delicate French silk chemises, nightgowns, slips, and robes from the twenties and thirties in fragile color. (See **Wedding Gowns and Evening Wear**, p. 180.)

CONTEMPORARY

The department stores offer a complete array of lingerie; Bergdorf Goodman, Bloomingdale's, Henri Bendel, and Saks Fifth Avenue selections are particularly noteworthy.

AM/PM
109 Thompson Street
219-0343
Daily: 12 noon–7 p.m.
All major

Lingerie goes from the demure to the outrageous in this tiny, well-stocked store. Among the attractive mix are Hanro's practical underthings, Sami's slinky bias-cut gowns, classic silk pajamas, flashy bustiers, relaxed silk boxer shorts, sexy garter belts, even real silk stockings and garters. Prices are good.

ENELRA
48½ East 7th Street
473-2454
Mon.–Wed.: 12 noon–9:30 p.m.; Thurs., Fri., Sat.: 12 noon–11:30 p.m.; Sun.: 12 noon–7:30 p.m.
AE, MC, V

The East Village might seem an unlikely spot for a store whose specialty is sensual lingerie, but even resident punks, it appears, must have the right undies. Bras run the gamut from practical sports kinds, to beautiful lacy numbers to jeweled bustiers. Teddies, slips, and nightgowns come in demure white cotton, sexy silk charmeuse, see-through lace, or body-hugging stretch fabrics. There are G-strings and garter belts suggestive enough for any porno star and, for men, silk T-shirts and boxer shorts. Prices are good.

JOOVAY
436 West Broadway

431-6386
Daily: 12 noon–7 p.m.
AE, MC, V

Barbara Cooke has stocked her vest-pocket-size store with lingerie that's feminine and romantic. You'll find a nicely edited selection of pretty nighties, camisoles, bikinis, and teddies, along with slinky silk nightgowns and robes. Colors are delicate, fabrics include cottons, silks, silk-satins, lace, and ribbed knits, and all the most popular names are here—Pluto, Lynn La Cava, Delorme, Christian Dior, Hanro, Lejaby, and Treesha. Prices are excellent.

L'AFFAIRE
226 Third Avenue, near 19th Street
254-1922
Mon.–Fri.: 11 a.m.–7 p.m.; Sat.: 11 a.m.–6 p.m.; closed Sat. in
summer
All major

Fanciful finds from France, England, Italy, and Switzerland are crammed into Barbara Wagh's small shop. Among the treasures are seductive tap pants, teddies, and bikinis, along with the best selection of garter belts around—more than sixty styles to choose from. There are luxurious silk slips, gowns, and robes as well, at prices that range from moderate to expensive.

LA GRANDE PASSION
1234 Lexington Avenue, near 83rd Street
570-9301
Mon.–Sat.: 11 a.m.–7 p.m.
All major

Although La Grande Passion is only a sliver of a shop, owner Elizabeth Hinden has managed to stock it with everything from practical cotton bikinis, to sexy silk G-strings, to funky Day-Glo bras, to lux chiffon peignoir sets. Among the designer names are Pierre Balmain, Calida, Lynn La Cava, Hanky Panky, Lejaby, Castellini, L'Indescrete, and Christine & Co. Prices range from inexpensive to costly.

LA LINGERIE
792 Madison Avenue, near 67th Street
772-9797
Mon.–Sat.: 9:30 a.m.–6:30 p.m.
All major

It's a toss-up whether La Lingerie or Montenapoleone is the city's most expensive lingerie store, since both stores' prices are shocking and it doesn't help to know that they use only the very finest European satins, silks, laces, and chiffons in their creations. Yet at La Lingerie it *is* possible to find a few affordable things—pretty mules, exquisite silk-

177

covered hangers, some lovely cotton panties, lacy bras. For the rest, even the very rich and famous might be hard-pressed to spend $950 for a teddy, $8,000 on a peignoir set.

LINGERIE DE NICOLLE
1046 Madison Avenue, near 79th Street
517-6160
Mon.–Fri.: 10 a.m.–5:30 p.m.; Sat.: 10 a.m.–6 p.m.;
Sun.: 12 noon–5 p.m.
MC, V

A mother-and-daughter-run operation that's only blocks away from the city's most-costly lingerie stores, Lingerie de Nicolle prides itself on its moderately priced intimate apparel. Robes and gowns are specialties in this tiny shop and you'll find them in a full range of styles and fabrics, along with teddies and chemises, bikinis and bras, slips and loungewear by all the most wanted names.

MONTENAPOLEONE
789 Madison Avenue, near 67th Street
535-2660
Mon.–Sat.: 10 a.m.–6 p.m.
All major

For more than fifteen years Montenapoleone has been New York's most famous name for lingerie. This Italian-owned boutique offers ladylike, rather than seductive, styling in the very finest Italian silk, lace, voile, georgette, cashmere, and cotton lingerie. Just about everything is heavily edged with lace or strewn with needlework; colors tend to old-fashioned creams and peaches. Although you can't help admiring the fabrics and fine workmanship, it's all a bit fussy and staggeringly expensive. Recently, however, the company has broadened its merchandise to appeal to a younger customer, so now there's a smattering of brighter colors and bolder styles, as well as less pricey items. Upstairs you'll find an exclusive collection of Italian swimwear for conservative sun worshipers.

PERESS
739 Madison Avenue, near 64th Street
861-6336
Mon.–Sat.: 10 a.m.–5:30 p.m.
All major

A family-run, old-time lingerie store, Peress offers nearly 100 quality labels—everything from Lore to Hunro to Vanity Fair to Calvin Klein. There's an in-depth selection of loungewear, more than eighteen lines of bras, and a helpful and attentive sales staff. Moderate to expensive.

ROBERTA
1252 Madison Avenue, at 90th Street

860-8366
Mon.–Sat.: 10 a.m.–6 p.m.
AE, MC, V

Roberta Liford's spacious store is as well-stocked with underthings as most of the large department stores. She carries everything from legwear, to loungewear, to swimsuits, to nursing bras by all the most wanted American and European names, and in styles that range from sexy to innocent. And unlike most department stores, Liford offers personal service, attention to fit, and a wide range of prices.

SAMANTHA JONES
1074 Third Avenue, near 63rd Street
308-6680
Mon.–Fri.: 11 a.m.–7 p.m.; Sat.: 11 a.m.–6 p.m.; Sun.: 1 p.m.–5 p.m.
All major

Samantha Jones has an eye for seductive lingerie, and she's filled her elegant shop—as comfortable as a lady's boudoir—with some of the most sexily romantic underthings in town. Among her beautiful indulgences are slinky bias-cut silk gowns, sensuous kimonos, lacy G-strings, teeny bikinis, sexy teddies, and luxurious peignoirs. Her color sense is keen, so you'll find tailored pajamas in shocking shades of yellow or periwinkle blue, and bras in unlikely prints and colors. Don't come here for the basics, come for treats, and for a staff that is expert at fit and attentive service.

WIFE/MISTRESS
1044 Lexington Avenue, near 75th Street
570-9529
Mon.–Sat.: 10 a.m.–6 p.m.
AE, MC, V

As the name suggests, the marvelous selection of underthings in this shop manages to encompass both the sensible and the sensuous. There are practical and thirsty chenille and terry bathrobes and pristine white nightshirts, along with sexy Merry Widows and slinky bias-cut gowns. Half of the stock is imported from France and Italy; the rest comes from the most popular American lingerie designers.

VICTORIA'S SECRET
34 East 57th Street
758-5592
Mon.–Fri.: 10 a.m.–7 p.m.; Thurs.: 10 a.m.–8 p.m.;
Sat.: 10 a.m.–6 p.m.; Sun.: 12 noon–5 p.m.
AE, MC, V

Victoria's Secret is virtually a department store devoted to lingerie, and on its two spacious floors there's ample room for an abundance of innocent cotton nighties; well-cut charmeuse slips; slinky nightgowns;

179

sexy G-strings; robes in cottons, silks, and satins; pajamas; panty hose; bras; and panties. The men's selection of robes, boxer shorts, briefs, pajamas, and undershirts is equally as impressive. From inexpensive to pricey.

WEDDING GOWNS AND EVENING WEAR

All the major department stores offer evening wear, and the selections at Bergdorf Goodman, Henri Bendel, Bloomingdale's, and Saks Fifth Avenue are outstanding. Saks and Bergdorf's also have fine bridal departments.

ANTIQUE AND VINTAGE

ANDY'S CHEE-PEE'S
Vintage wedding gowns, along with cocktail and beaded dresses that are as old as Victorian and as recent as the sixties. Much of it is in need of repair, but prices are cheap. (See **Antique and Vintage Women's Clothing,** p. 147.)

JEAN HOFFMAN/JANA STARR ANTIQUES
236 East 80th Street
861-8256
Mon.–Sat.: 12 noon–6 p.m.
AE, MC, V

In Jean Hoffman and Jana Starr's vest-pocket-size shop hundreds of gowns hang from the ceiling overhead, and linens are piled high on shelves and spill from boxes on the floor. Narrow and unbelievably cluttered, their shop is one of the city's best sources for pristine Victorian wedding gowns, twenties beaded flapper dresses, delicate bias-cut chiffons, opulent silk velvets, and exquisite lace frocks. Everything has been selected with care by the knowledgeable and friendly owners, and although the fashions are pricey, they're so much less so than the creations of today's top designers. Antique paisley and embroidered silk shawls, capes, frilly Victorian petticoats, lovely old lingerie, a sprinkling of vintage children's things, jewelry, and an enticing stock of vintage table and bed linens are among the other hard-to-resist temptations.

LIZA'S PLACE
132 Thompson Street
477-6027
Tues.–Sun.: 12 noon–6 p.m.
No credit cards

Antique and vintage evening and wedding gowns are Liza's specialty, and she's assembled a tantalizing collection of Victorian white confections (perfect for summer weddings), hand-beaded flapper dresses, luscious velvet gowns, and lacy frocks, all in excellent condition. She has antique evening shoes as well, along with a lovely array of beaded evening purses, and exquisite embroidered and gold-encrusted shawls. Expensive, but the quality is outstanding.

LORRAINE WOHL COLLECTION
150 East 70th Street
472-0191
Mon.–Sat.: 12 noon–6 p.m.; Sat.: 12:30 p.m.–5 p.m.
AE, DC, MC, V

Exquisite French couture gowns from the twenties and thirties are artfully displayed in Lorraine Wohl's tiny jewel of a shop. Lace tea dresses, French lawn frocks, bias-cut chiffons, and glorious beaded tunics, jackets and dresses are a few of the treasures, along with suits and dresses from Chanel, Lanvin, and Balmain. The vintage estate and costume jewelry is as tempting as the clothing, and the delicate French silk lingerie in fragile colors is winning. Expensive, but these are museum-quality fashions. Wohl has also an exemplary array of lamps, Deco furniture, and mirrors.

OPAL WHITE
131 Thompson Street
677-8215
By appointment only
AE

As much museum of wedding styles as vintage clothing store, Opal White is cluttered with more than 400 antique and vintage wedding dresses. Everything from pristine Victorian whites to opulent Edwardian satins, to twenties beaded chemises, to thirties sculptural silks, to fifties gossamer chiffons cram the double-tiered racks that circle the store. There are laces, velvets, and tulles, too, and all the gowns are in perfect condition. The quality of the fabrics and the styling are outstanding, and prices, although high, are actually reasonable in light of today's astounding wedding-gown costs.

PANACHE
525 Hudson Street
242-5115
Mon.–Sat.: 12 noon–7 p.m.; Sun.: 1 p.m.–6 p.m.
AE, MC, V

The stock is in such pristine condition and everything is so attractively organized and displayed that Panache looks like a fashionable boutique, not a vintage clothing shop. Silk, velvet, and chiffon evening gowns and cocktail dresses from the forties are a specialty, but there's always an appealing selection of beaded sweaters, silk lingerie, and evening bags. Equally tempting are the fashionable daytime and dressy jackets in fabrics that range from wool tweeds, to silk failles, to satins, many with exquisite dressmaker detailing, beadwork, or embroidery. For men there are never-worn wide ties in sedate or wild patterns, gabardine shirts, and good-looking sweaters. And the collection of floral-patterned drapery fabrics from the thirties and forties is an additional treat. Prices are reasonable for such high-quality clothing.

VICTORIA FALLS
Pristine Victorian white dresses and vintage gowns. (See **Contemporary Women's Clothing**, p. 158.)

CONTEMPORARY

ANITA PAGLIARO LTD.
1030 Lexington Avenue, near 73rd Street
737-2684
By appointment
AE, MC, V

For the past ten years Anita Pagliaro has been creating unusual and spirited wedding and evening gowns. Although lacy bridal confections are her specialty, she also does slim strapless formals, kicky cocktail dresses, voluminous ball gowns, along with gowns for bridesmaids, the mother of the bride, and second weddings. Pagliaro handles custom-made headdresses as well, and her prices are moderate in light of today's astronomical wedding gown costs.

BETSEY JOHNSON
Entertaining evening looks in Lycra and Spandex that are in keeping with Johnson's philosophy that dressing up should be fun. (See **Designer Women's Clothing**, p. 159.)

CAROL ROLLO/RIDING HIGH
Aggressively styled new wave gowns. (See **Cutting-Edge Women's Clothing,** p. 172.)

EMANUAL UNGARO
Outstanding party dresses in brilliant silk prints. (See **Designer Women's Clothing,** p. 160.)

GIVENCHY BOUTIQUE
Evening gowns are Givenchy's forte, and there are stunning examples here. (See **Designer Women's Clothing,** p. 161.)

JANET RUSSO
Wasp-waisted gowns perfect for proms or society balls in silk, velvets, taffeta, and laces. (See **Designer Women's Clothing,** p. 161.)

JONAL
Made-to-measure bridal and debutante gowns that are traditional yet sophisticated and come in such Old World fabrics as silk eyelet, cotton piqué, and delicate organza. (See **Contemporary Women's Clothing,** p. 154.)

KRIZIA
Sensuous evening gowns cut along ultra-simple lines. (See **Designer Women's Clothing,** p. 163.)

LANVIN
Eye-catching evening gowns of silk, satin, and chiffon. (See **Designer Women's Clothing,** p. 163.)

LINDA DRESNER
484 Park Avenue, near 58th Street
308-3177
Mon.–Sat.: 10 a.m.–6 p.m.; closed Sat. in summer
AE, DC, MC, V

Linda Dresner's spare minimalist space looks like a SoHo art gallery, not an uptown dress salon. A single dress graces a clothes rack that hangs near the window, and this, along with the on-duty guard, is the shop's sole window display. Once inside, however, you'll find tailored dresses, understated skirts and sweaters, along with Dresner's irresistible collection of dinner suits, cocktail dresses, and gowns by Romeo Gigli, Vicky Tiel, Sopriani, Mugler, Karl Lagerfeld, Gaultier, and Gaspar-Conran, along with the store's own private-label designs. There's an exciting array of jewelry, bags, and accessories as well. So don't be put off by the stark exterior; inside you'll find enticing fashions and a staff that's friendly and eager to help.

MARTHA
475 Park Avenue, at 58th Street

753-1511
Mon.–Sat.: 10 a.m.–6 p.m.

Trump Tower
725 Fifth Avenue, at 56th Street
826-8855
Mon.–Sat.: 10 a.m.–6 p.m.
AE, DC, MC, V

Martha, the doyenne of New York's elegant women's shops, is famous for Old World luxury and service. Park Avenue matrons sip coffee—or something stronger—while models slink by in the latest couture creations of Blass, Beene, De La Renta, Lagerfeld, Montana, Ferre, and Valentino. Since glorious evening wear is Martha's strength, it's not surprising that the stores offer Pat Kerr's elaborate wedding gown creations. There are day clothes, too—perfect suits and little black dresses—and sportswear that includes ski outfits and bathing suits. The atmosphere is plush, the dressing rooms elegant, the prices startling. But there's good news. Martha is opening an International Boutique at 473 Park Avenue, next door to her present emporium, and she will fill her new shop with more radical creations by young designers at more affordable prices. Blazers, suits, and cocktail dresses will be part of the mix.

OMO NORMA KAMALI
Sophisticated wedding gowns for brides who don't want to look like Scarlett O'Hara, along with crushable taffeta evening dresses in acidy colors, off-the-shoulder velvets, fringed strapless gowns, and elaborately embroidered evening skirts and blouses. (See **Designer Women's Clothing,** p. 164.)

SAINT LAURENT RIVE GAUCHE
Luxurious and lovely evening gowns. (See **Designer Women's Clothing,** p. 164.)

VALENTINO
The lavish evening gowns are outstanding, and three times a year couture wedding-gown designs are flown in from Rome for the very well-heeled bride-to-be. It's a very special collection and prices are exorbitant. (See **Designer Women's Clothing,** p. 165.)

MATERNITY CLOTHING

B. Altman & Co. and Bloomingdale's have well-stocked maternity departments, Macy's offers a wide choice of maternity underwear and separates, and Saks Fifth Avenue is a good source for stylish sportswear and fashionable dresses.

BALLOON
1321 Madison Avenue, at 93rd Street
831-7800
Mon.–Wed., Fri.: 10 a.m.–6 p.m.; Thurs.: 11 a.m.–7 p.m.;
Sat.: 11 a.m.–6 p.m.; Sun.: 12 noon–5 p.m.
AE, MC, V

Balloon is the American outlet of a popular European maternity chain that brings high fashion to the *enceinte* condition. It's the brainchild of Veronique Delachaux, a former fashion editor of a French parenting magazine, who was frustrated at not being able to find stylish maternity clothing when she was pregnant. So she set about creating maternity wear in the spirit of the avant-garde and *haute couture* French designers. Delachaux has dressed Princesses Di and Caroline, Isabelle Huppert and Jerry Hall, and she has separates for the casual life, functional designs for the office, and smashing things for formal occasions. Prices range from moderate to expensive.

JONAL
Society's darlings come to Jonal for pricey *haute couture* maternity wear in sumptuous fabrics; skirts, slacks, and dresses are designed with hidden panels so they easily convert from maternity to regular wear after Baby is born; and evening blouses, skirts, and gowns are luxuriously beaded and pailletted, or done up in the finest silks, velvets, laces, and taffetas. A few things are available off-the-rack, but most must be custom ordered. (See **Wedding Gowns and Evening Wear,** p. 183.)

LADY MADONNA
793 Madison Avenue, at 67th Street
Second floor
988-7173
Mon.–Wed., Fri.: 10 a.m.–6 p.m.; Thurs.: 10 a.m.–7 p.m.; Sat.:
10 a.m.–6 p.m.
AE, MC, V

Each season's fashionable looks are translated into maternity wear at Lady Madonna. In this well-stocked store slacks and skirts are often designed with little zippers or buttons (instead of panels) for expansion, and the store carries a good selection of styles for the executive woman, along with activewear and swimwear, and lingerie (including nursing bras and nightgowns). Prices can be steep.

MANOLA
1040 Lexington Avenue, near 74th Street
861-1227
Mon.–Fri.: 11 a.m.–7 p.m.; Sat.: 11 a.m.–6 p.m.
MC, V

Manola's maternity wear appeals to stylish mothers-to-be, and her airy and comfortable shop is filled with clothing imported from France, along with samples of custom designs that are made right in Manola's workrooms. Customers are welcome to bring their own fabrics or work with the store's own top-quality linens, cottons, and silks. Fantasy evening wear and party styles are a specialty, but there are chic silks, moderately priced casual dresses, along with business suits, sports separates, and lingerie. Prices range from moderate to costly.

MOTHERCARE
2305 Broadway, at 83rd Street
877-1044
Mon.–Wed., Fri.: 10 a.m.–6:45 p.m.; Thurs.: 10 a.m.–7:45 p.m.;
Sat.: 10 a.m.–5:45 p.m.: Sun.: 12 noon–5:45 p.m.
MC, V

Mothercare is a famed British maternity and children's clothing chain, and in the company's spacious Broadway emporium mothers-to-be can buy their maternity wear along with a layette for the new baby, and infant and toddler things. The casual maternity clothing in bright, bold colors and playful styles is especially appealing, but there are wool-blend knits in coordinating skirts, pants, and tops, and business suits in tweeds and twills. Among the styles for toddlers are classic blazers and short pants for little boys, sweet cotton dresses and bonnets for baby girls. Prices are moderate.

MOTHERHOOD
786 Madison Avenue, near 66th Street
988-5415
Mon., Tues., Sat.: 10 a.m.–6 p.m.; Wed., Thurs., Fri.: 10 a.m.–7 p.m.
AE, MC, V

The maternity designs in this well-stocked store range from preppy conservative to high fashion, and prices go from moderate to expensive. Career dressing is the shop's forte, and there's a wide selection of comfortable dresses and suits in silks, wools, and synthetics. Trio, Sweet Mama, Ma Mère, Judy Loeb, and Mama Jeune are a few of the names you'll find, but the majority of the stock is Motherhood's own label.

MOTHER'S WORK
52 West 57th Street
Second floor
399-9840
Mon.–Wed., Fri.: 10:30 a.m.–6:30 p.m.; Thurs.: 10:30 a.m.–7:30 p.m.;
Sat.: 10:30 a.m.–6 p.m.
MC, V

Maternity wear for the working woman is Mother's Work's chief attraction, and its most popular item is the "adjuster skirt." It comes in a pleated or straight version in a range of colors and fabrics, and it's designed so blouses can be tucked in and it can be worn through the fifth month of pregnancy. Dozens of conservative suits with blouses, and jumpers with matching jackets, fill the large showroom, but there are also lots of casual weekend separates, swimsuits, and lingerie, too. Fabrics are often blends, and everything is moderately priced.

PARENT PENDING
1178 Lexington Avenue, near 80th Street
988-3996
Mon.–Wed., Fri.: 11 a.m.–7 p.m.; Thurs.: 11 a.m.–8 p.m.;
Sat.: 10 a.m.–6 p.m.; Sun. 12 noon–5 p.m.

2007 Broadway, near 68th Street
769-2232
Mon.–Wed., Fri.: 11 a.m.–7 p.m.; Thurs.: 11 a.m.–8 p.m.;
Sat.: 10 a.m.–6 p.m.; Sun.: 12 noon–5 p.m.
AE, MC, V

Parent Pending is crowded with trendy fashion looks transformed into maternity clothing. Sportswear is a specialty, but the stores carry dresses for the boardroom or partying, and there's a full selection of activewear, swimwear, lingerie, and nursing accessories, including lacy nursing bras. Prices are moderate.

REBORN MATERNITY
1449 Third Avenue, near 82nd Street
737-8817
Mon.–Wed., Fri.: 10:30 a.m.–6:45 p.m.; Sat.: 10 a.m.–5:45 p.m.;
Sun.: 11 a.m.–4:45 p.m.

564 Columbus Avenue, at 87th Street
362-6965
Mon., Tues., Thurs.–Sat.: 10 a.m.–5:45 p.m.; Wed.: 10 a.m.–8:15 p.m.;
Sun.: 11 a.m.–4:45 p.m.
AE, MC, V

Reborn Maternity prides itself on offering the same styles and fabrics in maternity wear that a woman would want if she weren't pregnant. Belle France rayon dresses printed in tiny florals are exclusive to the stores, and they carry washable silks, denims, miniskirts, wool jersey pull-on pants with oversized tops, and black velvet evening dresses. Prices range from moderate to costly.

Department Stores

B. ALTMAN & CO.
361 Fifth Avenue, at 34th Street
679-7800
Mon.–Wed., Fri., Sat.: 10 a.m.–7 p.m.; Thurs.: 10 a.m.–8 p.m.;
Sun.: 11 a.m.–5 p.m.
All major

Staid and traditional with its white columns and lofty ceilings, Altman's has a charming faded elegance. All this may change under its new owners, who plan to spruce up the store and who have already closed the Art Gallery (once filled with paintings, antique maps, rare books, and vintage autographs) and are in the midst of shrinking the store still further. Altman's strength has always been in its fine selection of china, housewares, kitchenwares, traditional furniture, and rugs, and at the present writing these are still around. Once a somewhat secret and serene spot for picking up designer clothing by Calvin Klein, Versace, Fendi, Anne Klein, and Krizia long after the trendier stores have sold out, it's too early to know if these top designers will remain in residence. Recently Altman's has been discovered by Yuppies co-oping on lower Fifth Avenue and the Flatiron district, who've come to value it for its old-fashioned service, so now you are as apt to see trendy young things as blue-haired grandmothers on its floors.

BARNEYS NEW YORK
106 Seventh Avenue, at 17th Street
929-9000
Mon.–Thurs.: 10 a.m.–9 p.m.; Fri.: 10 a.m.–8 p.m.;
Sat.: 10 a.m.–7 p.m.; Sun.: 12 noon–6 p.m.

225 Liberty Street
945-1600
Mon.–Wed.: 10 a.m.–7 p.m.; Thurs.: 10 a.m.–9 p.m.;
Fri. & Sat.: 10 a.m.–7 p.m.; Sun.: 12 noon–6 p.m.

2 World Financial Center
945-1600
Mon.–Wed., Fri., Sat.: 9:30 a.m.–7 p.m.; Thurs.: 9:30 a.m.–9 p.m.;
Sun.: 10 a.m.–6 p.m.
AE, MC, V

In the world's largest men's store a customer can choose between 40,000 suits in styles that range from ultraconservative British cuts, to classic American, to cutting-edge Japanese. Every current direction is represented not only in suits, but in shirts, sweaters, shoes, sportswear, formal wear, and accessories. A white marble stairway curls through the women's section (housed in what was once six adjacent brownstone buildings) where, under a skylight dome, you'll find six floors filled with the trendiest names in fashion. Here, among the Art Deco and Wiener Werkstätte furnishings, you can admire the hot looks from Mugler, Montana, Gaultier, Alaïa, Matsuda, Yamamoto; the funky English designers; as well as the more sedate styles from the grand houses of Chanel, Valentino, Yves Saint Laurent, and Rykiel. The Co/Op houses the casual, younger, and less pricey fashions by Basco, Kenzo, Workers for Freedom, and Vass. Shoe departments for both men and women are excellent, there's a Bonpoint boutique filled with pricey infant's things, and a well-stocked boys' department that carries sporty separates in a complete range of sizes (even husky). But most exciting of all is Chelsea Passage on the main floor with its small stalls of dazzling things for the home. Right next to the Herend, Ceralene, Longchamps, and Bernardaud china—all lovingly selected—is the Baccarat, Lalique, and de Sèvres crystal and the Jensen and Christofle silver plate. Cartier and Van Cleef Art Deco jewelry, Clarice Cliff pottery, Anachini antique bed linens, and Paul Vogel leather desk accessories are here as well. And service at Barneys is so attentive it's difficult to believe you're shopping in a New York department store. Barneys' Liberty Street and World Financial Center addresses are filled with the best of the men's fashions.

BERGDORF GOODMAN
754 Fifth Avenue, at 57th Street
753-7300
Mon.–Wed., Fri., Sat.: 10 a.m.–6 p.m.; Thurs.: 10 a.m.–8 p.m.
AE

The carriage trade and the newly affluent flock to Bergdorf Goodman. This elegant store with its marble floors, crystal chandeliers, Art Deco touches, and roomy dressing rooms has been at the same location since 1928, but a much-needed escalator, trendy young designers, and a newly created home furnishings floor have added new life. Italian designers are represented by Armani, Versace, and Krizia; the French by Gaultier, Lacroix, Karl Lagerfeld, Chanel, and Givenchy; the Americans by Beene, Lauren, and Klein; and the hot young designers by Pomodoro and Kors. There's a fine bridal department and a fur department that offers some of the city's most beautiful skins worked into classic or trendy fur styles. For men there's Turnball & Asser's distinctive shirts and ties, conservative Oxxford suits and topcoats, as well as Gaultier and Versace's more radical fashions. In the Home Department, on seven, Bergdorf's has assembled old and new treasures and displays them in elegant settings. Splendid linens for bed, bath, and table; antique and modern tableware and accessories, as well as things for the library and game room are among the temptations.

BLOOMINGDALE'S
1000 Third Avenue, at 59th Street
705-2000
Mon., Thurs.: 10 a.m.–9 p.m.; Tues., Wed., Fri.,
Sat.: 10 a.m.–6:30 p.m.; Sun.: 12 noon–6 p.m.
AE, DC, MC, V

Bloomingdale's has recently been purchased by the Canadian real-estate and retailing magnate Robert Campeau, so major changes may be in the works, and although Bloomingdale's has lost something of its old luster, it still offers an amazing array of things to wear, sit on, eat, or apply. On the main floor you'll find just about every name brand cosmetic and perfume, the furniture department features trendy model rooms, and the snappy fourth floor the latest in designer fashions to be ogled, touched, and tried on. Among the international set you'll find Chanel, Valentino, Armani, Ricci, Montana, Rykiel, and Mugler and among the Americans, Lauren, Blass, De La Renta, Karan, Herrara, and both Kleins. There's a well-stocked lingerie and shoe department, too, as well as an infant and children's section with all the necessities and frivolities. In the very complete men's furnishings department the fashions are by Armani, Versace, Lauren, Blass, Klein, and Ellis, along with Bloomingdale's' own. The Main Course covers kitchen and table needs, and this floor also boasts all the most wanted names in glassware, china, and silver.

BONWIT TELLER
4 East 57th Street
593-3333
Mon.–Wed., Fri.: 10 a.m.–6 p.m.; Thurs.: 10 a.m.–7 p.m.;
Sat.: 10 a.m.–6 p.m.; Sun.: 12 noon–5 p.m.
All major

Conservative and somewhat suburban, Bonwit Teller's offers a selection of "safe" designs in its women's clothing and accessories, and although you'll find things by Ralph Lauren, Anne Klein, Liz Claiborne, and Albert Nipon, they're either tailored for business or sweet and romantic. Recently, however, Bonwit's has been updating its fashion image and has introduced more radical fashion looks. The lower level of Trump Tower houses Bonwit's fine men's furnishings department. Besides the expected Ralph Lauren, Calvin Klein, and Giorgio Armani labels in sweaters, shirts, slacks, and ties, there's an exclusive collection of Battistoni things from Italy—silk ties, cashmere sweaters cut like sweats, robes, and quietly elegant shirts. But you'll find John

191

Weitz's exuberant shirts here, too, and luxurious paisley and brocade smoking jackets.

HENRI BENDEL
10 West 57th Street
247-1100
Mon.–Wed., Fri., Sat.: 10 a.m.–6 p.m.; Thurs.: 10 a.m.–8 p.m.;
Sun.: 12 noon–5 p.m.
AE, MC, V

Leslie Wexner of the Limited now owns Henri Bendel, and at this writing the store isn't what it used to be. The look, the clothing, and the customer who shops there have all changed. Gone is the Bridal Shop, the stationery section, and such familiar labels as Sonia Rykiel, Jean Muir, Ralph Lauren, and Perry Ellis, and gone too are many of the store's former customers who have defected to Bergdorf Goodman or Madison Avenue boutiques. On a recent visit the fashions looked more mainstream—updated Limited—less trendy and cutting edge. However the Street of Shops, where you can purchase everything from cosmetics to sweaters, to jewelry, to hats, to handbags, to candlesticks, still looks fine, and a few of the shops, like Frank McIntosh's greatly expanded tabletop corner, sparkle. The Leg Shop has panty hose in seductive shades that never sag around the ankles, and the lingerie department, although not the largest in town, offers exciting finds and it's a civilized and quiet oasis manned by a sales staff downright eager to coddle customers.

LORD & TAYLOR
424 Fifth Avenue, at 38th Street
391-3344
Mon.–Thurs.: 10 a.m.–8:30 p.m.; Tues., Wed., Fri.,
Sat.: 10 a.m.–6:45 p.m.; Sun.: 12 noon–6 p.m.
AE

Lord & Taylor has been in New York since 1926, and it's another of the city's department stores that is in the midst of radical changes since its purchase and merger with the Mays Department Store chain. The rug section, decorative fabrics, and the antique furniture department are no longer around. But this store's strength has always been in its collection of classic American designers, and these remain. You'll find Blass, Klein, Lauren, Ellis, Brooks, McClintock, and Sachs here, and a nicely expanded menswear section. Lord & Taylor has always been a store known for its lack of hype, its good taste and great service, and at the present writing these have not changed.

MACY'S
151 West 34th Street, at Herald Square
695-4400
Mon., Thurs., Fri.: 9:45 a.m.–8:30 p.m.; Tues., Wed.,
Sat.: 9:45 a.m.–6:45 p.m.; Sun.: 10 a.m.–6 p.m.
AE, MC, V

Macy's, the world's largest department store, has its own pharmacy, post office, pet accessories shop, branch of the Metropolitan Museum of Art's gift shop, five eateries, and an extraordinary mix of merchandise. Recently restored, the main floor (devoted to handbags and accessories) now shines with an Art Deco elegance. In the cavernous Cellar you'll find a bustling market (with meats, fresh vegetables, cheeses, and take-out food) and everything for the kitchen, from appliances to tableware. The fashion floors offer a similarly astonishing array of things from all the established—and many of the trendy—European and American designers. There's a juniors department, replete with blaring disco music and TV screens, that's stocked with exciting fashions for the younger set, and a quieter, but fine, linen department. In fact at Macy's you can buy everything from David's Cookies, to a souvenir Statue of Liberty mug, to Pratesi linens, to a Vuitton handbag.

SAKS FIFTH AVENUE
611 Fifth Avenue, at 49th Street
753-4000
Mon.–Wed., Fri., Sat.: 10 a.m.–6:30 p.m.; Thurs.: 10 a.m.–8 p.m.
AE, DC, MC, V

Saks Fifth Avenue, the quintessential New York department store, mixes old-fashioned charm with urban sophistication. The floors, designed around a central core, are a delight to shop in, and each floor offers a great depth of merchandise. You'll find one of the city's best selections of designer ballgowns and evening wear by Adolfo, Blass, De La Renta, Roehm, McFadden, and the like; furs by Revillon; a fine bridal department; designer sportswear by Calvin Klein, Donna Karan, Ralph Lauren, and Perry Ellis; and well-stocked infant and children's sections. The Men's Department is as spacious as a men's club with appointments to match—burnished wood trim, welcoming leather sofas, and comfortable fitting rooms—and here you'll find classic styles to please a traditionalist, as well as more radical-looking fashions.

Engravings, Prints, and Posters

ANTIQUE AND VINTAGE EUROPEAN PRINTS AND POSTERS

The Metropolitan Museum of Art and the Pierpont Morgan Library offer a large and varied assortment of reproductions of antique prints and posters.

ASSOCIATED AMERICAN ARTISTS
Etchings, lithographs, woodcuts, and serigraphs by old and modern masters that date from the fifteenth through the early twentieth centuries. (See **Early and Contemporary American Prints and Posters**, p. 199.)

BELGIS FREIDEL GALLERY
131 Thompson Street
475-0248
Tues.–Sun.: 12 noon–5 p.m.
AE

Belgis Freidel is a tiny gallery tucked away on Thompson Street, yet it offers one of the largest collections in the world of original Toulouse-Lautrec posters and lithographs. There are posters, too, by many other legendary artists dating from the late-nineteenth to the early-twentieth centuries, along with a fine selection of Art Deco and Art Nouveau works.

C. & J. GOODFRIEND
61 East 77th Street
Fifth floor
628-9383

By appointment only
No credit cards

The Goodfriends are private dealers known for their vast and extraordinary collection of drawings and prints that range from the fifteenth to the twentieth centuries. They offer an extraordinary mix of European and American artists that includes Rembrandt, Dürer, Whistler, and Buhot. French and English eighteenth- and nineteenth-century works are particularly well represented.

CARUS GALLERY
872 Madison Avenue, at 71st Street
879-4660
Tues.–Sat.: 11 a.m.–5 p.m.
No credit cards

Although the Carus Gallery is known for its very fine collection of German Expressionist and Russian Constructivist paintings it also offers a small but very select group of prints by such leading proponents of those movements as Kandinsky, Kirchner, Severini, and Balle. The owners are experts in the field and most helpful, and in addition to the paintings and prints, they stock a large inventory of art books by avant-garde artists working in the first half of the twentieth century.

CHISHOLM GALLERY
43 Greenwich Avenue, near Sixth Avenue
243-8834
Tues.–Sat.: 12 noon–7 p.m.; Sun.: 2 p.m.–6 p.m.
AE, MC, V

An eclectic mix of European and American posters fills Gail Chisholm's friendly gallery. Advertising posters that relate to food, wine, and travel are a chief attraction, but Chisholm also has a good inventory of propaganda posters of World War I and World War II. All her posters are original printings and date from 1890 to 1950.

CHISHOLM PRATS GALLERY
145 Eighth Avenue, near 17th Street
741-1703
Tues.–Sat.: 11 a.m.–6 p.m.
AE, MC, V

Rare and decorative original posters from 1890 to 1940 crowd this pleasant gallery co-owned by Gail Chisholm's brother (hence the name) but with no other connection to the Chisholm Gallery. It's a good place to go for twenties and thirties Art Deco and Art Nouveau posters and for original lithographs of fashion, travel, liquor, and cabarets. But there's a fine array of movie and circus posters, too, along with unusual ones from the Spanish Civil War and World War I and World War II.

DAVID TUNICK, INC.
12 East 81st Street
570-0090
Appointment advisable
No credit cards

In his elegant, exquisitely furnished town house David Tunick exhibits the finest, rarest, and most costly Old Master prints and drawings, along with a very select group of first strikes by modern artists. The serious collector will find the work of Rembrandt, Dürer, Canaletto, Tripolo, and Piranesi represented here, as well as that of Delacroix, Goya, Pissaro, Millet, Watteau, Boucher, Kirchner, and Fragonard, not to mention first strikes by Cézanne, Degas, Picasso, Toulouse-Lautrec, and Matisse.

EAGLES ANTIQUES
Seventeenth- and eighteenth-century English botanical and animal prints. (See **Furniture,** p. 242.)

E. WEYHE
The second floor is crammed with hundreds of prints and engravings—twentieth century works are the strength, but there are earlier examples, too—along with decorative and architectural prints. (See **Books,** p. 22.)

EX LIBRIS
A brilliant array of early-twentieth-century avant-garde graphics—Dada, Surrealism, Russian Constructivism, the Bauhaus, German Expressionism, and Futurism are all represented. (See **Books,** p. 22.)

FITCH-FEBVREL GALLERY
5 East 57th Street
Twelfth floor
688-8522
Tues.–Sat.: 11 a.m.–5:30 p.m.; August: By appointment
No credit cards

Andrew Fitch and his wife, Dominique Febvrel, specialize in exceptionally fine master prints and drawings by such late-nineteenth-century artists as Bresdin, Redon, Besnard, and Klinger. But their small and attractive gallery is stocked with twentieth-century drawings, too, along with prints by contemporary American and French artists.

GALERIE ST. ÉTIENNE
24 West 57th Street
245-6734
Tues.–Sat.: 11 a.m.–5 p.m.
No credit cards

As much small museum as gallery, St. Étienne is sober, serious, and scholarly. The owners are considered leading experts on Egon Schiele, Käthe Kollwitz, and Grandma Moses, and their gallery is stocked with fine examples of Austrian and German Expressionism and international folk art. Paintings, drawings, and prints by Gustav Klimt, Oskar Kokoschka, Schiele, and Käthe Kollwitz—along with the work of John Kane and Grandma Moses—fill the glass cases and cover all the walls.

ISSELBACHER GALLERY
41 East 78th Street
472-1766
Tues.–Sat.: 10 a.m.–5 p.m.
No credit cards

The Isselbacher Gallery is small, but it's a first-rate source for late-nineteenth- and twentieth-century prints, woodcuts, and etchings. Among the collection of important master prints you'll find such names as Cassatt, Beckman, Chagall, Matisse, Miró, Signac, and Renoir.

JAMES WILSON
146 East 74th Street
772-6338
Tues.–Sat.: 10 a.m.–5:30 p.m.
No credit cards

James Wilson has filled his quiet and serene town house, located just off Lexington Avenue, with European and English decorative prints and drawings dating from 1730 through 1860. Among the varied fields of interest Wilson has collected are topographical, sporting, dog, and flora and fauna examples. All his prints have original hand-coloring, and they're all presented in hand-washed French mats.

MURIEL KARASIK GALLERY
A small but select group of Art Deco posters. (See **Furniture,** p. 257.)

PAGEANT BOOK & PRINT SHOP
The vast collection of prints, etchings, and illustrations range from the fifteenth to the nineteenth centuries, and among the varied selection you'll find examples from every field of interest—heraldry, architecture, decorative arts and ornamentation, topography, fashion, botany, travel, sports, science, music, fauna, and mathematics. (See **Books,** p. 17.)

POSTER AMERICA
138 West 18th Street
206-0499
Tues.–Sat.: 11 a.m.–6 p.m.; Sun.: 1 p.m.–5 p.m.
AE, DC, MC, V

Collectors come to Poster America for its eclectic mix of original European and American posters that are as early as the turn of the century and as recent as the fifties. Art Nouveau and Art Deco are the shop's specialties, but you'll find movie and opera posters, rare Holland-America Line ship examples, and early Erté's of the Folies Bergère, as well as a large stock of propaganda posters from World War I and World War II.

RHEINHOLD-BROWN GALLERY
26 East 78th Street
734-7999
Tues.–Sat.: 10:30 a.m.–5 p.m
No credit cards

Rheinhold-Brown specializes in graphic design from 1900 to the present, and this gallery is known for its collection of rare and hard-to-find European posters based on design and illustrative criteria. You'll find 1910 Swiss posters, others of twenties avant-garde movements, along with contemporary posters by American, Swiss, and Japanese graphic designers. The gallery has a fine stock of travel, cultural, and product posters from all periods and from each major country.

STAIR AND COMPANY
An exquisite collection of seventeenth-through-the-early-nineteenth-century English paintings and engravings. (See **Furniture,** p. 245.)

SYLVIA TEARSTON ANTIQUES
An appealing array of European prints from the eighteenth and early nineteenth centuries that might include botanicals and sporting and topographical subjects. (See **China and Glassware,** p. 71.)

THEODORE B. DONSON, LTD.
24 West 57th Street
Third floor
245-7007
Tues.–Sat.: 10 a.m.–5:30 p.m.
No credit cards

Theodore B. Donson is a writer and recognized authority in the print field, and only the finest quality prints from the fifteenth through the twentieth centuries appear in his gallery. Among the old masters you're likely to find works by Rembrandt, Dürer, and Hogarth, and among the modern masters Matisse, Renoir, Whistler, Toulouse-Lautrec, and the German Expressionists.

URSUS BOOKS & PRINTS
The outstanding collection of more than 2,500 prints and watercolors, mostly from the eighteenth and nineteenth centuries, includes the very best that England, France, Italy, and America have to offer. There are export and fabric design watercolors along with decorative prints cover-

ing a wide range of interests: botanicals, Art Deco, fashion, natural history, interior design, architecture, carriages, gardens, equestrian, the American Indian, as well as dozens more. (See **Books,** p. 19.)

WILLIAM H. SCHAB GALLERY

11 East 57th Street
Fifth floor
758-0327
Mon.–Sat.: 9:30 a.m.–5:30 p.m.; closed Sat. in summer
No credit cards

Serene and sedate, the William H. Schab Gallery is known for its superior selection of old and modern master drawings and prints that range from the fifteenth through the twentieth centuries. You'll find works by Rembrandt, Dürer, Goya, Tiepolo, and Tintoretto, along with an appealing group of lithographs, woodcuts, engravings, and etchings by more recent artists. Italian Renaissance drawings, Dutch perspectives, unusual and small-scale Boucheron prints, and rare books are among Schab's other delights.

EARLY AND CONTEMPORARY AMERICAN PRINTS AND POSTERS

The Museum of American Folk Art carries a selection of prints and posters of past and present exhibits, and the New-York Historical Society offers early Americana and Currier & Ives prints, along with Audubon botanicals.

ARGOSY BOOK STORE

Prints of early American scenes, including views of New York Harbor, Central Park, lower Manhattan, as well as Currier & Ives prints. (See **Books,** p. 15.)

ASSOCIATED AMERICAN ARTISTS

20 West 57th Street
Sixth floor
399-5510
Tues.–Sat.: 10 a.m.–6 p.m.; Summer, Mon.–Fri.: 10 a.m.–5 p.m.
MC, V

America's largest print dealer offers original etchings, lithographs, woodcuts, and serigraphs that span the fifteenth through the twentieth centuries. Although the old masters, as well as more recent European artists, are represented here, most of the prints are American. So Associated is an excellent source for the work of such thirties and forties painters as Avery, Benton, Curry, Davis, Marsh, and Wood, not to mention that of Frankenthaler, Katz, Barnet, Motherwell, and other major contemporary American artists.

THE OLD PRINT SHOP
150 Lexington Avenue, near 29th Street
683-3950
Mon.–Fri.: 9 a.m.–5 p.m.; Sat.: 9 a.m.–4:30 p.m.;
closed Sat. in summer
MC, V

The Old Print Shop was founded in 1896, and this enchantingly old-fashioned shop with its burnished wood-paneled walls and shelves is where museum directors and collectors go for original Currier & Ives, first-edition Audubon bird prints engraved by Robert Havell, and other rarities. The present owner, Kenneth Newman, carries a superb selection of city views, original old American maps, marine scenes, and landscapes, along with some fine nineteenth-century French and English engravings.

PHYLLIS LUCAS GALLERY & OLD PRINT CENTER
981 Second Avenue, at 52nd Street
755-1516
Tues.–Sat.: 9 a.m.–5:30 p.m.; closed Sat. in summer
and first two weeks of July
No credit cards

The Phyllis Lucas Gallery looks as though it could easily be pictured in any of the early American prints that it sells, with its worn wooden floors, rickety old shelves, and old-fashioned-style holders for displaying prints. New York scenes are the shop's main attraction, and these include both originals and Phyllis Lucas's own reproductions, since Lucas is both a dealer in old prints and a publisher of engravings and lithographs. She carries Currier & Ives and Audubon prints, along with those of ships, sporting and equestrian scenes, cowboys and Indians, even early maps, and everything is neatly classified by subject. Lucas is also known for her Art Deco prints, modern graphics, and signed limited-edition Dali lithographs.

POSTER AMERICA
Original American posters that are as early as 1890 and as recent as the fifties—film, travel, and military posters are specialties. (See **Antique and Vintage European Prints and Posters**, p. 197.)

JAPANESE PRINTS

AZUMA GALLERY
50 Walker Street
925-1381
Tues.–Sun.: 12 noon–6 p.m.
No credit cards

The Azuma Gallery is small and serene, and it's best known for its outstanding collection of early Japanese ceramics. But the gallery also boasts a select group of Japanese woodcut prints of the Ukiyo-E period. The owners are obliging and knowledgeable in both the ceramic and print fields.

GLASS GALLERY
315 Central Park West, near 91st Street
Eighth floor
787-4704
Wed.–Sat.: 1 p.m.–5:30 p.m.; or by appointment
No credit cards

Comfortable and homey, the Glass Gallery occupies four large rooms whose walls are filled with works on paper. Japanese woodcut prints—especially those from the Ukiyo-E period—are a chief attraction, yet there are examples that are as early as 1770 and as recent as the twenties. In addition to the large array of Japanese woodcuts, there are prints by such American and European artists as Chaim Gross, Raphael and Moses Soyer, Max Weber, Frank Kleinholz, Benny Andrews, and Soulages.

JAPAN GALLERY
1210 Lexington Avenue, at 82nd Street
288-2241
Tues.–Sat.: 10:30 a.m.–6 p.m.
AE, MC, V

Small and somewhat sober, the Japan Gallery is where serious collectors come for woodcut prints. Although exceptionally fine eighteenth-, nineteenth-, and twentieth-century examples fill its well-stocked shelves, prints from the 1830s to the 1840s are the gallery's specialty. The staff is friendly and well-informed.

RONIN GALLERY
605 Madison Avenue, near 57th Street
Second floor
688-0188

Mon.–Sat.: 10 a.m.–6 p.m.; closed Sat. in summer
AE, MC, V

George Nakashima furniture, rice paper screens, Noguchi paper lanterns, and pebble planters transform the Ronin Gallery into a serene Japanese haven on Madison Avenue. The gallery is famed for its superior collection of museum-quality Japanese art from the seventeenth through the twentieth centuries, and it stocks an outstanding selection of Japanese woodcut prints from those periods.

THINGS JAPANESE
A fine array of woodcut prints from the eighteenth and nineteenth centuries. (See **Ethnic Items,** p. 213.)

MILITARY PRINTS
AND POSTERS

CHISHOLM GALLERY
A large assortment of World War I and World War II propaganda posters. (See **Antique and Vintage European Prints and Posters,** p. 195.)

CHISHOLM PRATS GALLERY
A small but unusual selection of posters from the Spanish Civil War, along with World War I and World War II propaganda posters. (See **Antique and Vintage European Prints and Posters,** p. 195.)

THE MILITARY BOOKMAN
Rare prints of military conflicts, including World War I and World War II. (See **Books,** p. 36.)

POSTER AMERICA
A fine collection of World War I posters. (See **Antique and Vintage European Prints and Posters,** p. 197.)

THE SOLDIER SHOP
A select group of prints of soldiers and military conflicts. (See **Books,** p. 37.)

EQUESTRIAN AND WILDLIFE PRINTS AND POSTERS

ARGOSY BOOK STORE

An appealing inventory of eighteenth- and nineteenth-century English jumping, steeplechase, and fox hunting prints. (See **Books**, p. 15.)

ARTHUR ACKERMAN & SON, INC.

A fine selection of sporting and equestrian prints. (See **Furniture**, p. 241.)

SPORTSMAN'S EDGE LTD.

136 East 74th Street
249-5010
Mon.–Sat.: 10 a.m.–6 p.m.
AE, MC, V

Sportsman's Edge is a good place to come for signed and limited-edition prints by contemporary sporting and wildlife artists. Displayed in an appropriately masculine gallery outfitted with polished mahogany paneling and shelves, are the works of Robert Abbett, Francis Golden, Bod Kuhn, and Chet Reneson, along with prints by famous British wildlife artist David Shepherd.

ARCHITECTURAL DRAWINGS AND PRINTS

PAGEANT BOOK & PRINT SHOP

An eclectic and extensive collection of antique and vintage architectural engravings and prints of all kinds. (See **Books**, p. 17.)

STUBBS BOOKS & PRINTS, INC.

The city's largest array of European eighteenth- and nineteenth-century architectural drawings, engravings, and prints by all the legendary names. (See **Books**, p. 20.)

URSUS BOOKS & PRINTS

An excellent source for eighteenth- and nineteenth-century architectural drawings, engravings, and prints. (See **Books,** p. 19.)

WILLIAM H. SCHAB GALLERY

Italian architectural drawings, Dutch perspectives. (See **Antique and Vintage European Prints and Posters,** p. 199.)

PERFORMING ARTS POSTERS AND PRINTS

JERRY OHLINGER'S MOVIE MATERIAL STORE

242 West 14th Street
989-0869
Daily: 1 p.m.–7:45 p.m.
No credit cards

Still photos of old movie stars, stacks of old movie magazines, and hundreds of original movie posters fill this cluttered store to overflowing. Jerry Ohlinger's collection dates from the twenties to the present, and includes just about every major or minor actor or actress and every film. Many of the posters are rare, most are hard-to-find, and Ohlinger's amazing collection includes everything from the original poster for *Enter the Dragon* to the British, French, and Italian posters for *The Empire Strikes Back*.

MEMORY SHOP

109 East 12th Street
473-2404
Daily: 10 a.m.–6 p.m.
No credit cards

Stashed away in the Memory Shop's cluttered basement are thousands of posters, movie stills, press books, and movie momentos that are as early as the thirties and as recent as current film releases. It's best to know exactly what you want, browsing is not encouraged since this is primarily a telephone and mail order operation.

MOTION PICTURE ARTS GALLERY

133 East 58th Street
Tenth floor
223-1009
Tues.–Fri.: 11 a.m.–5:30 p.m.; Sat.: 12 noon–5 p.m.
MC, V

Ira Resnick believes that the finest movie posters—especially vintage ones—have achieved the status of art, and in his handsome, tidy, and well-organized gallery they're treated with the respect they deserve. The gallery is outfitted with plush carpeting, tables hold albums filled with photographs of the posters in stock, and there are cozy sofas to sit on while making selections. Resnick has put together a collection of more than 10,000 original American and European posters and lobby cards, from the Silent Era through the fifties—considered by experts the end of the golden age of posters. He has rare posters of the Marx Brothers together in one shot, the Three Stooges in color, and one of Fred Astaire solo. But the centerpiece of his collection is an Austrian poster of Louise Brooks in *Diary of a Lost Girl* which has a price tag of $50,000. Still, many of Resnick's posters are in the two-hundred-dollar range, and his lobby cards are very affordable.

MOVIE STAR NEWS

134 West 18th Street
620-8160
Mon.–Sat.: 10 a.m.–6 p.m.
AE, MC, V

Movie Star News claims to have one of the largest collections of movie star photographs in the world. They carry thousands of original and reissue photos, and their inventory of posters is almost as impressive. Posters in black-and-white and color capture eighty years of movie making, and you'll find just about every movie—and every star—past and present represented. The shop is crowded with press books, publicity materials, and scene stills, too.

NOSTALGIA . . . AND ALL THAT JAZZ

A large inventory of posters from old movies. (See **Records,** p. 415.)

TRITON GALLERY

323 West 45th Street
765-2472
Mon.–Sat.: 10 a.m.–6 p.m.
AE, MC, V

Triton Gallery offers just about every theater poster that has ever been produced for any Broadway, Off-Broadway, or Off-Off-Broadway production. It even stocks posters created for productions on London's West End. Robert Puckett, the owner of this beguiling shop, doesn't limit his stock to the theater. He carries posters for Masterpiece Theater, the PBS Mystery Series, and dance performances, along with a selection of rare movie ones. Hard-to-find and out-of-print original and second-edition show cards are also among Puckett's vast inventory, as well as photographic reproductions of the show cards and posters in his archives.

CONTEMPORARY PRINTS AND POSTERS

The Guggenheim Museum, the Metropolitan Museum of Art, the Museum of Modern Art, the New Museum of Contemporary Art, and the Whitney Museum stock an extensive selection of prints and posters by contemporary artists.

BROOKE ALEXANDER, INC.
59 Wooster Street
Second floor
925-4338
Tues.–Sat.: 10 a.m.–6 p.m.; summer, Mon.–Fri.: 10 a.m.–5 p.m.
No credit cards

Brooke Alexander is known for exhibiting the important names in European and American painting, and she also publishes prints of post-fifties American artists. So her spacious gallery is stocked with superior-quality prints of the work of Albers, Haas, Beal, Katz, Pearlstein, Bartlett, and many others.

CASTELLI GRAPHICS
578 Broadway, near Prince Street
941-9855
Mon.–Sat.: 10 a.m.–6 p.m.; closed July and August
No credit cards

The top contemporary American printmakers are represented by Castelli Graphics, so this gallery is a good place to go for graphics by such contemporary artists as Lichtenstein, Oldenburg, Serra, Stella, Flavin, Rauschenberg, Kelly, Judd, Twombly, and Warhol.

CIRCLE GALLERY LTD.
468 West Broadway
677-5100
Mon.–Fri.: 10 a.m.–6 p.m.; Sat.: 11 a.m.–7 p.m.; Sun.: 10 a.m.–6 p.m.

Trump Tower
725 Fifth Avenue, at 56th Street
980-5455
Mon.–Sat.: 10 a.m.–6 p.m.

203 Front Street
South Street Seaport
732-8707
Mon.–Sat.: 11 a.m.–7 p.m.; Sun.: 11 a.m.–6 p.m.
AE, D, MC, V

Since the Circle Gallery publishes original signed and numbered limited-edition graphics, it offers one of the largest collections of graphic arts in the city. Circle's spacious SoHo shop is filled with the work of 100 artists—some young, some up-and-coming, some established masters—working in a range of styles, from realistic to abstract. Barnet, Erté, Agam, Gallo, and Wyeth are just a few of the artists represented. The smaller Trump Tower and South Street Seaport shops stock edited selections of the gallery's vast inventory, along with a selection of artists' jewelry.

CROWN POINT PRESS
568 Broadway, near Prince Street
226-5476
Tues.–Fri.: 9:30 a.m.–5:30 p.m.; Sat.: 11 a.m.–6 p.m.;
closed Sat. in summer
MC, V

Crown Point Press is known as the best etching studio in the country, and it publishes prints by established European and American artists. Its huge loft space, designed by Denise Hall, is filled with prints displayed in natural light. Richard Diebenkorn, John Cage, Francesco Clemente, Alex Katz, Robert Kushner, Ed Ruscha, Pat Steir, and Wayne Thiebaud are all represented, and although the prints are pricey, the quality is exceptional.

PACE PRINTS
32 East 57th Street
Third floor and tenth floor
421-3237
Tues.–Sat.: 10 a.m.–5:30 p.m.; closed Sat. in summer
No credit cards

The Pace Gallery is famed the world over for its extraordinary stable of modern artists and its fine collection of American Indian, African, and Oceanic art. In the handsome Pace Prints gallery are scores of signed and numbered limited-edition prints and multiples by many of the Pace artists. All the graphics are beautifully displayed, and among the illustrious names are Matisse, Picasso, Avery, Dine, Nevelson, and Held.

POSTERS ORIGINALS LIMITED
924 Madison Avenue, near 73rd Street
861-0422
Mon.–Sat.: 10 a.m.–5:45 p.m.; closed Sat. in summer

158 Spring Street
226-7720
Tues.–Sun.: 10 a.m.–6 p.m.; summer: Tues.–Sun.: 12 noon–7 p.m.
AE, MC, V

These dramatic galleries designed by Gwathemey Siegel are crowded with American and European contemporary art posters. But contrary to what the name of the gallery suggests, these posters are reproductions, not originals. Art exhibition announcements are the chief attraction, and among the European artists are such illustrious names as Klee, Braque, Matisse, Picasso, Hockney, Klimt, and Chagall. Among the Americans: Calder, Lichtenstein, and Warhol. There are Olympic posters, as well as circus, zoo, comic book, and pop culture ones.

REINHOLD-BROWN GALLERY
Posters by contemporary European, American, and Japanese graphic designers. (See **Antique and Vintage European Prints and Posters,** p. 198.)

Ethnic Items

See **Museum Gift Shops;** see also **Furniture, Country** and **Orientalia.**

AMIGO COUNTRY
Among the Mexican treasures are colonial-style furniture, nubby wool rugs, tin mirrors, glazed terra-cotta pottery, and bright cotton placemats. (See **Furniture,** p. 272.)

ARTESANIA COLUMBUS AVENUE
274 Columbus Avenue, near 72nd Street
769-9377
Mon.–Wed.: 11 a.m.–9 p.m.; Thurs.: 10 a.m.–10 p.m.; Fri. & Sat.: 10 a.m.–11 p.m.; Sun.: 11 a.m.–10 p.m.
AE, MC, V

A tiny sliver of a shop, Artesania is crammed with stylish clothing fashioned from ethnic fabrics. Men's oversized shirts come in a range of vibrantly patterned Mexican cottons—some new, some vintage. Pants, skirts, and shorts are stitched from colorful Guatemalan weaves, and there are bold hand-knit sweaters, colorful shawls and scarves, woven handbags and duffles with leather trim.

BACK FROM GUATEMALA
306 East 6th Street
260-7010
Mon.–Sat.: 12 noon–11 p.m.; Sun.: 3 p.m.–10 p.m.
AE, MC, V

Susan Kaufman and Joe Grunberg have managed to stock their closet-size shop with dozens of bold and colorful treats. Brightly colored hand-woven clothing, wall hangings, masks, and puppets from Guatemala share the space with chiffon scarves from the Middle East, handmade sweaters from South America, and hundreds of cloisonné earrings from

China. And there are artifacts from Bali, Afghanistan, and Tibet as well.

BUEN DIA
108 West Houston Street
673-1910
Daily: 1 p.m.–9 p.m.
AE, MC, V

Every inch of this well-stocked and friendly store is filled with imports from Mexico and Guatemala. Among the exuberant mix are colorful cotton shirts and rebozos, elaborately embroidered dresses, leather sandals, tin mirrors, and hand-blown glasses in every size and shape. Buen Dia also offers the city's largest selection of handmade hammocks.

THE COMMON GROUND
50 Greenwich Avenue, near 11th Street
989-4178
Mon., Tues., Thurs., Fri., 11:30 a.m.–7:30 p.m.; Wed. 11:30 a.m.–6:30 p.m.; Sat., 11 a.m.–6:30 p.m.: Sun. 1 p.m.–6 p.m.
AE, DC, MC, V

The Common Ground has been on Greenwich Avenue for more than a dozen years and this narrow little shop is a favorite with those looking for authentic Native American wares. It offers a superb selection of jewelry, old and new, including antique turquoise-and-silver pieces, squash blossom necklaces, and designs by contemporary Indian and Mexican artists. And it has a fine stock of collectibles—old Zuñi, Hopi, and Acoma pottery; twenties and thirties Navaho rugs; old Pendleton blankets; vintage kachina dolls; and Seminole jackets.

CRAFT CARAVAN
63 Greene Street
431-6669
Tues.–Fri.: 10 a.m.–6 p.m.; Sat., Sun.: 11 a.m.–6 p.m.
MC, V

Craft Caravan is popular with stylists for fashion magazines who raid the store for vivid shirts, colorful straw bags, bright woven sashes, patterned scarves, and the shop's irresistible array of bold jewelry. Standouts are the chunky amber and silver-bead necklaces, ivory cuff bracelets, and African trading-bead pieces. But in the store's spacious location on Greene Street, there's ample room for a trove of traditional African crafts, terra-cotta jugs and pots, intricate European carved chains, hand-painted barbershop signs, handmade toys, hand-loomed fabrics, leather work, and baskets of all kinds. Although Craft Caravan's specialty is African household and utilitarian objects, everything has a pop edge and a touch of humor.

FIVE EGGS

Among the winning Japanese products are cozy cotton-flannel kimonos for children and adults, sake sets, lacquered and hand-carved chopsticks, flower-arranging tools, tea ceremony accoutrements, origami kits, and writing instruments. (See **Gifts,** p. 303.)

FOLKLORICA

89 Fifth Avenue, near 16th Street.
255-2525
Mon.–Fri.: 10 a.m.–7 p.m.; Sat.: 11 a.m.–6 p.m.; Sun.: 1 p.m.–6 p.m.
AE, MC, V

The exceptionally fine quality of the handcrafts from Africa, South America, and Asia distinguishes Folklorica. Cavernous, serene, and well-appointed, it's filled with traditional baskets, rugs, musical instruments, tapestries, masks, textiles, dolls, jewelry, and fine examples of primitive art. Everything has been chosen with care by owners Pamela Levy and Jack Bregman, and the staff is knowledgeable, friendly, and obliging.

GRASS ROOTS GALLERY

131 Spring Street
431-0144
Tues.–Sat.: 12 noon–6 p.m.
AE, MC, V

Margery Nathanson has turned her passion for Latin American folk art into a gallery whose white stucco walls are an appropriate foil for the exuberance of the art. Everywhere in her wonderful gallery hang papier-mâché, pottery, and wood figures, and Nathanson's shelves are stacked with displays of Day of the Dead skeletons, whimsical animals, and amusing toys. From tiny ceramic buses piled high with people, to handsome Santa Clara del Cobre copper urns, to exquisite lacquered wedding chests, to crèches both pious and whimsical, the Grass Roots Gallery offers a vivid world.

HANDBLOCK

487 Columbus Avenue, near 83rd Street
799-4342
Mon.–Sat.: 10 a.m.–7 p.m.; Sun.: 11 a.m.–7 p.m.; summer,
Mon.–Fri.: 10 a.m.–8 p.m.; Sat.: 10 a.m.–7 p.m.; Sun.: 11 a.m.–7 p.m.
AE, MC, V

Hand-blocking, the ancient art of India, gives this winning shop its name, and accounts for 50 percent of its wares. Hand-blocked Indian cotton, in dozens of patterns and in colors both pale and intense, appears in everything from clothing, to tablecloths, to duvet covers, to shower curtains—or can be purchased by the yard. Pottery, glassware, antique carved-wood boxes, rugs, wicker furniture, and hand-carved tables are among the other Indian (or Indian inspired) temptations. Prices are good.

JACQUES CARCANAGUES
114 Spring Street
925-8110
Tues.–Sun.: 11:30 a.m.–7 p.m.
AE, MC, V

Frenchman Jacques Carcanagues has traveled worldwide and has picked up artifacts from Southeast Asia, Panama, and Guatemala, and these ethnic finds are attractively displayed in his SoHo shop. Although much of his stock is antique and one-of-a-kind, you're likely to find handsome red-lacquer Indian chests and settees, rugs from the Near East, drum tables, Tanzu chests, and Indonesian textiles. Glass-topped cases hold an enticing collection of jewelry old and new—elaborately worked Indian sterling-silver belts, ivory cuff bracelets, Afghan pieces, and amber necklaces, along with a group of chunky silver bangle bracelets that are surprisingly affordable.

NUSRATY AFGHAN IMPORTS
215 West 10th Street
691-1012
Daily: 12 noon–8 p.m.
AE, MC, V

Abdul Nusraty's shop is cluttered with antiques from Afghanistan, the Middle East, and Asia. Stacks of antique and vintage kilims are piled on the floor, and hanging from racks overhead are elaborately embroidered nineteenth-century native dresses. Nearby counters hold old silver, early handwritten books, and sixteenth- and seventeenth-century bronzes and clay pots. Ancient turquoise necklaces, old-ivory bracelets, and amber beads fill the glass-topped cases, and Nusraty offers contemporary jewelry and handcrafts from Africa and Indonesia as well.

PAN AMERICAN PHOENIX
Citicorp Center
153 East 53rd Street
355-0590
Mon.–Fri.: 10:30 a.m.–6:30 p.m.; Sat.: 10 a.m.–6 p.m.
MC, V

Pan American Phoenix transforms a small corner of Citicorp Center into a vibrant Mexican bazaar. Bolts of brightly colored Mexican fabric fill the window, along with an appealing mix of Mexican and Guatemalan handcrafts and folk art. The cotton fabric is sold by the yard and comes in solids and stripes, and the shop is crammed with richly embroidered Mexican blouses and dresses, silver jewelry, glazed terracotta pottery, hand-woven shawls, cotton place mats, hand-blown glassware, tin mirrors, flower-and-fauna-bedecked clay candelabra, tiny dolls, and hand-carved wooden animals.

THE PERSIAN SHOP
534 Madison Avenue, near 54th Street
355-4643
Mon.–Sat.: 11 a.m.–6:30 p.m.
All major

Although Persia no longer exists, this small shop is crammed full of the riches Persia once offered the world. Eighteenth- and nineteenth-century Islamic art, antique Oriental jewelry, Persian rugs, icons, precious stones, rich brocades, and caftans are among its treasures.

PUTUMAYO
Dresses, blouses, skirts, and pants are made in Mexico, South America, and India from native fabrics, but the styling is very casual with an American country look. (See **Clothing,** p. 156.)

SERMONETA
Pretty dresses, hand-knit sweaters, innocent nightgowns, and classic straw bags from Peru, Ecuador, and India. (See **Clothing,** p. 157.)

SURMA
11 East 7th Street
477-0729
Mon.–Sat.: 11 a.m.–6 p.m.; Sun.: 11 a.m.–2 p.m.; closed Mon. in summer
AE

Since 1918 Myron Surmach has sold things from the "old country" in his East Village shop, and it's now crammed with an astonishingly eclectic mix of traditional Ukrainian and Rumanian wares. Racks of sheet music and stacks of books (Surma is also known as the Surma Book and Music Company) share the space with eggs and egg-decorating tools, imported Ukrainian honey, stationery, Cossak tunics, traditionally embroidered linens, hand-painted pottery, hand-tooled leather shoes, and exquisite hand-embroidered peasant blouses, vests, and dresses.

THINGS JAPANESE
1109 Lexington Avenue, near 77th Street
Second floor
249-3591
Tues.: 11 a.m.–7 p.m.; Wed.–Sat.: 11 a.m.–5 p.m.
AE, MC, V

Japanese porcelains, vintage silk kimonos, lacquerware, books, ivory carvings, dolls, scrolls, and woodblock prints are attractively displayed in this serene and tidy shop. The prints are first rate and include originals from the eighteenth and nineteenth centuries, as

213

well as those by contemporary artists, and you'll find the owners knowledgeable and expert at helping would-be collectors put together a grouping.

YUZEN

318 East 6th Street
473-3405
Mon.–Sun.: 2 p.m.–10 p.m.
AE, MC, V

Donal Walker is a devotee of antique Japanese textiles and folk crafts and he's assembled a very special collection of silk kimonos and haoris (short jackets) from the turn of the century through the fifties in his tiny shop. Walker also carries the richly patterned blue-indigo cotton clothing worn by today's Japanese farmers, along with Mingei antiques, tanzu chests, and a delightful assortment of folk crafts. Prices are excellent.

Fabrics And Trimmings

ANTIQUE AND VINTAGE

COBWEB
Ornate nineteenth-century silk drapery tassels on braided cords. (See **Furniture**, p. 273.)

DORIS LESLIE BLAU GALLERY
An exquisite collection of museum-quality woven fragments. (See **Carpets and Tapestries**, p. 56.)

JUAN PORTELA ANTIQUES
A very special group of antique drapes and curtains. (See **Furniture**, p. 250.)

L'ANTIQUAIRE & THE CONNOISSEUR
Museum-quality medieval and Renaissance textiles. (See **Furniture**, p. 254.)

TURKANA GALLERY
Old textiles from Japan, Central Asia, China, the Ottoman Empire, and Africa. (See **Carpets and Tapestries**, p. 59.)

CONTEMPORARY

ART-MAX FABRICS
250 West 40th Street
398-0755

Mon.–Fri.: 8:30 a.m.–5:45 p.m.; Sat.: 9 a.m.–4:45 p.m.
AE, MC, V

Art-Max occupies three large floors, and for more than forty years this company has been selling fine French laces, brocades, metallics, cut velvets, beaded and jeweled chiffons, Sposabella embroideries, and Italian silks. But Art-Max dazzles in its selection of fabrics for weddings. There are Swiss embroideries; French Alençon, Lyon, and Chantilly laces; and laces embellished with imported pearls, beads, and sequins; along with dozens of types of netting and tulles for veils.

CHARLOTTE MOSS & CO.
A colorful assortment of Victorian-style silk and satin tassel pulls and drapery ties. (See **Gifts,** p. 294.)

CHERCHEZ
Old-fashioned silk and moiré tassel pulls in solids or lush color combinations. (See **Gifts,** p. 300.)

FAR EASTERN FABRICS
171 Madison Avenue, near 33rd Street
Second floor
683-2623
Mon.–Fri.: 9 a.m.–5 p.m. (closed 12 noon–1 p.m.)
No credit cards

Far Eastern is primarily a wholesale operation that imports fabrics from the Far East and Holland, but the company will sell retail on purchases of five yards or more. It stocks rich brocades and luscious silks (including jacquard tussah), along with batiks, ikats, madras, and cotton prints that can be purchased by the yard. Equally tempting is the array of silk pillows, sarongs and silk saris, stoles, scarves, ribbons, and braids. Prices are excellent.

HOME TEXTILES
132-A Spring Street
431-0411
Mon.–Fri.: 11 a.m.–7 p.m.; Sat., Sun.: 12 noon–5:30 p.m.
AE, MC, V

Anne Helverson has filled her vast, sun-drenched loft with 50,000 yards of fabric that she sells by the yard. She stocks all the weaves you'd ever want: opulent silks, brocades, and tapestries; nubby wools and linens; gossamer voiles and laces; cheerful chintzes. Helverson has a staff of professionals who can suggest ideas and come up with decorating solutions, and best of all, a competent workroom crew that can turn those ideas and solutions into window treatments and upholstered furniture.

HOWARD KAPLAN'S FRENCH COUNTRY STORE

A charming selection of cottons in tiny provincial prints as well as oversized florals; also upholstery-weight cottons. (See **Furniture**, p. 274.)

HYMAN HENDLER & SONS

67 West 38th Street
840-8393
Mon.–Fri.: 9 a.m.–5:30 p.m.
No credit cards

Hyman Hendler was established in 1900, and this shop is best known for its extraordinary collection of ribbons from France and Switzerland. But it also has a fine stock of luxurious European tassels and tiebacks fashioned after Victorian ones. There are key tassels of silk, cotton, or metallic threading—in solid colors or exuberant combinations—and a large assortment of cording for pillows.

JERRY BROWN IMPORTED FABRICS

37 West 57th Street
753-3626
Mon.–Fri.: 9 a.m.–6 p.m.; Sat.: 9 a.m.–5:30 p.m.
AE, MC, V

Sumptuous cottons, silks, wools, cashmeres, and linens are all neatly wrapped in paper and carefully stacked in this orderly shop. Jerry Brown specializes in clothing fabrics from France, Italy, and Switzerland, and many of the same manufacturers that Brown buys from supply the grand French and Italian couture houses.

LAURA ASHLEY

Delicate floral and geometric fabrics with the English country look come in weights suitable for upholstery, draperies, or clothing, and the company also carries quilted cottons that can be transformed into bedspreads. (See **Clothing**, p. 275.)

LIBERTY OF LONDON

630 Fifth Avenue, at 51st Street
459-0080
Mon.–Sat.: 10 a.m.–6 p.m.
AE, MC, V

In Liberty of London's very English and very charming New York outpost you'll find bolts of this company's signature tiny-print florals and graceful Art Nouveau–style fabrics in weights suitable for sofas, drapes, or dresses. There are cotton, glazed chintz, linen, silk, wool, and challis to choose from in an appealing range of pastels and jewel tones. The shop also has ready-to-sew skirts in wools, challis, and country cottons, along with a wide range of clothing, bed linens, and gift items—

cosmetic cases, ties, desk accessories, dolls, stuffed animals, and little girls' smocked dresses.

MARIMEKKO
7 West 56th Street
581-9616
Mon.–Fri.: 10 a.m.–6:30 p.m.; Thurs.: 10 a.m.–8 p.m.;
Sat.: 10 a.m.–6 p.m.
AE, MC, V

Marimekko is Finnish for "Mary's frock," and the company was founded in Finland in 1951 by the late Arwi Ratia as a textile printing company. In the sixties it became known world-wide for simply styled shift dresses that were worn by the rich and famous of that era, and for fabrics that featured brightly colored, large-scale graphic patterns. Its New York shop—replete with blond-wood floors and furnishings, brilliant colors, and clean lines—re-creates the look of Finland, and it's filled with bold and graphic fabrics in colors that range from subdued to exuberant. There are bolts of playful and whimsical cottons ideal for children's rooms, flowers in sorbetti colors, along with sophisticated geometrics, and many patterns come vinyl coated for turning into tablecloths, place mats, or shower curtains. Marimekko also offers bed linens, simply cut and understated dresses and blouses for women, and clothing for children in the same strong prints, along with a handsome line of hand-woven wool coats.

M. & J. TRIMMINGS COMPANY
1008 Avenue of the Americas, near 38th Street
391-9072
Mon.–Fri.: 9 a.m.–6 p.m.; Sat.: 10 a.m.–5 p.m.
AE, MC, V

Shoppers for the Metropolitan Opera and Seventh Avenue design houses come to M. & J. Trimmings—the largest trimming source in the city—for braid, tassels, beaded fringes, cordings, and weltings. A clutter of these Victorian favorites are piled high everywhere in this crammed-full store, but there are also feather boas, sequins, sea beads, rhinestones, crystals, ribbons, beaded appliqués, buttons, and buckles.

PAN AMERICAN PHOENIX
Bolts of hand-woven Mexican cottons come in primary colors, pastels, and earth tones, and in solids and stripes. (See **Ethnic Items,** p. 212.)

PARON FABRICS
60 West 57th Street
247-6451
Mon.–Sat.: 9 a.m.–5:45 p.m.; Sun.: 1 p.m.–3 p.m.
AE, MC, V

Paron features designer cuts of cloth, so this well-stocked and neatly organized store is crammed with the same high-quality fabrics that the top designers use to create their costly creations. There's an appealing inventory of natural fabrics—silks, woolens, cottons, and linens—in each season's most wanted patterns and colors, and each bolt of cloth is labeled with the fiber content and price.

PIERRE DEUX

The famous Souleiado fabrics, hand-screened in traditional Provençal patterns, are beautifully displayed and sold by the yard. (See **Furniture**, p. 277.)

SAINT RÉMY

Tiny floral-print cottons, jacquards, linen and cotton toweling fabrics, and woven tapestries that are reproductions of medieval masterpieces are available by the yard. (See **Gifts**, p. 309.)

TINSEL TRADING COMPANY

47 West 38th Street
730-1030
Mon.–Fri.: 10:30 a.m.–5 p.m.; Sat.: 1 a.m.–5 p.m. (except summer)
MC, V

Sift through the mounds of trimmings in this cluttered store and you're likely to find antique galloon trims and elaborate silk tiebacks, along with braids, fringes, cords, gimps, soutaches, medallions, and edgings. Most of the tassels are from the twenties and thirties, and they're made of gold and silver metallic threadings. There's also a large collection of military braids, appliqués for blazer pockets, and sword knots.

WILLIAM N. GINSBURG COMPANY

242 West 38th Street
244-4539
Mon.–Fri.: 9 a.m.–5 p.m.
No credit cards

William N. Ginsburg is known as a fine source for top-quality dressmaker fabrics, and this tidy shop carries an excellent selection of all the most wanted silk, cotton, and woolen fabrics in all the trendy colors. But it is also brimful of unusual tassels, fringes, braids, gimps, and rope trims, and the owner will create custom braids, ropes, and cords to match a fabric.

WOLFMAN GOLD & GOOD COMPANY

The appealing selection of fabrics available by the yard includes laces, bold stripes, florals, and cotton mattress-ticking. (See **China and Glassware**, p. 80.)

Fireplace Equipment

ANTIQUE

BOB PRYOR ANTIQUES
Handsome eighteenth- and nineteenth-century brass fire tools. (See
Gifts, p. 293.)

DANNY ALESSANDRO LTD./EDWIN JACKSON, INC.
307 East 60th Street
421-1928/759-8210
Mon.–Fri.: 10 a.m.–6 p.m. (closed 1 p.m.–2 p.m.)
AE, MC, V

Danny Alessandro and Edwin Jackson are two legendary companies
that have been supplying New Yorkers with mantels and fireplace accessories since 1879. They joined forces several years ago and recently
moved to new headquarters around the corner from their old showroom, where they have six floors filled with equipment. Antique mantels of wood, marble, and stone are a specialty, and these range from
simple Early American to ornate eighteenth-century Louis XV, to graceful Art Deco beauties. And there are antique andirons, screens, and
tools, even Victorian bed warmers. In addition to the antiques you'll
find a large selection of reproductions, as well as a complete stock of
ultramodern contemporary ones in just about every material. Tools,
too, range from antiques, to reproductions of old sets, to Plexiglas and
chrome examples. Alessandro and Jackson also handle custom orders
on mantels and accessories.

EVE STONE & SON ANTIQUES
Andirons, tools, and screens from the seventeenth through the nineteenth centuries. (See **Kitchenware,** p. 364.)

GREAT AMERICAN SALVAGE COMPANY
An ever-changing collection of antique wood and marble fireplace mantels. (See **Furniture,** p. 231.)

220

IRREPLACEABLE ARTIFACTS
Marble, stone, and wood mantels salvaged from old buildings. (See **Furniture**, p. 231.)

JAMES II GALLERIES
Nineteenth-century English brass fire tools, bellows, and andirons. (See **China and Glassware**, p. 67.)

JUDITH AMDUR
Eighteenth- and nineteenth-century English brass fire tools. (See **Furniture**, p. 289.)

NEWEL ART GALLERIES INC.
A large selection of marble, wood, and stone mantels, as well as a vast assortment of eighteenth- and nineteenth-century brass fire tools, bellows, screens, and andirons. (See **Furniture**, p. 251.)

URBAN ARCHAEOLOGY
Marble, wood, and stone mantels that are as early as Victorian, as recent as the thirties. (See **Furniture**, p. 232.)

WILLIAM H. JACKSON
A fine inventory of antique mantels, tools, and andirons. (See **Contemporary Fireplace Equipment**, below.)

CONTEMPORARY

THE BRASS LOFT
A large stock of brass fire tools, screens, and andirons. (See **Gifts**, p. 299.)

DANNY ALESSANDRO LTD./EDWIN JACKSON, INC.
Mantels, tools, screens, and andirons in a variety of materials to complement contemporary interiors. (See **Antique Fireplace Equipment**, p. 220.)

WILLIAM H. JACKSON
3 East 47th Street
753-9400
Mon.–Fri.: 9 a.m.–4:30 p.m.; Sat.: 12 noon–4:30 p.m.;
closed Sat. in summer
AE, MC, V

William H. Jackson is the city's oldest fireplace company. It's been in business since 1827, and many of the antique mantels it sells are ones that this company had originally installed. There are hundreds of mantels on display, including scores of early ones in marble, stone, and wood, but the shop features reproductions, too, as well as stark contemporary models. Among the vast assortment of accessories—antique, reproduction, and new—are tools, screens, andirons, and bellows.

Frames

ANTIQUE
AND VINTAGE

See **Silver, Antique,** and **Gifts, Antique.**

AFFORDABLE ANTIQUE FRAMES
324 East 81st Street
570-5652
Mon.–Sat.: 10 a.m.–6 p.m.
AE

Affordable Antique Frames is the bright idea of Eli Wilner, whose original gallery is crowded with rare and costly frames too pricey for the average customer. Wilner has filled his long and narrow, brick-walled second shop with scores of one-of-a-kind nineteenth- and early twentieth-century frames that are more affordable because their styles are not as rare and their finishes are not as perfect as those in his other shop. Most of the seductive array are American, many are Victorian, and styles range from stark beauties, to fluid Art Nouveau gems, to ornate Italian treasures. The gallery also offers a stunning selection of mirrors.

BOB PRYOR ANTIQUES
A splendid group of eighteenth- and nineteenth-century double-ring brass wedding frames in a wide range of sizes. (See **Gifts,** p. 293.)

ELI WILNER & COMPANY
1525 York Avenue, near 80th Street
Second floor
744-6521
Mon.–Sat.: 9:30 a.m.–5:30 p.m.
AE

High ceilings, white walls, a spare amount of furniture, and more than 200 frames hanging within frames is the setting of Eli Wilner's irresistible gallery that reflects his special vision and his love for antique carved-wood frames. Wilner began by collecting frames that many of the museums were tossing out—replacing them with Robert Kulike's minimal modern "float frames"—and Wilner has now built an inventory of 1,500 of them, mostly American and mostly from the nineteenth and early twentieth centuries. Some are signed and dated by the makers, and he has examples by such leading framers as Winslow Homer, Frederick Church, James Whistler, Murphy, and Prendergast. Some are opulently carved and gilded, others starkly simple, and styles range from baroque, to Art Nouveau, to modern. Wilner also transforms antique frames into dazzling mirrors.

GLORIA BOSCARDIN
Manhattan Art & Antiques Center
1050 Second Avenue, at 55th Street
980-3268
Tues.–Sun.: 11:30 a.m.–5:15 p.m.
All major

Gloria Boscardin carries boudoir and desk frames of every kind in her tiny, cluttered shop. Sterling silver, brass, bronze, shagreen, wood, enamel, and ivory beauties from the Victorian and Edwardian eras crowd the shelves and fill the cabinets. Seductive Victorian, Art Nouveau, Art Deco, and forties beaded and mesh evening bags, estate jewelry, perfume bottles, paisley shawls, needlepoint samplers, and exquisite antique fans add to the shop's delightful disarray.

THE HOUSE OF HEYDENRYK
417 East 76th Street
249-4903
Mon.–Fri.: 9:30 a.m.–5 p.m.; Sat.: 9:30 a.m.–3 p.m.
No credit cards

More than 3,000 hand-carved French and Italian frames that date from the fourteenth century through the Art Deco period are available in this attractive and friendly gallery. Although most are very large, heavily gilded, and rococo, there are others in a range of styles and sizes. The gallery can handle complicated restoration jobs and can cut frames to fit a painting, and it also offers fine English, Spanish, and American reproductions.

JAMES II GALLERIES
English Victorian-silver frames in all sizes, from tiny ones to large desk-size versions; also brass double-ring wedding frames, along with others of ivory, tortoise, shagreen, and treen. (See **China and Glassware,** p. 67.)

JUDITH AMDUR

Eighteenth- and nineteenth-century sterling-silver and brass frames in a range of sizes, including double-ring wedding frames. (See **Furniture,** p. 289.)

JULIUS LOWY FRAME & RESTORING CO., INC.

28 West End Avenue, near 60th Street
586-2050
Mon.–Fri.: 8:30 a.m.–5 p.m.
No credit cards

Framers are quick to claim that their work is museum quality, but Lawrence Shar, the president of this seventy-five-year-old company, has framed Manets for the Met, Hoppers for the Whitney, and Sargents for the Smithsonian. In the company's cavernous old Firestone warehouse you'll find more than 8,000 period frames that range from nonsecular Renaissance, to ornate eighteenth-century French, to Art Nouveau, to forties modernist examples. Shar also manufactures reproductions of antique frames, as well as crafting contemporary ones. Oversized frames can be reduced here, small ones enlarged, and the shop does gilding and conservation, but the emphasis is always on preserving the integrity of the original work.

LINDA HORN ANTIQUES

Rare and exotic picture frames of tortoise, shagreen, shell, antler, and horn. (See **Furniture,** p. 251.)

MOOD INDIGO

Art Deco crystal and glass frames from the thirties and forties at excellent prices. (See **Furniture,** p. 256.)

NEWEL ART GALLERIES INC.

The selection of antique frames is as varied as the galleries' other treasures and includes everything from Venetian to Art Deco examples in sizes that can accommodate large-scale paintings or tiny miniatures. (See **Furniture,** p. 251.)

TUDOR ROSE ANTIQUES

Ornate Victorian sterling-silver frames, along with less pricey silver reproductions. (See **Silver,** p. 443.)

CONTEMPORARY

A. P. F. INC.

136 East 70th Street

Parlor floor
988-1090
Mon.–Fri.: 9:30 a.m.–5:30 p.m.; Sat.: 10 a.m.–5 p.m.
AE, MC, V

A. P. F. makes museum-quality reproduction frames in its own factory, and it offers more than 200 styles to choose from. Although ornate gilt frames are the chief attraction, you'll find reproductions of fifteenth-century frames as well as sleek contemporary examples in this pleasant showroom. German, Dutch, French, Spanish, Early American, and English styles are all represented. The staff is helpful and extremely knowledgeable, and the workmanship is excellent.

G. ELTER
740 Madison Avenue, near 64th Street
734-4680
Mon.–Sat.: 10:30 a.m.–6 p.m.
AE, MC, V

Constantly crowded with customers, G. Elter is a tiny, comfortably cluttered store that offers a tantalizing array of desk, boudoir, and tabletop frames. Styles range from Victorian reproductions, to Art Deco and Art Nouveau styles, to sleek modern versions, and come in sterling silver, inlaid woods, *faux marbre*, brass, and enamel.

JINPRA NEW YORK PICTURE FRAMING
1208 Lexington Avenue, at 82nd Street
988-3903
Wed.–Thurs.: 12 noon–7 p.m.; Fri. & Sat.: 12 noon–8 p.m.;
Sun.: 12 noon–5 p.m.
AE, MC, V

Wellington Chiang, owner of this sunny shop, makes the fine-quality frames he sells, and he offers more than 500 styles. Stacks of frames and sample corners of reproduction styles fill the shop, and although most of them are elaborately gilt and hand-carved, there are others that are spare and starkly modern. Chiang will also restore and gild antique frames.

JOSEF FRAMING
113 Prince Street
475-3815
Tues.–Fri.: 9 a.m.–5:30 p.m.; Sat.: 11 a.m.–5 p.m.
AE, MC, V

Styles in custom framing in this friendly, cozy shop range from ornate antique reproductions to stark contemporary designs. Many of the moldings are handmade right in the shop, and there's a striking selection of unusual American frames. Josef also handles restoration of antique frames.

J. POCKER & SON
824 Lexington Avenue, at 63rd Street
838-5488
Mon.–Fri.: 9 a.m.–5:30 p.m.; Sat: 10 a.m.–5:30 p.m.
AE, MC, V

At J. Pocker & Son the custom frame moldings include everything from reproductions of seventeenth-century beauties to today's most popular styles. Hand-carved gilt Louis XVI frames are a specialty, but there are examples of every period and style, including minimal "float frames" and Plexiglas box ones. This family-run company, now in its third generation, also offers a vast selection of new and vintage prints and posters in its spacious two-level gallery.

THE OLD PRINT SHOP
The shop excels in framing prints and stocks a selection of nicely executed reproduction frames along with contemporary framing materials. (See **Engravings, Prints, and Posters,** p. 200.)

TIFFANY & COMPANY
Sterling-silver and crystal frames for desks or dressing tables, as well as a charming selection of small sterling-silver frames adorned with rabbits and chickens for children's rooms. (See **Jewelry,** p. 358.)

VERNE GALLERY
1680 First Avenue, near 87th Street
722-4984
Tues.–Fri.: 10 a.m.–7 p.m.; Sat.: 10 a.m.–5:30 p.m.
No credit cards

A tiny shop, Verne Gallery is owned by knowledgeable people who are expert at choosing the right mat and frame for a painting or print. They carry museum-quality reproduction frames in a wide range of styles, both ornate and simple.

Furniture

ANTIQUES
AMERICAN

AMERICA HURRAH

An ever-changing selection of Early American grain-painted furniture
that might include a corner cupboard, a blanket chest, a table, a few
chairs. (See **Linens and Quilts,** p. 384.)

BERNARD & S. DEAN LEVY

24 East 84th Street
628-7088
Tues.–Sat.: 10 a.m.–5:30 p.m.; summer: Mon.–Fri.: 10 a.m.–5:30 p.m.
No credit cards

Serious collectors consider Bernard & S. Dean Levy's array of American
furniture from the seventeenth through the eighteenth centuries one of
the best in the world, and many of the Levys' treasures are now in the
permanent collections of major museums. The firm is a father-and-son
team and their antiques are housed on five floors of an elegant town
house whose rooms evoke the graciousness of the Colonial and Federal
periods. New York furniture is the Levys' specialty, yet they have offered
such rarities as a brilliantly carved Philadelphia lowboy, a Townsend
Chippendale kneehole desk, and chairs and tables from several of the
colonies. Although most of the pieces are formal, they're not the highly
polished, never-touched kind, but rather those whose surfaces have the
rich patina of age and reflect years of loving use. You'll find dozens of
tables of all kinds, chests, highboys and lowboys, servers, desks, even
sofas, settees, and chairs. There's a sprinkling of long-case clocks, as
well as export porcelain, silver, pottery, and paintings, but the furniture takes center stage. Prices range from moderate for some of the
decorative objects to very expensive for the investment-quality pieces.
But equally as rare as the furniture is the warmth and friendliness of
the staff.

EAGLES ANTIQUES
An edited selection of formal eighteenth- and nineteenth-century American furniture. (See **English Period Furniture,** p. 242.)

JAMES M. HANSEN
Important American furniture from the seventeenth through the nineteenth centuries, along with weather vanes and long-case clocks. (See **French and European Furniture,** p. 250.)

HIRSCHL & ADLER FOLK
851 Madison Avenue, at 70th Street
Second floor
988-3655
Tues.–Fri.: 9:30 a.m.–5:30 p.m.; Sat.: 10 a.m.–4:45 p.m.; summer by appointment
No credit cards

The original Hirschl & Adler Galleries specializes in pedigreed examples of American paintings dating from the seventeenth through the twentieth centuries. But a few years ago this prestigious company opened Hirschl & Adler Modern and more recently Hirschl & Adler Folk. Here, in an elegant and restrained setting, you'll discover museum-quality folk furniture tucked in among the paintings, quilts, needlework, weather vanes, and sculptures. Corner cupboards, unusual blanket chests, tables, and Windsor chairs are among the appealing selection.

ISRAEL SACK INC.
15 East 57th Street
Third floor
753-6562
Mon.–Fri.: 10 a.m.–4:30 p.m.; Sat.: 10 a.m.–3 p.m.
No credit cards

Experts will tell you that there is nothing like an Israel Sack provenance on a piece of furniture, and the gallery, now run by the founder's three sons and a grandson, has had its premium pieces in the permanent collections of every major museum in the country. The Sacks' elegant shop is brimful of the very best and rarest seventeenth, eighteenth, and early-nineteenth-century furniture: important Queen Anne, Chippendale, Federal, Sheraton, and Hepplewhite highboys, chests of drawers, tables, desks, sofas, and chairs all in pristine condition. Very expensive.

JUDITH JAMES MILNE INC.
506 East 74th Street
Second floor
472-0107
Mon.–Fri.: 9:30 a.m.–5:30 p.m.; or by appointment
MC, V

Early American furniture with a rustic country look fills Judith Milne's spacious gallery. Many of the pieces have their original paint, and Milne carries blanket chests, cupboards, desks, and tables of all sizes, along with a sprinkling of chairs. Quilts are one of Milne's passions, and she offers a winning collection of nineteenth- and twentieth-century examples, along with hooked rugs and folk art from the same period.

LEIGH KENO AMERICAN FURNITURE

19 East 74th Street
Fourth floor
734-2381
By appointment
AE

Leigh Keno is known for his collection of important eighteenth-century American furniture. Sculptural Queen Anne, Chippendale, and Philadelphia pieces are the gallery's specialty, and all the furniture has its original finish. You might find a Chippendale mahogany card table, a Hepplewhite desk, a Sheraton serving table, and a chest of drawers with claw-and-ball feet.

RUTH BIGEL ANTIQUES

743 Madison Avenue, near 64th Street
Second floor
734-3262
Mon.–Fri.: 12 noon–5 p.m.; Sat. by appointment
No credit cards

A beguiling mix of American country furniture, folk art, weather vanes, and Canton porcelains crams Ruth Bigel's charming gallery. Most of the furniture is painted, and cupboards (many grain-painted) are a specialty, but there are tables, a few chairs, and chests of drawers as well. Bigel's collection of colorful blue-and-white exportware fills all the cupboards' shelves, and her walls are crowded with folk paintings.

THOS. K. WOODARD AMERICAN ANTIQUES & QUILTS

Painted and unpainted chairs, stools, cupboards, blanket chests, and beds, as well as a fine selection of Shaker pieces. (See **Linens and Quilts**, p. 387.)

ARCHITECTURAL

GREAT AMERICAN SALVAGE COMPANY
34 Cooper Square
505-0070
Mon.–Sat.: 9:30 a.m.–6 p.m.
AE, MC, V

Steve Israel has a warehouse and a shop in Vermont, and he carts down to his 16,000-square-foot city showroom an ever-changing array of splendid treasures from buildings that are no longer around. Here you might find, displayed in appropriate splendor, the entire façade of a thirties movie theater; wood paneling from an old library; staircases; marble and wood fireplace mantels; stained glass windows; carved front doors; claw-footed bathtubs and pedestal sinks; the occasional carousel horse or one-armed bandit; lighting fixtures; and elaborate mirrors. There's a Stone Room with limestone gargoyles and terra-cotta and granite ornaments, as well as pedestals and columns, cast-iron chimney pots, and stone urns. And since Israel collects small things, too, you'll find dozens of old brass doorknobs and hinges.

IRREPLACEABLE ARTIFACTS
14 Second Avenue, at Houston Street
777-2900
Mon.–Fri.: 10 a.m.–6 p.m.; Sat.: 11 a.m.–5 p.m.
MC, V

Terra-cotta griffins that once watched over 42nd Street, a neon marquee from a Broadway theater, iron gates that once guarded a country mansion have all, at one time or another, been on display in Evan Blum's seven-story warehouse that's filled with the country's detritus. Since Blum salvages entire buildings, his gallery is a mix of interior and exterior ornamentation. You're likely to find counters and walls from a barbershop; a complete ice cream parlor; paneled rooms; marble, stone, and wood fireplace mantels; stained-glass windows; limestone Corinthian capitals; and Art Deco streetlights. In a lot on Sixth Avenue and 28th Street Blum offers antique cast-iron garden benches and chairs, along with new aluminum ones that he's made from original Victorian molds. Here, too, is Blum's stock of stone statues and fountains.

LOST CITY ARTS
275 Lafayette Street
941-8025
Mon.–Fri.: 10 a.m.–6 p.m.; Sat. & Sun.: noon–6 p.m.
AE

Leftovers from the world of commercial advertising are Jim Elkind's passion. He's rescued the original Mobil Oil Pegasus, subway scrolls from the fifties, Victor Record's dog Nipper, Champion Spark Plug signs, and Goodyear's Winged Foot, along with sugar bowls from the old Lundy's in Sheepshead Bay. But Elkind has architectural ornamentation as well— three-foot-tall lion's heads, Art Deco panels from building façades, and elaborate wrought-iron grillwork. Among Elkind's scaled-down treasures are '39 World's Fair memorabilia and cast-iron banks of the Flatiron and Empire State buildings.

TIM MCKOY GALLERY
318 Bleecker Street
242-2352
Daily: 12 noon–6 p.m.
No credit cards

Lovers of the neoclassic will take delight in Tim McKoy's tantalizing shop filled with details from New York City buildings. His treasures tend to be small-scale, like his shop, and appropriately sized for city apartments, and he has a large stock of pedestals that can double as table bases, and corbels that can be used as wall brackets. He collects capitals, statuary, garden figures, and cherubs, too.

URBAN ARCHAEOLOGY
285 Lafayette Street
431-6969
Mon.–Fri.: 9 a.m.–6 p.m.; Sat., Sun.: 12 noon–7 p.m.; closed Sun. in summer
AE, MC, V

At Urban Archaeology it's possible to buy a Victorian doorknob or the complete interior of a turn-of-the-century New York saloon. In fact anything that's salvageable from old buildings, whether exterior stone gargoyles or interior oak paneling, is apt to find itself in Gil Shapiro, Leonard Schechter, and Allan Reiver's cavernous multilevel 54,000-square-foot showroom. So, in addition to the saloon, you're likely to find ice cream parlors and barbershops, banks and drugstores. Some of the treasures are as early as the 1850s, others as recent as the 1950s. Art Deco mirrors stand next to Corinthian columns, and next to them claw-footed Victorian tubs; and Edwardian oak bookcases share the space with marble and stone fireplace mantels from the twenties, and pinball machines from the forties. There are iron gates, stained-glass windows, pool tables, old paneled doors, vitrines from the French department store Au Bon Marché, stonework urns, keystones, garden benches, and columns. Scores of Victorian, Art Deco, and Art Nouveau chandeliers and milk-glass lighting fixtures hang overhead, and the walls are covered with brass and glass sconces, vintage medicine chests, and brass bathroom fixtures. Recently the owners have added to this vast inventory affordable reproductions of their antique lighting fixtures, bathroom accessories, and garden furniture and urns.

ART DECO/ ART NOUVEAU FURNITURE AND *OBJETS*

ALAN MOSS
88 Wooster Street
219-1663
Mon.–Fri.: 11 a.m.–6 p.m.; Sat.: 12 noon–6 p.m.
No credit cards

Alan Moss's large, glitzy gallery is brimful of classics of twentieth-century modern design. American and European Art Deco pieces share the space with Art Moderne furniture and decorative objects. You'll find furniture by such stellar names as Donald Deskey, Jules Bouy, Paul T. Frankl, Frank Lloyd Wright, Noguchi, and a host of others, along with Viennese ceramics, period lighting, screens, rugs, and metalwork.

ALICE'S ANTIQUES
552 Columbus Avenue, near 87th Street
874-3400
Mon.–Sat.: 12 noon–7 p.m.; Sun.: 2 p.m.–6 p.m.
AE, MC, V

The Alice in Alice's Antiques is actually Bill Hemingway, who in the early years of the store supplied West Siders with cast-iron beds, country pine armoires, and Victorian wicker chairs. Hemingway now focuses on Art Deco furniture, so Alice's Antiques is cluttered with a splendid mix of European and American Art Deco and Art Nouveau treasures: armoires, bureaus, hall stands, torchères, dining sets, bed suites, screens, and mirrors. But Hemingway still carries antique American beds, and he always has dozens of brass, wood, and iron beauties in every size, from king to daybed to crib.

ARTISAN ANTIQUES
Mostly French Art Deco furniture from the twenties and thirties that includes dining tables, chairs, and desks. (See **Lighting Fixtures,** p. 371.)

DECO DELUXE
Place des Antiquaires
125 East 57th Street
751-3326

233

Mon.–Sat.: 11 a.m.–6 p.m.
AE

Since gallery owner Sandi Berman specializes in unexpected Art Deco antiques, her classy gallery offers such oddities as stainless-steel armoires and lacquered pianos, leather bars and mirrored vanities. But there's a wealth of appealing Art Deco accessories—telephones, perfume bottles, lamps, sterling-silver jewelry, Deco cigarette boxes— along with the larger pieces.

DELORENZO
958 Madison Avenue, near 75th Street
249-7575
Mon.–Sat.: 9:30 a.m.–5:30 p.m.
No credit cards

Anthony Delorenzo is a collector-turned-dealer who opened this elegant Madison Avenue gallery in 1980. Since he's a man of impeccable taste, he's assembled a stunning collection of pedigreed pieces by all the top French names. From Armand-Albert Rateau you might find an exceptional chaise longue; from Émile-Jacques Ruhlmann opulent wardrobes and cabinets of ebony inlaid with ivory; from Diego Giacometti an anorectic metal table; from Albert Cheuret, bronze and alabaster sculptures and lighting fixtures; and from Jean Durand spectacular lacquered and hammered-metal vases. Designs by Eileen Gray, Jean-Michel Frank, Edgar Brandt, and Pierre Chareau are often in residence, and in addition to furniture, the gallery carries rugs and lighting fixtures. Very expensive.

D. LEONARD AND GERRY TRENT
950 Madison Avenue, near 74th Street
737-9511
Mon.–Sat.: 10:30 a.m.–6 p.m.
AE

Dennis Leonard and Gerry Trent have an eye for line and form and a passion for Louis Comfort Tiffany, so they've filled their sedate gallery with resplendent examples of Art Nouveau and Art Deco furniture and accessories, along with anything designed by Tiffany. Assorted ravishing tables, desks, and vanities hold Tiffany lamps, French cameo glass, and bronze sculptures. Alphonse Mucha posters hang on the walls, and glass-fronted cabinets display a notable collection of turn-of-the-century Art Nouveau and Art Deco jewelry and Georg Jensen sterling-silver pieces.

FIRST 1/2
131 Thompson Street
533-2519
Wed.–Sun.: 12 noon–7 p.m.
AE, MC, V

Since First 1/2 is a tiny sliver of a shop, most of its stock is small-scale and just right for city apartments. Streamlined American metal and chrome designer furniture from the first half of the twentieth century is the specialty, and on a recent visit the store was cluttered with Norman Bel Geddes's metal bureaus in soft pastels, chrome vanities, assorted tiny tables, settees, and slim chairs, not to mention such odd pieces as standing ashtrays and chrome towel racks. There's always a smattering of fifties furniture and lighting, along with Deco and Retro flatware and serving pieces. Prices are good.

JOIA INTERIORS, INC.
149 East 60th Street
759-1224
Mon.–Fri.: 10 a.m.–6 p.m.
AE, MC

Joia is known as a good source for vintage Art Deco furniture, but in addition to the real thing, owner Oswaldo Novaes offers well-executed reproductions that he makes in his own factories. He carries chairs, sofas, dining room tables, desks, and bedroom suites both old and new, along with glass vases and bowls, paintings and sculptures, and accessories by such luminaries as Lalique and Lorentz.

LILLIAN NASSAU LTD.
220 East 57th Street
759-6062
Mon.–Fri., 10 a.m.–5 p.m.; Sat.: 10:30 a.m.–5 p.m.; closed Sat. in summer
AE, MC, V

Long considered the doyenne of Art Nouveau, the name Lillian Nassau has become synonymous with Tiffany lamps, even though her shop has always offered scores of other Art Nouveau and Art Deco treasures. Lillian is now retired, and the shop bearing her name is owned and run by her son Paul, who continues the Tiffany tradition but has broadened the inventory to include an even wider inventory of Art Nouveau furniture, glass, ceramics, and silver, as well as American and European Art Pottery. Paul also has a handsome group of Wiener Werkstätte furniture and *objets*, along with vintage Steuben glass pieces.

MACKLOWE GALLERY & MODERNISM
667 Madison Avenue, near 60th Street
644-6400
Mon.–Sat.: 10:45 a.m.–5:45 p.m.
AE, MC, V

Barbara and Lloyd Macklowe have amassed one of the largest collections of Art Nouveau furniture in the world, and it's shown to advantage in their serenely elegant two-level gallery. Louis Majorelle, Émile Gallé, Victor Horta, and Georges de Feure are some of the illustrious names you'll find here, and there are glistening dining tables and chairs, desks, vanities, armoires, and bedroom suites. The Wiener Werkstätte is richly represented by such leading lights as Hoffman, Wagner, and Olbrich. And there's a wealth of Tiffany lamps, pre-thirties modern furniture, and exquisite jewelry that spans all periods from late-Victorian to the fifties and includes the works of Lalique, Fouquet, Cartier, and Van Cleef & Arpels.

MAISON GERARD
36 East 10th Street
674-7611
Mon.–Fri.: 11 a.m.–6 p.m.; 1 p.m.–5 p.m.; or by appointment
AE

Owner Gerard Widdershoven, a collector of Art Deco for more than twenty years, believes that the very best in Art Deco furniture was made in France, and so 90 percent of his shop is filled with the top names in French design. Gleaming dining tables, cabinets, chairs, and desks are topped with the striking accessories of the period, and Widdershoven has amassed splendid rugs, standing and table lamps, china, shagreen boxes, *objets d'art*, and tantalizing jewelry.

MINNA ROSENBLATT
844 Madison Avenue, near 69th Street
288-0257
Mon.–Sat.: 10 a.m.–5:30 p.m.
No credit cards

Minna Rosenblatt favors small-scale Art Nouveau and Art Deco trea-sures, and her shop glistens with row upon row of Daum and Gallé French cameo glass, jewel-toned Tiffany lamps and vases, and translu-cent *pâté de verre* delights.

MURIEL KARASIK
Art Deco screens and panels along with a well-edited collection of Deco furniture and accessories. (See **Retro Furniture,** p. 257.)

OLDIES, GOLDIES & MOLDIES
1609 Second Avenue, near 83rd Street
737-3935
Mon.–Fri.: 12 noon–8 p.m.; Sat.: 11 a.m.–7 p.m.; Sun.: 11 a.m.–6 p.m.
MC, V

Lior Grinberg's cluttered two-story gallery is a maze of shops, each with a different focus. One is crammed with Art Deco finds, another with Victoriana, yet another with Art Moderne treats. Most of the antiques are small-scaled and closer to flea market finds than important pieces, but they're pleasantly affordable, and there are scores of dressers and doz-ens of assorted tables, vanities, desks, vintage office furniture, and dining chairs to choose from. Grinberg admits to an obsession with lighting (he restores and installs vintage neon clocks), and so his shop is overflowing with everything from Art Deco chandeliers to torchères from the twenties, to green-glass Edwardian desk lamps to old porcelain vases converted into lamps. Vintage radios, old clocks, glitzy forties jewelry, china, glassware, pottery, even handbags, shawls, and gloves complete the mesmerizing array.

PRIMAVERA GALLERY

European Art Deco furniture by such formidable artists as Eileen Gray, Jean-Michel Frank, Jean Durand, Pierre Chareau, and Eugene Printz, along with art glass by Lalique, Jean Luce, Daum, and Maurice Marinot. (See **Jewelry,** p. 347.)

ARTS AND CRAFTS MOVEMENT

CATHERS & DEMBROSKY

1000 Madison Avenue, near 77th Street
Second floor
737-4466
Tues.–Sat.: 11 a.m.–6 p.m.
No credit cards

In a handsome second-story space Beth Cathers and her partner Nick Dembrosky offer superb examples of the American Arts and Crafts Movement. Their gallery is unique in that it's stocked with an in-depth selection of lighting, metal work, ceramics, textiles, and rugs in addition to the furniture. Most of the pieces are signed and were crafted by such illustrious proponents of the movement as Gustav Stickley, Frank Lloyd Wright, Dirk van Erp, William Grueby, Harvey Ellis, and Charles Rohlfs. You'll find Stickley's ladder-back, spindle-back, and slat-back chairs, and his spare library tables, desks, and bookcases; Harvey Ellis's armchairs; American Academic paintings; and lamps from the Tiffany and Roy Croft studios. Cathers, who has co-authored *Treasures of the American Arts and Crafts Movement—1890–1920,* is an expert in the field, and she and Dembrosky are enthusiastic and enjoy sharing their knowledge.

HOFFMAN GAMPETRO ANTIQUES

One of the city's most extensive collections of American Arts and Crafts Movement silver. (See **Silver,** p. 440.)

KURLAND-ZABAR

19 East 71st Street

237

517-8576
By appointment only
No credit cards

Catherine Kurland and Lori Zabar are knowledgeable dealers educated in art history and preservation who teamed up four years ago because of a joint passion for the English Aesthetic and Arts and Crafts movements. Their attractive gallery is the only one in New York devoted to the English designers who inspired the American movement, so among their important pieces you might find E. G. Punnett's rush-seated armchair with ebony inlay, or a rare Archibald Knox "Tudric" pewter clock inlaid with abalone. But Kurland and Zabar also carry a compelling selection of nineteenth- and twentieth-century decorative arts that are less extraordinary and thus more affordable.

MICHAEL CAREY
107 Spring Street
226-3710
Tues.–Sat.: 11 a.m.–6 p.m.
No credit cards

Michael Carey has a reputation for collecting only the best of twentieth-century design, and his cluttered gallery is crammed with a superb array of Stickley pieces, including some rarely seen examples. You'll find daybeds, buffets, lamps, and dining tables, and Carey always has some choice Josef Hoffmann, Le Corbusier, and Thonet designs, as well as early-twentieth-century pottery.

PETER ROBERTS ANTIQUES
134 Spring Street
226-4777
Mon.–Sat.: 11 a.m.–7 p.m.; Sun.: 12 noon–6 p.m.
No credit cards

Signed and unsigned examples of American Arts and Crafts and Mission furniture and accessories crowd Peter Smorto and Robert Melita's loftlike SoHo shop. There are tables, chairs, buffets, and daybeds signed by such masters as Stickley, Ellis, Limbert, and Roycroft, along with a tempting selection of Arts and Crafts lighting, pottery, and copper.

EMPIRE AND BIEDERMEIER

Macy's Corner Shop offers a notable inventory of Biedermeier sofas, chairs, settees, armoires, and vitrines.

THE BIEDERMEIER HOUSE LTD.
1 Patchin Place, near 10th Street
463-0429
By appointment only
No credit cards

The Biedermeier House, a New York branch of a famous Austrian company, has opened a showroom in a gracious town house in Greenwich Village and filled three floors with fine Viennese furniture, paintings, and accessories. Upholstered pieces are a main attraction, along with assorted tables, vitrines, armoires, and desks. The gallery also offers an impressive selection of Jugendstil, Wiener Werkstätte, and Art Deco furniture and furnishings.

EILEEN LANE ANTIQUES
150 Thompson Street
475-2988
Daily: 11 a.m.–7 p.m.

52 East 11th Street
982-6067
Mon.–Fri.: 11 a.m.–5:30 p.m.; Sat.: 12 noon–5 p.m.
AE, MC, V

Each month Eileen Lane gets a fresh shipment of antiques from France, Sweden, and Austria, and although her stock is ever-changing, at any time you're sure to find an in-depth array of Biedermeier and Empire pieces. Burnished blond-wood arm and club chairs, vanities, desks, bureaus, beds, and tables, along with upholstered suites and Empire mirrors, crowd the smaller store on 11th Street. In the warehouse-sized Thompson Street gallery, there's ample room for all of the above, plus Art Deco armoires, Art Nouveau chandeliers, Biedermeier sofas, French and Flemish furnishings, iron beds, Napoleon III settees, Swedish country trunks, Jugendstil lamps, art glass, and Viennese china. The stock turns over quickly, since Lane's prices are good.

MALMAISON
253 East 74th Street
288-7569
Mon.–Fri.: 10 a.m.–6 p.m.
No credit cards

Malmaison is a spare, but pleasant, shop that's crammed with an impressive selection of Neoclassic French furniture that includes Directoire, Empire, and Biedermeier, along with Napoleonic memorabilia. Dozens of small writing tables, settees, chairs, bed frames, dressers, marble busts, cupboards, mirrors, bronze d'ore mantel clocks, and assorted tables are piled everywhere, yet the owners have even more stored in a nearby warehouse.

NIALL SMITH
344 Bleecker Street
255-0660
Mon.–Sat.: 2 p.m.–6 p.m.

96 Grand Street
941-7354
Mon.–Sat.: 1 p.m.–6 p.m.
No credit cards

In his attractive galleries, Niall Smith offers an enticing array of Biedermeier furniture, mixed with pieces from many other periods picked up on numerous buying trips to Europe. You might find a Biedermeier desk or a gilt-wood chandelier, a lacquered Napoleon III sofa with gargoyle arms or a Charles II console, a nineteenth-century garden chair with lion's tails, or a table inlaid with a mosaic top. The inventory is impressive and ever-changing.

RITTER ANTIK
1166 Second Avenue, at 61st Street
644-7442
Mon.–Fri.: 1 p.m.–4 p.m.; or by appointment
No credit cards

Although the name Ritter Antik is well-known in Germany, it's new to the New York antiques scene, but it's quickly gaining a reputation for superb quality Biedermeier furniture. Among the recent sightings were shovel chairs, a lyre console table, a globe-shaped worktable, a secretaire inlaid with brass, a column cupboard, and a pedestal dining table. There are vitrines, desks, and sofas, too, along with fine Continental furniture.

VICTOR ANTIQUES
135 Sullivan Street
995-9491
Mon.–Fri.: 9:30 a.m.–6:30 p.m.; Sat.–Sun.: 12:30 p.m.–6:30 p.m.
AE

In a shop that's not much bigger than an alleyway, Victor Antiques manages to stock a delightful clutter of both Biedermeier and Swedish treasures. Among the handsome blond Austrian Biedermeier pieces, there's likely to be chairs, desks, vanities, lamps, and assorted tables.

These are artfully arranged with antique wooden picture frames, old leather-bound books, and boudoir and desk accessories from Sweden.

ENGLISH PERIOD

AGOSTINO ANTIQUES LTD.
808 Broadway, near 10th Street
533-3355
Mon.–Fri.: 9 a.m.–5:30 p.m.; Sat.: 10 a.m.–2 p.m.
No credit cards

Until recently antiques stores on lower Broadway sold only to the trade; now many have opened their doors to the public so this area has become an important source for antiques. Agostino Antiques occupies two enormous floors in this prime location and offers a constantly replenished inventory of eighteenth- and nineteenth-century English furniture. Pembroke tables, lowboys and highboys, bachelor's chests and linen presses, dining and living-room chairs, dressers, and servers fill every inch of showroom space. Although the gallery specializes in English antiques, it carries a few select pieces from Europe, as well as a vast assortment of candelabra, mirrors, urns, and other decorative accessories.

ARTHUR ACKERMAN & SON, INC.
50 East 57th Street
753-5292
Mon.–Fri.: 9 a.m.–5 p.m.; Sat: 9 a.m.–4 p.m.;
closed Sat. in summer
No credit cards

Pedigreed eighteenth-century English furniture is displayed in a warm and gracious town house setting at Arthur Ackerman & Son. The handsome old oak furniture and furnishings reflect the owners' hunting and equestrian interests, and even the decorative accessories reflect these themes. Scores of Royal Worcester porcelains of racehorses, as well as fine English sporting paintings and prints, fill the shop.

BARBARA STEINBERG ANTIQUES UNLIMITED
964 Lexington Avenue
439-9600
Mon.–Fri.: 10:30 a.m.–6 p.m.; Sat.: 11 a.m.–5 p.m.;
closed in summer
AE, MC

Barbara Steinberg's interest in antiques began while she was married to multimillionaire Saul Steinberg—she collected extensively to furnish their assorted homes. After her divorce Steinberg sold privately for a number of years before opening her handsome shop that reflects her passion for eighteenth- and nineteenth-century English furniture. Among the highly polished stock are dining tables, chairs of all kinds, writing tables, highboys and lowboys, and assorted small-scale cabinets. There's the occasional French piece and an eclectic mix of English, Oriental, and European *objets*—screens, mirrors, paintings, candlesticks, porcelains, and decanters.

DIDIER AARON, INC.

Exotic and unusual English furniture from the eighteenth and nineteenth centuries, including a collection of pieces from about 1830 that are massive, powerful, and overscaled. (See **French and European Furniture,** p. 248.)

EAGLES ANTIQUES

1097 Madison Avenue, at 83rd Street
772-3266
Tues.–Fri.: 10 a.m.–5 p.m.; Sat.: 10:30 a.m.–5:30 p.m.
No credit cards

Formal eighteenth- and early nineteenth-century English furniture, along with a well-edited selection of American pieces from the same period, are attractively displayed in this friendly shop. Chippendale and George III are well represented, and Eagles Antiques offers a myriad of dining tables and chairs, desks, highboys, sideboards, and occasional tables. Among the small-scale temptations are porcelains (including Chinese vases mounted as lamps), mahogany and brass candlesticks, antique needlepoint and tapestry pillows, and seventeenth-, eighteenth-, and nineteenth-century hand-colored engravings.

FLORENCE DE DAMPIERRE

Japanned tables, papier-mâché, and English painted furniture. (See **French and European Furniture,** p. 248.)

FLORIAN PAPP

962 Madison Avenue, near 76th Street
288-6770
Mon.–Fri.: 9:30 a.m.–5:30 p.m.; Sat.: 10 a.m.–5 p.m.;
closed Sat. in summer
No credit cards

Florian Papp has the distinction of being the city's first antiques store. It opened in 1900, and since then three generations of Papps have supplied museums and collectors with extremely fine seventeenth-, eighteenth-, and nineteenth-century English furniture. Rare examples of Queen Anne and George II and III styles—in everything from writing tables to highboys to four-poster beds—fill the gallery's three graciously appointed floors. Long-case clocks, game tables, mirrors, papier-mâché tray-tables, and library globes, as well as a few excellent European pieces, are displayed as well. Recently the Papps broadened their inventory, and they now offer furniture from the English Aesthetic Movement and the Victorian era.

FREDERICK P. VICTORIA AND SON, INC.
Exceptionally fine English furniture. (See **French and European Furniture**, p. 249.)

FRENCH & COMPANY
Museum-quality nineteenth-century English furniture. (See **French and European Furniture**, p. 249.)

GUILD ANTIQUES
A selection of small-scale antique English furniture. (See **China and Glassware**, p. 66.)

HYDE PARK ANTIQUES
836 Broadway, near 12th Street
477-0033
Mon.–Fri.: 9 a.m.–5:30 p.m.; Sat.: 10 a.m.–2:30 p.m.;
closed Sat. in summer
No credit cards

Hyde Park Antiques occupies two spacious floors of an historic cast-iron building, and it offers one of the most comprehensive collections of eighteenth- and early-nineteenth-century English furniture in the country. Whether you are looking for a George I kneehole desk or a Carlton House writing table, you're likely to find it here, as well as Georgian sideboards and lacquered and painted pieces. Everything dates from William and Mary through Regency and in addition to furniture there's a profusion of paintings, mirrors, and English and Chinese export porcelains.

JUAN PORTELA ANTIQUES
Unique and offbeat nineteenth-century English furniture. (See **French and European Furniture**, p. 250.)

KENTSHIRE GALLERIES
37 East 12th Street
673-6644
Mon.–Fri.: 9 a.m.–5 p.m.; Sat.: 10 a.m.–2 p.m.
AE

For years decorators have come to Kentshire Galleries—they knew that it was one of the city's best sources for fine English antique furniture, porcelains, and accessories. It is no longer exclusively "to the trade," so now everyone can indulge in Kentshire's Queen Anne, Georgian, and Regency treasures. The showroom occupies seven huge floors **243** (there's an additional one devoted to cabinetry and restoration), and here you'll discover one of the city's largest selections of chairs— dozens of sets of dining chairs, as well as wing, side, and arm chairs, even child-size versions—and they share the space with scores of partner's desks, lowboys and highboys, secretaires, tables of all persuasions, sideboards, servers, and commodes. On the third floor is the Collector's Gallery, a veritable treasure trove of "smalls" and collectibles displayed in a series of charming vignettes against a backdrop of eighteenth-century wood paneling. Among the tantalizing mix is antique and vintage jewelry, old leather luggage and vanity cases, wine decanters, humidors and cigarette cases, desk accessories, Staffordshire china and majolica, as well as Chinese export porcelain, picture frames, candlesticks, and all the other whatnots needed to re-create the look of an old English country home.

LENOX COURT ANTIQUES
972 Lexington Avenue, near 70th Street
772-2460
Mon.–Fri.: 11 a.m.–6 p.m.; Sat.: 11 a.m.–5:30 p.m.
AE, V

Diane Solomon began as a collector with a background in the museum world, but when her collection began overwhelming her living space, she opened Lenox Court Antiques. Although modest in size, Solomon has managed to fill it with a select group of eighteenth- and nineteenth-century English furniture that includes Queen Anne and Regency tables, chairs, consoles, and lowboys. There's a sprinkling of Charles X, Neoclassic, and Gothic styles, too, and her carefully chosen decorative accessories should not be overlooked. Pillows, paisley shawls, candlesticks, crystal decanters, export porcelains, engravings, and Liberty pewter are among the outstanding array, and Solomon has put together the city's largest selection of Palissy pottery, those macabre collectibles embellished with slithering snakes, alligators, and bugs.

LINDA HORN ANTIQUES
Unique, ornate, whimsical, and dramatic English furniture. (See **French and European Furniture,** p. 251.)

MALCOLM FRANKLIN, INC.
15 East 57th Street
Second floor
308-3344
Mon.–Fri.: 10 a.m.–5:30 p.m.; Sat.: 10 a.m.–4 p.m.; closed Sat. in summer
No credit cards

Malcolm Franklin opened his first antiques shop in Chicago in 1947, and this New York branch, run by knowledgeable family members, is a friendly and charming gallery that's filled with English furniture from the seventeenth through the early nineteenth centuries. Queen Anne walnut pieces are a chief attraction, but there's a fine stock of William and Mary and Georgian styles, too. Oak and walnut chairs, tables, bureau–bookcases, chests of drawers, and fine accessories fill the shop, and the Franklins take pride in pointing out that their pieces have not been refinished but have their original skin.

NEWEL ART GALLERIES INC.
A vast selection of English period furniture, including English wicker and bamboo. (See **French and European Furniture,** p. 251.)

PHILIPPE FARLEY
Fine examples of furniture from the Georgian and English Regency periods. (See **French and European Furniture,** p. 252.)

PHILLIP COLLECK OF LONDON LTD.
830 Broadway, near 12th Street
505-2500
Mon.–Fri.: 9:30 a.m.–5:30 p.m.; closes at 5:00 p.m. in summer
No credit cards

Rare and important eighteenth-century formal English furniture is displayed in a shop that's as proper and elegant as the furniture it sells. Queen Anne, Chippendale, and Adam styles are a specialty, and this spacious gallery is filled with a grand profusion of formal chairs, dining tables, desks, bureaus, and commodes, along with decorative accessories from the same period. And collectors come to Colleck for mirrors; they know that the shop always has a selection of magnificent, museum-quality carved and gilded beauties.

STAIR AND COMPANY
942 Madison Avenue, at 74th Street
517-4400
Mon.–Fri.: 10 a.m.–5:30 p.m.; Sat.: 11 a.m.–5 p.m.;
closed Sat. in summer
No credit cards

Stair and Company's extremely fine eighteenth- and early nineteenth-century English furniture is housed on two floors of a landmark English Renaissance building. The gallery is set up as a series of gracious rooms decorated with the company's William and Mary through Regency furnishings. Among the notable hoard are simple seventeenth-century pieces, formal and conservative eighteenth-century examples, as well as dramatic and flamboyant furniture from the late-eighteenth and early-nineteenth centuries. Queen Anne and Chippendale are represented by chairs, chests of drawers, cabinets, and desks, but there's a grand inventory of game tables, sofas, dining tables, commodes, and secretaires from all periods, and Stair's collection of paintings and engravings, carpets, Chinese export porcelains, screens, mirrors, and chandeliers is as exquisite as the furniture.

SYLVIA TEARSTON ANTIQUES

A notable stock of English, American, and French period furniture. (See **China and Glassware**, p. 71.)

TILLER & KING LTD.

1058 Madison Avenue, at 80th Street
988-2861
Mon.–Sat.: 10 a.m.–5:30 p.m.; closed Sat. in August
AE, MC, V

Tiller & King, a comfortably cluttered shop, is crammed with fine eighteenth- and nineteenth-century English and American furniture, and it's run by obliging and knowledgeable people. Chairs, sofas, settees, tables of all kinds (including scores of tray, tilt-top, tea, nesting, and game varieties), commodes, secretaires, and small chests of drawers occupy every available bit of space. And on every exposed surface you'll find the gallery's winning collection of antique vases that have been converted into lamps, eighteenth-century salt-glaze pottery, mirrors, and American clocks.

TREVOR POTTS ANTIQUES

1011 Lexington Avenue, at 72nd Street
737-0909
Mon.–Fri.: 10 a.m.–5 p.m.
No credit cards

Englishman Trevor Potts has filled his shop with an exuberant array of largely English Regency painted and gilded furniture. He favors pieces with flair, so you're likely to find ebonized and gilded armchairs, gilt torchères, decorative commodes, and chinoiserie writing tables. Lacquerware and bamboo are favorites, along with dogs—primarily pugs and spaniels—and they are captured in paintings and as porcelain figurines.

VERNAY & JUSSEL, INC.

625 Madison Avenue, near 58th Street
Second floor
879-3344
Mon.–Fri.: 9:30 a.m.–5:30 p.m.
AE

Highly respected as one of New York's oldest antiques dealers, Vernay & Jussell is known for its splendid eighteenth- and early-nineteenth-century furniture. Among the small and very select inventory of unusual pieces are William and Mary, Queen Anne, Chippendale, Georgian, and Regency examples. Mirrors are a specialty, and the gallery offers a marvelous assortment, as well as rare and extremely fine clocks that include everything from table to mantel to long-case varieties.

FRENCH
AND EUROPEAN

À LA VIEILLE RUSSIE
Eighteenth-century French and Russian furniture in the grand style, along with *objets d'art*. (See **Jewelry,** p. 342.)

BERNARD STEINITZ ET FILS
Place des Antiquaires
125 East 57th Street
832-3711
Mon.–Sat.: 11 a.m.–6 p.m.
No credit cards

Considered the jewel of the Place des Antiquaires, Bernard Steinitz et Fils occupies two double-story galleries flanking the entrance to the center. One side is devoted to the seventeenth century and the other to the eighteenth, and in each the floors, walls, chandeliers, and *objets d'art* are true to the period. Steinitz is regarded by experts as the foremost specialist in eighteenth-century French furniture, and he has an unrivaled reputation among museum curators and serious collectors. In his elegant salons you might find an exceptional Louis XVI commode signed by Pierre Foullet, lavishly carved consoles, painted chairs, imposing desks, crystal and ormolu chandeliers, gilt sconces, richly carved boiseries, rare provincial pieces, and exquisite *objets*, along with a host of other grand-style treasures of peerless pedigree. Very expensive.

BRINKMAN GALLERIES, INC.
Place des Antiquaires
125 East 57th Street
319-1002
Mon.–Sat.: 11 a.m.–6 p.m.
AE

The Brinkman family is well-known in the Netherlands as purveyors of the finest-quality antiques. They specialize in seventeenth- through nineteenth-century Dutch and French furniture and paintings as well as Oriental porcelains. On a recent visit their tiny New York gallery held such assorted treats as gilt-wood mid-eighteenth-century armchairs with original Aubusson needlepoint, a mahogany dining table with carved dolphin feet, nineteenth-century bronze-and-ormolu candelabra, and an extremely fine seventeenth-century French chest-on-chest.

DALVA BROTHERS
44 East 57th Street

758-2297
Mon.–Fri.: 9:30 a.m.–5:30 p.m.; Sat.: 10 a.m.–5:30 p.m.;
closed Sat. in summer
No credit cards

Dalva Brothers occupies five floors of showroom space, and the gallery's handsome carved wood-paneled rooms are filled with extremely fine eighteenth-century French furniture. Collectors come for the resplendent marquetry pieces and the rare Sèvres porcelains, but the store is also known for its selection of chairs, settees, and recamiers (many covered in brocades and petit-point tapestries) and for its eighteenth-century bronze, marble, and porcelain clocks. Although prices are high, they're not outlandish for pieces of such top quality.

DIDIER AARON, INC.
32 East 67th Street
988-5248
Mon.–Fri.: 10 a.m.–6 p.m.
No credit cards

An elegant turn-of-the-century brownstone houses Didier Aaron's exotic mix of eighteenth- and nineteenth-century furniture. Although still thought of as predominantly French, Aaron offers an eclectic assortment of Irish, English, Russian, Italian, and Anglo-Indian pieces, along with an outstanding selection of Old Master and nineteenth-century paintings. Didier and his son Hervé favor the unusual, so you might find a French neo-Gothic writing desk with carved tracery, a Louis XV rosewood corner cabinet with gilt bronze mounts, a marble Alexandrian head from the first century A.D., a coconut-embellished commode. Also in evidence are Austrian Biedermeier and nineteenth-century English pieces (massive, powerful, and overscaled), as well as splendid Art Deco furnishings and Oriental art and *objets*.

FLORENCE DE DAMPIERRE
16 East 78th Street
734-6764
Mon.–Fri.: 10 a.m.–6 p.m.
No credit cards

Florence de Dampierre has turned a passion for painted furniture into a stunning, red-walled salon. Extremely fine French lacquerware shares the space with English satinwood and japanned tables, Italian trompe l'oeil, papier-mâché from England and France, and painted country scenes from Denmark, Holland, and Germany. In fact this jewel of a shop mixes all genres of European painted furniture from the eighteenth and nineteenth centuries. There are exquisite screens, lacquered and enameled trays, and dummy-board ladies and gentlemen (with which the super-rich once peopled their cavernous drawing rooms). Expensive.

FREDERICK P. VICTORIA AND SON, INC.
154 East 55th Street
755-2581
Mon.–Fri.: 9 a.m.–5 p.m.
No credit cards

Frederick P. Victoria and Son's pedigreed eighteenth-century French furniture fills a gracious town house that's somewhat off the beaten antiques paths, yet it still attracts serious collectors. Chairs, settees, and occasional tables are Victoria's specialty, but there are magnificent mantel and figural clocks as well as whimsical items, which might include cabbage-shaped porcelain tureens. In addition to the French pieces you'll find furniture from England, Austria, and Italy, along with Oriental works of art. An upstairs workshop turns out very fine handmade facsimile reproductions of the gallery's antique stock. Very expensive.

FRENCH & COMPANY
17 East 65th Street
535-3330
By appointment only
No credit cards

French & Company has been around for more than eighty years, and although it now operates on a small scale, it still offers a very splendid inventory of museum-quality French and English eighteenth-century furniture, as well as French Art Deco pieces and Old Master paintings. Among the recent treasures was a pair of rare gilt eighteenth-century English torchères, a Louis XV commode, a partner's desk, an Art Deco bed, as well as bronzes, and exquisite tapestries.

GARRICK C. STEPHENSON
625 Madison Avenue, near 58th Street
Second floor
753-2570
Mon.–Fri.: 10 a.m.–5 p.m.
No credit cards

Garrick Stephenson personally selects the antiques that he sells, and he's known for superior furniture that is tasteful, yet often fanciful and unique. French is a specialty, but it's generously mixed with pieces of English, Italian, Russian, and Swedish origin. Most of Stephenson's antiques date from the eighteenth through the nineteenth centuries, but there are seventeenth-century Chinese lacquered tables and a few turn-of-the-century things. Leather and lacquer screens, *objets*, and Venetian, lacquer, and eighteenth- and nineteenth-century mirrors are among the small-scale delights.

JAMES M. HANSEN

Place des Antiquaires
125 East 57th Street
888-4687
Mon.–Sat.: 11 a.m.–6 p.m.
No credit cards

This cozy gallery is stocked with a mix of seventeenth- and eighteenth-century European and American mahogany and walnut furniture, silver, porcelains, and paintings. A Regency walnut taboret, a Queen Anne wing chair with cabriole legs and original needlepoint upholstery, splendid Adam mahogany urns, as well as seventeenth-century English stump-work embroidery were among the recent offerings.

JUAN PORTELA ANTIQUES

138 East 71st Street
650-0085
Mon.–Fri.: 10 a.m.–6 p.m.
No credit cards

Juan Portela's town house is a mélange of unique nineteenth-century furniture that's whimsical, decorative, and far less traditional than what's commonly around. Many of his offbeat pieces are from France, but he carries examples from England, Austria, Russia, and Germany, too. Since Portela favors fantasy in his furniture, you might find a pair of exceptional neoclassical mahogany bookcases, a Gothic revival Charles X cabinet rich in cathedral detailing, a high-backed armchair with arches and finials, a Gothic commode. Portela's accessories are just as exceptional as his furniture and include antique drapes, curtains, table throws, rugs, and candelabra.

L'ANTIQUAIRE & THE CONNOISSEUR

Early French and Spanish furniture, paintings, and decorative accessories, as well as eighteenth-century Italian furniture that includes Venetian painted pieces. (See **Medieval and Renaissance Furniture**, p. 254.)

LE CADET DE GASCOGNE

1015 Lexington Avenue, at 73rd Street
744-5925
Mon.–Fri.: 10 a.m.–6 p.m.
No credit cards

Gilbert Gestas is a native of Gascony, hence the name of his handsome shop, and he's partial to Louis XIV, XV, and XVI styles, along with the Regency, Directoire, and First Empire periods. Many of the top names in cabinetmaking are represented, and many of his pieces are signed and have not been restored. Gestas is particularly proud of his myriad fauteuils and bergères and his splendid collection of candelabra, sconces, paintings, and *objets d'art*.

LINDA HORN ANTIQUES

1015 Madison Avenue, near 78th Street
772-1122
Mon.–Sat.: 10 a.m.–6 p.m.
AE, MC, V

Stepping into Linda Horn's shop is like stepping into a Boucher painting; lush and romantic, it's a stunning setting for Horn's dramatic French, European, and English nineteenth-century antiques. Everywhere you look you'll see intricately carved and inlaid desks and chairs, bamboo pieces, marble tables on gargoyle bases, chinoiserie chests, horn chairs, and swan daybeds. Horn carries bamboo, lacquer, and papier-mâché furniture as well as pieces covered in exotic skins, and each is unique, ornate, whimsical, or downright bizarre. There are animals in every guise and an incredible array of accessories—everything from sterling-silver picture frames to crystal decanters, to shagreen desk accessories, to rococo candelabra, to majolica plates and bowls.

MALMAISON ANTIQUES

An impressive selection of Neoclassic French furniture that includes Directoire, Empire, and Biedermeier. (See **Empire and Biedermeier Furniture**, p. 239.)

MATTHEW SCHUTZ LTD.

1025 Park Avenue, near 85th Street
876-4195
By appointment only
No credit cards

As much museum as antiques shop, the Matthew Schutz gallery is set in a landmark mansion, and it's filled with extremely fine French, European, and English furniture and decorations, with Louis XIV through Empire a specialty. Although the furniture takes center stage, this shop is an excellent source for chinoiserie, clocks, Japanese and Chinese art works, Russian chandeliers, and Chinese export porcelain, and prices are fair considering the exceptional quality of the antiques.

NEWEL ART GALLERIES INC.

425 East 53rd Street
758-1970
Mon.–Fri.: 9 a.m.–5 p.m.
No credit cards

If it's unique, hard to find, whimsical, or slightly bizarre, you're likely to find it on Newel Art Galleries' six floors. Owner Bruce Newman has assembled the city's most comprehensive collection of antique furniture and decorative arts and it ranges from the Renaissance through the Art Deco periods. Since Newman favors fantasy pieces, you're likely to find Venetian Grotto chairs, realistically carved Black Forest bear coat racks,

251

palm tree candelabra and tables, altars from abandoned temples, and royal thrones. English bamboo and wicker appear in desks, tables, vanities, lamps, chairs, settees, and bureaus. There are headboards from every period in brass, wood, and iron, as well as a complete array of sleigh beds, chaise longues, and recamiers. And chairs, dining tables, and breakfronts rival all the rest in number and variety. Newman's hoard of outdoor furniture in iron, wire, and stone is impressive, and his stock of decorative pieces is staggering. Hundreds of frames, mirrors, mantel clocks, vases, decanters, desk accessories, boxes, andirons and fireplace tools, candlesticks, wall sconces, chandeliers, bookends, and lamps cram the first-floor gallery. It's no wonder that magazine stylists turn to Newel Art Galleries as their prime source for props.

PHILIPPE FARLEY
157 East 64th Street
472-1622
Mon.–Fri.: 9:30 a.m.–6 p.m.
No credit cards

Large-scale, richly decorative furnishings give Philippe Farley's four-story gallery the look of a Napoleonic salon. A Canadian dealer, Farley has stocked his shop with grand eighteenth- and nineteenth-century French pieces that include Louis XV and XVI, Directoire, and Empire, as well as ornate examples from the Georgian and English Regency periods. He carries Chinese lacquered cabinets and tilt-top tables, embossed and painted leather screens, decorative paintings from the seventeenth, eighteenth, and nineteenth centuries, Chinese export porcelains, handsome mirrors, and exquisite crystal chandeliers.

PROVENCE ANTIQUES
35 East 76th Street
288-5179
Mon.–Fri.: 10 a.m.–4:30 p.m.
No credit cards

Provence Antiques is located in the Carlyle Hotel, and this elegant gallery offers premier-quality eighteenth-century French furniture and *objets d'art*. There's a splendid group of fauteuils and bergères, and the gallery specializes in early and rare European and Oriental lacquered pieces, as well as Chinese and Japanese works of art.

REYMER-JOURDAN ANTIQUES
43 East 10th Street
674-4470
Mon.–Fri.: 10 a.m.–6 p.m.; Sat.: 11 a.m.–4 p.m.
No credit cards

Directoire, Empire, Charles X, and Biedermeier furniture are the chief attractions at Reymer-Jourdan Antiques, and the gallery is crowded with some first-rate examples. There are earlier pieces, too—an inlaid brass and tortoiseshell desk attributed to André-Charles Boulle—along with a few Art Deco treasures and neoclassic *objets d'art*.

R. J. KING & COMPANY
370 Bleecker Street
645-6978
Mon.–Fri.: 12 noon–6 p.m.; Sat.: 12 noon–6:30 p.m.
AE, MC, V

Eighteenth- and nineteenth-century French furniture that is mostly formal, carved, and highly polished fills R. J. King & Company's spare shop. Known as a good source for armoires, side tables, and consoles of cherry, chestnut, and mahogany, this gallery also offers furniture with a rustic country look, along with a sprinkling of upholstered sofas and chairs. There's an annex just around the corner that is filled with farm tables, benches, and other country furniture.

ROSENBERG & STIEBEL, INC.
32 East 57th Street
Fifth floor
753-4368
Tues.–Sat.: 10 a.m.–5 p.m.; Mon. by appointment
No credit cards

For four generations the Rosenberg and Stiebel families have handled the world's finest treasures, and museum curators and leaders in banking and industry come to their graciously appointed gallery for the very best in eighteenth-century French furniture whose authenticity and provenance are unimpeachable. You're likely to find a cabinet crafted by famed *ébéniste* Roger Vandercruse or one by Jean-Pierre Latz; an unusually large Louis XV *bureau plat;* a breathtaking collection of Old Masters paintings and drawings; Meissen and Sèvres and other famed German and French porcelains; and medieval and Renaissance bronzes. Very expensive.

RUSSISIMOFF
Place des Antiquaires
125 East 57th Street
752-1284
Mon.–Sat.: 11 a.m.–6 p.m.
No credit cards

Parisian Didier Rabes, who has a showroom in the Louvre des Antiquaires in Paris, has filled his tiny New York outpost with rare eighteenth- and nineteenth-century antiques from the French and Russian courts, along with a few Italian pieces of the same period. Unusual suites of furniture, graceful torchères, and richly inlaid cabinets, many with ormolu mounts, are among his treasures.

253

MEDIEVAL AND RENAISSANCE ANTIQUITIES

BLUMKA
101 East 81st Street
734-3222
By appointment only
No credit cards

Step through the black-wood door simply adorned with the Blumka name, and you'll discover a delightful two-story gallery graced with the opulent trappings of medieval castles. Leopold Blumka opened the shop in 1942, and now it's run by his widow, Ruth, and their daughter, Victoria. Massive and heavily carved tables, chairs, and cupboards share the space with Medieval and Renaissance tapestries. But not everything in this beguiling shop is on the grand scale. The Blumkas offer early Venetian glass goblets, delicate French ivories, Renaissance keys, and medieval helmets, along with relics from medieval monasteries.

L'ANTIQUAIRE & THE CONNOISSEUR
36 East 73rd Street
517-9176
Mon.–Fri.: 9 a.m.–5:30 p.m.; Sat., Sun. by appointment
No credit cards

Experts consider L'Antiquaire & the Connoisseur one of the best sources in the country for treasures from the Middle Ages and the Renaissance. Museum-quality Roman and Byzantine antiquities, ancient architectural elements, and fifteenth-, sixteenth-, and seventeenth-century French and Spanish furniture, paintings, and decorative accessories fill this elegant gallery. Most of the pieces have little or no restoration, and their condition and quality are exceptional. In addition to medieval and Renaissance antiques, L'Antiquaire offers a sumptuous collection of eighteenth-century Italian furniture (including Venetian painted pieces), Old Masters paintings and drawings, tapestries, and period textiles.

NEWEL ART GALLERIES INC.
Medieval and Renaissance tables, cupboards, and chairs. See **French and European Furniture**, p. 251.)

ROSENBERG & STIEBEL, INC.
Medieval and Renaissance bronzes. (See **French and European Furniture**, p. 253.)

RETRO

CLASSIC AGE
41 East 11th Street
Eleventh floor
353-3450
Mon.–Fri.: 10 a.m.–6 p.m.; Sat.: 12 noon–6 p.m.
AE

Sunny and cavernous, Classic Age is crowded with reissues of modern furniture classics that have been made to the same specifications as the originals. Indeed, in some cases they've been made by the companies that first manufactured them. All the legendary names are here: Josef Hoffmann, Charles Rennie Mackintosh, Marcel Breuer, Le Corbusier, Ludwig Mies van der Rohe, and Frank Lloyd Wright. There are chairs, tables, beds, sofas, wall units, and cabinets and the designs are as early as the turn of the century, as recent as the sixties. Classic Age also stocks reissues of modern lighting, wallpapers, fabrics, rugs, and accessories for a total Retro look.

DELORENZO 1950
965 Madison Avenue, near 75th Street
535-8511
Mon.–Sat.: 9:30 a.m.–5:30 p.m.
No credit cards

Anthony Delorenzo exhibits his collection of French designs from the fifties in a shop across the street from his gallery filled with Art Deco treasures. Since Delorenzo favors the works of Jean Prouvé and Serge Mouille, you'll find an in-depth selection of the former's tables, desks, bookcases, and bent-plywood chairs and the latter's industrial-looking floor and table lamps. Sonia Delaunay, Charlotte Perriand, and Mathieu Mategot are also represented. Expensive.

DEPRESSION MODERN
150 Sullivan Street
982-5699
Wed.–Sun.: 12 noon–7 p.m.
No credit cards

Each week Depression Modern takes on a new look. Owner Michael Smith scours the country for treasures from the thirties and forties, and every week he redecorates his store. One week everything might be chrome and covered in black; another it's in boudoir shades of pinks and mauves, still another and everything is bar related. But whatever the transformation, Smith always offers exciting examples of spare and streamlined furniture, and his selection of lamps, rugs, and decorative accessories are not to be missed. He has a garden filled with vintage summer furniture, and at Christmas his shop is a wonderland of unusual ornaments. Prices are reasonable.

FIFTY/50
793 Broadway, near 10th Street
777-3208
Mon.–Fri.: 11 a.m.–6 p.m.; Sat.: 12 noon–5 p.m.
All major

Although a somewhat seedy-looking, unprepossessing shop, Fifty/50 is stocked with all the important American and European designers of the mid-twentieth century. You'll find Eames plywood chairs, Noguchi coffee tables, Nelson slatted benches, Alvar Aalto stools, and hanging pieces by Herman Miller and Knoll. Recently the owners have broadened their inventory to include Donald Deskey, Gilbert Rohde, and Paul Theodore Frankl's American designs from the twenties through the fifties. In addition to furniture the gallery always has wonderful examples of fifties ceramics, Venini glassware, and jewelry by all the illustrious Retro names. Pricey.

FIRST 1/2
Fifties chairs, tables, and accessories. (See **Art Deco/Art Nouveau Furniture,** p. 235.)

MOOD INDIGO
181 Prince Street
254-1176
Tues.–Sat.: 12 noon–7 p.m.; Sun.: 1 p.m.–6 p.m.
AE, MC, V

Mood Indigo is a favorite with collectors who raid this tidy shop for decorative accessories from the thirties and forties with a Retro look. Although mostly tabletop collectibles, there are always a few choice pieces of furniture that might include a rattan porch set, sleek chrome towel racks, small Deco tables, and assorted chairs. The store carries the largest selection of Frederick H. Rhead FiestaWare in the city; along with Russel Wright china; chrome bar accessories; kitschy thirties glassware; streamlined toasters and irons; forties kitchen clocks; wood-handled kitchen utensils from the twenties and thirties; and Art Deco and Bakelite jewelry.

THE MOMA DESIGN STORE (Museum of Modern Art)
Reissues of the furniture designs by the top designers of the thirties, forties, and fifties. (See **Museum Gift Shops,** p. 406.)

MURIEL KARASIK GALLERY
1094 Madison Avenue, at 82nd Street
535-7851

Mon.–Sat.: 10 a.m.–6 p.m.; closed Sat. in summer
AE

An ever-changing and eclectic mix of twentieth-century decorative arts treasures, Muriel Karasik's gallery reflects her acquisitive nature and her delight in the witty and offbeat. Among the potpourri are *objets* from the Arts and Crafts, Deco, and postwar eras. High-style Art Deco furniture shares the space with such quirky Retro pieces as a chair shaped like a boxing glove, a chaise longue that looks like a baseball mitt, a golf-bag floor lamp. Handbags masquerade as telephones or poodles or champagne bottles, and compacts are disguised as soccer balls or dancing girls. But Karasik also carries such gems as Venini glassware, Bakelite radios, jigsawed animal doorstops from the thirties, a fine selection of lamps, perfume bottles, along with table and bar accessories in sterling silver or chrome. The shop always has at least a dozen children's chairs, and these date from the turn of the century to the fifties and might include a Queen Anne wing chair or a molded plywood rocker. And since Karasik's collection of costume jewelry covers all bases, you're likely to find designs by Hattie Carnegie and Miriam Haskell, early Olympic sporting medals, vintage Mexican sterling-silver pins and earrings, silly cowboy and Indian pieces, Czechoslovakian bead bracelets and brooches, as well as Bakelite and paste jewelry. Expensive.

THE SECOND COMING

72 Green Street
431-4424
Mon.–Sat.: 12 noon–7 p.m.; Sun.: 1 p.m.–6 p.m.
AE, MC, V

The Second Coming calls itself "a vintage department store," and on its two spacious floors you'll find an exuberant mix of just about everything and anything that's old: furniture, clothing, shoes, linens, fifties wallpaper, housewares, jewelry, and decorative accessories of all kinds. Victorian wicker shares the space with turn-of-the-century oak armoires and vanities, streamlined Art Deco chairs and sofas, twenties bamboo bars and stools, and living room, bedroom, and dining-room suites from the thirties and forties. There's an attractive selection of vintage clothing that includes printed day frocks, forties broad-shouldered dresses, and beaded blouses and sweaters for women; shirts, slacks, and jackets for men. Among the large assortment of never-worn old shoes are forties two-tone saddles and fifties pointy flats. The second floor is brimful of vintage table and bed linens, kitschy glassware, china, and housewares from the thirties, as well as nicely done reproductions of vintage brass and iron bed frames that are made from old molds. Prices are good.

SECOND HAND ROSE

270 Lafayette Street

431-7673
Mon.–Sat.: 10 a.m.–6 p.m.; closed Sat. in summer
No credit cards

Suzanne Lipschutz was one of the city's first dealers to carry Retro
forties and fifties furniture along with Deco pieces, and she now has a
fine collection of both and a 5,000 square foot space in which to display
them. Furniture by the top names of the twenties and thirties—Donald
Desky, Norman Bel Geddes, P. T. Frankel, Gilbert Rohde, and Frank
Lloyd Wright—coexist with the molded-plywood, steel, and plastic designs of Eames, Bertoia, and Nelson. Fifties bamboo is one of Lipschutz's passions, so she always has a few bamboo, wicker, and reed
chairs, settees, and tables in her shop. And Lipschutz admits to a weak-
ness for old thirties, forties, and fifties wallpapers (the kind adorned
with silly fish, flamingos, plaids, huge florals, and French bistro
scenes), so she offers the city's largest supply, along with luggage from
the thirties and forties (including matched sets), vintage fabrics and
drapes and hard-to-find linoleum rugs. When her son was born, Lipschutz began collecting antique children's furniture, and although he's
now a teenager, she's still a collector and usually has a turn-of-the-
century Thonet chair or settee, as well as molded plastic or plywood
chairs and stools from the fifties. Prices are good.

WAVES

32 East 13th Street
989-9284
Tues.–Fri.: 12 noon–6 p.m.; Sat.: 12 noon–5 p.m.
MC, V

Bruce and Charlotte Mager's beguiling little shop is a throwback to an
earlier era. Cathedral-style radios from the thirties sit next to funny-
looking red-and-white plastic ones from the fifties, and the floor and
shelves are crowded with gramophones, old telephones, neon clocks,
and early television sets. Everything is in good working order with
surprisingly clear sound. The Magers also carry such radio-related
objects as radio-shaped cigarette lighters, as well as a selection of old
disks for crank-handled phonographs.

VICTORIAN

See also **Wicker, Bamboo, Bentwood, Twig, and Rattan Furniture.**

ABC ANTIQUES

Formal American and English Victorian and Edwardian walnut and oak furniture, including armoires, chairs, desks, chests, and tables, along with a sprinkling of wicker pieces. (See **Furniture,** p. 272.)

BARDITH I

1015 Madison Avenue, near 78th Street
737-6699
Mon.–Fri.: 11 a.m.–5:30 p.m.; Sat.: 11 a.m.–5 p.m.
No credit cards

Owner Edith Wolf is a prodigious shopper. Her tiny china shop, Bardith Ltd., is crammed floor to ceiling with antique china, and although Bardith I, by comparison, seems almost austere, it's one of the city's best sources for Victorian sofas, chairs, and settees. Most of the stock is from England, and Wolf has refurbished and upholstered her pieces in muslin. She's assembled earlier pieces, too—eighteenth-century linen presses, Pembroke and tripod tables, and oak sideboards—along with a tempting array of Victorian accessories. There are enough needlepoint cushions and footstools, lamps and chandeliers, papier-mâché tray tables, and assorted other whatnots to transform a bare apartment into an appropriately cluttered Victorian gem.

CHARLOTTE MOSS & CO.

Although her collection of Victorian furniture is small—a few frame chairs and end tables—Moss offers a full range of Victorian decorative accessories that includes screens, beribboned lamp shades, chintz picture bows, needlepoint panels, tapestry cushions, china, luggage racks, tole trays, and chintz-covered hatboxes. (See **Gifts,** p. 294.)

FLORIAN PAPP

A small but very special selection of furniture from the Victorian era.
(See **English Period Furniture,** p. 242.)

HAMILTON-HYRE LTD.

Victorian *faux*-bamboo is a specialty, so you're likely to find standing mirrors, Davenport desks, vanities, writing tables, bookcases, and chests of drawers. (See **Furniture,** p. 288.)

JUDITH AMDUR

Small-scale Victorian antiques and accessories, including one of the city's largest selections of *faux*-bamboo—desks, tables, bookcases, vanities, mirrors, and bureaus. (See **Furniture,** p. 289.)

MARGOT JOHNSON, INC.

18 East 68th Street
794-2225
By appointment only
No credit cards

Margot Johnson was a pioneer in Victorian American furniture when she began collecting wicker pieces in the seventies. She has since **259** moved on from wicker to more formal furniture crafted by the best cabinetmakers of the time. So her beguiling gallery, located in a turn-of-the-century mansion, is filled with such names as Herter Brothers, R. J. Hornet, Pottier & Stymus, Alexandre Roux, and George Hunzinger. Johnson favors works in the Revival styles and furniture that is whimsical, and yes, she still carries a few select, important wicker pieces.

NEWEL ART GALLERIES INC.

A large stock of English and American Gothic Revival furniture from the Victorian era—sideboards, club chairs, dining tables, desks, headboards, and bureaus—along with English and American Victorian *faux*-bamboo and wicker pieces. (See **French and European Furniture,** p. 251.)

OLDIES, GOLDIES & MOLDIES

Among the small-scale Victorian pieces you'll find bureaus, vanities, desks, chairs, and assorted tables, along with lighting and accessories from the same period. (See **Art Deco/Art Nouveau Furniture,** p. 236.)

PENWOOD ANTIQUES

470 Broadway, near Broome Street
925-7589
Mon.–Sat.: 11 a.m.–7 p.m.
AE

In a cavernous, no frills space, Penwood Antiques offers a nostalgic array of Victorian and Edwardian treasures. Walnut and oak furniture are specialties, so come here for those hard-to-find rolltop desks, oak filing cabinets, glass-fronted bookcases, brass and iron bedframes, and round pedestal-based dining tables. But there are other fascinating finds—wicker wheelchairs, vintage dental cabinets, antique industrial storage cabinets, and a good stock of Victorian wicker that includes settees, chairs, and tables. The lighting is as eclectic as this shop's other treasures, but there's always a large selection of desk and table lamps, torchères, and chandeliers.

R. BROOKE LTD.

In addition to a few select pieces of Victorian furniture—small chairs and assorted tempting tables—R. Brooke is crammed with a heady jumble of tea caddies, cushions, papier-mâché trays, tole boxes, sterling-silver frames, desk accessories, and lamps. (See **Gifts,** p. 297.)

VAUGHN ANTIQUES

630 Hudson Street
243-0440
Tues.–Sat.: 11:30 a.m.–7 p.m.; Sat., Sun.: 11:30 a.m.–6 p.m.

AE, MC, V

Vaughn Antiques is a good place to search for those increasingly hard-to-find Victorian and Edwardian walnut and oak furniture pieces. There are usually a few rolltop desks, file cabinets, bookcases, bed frames, or round pedestal-based tables, but if Vaughn doesn't have what you're looking for, he'll try to find it for you. And although some pieces may need work, prices here are good.

THE WICKER GARDEN

Among the lacy Victorian wicker confections are natural and white-painted chairs, settees, étagères, plant stands, tea carts, and assorted small tables. (See **Wicker Furniture,** p. 290.)

WIENER WERKSTÄTTE

BARRY FRIEDMAN LTD.

1117 Madison Avenue, near 83rd Street
794-8950
Mon.–Sat.: 10 a.m.–6 p.m.
No credit cards

Barry Friedman's stark, all-white gallery is an appropriate setting for his splendid and important collection of furniture, *objets*, paintings, and posters from the Vienna Secession movement. Friedman features the works of Josef Hoffmann, Otto Wagner, and Kolomon Moser, but he also stocks original works from the Bauhaus and DeStijl movements, including pieces by Rietveld. There's always a handsome assortment of chairs, along with tables, desks, and cabinets, and the gallery abounds in decorative accessories and tableware as well as paintings, drawings, and posters by avant-garde and Art Deco artists. The designs of Charles Rennie Mackintosh and Italian Moderne pieces from the fifties and sixties are also generously represented. Pricey.

THE BIEDERMEIER HOUSE LTD.

An impressive selection of Jugendstil and Wiener Werkstätte furniture. (See **Empire and Biedermeier Furniture,** p. 239.)

GALERIE METROPOL

927 Madison Avenue, near 73rd Street
Second floor
772-7401
Tues.–Sat.: 1 p.m.–6 p.m.; and by appointment
No credit cards

The meticulously designed furniture and accessories by the top names in the Vienna Secession, the Wiener Werkstätte, and the Bauhaus are

261

represented in this stark, white gallery. Tables, chairs, sofas, settees, desks, and bureaus by such illustrious artists as Mies van der Rohe, Hans Hoffman, Marcel Breuer, Koloman Moser, and Le Corbusier come and go surprisingly quickly, considering the price tags, and there's an ever-changing selection of ceramics, glass, metalware, and lamps as well.

MACKLOWE GALLERY & MODERNISM
Furniture and decorative objects from the Vienna Secession, including some exceptional pieces by the top names. (See **Art Deco/Art Nouveau Furniture**, p. 235.)

MICHAEL CAREY
A special group of Josef Hoffmann pieces. (See **Arts and Crafts Movement Furniture**, p. 238.)

THE MUSEUM OF MODERN ART
A select group of Wiener Werkstätte furniture and accessories. (See **Museum Gift Shops**, p. 406.)

CHILDREN'S FURNITURE
ANTIQUE AND VINTAGE

BACK PAGES ANTIQUES
The eclectic mix of antique children's furniture might include the occasional wicker carriage, bouncing oak swing, high chair, rocking horse. (See **Toys**, p. 489.)

MURIEL KARASIK
The selection of antique children's chairs range in style from Victorian, to pierced wood, to Adirondack twig, to Retro. (See **Retro Furniture**, p. 256.)

NEWEL ART GALLERIES INC.
Chippendale, Shaker ladder-back, and French wire-scroll armchairs suggest the eclectic variety of antique children's chairs. (See **French and European Furniture**, p. 251.)

SECOND HAND ROSE
An ever-changing collection that might include molded plastic buck-

ets, Eames molded-plywood, and Breuer cane-seated chairs. (See **Retro Furniture**, p. 257.)

THOS. K. WOODARD AMERICAN ANTIQUES & QUILTS
Among the small but very select inventory of Early American children's furniture, you're apt to find a Shaker rocking chair, an early crib, tables, and chairs. (See **Linens and Quilts**, p. 387.)

THE WICKER GARDEN
The selection of one-of-a-kind children's antique wicker pieces includes chairs and tables, high chairs, an occasional crib, carriage, or cradle. (See **Furniture**, p. 290.)

CONTEMPORARY

AU CHAT BOTTÉ
Enchanting fabric-wrapped bassinets, along with hand-painted children's furniture with cavorting barnyard or jungle animals that can be custom-ordered from the samples on display. (See **Clothing**, p. 88.)

BELLINI
1305 Second Avenue, at 68th Street
517-9233
Mon.–Wed., Fri.: 10 a.m.–6 p.m.; Thurs.: 10 a.m.–8 p.m.; Sat.:
10 a.m.–5:30 p.m.

473 Columbus Avenue, near 83rd Street
362-3700
Mon., Wed., Fri.: 10:30 a.m.–6:30 p.m.; Sat.: 10 a.m.–6 p.m.; Thurs:
10 a.m.–8 p.m.; Sun.: 12 noon–5 p.m.
AE, MC, V

Sleek, contemporary, and European-made cribs color-coordinate with armoires and changing tables for a pulled together, designer look for Baby's room. The furniture is designed to grow with the child, so cribs convert to junior beds and changing tables transform into dressers. Colors are sophisticated, and the stores carry a full range of matching decorative accessories, such as lamps, wastebaskets, clocks, toy chests, hampers, linens, and wall hangings. You'll find Silver Cross and Inglesina carriages, Aprica strollers, and high chairs, as well as bunk beds and bureaus for the older child.

BEN'S FOR KIDS
1380 Third Avenue, near 78th Street
794-2330

Mon.–Wed., Fri.: 10 a.m.–5 p.m.; Thurs.: 10 a.m.–8 p.m.; Sat.:
11 a.m.–5 p.m.
AE, MC, V

A friendly neighborhood store, Ben's is filled with a seemingly endless
selection of sturdy, practical, well-made, and affordable children's furniture. Not high-style or top-of-the-line pieces, these are the standards
in cribs, bassinets, high chairs, and wardrobes. Ben's carries carriages
and strollers, too, along with accessories such as lamps, crib bumpers,
quilts, and linens for Baby's bed. And stacked floor to ceiling in the
front of the store, there's a staggering array of Fisher-Price, Playskool,
and Little Tikes toys, puzzles, and games.

BONPOINT
Scaled-down chairs and sofas are replicas of antique designs—a Louis
XV upholstered armchair is an exact copy of an eighteenth-century
piece, and there are clones of Edwardian club chairs—but you'll also
find more ordinary children's things, such as glossy white high chairs
and cribs. (See **Clothing,** p. 88.)

THE CHILDREN'S ROOM
318 East 45th Street
687-3868
Mon.–Fri.: 10 a.m.–5:30 p.m.; Sat.: 10 a.m.–5 p.m.
MC, V

Scandinavian good design that avoids the trendy is the hallmark of this
refreshing children's furniture store. Most of the pieces are geared to
the older child—although there's a splendid crib on wheels—and you'll
find flexible and expandable units perfect for apartment living. An all-
in-one loft bed, storage, and desk unit; bunk and trundle beds with
massive storage drawers; modular storage systems; table-and-chair
sets; desks; and some clever lamps are among the fine ideas.

CONRAN'S HABITAT
The appealing selection of furniture for the older child includes bunk
beds of tubular steel or wood, captain's beds with storage drawers,
table-and-chair sets, oak rockers, wardrobes, dressing tables, and
desks. (See **Contemporary Furniture,** p. 267.)

E.A.T. GIFTS
Armoires, changing tables, and cribs adorned with Babar or pastoral
scenes; child-size settees, rockers, chairs, and tables; and Peter Rabbit
nursery accessories such as lamps, pajama bags, and tissue holders.
(See **Gifts,** p. 302.)

F. A. O. SCHWARTZ
Marcel Breuer-style chair-and-table-sets, along with Laura Dabrow-
ski's fanciful hand-painted animal-shaped chairs, tables, and rockers.
(See **Toys,** p. 496.)

HUSH-A-BYE
1459 First Avenue, at 76th Street
988-4500
Mon.–Wed., Fri., Sat.: 10 a.m.–6 p.m.; Thurs.: 10 a.m.–9 p.m.; Sun.:
12 noon–5 p.m.
AE, MC, V

Hush-A-Bye is cluttered with matching sets of cribs, dressing tables, and
wardrobes in everything from contemporary Mica to traditional wood,
yet the store also manages to stock a vast assortment of bassinets, high
chairs, strollers, and carriages. All the accessories (wastebaskets,
lamps, wall hangings, toy chests, and hampers) are here as well, along
with furniture for the older child in styles that range from Victorian
wrought-iron daybeds to space-saving all-in-one bed, desk, and storage
units, to twin-sized racing-car beds in circusy colors.

JENSEN-LEWIS
Cheery red tubular steel or wood bunk beds, with matching desks,
wardrobes, and chests of drawers. (See **Contemporary Furniture**, p.
269.)

LEWIS OF LONDON
215 East 51st Street
688-3669
Mon.–Wed., Fri., Sat.: 10 a.m.–6 p.m.; Thurs.: 10 a.m.–8 p.m.
AE, MC, V

For more than forty years Lewis of London has been supplying well-
heeled parents with stylish and pricey nursery furniture. The pieces
are imported and exclusive to the store, and the look, for the most part,
is sleek, modern, and color-coordinated. Cribs come in everything from
simple wood laminates to gold-plated versions, and there are sets designed for the growing youngster, along with bunk beds and furniture
for the older child. Unique and costly carriages, strollers, high chairs,
changing tables, and all the appropriate accessories—mirrors, lamps,
toy boxes, hampers, and wall hangings—are here as well.

MABEL'S
Child-size chairs in every imaginable animal shape, from zebras to
frogs. (See **Gifts**, p. 307.)

SCULLY & SCULLY
Among the classic chairs scaled to kiddie size are Queen Anne styles
and Chippendale corner ones, and they're beautifully made and upholstered in traditional fabrics and fit for the most elegant drawing room.
(See **Gifts**, p. 310.)

THE WICKER GARDEN
The infant furnishings on the second floor are guaranteed to make a
baby's room look right for a baby: Iron cribs are adorned with brass or

porcelain finials and canopies, and bureaus and armoires are hand-painted with pastoral scenes. (See **Wicker Furniture,** p. 290.)

WORKBENCH
The selection of practical and space-saving furniture for children in-cludes bunk and trundle beds, desks, storage units, bureaus, and toy chests in at least a dozen finishes and colors. (See **Contemporary Furniture,** p. 271.)

CONTEMPORARY FURNITURE

B. Altman & Co., Bloomingdale's, and Macy's carry a very complete selection of contemporary furniture.

BON MARCHÉ
55 West 13th Street
Sixth floor
620-5550
Mon.–Sat.: 10:30 a.m.–6:30 p.m.

1060 Third Avenue, near 63rd Street
620-5592
Mon.–Sat.: 10:30 a.m.–6:30 p.m.
MC, V

Bon Marché is known for its nicely designed, moderately priced mod-ern furniture. Chairs are a specialty, and these range in style from Breuer-inspired classics, to whimsical variations on the latest Italian designs, to Mallet Stevens's stacking beauties. Others are made of tubular steel, black lacquer, leather, and chrome. Much of the furniture is scaled to New York apartments, so you'll find bookcases and wall units with a built-in look, small-size sofas, desks and tables that fold, storage cabinets and bookshelves of all kinds, along with a first-rate selection of lighting fixtures for every room in the house.

CARDARELLI
205 West Houston Street
924-2040
Mon.–Fri.: 9 a.m.–5 p.m.; Sat.: 9 a.m.–5 p.m.
MC, V

Since 1900 Cardarelli has offered New Yorkers fine-quality reproduc-tions of traditional furniture. Its handsome showroom, well off the beaten furniture track, is filled with reproductions of eighteenth-century Newport chests (with escutcheons and solid brass pulls), three-leg drop-leaf tables, traditional secretaires, consoles, and claw-and-ball Chippendale sofas. Those who can't afford originals come to Cardarelli for pleasing alternatives by such experts in the field as Drexel-Heritage, Henredon, Century, Kindel, Harden, and Hickory Chair.

CONRAN'S HABITAT
Citicorp Center
160 East 54th Street
371-2225
Mon–Fri.: 10 a.m.–9 p.m.; Sat.: 10 a.m.–7 p.m.; Sun.: 11 a.m.–6 p.m.

2-8 Astor Place
505-1515
Mon.–Sat.: 10 a.m.–9 p.m.; Sun.: 12 noon–7 p.m.

2248 Broadway, near 81st Street
873-9250
Mon.–Fri.: 10 a.m.–8 p.m.; Sat.: 10 a.m.–9 p.m.; Sun.: 11 a.m.–6 p.m.
AE, MC, V

Everything is attractive and appealing in Terence Conran's New York outposts, Americanized versions of his English Habitat stores. Cavernous housewares supermarkets—they're bi-level, high-tech, and well-organized, and they offer nicely executed versions of au courant trends. Styles range from starkly modern, to rustic country, to Arts and Crafts looks, to sophisticated Wiener Werkstätte-inspired pieces. The selection of convertible sofa beds is noteworthy for styling, sturdiness, and comfort, and the shops carry furniture for every room of the house, including the kitchen. There's always a selection of porch and outdoor furniture, too—everything from Tennessee rockers to Kensington Park benches, Adirondack chairs to market umbrellas, canvas beach chairs to Lloyd Loom examples, and Victorian wicker to French bistro sets. No less attractive is Conran's children's furniture that consists of bunk beds, bureaus, chairs, and desks. Generously mixed with the furniture is a very complete stock of lighting fixtures in a broad range of styles; rugs of all kinds (from rag versions to straw ones); and an enormous and irresistible stock of china, glassware, cutlery, linens, fabrics, window shades, and toys. Best of all, prices are excellent.

DOOR STORE
1 Park Avenue, at 32nd Street
679-9700
Mon.–Wed., Fri.: 9:30 a.m.–7 p.m.; Thurs.: 9:30 a.m.–8 p.m.;
Sat.: 10 a.m.–6 p.m.; Sun.: 12 noon–5 p.m.

1201 Third Avenue, near 69th Street
772-1110
Mon.–Wed., Fri.: 10 a.m.–7 p.m.; Thurs.: 10 a.m.–8 p.m.;
Sat.: 10 a.m.–6 p.m.; Sun.: 12 noon–5 p.m.

123 West 17th Street
627-1515
Mon.–Wed., Fri., Sat.: 10 a.m.–6 p.m.; Thurs.: 10 a.m.–8 p.m.;
Sun.: 12 noon–5 p.m.

134 Washington Street
267-1250
Mon.–Wed., Fri., Sat.: 10 a.m.–6 p.m.; Thurs.: 10 a.m.–8 p.m.;
Sun.: 12 noon–5 p.m.
MC, V

The Door Store began as a shop that reflected a fifties craze—transforming doors into tables, desks, and sofas—but in the eighties it has become a source for simply styled and affordable furniture. Country pine pieces include wardrobes, headboards, dressers, and farm tables; there are elegant beechwood reproductions of Louis XV and Chinese Chippendale chairs; comfortable sofas and loveseats with a country look; along with sophisticated black dining tables and sleek Italian-inspired leather furniture. The shop's flexible wall systems that can double as a closet, home office, bookcase, or entertainment center are boons for city apartment dwellers.

GRANGE

831 Madison Avenue, near 69th Street
737-8080
Mon.–Wed.: 10 a.m.–6 p.m.; Thurs.: 10 a.m.–7 p.m.;
Fri. & Sat.: 10 a.m.–6 p.m.
MC, V

Grange is a century-old French furniture manufacturer that specializes in handmade reproductions of traditional styles. The company's flagship store on Madison Avenue is housed on three floors of a handsome limestone building, and it's filled with Art Deco, Biedermeier, Louis Philippe, Empire, and Directoire inspired pieces. Sleigh beds in solid cherry or wicker, elegant chaises, campaign chairs, sofas, Ultra-Suede bergères, and rattan tables are among the large-scale offerings, but the shop also carries tapestry pillows, baskets, mirrors, and botanical prints.

J & D BRAUNER BUTCHER BLOCK

316 East 59th Street
421-1143
Mon.–Thurs., Fri.: 10 a.m.–8 p.m.; Tues., Wed., Sat.: 10 a.m.–6 p.m.;
Sun.: 11 a.m.–5 p.m.

181 Amsterdam Avenue, at 68th Street
496-6447
Mon., Wed., Thurs., Fri.: 10 a.m.–8 p.m.; Tues., Wed., Sat.: 10 a.m.–6 p.m.; Sun.: 11 a.m.–5 p.m.

298 Bowery, near Houston Streeet
477-2830
Mon.–Sat.: 10 a.m.–6 p.m.; Sun.: 11 a.m.–5 p.m.

1522 Second Avenue, at 79th Street
535-0984
Mon., Thurs., Fri.: 10 a.m.–8 p.m.; Tues., Wed., Sat.: 10 a.m.–6 p.m.;
Sun.: 11 a.m.–5 p.m.
AE, MC, V

Famous since 1946 as a source of customized solid maple and oak kitchen counters and tabletops, J & D Brauner has expanded its business and transformed butcher block into a complete line of contemporary furniture. Now, in addition to sturdy butcher-block counters, the shops stock everything from chairs and tea carts, to desks, headboards, and hutches. Prices are good.

JENSEN-LEWIS
89 Seventh Avenue, at 15th Street
929-4880
Mon.–Wed., Fri., Sat.: 10 a.m.–7 p.m.; Thurs.: 10 a.m.–8 p.m.;
Sun.: 12 noon–5 p.m.

1496 Third Avenue, at 84th Street
439-6440
Mon.–Wed., Fri., Sat.: 10:30 a.m.–7 p.m.; Thurs.: 10:30 a.m.–8 p.m.;
Sun.: 12 noon–5 p.m.
AE, MC, V

When Jensen-Lewis opened in 1932, it supplied New Yorkers with canvas awnings, but in 1968 the company began producing canvas sofas and director's chairs, and the awnings became a thing of the past. Although Jensen-Lewis still makes canvas furniture—along with bright canvas totes in thirty-two colors—it now carries furnishings for every room in the house. Much of the stock is geared to city living, so there are drop-leaf and extension tables, sectional sofas, room dividers, and platform beds with pull-out storage units. Also in evidence is a large selection of standing lamps and desk lights, along with housewares and kitchen accessories. Colorful bunk beds, small-scale bureaus, and animal standing lamps are among the attractions for children's rooms, and for summer homes the stores offer carefree and durable porch and patio furniture, as well as a full line of canvas umbrellas.

LAYTNER'S HOME FURNISHINGS
2394 Broadway, near 88th Street
769-1900
Mon.–Sat.: 10:30 a.m.–7 p.m.; Sun.: 12 noon–5 p.m.
AE, MC, V

A pleasant neighborhood store, Laytner's is well-stocked with contemporary furniture generously mixed with reproductions of old-time favorites. Sturdily crafted, hand-woven wicker chairs, ottomans, sofas, and tables are inspired by classic twenties pieces and come in earth tones or warm pastels. The Shaker pine collection—for dining, bedroom, and living rooms—is made the old-fashioned way, using mortise and tenon joints and dovetailed drawers.

MAURICE VILLENCY
200 Madison Avenue, near 35th Street
725-4840
Tues., Wed., Fri., Sat.: 10 a.m.–6 p.m.; Mon., Thurs.: 10 a.m.–9 p.m.;
Sun.: 12 noon–5 p.m.
AE, MC, V

An eclectic mix of styles is on display in Maurice Villency's large and pleasant showroom. Simple, somewhat stark Scandinavian pieces share the space with glitzy marble consoles and dining tables, and sleek, stylized lacquer bedroom suites from Italy. There are wall units, sectional sofas, and leather recliners, and everything is well-made.

NORSK
114 East 57th Street
752-3111
Mon.–Wed., Fri., Sat.: 10 a.m.–6 p.m.; Thurs.: 10 a.m.–8 p.m.;
Sun.: 12 noon–5 p.m.
All major

Scandinavian designs similar to the styles that were popular in the fifties and sixties are still available at Norsk. Spare teak tables, cabinets, and dressers; the Norwegian Falcon chair; stressless leather recliners; unadorned sofas; Scandinavian wool rugs; and hanging wall units that bring high prices in vintage furniture stores can be bought new at Norsk for less.

OMO HOME
113 Spring Street
334-9696
Mon.–Sat.: 10 a.m.–6 p.m.
AE, MC, V

Fashion designer Norma Kamali has applied her flair and sense of style to the home and created a line of opulent and dramatic furniture. Her exuberant designs, along with her collection of Empire and rococo antiques (also for sale) are ensconced in a cavernous gold-painted loft. She does overstuffed club chairs and Chesterfield sofas, along with dining tables, consoles, and end tables with beveled-mirrored bases. Fabrics include velvets, satins, brocades.

WIM & KAREN SCANDINAVIAN FURNITURE
319 East 53rd Street

758-4207

Mon.–Wed., Fri.: 10 a.m.–6 p.m.; Thurs.: 10 a.m.–7:30 p.m.;
Sat.: 10 a.m.–5 p.m.
MC, V

Wim & Karen imports oak, teak, and rosewood furniture that's designed in Scandinavia and made in the company's factories abroad. Everything is light in feeling, yet extremely functional, and the showroom offers furnishings for every room. Teak pedestal tables, chairs with upholstered seats, bed frames, desks, plant stands, and bureaus are among the attractions, but the shop's specialty is wall units that can be customized to accommodate books, glassware, entertainment centers, sound systems, or art objects. Recently the company has added innovative pieces to their line—headboards upholstered in black leather and night tables outfitted with unique swing mechanisms.

WORKBENCH
470 Park Avenue, at 32nd Street
481-5454
Mon.–Wed., Fri., Sat.: 10 a.m.–6 p.m.; Thurs.: 10 a.m.–8 p.m.;
Sun.: 12 noon–5 p.m.

2091 Broadway, near 72nd Street
724-3670
Mon., Thurs.: 10 a.m.–8 p.m.; Tues., Wed., Fri.: 10 a.m.–6:30 p.m.;
Sat.: 10 a.m.–6 p.m.; Sun.: 12 noon–5 p.m.

1320 Third Avenue, near 75th Street
734-5106
Mon.–Wed., Fri.: 10 a.m.–6:30 p.m.; Thurs.: 10 a.m.–8 p.m.;
Sat.: 10 a.m.–6 p.m.; Sun.: 12 noon–5 p.m.

161 Avenue of the Americas, near Spring Street
675-7775
Mon.–Wed., Fri.: 9:30 a.m.–6:30 p.m.; Thurs.: 9:30 a.m.–8 p.m.;
Sat.: 10 a.m.–6 p.m.; Sun.: 11 a.m.–5 p.m.
AE, MC, V

Functional furniture that's attractively styled accounts for the Workbench's popularity. Melamine wardrobes, desks, folding tables, and multiple-purpose storage units are scaled to apartment living, and the showrooms offer beautifully spare cherrywood furniture inspired by the clean styling of Shaker pieces. There's a large selection of sturdy bookcases and appealing children's things—dressers, desks, bunk and trundle beds—in bright primary colors or wood veneers, and the Workbench's prices are good.

COUNTRY FURNITURE

B. Altman & Co., Bloomingdale's, and Macy's offer a selection of country pine furniture.

ABC ANTIQUES
888 Broadway, at 19th Street
254-7171
Mon., Thurs.: 10 a.m.–8 p.m.; Tues., Wed., Fri.: 10 a.m.–7 p.m.;
Sat.: 10 a.m.–6 p.m.; Sun.: 11 a.m.–6 p.m.
All major

ABC Antiques occupies the fourth floor of the block-long building that houses ABC Carpets, and its barnlike space is brimful of country pine furniture from Scandinavia, England, and France. Dozens of pine farm tables, hutches, armoires, cabinets, chairs, headboards, and commodes share the space with Victorian wicker, Edwardian oak corner cabinets, formal French armoires, chiffoniers, and Louis Philippe sleigh beds. Also in evidence are decorative accessories from around the world that include clocks, porcelains, lighting fixtures, and glassware. On the cavernous third floor, displayed in vignette bedroom settings, is ABC's linen department, and it's filled with a well-chosen selection of all-cotton bed linens in pristine whites, appealing prints, and a full range of solids. All the top companies and designers are represented, and there's a good supply of duvet covers and mohair throws, too, along with a winning array of table linens.

AMIGO COUNTRY
19 Greenwich Avenue, at 10th Street
620-5796
Mon.–Sat.: 11 a.m.–7:30 p.m.; Sun.: 12 noon–6 p.m.
AE, MC, V

Bill Harris and Tom Doane have a passion for things Mexican, and they haunt *mercados* and trek through out-of-the-way villages to hunt for treasures for their spacious store. Carved pine tables, settees, and cupboards with a rustic charm; pigskin chairs; tin mirrors; brilliant papier-mâché fruits and vegetables; nubby wool rugs; and glistening copper lanterns are among the exuberant stock. The owners carry glazed terra-cotta pottery and bright cotton place mats for the table, too, along with graceful hand-painted porcelain washbasins for the bath, and vivid paintings for the walls.

BETTER TIMES ANTIQUES, INC.
500 Amsterdam Avenue, near 84th Street
496-9001

Mon., Tues., Thurs.–Sun.: 12 noon–6:30 p.m.
MC, V

A cozy shop, Better Times is comfortably cluttered with honey-toned
nineteenth-century English and Irish country-pine furniture that has
not been vat stripped, but lovingly refurbished. The owners select and
directly import their wares from England, so there's always a profusion
of cupboards, armoires, chests of drawers, chairs, and farm tables. In
addition to pine, they also import more formal hardwood pieces (including mahogany and oak), Edwardian upholstered sofas and chairs, and
the occasional wicker. Prices are good.

CLAIBORNE GALLERY
366 West 15th Street
727-7219
By appointment only
No credit cards

Claiborne Gallery is the cavernous branch of a Santa Fe emporium. Co-
owner Leslie Cozart grew up in Mexico City, where she fell in love with
the furnishings around her, and her collection of rare nineteenth-century
Mexican antiques reflects that love. Since Mexican artisans reinter-
preted the European furniture that foreigners brought with them, Cozart
has splendid examples that reflect Victorian, Chippendale, and Spanish colonial influences. Cupboards, armoires, stools, *trasteros* (for stor-
ing plates), and dining, corner, and work tables fill the warehouselike
space. Cozart carries reproductions of antique wooden chairs—the originals, it seems, were often used for firewood—along with hand-forged
iron benches, chairs, and tables. And the selection of hand-carved
wooden crosses, vintage ceramics (many examples of airport art), candlesticks, and *retablos*—religious paintings on tin—are as tempting as
the larger treats.

COBWEB
116 West Houston Street
505-1558
Mon.–Fri.: 12 noon–7 p.m.; Sat.: 12 noon–5 p.m.
AE

Cobweb was launched by Catherine Holt, who lived in Spain for a
number of years, and her sweeping two-story shop is filled with an
enchanting mix of antique Spanish and Portuguese rustic and formal
furniture that she personally selects on buying forays in Spain and
Portugal. Deliciously cluttered, the store offers all manner of serendipitous finds. Dozens of brass, iron, and painted wood bed frames share
the space with pine cupboards, armoires, small chests, garden chairs,
dining tables, marble-topped commodes, elaborately carved old doors,
benches in all sizes, iron washstands, chairs, wood plant stands,
earthen water jugs, hundreds of antique tiles, terra-cotta bowls, and
hand-painted ceramic plates. Overhead hang a dazzling array of chan-

deliers, and there's an entire room devoted to vintage kilim rugs. Most of Holt's treasures are turn-of-the-century, but some are as old as the seventeenth century, others as recent as the thirties. Holt's prices for country furniture are the best in town, and her shop is a personal favorite.

ERIC SERVAN ANTIQUES LTD.
Place des Antiquaires
125 East 57th Street
752-1521
Mon.–Sat.: 11 a.m.–6 p.m.
MC, V

Exceptionally fine eighteenth-century country furniture from the French provinces graces Eric Servan's handsome gallery. He favors large-scale country tables, armoires, chairs, and commodes made of fruitwood and ornamented with carvings of fruits and leaves, and his pieces are finished with beeswax and glow with a rich patina. Although pricey, the quality of Servan's collection is first-rate.

EVERGREEN ANTIQUES
1249 Third Avenue, at 72nd Street
744-5664
Mon.–Fri.: 11 a.m.–7 p.m.; Sat.: 11 a.m.–6 p.m.

120 Spring Street
966-6458
Daily: 11 a.m.–6 p.m.
AE, MC, V

Paul Siegenlaub's two-story shops hold a beguiling mix of rustic eighteenth- and nineteenth-century Scandinavian country furniture. Many of the primitive pine pieces have their original paint, and there are hard-to-find corner cupboards, as well as assorted tables, blanket chests, cabinets, sideboards, chairs, and armoires. Generously mixed with the furniture are appealing rag rugs (some old, some new), in a range of sizes, salt-glaze pottery, and antique hand-carved wooden bowls and boxes.

HOWARD KAPLAN'S FRENCH COUNTRY STORE
35 East 10th Street
529-1200
Mon.–Sat.: 10 a.m.–6 p.m.
AE, MC, V

Howard Kaplan was one of the first antiques dealers to recognize the commercial importance of the French Country look. Although his original store, on 10th Street, no longer offers antiques, it is now well-stocked with Kaplan's line of reproductions. He does floral fabrics and wallpapers, china with a country look, iron benches, children's chairs, and a wide array of decorative accessories that includes lacy covers for lamps, bistro ware, and table linens. At the newer Broadway store everything is old, but this gallery is open only to the trade.

JENNY BAILEY ANTIQUES
1326 Madison Avenue, at 94th Street
Lower level
831-6432
Mon.–Sat.: 10 a.m.–6 p.m.; Sun.: 11 a.m.–6 p.m.
AE

Jenny Bailey Antiques occupies a basement space that's a labyrinth of rooms comprising more than 2,000 square feet, and if you can find your way through this maze you'll discover French Country armoires, tables, and chairs; English pine chests, linen presses, wardrobes, and tables; along with a sprinkling of formal mahogany pieces and some fine decorative accessories. Most of the antiques date from the nineteenth century, but there are a few earlier pieces as well.

LAURA ASHLEY HOME FURNISHINGS
714 Madison Avenue, near 64th Street
735-5000
Mon.–Wed., Fri., Sat.: 10 a.m.–6 p.m.; Thurs.: 10 a.m.–7 p.m.
AE, MC, V

Laura Ashley's fashions for the home are attractively displayed in this handsome Madison Avenue townhouse. The first floor houses bed linens, blankets, quilts, duvet covers, and bath towels in soft pastels. There's a darling selection of linens for baby's crib, too, including sheets, pillowcases, comforters, bumper guards, and dust ruffles. On the second floor bolts of fabrics sold by the yard come in the signature Ashley prints, along with an assortment in bold stripes and dark florals. Here, too, is the company's large selection of wallpapers, lacy curtains, paints, and tiles, as well as lamps, china, pillows, and needlepoint rugs with a country look. Room vignettes on the third floor pull the Ashley look together. The company's line of upholstered furniture by Baker—overstuffed chairs, settees, sofas, and chaise longues—is covered in Ashley fabrics and they're accessorized with furnishings from the store.

LE FANION
299 West 4th Street
463-8760
Mon.–Sat.: 12 noon–7 p.m.
AE

Antiques and ornaments from the south of France are appealingly displayed in Claude-Noëlle's charming little shop. Eighteenth- and nineteenth-century walnut armoires, tables, buffets, tall-case clocks, and chairs share the tiny space with antique earthenware and contemporary handmade pottery, hand-painted tiles from Provence, and copper weather vanes. It's a pleasing shop presided over by a warm, obliging, and knowledgeable owner.

L'ÉPOQUE

30 East 10th Street
353-0972
Mon.–Fri.: 10 a.m.–6 p.m.; Sat.: 11 a.m.–5 p.m.
No credit cards

L'Époque specializes in rare seventeenth- and eighteenth-century country armoires, tables, desks, buffets, vaisseliers, and chests that are authentic examples from the time of Louis XIII to Louis XVI. Made of cherry, walnut, and oak, the massive pieces fill L'Époque's spare and cavernous space. But owners Pete and Sandor Balint have smaller-scale furniture, too, along with exquisite reproductions of medieval tapestries that are hand-finished in France on nineteenth-century looms, bolts of provincial cotton fabrics that are sold by the yard, and charming rustic ceramics and dinnerware.

MAISON JEAN-FRANÇOIS

359 Bleecker Street
645-4774
Mon.–Fri.: 12 noon–6:30 p.m.; Sat: 12 noon–6 p.m.
MC, V

Come to Maison Jean-François for large-scale country pieces, Quimper faïence, and reproduction bronze Bouillotte lamps. The owner imports his French Country wares directly from France and always has a number of old farm tables, buffets, cupboards, and commodes, as well as a few smaller pieces and dining chairs. Jean-François's collection of Quimper is one of the most complete around, and he also offers a charming assortment of baskets and kitchen accessories, some old, some new.

MARTELL ANTIQUES

53 East 10th Street
777-4360
Mon.–Fri.: 10 a.m.–5:30 p.m.; Sat.: 11 a.m.–5 p.m.
No credit cards

Martell's large barnlike store is filled with eighteenth- and early-nineteenth-century country furniture from Normandy, Brittany, and Arles that's more formal and elaborate than what's generally thought of as "country." Buffets, servers, commodes, settees, cupboards, and armoires are handsomely carved from oak, walnut, cherry, and fruitwood, then rubbed till they glow.

PIERRE DEUX

369 Bleecker Street

243-7740
Mon.–Sat.: 10 a.m.–6 p.m. (Closed Sat. in summer)
No credit cards

870 Madison Avenue, at 71st Street
570-9343
Mon.–Sat.: 10 a.m.–6 p.m.
AE, MC, V (uptown only)

The two Pierres, Pierre LeVec and Pierre Moulin, have filled their irresistible shops with eighteenth- and nineteenth-century French Country furniture (mostly from Provence), decorative accessories, and pretty printed-cotton Souleiado fabrics (also from Provence). The original store (at 369) carries the antique furniture: honey-colored loveseats, cupboards, armoires, chests, commodes, tables, and chairs. At the uptown store you'll find the tiny-patterned Souleiado fabrics transformed into an exuberant array of dresses, tablecloths, place mats, napkins, pillows, makeup cases, and statusy handbags. Also in evidence are reproduction pewter serving plates, mugs, and candlesticks, charming faïence dishes by Moustier, and bolts of the Souleiado fabrics that can be purchased by the yard.

RENÉ
Hand-painted Swedish country-pine furniture can be custom-ordered. (See **Gifts**, p. 309.)

R. J. KING & COMPANY
Farm tables, benches, and armoires. (See **French and European Furniture**, p. 253.)

T & K ANTIQUES
120 Wooster Street, near Prince Street
219-2472
Mon.–Fri.: 11 a.m.–6 p.m.; Sat.: 12 noon–6 p.m.
All major

Gregory and Annick Kerwin's sunny, loft-size shop is crowded with splendid examples of eighteenth- and nineteenth-century French country antiques. So come here for oversized armoires from Normandy or smaller-size wedding chests from Bressane in warm woods such as walnut, cherry, and chestnut. Or for refectory tables, cupboards, and buffets, polished wrought-iron chairs and tables made from vintage molds, or classic rattan bistro chairs. But come, too, for the Kerwins' unique, one-of-a-kind treasures: grape baskets from Burgundy, brass dental cabinets from the twenties, porcelain sinks, copper bathtubs, doll beds and carriages, wicker and iron bird cages, trade signs from the eighteenth century, nineteenth-century tile stoves, cheese draining racks with their original paint, and wicker holders for baguettes.

UMBRELLO

379 West Broadway
941-7800
Mon.–Sat.: 11:30 a.m.–7 p.m.; Sun. 12 noon–6 p.m.
AE, MC, V

Umbrello stretches from West Broadway to Wooster Street and swallowed up in this cavernous space is one of the largest selections of Southwestern furniture in the city. Here, among walls mottled and glazed in desert colors, are antique armoires and cupboards—many with their original paint—along with the store's exclusive line of Santa Fe Heritage pieces that includes everything from overstuffed sofas to rocking chairs, bed frames, and children's furniture. Old drying racks hung with woven carriage blankets and rustic wooden tables set with terra-cotta jugs reinforce the look of the Old West. Among the small-scale finds are handsome paper-covered bandboxes, iron candlesticks, a fine selection of candles, corn chips and salsa dips, potpourri, and wooden bowls.

CUTTING-EDGE FURNITURE

ARCHETYPE

411 East 9th Street
529-5880
Wed.–Sun.: 1 p.m.–6 p.m.
MC, V

Architectural designers Robert J. Gaul and Iris de Mauro have created an appropriate setting for their gallery's avant-garde furnishings. They made floors and counter tops out of particle board, punched lighting fixtures out of galvanized sheet metal, and used steel and bronze washers they picked up for pennies as detail elements on the cabinets and walls. The gallery features the work of fifteen furniture and five jewelry designers, and everything is handcrafted and one-of-a-kind. You might find Kate Loye's "house" chair with an Astroturf "lawn" seat, a coffee table of solid granite, wool rugs by Vlasta Volcano and Gaul, a cabinet of bird's-eye maple, over-scaled torchères and sconces of spun aluminum, or a red aluminum "R" table lamp. The accessories are as assertive as the furniture and include sandblasted barware, patinated metal bowls, medieval-looking spoons, and stone candlesticks.

CIVILIZATION

A well-edited selection of small-scale furniture that might include funky guitar-shaped coffee tables and wild chairs. (See **Handcraft Galleries,** p. 323.)

CLODAGH, ROSS, AND WILLIAMS
122 St. Marks Place
505-1774
Mon.–Wed., Sun.: 12 noon–7 p.m.; Thurs.–Sat.: 12 noon–8 p.m.
AE, MC, V

Ivy Ross, Clodagh, and Sherry Jo Williams's shop wittily mirrors the spirit of the East Village with its scratched windows, graffiti-covered walls, and rough cement floor, and they've filled this exciting architectural space with the best of the new-wave designers. Among the inspired stock you might find Mark Schaeffer's cast-concrete and stainless-steel cone table, and Steve Buss's sanded aluminum and brass coffee table. There are Furniture Club's tinted concrete lamps and mirrors, James Evanson's skyscraper lighting, and a host of aggressive tabletop items—pewter vases, anodized aluminum flatware, *faux* concrete candleholders, sandblasted serving trays, and oxidized copper bowls and candlesticks. The jewelry is as unique as the furnishings, mostly because of the unexpected mix of materials, and might include earrings of sterling silver and sandblasted Plexiglas, butterfly-wing brooches, rubber and 24-karat-gold bracelets, and colored plastic-and-gold leaf necklaces.

D. F. SANDERS
An arresting assortment of mostly black, minimalist furniture that includes dining tables and chairs, webbed chaise longues, assorted folding stools, and rolling carts. (See **Housewares and Hardware,** p. 337.)

FURNITURE OF THE TWENTIETH CENTURY
227 West 17th Street
Second floor
929-6023
Mon.–Fri.: 10 a.m.–6 p.m.
No credit cards

Furniture of the Twentieth Century is a wholesale operation that also sells to individuals, and in its no frills warehouse the company carries the very best examples of twentieth-century design. Philippe Starck's skeletal pieces—his leggy "Sarapis" stool and his "Mickville" folding table—share the space with Zanotta furniture, Pierre Chareau's fan table, and the "Teulada" television trolley. There's an appealing selection of reissues of classic carpets from the thirties as well as rugs by contemporary artists that were inspired by the Russian Constructivists and the Art Deco and Art Nouveau movements.

GILES & COMPANY
444 Columbus Avenue, near 81st Street

362-5330
Mon.–Fri.: 11 a.m.–7:30 p.m.; Sat.: 11 a.m.–7 p.m.; Sun.: 12 noon–
6 p.m.

Giles & Lewis
464 Columbus Avenue, near 82nd Street
362-5330
Mon.–Fri.: 10 a.m.–7:30 p.m.; Sat.: 11 a.m.–7 p.m.; Sun. 12 noon–
6 p.m.
AE, MC, V

Giles & Company is a multilevel gallery stocked with an eclectic mix of classic and trendy modern furniture designs. You'll find Charles Rennie Mackintosh's "Hill House" chair, Frank Lloyd Wright's "Allen" dining table, and chairs and tables by Alvar Aalto and the Saarinens (Eliel and Eero). Among the cutting-edge new designers are Pascal Mourgue and his textured-metal table, Philippe Starck's leggy stools, and Charles Jenck's trend-setting skinny cabinets. Generously mixed with the furniture are rugs, tabletop accessories by such illustrious names as Alessi, Swid-Powell, and Georg Jensen, and an artful array of sterling-silver and gold jewelry and watches. Just up the street is **Giles & Lewis,** the company's smaller shop that offers less furniture, but a good selection of tabletop, desk, and gift items.

MELODROM FURNITURE
525 Broadway, near Spring Street
Eighth floor
219-0013
Mon.–Fri.: 10 a.m.–5 p.m.; Sat. by appointment
AE, MC, V

Melodrom represents nearly a dozen advanced designers, and its cavernous loft is filled with a host of radical European designs rarely seen in this country. There's Stefan Wewerka's three-legged chair and his complete kitchen that's mounted on a single pole, along with iron and stone coffee tables. But Melodrom also carries the best of the classics—re-editions of Jean Prouvé's metal folding chair, Marcel Breuer's Bauhaus vitrine, and Gerrit Rietveld's hanging lamp.

MODERN AGE
795 Broadway, near 10th Street
674-5603
Mon.–Fri.: 10 a.m.–6 p.m.; Sat.: 11 a.m.–6 p.m.
AE, MC, V

In its early years Modern Age was a source for Art Moderne furniture produced between the wars, but now the gallery carries cutting-edge new designs. Although some of the pieces look Retro, most reflect the minimalist sensibility of Italian designers, so you'll find Zeus's stackable rubber-and-leather chairs, along with skinny Italian tables, dressers, vanities, and desks. Among the sleek accessories are black-lacquer clothes trees and umbrella stands, lighting, appealing tabletop items such as oxidized copper bowls and etched crystal vases and barware, standing and table lamps and a compelling group of artist-designed, hand-crafted carpets.

NOLTE
110 Wooster Street
431-0162
Mon.–Fri.: 11 a.m.–5 p.m.; Sat.: 2 p.m.–5 p.m.
AE

Nolte's rusted iron columns and dark wood floors are an appropriate backdrop for its mostly German furniture of strong design. You might find Thomas Wendtland's starkly sculptural stainless-steel and patinated-copper tables, Torsten Neeland's rugged steel-frame chairs upholstered in hand-painted suede, and Alexander Vether's dramatic stone-and-steel screens, along with a chaise longue of steel mesh, and assorted decorative accessories—candlesticks, dishes, and vases—that are as original as the furniture.

SEE, LTD.
118 Spring Street
226-0038
Tues.–Sat.: 11 a.m.–7 p.m.; Sun.: 12 noon–7 p.m.
MC, V

SEE stands for Spatial Environmental Elements, and it's the brainchild of two architects, Leora Douek and Carolyn Walton, who wanted to make avant-garde furniture available to customers without the need for a decorator. Much of the collection comes from Spain and Italy, most of it is scaled to apartment living, and many of the pieces are multifunctional—a handsome leather sofa converts to a bed, a table rises from coffee-table to dining height, and a ladder-back desk chair turns into a high stool. Aficionados of inventive design will find Philippe Starck's skeletal chairs and tables, Vicente Martinez's rolling bookcase, and Stan Magnan and Gary Payne's innovative lighting.

URBAN BOB-KAT
130 Spring Street
925-7170
Tues.–Sun.: 12 noon–6 p.m.
No credit cards

Kathy and Bob Flora are the design team behind Urban Bob-Kat, and they offer custom-made "fantasy" furniture. Plywood or composition board cabinets and entertainment units are the Floras' specialty, and they make them to the customer's specifications, then paint them with any number of opulent *faux* finishes. Styles range from Memphis to "Miami Vice" to Classic Revival.

UZZOLO
565 Broadway, at Prince Street
219-2225
Mon.–Sat.: 11 a.m.–6 p.m.; Sun: 12 noon–6 p.m.
All major

Uzzolo means whimsical or capricious in Italian and this home furnishings emporium is true to its name. It's housed in a 11,000-square-foot landmark building in which the original architectural elements have been retained—white marble, fluted columns, and wide wooden-planked floors—and it's filled with everything in black: upholstered furniture, tables, lighting, housewares, and gifts. Even the men's clothing comes in basic black-and-white. There's a witty catacomb-like entrance to the downstairs display area, where you'll find the larger upholstered pieces, along with beds and dining sets. Upstairs is the impressive selection of floor, desk, and table lamps; the occasional tables; and the tabletop and desk accessories. Here, too, is the jewelry and men's clothing. Uzzolo carries Charpentier's Spider Chair, Amisco's eccentric Bicycle Chair, as well as accessories that are equally light-hearted. A tiny espresso maker resembles a faucet, salt and pepper shakers look like crushed paper, and rough-cut marble slabs are sushi servers.

ORIENTALIA

ART ASIA
1086 Madison Avenue, near 81st Street
249-7250
Mon.–Sat.: 10 a.m.–6 p.m.; Sun.: 12 noon–6 p.m.
AE, D, MC, V

Art Asia offers few surprises, yet this small shop's mix of Oriental antiques is appealing. There's a nicely edited selection of small-scale Tanzu chests, along with antique silk kimonos, early Imari and export porcelains, lacquerware boxes and bowls, and fine Japanese woodblock prints. Vintage ivory bracelets, chunky cinnabar necklaces, and a stylish group of contemporary Asian jewelry fill the glass cases.

ASIAN ART GALLERY
5 East 57th Street
Seventh floor
688-7243
Mon.–Fri.: 9:30 a.m.–5 p.m; or by appointment

Despite its name, the Asian Art Gallery specializes in furniture, not art, and fine examples of nineteenth-century Chinese, Japanese, and Korean furnishings are attractively displayed in this pleasant shop. There's a myriad of lacquer coffee tables, rosewood chairs, and storage cabinets, along with an exemplary selection of antique screens. Also in evidence are early porcelains, pottery, and Korean celadons.

THE CHINESE PORCELAIN COMPANY
822 Madison Avenue, near 68th Street
Second floor
628-4101
Mon.–Fri.: 10 a.m.–5:30 p.m.; Sat.: 11 a.m.–5 p.m.; closed Sat. in summer
AE

At the Chinese Porcelain Company exquisite examples of Chinese works of art, furniture, and ceramics are displayed in an elegant setting. Among the pedigreed export porcelains from the seventeenth and eighteenth centuries are such rare pieces as a blue-and-white porcelain *kendi* from the late Ming dynasty, and blue-and-white porcelain Monteith bowls. The furniture is just as splendid and might include a Chinese export lacquer davenport, a seventeenth-century altar coffer, an unusual Huang Huali painting table, and a nineteenth-century cane settee. There are exceptional carpets from China and the border regions; lacquer boxes; China trade pictures, maps, and engravings; along with intricately carved brush pots, handsome table screens, and small jade and ivory works of art suitable for a scholar's table.

DIDIER AARON, INC.
An eclectic mix of Oriental *objets* and furniture. (See **French and European Furniture**, p. 248.)

E. & J. FRANKEL LTD.
1040 Madison Avenue, near 78th Street
879-5733
Mon.–Sat.: 10 a.m.–5:30 p.m.
V

Edith and Joel Frankel's spacious gallery is one of the three oldest in the city specializing in Oriental antiques, and it houses splendid Chinese, Japanese, and Oriental furniture, art, and *objets*. Edith Frankel chaired the department of Far Eastern studies at the New School, and she and her husband's lifelong dedication to Oriental arts has enabled them to put together an outstanding collection. Chinese pieces date from the Shang to the Ching dynasties, and Japanese treasures from the Fugiwara to the Meiji periods. Among the temptations are screens, rugs, jades, jewelry, kimonos, bronzes, lacquerware, paintings, ivory netsuke, and priceless porcelains and pottery.

FLYING CRANES ANTIQUES
Manhattan Art & Antiques Center
1050 Second Avenue, near 55th Street
223-4600
Mon.–Sat.: 10:30 a.m.–6 p.m.
All major

Japanese arts of the eighteenth and nineteenth centuries fill every corner of this cluttered gallery. Small-scale furniture, ivories, cloisonné (including massive cloisonné palace vases), satsuma, bronzes, and silver are the main attractions, but Imari ware and Chinese export porcelains are here as well.

FRANK CARO GALLERY
41 East 57th Street
Second floor
753-2166
Tues.–Sat.: 10 a.m.–5:30 p.m.; closed during August
No credit cards

Frank Caro offers an excellent collection of Indian, Southeast Asian, and Chinese art that includes traditional furniture, paintings, bronze ware, screens, decorative objects, porcelains, and ceramics. Among the ever-changing furniture you'll find rosewood chairs, tables, and lacquer pieces. Although most of Caro's treasures date from the Shang dynasty to the eighteenth century, he carries a few contemporary Chinese things as well.

GARRICK C. STEPHENSON
Seventeenth-century Chinese lacquer tables and screens. (See **French and European Furniture,** p. 249.)

J. J. LALLY & COMPANY ORIENTAL ART
42 East 57th Street
Third floor
371-3380
Mon.–Fri.: 9 a.m.–5 p.m.
No credit cards

James J. Lally formerly headed up Sotheby's Chinese Art Department, and he went on to serve as president of Sotheby's in New York for four years, but in 1986 Lally left the auction world to open his own Asian art gallery. As might be anticipated, he's filled it with magnificent objects of the finest pedigree. Quietly displayed, in two serene rooms, are ceramics and ancient works of art that include pottery, jade, lacquer, silver, gold, and bronzes from the neolithic period to the eighteenth century. You might find an archaic bronze wine vessel from the Shang dynasty, a glorious pair of stools, a pottery Han horse, and ancient jade disks. Although costly, Lally's offerings are of museum quality.

KOREANA ART AND ANTIQUES
963 Madison Avenue, near 75th Street
249-0400
Mon.–Sat.: 11 a.m.–6 p.m.
All major

A serious but friendly shop, Koreana Art and Antiques offers the usual and the unusual in Korean antiques. Everything dates to the eighteenth and nineteenth centuries, and among the beguiling mix are magnificent Korean cabinets of gingko and elm with brass fittings, irresistible hand-carved "wedding" ducks, hand-painted papier-mâché bridal boxes, handsome lacquerware, splendid small tables, along with paintings, traditional ceramics, and charming examples of Korean folk art.

KRISHNA GALLERY OF ASIAN ARTS, INC.
Place des Antiquaires
125 East 57th Street
249-1677
Mon.–Sat.: 11 a.m.–6 p.m.
AE

For years Krishna Nathan's shop, Vajra Arts, was a fixture on Madison Avenue, but Nathan has now installed his Asian art works in the Place des Antiquaires. His attractive gallery offers the arts of Tibet, Nepal, and India that date from the second century B.C. to the nineteenth century A.D., and it's crowded with powerful bronze and terra-cotta sculptures and colorful Tibetan Tanka paintings, with temple carvings, and bold tribal and folk jewelry.

MATTHEW SCHUTZ LTD.
Pedigreed Chinese export porcelains, Japanese and Chinese lacquer furniture, and Oriental bronzes that date from the seventeenth to the early nineteenth centuries. (See **French and European Furniture,**p. 251.)

MICHAEL B. WEISBROD, INC.
987 Madison Avenue, near 76th Street
734-6350
Mon.–Fri.: 9:30 a.m.–5 p.m.
No credit cards

Collectors come to the Michael Weisbrod gallery in the Carlyle Hotel for museum-quality Oriental antiques that date from the neolithic period to the nineteenth century. Ancient Chinese bronzes, famille-verte and blue-and-white porcelains from the Ming dynasty, early cloisonné, Buddhist sculptures, furniture, jade, ivory, Chinese glass, and pottery are among Weisbrod's broad range of specialties. You'll find Ming and early-Ching exotic-wood pieces among the furniture selection, and such rare pottery treasures as an eighteenth-century teadust-glazed vase and a Sung-dynasty celadon censer.

285

NAGA ANTIQUES LTD.
145 East 61st Street
593-2788
Mon.–Fri.: 10 a.m.–5 p.m.
No credit cards

Naga Antiques is a serene gallery that is located in a handsome town house complete with a Japanese garden, and it offers an eclectic mix of Japanese collectibles. In addition to a large and comprehensive selection of Japanese art, you'll discover antique furniture, fine lacquerware, rare hand-painted eighteenth-century screens, tables, jars, dolls, baskets, and tea ceremony accoutrements. From an exquisitely detailed six-fold screen to a humorously carved fifteenth-century life-sized lion, the range is broad, and it is all temptingly displayed.

NURI FARHADI, INC.
920 Third Avenue, near 55th Street
355-5462
Mon.–Fri.: 10 a.m.–5 p.m.
No credit cards

Nuri Farhadi is a dusty, cluttered gallery that does not welcome browsers, but if you're a serious shopper and know what you want, you're sure to find it on Farhadi's three crammed-full floors. This shop stocks the city's largest collection of Chinese porcelains, and in addition to endless stacks of plates, platters, and bowls it carries dozens of porcelain vases, teapots, and lamps. Jade and hard-stone carvings, antique Chinese paintings, furniture, bronzes, and ivories are also part of this gallery's enormous stock.

ORIENTATIONS ORIENTAL ART LTD.
Place des Antiquaires
125 East 57th Street
371-9006
Mon.–Sat.: 11 a.m.–6 p.m.
AE, MC, V

Opulent eighteenth- and nineteenth-century Japanese decorative arts fill every corner of this well-stocked gallery. Cloisonné enamels, Satsuma, Okimono, vibrant lacquers, and intricately carved netsuke are among the attractive mix.

PHILIPPE FARLEY
Chinese export lacquer furniture and screens made for the European market, along with Japanese lacquerware. (See **French and European Furniture**, p. 252.)

RALPH M. CHAIT GALLERIES
One of the city's oldest sources for period Oriental antiques: porcelains, pottery, silver, jade, crystal, bronzes, and paintings from the

Neolithic period to the nineteenth century. (See **China and Glassware,** p. 70.)

THE REGAL COLLECTION
5 West 56th Street
582-7696
Mon.–Sat.: 9 a.m.–6 p.m.
All major

The Regal Collection has been assembled by Albert Harari, an inveterate collector, and it consists of nineteenth-century *objets d'art*, porcelains, netsuke, and carved jades. Everything is attractively displayed in this large and spacious store, and among the finds are exquisite hand-carved Chinese snuffboxes in unusual shapes, rock crystal bowls, Chinese porcelain urns, and pedestal tables in exotic woods.

STAIR AND COMPANY
A comprehensive selection of very fine Oriental furniture and lacquerwork. (See **English Period Furniture,** p. 245.)

SUGIMOTO WORKS OF ART
120 East 64th Street
431-6176
By appointment only
No credit cards

Understated and serene, Hiroshi Sugimoto's gallery is perhaps the best source outside of Japan for museum-quality period Japanese ceramics, paintings, and sculptures. The treasures span 3,000 years, and range from Japanese calligraphy, to Shigaraki clay storage jars, to contemporary bamboo baskets.

THINGS JAPANESE
Scroll paintings, nineteenth-century Imari and Kutani porcelains and pottery, old Japanese and Korean chests and boxes. (See **Ethnic Items,** p. 213.)

WICKER, BAMBOO, BENTWOOD, TWIG, AND RATTAN FURNITURE
ANTIQUE

ALICE'S ANTIQUES

A small well-edited collection of Victorian wicker furniture, along with thirties bamboo pieces. (See **Art Deco/Art Nouveau Furniture and Objets**, p. 233.)

ANN LAWRENCE ANTIQUES

Scores of antique English bamboo-and-lacquer tables, armoires, bureaus, along with wicker chaise longues. (See **Linens and Quilts**, p. 381.)

ANTIQUE CACHE

Manhattan Arts and Antiques Center
1050 Second Avenue, near 55th Street
752-0838
Mon.–Sat.: 10:30 a.m.–5:30 p.m.
AE

Antique English bamboo and lacquer furniture is increasingly hard to find, but Tillie Steinberg scours England for pieces to add to her inventory, and she has one of the city's largest collections. Her tiny gallery is crammed with bookcases, desks, étagères, chests of drawers, and assorted ravishing tables. Most are Victorian, many have chinoiserie lacquered panels, and almost all are in pristine condition. Steinberg also has a passion for pens and inkwells, letter boxes and letter scales, tea caddies and snuffboxes. Her shop offers an enticing array, and Steinberg's prices are excellent.

THE GAZEBO

Antique and reproduction Victorian wicker furniture that includes rocking chairs, love seats, settees, tables, étagères, and lamps. (See **Linens and Quilts**, p. 385.)

HAMILTON-HYRE LTD.

413 Bleecker Street
989-4509
Mon.–Fri.: 12 noon–7 p.m.; Sat.: 12 noon–6 p.m.; closed Sat. in summer
No credit cards

A tiny friendly shop, Hamilton-Hyre specializes in European and American faux-bamboo furniture, and the shop always has a small but well-chosen collection. On a recent visit there was a handsome cheval dressing mirror by Horner, a nineteenth-century bamboo and bird's-eye maple Davenport desk, assorted tables, a few bureaus, along with chairs and a table made of antlers; majolica, and antique crystal lamps.

HUBERT DES FORGES
Among the selection of small-scale bamboo pieces you'll find desks, assorted tables, bureaus, and étagères. (See **Gifts**, p. 294.)

JUDITH AMDUR
1193 Lexington Avenue, near 80th Street
879-0653
Mon.–Sat.: 11 a.m.–6 p.m.

950 Lexington Avenue, near 69th Street
472-2691
Mon.–Sat.: 11 a.m.–6 p.m.

Pimlico Way
1028 Lexington Avenue, near 73rd Street
439-7855
Mon.–Sat.: 11 a.m.–6 p.m.
AE, MC, V

Judith Amdur was one of the first antiques dealers in the city to bother with Victoriana, and her spacious uptown shop and her newer gallery, **Pimlico Way**, are crammed with one of the city's largest collections of English Victorian bamboo furniture. Many have lacquered chinoiserie panels, and Amdur carries everything from side tables to desks, to whatnots, to chests of drawers. Mixed in with the bamboo pieces are scores of sterling-silver picture frames in all sizes, tea caddies, desk accessories, blue-and-white export china, lamps made from antique Japanese and Chinese vases, candlesticks, snuffboxes, and other irresistibles. Her smaller store at 950 Lexington Avenue offers eighteenth- and nineteenth-century brass, so you'll find fire tools, andirons, and screens, telescopes, picture frames, wooden coal buckets, boxes, corkscrews, and lots of other handsome gifts.

MURRAY HILL ANTIQUE CENTER
201 East 31st Street
686-6221
Mon.–Fri.: 12 noon–7 p.m.; Sat.: 12 noon–6 p.m.; Sun. by appointment
AE, MC, V

A small-scale antiques center, Murray Hill is run by Larry Dupuis, and he and eight dealers offer a cozy mix of late nineteenth century through forties antique and vintage collectibles. Natural rattan, bamboo, wicker, and split-reed furniture fills the shop, and you might find a wicker daybed, a rattan chaise, bamboo sofas and chairs, and assorted tables among the ever-changing inventory. The center is also well-stocked with advertising collectibles, as well as formal and kitschy china and glassware that dates from Victorian times through the thirties. There's a winning selection of bed and table linens from the same period as well.

NEWEL ART GALLERIES INC.
Antique English bamboo furniture in every size and style—dozens of cabinets, desks, whatnots, chairs, chaise longues, chests of drawers, small end tables, and settees. (See **French and European Furniture,** p. 251.)

PIMLICO WAY
See **Judith Amdur,** p. 289.

R. BROOKE LTD.
A small but very special collection of Victorian bamboo furniture. (See **Gifts,** p. 297.)

SECOND HAND ROSE
Bamboo chairs, sofas, love seats, and tables from the thirties and forties. (See **Retro Furniture,** p. 257.)

T. & K. ANTIQUES
French rattan café chairs and tables from the twenties and thirties, along with reproductions by the company that originally made them. (See **Country Furniture,** p. 277.)

TREVOR POTTS ANTIQUES
Excellent examples of English bamboo furniture, many with chinoiserie lacquer-work panels. (See **English Period Furniture,** p. 246.)

THE WICKER GARDEN
1318 Madison Avenue, near 93rd Street
410-7000
Mon.–Sat.: 10 a.m.–5:30 p.m.
AE, MC, V

Pamela Scurry's shop resembles the lovely Victorian rooms she helps others re-create. It's replete with frothy confections of Victorian wicker, frilly pillows, fanciful boudoir mirrors, patchwork quilts, old doorstops, and other irresistible treasures. Among the top-notch nineteenth- and early-twentieth-century white and natural wicker are signed Heywood-Wakefield pieces, and Scurry offers everything from spectacular love-seats to chairs with bird-cage legs, to curlicue tea carts, to delicately scrolled planters, to corner chairs with cornucopia backs. The upstairs gallery is a nursery filled with a delectable array of cribs, dressers, changing tables, and accessories fit for a tiny prince or princess, with prices to match. Upstairs, too, you'll find Scurry's exquisite collection of linens, some of which are antique, others that only look old.

CONTEMPORARY

B. Altman & Co., Bloomingdale's, Lord & Taylor, and Macy's offer re-creations of Victorian white-wicker furniture, as well as more contemporary stained-wicker pieces.

ABC ANTIQUES
A vast stock of chairs, chaise longues, love seats, and coffee tables in white, natural, and pastel-stained wicker, as well as handcrafted willow granny rockers, chairs, coffee tables, and love seats. (See **Country Furniture,** p. 272.)

AZUMA
251 East 86th Street
369-4928
Mon.–Sat.: 10 a.m.–8 p.m.; Sun.: 11 a.m.–7:30 p.m.
AE, MC, V

Azuma no longer carries the large stock of wicker furniture it once did, yet it's still possible to find very functional and inexpensive pieces on the downstairs level of the 86th Street store. Small tables, bed frames, trunks, étagères, chests of drawers, trunks, and bookcases, in both white and natural wicker, were among the recent mix.

CONRAN'S HABITAT
An appealing array of white-wicker furniture, along with Lloyd Loom–style wicker chairs, and stained-wicker pieces. (See **Contemporary Furniture,** p. 267.)

DEUTSCH
31 East 32nd Street
683-8746
Mon.–Fri.: 9 a.m.–5 p.m.; Sat: 10 a.m.–4 p.m.; closed Sat. in summer
No credit cards

Deutsch has been in the business of selling wicker for more than thirty years, and although this family-run company is primarily a wholesale operation, current owner Roger Deutsch sells retail, too. There are more than 800 rattan, wicker, and bamboo designs imported from Italy, Hong Kong, the Philippines, and Indonesia displayed in Deutsch's cavernous showroom, and styles range from classic Victorian, to Indian Raga, to simple contemporary. Dressers, bookcases, headboards, chaise longues, settees, chairs, tables, sofas, trunks, bar stools, mirrors, even children's chairs are available in natural wicker, white, or painted any color desired.

THE GAZEBO

The large selection of Victorian-style white and natural wicker furniture includes rocking chairs, love seats, tables, étagères, hassocks, and standing lamps. (See **Linens and Quilts,** p. 385.)

HANDBLOCK

A small, well-edited collection of Victorian-style white wicker furniture, along with stained-wicker pieces. (See **Ethnic Items,** p. 211.)

LAYTNER'S HOME FURNISHINGS

Twenties-style hand-woven wicker chairs, ottomans, couches, and tables in natural or pastels. (See **Contemporary Furniture,** p. 270.)

T. & K. ANTIQUES

Reproductions of vintage French bistro chairs by the company that originally made them. (See **Country Furniture,** p. 277.)

THE WICKERY

342 Third Avenue, at 25th Street
889-3669
Mon.–Sat.: 10:30 a.m.–6:30 p.m.
AE, MC, V

Wicker and rattan furniture, accessories, and baskets fill every corner of this cluttered store. Among the mix are both Victorian-inspired and contemporary pieces in everything from oversized sofas to small end tables. White Victorian-style rockers, natural-wicker love seats and sofas, and stained-wicker sofas and chairs are among the Wickery's popular stock. Prices are good and the sales staff helpful.

ZONA

A small but winning collection of stained-wicker chairs, ottomans, and love seats. (See **Handcraft Galleries,** p. 328.)

Gifts

ANTIQUE

See also **China and Glassware, Antique; Silver, Antique; and Jewelry, Antique.**

ALIX & ALIXIS
956 Lexington Avenue, near 69th Street
772-8867
Mon.–Tues., Fri.: 10 a.m.–6 p.m.; Wed., Thurs.: 10 a.m.–6:30 p.m.;
Sat.: 11 a.m.–5:30 p.m.
AE, MC, V

Barbara Sela's vest-pocket-size shop is a mix of treasures new and old.
Antique and vintage pitchers, dresser trays, and perfume bottles share
this tiny space with custom-made tablecloths, mirrors with *faux*-ivory
frames made from aged molds, and opera scarves that only look old.
There are Beatrix Potter and Kate Greenaway illustrations (the prints
are new, the maple frames vintage), unusual dried-flower arrangements, silk-moiré-covered photo albums, lace-trimmed towels, rag
rugs, and kittens, dogs, and bears made from antique linens. But there
are also the occasional small antique scrubbed-pine dresser, blanket
chest, or wicker table.

ANTIQUE CACHE
A handsome group of antique pens, brass scales, Victorian wood letter boxes, brass and tortoiseshell snuffboxes, mahogany humidors,
ivory-handled magnifying glasses and paper knives, crystal inkwells,
wooden candlesticks. (See **Furniture,** p. 288.)

BOB PRYOR ANTIQUES
1023 Lexington Avenue, near 73rd Street
688-1516
Mon.–Sat.: 11 a.m.–5:30 p.m.; closed Sat. in summer
AE, MC, V

Bob Pryor's tiny treasure box teems with collectibles from the eighteenth and nineteenth centuries. The shop is best known for its abundance of brass and copper, and these metals are seen to advantage in the fine old candlesticks, sconces, jelly molds, fire tools, saucepans, skimmers, and ladles. But there are other treats as well: unusual examples of English treen snuffboxes and nutcrackers, antique hand-carved corkscrews, ivory-handled magnifying glasses, silver and mother-of-pearl card cases, Bristol blue glass, match strikers, and inkwells.

CHARLOTTE MOSS & CO.
131 East 70th Street
772-3320
Mon.–Fri.: 10 a.m.–5:30 p.m.; Sat.: 11 a.m.–5 p.m.
AE, MC, V

Charlotte Moss is an ex-banker who decided to give up banking for business, and she's created a warm and cozy shop that resembles an old English country house. Victorian papier-mâché tables, Chinese export porcelains, brass and wood candlesticks, and lacquer tea caddies are everywhere, joined by enough mahogany-urn lamps, needlepoint cushions, botanical prints, leather-bound volumes, picture frames, and sundry other smallish English bibelots to re-create the fashionable look of Victorian clutter. Mixed in with the antiques are Moss's newly crafted classics—mirrored wall sconces, obelisk book cabinets, chintz-rosette picture bows, painted fire screens, all manner of drapery tassels, and fabric-covered luggage racks. There are a few important pieces of furniture as well, along with reproduction four-poster beds that can be custom ordered.

HUBERT DES FORGES
1193 Lexington Avenue, at 81st Street
744-1857
Mon.–Fri.: 10 a.m.–6 p.m.; Sat.: 11 a.m.–5 p.m.;
closed Sat. in summer
AE, MC, V

Hubert des Forges's windows and store are piled high with attractive small-scale treasures. Victorian bamboo pieces—tables, chests, secretaires, and cabinets—account for most of the clutter, but they're joined by vintage bird cages, hand-carved Black Forest bear umbrella stands, tole watering cans, needlepoint pillows, and framed prints. There are treats for the table—antique French majolica, cookie jars both old and new—along with an exuberant array of brightly printed tablecloths from the thirties and forties, and such new things as dishes and platters with a country look.

JAMES II GALLERIES
Among the riches are Victorian silver trays; crystal candlesticks; silver stuffing spoons, ladles, and berry spoons; ivory-handled magnifiers;

silver and ivory paper knives; crystal boudoir jars; and crystal decanters. (See **China and Glassware,** p. 67.)

J. MAVEC & COMPANY, LTD.
Sterling-silver baby spoons and mugs, Bilston enamel boxes, Edwardian cuff links, sterling-silver frames, tartanware, and treen. (See **Silver,** p. 441.)

JUDITH AMDUR
Trays, brass candlesticks, vases, brass and silver frames, tortoiseshell and treen boxes, tea caddies, match strikes, and assorted whatnots. (See **Furniture,** p. 289.)

JULIAN GRAHAM-WHITE, LTD.
957 Madison Avenue, near 75th Street
249-8181
Mon.–Sat.: 10 a.m.–6 p.m.
AE, MC, V

Julian Graham-White, an English nobleman and the shop's namesake, peers down from a painting over a mantel rescued from a Park Avenue home, and this gallery has a banister from Barbara Hutton's home and architectural fittings from the Carnegie mansion. The antiques are as eclectic as the interior, as distant as the eighteenth century, and as recent as the twenties. There's a sumptuous collection of tea caddies, decanters, treen boxes, fitted alligator suitcases, newel posts, crystal bibelots, and inkwells. But there are larger finds, too—a Carlton House desk and a rich assortment of cabinets, chairs, and tray tables. Best of all, the owners offer a 72-hour search service: if you can't find the *objet* you're looking for, they will locate the treasure and clear it through Customs within seventy-two hours—at no extra charge.

KENTSHIRE GALLERIES
In the Collector's Gallery are scores of cut-crystal decanters, silver and shagreen frames, ivory-handled magnifying glasses and letter openers, wood candlesticks, mahogany humidors, and lacquer tea caddies. (See **Furniture,** p. 243.)

KOGAN AND COMPANY
971 Madison Avenue, at 76th Street
Mezzanine
288-8523
Mon.–Sat.: 10:30 a.m.–6 p.m.
AE, MC, V

Barbara Kogan's gallery of decorative arts and home accessories encompasses eight rooms and it's chockful of predominantly English treasures, new and old. She has eighteenth-century chairs, Georgian paste jewelry, antique Spode and Derby china, and Victorian colored glass, as well as contemporary sterling-silver flatware, dried floral designs by Robert Day, Viscount Linley's porcelains, and stationery and leather goods from Smythson, in London. Sterling-silver frames, tea caddies, botanical prints, desktop accessories, and assorted Colefax and Fowler treats are among the other luxury items.

LINDA HORN ANTIQUES

Cut-crystal decanters; silver-topped crystal boudoir jars; shagreen, horn, tortoiseshell, and sterling-silver frames; ivory-handled magnifying glasses; horn mugs; and shell-encrusted boxes. (See **Furniture**, p. 251.)

MAN-TIQUES LTD.

Manhattan Art & Antiques Center
1050 Second Avenue, at 55th Street
759-1805
Mon.–Sat.: 11 a.m.–5:30 p.m.; Sun.: 12 noon–5:30 p.m.
AE

True to its name, this tiny gallery offers antique treasures for men. If he's a lover of ocean liners, Dickens, or polo, you'll find something appropriate here. But even if he's not, there's sure to be something among the intriguing assemblage of commemorative coronation ashtrays, scientific instruments, German beer steins, porcelain shaving mugs, brass scales and binoculars, ceramic match strikes, vintage cameras, and hand-carved or ivory- or silver-handled canes and walking sticks to please that hard-to-please gentleman.

MARCO POLO

1135 Madison Avenue, near 85th Street
734-3775
Mon.–Fri.: 10:30 a.m.–5:30 p.m.; Sat.: 12 noon–5 p.m.
AE, D, MC, V

A tempting selection of gifts—mostly antique and mostly English—crams every corner of this charming little shop. Counters and display cases are crowded with brass telescopes and binoculars, pens and inkwells, and magnifying glasses, not to mention letter openers, snuffboxes, sterling-silver picture frames, crystal-and-sterling-silver boudoir jars, and Battersea boxes.

M. H. STOCKROOM LTD.

654 Madison Avenue, near 60th Street
21st floor
752-6696
By appointment only
No credit cards

M. H. Stockroom is owned by Duane Hampton, wife of well-known interior designer Mark Hampton, and when she's not appearing at various social do's you'll find her ensconced in her snug little aerie high above Madison Avenue. Here she offers antique boxes of ivory, tortoise, and treen; Victorian silver-plate fruit knives and crumbers; antique majolica; framed botanicals; and wood and brass candlesticks. She stocks an enchanting selection of what English antiques dealers call "smalls"—old match strikers, lusterware pitchers, perfume bottles, vases. And items with a bookish slant: library steps, small bookcases, ivory-handled page turners, bookends, inkwells, even leather-bound books.

PISTON'S
Manhattan Art & Antiques Center
1050 Second Avenue, near 55th Street
753-8322
Mon.–Fri.: 10 a.m.–4 p.m.; Sat. by appointment
No credit cards

Collectors come to Fay Piston's tidy gallery for her museum-quality seventeenth- to nineteenth-century pewter, copper, and brass and for her vast knowledge of the field. Brass candlesticks, copper kettles, pewter platters and tankards, bell-metal andirons, and brass fire tools are all neatly arranged here. And Piston's collection of Victorian curtain tiebacks in metal and glass is one of the best and largest in the city.

R. BROOKE LTD.
138½ East 80th Street
628-3255
Mon.–Sat.: 10 a.m.–6 p.m.

960 Lexington Avenue, at 70th Street
535-0707
Mon.–Sat.: 10 a.m.–6 p.m.; closed Sat. in summer
AE

Hethea Nye's impeccable taste is everywhere apparent in the rich and varied jumble of the mostly English nineteenth-century country furniture and accessories that you'll find in both her East Side shops. Among her trove of treasures designed to help you re-create the look of Victorian clutter are antique papier-mâché tables, old bird cages, small-scaled bamboo furniture, tea caddies, oak and brass twist candlesticks, a myriad of needlepoint pillows, and export porcelains. Nye stocks tortoiseshell and silver frames, paisley shawls, and sterling-silver and crystal dressing table jars for the boudoir. Brass student lamps, mahogany trays with brass fittings, botanical engravings, horn mugs, and ivory-handled magnifying glasses for the library. And for the dandy—ivory- or silver-handled walking sticks.

T. J. ANTORINO
152 East 70th Street

297

628-4330
Mon.–Fri.: 12 noon–6 p.m.
AE, MC, V

Artfully arranged in a space no bigger than an alleyway, Thomas Antorino's shop offers an ever-changing assortment of seductive treasures. You might find French chintz pillows and drapes, Art Deco jewelry, vintage perfume bottles, and framed nineteenth-century paintings and illustrations. And since alligator and crocodile skins are one of Antorino's loves, there's always a striking assortment of billfolds, card cases, handbags, frames, and portmanteaus in these prized skins.

VITO GIALLO ANTIQUES
966 Madison Avenue, near 75th Street
535-9885
Mon.–Sat.: 10 a.m.–6 p.m.
AE, MC, V

Vito Giallo has a passion for everything from Victorian trade cards to Chinese porcelains, so his tiny store is a jumble of unexpected treats. Vintage fountain pens are a particular obsession, so you'll find handsome American, Japanese, Chinese, and French examples that are as early as the eighteenth century and as recent as the thirties, and his collection includes rare Watermans, Sheaffers, and Parkers—all in working order. Eighteenth-century paisley shawls; sterling-silver compotes, napkin rings, salt cellars, and tea strainers; antique lamps; match strikers; and magnifying glasses are among his other enthusiasms.

CONTEMPORARY

The department stores offer a wide selection of gift items. See also **Handcraft Galleries** and **Museum Gift Shops** sections.

ARCHETYPE
Cutting-edge glassware, carving sets, china, frames, vases, and desk accessories. (See **Furniture,** p. 278.)

ARIS MIXON
381 Amsterdam Avenue, near 79th Street
724-6904
Mon.–Fri.: 12 noon–7 p.m.; Sat.: 11 a.m.–6 p.m.;
Sun.: 1 p.m.–5:30 p.m.
MC, V

This friendly shop is a favorite with West Siders who come here for tasteful gifts both old and new. They come for the antique and vintage stemware and barware, whimsical thirties salt-and-pepper shakers, Victorian lusterware, cut-crystal vases, and old match strikers. And they come for cutting-edge ceramics, hand-crafted toys, hand-woven baskets, terra-cotta angels, and assorted small temptations. At Christmas this tiny shop dazzles with an abundance of winning tree ornaments and gifts.

ASPREY LIMITED
Trump Tower
725 Fifth Avenue, at 56th Street
688-1811
Mon.–Sat.: 10 a.m.–5:30 p.m.; closed Sat. in summer
All major

Asprey has been a British institution for more than 200 years, and in its New York outpost, as in London, it will make *anything* a customer wishes. But this venerable house's stock of ready-made items is so vast and eclectic it's difficult to name anything that's not already displayed on its three elegant floors. Handsome luggage; wool and cashmere throws; leather-bound books, photo albums, and cassette holders share the space with ivory bar tools and hairbrush sets; desk accessories; mother-of-pearl caviar servers; crystal claret jugs; silver frames; animals carved from semiprecious stones; and sterling-silver flatware. Equally broad is the selection of timepieces that ranges from brass carriage clocks, to shagreen quartz mantel examples, to tiny traveling alarm ones, to Victorian gold pocket watches, to Baume & Mercier wristwatches. And Asprey's gleaming counters hold a small but exquisite selection of antique jewelry that includes diamond brooches, intricately worked gold and diamond bracelets, and cuff links, along with nicely executed contemporary baubles.

BEN KARPEN BRASS CORPORATION
212 East 51st Street
755-3450
Mon.–Fri.: 9:15 a.m.–5:45 p.m.; Sat.: 10 a.m.–4 p.m.;
closed Sat. in summer
No credit cards

You may be blinded by the gleam of polished metal when you enter Carole and Gerry Benson's long and narrow shop that's crammed floor to ceiling with shiny brass. Umbrella stands, candlesticks, frames, fire tools, mirrors, coatracks, lamps, hooks, house numbers, and screens fill every bit of space. Larger pieces—coffee tables, tea and bar carts, brass headboards, planters, and baker's racks—can be custom-ordered.

THE BRASS LOFT
20 Greene Street

226-5467
Tues.–Sun.: 11 a.m.–5:30 p.m.;
July–Aug., Mon.–Fri.: 11 a.m.–5:30 p.m.
MC, V

In their large loft space Ruth and Gayle Hoffman stock myriad small
brass gift items, along with furniture and custom-made railings. A
family-run business, the Brass Loft has been around for forty years, and
among the eclectic mix are sconces, coatracks, fireplace screens, fire
tools, frames, candlesticks, umbrella stands, planters, hooks, hurricane lamps, and chandeliers.

CABBAGES & KINGS

Barbizon Hotel Arcade
813 Lexington Avenue, near 62nd Street
355-5513
Mon.–Sat.: 10 a.m.–6 p.m.
AE, MC, V

Cabbages & Kings calls itself a gift shop for executives, and it's brimful of small antiques and reproductions for the home or office. Pictures
are a specialty, so etchings of the hunt, sailing, polo, and other physi-
cal and outdoor pursuits (along with early maps) crowd the walls. And
dozens of humidors, cigar cases, and crystal decanters old and new,
desk accessories, glasses etched with birds and animals, trays with
hunting scenes, barware, and ice buckets are everywhere. True to the
shop's name, the collection of walruses in stone, brass, marble, faux
ivory, plush, and wood is mind-boggling.

CASA MAIA

1143 Park Avenue, near 91st Street
534-3615
Tues.–Fri.: 10:30 a.m.–6 p.m.; Sat.: 10 a.m.–6 p.m.;
closed Sat. in summer
AE, MC, V

Turquoise walls and latticework are the backdrop to floral designer
Ronaldo Maia's charming retail store that's filled with gifts and treats
for the home. Among the mix are faux marble trays, tin picnic baskets,
bowls and plates, and a variety of vases in pewter, copper, and brass.
Bath and table linens occupy one section of the shop, and these include
pillowcases, tea towels, and place mats. There's an unusual assortment of mirrors, scented rice paper fans wrapped in tiny cotton
scarves, a smattering of small-scale antiques, and, of course, a splendid stock of dried flowers and topiaries.

CHERCHEZ

862 Lexington Avenue, near 64th Street
737-8215

Mon.–Fri.: 11 a.m.–6 p.m.; Sat.: 11 a.m.–5 p.m.
AE, MC, V

Barbara Ohrbach's sweet-smelling store—redolent of herbs, sachets, and potpourri—is filled with gifts that are sweet as the scents. The owner's impeccable taste is apparent in the little girls' smocked dresses stitched from Liberty of London fabrics, in the antique English pottery and the white ironstone vases, the Colefax and Fowler floral chintz tablecloths, and the frothy Victorian linens for bed and table. Ohrbach has amassed a first-rate collection of antique paisley shawls, but she offers small treats as well—soap and soap dishes, beeswax candles, gardening books, diaries and agendas.

CIVILIZATION
Ceramics by Tom Garson and Susan Pakele, jewelry by Linda Hesh, tiny photo albums by Kathy Troup Greenberg, and witty candle holders. (See **Handcraft Galleries,** p. 323.)

CLODAGH, ROSS, AND WILLIAMS
Among the forward-look accessories you'll find sandblasted vases, woven metal baskets, jewel-toned anodized aluminum flatware, patinated candlesticks, and witty jewelry. (See **Cutting-Edge Furniture,** p. 279.)

CONTRE-JOUR
190 Columbus Avenue, near 68th Street
877-7900
Mon.–Sat.: 11 a.m.–8 p.m.; Sun.: 12 noon–6:30 p.m.
AE, MC, V

Bill Roach's small, airy store with its "floating" black-trimmed glass display cases once looked like an ultra-modern art gallery. But recently its high-tech interior has been softened by French floral tablecloths, antique majolica, and china with a Victorian air. The eclectic mix of merchandise ranges from machine-made to handmade items and includes hand-blown glass vases, Art Deco-inspired silver ice tongs, anodized aluminum napkin rings, candlesticks, picture frames, and clocks. Among Roach's small but very select assortment of jewelry is Ole Mathiesen's Swiss-made black leather wristwatch and the high-tech Pictowatch, Linda Hesh's silver-and-brass earrings and pins, and Peggy Johnson's sterling-silver "kitchen" jewelry.

CRYPTOGRAPHICS
40 East 32nd Street
685-3377
Mon.–Fri.: 9 a.m.–5 p.m.
MC, V

For the truly personal gift you might want to check out Crypto-graphics. This company engraves and silk-screens signs, shirts, and baseball hats, plaques, trophies, and awards with names or mes-sages and does them in any quantity. Cryptographics also carries a large selection of gifts—paperweights, mugs, bowls, and trays—that can be personalized.

DOT ZERO
165 Fifth Avenue, at 22nd Street
533-8322
Mon.–Fri.: 11 a.m.–7 p.m.; Sat.: 11 a.m.–6 p.m.; Sun.: 12 noon–5 p.m.;
closed Sun. in summer
AE, MC, V

Owners Kevin Brynan and Harvey Berstein have taken an unlikely mix—modern mat-black and stainless steel items of *good* design and quirky, nostalgic treats—and turned it into a success story. In their always crowded black high-tech mini-department store, sleek glass-and-steel tables, black leather attaché cases, and stainless steel desk accessories share the space with Slinkys and Lava lamps, model kits of the Invisible Man, square dice, basketballs that look like globes, and acid-colored roller skates. Bryan and Berstein carry lots of Lilliputian things as well: razors no bigger than a matchbook, credit card-size sewing kits and folding rulers, and tiny cameras.

E.A.T. GIFTS
1062 Madison Avenue, near 80th Street
861-2544
Mon.–Sat.: 10 a.m.–6 p.m.; Sun.: 12 noon–5 p.m.
AE

Once a sliver of a gift shop filled only with tiny treasures—inch-high Austrian candles, doll-size armoires stocked with linens, little French pincushions—E.A.T. Gifts has recently doubled in size and now also offers large-scale treats. The creation of Kim Staller, who has a talent for combining toys and foods in a way that's both childlike and sophisti-cated, shelves are artfully crammed with things for newborns, amus-ing gifts for traveling friends, games, puzzles, whimsical stuffed ani-mals, party favors, and unique place and menu cards. But there are practical things as well: mustards, teas, jams, and herbs, and splendid gift baskets. And for Baby: armoires, chests, and cribs hand-painted with Babar or pastoral scenes, kiddie-size furniture, and lamps, coatracks, and nursery room accessories.

THE ELDER CRAFTSMAN
Handmade picture frames and photo albums, desk accessories, needle-point pillows, crib quilts, and hand-carved toys. (See **Handcraft Galler-ies,** p. 324.)

FIVE EGGS
436 West Broadway
226-1606
Daily: 12 noon–7 p.m.
AE, MC, V

Elaine McKay's serene little shop, manned by a friendly staff, offers a winning array of Japanese products. Cozy cotton and cotton-flannel kimonos for adults and children are a chief attraction, but there are other traditional things as well: sake sets, lacquered and hand-carved chopsticks, sushi knives and cooking equipment, flower-arranging tools, tea ceremony accoutrements, calligraphy pens, and origami kits. There's a well-edited selection of antiques as well—old Japanese work jackets, antique obi sashes, and miniature Tansu chests. At Christmas McKay fills her shop with enchanting origami tree ornaments and unusual stocking stuffers.

FLIGHTS OF FANCY
450 East 78th Street
772-1302
Tues., Thurs., Fri.: 12 noon–7 p.m.; Wed.: 12 noon–8 p.m.;
Sat.: 10 a.m.–6 p.m.; Sun.: 1 p.m.–6 p.m.
AE, MC, V

Don Detrick is a pro at ferreting out the unusual, and he's assembled seductive American-made treasures—some old, some new—that he displays in a charming Victorian-parlor setting. Many of the gifts in his small shop are handmade and exclusive, and among the mix are cuddly animals, terra-cotta vases and planters, leather baseballs in riotous colors, "rabbit" tureens and "fish" platters, reproduction Victorian and Art Deco jewelry, and enchanting dolls, some with bisque faces.

THE GAZEBO
Floral-painted china, sweaters with country scenes, pastel rag rugs, little girls' smocked dresses. (See **Linens and Quilts,** p. 385.)

GILES & COMPANY
Plexiglas bookends, earth-toned vases, magazine racks, dinnerware and frames from Swid-Powell, and condiment sets and espresso makers by Alessi. (See **Cutting-Edge Furniture,** p. 280.)

GLORIOUS BASKETS
326 East 81st Street
772-7400
Mon., Wed., Fri., Sat.: 10 a.m.–5 p.m.; Tues.–Thurs.: 10 a.m.–7 p.m.
AE, MC

This closet-size shop is filled with myriad treats so customers can pick and choose to create personalized gift baskets. There are dolls and toys

303

for newborns, gourmet foods for the gourmand, handsome pens and stationery for the literati, and enchantments for homebodies. The selection of baskets is as wonderful as the goodies, but if you don't have time for a visit, the owners, Gloria Gibson and her daughter-in-law, Martha, will assemble a basket for you and ship it anywhere in the country.

GOLDUST MEMORIES
386 Second Avenue, near 22nd Street
677-2590
Mon.–Wed., Fri.: 11 a.m.–7 p.m.; Thurs.: 11 a.m.–8 p.m.; Sat.:
11 a.m.–6 p.m.
AE, MC, V

Jewelry, antiques, and gifts with a Victorian or Deco flavor are attractively displayed in this large and airy store. Originals from the turn-of-the-century through the fifties join with reproductions cast from original European molds. The mix is eclectic and includes everything from old Parrish prints, to forties rosegold-over-sterling-silver jewelry, to Art Deco vases, to new martini shakers. Antique and new silk scarves and kimonos, pewter flasks, china and glassware, and rhinestone and marcasite jewelry are here as well.

HERMÉS
An elegant selection of luxurious leathers—from the tiniest of notebooks, to lizard agendas, to the legendary Kelly bag, to luggage custom-made for your Lear jet—along with silk scarves, gloves, and attractive china and handsome bar tools. (See **Contemporary Handbags,** p. 318.)

HUDSON STREET PAPERS
581 Hudson Street
243-4221
Mon–Sat: 10 a.m.–8 p.m.

234 Third Avenue, near 19th Street
529-9748
Mon.–Fri.: 11 a.m.–7 p.m.; Sat.: 11 a.m.–6 p.m.
AE, MC, V

Hudson Street Papers are mini-department stores filled with paper and paper-related gifts. Fine imported Italian, French, and English stationery, dictionaries and desk accessories, diaries and photo albums, organizers and hatboxes covered in marbleized papers fill the tiny Hudson Street store to overflowing. The more spacious store on Third Avenue offers tabletop items as well—romantic chintz tablecloths and pillows, English teapots, along with Liberty of London scarves, Crabtree & Evelyn soaps, sachets, and lotions, beach umbrellas, wicker furniture, even children's chairs.

JEAN LAPORTE L'ARTISAN PARFUMEUR
870 Madison Avenue, near 71st Street
517-8665
Mon.–Sat.: 10 a.m.–6 p.m.
AE, D, MC, V

Jean Laporte offers unique all natural fragrances along with a tantalizing selection of small gift items in a tiny jewel of a store, replete with lush green-silk walls, a Venetian-crystal chandelier, an antique French gilt desk, and black lacquer accents. There are noncommercial aftershaves and shower gels for men, antique perfume bottles and French jewelry for women, and for the home, perfumed candles, rose-scented linen sprays, and fragrant potpourri.

JENNY B. GOODE
1194 Lexington Avenue, near 81st Street
794-2492
Mon.–Fri.: 10 a.m.–6:30 p.m.; Sat.: 10 a.m.–6 p.m.

11 East 10th Street
505-7666
Mon.–Fri.: 11 a.m.–7 p.m.; Sat.: 10 a.m.–6 p.m.
All major

Whatever tempts Jenny and her daughter Elizabeth on their frequent European buying forays is quickly added to their basic stock of goodies in these appealing stores. So in addition to such standards as stationery, hand-painted ceramics, teapots, trivets, perfume bottles, pristine white pillowcases, hand-knit sweaters, and hand-woven scarves, you might find vintage crystal-and-silver necklaces, Clarice Cliff pottery from the twenties, reproduction Art Deco travel clocks, French inlay wood frames, or hand-painted French porcelains. There's always a winning selection of children's things, too: wing-back chairs, small work tables, silver mugs, wooden toys, and charming tea sets.

KEESAL & MATTHEWS
1244 Madison Avenue, near 90th Street
410-1800
Mon.–Sat.: 11 a.m.–6 p.m.; Sun.: 1 p.m.–5 p.m.
AE

Susan Vasillov and her financial partner, David Clark, named their seductive home-furnishings shop after their respective mothers, and they've filled it with some fine, offbeat finds. Classic china, table linens, and glassware are artfully arranged in antique cupboards and on vintage servers, tables hold candlesticks and dried flower topiaries, and the walls are hung with botanical prints and engravings. Cotton-jacquard coverlets, handsome desk accessories, planters, mirrors, teapots, and porcelain boxes are among the other irresistibles.

THE H. LEXINGTON COLLECTION
907 Madison Avenue, near 72nd Street
570-0060
Mon.–Fri.: 10 a.m.–6:30 p.m.; Sat.: 10 a.m.–6 p.m.
Sun.: 12 noon–6 p.m.
AE, MC, V

Gifts inspired by a more romantic age—the Edwardian era—fill this sweet-smelling store. Fine English men's toiletries, pressed-flower cards and stationery, dried flowers, and potpourri are everywhere, joined by frilly English lace pillows, desk accessories, porcelain tea sets, silver frames, cuddly patchwork teddy bears, floral-covered boxes, and hand-decorated confections. There's a tempting assortment of English food items as well—mustards and vinegars, jams, and fudge sauces.

LEXINGTON GARDENS
1008 Lexington Avenue, near 72nd Street
861-4390
Mon.–Sat.: 10 a.m.–6 p.m.
AE, MC, V

Lexington Gardens is an unexpected delight, like discovering a lush garden hidden behind forbidding walls. Its whitewashed terra-cotta floor and pale-celadon walls provide the backdrop to the jumble of antiques and new garden ornaments that artfully cram the cupboards and occupy every inch of floor space. Aluminum garden benches, chairs, and tables made from old castings coexist with planters, jardinieres, and garden seats; birdhouses, feeders, and cages; and small-size hoes and rakes for children. And, although you won't find plants or flowers, you will find a smattering of practical stuff like gardening books, English-made clippers, watering cans, and potting gloves, along with Kenneth Turner candles and potpourri, framed antique botanicals, and assorted floral- and vegetable-adorned china.

LITTLE RICKIE
This playground for nostalgia buffs is packed floor to ceiling with zany and kitschy delights: Gumby and Pokey, Lava lamps, fifties friction convertibles, Mouseketeer hats, sixties space-age watches, vintage wind-up toys. (See **Toys,** p. 497.)

L. S. COLLECTION
765 Madison Avenue, near 65th Street
472-3355
Mon.–Sat.: 10 a.m.–6 p.m.
AE

L. S. Collection is owned by Japanese brothers Yoshikazu and Masahiko Kasuga and the shop's rough stone floor and high-glass lacquered walls are a fitting setting for its stock of modern china, flatware, glassware, and leather accessories. Among the vast international inventory are sterling-silver vases, champagne buckets, and desk accessories by Zucchi & Pampaloni; structural perfume bottles by Canadian sculptor Max Leser; handsome Italian fountain pens; vases, candlesticks, stemware, and barware from Murano, Italy; stark sterling-silver flatware from West German silversmiths Robbe & Berking; china from Italian architect Paolo Portoghesi; along with walking sticks, alabaster chess sets, alderwood bowls, and such gourmet treats as a rechargeable electronic peppermill.

MABEL'S
849 Madison Avenue, near 70th Street
734-3263
Mon.–Sat.: 10 a.m.–6 p.m.
AE, MC, V

Peaches Gilbert named her whimsical shop after her departed black-and-white cat Mabel, and in keeping with its inspiration she's filled it with a menagerie of handmade treasures. Hand-tooled piglet leather belts, English bulldog foot rests, kitty doorstops, puppy cushions, life-size papier-mâche dogs, lamb vases, and mohair sweaters with barn-yard scenes are among the small delights. But there's furniture, too, and rugs; assorted wooden chests and tall bureaus hand-painted with animals in many guises, adult and child-size chairs in every imaginable animal shape, and Preston MacAdoo's winning hooked beauties adorned with marching holstein or Canada geese in flight.

MARK CROSS
645 Fifth Avenue, 51st Street
421-3000
Mon.–Sat.: 10 a.m.–6 p.m.

World Financial Center
945-1411
Mon.–Fri.: 10 a.m.–7 p.m.; Sat. & Sun.; 12 noon–5 p.m.
All major

Mark Cross originally was a saddle and harness maker, but when the horse and carriage gave way to the car, Cross turned his attention to luggage, wallets, and toiletry cases. The store that bears his name still carries some of the finest crafted leather goods around, but now in its elegant wood-paneled Fifth Avenue home, there's a bevy of handsome gift items as well. So in addition to high-quality luggage and brief-cases you'll find both classic and high-fashion handbags, beautifully executed leather desk accessories, enamel boxes, brass clocks, pens, exquisite evening purses, and antique jewelry. The smaller shop in the World Financial Center carries a well-edited selection of Mark Cross merchandise.

MATT MCGHEE
18 & 22 Christopher Street
741-3138
Tues.–Fri.: 12 noon–7 p.m.; Sat. & Sun.: 12 noon–6 p.m.
AE, MC, V

Discriminating denizens of the Village put their trust in the expert hands
of Matt McGhee. They know that if they're searching for a special gift,
he's sure to have it. Stuffed animals of every species, beguiling German
pewter figures in Old World skating and garden scenes, hand-painted
baskets, porcelains and ceramics, pillows, and hand-woven mohair
throws in delicious colors merely suggest the seemingly endless gifts
that are seductively displayed in McGhee's twin stores. At Christmas
these shops dazzle with old-fashioned-looking German glass tree ornaments and stocking stuffers.

MOVADO DESIGN COLLECTION
625 Madison Avenue, at 59th Street
688-4002
Mon.–Sat.: 10 a.m.–6 p.m.
AE, MC

The Movado Collection represents a departure from tradition. While
many designers have gone from fashion into the watch industry, Movado
has gone from watches into accessories. Like the company's famous
Museum Watch (part of the permanent design collection of the Museum
of Modern Art), Movado's new accessories are also modern classics.
There are Cortina calf handbags, luggage, and desk accessories crafted
with subtle elegance, sunglasses with patented nose pieces, and distinctive woven silk-twill scarves.

MYTHOLOGY
370 Columbus Avenue, near 77th Street
874-0774
Mon.–Sat.: 11 a.m.–11 p.m.; Sun.: 11 a.m.–6 p.m.
AE, MC, V

If it's whimsical, nostalgic, cutting edge, or way out you're likely to find
it in this amusing shop. Folk-art masks line the walls, and neatly arranged shelves hold thousands of rubber stamps, Voodoo flags, dozens
of vintage wind-up toys and tin beach pails, scores of robots, all manner
of mini-erasers and magnets, not to mention old postcards, posters,
books on architecture and design, barnyard butter dishes, colorful kites,
whimsical jewelry, and plastic lettuce heads for stashing jewels. Among
the large-size treats are lamps that look like daffodils and child-size
tables with giant crayon legs.

THE NATURE COMPANY
8 Fulton Street
South Street Seaport

422-8510
Mon.–Sat.: 10 a.m.–9 p.m.; Sun.: 12 noon–8 p.m.
AE, MC, V

In 1973 Tom and Priscilla Wrubel opened a small store in California devoted to the observation, understanding, and appreciation of nature. It soon became a West Coast phenomenon and spawned a catalogue and an East Coast branch. The New York emporium, devoted to the Wrubels' original principles, is crammed with such unlikely delights as a real pachydiscus fossil, a ten-foot amethyst crystal, meticulously detailed inflatable snakes, a clock that runs on potatoes. But there are objects of more general appeal: Wolfard oil lamps, celestial charts, hikers' plant presses, binoculars, Japanese gardening shears, bronze birdbaths, and bird feeders, and, for children, puzzles, fossil collectors' kits, battery-powered planetariums, and lightsticks.

PLANET EARTH
23 Lexington Avenue, near 23rd Street
677-7005
Mon.–Sat.: 11 a.m.–9 p.m.; Sun.: 12 noon–7 p.m.
AE, MC, V

Lorraine Simone and Robert Werner's soothing shop has piped-in celestial electronic music and a ceiling aglow with spotlit planets, and it's stocked with "gifts from the earth and beyond." This supermarket of celestial things offers maps of the stars and planets, prisms and minerals, binoculars and telescopes, shells and fossils, clocks that run on solar, water, or potato power, and New Age music. For children there are robots, gyroscopes, dinosaurs in every form, refraction glasses, toys and games, even an erupting volcano. And for those less earthbound, healing quartzes, crystals for meditation, ion fountains, and subliminal tapes.

RENÉ
1188 Madison Avenue, near 87th Street
860-7669
Mon.–Sat.: 10 a.m.–6 p.m.
AE, D, MC, V

A pleasing mix of furniture, linens, and gifts fills this friendly duplexshop. Hand-painted Swedish country-pine armoires that can be customordered are stacked high with lacy bed and table linens that are mostly reproductions of Victorian whites. Painted tables hold splendid arrangements of antique and new silver frames, crystal and silver boudoir jars, and hand-painted candlestick lamps; and cabinets are filled with all manner of decorative treats.

SAINT RÉMY
818 Lexington Avenue, near 62nd Street
759-8240

309

Mon.–Sat.: 10 a.m.–6:30 p.m.
AE, MC, V

Saint Rémy was once a tiny herb shop crowded with bins of dried herbs. Although this outpost of Provence still sells sweet-smelling things— potpourri, sachets, wreaths, scented drawer liners, and dried flowers— it's now crammed with tapestry pillows, vinegars and jams, hand-painted French country pottery, Limoges collectibles, and a winning selection of fabrics. Floral chintzes, cotton and linen toweling, and machine-woven reproductions of fifteenth-century tapestries are available by the yard.

SCULLY & SCULLY
506 Park Avenue, near 59th Street
755-2590
Mon.–Fri.: 9 a.m.–6 p.m.; Sat.: 9 a.m.–5:30 p.m.
All major

Scully & Scully manages to cram into a smallish space a heady assortment of English- and American-made furniture, furnishings, and accessories both large and small. A reproduction eighteenth-century Chippendale secretary stands next to a mahogany game table, and shelves and tabletops are laden with leather party planners, and photo albums, Halcyon Day enameled boxes, staghorn-handled steak knives and carving sets, and desk accessories. Brass fire tools and umbrella stands, library globes, stemware, and china by Ceraline, Royal Crown Derby, Wedgwood, Haviland, and Herend are here as well. Among the winning children's furniture you'll find a hand-carved walnut Chippendale-style armchair, a solid walnut desk with brass hardware, and a King George II reproduction corner chair.

SERENDIPITY
225 East 60th Street
838-3531
Mon.–Fri.: 11:30 a.m.–1 a.m.; Sat.: 11 a.m.–2 a.m.; Sun.: 11:30 a.m.–12 midnight
AE, DC, MC, V

Celebrity watchers come to Serendipity to spot their favorite movie star indulging in the store's famous chili, hot chocolate, or ice cream sundaes. But the front of the store offers less caloric treats: hand-painted T-shirts, coffee mugs, hand-blown wine goblets, character dolls, gargoyle-adorned mirrors, and exuberant jewelry.

SOINTU
20 East 69th Street
570-9449
Mon.–Sat.: 11 a.m.–6 p.m.
AE, MC, V

Sointu is Finnish for harmony and balance, and it aptly describes this tiny jewel of a store. Since the very best in modern design is in residence here, you'll find mass-produced wares of Alessi and Braun, the work of small design studios and crafts people, as well as the store's own sleek stainless-steel high-tech watches, tableware, and stemware. Hand-thrown porcelain dinnerware by Ikuzi Teraki, crystal decanters, wine coolers, nutmeg and cheese graters, bar tools, and candlesticks are among the tempting stock of tabletop accessories. The city's most extensive line of mat-black desk and personal accessories are here as well, along with buttery-soft luggage and attaché cases and state-of-the art telephones and calculators. Also hand-carved ivory jewelry, minimalist fireplace tools and magazine racks, and just for the fun of it, adult games and toys.

STAR MAGIC
743 Broadway, near 8th Street
228-7770
Mon.–Sat.: 10 a.m.–10 p.m.; Sun.: 11 a.m.–9 p.m.

275 Amsterdam Avenue, at 73rd Street
769-2020
Mon.–Sat.: 10 a.m.–10 p.m.; Sun.: 12 noon–8 p.m.
AE, MC, V

Midnight black ceiling, grid floor, spacecraft-like walls, and out-of-space music enhance the selection of other-worldly merchandise that owners Robert Hanfling, Shlomo Ayel, and Justin Moreau have assembled. Among the celestial treats are minerals and prisms, telescopes in all sizes, meditation crystals, maps of the stars, and constellations, electronic music, books, science kits, and scientific-inspired games and toys.

STATE OF THE ART
47 Greenwich Avenue, near 7th Street
924-8973
Mon.–Sun.: 1 p.m.–8 p.m.

4 World Financial Center
945-4400
Mon.–Fri.: 10 a.m.–6 p.m.; Sat. & Sun.: 12 noon–5 p.m.
AE, MC, V

If they're not "state-of-the-art," they're certainly the very latest in intelligently designed functional products for the home and office. Alessi, Swid-Powell, Richard Sapper, Ettore Sottsass, Rossi, Porsche, Michael Graves, are some of the international names you'll find in these sleek high-tech stores. Porcelain dinnerware, razors, wooden trays, telephones, frames, espresso makers, metal bowls, candlesticks, stemware, condiment sets, electronic toasters, vases, desk accessories, and attaché cases are some of the items.

S. T. DUPONT

680 Madison Avenue, near 61st Street
593-4224
Mon.–Fri.: 10 a.m.–6 p.m.; Sat.: 10 a.m.–5:30 p.m.
AE, MC, V

S. T. Dupont has supplied kings, maharajas, sheiks, and captains of industry with writing instruments and small leather goods for more than 200 years. Today, just as in the past, Dupont's products are made to exacting standards in their own factory-workshop in the Swiss Alps, and now the complete collection is available in their small sparkling New York store. The statusy S. T. Dupont pen, handsomely lacquered and with gold fittings, is the chief attraction, but equally classy are the watches, lighters, stationery, wallets, scarves, and assorted small leather accessories.

SURA KAYLA

484 Broome Street
941-8757
Daily: 11 a.m.–7 p.m.
AE

Owner Sura Kayla has turned a love for botanicals and found objects into a delightful store that's a herbaceous wonderland filled with nosegays, topiaries, and bunches and baskets of dried flowers. Wreaths, tiny framed antique silhouettes, and prints new and old hang on the walls; the shelves are crammed with birdhouses, hand-painted columns and candlesticks, as well as the occasional antique *objet d'art*. There are fresh flowers, too, along with hand-blown glass vases from Italy, herb bouquets, handmade cornhusk napkin rings, and old-fashioned potpourri. Best of all are Kayla's custom-made pine dining and end tables with white birch legs.

SWEET NELLIE

1262 Madison Avenue, near 90th Street
876-5775
Mon.–Fri.: 10 a.m.–6 p.m.; Sat.: 11 a.m.–6 p.m.
AE, MC, V

As charming as its name, Pat Ross's country store is brimful of vintage patchwork, appliqué quilts, and Marseilles bedspreads, along with newly hooked pictorial rugs, mohair throws in luscious shades, majolica-inspired bowls and vases, and hand-dipped candles in a rainbow of colors. Bandboxes covered in vintage wallpapers vie for attention with grain-painted frames, hand-painted pottery, and baskets. At Christmas Sweet Nellie boasts old-fashioned-looking tree ornaments and Christmas stockings.

THINK BIG

390 West Broadway

925-7300
Mon.–Sat.: 10 a.m.–7 p.m.; Sun.: 12 noon–6 p.m.

313 Columbus Avenue, near 74th Street
769-0909
Daily: 11 a.m.–7 p.m.
AE, MC, V

Oversized versions of everyday objects fill these popular stores. The witty stock includes baseball-glove sofas, alphabet-block toy chests, giant-sized pencils, salt shakers that double as vases, and crayons taller than a child. Kids love it.

A VICTORIAN HOLIDAY
141 East 62nd Street
755-5327
Mon.–Fri.: 10 a.m.–6:30 p.m.; Sat.: 11 a.m.–5:30 p.m.
No credit cards

Molly Blayney is a voracious collector of Christmas Victoriana, and in 1986 she left her job in advertising and opened a small Christmas boutique. Her shop proved so successful she decided to broaden her original concept and devote herself full-time to her holiday obsessions. So for each of the holidays her snug little shop is stocked floor to ceiling with a delightful mix of appropriate merchandise—in between holidays it's jammed with lacy treats, wreaths, soaps, and jellies. Hearts and flowers, vintage books of love poems, Victorian cards, and old sheet music with love songs fill the shop for Valentine's Day. Easter it's crammed with rabbits, old and new, early Beatrix Potter illustrations, ceramic bird-house music boxes, and eggs in every guise. And at Christmas it's transformed into a wonderland with Victorian ornaments, sleds, hobbyhorses, dolls and dollhouses, not to mention Christmas books, cookies, custom wreaths, and, of course, stockings.

WEST TOWN HOUSE
2276 Broadway, at 82nd Street
724-5000
Mon.–Sat.: 10:30 a.m.–6:30 p.m.; Sun.: 12 noon–5 p.m.
AE, MC, V

A friendly, neighborhood shop, West Town House is popular with West Side co-opers who come here for home accessories, furniture, and an attractive assortment of gifts. Antique and new quilts, pine furniture, rag rugs, and rustic Italian pottery have a country look, but there are trendy tablewares and high-tech desk accessories, along with linens for bed, bath, and table, candles in every size and color, and bath products.

ZONA
Tiny papier-mâché finger puppets, Smith & Hawkins's garden tools,

313

Centro Botanicos soaps and fragrances, leather backpacks, linens, pottery, brushes in all sizes, natural sea sponges, metal candleholders, beeswax candles, and much more. (See **Handcraft Galleries,** p. 328.)

Handbags

VINTAGE

Many vintage clothing stores have a fine selection of old handbags; below are a few whose collections are particularly noteworthy.

FDR DRIVE
An exceptionally fine collection of antique beaded and tapestry evening purses. (See **Clothing**, p. 153.)

ILENE CHAZANOF
An enticing group of vintage handbags from the twenties through the fifties, many with unusual clasps, at fantastic prices. (See **Jewelry**, p. 345.)

JAMES II GALLERIES
Unusual antique evening purses in shagreen, alligator, crocodile, and lizard. (See **China and Glassware**, p. 67.)

LORRAINE WOHL COLLECTION
A small but very special group of alligator and crocodile bags, and evening purses with exquisite jeweled clasps. (See **Clothing**, p. 181.)

SYLVIA PINES—UNIQUITIES
1102 Lexington Avenue, near 77th Street
744-5141
Mon.–Sat.: 10:30 a.m.–6 p.m.
No credit cards

Sylvia Pines's closet-sized shop is crammed with the most spectacular collection of beaded, jeweled, and tapestry evening purses in the city. Pines carries Victorian, Edwardian, Art Deco, and Art Nouveau bags, many with exquisite precious- or semiprecious-stone frames, and they're all in pristine condition. Marcasite and estate jewelry from the same period is equally irresistible, as are the antique silver mirrors in

315

every size and shape, and her crystal and silver perfume bottles. Expensive.

T. J. ANTORINO
Twenties and thirties alligator, crocodile, and lizard handbags and wallets in excellent condition, as well as exquisite needlepoint evening purses. (See **Gifts,** p. 297.)

CONTEMPORARY

All the department stores carry a large selection of handbags and evening purses in a wide range of prices. See also **Shoes, Women's.**

BOTTEGA VENETA
635 Madison Avenue, near 59th Street
371-5511
Mon.–Wed., Fri.: 10 a.m.–6 p.m.; Thurs.: 10 a.m.–7 p.m.; Sat.:
11 a.m.–6 p.m.
AE, MC, V

In its spacious and elegant duplex quarters on Madison Avenue, Bottega Veneta boasts a full complement of the buttery-soft Italian leathers that once made a trip to Italy mandatory. Woven-leather handbags in luscious colors share the plushly carpeted space with practical (yet beautiful) bags in vinylized-print fabrics in all the most-wanted shapes; tasteful luggage; slim women's lizard and calfskin attaché cases in unexpected shades; men's briefcases in conservative black and brown; and classic shoes in normal and narrow widths. There's a small but noteworthy stock of gloves, ties, scarves, and small leather goods, too.

BREE
610 Fifth Avenue, near 50th Street
315-5925
Mon.–Wed., Fri.: 10 a.m.–6:30 p.m.; Thurs.: 10 a.m.–7 p.m.; Sat.:
10 a.m.–6 p.m.

World Financial Center
406-7105
Mon.–Sat.: 10 a.m.–7 p.m.; Sun.: 12 noon–5 p.m.
AE, MC, V

Bree's trademark is "classic simplicity in natural leather," and the company's large and sunny emporium located on the Promenade at Rockefeller Center is as spare and blond as the merchandise. Bags and luggage are crafted from hand-brushed leathers that are pale when purchased but become burnished with age, and they're sturdy, long-lasting, and come in traditional shapes. Shoulder bags, clutches, back-packs, duffels, camera cases, overnighters, belts, and small leather goods are among the attractions. The smaller shop in the World Financial Center carries a similar mix of leather goods.

CHANEL BOUTIQUE
Coco's coveted gold-chained handbags—classic and costly—in velvets and quilted leathers in a range of pastels or jewel-tones and in standard and tiny versions. (See **Clothing,** p. 160.)

THE COACH STORE
710 Madison Avenue, at 63rd Street
319-1772
Mon.–Wed., Fri., Sat.: 10 a.m.–6 p.m.; Thurs.: 10 a.m.–7 p.m.

193 Front Street
South Street Seaport
947-1727
Mon.–Sat.: 10 a.m.–7 p.m.; Sun.: 11 a.m.–6 p.m.
AE, MC, V

In the marble-and-mahogany interior of Coach's newest store, a two-story building with an atrium and gallery of leather art, bags are displayed on shelves like library books and there's a sliding wooden ladder to reach them. Known for simple, classic handbags crafted of natural, long-lasting leathers, Coach styles have stayed substantially the same for more than thirty years. Recently, however, the company has introduced softer, lighter-weight leather bags with a more fashionable silhouette. In addition to the popular purses, both stores offer briefcases, wallets, diaries, belts, and small accessories that are exceptionally durable and timeless in their simplicity.

CROUCH & FITZGERALD
Among the vast number of classically styled handbags in leathers and exotic skins are all the better-known domestic and imported labels. (See **Luggage and Briefcases,** p. 396.)

DINOFFER INC.
A noteworthy selection of classically styled handbags in leathers and exotic skins. (See **Luggage and Briefcases,** p. 397.)

FURLA
705 Madison Avenue, near 63rd Street
755-8986
Mon.–Fri.: 10 a.m.–6 p.m.; Sat.: 11 a.m.–5 p.m.

159A Columbus Avenue, near 67th Street
874-6119
Mon.–Sat.: 12 noon–7 p.m.; Sun.: 1 p.m.–6 p.m.
AE, MC, V

Attractively displayed in Furla's dramatic little shops, New York branches of an Italian bag and accessory company, are scores of handsome leather handbags. Once known for attention-getting leathers, the shapes—though still trendy—are now classic and the colors subtle. You'll find hatboxes, pouches, and envelopes in suedes and such soft colors as blues, beiges, and browns.

GUCCI
A full complement of ladylike handbags in leathers and exotic skins. (See **Clothing,** p. 154.)

HERMÉS
11 East 57th Street
751-3181
Mon.–Wed., Fri., Sat.: 10 a.m.–6 p.m.; Thurs.: 10 a.m.–8 p.m.
AE, MC, V

Polished mahogany counters and brass-filled display cases are the elegant setting for the legendary Hermés Kelly bag. Along with this prized purse you'll find the illustrious house's complete line of classic handbags—once considered high-fashion, then dowdy, now *très* au courant—in a range of luscious shades and in fabulous leathers. There are exotic-skin agendas and jotters in a dozen colors; key rings; brass whistles; and fantastic gloves; and these vie for attention with the Hermés silk scarves; shoes; linens; china; and sports separates. Hermés' coveted jodhpurs and hunting pinks and the exceptionally fine saddles that the company has been making for more than 150 years, and all the horsey accessories are of course here as well. Very expensive.

HUNTING WORLD/ANGLER'S WORLD
The popular battue-cloth bags in a range of colors and shapes and in sizes that range from a small camera-case shoulder bag to an oversized duffel. (See **Sporting Goods,** p. 460.)

IL BISONTE
72 Thompson Street
966-8773
Tues.–Sun.: 12 noon–6:30 p.m.
AE, MC, V

Spare and spartan, Il Bisonte is filled with Wanny di Filippo's complete line of bison-inspired Italian leather goods that are stamped with his bison logo—a symbol of the peace and strength of nineteenth-century America. Each piece looks and smells as if it just emerged from the tannery, and the bags are soft, simply styled, unlined, and come in natural leathers. Shelves are laden with drawstring pouches, large doctor's bags, binocular and camera cases, along with leather agendas, briefcases, flasks, wallets, and handsome luggage. Prices range from moderate to costly.

JACOMO
25 East 61st Street
832-9038
Mon.–Fri.: 10 a.m.–5 p.m.; Sat.: 12 noon–4:30 p.m.
AE, MC, V

Jacomo, a tiny salon of a shop, has gilt moldings, a crystal chandelier, and elegant antique French sofas and chairs to relax on while ogling pricey evening purses. These have been created from exquisite turn-of-the-century-through-the-forties handbag frames that have been refitted with bodies of silk, satin, or exotic skins. In addition to these one-of-a-kind purses the boutique carries tempting day bags, many designed by owner Jim Kaplan, that are beautifully styled and more affordable.

J. & F. MARTELL
897 Madison Avenue, near 72nd Street
744-6135
Mon.–Sat.: 10 a.m.–6 p.m.
AE, MC

J. & F. Martell is owned by the venerable French cognac company, and its spiffy New York showroom is filled with beautifully made, hand-stitched handbags, handsome briefcases, and buttery-soft suitcases and travel cases (discreetly stamped with the J. & F. Martell seal). Although the bulk of the stock is classic in shape and color and comes in textured Indian kid or ecru calfskin, the shop carries well-known architect Martine Bedin's witty designs inspired by New York City. Her intriguing bags are constructed of such unlikely shapes as arches, half-circles, and triangles and in such colors as malachite, onyx, slate, and bronze. Handsome briefcases, agendas, and business-card holders can be found at Martell as well. Expensive.

JILL STUART
22 East 65th Street
535-2200
Mon.–Sat.: 10:30 a.m.–5:30 p.m.
AE, MC, V

Jull Stuart is a young American designer who has created high-fashion accessories for the past seven years. Eager for a place to show her complete line, she opened a snug little shop fashioned after a French boudoir. Her classic but somewhat whimsical designs include handbags in unlikely color combinations, oversize pig-suede pouches, and exquisite tapestry evening purses. Stuart does gloves adorned with one-of-a-kind buttons, suede trouser belts in sherbety hues, and she stocks softly tailored cashmere sweaters and thick shawls.

LA BAGAGERIE

727 Madison Avenue, near 64th Street
758-6570
Mon.–Sat.: 10 a.m.–6:30 p.m.

412 West Broadway
941-1172
Tues.–Sat.: 10:30 a.m.–7 p.m.; Sun.: 11 a.m.–6 p.m.
AE, MC, V

Hundreds of handbags in high fashion styles, every possible size, and in scores of colors crowd these well-organized outposts of a French leather manufacturing company. La Bagagerie is an especially good source for small leather clutches in simple shapes and a rainbow of colors, and tapestry evening purses; wallets in unlikely colored leathers; classic briefcases; garment bags; and luggage. From moderate to expensive.

LANCEL

690 Madison Avenue, at 62nd Street
753-6918
Mon.–Sat.: 10 a.m.–6 p.m.
All major

Lancel was once known for its monochromatic polyurethane-canvas bags adorned with a signature "L," but this French company has moved on to handbags, totes, and luggage in bold colors and exotic skins. Mammoth totes come in acidy greens and red, shoulder bags in pristine white or lavender, green, or red suede, and classic hard-frame luggage in rich shades of brown and black. Lancel's newest collection, "Jet Set," offers polyurethane carry-ons trimmed in natural leathers that are soft, unconstructed, and incredibly lightweight. And there are small leather goods, umbrellas, jewelry, and silk scarves.

LEDERER DE PARIS, INC.

613 Madison Avenue, at 58th Street
355-5515
Mon.–Sat.: 9:30 a.m.–6 p.m.
AE, MC, V

Lederer opened in Paris more than 75 years ago as a women's handbag store, and although men now account for nearly half of the company's New York business, it's still a fine source for ladylike handbags from France and Italy. Styles are classic and suggestive of Chanel and Hermés. The leathers and exotic skins are top-notch, and Lederer's one-of-a-kind crocodile handbags are made from perfectly centered skins. Understated and elegant attaché cases and portfolios for men and women are a specialty, and there's a fine selection of wallets, canvas and leather carry-on luggage, canvas hunting bags, business card holders, small leather goods, and well-made standard and folding umbrellas. The store supplies the city's gentry with Barbour shooting and riding jackets and Wellington boots. Prices are good.

THE LIMITED
Leather handbags in all the most up-to-the-minute shapes and colors at very good prices. (See **Clothing,** p. 168.)

LOEWE
Glove-soft leather handbags in muted colors and classic shapes. (See **Clothing,** p. 109.)

LOUIS VUITTON
In addition to the signature line of handbags made of laminated-vinyl on Egyptian cotton canvas and adorned with the world-famous logo, Vuitton offers the Epi collection crafted of real leather in exciting colors that come with a mere hint of "V"s. (See **Luggage and Briefcases,** p. 398.)

MARK CROSS
Ladylike handbags in fine-quality calfskin, lizard, alligator, and crocodile, as well as beautifully crafted updates of the classic feedbag, camera case, and hatbox styles that appeal to a younger audience; also exquisite needlepoint and tapestry evening purses. (See **Gifts,** p. 307.)

MCM
Resinated-canvas bags stamped all over with the company's logo come in all the classic shapes. (See **Luggage and Briefcases,** p. 398.)

PETER HERMAN LEATHER GOODS
118 Thompson Street
966-9050
Daily: 1 p.m.–6:30 p.m.
AE, MC, V

Peter Herman's simple yet elegant sliver of a shop is filled with mostly European cutting-edge handbags and luggage. Sleek black predominates, but it's livened by bags in splashy colors. The clean-looking and tailored luggage, mostly black leather or rubber, includes soft satchels, oversized hatboxes, and carry-ons. Herman also carries John Jacobus's fashionable silk scarves, along with unique watches.

POLO/RALPH LAUREN
The wide selection of handbags includes tiny minis and oversized travel totes in everything from canvas, to calf, to exotic skins; Lauren's old-fashioned alligator and crocodile clutch-purses with sterling-silver fittings are the stuff of dreams. (See **Clothing,** p. 124.)

PRADA
45 East 57th Street
308-2332

Mon.–Sat.: 10 a.m.–6 p.m.
AE, MC, V

Italian royalty has toted Prada bags since Mario Prada opened his deluxe leather goods shop in Milan's famed Galleria in 1913, and in more recent times everyone from Grace Kelly to contemporary princesses have been seen swinging a Prada purse. The company's black-lacquer and polished-nickel New York shop is outfitted with re-creations of the Old World furnishings and display cases of the original store, and it offers the company's high-quality and exquisitely crafted goods made from sophisticated leathers. In addition to the classic and conservative collection, Miuccia Prada—the founder's great-granddaughter—has introduced updated, fashion-forward bags and shoes that bring a touch of the avant garde to traditional styling. So classic handbags in calfskin, lizard, crocodile, alligator, and ostrich share the elegant space with Miuccia's embossed leather and quilted bags; and her nylon totes and sophisticated satin heels are here along with sporty-chic ostrich loafers. You'll also find beautifully made luggage, belts, along with a smattering of briefcases, umbrellas, and small leather goods. Very expensive.

T. ANTHONY
Ladylike handbags in leathers and exotic skins. (See **Luggage and Briefcases,** p. 399.)

TIFFANY & COMPANY
Finely crafted handbags of sophisticated leathers in classic and high-fashion styles. (See **Jewelry,** p. 358.)

TONY BRYANT DESIGNS
339 Lafayette Street, near Bleecker Street
254-5743
Mon.–Sat.: 12 noon–7:30 p.m.; Sun.: 12 noon–7 p.m.
AE, MC, V

Tony Bryant's sunny shop is crammed with well-priced, handcrafted leather and canvas bags in a range of fashionable styles and in all the most wanted colors. Roomy totes, soft backpacks, leather-trimmed canvas satchels in brights and pales, multizippered leather shoulder bags, tempting belts, and a friendly staff make a visit here worthwhile.

Handcraft Galleries

ARCHETYPE

Up-to-the-minute hand-crafted lighting, glass, and jewelry. (See **Furniture,** p. 278.)

CARLYN GALLERY

1145 Madison Avenue, at 85th Street
879-0003
Mon.–Fri.: 11 a.m.–6 p.m.; Sat.: 11 a.m.–5 p.m.;
closed Sat. in summer
AE, MC, V

Carlyn is a sunny gallery brimming with the exuberant work of nationally known and emerging American artisans. Clay, glass, wood, metal, and papier-mâché decorative accessories and art objects are attractively displayed on bleached-wood platforms and in cozy nooks. There's a profusion of ceramic tableware, along with unusual and one-of-a-kind jewelry crafted from a mix of metals, often set with precious stones or antique findings. Periodically owners Carole Soling and director Roslyn Tunis mount exhibits, and among the recent shows was "Ancient Inspirations" with weavings, sculptures, hand-crafted jewelry, and functional pieces inspired by ancient or primitive civilizations.

CIVILIZATION

78 Second Avenue, near 4th Street
254-3788
Sun.–Mon.: 12 noon–6 p.m.; Tues.–Sat.: 11 a.m.–7 p.m.
AE, MC, V

Evie McKenna and Mitchell Soble met in graduate school at New York University, and there's no mistaking their art background in the mix of cutting-edge artist-made crafts in their lively store. Funky guitar-shaped coffee tables, jigsawed "fish" chairs, concrete clocks, a martini shaker inlaid with olives, Acme Robots stick-figure candle holders, and quirky lights made from cheese graters and old tin cans are sure to

323

elicit smiles. And although the appealing glassware and ceramics are less wild, they're still whimsical. Watches by M & Company, and jewelry by Catherine Butler, Erica Peterson, Meryl Waitz, and a host of others occupy at least a third of the shop, and like almost everything else in this shop, they are witty and affordable.

CLODAGH, ROSS, AND WILLIAMS

Assertive furniture, decorative accessories, and tabletop items by the best of the new wave crafts people. (See **Furniture,** p. 279.)

CONTEMPORARY PORCELAIN

Beautifully executed ceramics by the world's most innovative ceramic artists. (See **China and Glassware,** p. 73.)

DISTANT ORIGIN

153 Mercer Street
941-0024
Tues.–Sat.: 11 a.m.–6 p.m.; Sun.: 12 noon–6 p.m.
AE, MC, V

Owners Julio Hernandez and Alberto Ortega were attracted to cultures where art and utility are synonymous. So they decided to bring the work of Santa Fe, Mexican, and South American artists and artisans to New York. Their cavernous whitewashed gallery boasts psychedelic hand-beaded bowls and masks from the Huichol Indians, clay pots and hand-carved wooden spoons, hand-painted Mesa Verde–style pottery by Santa Fe artist Joan Mesznik, antique Navaho weavings, folk art, and old colonial tables, and benches and pie safes from Mexico and the American Southwest (many of the pieces with original paint). It's an enchanting mix of wares, and the owners are friendly and knowledgeable.

THE ELDER CRAFTSMAN

846 Lexington Avenue, at 64th Street
535-8030
Mon.: 11 a.m.–5:30 p.m.; Tues.–Fri.: 10 a.m.–5:30 p.m.;
Sat.: 10 a.m.–4 p.m.
MC, V

Everything in this captivating nonprofit shop is made by over-sixty-years-old citizens, and much of it has a country look. Patchwork crib quilts, crocheted bed throws, knit pillow slips, delicately smocked little-girls' dresses, sweaters for children and adults (many embellished with animals or country scenes), and sturdy hand-carved trucks, trains, and animals are all appealingly displayed. And the lavish stock of nostalgic dolls and stuffed animals—tiny sock babies, Raggedy Ann and Andy, Pinocchio, monkey-stocking dolls—makes a stop here worthwhile. And the shop sparkles with old-fashioned hand-made tree ornaments, hand-knit Christmas stockings, doll-houses, and rocking horses at holiday time.

HOSHONI
309 East 9th Street
674-3120
Daily: 12 noon–8 p.m.
AE, MC, V

Walk into Hoshoni and it's like entering an adobe, and this exciting shop displays the work of Santa Fe artisans. Brandon Santos's chairs, tables, shelves, and mirrors are jigsawed from gray wood, then hand-painted with traditional Southwestern graphics in delicious shades of lavender, turquoise, and peach. There are hand-tooled belts from Cerrillos, colorful wooden snakes, Taos mica clay pottery, wonderful buffalo-hide handbags, twig and birch baskets, bark-paper waste baskets, rustic wooden crosses, and assorted turquoise-and-silver jewelry. Prices are excellent.

INCORPORATED GALLERY
1200 Madison Avenue, near 87th Street
831-4466
Mon.–Tues., Thurs.–Sat.: 10 a.m.–6 p.m.; Wed.: 11 a.m.–8 p.m.
AE, MC, V

The work of more than 300 American crafts people is at the Incorporated Gallery. Although handcrafted ceramics are the chief attraction with dozens of boldly colored and monochromatic vessels, bowls, platters, and jugs on display, you'll find nicely executed fiber wall hangings, hand-carved wooden bowls and boxes, and sculptures, too. Many of the pieces are functional (such as teapots, butter dishes, and vases); others are fanciful or purely decorative art objects. There's a selection of glassware, puzzles, metal and ceramic chess sets, and jewelry crafted from a mix of metals and semiprecious stones.

JORICE
1057 Second Avenue, near 55th Street
752-0129
Mon.–Fri.: 11 a.m.–6 p.m.; Sat.: 11 a.m.–6 p.m.
AE, MC, V

A tiny jewel of a store, Jorice is known for hand-blown signed studio glass. Everything is one-of-a-kind and vividly colored. Intricately worked paperweights are a specialty, but there's a lovely selection of vases, lamps, plates, perfume bottles, goblets, and fused-glass jewelry, too. At Christmas Jorice sparkles with exquisite hand-blown ornaments.

JULIE: ARTISAN'S GALLERY
687 Madison Avenue, near 61st Street
688-2345

325

Mon.–Sat.: 11 a.m.–6 p.m.
AE, D, MC, V

Clothing as an art form is the focus in this well-known gallery, and the unique works of these American artists are meant to be worn. Those who like individuality and flair in their fashion come here for handsome woven jackets, exuberantly patterned sweater coats, as well as exquisite hand-painted silk kimonos. Most of the clothing is one-of-a-kind, and the mix is ever-changing, and it's not meant for the faint of heart. Cutting-edge jewelry is crafted from exotic materials, and you might find Pier Voulkos's "Lollipop Necklace" made from oven-baked plastic, or Carol Motty's clusters of amethysts that are actually molded silicone.

LIGHTHOUSE CRAFT SHOP
111 East 59th Street
355-2200, ext. 203
Mon.–Fri.: 10 a.m.–5 p.m.; in Dec., Sat.: 10 a.m.–5 p.m.
MC, V

Crafts made by the blind are featured in this bleached-wood shop affiliated with the Lighthouse for the Blind. Among the mix of handcrafted things are hand-knit infants' clothing, cuddly-soft knit dolls, boldly patterned sweaters for children, Afghans, handmade toys, and colorful wool gloves. And those in the know come to the Lighthouse for its outstanding selection of sturdy and long-lasting household brushes of all kinds.

NEW YORK EXCHANGE FOR WOMEN'S WORK
660 Madison Avenue, near 60th Street
753-2330
Mon.–Sat.: 10 a.m.–6 p.m.
AE, MC, V

The New York Exchange for Women's Work has been around for more than 110 years, and it began as a place for Civil War widows to discreetly sell their handiwork. Today it still carries handmade objects done by crafts people working in their homes. Particularly appealing is the Exchange's fine collection of infants' and children's things—exquisite hand-knit sweaters, buntings, bonnets, and mittens; delicate hand-smocked dresses, cuddly-soft dolls and animals. But on two floors set up as tiny boutiques, you'll find clothing for grown-ups, as well as vintage and new linens and jewelry, lingerie, sweet-smelling sachets, floral-printed toiletry cases, and such gift items as picture frames, fabric-covered hangers, and hand-knit socks. Surprisingly, the Exchange also offers a pleasing and ever-changing array of antique furniture that might include Early American chairs and Victorian vanities.

PERFORMER'S OUTLET
222 East 85th Street
249-3088
Mon.–Sat.: 3 p.m.–6:30 p.m.
AE, MC, V

When Performer's Outlet first opened nineteen years ago, it carried handmade items crafted by performers with time on their hands and a need for a little extra cash. Although everything in this maze of shops is still handmade, it's now the work of a broad range of crafts people. Hand-loomed rag rugs that can be custom-ordered in a vivid array of colors and in a range of sizes, rainbow-colored glass picture frames, hand-carved wooden cars, candlesticks, pottery, and glassware are among the domestic temptations. From France there's rustic faïence-ware, bright jewelry, hand-screened or woven scarves, and Gothic stained-glass hangings. The candle collection, one of the best in the city, offers candles in dozens of colors and in shapes both chunky and skinny, along with hand-dipped tapers, votives, and twists.

POTTERS GALLERY
168 Thompson Street
995-0997
Tues.–Sat.: 1 p.m.–8 p.m.; Sun.: 1 p.m.–5 p.m.
AE, MC, V

Owner Kee Cho has traveled the Northeast, to the West Coast, and South Korea to assemble one-of-a-kind pieces by leading potters for her charming gallery devoted to functional pottery. Among her stellar artists are Karen Karnes, Ken Pick, Dan Lasser, Jean Cohn, and Susan Macmillan, and they've contributed tea sets and coffee mugs, vases and table lamps, planters and casserole dishes.

A SHOW OF HANDS
531 Amsterdam Avenue, near 85th Street
787-1174
Mon.–Sat.: 11 a.m.–7 p.m.; Sun.: 11 a.m.–5 p.m.
AE, MC, V

A Show of Hands is an artist's collective, and it features the work of its twenty-five members in an airy, bleached-wood two-level store. Although there are few surprises, everything is beautifully executed. Hand-woven chenille mufflers in pastel or jewel tones, comforting mohair blankets, raw silk ties, and boldly patterned pottery coexist with anodized aluminum clocks, hand-carved wooden trains and trucks, whimsical jack-in-the-boxes, hand-blown vases, hand-dipped candles, and brightly colored metal and ceramic jewelry.

TREADLES
351 Bleecker Street
633-0072

Mon.–Sat.: 12 noon–6 p.m.; Sun.: 12 noon–5 p.m.
AE, MC, V

In her sunny gallery Lisa Wagner offers a sumptuous collection of hand-woven goods (made by seventy artisans) that are beautiful yet functional—rugs, blankets, place mats, napkins, pillows, and shawls. Elsa Diehl's "quilt" rug of double-woven cotton, Jane Doyle's reversible geometric rug, hand-dyed silk ikat shawls, Scandinavian damask table linens, and hand-loomed baby blankets are just a few of the temptations.

WALLENGREN USA
75 Thompson Street
966-2266
Wed.–Sun.: 12 noon–6 p.m.
AE

Henry Wallengren concentrates on the very best in American crafts in his spartan shop. He mounts seasonal shows of mostly glass, clay, and metal work, and among his recent exhibits were Nicholas Bernard's raku vessels inspired by Native American pottery; Steven Tatar's fused glass, copper, and slate pieces; and Louise Block's sensual sculpted vessels; along with lead-crystal and twenty-karat-gold vases, and Victoria Kroll's hand-painted porcelains. Although Wallengren's stock of handcrafted one-of-a-kind crafts is not lavish, everything is so splendid and lovingly selected it's well worth a visit.

THE WORKS GALLERY
1250 Madison Avenue, near 89th Street
996-0300
Mon.–Sat.: 10 a.m.–6 p.m.; Sun.: 12 noon–5 p.m.
AE, MC, V

If the phrase "handcrafts gallery" has a frightening macramé ring to it, the Works Gallery will put your fears to rest. Tiny and jewel-like, it offers a collection of handcrafts that steer away from the trendy— classic design and fine craftsmanship are the basis for inclusion. Among the seductions are exquisite hand-turned boxes, blown-crystal goblets and vases, one-of-a-kind decorative ceramics, clocks, fine gold and silver jewelry (many pieces set with precious or semiprecious stones), and a handsome assortment of watches. Almost everything is one-of-a-kind or in limited editions, and there is a constantly changing mix.

ZONA
97 Greene Street
925-6750
Tues.–Wed., Fri., Sat.: 11:30 a.m.–6 p.m.; Thurs.: 11:30 a.m.–7 p.m.;
Sun.: 12 noon–5:30 p.m.
AE, MC, V

The sun-dappled, spare, and airy look of the American Southwest is captured in Zona's seductive interior, so it's the perfect setting for the shop's splendid wares of Native American, Mexican, and Tuscan artisans. A true New York success story—at Christmas the lines outside rival those for the city's hottest flick—Zona is richly deserving of its popularity for the sheer beauty, quality, and presentation of its treasures. Pastel-tinted wicker furniture shares the whitewashed space with enchanting hand-painted Taos cabinets, steel coffee tables with Mexican cutouts, three-foot-tall iron candlesticks, unglazed terra-cotta plates, Smith & Hawkens's fine gardening tools, old Indian cornhusk bags, sturdy cowhide backpacks, fragrances from Santa Maria Novella, and tiny papier-mâché finger puppets. Indeed, there are so many enticements it's impossible to leave this shop empty-handed.

Hats

The department stores offer a full-range of fashionable hats for men and women. See also **Clothing, Vintage,** for stores that sell classic men's and women's hats, often at prices considerably below designer updates.

ANNE MOORE BOUTIQUE
132 East 61st Street
Second floor
755-0048
Mon.–Fri.: 10 a.m.–6 p.m.; Sat.: 11 a.m.–6 p.m.
AE

Anne Moore is a young accessory designer whose hats, gloves, and hair ornaments have been featured in all the glossy fashion magazines. In her vest-pocket-size shop you'll find all of her beguiling creations. One-of-a-kind hats are fur-trimmed, beaded, feathered, or covered with buttons. Styles range from stovepipes to berets to straw mini-hats adorned with silk asparagus or twigs. Moore also carries gloves, shawls, and purses.

DON MARSHALL
465 Park Avenue, near 57th Street
Third floor
758-1686
Mon.–Fri.: 10 a.m.–5 p.m.
No credit cards

Don Marshall has been creating custom-made women's hats (along with custom-made ladies' suits) for more than forty years. His specialty is matched hat and suit ensembles, but in addition to working in fabric, Marshall makes straw, fur, and felt hats, too. The quality of materials and his workmanship is top-notch. Expensive.

JOSEPHINE TRIPOLI
237 East 59th Street
421-5667
Tues.–Sat.: 11 a.m.–6 p.m.
AE, MC, V

Tiny and old-fashioned—it was founded in 1937—Josephine Tripoli may look like an anachronism today, with its stack upon stack of hats and its floor-to-ceiling clutter of floral hatboxes, but with the recent millinery revival (thanks in part to Princess Di) young fashionables are seeking this shop out for its fine selection of timeless and classic hat shapes. There are felts, straws, furs, and velours designed by Josephine Tripoli (the original owner), as well as styles created by current owner Suzanne Newman, who also makes custom creations and handles alterations.

LOLA MILLINERY
102 St. Marks Place
979-1005
No credit cards

Lola Ehrlich's bright little shop—pink and blue and as exuberant as a Lacroix gown—is filled with some of the most whimsical hats in town. Ehrlich, a Vogue knitting editor for fifteen years, began making hats after studying at F.I.T., and she blocks her hats right in the back of the shop. Each wonderfully wearable, one-of-a-kind creation is a delight of color, shape, and texture. Ehrlich does awning-stripe turbans, tiny Panama bowlers, and very French-looking felts. Her charming store is definitely worth a visit.

NATASHA L. G.
59 Thompson Street
925-7335
Tues.–Sat.: 12 noon–7 p.m.; closed Sat. in summer
MC, V

Natasha's shop is as cozy as a small salon, and customers are encouraged to sit and try on all the hats, since Natasha designs each one differently for each woman, and many of her things are custom-made. She does very feminine and sexy styles, straws, and slouchy turbans, along with cutting-edge creations.

PAUL STUART
A fine assortment of men's wool caps and tweedy casual styles, along with a well-edited selection of classic fedoras and fur felts. (See **Clothing,** p. 118).

VICTORIA DINARDO
68 Thompson Street
334-9615

331

Tues.–Fri.: 11 a.m.–7 p.m.; Sat.: 12 noon–7 p.m.; Sun: 12 noon–6 p.m.
AE

This shop is no bigger than a closet, it's lined with handsome black-striped hatboxes and hat forms, and it's filled with Victoria Dinardo's irresistible classics. Her hats are made the old-fashioned way—each one is hand-sewn and hand-blocked—and custom work and bridal headwear are specialties. Dinardo has designed high-fashion looks for Donna Karan, and she does little cocktail hats, classic straws, rakish cloches, and linen berets. Prices are excellent.

WORTH & WORTH
331 Madison Avenue, near 42nd Street
867-6058
Mon.–Fri.: 9 a.m.–6 p.m.; Sat.: 10 a.m.–6 p.m.
All major

Tidily arranged by style and size on burnished mahogany shelves are all the top names in hats—Borsalino, Stetson, Cavanaugh, and Christy's of London. For more than fifty years Worth & Worth, the oldest hat shop in New York, has supplied New Yorkers with hats, and it carries everything from English trilbys to Australian range hats, silk top hats to Irish walkers, and real Panamas to luxurious furs. All the hats are still hand-shaped the old-fashioned way, and the staff is obliging and expert at proper fit. Don't overlook the splendid selection of Briggs of London umbrellas (considered the finest in the world), the handsome leather gloves, and the English schoolboy scarves.

Hosiery

Bloomingdale's and Macy's offer a good selection of panty hose and socks for men and women, Barneys New York has an extensive array of both classic and fashionable socks for men, and Bergdorf Goodman and Henri Bendel carry well-fitting panty hose in fashion-forward colors and patterns.

BROOKS BROTHERS
Hundreds of conservative dress socks in a range of lengths, weights, and colors fill the glass cases on the main floor. (See **Men's Clothing,** p. 116.)

CHARIVARI
An abundant selection of haute hosiery for men. (See **Men's Clothing,** p. 126.)

FOGAL
680 Madison Avenue, near 61st Street
759-9782
Mon.–Sat.: 10 a.m.–6 p.m.

510 Madison Avenue, at 53rd Street
355-3254
Mon.–Sat.: 10 a.m.–6 p.m.
AE, DC, MC, V

Fogal, a Swiss hosiery specialist, offers fabulous legwear in more than 200 styles and colors in its spiffy and neatly organized stores. Choose from 100% silk stockings, stockings with seams, or select from sexy body stockings, high-cut lacy bikini panty hose, or panty hose textured like tweeds, patterned with polka dots, or flecked with silver, gold, or rhinestones. Opaques and sheers come in all the most wanted and hard-to-find shades (and in sizes from extra-small to extra-large), and socks and thigh-highs come in every conceivable color. Although prices are higher than department-store brands, this legwear is wonder-

333

fully long-wearing. For men there are ankle and over-the-calf socks in cottons, wools, silks, and cashmere-silk blends in dozens of colors.

LEGGIADRO
700 Madison Avenue, near 62nd Street
753-5050
Mon.–Sat.: 10 a.m.–6 p.m.
AE, MC, V

Displays of panty hose, stockings, and leggings stretch from floor to ceiling in this tiny shop, and baskets overflowing with socks nestle on the floor. In addition to Leggiadro's own label, there are Italian, German, Japanese, French, and Austrian panty hose in pure silk, cotton, cashmere, wool, nylon, and Lycra, that come in an endless array of colors. Funky socks in Day-Glo colors, and luxurious cashmere-ribbed knits, fill the baskets. Prices are good.

THE LEG MARKET
1427 Lexington Avenue, near 93rd Street
831-3500
Mon.–Fri.: 12 noon–8 p.m.; Sat.: 11 a.m.–7 p.m.
AE, MC, V

A friendly little neighborhood store, the Leg Market stocks hundreds of socks for men, women, and children in all the most wanted colors, patterns, and textures. Calvin Klein, Christian Dior, Hanes, and Burlington are just a few of the designer names you'll find here. Socks come in ankle, over-the-calf, and knee-high versions and in cottons, wools, silks, and silk-and-cotton blends. Prices are pleasantly affordable.

PAUL STUART
Classic men's dress socks in fine cottons, wools, cashmeres, and silk blends, along with a good selection of cotton sports socks. (See **Men's Clothing,** p. 118.)

POLO/RALPH LAUREN
A stellar collection of hosiery for men and women in handsome menswear patterns—paisleys, chevrons, herringbones, chalk stripes, and Prince of Wales plaids. (See **Men's Clothing,** p. 124.)

SOCK EXPRESS
201–203 East 59th Street
888-4162
Mon.–Sat.: 11 a.m.–8 p.m.; Sun.: 12 noon–6 p.m.

349 Sixth Avenue, near West 4th Street
929-7613
Mon.–Sat.: 11 a.m.–8 p.m.; Sun.: 12 noon–6 p.m.

H
O
S
I
E
R
Y

265 Columbus Avenue, near 72nd Street
769-3610
Mon.–Fri.: 10 a.m.–8 p.m.; Sat.: 10 a.m.–9 p.m.; Sun.: 12 noon–7 p.m.

1314 Broadway, near 34th Street
695-0027
Mon.–Sat.: 11 a.m.–8 p.m.; Sun.: 12 noon–6 p.m.
AE, MC, V

The tiny Sock Express stores afford a pleasant alternative to the long lines at department store checkout counters. Open seven days a week, with free delivery service on purchases of $25 or more, this chain features panty hose and socks by such top European and American designers as Givenchy, Calvin Klein, Bill Blass, Alexander Julian, and Oscar De La Renta, as well as the company's own novelty hosiery that's painted, fringed, appliquéd, and jeweled. There are stockings, sheer knee-highs, thigh-highs, garter belts, and socks for women; dress and sports hosiery for men; and practical and silly socks for children. Prices are excellent.

TO BOOT
Dress, casual, and sports socks for men in solids, traditional patterns, and funky prints. (See **Shoes,** p. 427.)

Housewares and Hardware

ANTIQUE

AMERICAN STEEL WINDOW SERVICE
111 West 17th Street
242-8131
Mon.–Fri.: 7:30 a.m.–4 p.m.
No credit cards

In a warehouse filled with thousands of crusty old locks and latches, Daniel Weinberger and his son Peter carry on the family's seventy-six-year-old window-hardware business. Weinberger will try to match missing or broken window hardware from his vast stock of vintage pieces, but if he doesn't have a duplicate he'll supply a reproduction or have a new one made.

FRANÇOISE NUNNALLE
A small and first-rate assortment of antique drapery tiebacks in porcelain, Battersea enamel, brass, bronze, and glass. (See **Linens and Quilts,** p. 382.)

GREAT AMERICAN SALVAGE COMPANY
A large collection of antique and vintage doorknobs and latches in brass, copper, and crystal. (See **Furniture,** p. 231.)

IRREPLACEABLE ARTIFACTS
Antique and vintage doorknobs and latches in brass, copper, and crystal. (See **Furniture,** p. 231.)

PISTON'S
The city's largest collection of vintage drapery tiebacks includes bronze, brass, and porcelain examples, as well as rare ones of American Sandwich glass on pewter. (See **Gifts,** p. 297.)

URBAN ARCHAEOLOGY

Antique, vintage, and reproduction doorknobs, latches, and towel racks in brass and copper. (See **Furniture**, p. 232.)

CONTEMPORARY

B. Altman & Co., Bloomingdale's, and Macy's have well-stocked housewares departments.

BROOKSTONE & CO.

South Street Seaport
18 Fulton Street
344-8108
Mon.–Sat.: 10 a.m.–7 p.m.; Sun.: 12 noon–6 p.m.
AE, MC, V

Brookstone, the New Hampshire vendor of hard-to-find tools, has brought its mail-order catalogue to life in this South Street Seaport store. Pick up a clipboard, choose from among the sample goods on display, mark what you want, and in minutes a conveyor-belt sends down your selection from the storerooms above. The shop features everything from hammers to feather dusters, cassette holders to garden hoses, badminton sets to room humidifiers.

CONRAN'S HABITAT

Mops, dusters, pails, and brooms in primary colors; hooks of all kinds, shelving; and pots, pans, and kitchen utensils and gadgets. (See **Furniture**, p. 267.)

D. F. SANDERS

386 West Broadway
925-9040
Mon.–Sat.: 11 a.m.–7 p.m.; Sun.: 12 noon–5:30 p.m.

125 East 57th Street
753-2121
Mon.–Sat.: 10 a.m.–6 p.m.; Sun.: 12 noon–6 p.m.

952 Madison Avenue, near 74th Street
879-6161
Mon.–Sat.: 10 a.m.–6 p.m.; Sun.: 12 noon–5 p.m.
AE, DC, MC, V

Housewares stores have shed their low-rent image ever since D. F. Sanders opened a flagship store next to the Place des Antiquaires—home to the city's priciest antiques shops. This strikingly handsome

3,500 square-foot, multilevel space was designed by Craig Logan Jackson (responsible, also, for the company's sleek Madison Avenue shop). Happily, D. F. Sanders has not forsaken its housewares roots (top-of-the-line ironing boards, Italian vacuum cleaners, dusting brushes in acid colors, and industrial shelving) or the modern classics it's known for (Alessi bowls and candlesticks, Swid-Powell china, Sasati flatware, and cutting-edge furniture). But now the shops have splashes of color and touches of luxuriousness. Among the new additions are art glass, sterling-silver flatware, fine linens, and designer jewelry. The furniture remains black and minimalistic and includes dining tables and chairs, webbed chaise longues, rolling carts, lamps, and in the warm months, lawn furniture and umbrellas.

GARRETT WADE
161 Sixth Avenue, at Spring Street
Mezzanine
807-1155
Mon.–Fri.: 9 a.m.–5:30 p.m.; Sat.: 10 a.m.–3 p.m.
AE, MC, V

The finest woodworking tools from all over the world are available in Garrett Wade's spare warehouse that's staffed by knowledgeable, helpful, and friendly salespeople. Every type of implement—from Japanese pruning saws to "Norris-Style" long-bed finishing tools—is neatly displayed in this tidy and well-organized showroom. Recently the company enlarged its hardware department, so now, in addition to tools, it carries an overwhelming assortment of hardware in traditional styles. Escutcheons, door locks and latches, table slides, double-post bureau handles, decorative pulls, casters, and hinges—for everything from folding screens to butler's trays—come in cast, forged, extruded, pressed, or spun brass.

GRACIOUS HOME
1220 Third Avenue, at 70th Street
517-6300
Mon.–Sat.: 9 a.m.–7 p.m.; Sun.: 10:30 a.m.–5:30 p.m.

1217 Third Avenue
988-8990
Mon.–Sat.: 9 a.m.–7 p.m.; Sun.: 11 a.m.–5 p.m.
AE, DC, MC, V

The ad reads "everything you need to make your home more liveable" and Gracious Home doesn't disappoint. Large, well-organized, and well-stocked, it offers everything from nails and screws, to pedestal sinks, to stacking washers and dryers. Closet organizers, paints, venetian blinds, wall coverings, bath accessories, vacuum cleaners, pots, pans, kitchen gadgets, curtain rods, tape recorders, clocks, barbecues, picnic baskets, pool floats, and outdoor furniture merely suggest the range. If it's for the home, be assured that Gracious Home will have it.

Recently the owners opened a second shop directly across the street (1217 Third Avenue), and they've filled this new annex with a lavish supply of bed and bath treats—linens, shower curtains, hampers, rugs, bathroom hardware, and wallpapers.

HAMMACHER SCHLEMMER
147 East 57th Street
421-9000
Mon.–Sat.: 10 a.m.–6 p.m.
AE, MC, V

Hammacher Schlemmer is paradise for the gadget-minded. In this unique store it's possible to purchase a minus gravity plant-feeding system or a jet-propelled pedal boat, a portable dry-ice maker or a squirrel-resistant bird feeder, an ultrasonic denture cleaner or an electronic auto compass. But there are things here, too, for those whose needs are simpler—toaster ovens, vacuum cleaners, clock radios, and barbecues.

KRAUS HARDWARE
1127 Third Avenue, near 65th Street
753-3366
Mon.–Tues.: 8:30 a.m.–7 p.m.; Wed.–Fri.: 8:30 a.m.–8 p.m.; Sat.: 9 a.m.–6 p.m.; Sun.: 11 a.m.–6 p.m.

1498 Third Avenue, near 84th Street
288-5235
Mon.–Tues.: 9 a.m.–7 p.m.; Wed.–Fri.: 9 a.m.–8 p.m.; Sat.: 9 a.m.–6 p.m.; Sun.: 11 a.m.–6 p.m.

1781 Second Avenue, at 93rd Street
348-9402
Mon.–Sat.: 9 a.m.–6 p.m.; Sun.: 11 a.m.–6 p.m.
AE, DC, MC, V

Kraus stores are as spacious and well-stocked as suburban hardware stores, and they number among their customers building maintenance crews and co-opers. In addition to the expected—nails and screws, hand- and power-tools, plumbing and electrical supplies, and paints and brushes—they carry a fine selection of decorative hardware, kitchen housewares, small appliances, and cleaning supplies, and they're well-organized and manned by an obliging staff.

M. WOLCHONOK & SON
155 East 52nd Street
755-2168
Mon.–Fri.: 8:45–5:45 p.m.; Sat.: 9 a.m.–4 p.m.; closed Sat. in summer
AE, MC, V

The Wolchonoks have been selling furniture hardware for more than fifty years, and legs and decorative hardware are their specialty. They carry an enormous selection of chair legs and bureau pulls, but if what you're looking for is not in stock, they'll make it up to order. There's also an appealing assortment of authentic reproduction Victorian plumbing fixtures, brass towel racks, and soap baskets, as well as sleekly modern ones in chrome and lucite.

PUTNAM ROLLING LADDER COMPANY
32 Howard Street
226-5147
Mon.–Fri.: 8 a.m–4:30 p.m.

New Yorkers have come to the Putnam Rolling Ladder Company since 1905. The company manufactures extension ladders, step stools, and pulpit ladders, along with steel ones for industry and those used for window cleaning, but Putnam is perhaps most famous for its handsome rolling library ladders. Although the standard is made of red oak, Putnam will make it of any hardwood, including mahogany, ash, and cherry.

RELIABLE HARDWARE
303 Canal Street
966-4166
Mon.–Fri.: 8 a.m.–5:30 p.m.; Sat.: 9 a.m.–5 p.m.; Sun.: 10 a.m.–4 p.m.
AE, MC, V

Reliable Hardware is where serious home builders shop. The cluttered and always crowded store carries an impressive inventory of power and hand tools; electrical, plumbing, and janitorial supplies; paints of all kinds; and nails and screws in every shape and size; along with all the usual hardware-store items. The staff is helpful and expert at many trades and can advise customers on how to build or repair just about anything.

SIMON'S HARDWARE
421 Third Avenue, near 29th Street
532-9220
Mon.–Fri.: 8 a.m.–5:30 p.m.; Sat.: 10 a.m.–4:30 p.m.
AE, MC, V

Whether you're looking for casters and hinges, lock sets, decorative pulls, or bathroom faucets, you'll find it at Simon's. This company has supplied New Yorkers with hardware since 1909, and today the store glows with hundreds of decorative pieces for doors, windows, bathrooms, and furniture. Styles range from antique brass reproductions, to modern chrome and stainless steel, to futuristic lucite examples.

W. G. LEMMON
755 Madison Avenue, near 65th Street
734-4400

Mon.–Fri.: 9 a.m.–6 p.m.; Sat.: 9 a.m.–5:30 p.m.
MC, V

W. G. Lemmon is a neighborhood hardware store and it carries all the things you'd expect to find in such a store—paints, brushes, tools, screws, and nails. But given the neighborhood—posh Madison Avenue—W. G. Lemmon is also well-stocked with the best names in small electric appliances, pots and pans, dishes and glassware, kitchen utensils and gadgets, and cleaning supplies.

WILLIAM HUNRATH CO.
153 East 57th Street
758-0780
Mon.–Fri.: 9 a.m.–5:45 p.m.; Sat.: 9 a.m.–4 p.m.; closed Sat. in summer
AE, MC, V

William Hunrath is one of the city's oldest hardware stores, and it's far from the ordinary neighborhood variety. It boasts one of the largest selections of decorative furniture and cabinet hardware in the country, and on the walls, all neatly displayed, are hundreds of doorknobs, hinges and knockers, drawer slides and pulls, casters, stair rods, switch plates, drapery tiebacks, and bathroom fixtures. Most come in brass or chrome, but Hunrath carries Lucite, high-tech rubber, and bright-colored enamels, and the store stocks brass and onyx nameplates, and brass candelabra and lamp bases, too.

Jewelry

ANTIQUE AND ESTATE JEWELRY

All the major department stores have antique or estate jewelry departments. The Metropolitan Museum of Art carries excellent reproductions of ancient, antique, European, and American jewelry. See **Clothing, Women's, Antique and Vintage.**

AARON FABER GALLERY
Along with bold modern designs you'll find estate and Art Deco jewelry, as well as Retro-Modern pieces from the forties and fifties and early Georg Jensen sterling-silver classics. (See **Fine Jewelry,** p. 349.)

À LA VIEILLE RUSSIE
781 Fifth Avenue, at 59th Street
752-1727
Mon.–Sat.: 10 a.m.–5 p.m.; closed Sat. in summer
AE, V

À La Vieille Russie's tiny display windows offer tantalizing vignettes of the treats within—eighteenth-century jeweled cuff links in their original boxes, a carved agate kiwi on gold legs, a miniature picture of a Romanov princess in an enameled frame, a gold bonbonnière— all arranged like delicate still lifes. Inside you'll discover a palatial and somewhat intimidating interior of rose-colored walls and plush carpeting, set off by the sweep of an elegant staircase. This illustrious house is known the world over for its extraordinary collection of *objets* and jewelry crafted by Peter Carl Fabergé (jeweler, goldsmith, and designer to the Russian court), yet the shop offers many other dazzling delights. Chief among these is the selection of eighteenth- and nineteenth-century European jewelry, one of the largest and most exquisite around. Finely worked cuff links, bracelets, necklaces, rings, and brooches, many set with diamonds and precious stones, are marvels of intricate detailing. Snuffboxes—some crafted of tiny mosaics, others of gold and enameling, still others of bloodstones mounted in gold—are another of the store's specialties, along with rare and gilded Russian icons, and enameled plique-à-jour goblets. Mount the staircase and on the second floor, as much museum as antiques shop, you'll find Russian paintings, porcelains, and candelabra, and a truly fine collection of Russian and French eighteenth-century furniture that once graced the palaces of Russian and French nobility. Very expensive.

AMETHYST
32 East 7th Street
979-9458
Tues.–Fri.: 12 noon–7 p.m.; Sat.: 12 noon–7 p.m.; Sun.: 12 noon–
6 p.m.
No credit cards

Lawyer Guy DeVille's favorite color is purple and amethyst is his favorite stone, so he combined his passions and opened a shop appropriately called Amethyst. Along with jewelry set with that semiprecious stone, DeVille's vest-pocket-size shop is brim full of purple, mauve, and lavender collectibles. He carries Victorian sash pins, Art Nouveau brooches, Art Deco cigarette holders, and designer jewelry from the thirties, forties, and fifties. Even the antique kimonos, beaded evening purses, hats, and evening wraps are in the royal shade.

THE ANTIQUE BUFF
321 1/2 Bleecker Street
243-7144
Mon.–Fri.: 12 noon–5:30 p.m.; Sat: 12 noon–5 p.m.
AE, MC, V

A tiny shop, the Antique Buff is filled to overflowing with Victorian, Georgian, Art Nouveau, and Art Deco jewelry. Cameo brooches are a specialty, but there are Victorian mourning pieces, as well as a wonderful array of rings, including engagement and wedding bands that are as early as the 1800s and as recent as the twenties. Also in evidence are antique silver and bric-a-brac, canes and walking sticks, cigarette cases, and gold pocket watches. Prices are good.

ARES RARE
961 Madison Avenue, near 75th Street
988-0190
Mon.–Sat.: 11 a.m.–5:45 p.m.; closed Sat. in July and August
AE, MC, V

Ares Rare's treasures span 4,000 years and encompass everything from Greek and Roman coin jewelry, to ancient Egyptian scarabs, to glamorous French creations of the twenties and thirties. In addition to an exquisite assortment of necklaces, bracelets, rings, brooches, and cuff links (many antique and set with large diamonds and precious stones), there are scores of cameos, intaglios, mosaics, enamels, and Victorian memorial jewelry. Salespeople are knowledgeable and helpful. Expensive.

ASPREY LIMITED
A small but pedigreed array of mostly eighteenth- and nineteenth-century jewelry that includes brooches, earrings, necklaces, rings, and cuff links, many set with diamonds, pearls, and precious stones. (See **Gifts,** p. 299.)

THE BELLE EPOCH
211 East 60th Street
319-7870
Mon.–Sat.: 11:30 a.m.–7 p.m.
All major

Alice San Germano and her husband, Felix, operate a wholesale antique furniture business, but the Belle Epoch is their tiny retail outlet for their hoard of antique and vintage jewelry. Bakelite bracelets, Victorian buttons transformed into dazzling clip-on earrings, marcasite brooches and pendants, crystal-and-silver ropes à la Chanel, sterling-silver Mexican jewelry from the forties and fifties, old pearl necklaces, and assorted bar pins are constants among the ever-changing treats.

EDITH WEBER & CO.
Place des Antiquaires
125 East 57th Street
688-4331
Mon.–Sat.: 11 a.m.–5 p.m.
AE, MC, V

Edith Weber is an internationally recognized expert in antique and estate jewelry, and in her glistening little shop she carries jewelry from the seventeenth through the nineteenth centuries. Her offerings are as diverse as a Fabergé pendant and a George Washington memorial ring containing a lock of hair. Rose-cut diamonds, semiprecious stones set in intricately worked settings, austere neoclassic earrings and pins, and intricately carved coral are among her stellar stock. Expensive.

FRED LEIGHTON
773 Madison Avenue, at 66th Street
288-1872
Mon.–Sat.: 10 a.m.–6 p.m.; closed Sat. in July

Trump Tower
725 Fifth Avenue, at 56th Street
751-2330
Mon.–Sat.: 10 a.m.–6 p.m.; closed Sat. in July
344 AE, DC, MC, V

Those who remember the Fred Leighton Greenwich Village clothing and jewelry store of the sixties filled with Mexican wedding dresses and American Indian jewelry will find it hard to believe that the Madison Avenue Fred Leighton, purveyor of fabulous Cartier, Fabergé, and Lalique antique jewels, is one and the same. But Murray Mondschein is the man behind both. His estate jewelry collection includes Art Nouveau brooches and necklaces of René Lalique, George Fouquet, and Paul and Henri Vever, along with the Art Deco designs of Cartier, Tiffany, and Van Cleef & Arpels. Although Mondschein is most known for his restrained Deco jewelry, he also carries Cartier and Van Cleef's exuberant and ornate pieces that were made for Indian potentates, along with a breathtaking selection of pearls that might include an elaborate Victorian choker or a rare and exquisite single strand. Some of his gems are as early as the 1800s, others as recent as the fifties. Very expensive.

GOREVIC & GOREVIC

Among the beguiling mix of estate jewelry are brooches set with precious stones, diamond and emerald pendant necklaces, beautifully worked diamond bracelets, and gold pocket watches. (See **Silver**, p. 439.)

ILENE CHAZANOF

7 East 20th Street
Fourth floor
254-5564
Mon.–Fri.: by appointment only; Sat.: 11 a.m.–6 p.m.

Ilene Chazanof started selling antique jewelry to earn a little extra cash while she attended graduate school, and her sideline soon burgeoned into a full-time business. Today Chazanof has a large showroom crammed with jewelry and *objets* from the 1880s to the fifties, all carefully organized by period or motif. One drawer is filled with Egyptian Revival jewelry, another with Victoriana, still others with Art Nouveau, Arts and Crafts, early Georg Jensen, silver Mexican pieces from the forties and fifties, and postwar Retro-Modern. Bird, fish, insect, beast, or cartoon character pins of Bakelite, paste, enamel, or silver fill dozens of drawers to overflowing. And vintage evening purses with exquisite handles are jammed into still others. Chazanof has put together a fine group of period glass from Orrefors, Kosta-Boda, and Venini along with American Art Pottery and a sprinkling of Mission furniture. And she has a winning collection of early Jensen sterling-silver serving pieces. Since Chazanof's prices are some of the best around, things come and go quickly.

JAMES ROBINSON

Exquisite eighteenth- and nineteenth-century brooches, bracelets, and rings (many set with premium diamonds and precious stones), delicate Victorian jewelry, along with intricately detailed and signed pieces from the twenties and thirties. (See **Silver**, p. 440.)

JAMES II GALLERIES

Nestled in glass-topped jewelry cases are beguiling examples of Victorian brooches, bracelets, and earrings made of piqué, cut-steel, marcasite, early paste, Scotch agate, and gold. (See **China and Glassware**, p. 67.)

J. MAVEC & COMPANY, LTD.

Among the eclectic mix of antique English jewelry you're likely to find Georgian diamond earrings; an important Victorian diamond, emerald, and gold bracelet; Victorian gem-set rings and earrings; Scottish agate brooches; a few piqué pieces; along with a collection of Edwardian cuff links set with pearls, diamonds, or precious stones. (See **Silver**, p. 441.)

JOSIE & PAUL

Place des Antiquaires
125 East 57th Street
838-6841
Mon.–Sat.: 11 a.m.–6 p.m.
AE, MC, V

In their elegant new quarters—they were formerly at the Manhattan Arts & Antiques Center—Josie Yoslowitz and Paul Marino now have ample space for their stunning jewelry collection. Edwardian is a specialty, mostly diamonds and precious stones set in gold, but they carry Retro pieces from the forties, along with a small selection of American silver, including Tiffany and Gorham. Prices are high and service can be cool.

KENTSHIRE GALLERIES

Each piece of jewelry is individually chosen by the owners, and although antique (mostly Georgian, Victorian, and Edwardian) the brooches, necklaces, bracelets, and earrings are bold and refreshingly simple in design. (See **Furniture**, p. 243.)

MACKLOWE GALLERY & MODERNISM

The jewelry, as impressive as the furnishings, includes signed pieces by Tiffany, Cartier, Boucheron, Fouquet, Van Cleef & Arpels, as well as exquisite Georgian and Victorian bracelets, brooches, and necklaces. (See **Furniture**, p. 235.)

MALVINA L. SOLOMON

Glass-topped cases are crammed with antique jewelry, mostly marcasite set with semiprecious stones, but there are Mexican sterling-silver designs from the forties, Bakelite bracelets and brooches, rhinestone earrings and necklaces from the fifties, and animal pins of all kinds. (See **China and Glassware**, p. 68.)

MASSAB BROTHERS

782 Lexington Avenue, at 61st Street

752-7139
Mon.–Sat.: 10 a.m.–6 p.m.
AE, MC, V

Collectors of antique jewelry come to this dusty, tiny sliver of a store that looks as if it had been around for hundreds of years, for its appealing and surprisingly extensive array of Georgian, Victorian, Art Deco, and Art Nouveau treasures. There are literally hundreds of earrings to choose from, almost as many brooches and bracelets, and scores of rings and cuff links. Also in evidence are pearl necklaces, ivory cuff bracelets, jade pendants, and a fine selection of gold pocket watches, and prices are as attractive as the jewelry.

MEISEL-PRIMAVERA
An enormous collection of Mexican silver jewelry from the forties and fifties (including the work of Pineda and Castillo), along with Georg Jensen, Ed Weiner, and Sam Kramer designs from the fifties. (See **China and Glassware,** p. 68.)

MURIEL KARASIK GALLERY
A witty collection of jewelry from the thirties, forties, and fifties, much of it inspired by sporting or Western themes—vintage Olympic medals; brooches and bracelets embellished with golfers, tennis pros, or polo players; and others in the shape of cowboy hats, saddles, or boots. Karasik also offers a fine group of Mexican sterling-silver jewelry from the thirties through the sixties, including designs by William Spratling. (See **Furniture,** p. 257.)

NATCON ART LTD.
Place des Antiquaires
125 East 57th Street
751-5422
Mon.–Sat.: 11 a.m.–6 p.m.
AE, MC, V

Natcon Art is the New York branch of Demner, a Viennese company that's internationally known for its fine collection of late-nineteenth- and early-twentieth-century jewelry by such great names as Cartier and Fabergé. Many of these rare and important pieces are set with diamonds and precious stones, but others are romantic Art Nouveau, Art Deco, and Retro creations of pearls, moonstones, and semiprecious gems. There's also a smattering of Wiener Werkstätte furniture and silver, including Josef Hoffmann designs.

PRIMAVERA GALLERY
808 Madison Avenue, near 68th Street
288-1569
Mon.–Fri.: 11 a.m.–6 p.m.; Sat.: 11 a.m.–6 p.m.; closed Sat. in summer
All major

347

All the great Art Deco and Art Nouveau jewelry artisans are represented in Audrey Friedman's sparkling gallery—Cartier, Van Cleef & Arpels, Bouchéron, René Lalique, George Fouquet, Tiffany. She carries a sprinkling of Georgian and Victorian pieces, too, along with exquisite cigarette and compact cases, jewel-like travel clocks, and gem-encrusted evening purses. There's glassware by such top Art Nouveau and Art Deco designers as Lalique, Marinot, Luce, and Daum, along with Retro pieces by Venini. Downstairs you'll find mostly European Art Deco furniture, including the work of Jean Durand, Jean-Michel Frank, Pierre Chareau, and Eileen Gray.

S. J. SHRUBSOLE

Although not generally known, Shrubsole's period jewelry is as choice as its silver. Each piece is individually selected, and among the rare treasures are exquisitely worked eighteenth- and nineteenth-century necklaces, bracelets, brooches, rings, earrings, and cuff links, many set with precious stones. (See **Silver,** p. 442.)

SMALL PLEASURES

Manhattan Arts & Antiques Center
1050 Second Avenue, at 55th Street
688-8510
Mon.–Sat.: 11 a.m.–5 p.m.; Sun.: 12:30 p.m.–5 p.m.
AE, MC, V

Joseph Caravella and Ralph Furst's small but well-stocked gallery is filled with Georgian through forties estate jewelry. Rubies, emeralds, and jade are the chief attraction. Particularly appealing are the diamond and ruby line bracelets, bow brooches set with precious stones, diamond and pearl circle pins, thirties cocktail rings, and Victorian cameos and earrings.

SYLVIA PINES—UNIQUITIES

An enormous and stunning stock of Art Deco marcasite jewelry that includes dozens of brooches, bracelets, earrings, and rings, along with an array of Victorian and Georgian pieces. (See **Handbags,** p. 315.)

V.Z.I., INC.

Place des Antiquaires
125 East 57th Street
319-1855
Mon.–Sat.: 11 a.m.–6 p.m.
AE

The leopard-patterned carpet seems an appropriate backdrop for Ilva Invernizzi's collection of fanciful antique jewelry. Since Invernizzi focuses on pieces that were crafted in Europe from the twenties through the forties, you might find an Art Deco ruby jabot pin by Janesich, a rare bumblebee diamond brooch from Van Cleef & Arpels, a pink-quartz and

348

Chinese green-agate inkstand by Cartier, along with inventive designs by less-well-known artisans.

FINE JEWELRY

All the department stores offer fine jewelry. Bergdorf Goodman carries Angela Cummings and Barry Kieselstein-Cord's imaginative designs; Bloomingdale's has an Artwear jewelry section. See also **Museum Gift Shops.**

AARON FABER GALLERY
666 Fifth Avenue, at 53rd Street
586-8411
Mon.–Wed., Fri.: 10 a.m.–6 p.m.; Thurs.: 10 a.m.–7 p.m.; Sat.:
10 a.m.–5 p.m.
AE, DC, MC, V

Aaron Faber specializes in jewelry from the twentieth century, so you'll find imaginative and boldly designed handcrafted gold pieces by modern artists, along with beautiful Cartier brooches from the twenties. There are constantly changing exhibitions of contemporary goldsmith's modern designs, as well as a permanent collection of their work, and these coexist with Art Deco treasures; Retro ones from the forties and fifties; and early Georg Jensen sterling-silver pieces. And Faber has a singularly fine group of antique and vintage pocket and wristwatches. Among the hundreds of unusual examples you might find an extremely rare Longines with a right-angle tank, a very rare Art Deco Gruen driver's watch, or a fifties Rolex with a sculptured case.

ALEX STREETER
152 Prince Street
925-6496
Wed.–Sat.: 12 noon–8 p.m.; or by appointment
AE

Tiny and spartan, this shop is a showcase for Alex Streeter's original designs in gold, silver, bronze, and brass. Streeter works in three distinctive styles—sleeky modern, historical, and futuristic. A skyline necklace includes such legends of the urban landscape as the Flatiron, Speer, Chrysler, and Empire State buildings; and Streeter crafts watches in the shape of spaceships, and belt buckles that look like streamlined trains. Streeter is famous for his surrealistic faceless "melted" watches.

349

ARTWEAR
456 West Broadway
673-3388
Mon.–Fri.: 11 a.m.–6 p.m.; Sat., Sun.: 12 noon–7 p.m.

A T & T Arcade
550 Madison Avenue, near 56th Street
593-3388
Mon.–Sat.: 11 a.m.–6 p.m.
AE, MC, V

ROBERT LEE MORRIS–ARTWEAR
409 West Broadway
431-9405
Mon.–Fri., Sun.: 11 a.m.–6 p.m.; Sat.: 12 noon–7 p.m.
AE, MC, V

Robert Lee Morris's Artwear gallery in SoHo looks like a glitzy archaeological dig. The two-story space is punctuated by two slabs of granite
jutting out at the entrance, a pool of water, and shafts of light from a
skylight above. Glass-fronted cases lining the walls house the daring
designs of Morris's stable of forty artists that might include Carol
Motty and her rubber-ribbed silk scarves, Ted Muehling's organically
inspired pieces, Cara Croniger's chunky rainbow-hued acrylic bracelets, along with Morris's own assertive designs. In addition to traditional gold, silver, and platinum, these artists are as likely to use
plastic, oxidized brass, wood, rubber, silicone, and other unconven-
tional materials in their work. In Artwear's uptown branch located in
the AT&T Arcade you'll find an edited selection of the SoHo stock, and
in the **Robert Lee Morris** shop the complete line of Morris's jewelry.

BALOGH JEWELERS
798 Madison Avenue, near 67th Street
517-9440
Mon.–Sat.: 10 a.m.–6 p.m.
AE, DC, MC, V

Balogh Jewelers has been around since 1910, and the company occupies an understated little shop that allows the jewels to dazzle.
Among its lavish stock are pearl necklaces in all sizes, beautifully
executed ruby and emerald designs, sapphire and diamond earclips,
and traditional and classic-looking one-of-a-kind pieces that incorporate large and rare gemstones. Many of the new designs have the look
of old estate jewelry with the lavish use of diamonds, rubies, pearls,
and sapphires, but Balogh also offers important antique treasures. An
in-house team of designers can create contemporary designs for those
who wish a high-style fashion look, and they can tackle custom work.

BLACK STARR & FROST
Plaza Hotel

768 Fifth Avenue, at 59th Street
838-0720
Mon.–Sat.: 10 a.m.–5:30 p.m.
AE, DC, MC, V

Black Starr & Frost is tucked away in the elegant lobby of the Plaza
Hotel, and these jewelers, on the New York scene since 1810, offer jewels to match the setting. Important gold and pavé diamond brooches
and earrings, pendant necklaces of emeralds or sapphires encrusted in
diamonds, chunky pavé-diamond-and-gold link bracelets, and romantic mabes circled with diamonds and worked into earrings, rings, and
necklaces are a few of the delights you'll find here. But this small shop
also offers witty diamond lapel pins in the shape of circles, curves, and
"X"s, Rolex and Baume & Mercier watches, as well as cufflinks, money
clips, and sterling-silver frames.

BORIS–LE BEAU JEWELERS
721 Madison Avenue, near 63rd Street
752-4186
Mon.–Sat.: 10 a.m.–5:30 p.m.
AE, MC, V

Madeline van Erde and Norman Le Beau's creations are not for the
timid. Among their extravagant and fanciful designs are chunky chain
necklaces of granulated gold and pavé diamonds, oversized gold bows
set with diamonds, intricately worked diamond and cabochon emerald
and sapphire necklaces, and chokers of large South Sea pearls and
gold links with matching earrings and rings. In fact rings and earrings
are the shop's specialty, and Erde and Le Beau will do custom orders or
transform an old ring by hand-crafting a custom-fit jacket of gold and
gem stones.

BUCCELLATI
Trump Tower
725 Fifth Avenue, at 56th Street
308-5533
Mon.–Sat.: 10 a.m.–6 p.m.
AE, MC, V

Mario Buccellati created his extraordinary jewelry in the twenties, and
it has never been surpassed. It was intricately worked, highly original,
and exquisitely crafted. Today the Buccellati family continues to inter-
pret Mario's designs and offers these, along with more modern creations by the firm's specially trained artisans, in their elegant Trump
Tower gallery outfitted with crystal chandeliers, a painted ceiling, and
ornate draperies. Imaginative artistry, fine craftsmanship, and an artist's way with gold still distinguish the jewelry, and the use of precious
stones—rubies, emeralds, sapphires, and diamonds—is extraordinary.
A fourth floor boutique offers smaller-scale gold and silver pieces,

351

mostly without stones, that are a shade more affordable than the very costly gem-encrusted creations.

BULGARI

Hotel Pierre
2 East 61st Street
486-0086
Mon.–Sat.: 10 a.m.–5:30 p.m.
AE, MC, V

Tucked behind ornate metal doors in the lobby of the Hotel Pierre you'll find Bulgari's tiny gallery filled with brooches, rings, earrings, necklaces, and cufflinks that display the distinctive Bulgari touch. Large, colorful precious stones set high on beautiful mountings and elaborate creations of diamonds, rubies, and emeralds are two of the famous looks. Cabochon-cut stones are another specialty at this branch of the Italian shop, and these are worked into handsome bracelets and rings. Bulgari also offers unlikely materials used in combination with precious stones and metals—diamonds and hematite, gold and stainless steel, fancy-colored diamonds and frosted crystal. This winter Bulgari opens a glistening new boutique on Fifth Avenue at 59th Street. Three times as large as the original gallery, it will offer a broader range of jewelry.

CARTIER

653 Fifth Avenue, at 52nd Street
753-0111
Mon.–Sat.: 10 a.m.–5:15 p.m.

Trump Tower
725 Fifth Avenue, at 56th Street
308-0840
Mon.–Sat.: 10 a.m.–6 p.m.

Westbury Hotel
Madison Avenue, at 70th Street
249-3240
Mon.–Sat.: 10 a.m.–5:30 p.m.
AE, MC, V

Cartier is housed in a landmarked neo-Italian marble and granite palazzo that, according to legend, was traded by the owner, Mrs. Plant, to Pierre Cartier for a string of natural pearls. True or not, this elegant mansion is an appropriate backdrop for the fabulous Cartier jewels, a name synonymous with jewelry since 1847. The Art Deco collection and the reproductions from Cartier's archives are breathtaking; there are classic gold creations, and necklaces, brooches, and bracelets of diamonds, precious stones, and gold combined in understated ways, so although they're "important" pieces, they're far from glitzy. Les Must de Cartier offers watches (including the famous Santos and the Panther), clocks, frames, sterling-silver tableware, scarves, handbags and briefcases, and small leather goods. Upstairs you'll find classic stationery, Limoges china, and crystal. The Madison Avenue and Trump Tower branches offer edited versions of Cartier's jewelry, but well-stocked Les Must departments.

CHAUMET
48 East 57th Street
371-3960
Mon.–Sat.: 10 a.m.–5:30 p.m.
AE

For more than 200 years the name Chaumet has been associated with jewelry and it's been a legendary fixture on Paris's Place Vendôme. In its glitzy New York store classic pieces share the space with innovative contemporary designs; bold necklaces and bracelets that combine hematite and pearls and a line of glamorous yellow-gold creations. In addition to jewels Chaumet stocks the city's largest collection of Breguet's exquisite and pricey hand-crafted watches.

DAVID WEBB
7 East 57th Street
421-3030
Mon.–Fri.: 10 a.m.–5:30 p.m.; Oct.–Dec., Sat: 10 a.m.–5 p.m.
AE, V

For years David Webb has been known for his opulent and extravagant designs, and his store is as grandiose as his jewelry. Enormous precious and semiprecious stones are set in tiers of pavé diamonds, a chunky carved emerald-bead necklace has a cabochon center surrounded by pavé diamonds and platinum, South Sea pearl earrings have pavé diamond wings. Many of Webb's bold designs incorporate animal images, and his creations are not for the timid; they're for those who enjoy being noticed.

FORTUNOFF
The mind-boggling selection of jewelry includes precious and semiprecious stone pieces set in fourteen- or eighteen-karat gold or sterling silver. The designs are rarely innovative or unusual but stick to the tried and true, but prices are good. You'll find hundreds of gold chains, pearl necklaces, scores of bracelets, rings (including diamond wedding rings), and earrings, as well as all the important brand-name watches. (See **Silver,** p. 440.)

FRED JOAILLIER
703 Fifth Avenue, at 55th Street
832-3733
Mon.–Sat.: 10 a.m.–5:30 p.m.
AE, MC, V

In this plush, thickly carpeted store Fred Joaillier, a Parisian jeweler, offers high-quality diamonds, rubies, sapphires, emeralds, and pearls in artfully designed settings. You'll find pendant necklaces set with rubies or emeralds and dripping diamonds, diamond and sapphire earclips along with Fred's signature Force 10 gold-and-stainless-steel nautical-rope collection of bracelets, necklaces, earrings, cufflinks, and pins. In addition to the company's own watches, the store carries such top names as Audemars Piguet, Baume & Mercier, Piaget, and Rolex.

GOREVIC & GOREVIC, LTD.

Appealing contemporary designs in eighteen-karat gold—chunky bracelets and necklaces of cabochon rubies and diamonds, gold chains encrusted with pavé diamonds, large stones in heavy gold settings. The handsome watch collection includes the Rolex Oyster and Audemars Piguet. (See **Silver,** p. 439.)

HANS APPENZELLER

426 West Broadway
941-7042
Tues.–Sat.: 11 a.m.–7 p.m.; Sun: 12 noon–4:45 p.m.
AE, MC, V

Hans Appenzeller began his career as a minimalist who was inspired by the Bauhaus tradition, and he created starkly beautiful geometric jewelry. Recently, Appenzeller's work has evolved along more sensuous and naturalistic lines, and he uses the lost wax process to sculpt extravagant pieces that are fluted like flower petals or fabric or filigree and to reinterpret antique forms. He crafts most of his pieces of eighteen-karat gold or sterling-silver mesh (sometimes set with diamonds or precious stones), and he does undulating bracelets, filigree brooches, and pleated neck pieces that are indeed works of art.

HARRY WINSTON

718 Fifth Avenue, near 56th Street
245-2000
Mon.–Sat.: 10 a.m.–5 p.m.

Trump Tower
725 Fifth Avenue, at 56th Street
245-2000
Mon.–Fri.: 10 a.m.–5 p.m.
AE

Harry Winston was known as the King of Diamonds, and his stores are still famous as sources for lavish diamonds and costly jewelry. Often huge stones of superb quality are mounted in hand-crafted and very classic settings. Even a pearl choker is likely to have an enormous emerald centerpiece. The smaller Trump Tower shop houses a slightly less costly collection, but since everything at Winston's is investment quality, it's all frightfully expensive.

HELEN WOODHULL
743 Fifth Avenue, near 57th Street
Eighth floor
826-1212
Mon.–Sat.: 10 a.m.–5 p.m.
AE, MC, V

Stepping into Helen Woodhull's gallery is like entering a charmed world. Overstuffed sofas, a wood-burning fireplace, plush carpeting, and classical music are the backdrop for Woodhull's intricately designed jewelry inspired by classic, romantic, and mythical themes. Diamonds, garnets, tourmalines, rubies, rhodolite, and chiastolite— often cabochon cut—are set into exquisite eighteen-karat gold, silver, or platinum settings. There are intaglios and cameos of mythical animals, and Woodhull's collection includes pendants, bracelets, necklaces, earrings, rings, and cufflinks. Woodhull also has a stunning group of framed antique embroideries.

H. STERN
645 Fifth Avenue, near 51st Street
688-0300
Mon.–Sat.: 10 a.m.–5:30 p.m.
AE, DC, MC, V

Hans Stern founded the company in Rio in 1946, and since then H. Stern has supplied the world with a dazzling collection of colored gemstones. It's the only company in the world that encompasses all stages of jewelry production, from mining to polishing, to designing, to merchandising, and H. Stern has more than 200 retail outlets. Diamonds, rubies, emeralds, sapphires, and Brazilian gems are worked into beautifully crafted contemporary settings. The second floor gallery is filled with gifts: agate-handled letter openers and magnifying glasses, boxes, cufflinks, and exquisite stone-carved animals.

ILIAS LALAOUNIS
4 West 57th Street
265-0600
Mon.–Sat: 10 a.m.–5 p.m.
All major

Internationally famous Greek jeweler Ilias Lalaounis designs modern interpretations of ancient Greek art. He uses age-old techniques such as granulation, martele, cisele, and filigree to create exquisite and intricate pieces. Everything is hand-finished in the company's workshop in Athens, and most of it is crafted in 18- or 22-karat gold.

MANFREDI

737 Madison Avenue, near 64th Street
734-8710
Mon.–Fri.: 10 a.m.–6 p.m.; Sat.: 11 a.m.–5:30 p.m.
AE, DC, MC, V

In his elegant little shop Giulio Manfredi, a young Italian jeweler, combines classic techniques with modern design to produce hand-crafted jewelry in unexpected shapes and colors. Precious and semiprecious stones are bezel-set into highly original and fluid pieces of eighteen-karat gold. A necklace might be half chain, the rest solid gold; a diamond might be set within a larger stone; earrings in a pair might be set with different-colored stones. Manfredi offers his own line of watches, along with a selection of crystal, silver, and wood tabletop items.

MARINA B

809 Madison Avenue, near 67th Street
288-9708
Mon.–Sat.: 10 a.m.–5:30 p.m.; closed Sat. in summer
AE, MC, V

Extravagant gems are treated playfully in Marina B's peach-colored gallery located in a lovingly restored Art Nouveau building. Her designs are mounted in 18-karat-gold settings and feature sleek and modern styling and such innovative features as reversible construction and interchangeable settings. Each piece is signed and one-of-a-kind or from a limited edition.

MIKIMOTO

608 Fifth Avenue, near 48th Street
586-7153
Mon.–Sat.: 10 a.m.–5:30 p.m.
AE, DC, MC, V

Kokichi Mikimoto was the originator of cultured pearls, and this tranquil branch of the Tokyo store is the city's best cultured pearl source. Necklaces in three lengths—choker, matinee, and opera—and in every size and color fill the glass cases, along with rings, bracelets, and earrings set with pearls. Quality ranges from good to superior, and the gallery stocks river, seed, and black South Sea pearls as well.

MISHON MISHON

410 Columbus Avenue, near 79th Street
769-2277
Mon.–Sat.: 11 a.m.–8 p.m.; Sun.: 11 a.m.–7 p.m.

899 Madison Avenue, near 72nd Street
288-7599
Mon.–Sat.: 11 a.m.–7 p.m.
All major

High-style jewelry is the passion of the Mishon brothers, Isaac and Edward, and the fashion magazines' favorite designers are in residence here: Wendy Gell, David Yurman, Mark Spirito, Patricia Von Musulin, Steve Vaubel, Robert Lee Morris, and the like. It's all up-to-the-moment and ever-changing. Most of the pieces are made in precious metals and set with semiprecious stones although the Mishons also offer one-of-a-kind fine jewelry designs featuring diamonds, emeralds, and sapphires. A collar of 18-karat gold is set with pavé diamonds and cabochon emeralds; a flexible panther bracelet mixes diamonds and sapphires. You'll find trendy watches, too, in sterling silver, gold, titanium, and rubber, as well as an array of sunglasses that are au courant, attractive handbags by Luc Benoit, and Patricia Underwood hats.

NEIL ISMAN GALLERY
1100 Madison Avenue, near 82nd Street
628-3688
Mon.–Sat.: 10:30 a.m.–6 p.m.; closed Sat. in summer
AE, DC, MC, V

Cutting-edge jewelry designs created by the country's most talented contemporary artists are this small shop's specialty. The owners mount seasonal shows of exciting new pieces, as well as stocking a permanent collection of artists' works. The hand-crafted pieces are mostly one-of-a-kind or produced in very limited editions, and the workmanship and quality are first-rate. Surprisingly, the gallery also offers a winning selection of antique jewelry, as well as a fine group of vintage watches that date from 1915 through the fifties.

PAVILLON CHRISTOFLE
A beautiful collection of necklaces, earrings, and bracelets that combine 18-karat gold, sterling silver, and precious stones. (See **Silver**, p. 444.)

REINSTEIN/ROSS
122 Prince Street
226-4513
Tues.–Sun.: 12 noon–6 p.m.

29 East 73rd Street
772-1901
Mon.–Sat.: 11:30 a.m.–6:30 p.m.
AE, MC, V

Although tiny and spartan the Reinstein/Ross shops sparkle with exquisite jewelry that manages to look cutting-edge and ancient at the same time. Granulated 22-karat gold is a chief attraction, and it's set with unusually colored cabochon sapphires, emeralds, or garnets. You might find carved emerald-bead necklaces with gold braiding, a freshwater pearl necklace embedded with multicolored sapphire beads, along with beguiling rings and enticing bracelets. The craftsmanship is superior, the designs outstanding.

ROYAL COPENHAGEN PORCELAIN/GEORG JENSEN SILVERSMITHS

The charm of flora and fauna are exquisitely captured in Georg Jensen's sterling-silver brooches, and his plaited necklaces and bold earrings are equally seductive. (See **China and Glassware**, p. 78.)

SAITY JEWELRY

Trump Tower
725 Fifth Avenue, at 56th Street
308-6570
Mon.–Sat.: 10 a.m.–6 p.m.
AE, MC, V

Come to Saity if you're looking for ivory or American Indian jewelry. Chunky ivory bangle bracelets are set with precious or semiprecious stones, and there are important-looking ivory bead necklaces along with squash-blossom belts, liquid sterling-silver necklaces, and turquoise-and-silver bracelets and rings. Although most of the jewelry is contemporary (and designed by the owner), there are turn-of-the-century treasures from the Navaho, Hopi, and Zuni tribes, as well as antique ivory pieces.

STEPHEN P. KAHAN LTD.

810 Madison Avenue, at 67th Street
772-7997
Mon.–Sat.: 11 a.m.–5:30 p.m.; closed Sat. in summer
AE, MC, V

Originally known as Cravetz Kahan, the partners separated a couple of years ago and Stephen Kahan now owns this warm and friendly shop that's not intimidating like so many Madison Avenue emporiums. Pearls and yellow diamonds are one of the gallery's chief attractions, and in addition to important-looking contemporary designs, Kahan offers treasures by such luminaries as Lalique, Mauboussin, Chaumet, and Van Cleef, along with early David Webb gems. Kahan handles custom work and will remodel old pieces.

TIFFANY & COMPANY

727 Fifth Avenue, at 57th Street
755-8000
Mon.–Sat.: 10 a.m.–5:30 p.m.
AE, MC, V

This legendary establishment, once a humble stationery and "fancy goods" store, is the name (and robin's-egg-blue gift box) that's sought by thousands to lend cachet to their purchases. The main floor holds the jewelry, which includes the store's own classics as well as Jean Schlumberger's sedate creations and the innovative designs of Elsa Peretti and Paloma Picasso. Here also is Tiffany's remarkable collection of diamond solitaire engagement rings, diamond and gold wedding bands, men's signet rings, and its vast selection of watches. In addition to Tiffany's exclusive timepieces there's Audemars Piguet, Patek Philippe, Breguet, and Baume & Mercier. Upstairs, on the second floor is silver (sterling-silver flatware, trays, and hollowware, along with an enormous selection of silver gift items, such as frames, pens, key rings, baby mugs, and spoons), and Tiffany's very traditional stationery department. The third floor, amidst table settings designed by the rich and famous, houses Tiffany's crystal department, with stemware, barware, bowls, candlesticks, and vases by the top manufacturers, and here also is the store's very fine and extensive array of china, porcelain, and earthenware. You'll find all the most wanted names as well as Tiffany's Private Stock, which is hand-painted in Paris and a Tiffany exclusive. Since Tiffany's prices are so surprisingly broad, there's sure to be something here that most people can afford.

UNDERGROUND JEWELER
147 East 86th Street, in the subway arcade
348-7866
Mon.–Fri.: 10 a.m.–8 p.m.; Sat.: 10 a.m.–7 p.m.
AE, MC, V

Although a subway arcade might seem an unlikely spot for buying jewelry, the Underground Jeweler carries an enormous selection from more than sixty countries. Most of it has an ethnic look, so you'll find scores of chunky beaded necklaces, but there are gold earrings, rings, and bracelets set with semiprecious stones, hand-worked sterling-silver pendants, along with a few vintage American and European pieces. Egypt, Africa, Israel, Rumania, Russia, France, and Italy are all represented, and prices are exceptionally good.

VAN CLEEF & ARPELS
744 Fifth Avenue, at 57th Street
644-9500
Mon.–Sat.: 10 a.m.–5:30 p.m.
AE, DC, MC, V

Tucked away in a lushly carpeted corner on Bergdorf Goodman's main floor is the legendary Van Cleef & Arpels, jewelers to royalty. Along with the signature pendant necklaces of emeralds or rubies or sapphires encrusted in diamonds, you'll find such baubles as gold necklaces with diamond baguettes; pearl necklaces centered with cabochon emeralds, rubies, sapphires, and diamonds; bracelets of diamond flowers; and platinum and diamonds worked into hair barrettes and clips. And this small boutique is well stocked with Van Cleef & Arpels's watches.

COSTUME JEWELRY

All the department stores have costume jewelry departments that offer a wide range of styles. See the **Museum Gift Shops** and **Handcraft Galleries** sections.

CIRO OF BOND STREET
711 Fifth Avenue, near 55th Street
752-0441
Mon.–Sat.: 10 a.m.–6 p.m.

6 West 57th Street
581-0767
Mon.–Sat.: 10 a.m.–6 p.m.

791 Madison Avenue, at 67th Street
628-1290
Mon.–Sat.: 10 a.m.–6 p.m.
All major

For more than fifty years Ciro has been providing New Yorkers with fantastic fakes, and among its *faux* treasures are good copies of jewels from such legendary houses as Harry Winston, Bulgari, and Tiffany. The stores offer a large assortment of cultured pearls in all lengths, cirolite made into rings and necklaces, and Ciro's own brand of watches. Alas, even the bogus gems are not cheap.

GLITZ BLITZ
72 Thompson Street
966-1710
Tues.–Sun.: 12:30 p.m.–6 p.m.
All major

Most of the funky bijous in this snug little SoHo shop are made by Parisian artisans, and they're stunningly displayed by the owners, who were once window dressers at Henri Bendel. Art Deco paste earrings and brooches made from vintage molds are artistically arranged on bird cages and wire torsos. Nooks contain giant yet delicate floral pins along with Diana Milia's romantic hand-painted, molded-leather face brooches. Lapel pins are painted, laquered, and embellished with beads from the forties, giant cuffs are made of papier-mâché and plaster, then painted medieval colors, and there are oversized watches, suede bracelets in deep greens and rich magentas, and earrings galore.

JOLIE GABOR FOR COUNTESS MADELINE LTD.
699 Madison Avenue, near 62nd Street
838-3193

Mon.–Sat.: 10 a.m.–6 p.m.; closed Sat. in summer
AE, MC, V

Although this tiny gilt salon furnished in imitation Louis XV is now owned by Madeline Herling, it still carries the opulent fakes that Jolie Gabor made famous. Victorian-style hand-knotted pearl chokers are set with *faux* rubies, and opulent bracelets and ear clips are made of ersatz diamonds and sapphires. You'll find good copies of Van Cleef & Arpels, Harry Winston, Bulgari, David Webb, Angela Cummings, even copies of Hungary's crown jewels. Much of the jewelry is hand-set, and the stones are from Czechoslovakia, Italy, and France. Even the copies are costly, but this store is worth a visit.

KENNETH JAY LANE
Trump Tower
725 Fifth Avenue, at 56th Street
751-6166
Mon.–Sat.: 10 a.m.–6 p.m.
AE, MC, V

The darling of the social set, Kenneth Jay Lane, the master of *faux*, is treasured for his fabulous fakes of important Tiffany, Bulgari, Van Cleef, and Harry Winston creations, along with copies of the Duchess of Windsor's gems. His glitzy Trump Tower boutique is artfully crammed with dozens of these ersatz baubles, along with his multi-strand *faux* pearl necklace favored by the First Lady bogus Art Deco creations, as well as his appealing original work. Prices are good for such quality copies.

REMINISCENCE
Cases are filled with jewelry that leans toward the funky—huge leopard-print earrings and lots of plastic—but there are some antique and vintage pieces along with one-of-kind designs by local artists. (See **Clothing**, p. 170.)

SALLY HAWKINS GALLERY
448 West Broadway
477-5699
Mon: 11 a.m.–6 p.m.; Tues.–Sun.: 11 a.m.–6 p.m.
AE, MC, V

A bold, vibrant mural announces Sally Hawkins's colorful gallery that features Bill Schiffer's energetic jewelry. Schiffer works in brightly painted layered plastics, mostly embedded with crystals, and his unusual, eye-catching brooches, necklaces, earrings, and cuff bracelets are artfully displayed here.

SAVAGE I
59 West 8th Street

473-8171
Mon.–Fri.: 11 a.m.–7:30 p.m.; Sat.: 1 p.m.–7 p.m.; Sun.: 1 p.m.–6 p.m.

Savage II
267 Columbus Avenue, near 72nd Street
724-4662
Mon.–Fri.:12 noon–8 p.m.; Sat.: 11 a.m.–7 p.m.; Sun.: 1 p.m.–6 p.m.
AE, MC, V

In the Columbus Avenue store *faux*-marble walls surround a mural of a nude bather, and a huge rhinestone-studded pair of horn-rimmed glasses graces another wall. Like the decor, Thelma Klein's jewelry tends to be outrageous. Mickey Mouse characters dangle from clunky necklaces, bracelets are a riot of plastic fruits, and earrings (made from every kind of material) come in every possible shape. You'll find designs by Marla Buck, Steve Rosen, and Glenda Arentzen, some wonderful African and Native American bead necklaces, along with a spectacular selection of rings.

THOMAS CHRISTIAN JEWELERS
172 Fifth Avenue, near 22nd Street
645-5769
Mon.–Fri.: 11 a.m.–6:30 p.m.
AE, MC, V

The owners of this tiny shop take pride in their beautiful reproductions of Art Deco and Art Nouveau jewelry. Sterling-silver earrings, brooches, and pendants are made from vintage molds, and many of the pieces are set with onyx, lapis, carnelian, and mother-of-pearl. There are a few authentic period pieces, too, and prices are excellent.

YLANG YLANG
806 Madison Avenue, near 67th Street
879-7028
Mon.–Fri.: 10:30 a.m.–6:30 p.m.; Sat.: 10:30 a.m.–6 p.m.

4 West 57th Street
247-3580
Mon.–Fri.: 10 a.m.–6:30 p.m.; Sat.: 10 a.m.–6 p.m.

324 Columbus Avenue, near 74th Street
496-0319
Mon.–Sat.: 11 a.m.–7 p.m.; Sun.: 12 noon–6 p.m.

Herald Center
1 Herald Square
279-1428
Mon.–Sat.: 10 a.m.–7 p.m.
All major

Ylang Ylang has sprouted flashy branches all over the city that cater to the mercurial tastes of the ultra-trendy. Huge hoop earrings, chunky-bead necklaces, mammoth rhinestone brooches, metal chains, clunky bangle bracelets, and riotous colors fill the windows and show-cases. Most of the baubles are European and exclusive to the store, as are the equally funky frames, gloves, handbags, and decorative pil-lows.

ZOE

1034 Third Avenue, near 61st Street
319-3033
Mon.–Sat.: 10 a.m.–5:45 p.m.
AE, MC, V

All mirrors and glitz, Zoe satisfies a range of tastes. The young and daring will be tempted by the shop's bold, colorful, and geometric jew-elry that might include brooches set with enormous Austrian colored stones, or the oversized glitter star pins; preps will love the delicately understated gold and silver pieces and the sweet antique-looking hearts; while Retro freaks will be attracted to the rhinestone pins set in silver and the jewelry "sets" of necklace, bracelet, and earrings that look as though they came straight from a forties movie.

Kitchenware

ANTIQUE

BOB PRYOR ANTIQUES
Eighteenth- and nineteenth-century copper skimmers, saucepans, and old copper jelly and pudding molds, along with elaborately hand-carved nutcrackers and corkscrews, and brass candlesticks in every size from tiny brass tapers to tall mahogany barley twists. (See **Gifts,** p. 293.)

COBBLESTONES
314 East 9th Street
673-5372
Tues.–Sat.: 12 noon–7 p.m.; Sun.: 12 noon–6 p.m.
AE, MC, V

Anyone with a passion for vintage kitchenware should head for Cobblestones, a tiny, old-fashioned neighborhood store. Here, hidden in the general clutter of mostly flea market treasures, are a trove of colorful wooden-handled rotary eggbeaters, potato mashers, mixing spoons, and knife sharpeners from the thirties, brightly printed kitchen towels and tablecloths from the same period, old cookie cutters, dozens of kitschy salt and pepper shakers, cookie jars, mixing bowls, depression glass, canister sets, and much more.

EVE STONE & SON ANTIQUES
Place des Antiquaires
125 East 57th Street
935-3780
Mon.–Sat.: 11 a.m.–6 p.m.
AE, MC, V

Eve Stone's emerald-green and marbleized terra-cotta gallery glistens with the glow from scores of highly polished antique brass and copper pots. Eighteenth- and nineteenth-century English and Dutch jelly molds, teapots, candlesticks, saucepans, and stockpots crowd the shelves, and the floor is crammed with such antique fireplace furnishings as and-irons, tools, and screens. Stone is not new to the antiques business; she has a shop in Woodbury, Connecticut, and another on Martha's Vineyard, and she is one of the largest dealers of antique copper and brass in the country. In addition to her treasures, the shop offers her son's selection of Federal sideboards, cupboards, and tables.

HUBERT DES FORGES
Vintage cookie jars, some old, some reproductions; and printed kitchen tablecloths from the thirties and forties. (See **Gifts,** p. 294.)

KALEIDOSCOPE ANTIQUES
Cookie jars from the forties through the sixties in the guise of kittens, owls, and fairy-tale characters. (See **Lighting Fixtures,** p. 373.)

MEISEL-PRIMAVERA
Dozens of shiny streamlined chrome toasters from the twenties and thirties, and scores of vintage irons. (See **China and Glassware,** p. 68.)

MOOD INDIGO
Unique toasters, cocktail shakers, Bakelite-handled kitchen utensils, kitchen clocks, and chrome sugars and creamers. (See **Furniture,** p. 256.)

PANTRY & HEARTH
121 East 35th Street
532-0535
By appointment only

Gail Lettick collected eighteenth- and nineteenth-century American kitchenware for over twenty years, but when her collection began to take over the entire first floor of her nineteenth-century Georgian town house, she converted it into a charming shop. Fine-quality sponge-ware, stoneware, redware, and yellowware are chief attractions, but she also offers whimsical apple corers that resemble Rube Goldberg inventions, old cutting boards, utensils, and cookie cutters, rare graters and coffee roasters, handsome wooden dough bowls, baskets of all kinds, along with table linens and beautifully worked show towels.

THE SECOND COMING
A whimsical collection of cookie jars from the thirties and forties. (See **Furniture,** p. 257.)

THOS. K. WOODARD AMERICAN ANTIQUES AND QUILTS
Early yellowware bowls, antique kitchen utensils, and a large selection of spatterware. (See **Linens and Quilts,** p. 387.)

CONTEMPORARY

B. Altman & Co., Bloomingdale's, and Macy's have well-stocked kitchenware departments.

BALDUCCI'S PICCOLA CUCINA
334 East 11th Street
982-7471
Mon.–Sat.: 12 noon–9 p.m.; Sun.: 12 noon–7 p.m.
AE, MC, V

Balducci's vest-pocket-size shop combines a sleekly modern interior with the rustic country charm of Italian kitchenware. Among the finds are the complete line of Vani stainless-steel pots and pans; olive oil containers; colorfully glazed plates, bowls, and platters; Anachini table linens; beeswax candles; teapots; and myriad kitchen utensils.

BRIDGE KITCHENWARE
214 East 52nd Street
688-4220
Mon.–Fri.: 9 a.m.–4:30 p.m.; Sat.: 10 a.m.–4:30 p.m.
MC, V

A fascinating but often overwhelming clutter of professional cookware covers every inch of wall, floor, and ceiling space at Bridge Kitchenware. The selection of copper pots, baking pans, cookie sheets, and unusual kitchen tools and gadgets is remarkable, and you'll find everything from earthenware dishes to French ovenproof porcelain casseroles, from woks to pâté crocks, and from stainless-steel paella pans to restaurant-size stockpots. Coffeepots and tea kettles, pastry equipment of all kinds, cutting boards and marble pastry slabs—if it has to do with cooking, you'll find it at Bridge. And the selection of professional knives is one of the best in the city. But it's wise to know exactly what you're looking for when you shop here; owner Fred Bridge sells to restaurants and professional cooks, so he's accustomed to dealing with the experts, and he can be gruff with novices.

BROADWAY PANHANDLER
520 Broadway, near Spring Street
966-3434
Mon.–Fri.: 10:30 a.m.–6 p.m.; Sat.: 11 a.m.–5:30 p.m.;
Sun.: 12 noon–5 p.m.; closed Sun. in summer
AE, MC, V

Thanks to Broadway Panhandler, owners of East Village apartments and SoHo lofts have a neighborhood source for top-quality kitchenware. Baking and pastry equipment is the store's chief attraction, so you'll find cake and muffin pans and cookie sheets in every size, and cake forms and decorations for everything from a child's birthday party to a five-tiered wedding extravaganza. Pots and pans range from basic to gourmet quality, and there's a fine selection of cutlery and kitchen gadgets, along with stainless-steel flatware (many with bright plastic handles), informal china and glassware, colorful cotton napkins, candles in every size and hue, and everything else needed for setting a pretty table.

CATHAY HARDWARE CORPORATION
49 Mott Street
962-6648
Mon.–Tues., Thurs.–Sun.: 10 a.m.–7 p.m.

Cathay has been located in the heart of Chinatown since 1928, and although it is primarily a hardware store, it has always stocked Chinese cooking equipment for the chefs of neighboring Chinese restaurants. They come for its vast stock of authentic woks in all sizes, bamboo strainers, ladles, and utensils. When the craze for home-cooked Chinese food hit New Yorkers in the seventies, this cluttered store became a favorite with gourmet cooks, and today it is still considered one of the city's best sources for fine-quality knives, woks, and utensils.

CONRAN'S HABITAT
This mini-department store carries all the essentials for outfitting a kitchen—pots and pans, cutlery, mixing bowls, spice and wine racks, cooking utensils, kitchen gadgets, and shelving. (See **Furniture**, p. 267.)

DEAN & DELUCA
560 Broadway, at Prince Street
431-1691
Mon.–Fri.: 11 a.m.–7 p.m.; Sat.: 10 a.m.–7 p.m.; Sun.: 10 a.m.–6 p.m.
AE, MC, V

Stroll past the herbs displayed as beautifully as flowers, the mouth-watering cakes and pies, and the luscious array of tiny roasted game birds, veal en croute, and other assorted irresistibles in this block-long store with its soaring pillars, and you'll find an impressive inventory of stainless steel, copper, porcelain, and earthenware in everything from stockpots to steamers to pâté crocks. It's all top-of-the-line and geared to the serious cook. There's baking equipment, cutlery, kitchen utensils, and gadgets, too, along with table linens and the best of the new cookbooks.

D. F. SANDERS
Fine-quality stainless-steel and matte-black kitchen appliances, utensils, and gadgetry with an industrial, high-tech look: food processors, toasters, electric mixers, timers, mixing bowls, cutlery, and coffeepots and tea kettles. (See **Housewares and Hardware**, p. 337.)

367

GRACIOUS HOME

The large selection of kitchen basics includes everything from pots to garlic presses, toaster ovens to mixing bowls, and canister sets to salt and pepper shakers. (See **Housewares and Hardware,** p. 338.)

HOFFRITZ FOR CUTLERY

331 Madison Avenue, near 43rd Street
697-7344
Mon.–Fri.: 8 a.m.–6 p.m.; Sat.: 9 a.m.–6 p.m.

203 West 57th Street
757-3431
Mon.–Sat.: 9 a.m.–5:45 p.m.

30 Rockefeller Plaza
757-3497
Mon.–Fri.: 8 a.m.–6 p.m.; Sat.: 9 a.m.–6 p.m.

324 World Trade Center
938-1936
Mon.–Fri.: 8 a.m.–6 p.m.; Sat.: 10 a.m.–5 p.m.

Grand Central Terminal
682-7808
Mon.–Fri.: 8 a.m.–6 p.m.; Sat.: 9 a.m.–6 p.m.

Penn Station Main Terminal
736-2443
Mon.–Fri.: 8 a.m.–6 p.m.; Sat.: 9 a.m.–6 p.m.
All major

Walk into any Hoffritz store and you will gaze in wonder at the amazing assortment of scissors and knives that are neatly arranged and displayed in glass cases. Scores of paring knives and meat cleavers, at least a dozen different kinds of cheese knives, and three types of clam openers share the glass case with barware, cherry pitters, and scissors for cutting everything from poultry to double-knit polyester, and from ribbons to nails. And Hoffritz offers the city's largest selection of Victorinox Swiss Army knives.

PLATYPUS

Espresso makers and pasta machines, cutlery, kitchen gadgets and utensils. (See **China and Glassware,** p. 76.)

POTTERY BARN

Everything needed for setting up a smooth-functioning kitchen is available at each of the Pottery Barn stores, and although you won't find dozens of brands to choose from, the selection of pots and pans is first-rate, and the cutlery, barware, kitchen utensils, and gadgetry offer quality at reasonable prices. (See **China and Glassware,** p. 76.)

THE VILLAGE CUPBOARD
10 Christopher Street
727-1578
Tues.–Sun.: 11 a.m.–8 p.m.
AE, MC, V

The Village Cupboard caters to those who like a kitchen to have a country look, and this sunny shop is crowded with a jumble of cookware and table accessories. Glistening copper pots, colanders, molds, skimmers, and ladles share the space with hand-painted china imported from France, Portugal, Italy, and England. There are dish towels and table linens in jacquard weaves and prints, chunky hand-blown glassware, reproduction Welsh cupboards, and hand-painted Windsor chairs.

WILLIAMS-SONOMA, INC.
20 East 60th Street
980-5155
Mon.–Fri.: 10 a.m.–7 p.m.; Sat.: 10 a.m.–6 p.m.; Sun.: 12 noon–5 p.m.
AE, MC, V

Williams-Sonoma has a casual California air with its white walls and terra-cotta tiled floors, and its cavernous space is filled with blond-wood tables and shelves neatly stacked with china and glassware. Gleaming copper and stainless-steel pots by all the top names, small electric appliances, and good-quality cutlery are piled next to cobalt blue or flowered china, chunky glassware, and such hard-to-find items as shrimp deveiners, tomato presses, fired-clay tiles for baking, spiral vegetable shredders, potato baskets, and tortilla fryers. There's a fine selection of utensils, gadgets, and cleaning equipment, as well as the best dish towels around, and the shop carries gourmet spices, oils and vinegars, baking chocolates, and vanilla along with a small but well-edited collection of cookbooks.

W. G. LEMMON
Well-stocked with all the kitchen utensils, small appliances, and gadgets needed for everyday cooking—coffeepots and tea kettles, pots and pans, toasters and mincers, timers and food scales, corkscrews and garlic presses. (See **Housewares and Hardware,** p. 340.)

ZABAR'S
2245 Broadway, at 80th Street
787-2000
First floor: Mon.–Fri.: 8 a.m.–7:30 p.m.; Sat.: 8 a.m.–midnight;
Sun.: 9 a.m.–7 p.m.
Second floor: Daily: 9 a.m.–6 p.m.
AE, MC, V

For more than fifty years the Zabar family has been supplying New Yorkers with lox, pickled herring, sturgeon, whitefish, and cheeses.

And in those fifty years the business has grown so popular that what was once a small shop has mushroomed into a block-long two-level store. On the second floor of Zabar's ersatz-Tudor building, you'll find a mini-supermarket of cookware and kitchen things. There are at least a dozen of the top names in pots and pans, espresso makers, and toaster ovens; microwaves both large and small; along with all the important food processors, stove-top and electric coffeepots, woks, and popcorn poppers. The stock of kitchen utensils and gadgets is equally strong. In fact, you'll find everything here for cooking anything from a simple down-home meal to gourmet extravaganzas, and Zabar's prices are some of the best in town.

Lighting Fixtures

ANTIQUE AND VINTAGE

ALICE'S ANTIQUES
Art Deco torchères, sconces, and table lamps. (See **Furniture,** p. 233.)

ARTISAN ANTIQUES
81 University Place, near 11th Street
353-3970
Mon.–Fri.: 10 a.m.–6 p.m.; Sun.: 12 noon–5 p.m.
AE, MC, V

A dazzling collection of authentic thirties etched- and frosted-glass lighting hangs from the ceilings, graces the walls, and decorates every available bit of floor and table space at Artisan Antiques. The store claims to have the largest selection of Art Deco art-glass lighting in the world, and most of the collection is French and from the thirties. Chandeliers, sconces, and floor and table lamps bear such legendary names as Lalique, Sabina, Daum, and Le Leu. Artisan is also the place to go for furniture from the same period. There's a full complement of Art Deco desks, vanities, pedestals, and tables and chairs, along with bronze sculptures.

BARRY OF CHELSEA ANTIQUES
154 Ninth Avenue, near 19th Street
242-2666
Tues.–Sun.: 12 noon–7:30 p.m.
AE, MC, V

A splendid hodgepodge of vintage lamps, all lovingly restored, fills this cluttered store. Art Deco milk-glass hanging lamps—etched in black and looking like inverted wedding cakes—hang overhead, and they share the space with schoolhouse globes from the thirties. There's a nice variety of desk, table, bridge, and boudoir lamps from the turn of the century through the forties, electrified chandeliers from the gaslight era, art-glass shades, along with Holophane shades with brass fittings—some of which are old, some reproductions. The owner knows a lot about lighting and is friendly and helpful.

COBWEB
An appealing selection of turn-of-the-century and Art Deco chandeliers: some are crystal and ornate, others are simple milk-glass shades, still others are rustic and have a country look. (See **Furniture**, p. 273.)

DELORENZO
Torchères, table lamps, and floor lamps by such Art Deco and Art Nouveau masters as Brandt and Chéret. (See **Furniture**, p. 255.)

DEPRESSION MODERN
Highly stylized floor and table lamps, along with the occasional Art Deco chandelier and sconce. (See **Furniture**, p. 255.)

D. LEONARD AND GERRY TRENT
A very fine and extensive collection of Tiffany lamps. (See **Furniture**, p. 234.)

EAGLES ANTIQUES
Antique Chinese porcelain and cloisonné vases that have been mounted as table lamps, along with electrified nineteenth-century wood candlesticks that come with pleated paper shades. (See **Furniture**, p. 242.)

EARLE D. VANDEKAR OF KNIGHTSBRIDGE
Eighteenth- and nineteenth-century crystal chandeliers. (See **China and Glassware**, p. 65.)

EILEEN LANE ANTIQUES
An unusual selection of Scandinavian and Austrian turn-of-the-century through thirties glass and brass chandeliers, table lamps, and torchères, along with nicely executed reproductions of Josef Hoffmann's Wiener Werkstätte desk lamp. (See **Furniture**, p. 239.)

FIFTY/50
Retro-modern hanging lights, and table and floor lamps from the forties through the sixties. (See **Furniture**, p. 256.)

FREDERICK P. VICTORIA AND SON, INC.
A glittering array of important crystal chandeliers, including fine Russian, French, and English beauties. (See **Furniture**, p. 249.)

GALLERIA HUGO
304 East 76th Street
288-8444

By appointment only
AE, MC, V

Gleaming with brass, cranberry glass, and crystal, Galleria Hugo is a delightfully cluttered shop filled with lovingly restored antique lighting. Owner Hugo Ramirez does his own restoration work, and his fixtures hang in Gracie Mansion and city museums and grace historic houses throughout the country. All his pieces are original and have not been plated, and among his tempting selection you'll find electrified gas and kerosene lamps, chandeliers, and desk and table lights in a wide range of styles that date from the eighteenth century through the twenties. Ramirez is a lighting expert who enjoys sharing his knowledge, and you'll find him friendly and obliging.

GREAT AMERICAN SALVAGE COMPANY
A large selection of chandeliers in crystal, brass, and milk glass. (See **Furniture**, p. 231.)

KALEIDOSCOPE ANTIQUES
636 Hudson Street
989-1036
Daily: 12 noon–7 p.m.
MC, V

Although Kaleidoscope Antiques carries oak furniture—some old, some reproductions—come here for the shop's notable stock of turn-of-the-century through thirties lighting and for its collection of vintage cookie jars. Among the large inventory you'll find old standing lamps, along with hundreds of old and new shades, including Holophane ones with brass rims, and milk glass, pressed-glass, and iridescent carnival-glass examples. Dozens of cookie jars from the forties through the fifties are stacked on shelves along the wall, and peering down are nursery-rhyme characters, animals, and little Dutch girls. Cookie jars have become a hot new collectible, thanks to last year's auction of Andy Warhol's collection, and Kaleidoscope offers a winning group.

LILLIAN NASSAU LTD.
Anyone with a passion for Tiffany lamps should make this gleaming shop the first stop, since it's filled with the world's largest selection—and finest examples—of those rainbow-hued beauties. (See **Furniture**, p. 235.)

LOUIS MATTIA
980 Second Avenue, near 52nd Street
753-2176
Mon–Fri: 9 a.m.–6 p.m.

An overwhelming clutter of sconces and chandeliers of every era and every style covers every inch of available wall and ceiling space in

Louis Mattia's remarkable store that's been around for thirty years. The sheer number of antique and vintage brass, crystal, and bronze fixtures and the volume of spare parts is mind-boggling. Mattia's small and narrow shop is where the city's top interior designers come to convert a priceless vase into a lamp or to electrify a gas light. Mattia handles custom mounting, electrical conversion, and lamp repairs, and Mattia and his staff are knowledgeable, friendly, and helpful.

MACKLOWE GALLERY & MODERNISM

A fine assortment of lamps by all the legendary Art Nouveau artists, including Tiffany, Gallé, and Daum. (See **Furniture,** p. 235.)

MINNA ROSENBLATT

Unusual examples of Tiffany lamps, along with lighting by other Art Deco and Art Nouveau masters. (See **Furniture,** p. 236.)

NESTLE

151 East 57th Street
755-0515
Mon.–Fri.: 9 a.m.–5 p.m.

Crystal glistens from every corner of this large and sparkling shop. Most of Nestle's stock is French and from the eighteenth and nineteenth centuries. In addition to exquisite chandeliers, candelabra, and girandoles, you'll find hurricane globes, brass lanterns, and sconces, and what was once candle-powered has been discreetly electrified.

NEWEL ART GALLERIES INC.

Antique chandeliers and sconces in a range of styles, along with scores of Edwardian green-shade desk lamps. (See **Furniture,** p. 251.)

OLDIES, GOLDIES & MOLDIES

Victorian, Edwardian, and Art Deco chandeliers, along with period table, desk, and floor lamps. (See **Furniture,** p. 236.)

PHILIP CHASEN GALLERY

Manhattan Art & Antiques Center
1050 Second Avenue, at 56th Street
319-3233
Daily: 12 noon–6 p.m.
AE, MC, V

Art Nouveau and Art Deco lamps, vases, and glass glow in Philip Chasen's shimmering gallery. In addition to Tiffany, Chasen has a fine array of Pairpointe's unique turn-of-the-century lamps with their melted look, along with others by such legendary glass masters as Handel, Daum, and Gallé. He carries Loetz glass and Rookwood pottery, too.

PRICE GLOVER

625 Madison Avenue, near 58th Street

Second floor
772-1740
Mon.–Fri.: 10 a.m.–5:30 p.m.
No credit cards

Price Glover shares its space with Vernay and Jussel, a store known for fine eighteenth- and nineteenth-century English furniture and clocks. Price Glover's specialty is eighteenth- and nineteenth-century English lighting that was made for the Indian market. Very special and select, it includes antique brass sconces, hurricane shades, and brass chandeliers, along with nicely executed reproductions. This gallery is also a good place to look for eighteenth-century English pottery and brass and pewter chargers and tankards.

R. BROOKE LTD.
Electrified Victorian wooden candlesticks with pleated shades, as well as vintage brass student lamps. (See **Gifts,** p. 297.)

UPLIFT, INC.
506 Hudson Street
929-3632
Daily: 1:30 p.m.–8 p.m.
AE, MC, V

More than 200 turn-of-the-century and Art Deco lamps are crammed into Uplift's unique store. Some are reproductions, but most are originals, and they are all in perfect working condition. Chandeliers and Deco milk-glass hanging lamps, torchères from the twenties and thirties, and Holophane-glass shades with brass rims are Uplift's specialty, but Uplift carries lots more, including hundreds of old and new glass shades.

URBAN ARCHAEOLOGY
A large array of Victorian and Art Deco sconces, chandeliers, and flush mounted wall and ceiling fixtures; some are antique, more are the company's own reproductions that they've made from original molds in their collection, and these come in bronze, copper, nickel, or baked-lacquer finishes. (See **Furniture,** p. 232.)

THE WICKER GARDEN
A small but very special selection of antique wicker floor and table lamps. (See **Furniture,** p. 290.)

CONTEMPORARY

B. Altman & Co., Bloomingdale's, and Macy's carry a good selection of traditional and modern lighting.

ARCHETYPE

Over-scaled torchères and sconces of spun aluminum in a range of metallic finishes, along with other new-wave lighting designs. (See **Furniture,** p. 278.)

BON MARCHÉ

A full stock of track lighting, as well as desk and table lamps in many colors and styles at good prices. (See **Furniture,** p. 266.)

CHELSEA LIGHTING, INC.
110 West 18th Street
242-4220
Mon.–Fri.: 8 a.m.–5 p.m.
AE, MC, V

High-tech, high-style lighting is this sleek store's specialty. Come here for Halo's black chrome Power-Track lamp holders, Atelier International's ceiling and wall-mounted Starbursts, the Mackinaw 900, Proteus track and surface mount fixtures, and Jav sconces. In fact, if it's on the cutting edge, Chelsea Lighting is sure to have it, along with Dove desk lamps and dozens of minimalist floor, table, and bed fixtures. Prices are good.

CONRAN'S HABITAT

Among the eclectic mix of very affordable lighting you'll find torchères, sconces, desk, bed and table lamps, and hanging lights in finishes and colors to suit any decor, from traditional to Art Deco, Retro to Country, and Contemporary to Cutting Edge. (See **Furniture,** p. 267.)

D. F. SANDERS

A fine selection of top-quality, high-tech, minimalist desk lights, along with a few floor and table models. (See **Housewares and Hardware,** p. 376.)

DOT ZERO

Isamu Noguchi's original Japanese-inspired paper lanterns, Lucasz Bogucki's folded fiberglass lamp shades, and Kevin Gray's black steel-and-aluminum floor lamps. (See **Gifts,** p. 302.)

GEORGE KOVACS LIGHTING
330 East 59th Street
838-3400

Mon.–Fri.: 10 a.m.–6:30 p.m.; Sat.: 10 a.m.–6 p.m.; Sun.: 12 noon–
5 p.m.
AE, MC, V

The lighting at George Kovacs tends to be high-tech and trendy, but the store also stocks a mix of more traditional styles. Many of the pieces are Kovacs's own designs, and he works in black, chrome, and brass, as well as exuberant colors. Chandeliers, floor lamps, track and recessed fixtures, along with desk, table, and bed lamps fill his sleek store. On a recent visit Kovacs's Wiener Werkstätte-inspired lamp in metal and glass, the "Mack" inspired by Rennie Mackintosh, Robert Sonneman's speckled gray "Taimatsu" standing light, and an Eileen Gray half-moon table lamp were particularly noteworthy.

JERRYSTYLE
23 East Fourth Street
353-9480
Tues.–Sat.: 12 noon–7 p.m.
AE, MC, V

"Ancient modern" lighting is how Jerry Van Deelen describes his unusual designs, and his work looks like the Flintstones crossed with the Jetsons. Van Deelen fashions patinated copper lamps and light fixtures that he finishes in verdigris so they look like archaeological findings; then he enhances them with a variety of gray, green, or gold bulbs. Table lamps, sconces, and chandeliers are among his whimsical or glamorous lighting creations, but he designs furnishings and accessories—curtain rods, door pulls, candlesticks, and candelabra— with a newly excavated look as well.

JUST BULBS
938 Broadway, near 22nd Street
228-7820
Mon.–Fri.: 8 a.m.–5 p.m.
AE, MC, V

Just bulbs, almost 3,000 of them and nothing else, fill this imaginatively designed store. Each of the bulbs, arranged by type, is displayed on a black switch box so you can turn it on to see the light before you buy. There are quartz halogen bulbs, globes, reflectors, Christmas lights, fluorescents, plant bulbs, spotlights, outdoor ones, and bulbs that can be used in old fixtures, or in European bases with American voltage or American bases with European voltage. There's also a huge selection of colored varieties, as well as fluorescent tubes in dozens of hues.

JUST SHADES
21 Spring Street
966-2757

Thurs.–Tues.: 9:30 a.m.–4 p.m.
No credit cards

For more than twenty-five years the Rakower family has been selling shades, and their small shop is crowded with hundreds of appealing examples to choose from. There are silk, linen, cotton, parchment, vinyl, tole, burlap, and just about any other material. The Rakowers are experts, and they'll help select the proper shade for a wide variety of lamps. They'll even re-cover an old shade or make one from a customer's own fabric.

LEE'S STUDIO GALLERY
211 West 57th Street
265-5670
Mon.–Sat.: 10 a.m.–6:15 p.m.

1069 Third Avenue, at 63rd Street
371-1122
Mon.–Sat.: 10 a.m.–6 p.m.
D, MC, V

At Lee's Studio Gallery trendy lighting by the top Italian designers shares the space with reproductions of Art Nouveau and Art Deco classics and Retro looks. Ceiling fixtures, sconces, track lights, floor, table, and desk lamps, neon lighting, and lights that look like sculptures, flowers, and vases are jammed into these well-stocked stores. You'll find such modern classics as Artemide's Tizio lamp, Koch & Lowy's Footsteps and Delta, Gobbo's "barely there" desk lamp, and Kovacs's updated banker's lamp, along with an excellent supply of halogen, fluorescent, and chandelier bulbs.

LET THERE BE NEON
38 White Street
226-4883
By appointment only
AE, MC, V

Interior decorators, architects, and lighting designers come to Let There Be Neon for the very special lighting effects this company is known for. It can neonize an aquarium, create a three dimensional neon sculpture, or border a picture frame or dressing table with neon. Everything is custom-made, and this company turns out some of the most creative designs, fabrications, and installations around.

LIGHTFORMS
168 Eighth Avenue, near 18th Street
255-4664
Mon.–Fri.: 11 a.m.–7 p.m.; Sat.: 10 a.m.–6 p.m.; Sun.: 1 p.m.–5 p.m.

510 Amsterdam Avenue, near 85th Street
496-2090

Mon.–Fri.: 11 a.m.–7 p.m.; Sat.: 10 a.m.–6 p.m.; Sun.: 1 p.m.–5 p.m.
All major

Some of the best of the new American and European lighting designs are available at both of the Lightforms locations. Most of the fixtures are black and minimalistic, and such top names as Artemide, Kovacs, Halo, Lightolier, Nessen, and Koch & Lowy are all represented. Lightforms offers floor, table, wall, and track lighting, along with Kovacs's halogen torchères, Artemide's Tizio desk lamp, halogen torchères with full-range dimmers, and table torchères that suggest the Wiener Werkstätte.

THE MUSEUM OF MODERN ART, THE MUSEUM STORE
Reproductions of Retro classics, along with such modern designs as Zelco's Micro-Halogen Lamp and Artemide's Tizio. (See **Museum Gift Shops,** p. 406.)

NEON MODULAR SYSTEMS/SAY IT IN NEON
430 Hudson Street
691-7977
Mon.–Sat.: 11:30 a.m.–6 p.m.
AE, DC, MC, V

As the name suggests, this shop serves a dual purpose. The owners are known for creating imaginative custom-neon lighting; they also carry a line of dramatic laser lights that look like ever-changing sculptures. Laser tubes, in such other-worldly colors as aura and uranium, and in earth-bound reds, purples, whites, and blues, are mounted on matte-black metal bases.

SAM FLAX
The functional and well-designed work lamps include the standards, along with such assertive lighting as Christopher Kyricos's black matte-finished steel-and-aluminum halogen desk lamp with a swivel arm and head, and the Mavro halogen desk lamp that has an infinitely variable dimmer and an infinite axis of rotation. (See **Art Supplies,** p. 6.)

SEE, LTD.
Among the very latest looks in lighting are George Seris's Aquiline Light and René Kemna's anorectic desk lamp. (See **Furniture,** p. 281.)

THUNDER & LIGHT
171 Bowery, near Delancey Street
219-0180
Daily: 10 a.m.–6 p.m.
MC, V

Thunder & Light manufactures and imports the beautifully designed and high-quality Italian lighting that it sells. Its selection of wall and

LIGHTING FIXTURES

ceiling lights, torchères, sleek track lighting, and halogen floor lamps—including the advanced Graal—are all inventive and very special.

UZZOLO
The starkly modern lighting includes a complete selection of halogen desk, table, and floor lamps. (See **Furniture,** p. 282.)

Linens
and Quilts

ANTIQUE
AND VINTAGE

Barneys New York offers an enticing stock of antique bed and table
linens; hand-embroidered and lace-edged pillows range in size from
neck rolls to oversized European squares.

ALICE UNDERGROUND
Tucked away in drawers, all carefully marked and sorted, are scores of
pillowcases, napkins, tablecloths, and runners, along with a smaller
assortment of sheets. There's an ever-changing collection of bedspreads (some early Bates, some vintage chenille), but most are from
the fifties and sixties. The collection of inexpensive kitchen towels and
tablecloths with fruit and floral motifs that date back to the thirties and
forties is winning. (See **Clothing**, p. 147.)

ANN LAWRENCE ANTIQUES
250 West 39th Street
Eighth floor
302-4036
By appointment
No credit cards

For the past thirteen years dress-designer Ann Lawrence has had a
passion for antique lace and in her shop, as cozy as a Victorian parlor,
it's all lovingly displayed. Valenciennes, Alençon, Battenburg, Brus-
sels, Normandy, Irish, Maltese, and point de Venise laces adorn curtains, table and bed linens, and dresses and gowns. But Lawrence's
collecting mania goes far beyond mere frothy finds. She offers scores of
antique English bamboo-and-lacquer tables, armoires, bureaus, and
wicker chaise longues; boudoir jars and dresser sets; nineteenth-
century majolica; delicate old ribbons by the yard; Victorian pillows;
tea sets and vintage tea cozies. One small room holds Lawrence's col-

lection of Palissy-style pottery, while others are crammed with vintage clothing: Victorian "whites," turn-of-the-century tea dresses, twenties batiste afternoon dresses and beaded gowns, and thirties lingerie.

CHERCHEZ

Pristine lacy and hand-embroidered antique bed and table linens, along with beautifully executed contemporary re-creations. (See **Gifts,** p. 300.)

COBBLESTONES

Exuberant thirties and forties kitchen towels, tablecloths, and napkins printed with fruits and flowers. (See **Kitchenware,** p. 364.)

FRANÇOISE NUNNALLE

105 West 55th Street
246-4281
By appointment only
No credit cards

French antique furniture, ornate silk drapes, gilt-framed paintings, huge vases filled with flowers, and the pervasive scent of potpourri provide the appropriate backdrop for Françoise Nunnalle's collection of exquisite antique linens. Many of her pieces are museum quality, and they're as early as the eighteenth century and as recent as the twenties. They come from Italy, France, Belgium, Germany, Russia, and America and they're hand-embroidered and edged with the very finest hand-tatted laces. Although sheets, blanket covers, pillow shams, and cases are Nunnalle's strength, she offers a selection of curtains, tablecloths, napkins, and runners that are also first-rate, along with a charming group of pillows made from antique Madeira handkerchiefs. Everything she sells is freshly starched, ironed, and in pristine condition, and although her things are pricey, the quality is exceptional.

HUBERT DES FORGES

Brightly printed tablecloths, napkins, and hand towels from the thirties and forties. (See **Gifts,** p. 294.)

JEAN HOFFMAN–JANA STARR ANTIQUES

Overflowing from baskets on the floor are hundreds of Victorian lace-trimmed napkins in dinner, lunch, and tea sizes, and piled high on all the shelves are stacks of antique lace doilies, linen runners, elaborately embroidered tablecloths, place mats, and bed linens, along with lacy curtains. (See **Clothing,** p. 180.)

THE SECOND COMING

The wide selection of bed and table linens ranges from lacy Victorian bedspreads to the exuberantly printed tablecloths of the thirties and forties. (See **Furniture,** p. 257.)

TROUVAILLE FRANÇAISE
737-6015
By appointment only
No credit cards

Muriel Clark has transformed the top floor of her Federal brownstone
into a tiny shop and filled it with the lacy confections she's collected on
repeated forays into flea markets and antiques shops in France and
Belgium. The elaborately embroidered sheets, decorative pillow shams,
turn-of-the-century lace curtains and valances, blankets and crib covers, finely worked tablecloths and runners, delicate guest towels and
handkerchiefs date from Victorian times to the thirties. Clark's children's clothing is equally winning. Among the irresistible array are
gossamer christening gowns, fleecy flannel pinafores, darling dotted-
Swiss dresses, turn-of-the-century buntings, infant caps, and cozy
flannel-lined dresses. And for boys there are little rompers and vintage
French farmer shirts. Everything at Trouvaille Française is starched,
ironed, and in excellent condition, and prices are surprisingly gentle.

THE WICKER GARDEN
In an upstairs, closet-sized room there's an appealing selection of antique Victorian pillowcases, shams, and bedsheets, along with a supply of bed linens that only look old; also sweet dust ruffles, sheets,
pillowcases, canopies, and quilts for Baby's crib. (See **Furniture,**
p. 290.)

PENDLETON
AND BEACON BLANKETS

KELTER-MALCE
The very best examples and the city's largest selection of Pendleton
blankets from the twenties through the forties. (See **Early American
Quilts,** p. 385.)

LAURA FISHER/ANTIQUE QUILTS & AMERICANA
A good source for early and later examples of Pendleton blankets as
well as Beacon blankets from the thirties and forties, all at good prices.
(See **Early American Quilts,** p. 386.)

MARSEILLES BEDSPREADS

Barneys New York has a small but fine collection of spreads, along with pillows covered in Marseilles remnants.

CHERCHEZ
A very special group of close-stitched, top-quality early Marseilles bedspreads, along with nicely executed reproductions. (See **Gifts,** p. 300.)

FDR DRIVE
A small but splendid selection of hand-stitched, trapunto-weave Marseilles spreads from the turn of the century, along with machine-made examples and early Bates spreads. (See **Clothing,** p. 153.)

LAURA FISHER/ANTIQUE QUILTS & AMERICANA
There's always at least two dozen Marseilles spreads on hand that range from Victorian hand-stitched trapunto weaves to machine-made examples from the twenties and thirties, and Fisher always has a charming selection of vintage hand-knit white-cotton coverlets. (See **Early American Quilts,** p. 386.)

EARLY AMERICAN QUILTS

AMERICA HURRAH
766 Madison Avenue, near 66th Street
Third Floor
535-1930
Tues.–Sat.: 11 a.m.–6 p.m.; closed Sat. in July and August
No credit cards

As much cozy museum as shop, Kate and Joel Kopp's welcoming third-floor gallery is filled with Americana. Early American folk paintings and sculpture, carousel figures, weather vanes, decoys, hooked rugs, and exuberantly patterned American Indian cornhusk bags decorate walls, shelves, and floor. Yet the gallery is best known for its extraordinary collection of antique patchwork quilts. Among the more than 400 examples—all in excellent condition—are rare museum-quality Amish and album quilts (including pictorial ones), but there's always an appealing group of more modestly priced spreads, along with a

selection of hard-to-find crib quilts. The Kopps also handle mounting
and some restoration.

FUNCHIES, BUNKERS, GAKS AND GLEEKS
Hundreds of patchwork and appliqué quilts from the turn of the century
through the thirties. (See **Toys,** p. 491.)

THE GAZEBO
660 Madison Avenue, at 61st Street
832-7077
Mon–Sat.: 9 a.m.–6:30 p.m.; Sun.: 1:30 p.m.–6 p.m.
AE, MC, V

The Gazebo brings Connecticut to Madison Avenue with its fresh country
stock of white wicker furniture, lacy pillows, patchwork quilts, hooked
rugs, and painted baskets. The owners claim to carry the largest selection of handmade patchwork quilts in the country, and there are hundreds neatly stacked on two floors. Although much of the stock is new,
handmade from traditional quilting patterns, the shop does offer an
attractive selection of antique and vintage patchwork and appliqué
quilts photographed and filed in albums for easy selection. Some are
from the turn of the century, many more are from the twenties and thirties, and most of the quilts, old and new, come in sorbetti colors. Rag
rugs rival the quilts in variety and number and there are scores of
hooked and braided rugs, too. Downstairs is crammed with an assortment of white and natural wicker furniture—some old, more new—that
includes chairs of all kinds, settees, tables, étagères, lamps, and cabinets, along with kiddie-size pieces. The Gazebo also offers an enchanting collection of Christmas ornaments handmade by a lady in upstate
New York.

KELTER-MALCE
361 Bleecker Street
989-6760
Mon.–Sat.: 11 a.m.–7 p.m.
AE, MC, V

Kelter-Malce is a snug little shop with old barn-siding walls, creaky
wood floor, and a beamed ceiling, and here you can browse among the
treasures and then share a cup of coffee with the knowledgeable owners who are passionate about antiques and enjoy sharing their knowledge with curious customers. Amish quilts are a specialty, but there's a
huge selection of patchwork quilts that date from the early nineteenth
through the twentieth centuries, as well as the city's largest and best
selection of early Pendleton blankets. Nineteenth-century painted furniture, samplers, baskets, hooked rugs, game boards, weather vanes,
folk art, and enchanting vintage Christmas ornaments year round are
among the other delights.

LAURA FISHER/ANTIQUE QUILTS & AMERICANA

Manhattan Art & Antiques Center
1050 Second Avenue, at 55th Street
838-2596
Mon.–Sat.: 11:30 a.m.–5:30 p.m.; or by appointment
AE, MC, V

An endearing collection of folksy treasures are displayed in every corner of Laura Fisher's cluttered gallery. Early American quilts, European bedspreads, paisley shawls, French Canadian Catalons (hand-woven bed rugs), Pendleton and Beacon blankets, Early American hooked and American Indian rugs, vintage Amish buggy robes, Marseilles and hand-knit bedspreads, and nineteenth-century woolen coverlets fill shelves and floor to overflowing. Fisher's dazzling quilt collection includes patchwork and appliqué examples that are as early as 1830 and as recent as the thirties in everything from dark Amish to bold Victorian crazy quilts, and from colorful eighteenth-century chintzes to Art Deco graphics—and in sizes that range from doll to king. Prices are excellent.

QUILTS OF AMERICA

431 East 73rd Street
535-1600
Mon.–Sat.: 10:30 a.m.–6:30 p.m.; or by appointment
AE

Elaine Sloan Hart has collected quilts for more than twenty years, and her cavernous store is crammed with a vivid hoard. Quilts hang from the walls, cover chairs and a bed, are draped over blanket racks, and are neatly stacked on the floor. Hart offers more than 500 examples that date from 1830 to 1930, and she has crib sizes and a few rare matched pairs, along with Baltimore album, patriotic, friendship, Amish, Mennonite, and every other important type of quilt ever stitched.

SEVENTEENTH STREET GALLERY

132 East 17th Street
260-3454
Tues.–Sun.: 12 noon–6 p.m.
No credit cards

The Seventeenth Street Gallery is a tiny spartan shop, and everything about it is neat and tidy. Quilts are lovingly displayed like works of art, and there are some fine nineteenth- and early-twentieth-century examples, vintage Amish buggy robes, and quilted pillows, along with new quilts made from traditional quilting patterns that include a good stock of hard-to-find crib and king-size spreads.

SUSAN PARRISH

390 Bleecker Street

645-5020

Mon.–Sat.: 1 p.m.–7 p.m.; or by appointment
AE, DC, MC, V

This appealing little shop is filled with American folk paintings and sculptures and examples of American Indian art, yet it's best known for its fine collection of antique American quilts. Parrish collects quilts from every state, and she has Amish, Mennonite, and pieced and appliquéd examples that are as early as 1820, as recent as the forties, and her quilts come in the somber shades of the Amish as well as the exuberant colors of crazy quilts.

SWEET NELLIE
Quilts from the nineteenth through the early-twentieth centuries in all the traditional patterns. (See **Gifts,** p. 312.)

THOS. K. WOODARD AMERICAN ANTIQUES AND QUILTS
835 Madison Avenue, near 69th Street
Second floor
988-2906
Mon.–Sat.: 11 a.m.–6 p.m.
AE, MC, V

Thomas K. Woodard and Blanche Greenstein's light and airy gallery is filled with the usual and unusual in Americana. Early American painted and Shaker furniture, baskets, folk art, country kitchenware and accessories, and hooked and rag rugs (some old, some new) are artfully displayed, but the owners' first love are the quilts, and they offer some unique examples. Patchwork and appliqué quilts date from the early nineteenth to the early twentieth centuries, many are museum-quality, and most, like a recent acquisition "Houses and Willow Trees," have highly original patterns. The shop also stocks early yellowware bowls, antique kitchen utensils, and a large selection of spatterware. Pricey.

CONTEMPORARY

B. Altman & Co., Bloomingdale's, Lord & Taylor, Macy's, and Saks Fifth Avenue have very complete linen departments; Barneys New York, Bergdorf Goodman, and Henri Bendel offer some unusual finds.

ABC ANTIQUES
More than 100 sheet patterns, including all the top brands and all the designer names—from Bill Blass to Laura Ashley to Kenzo—are displayed in attractive vignette settings, and you'll find everything from pristine lace-trimmed whites, to bold geometrics, to masculine pin-

stripes; the selection of table linens is equally eclectic. (See **Furniture,** p. 272.)

AD HOC SOFTWARES
410 West Broadway
925-2652
Mon.–Sat.: 11:30 a.m.–7 p.m.; Sun.: 11:30 a.m.–6 p.m.
AE, D, MC, V

Ad Hoc Software's high-tech origins have been gentled by its stock of lacy French curtains and sweet baby things, yet it's still a fine source for no-nonsense, practical bed linens and bath accessories. Come here for cozy flannel sheets in buffalo plaids, prints, and stripes; for comforting houndstooth, Tartan plaid, and updated Canadian "point" wool blankets; and for cool thermal-cotton ones in candy colors. There's always a good supply of hard-to-find thick white-cotton towels, top-quality plastic shower curtains in solid colors, as well as thirsty cotton bath mats. Toiletries, soaps, dish towels, glasses, and stationery, too.

BROOK HILL LINENS
698 Madison Avenue, near 62nd Street
Second floor
688-1113
Mon.–Fri.: 9:30 a.m.–6 p.m.
AE

Jan Dean Wechsler's airy shop is filled with the most romantic linens in town. Among the lacy confections are pillowcases and pillow shams crafted from a combination of antique and contemporary laces, but there are frothy coverlets, bed ruffles, and canopy covers, too. Sheets are lace-trimmed and embroidered, or they're made from floral cotton chintzes, tattersalls, jacquards, and eyelets and come in cotton-candy colors.

CHERCHEZ
In addition to some of the prettiest embroidered white linen place mats in town, the store carries lacy napkins, tablecloths that can be ordered in a range of sizes and fabrics (including Colefax and Fowler and Liberty of London's cotton chintzes), pristine-white sheets and pillowcases, Marseilles quilts, and blanket covers in organdy, linen, and plissé. (See **Gifts,** p. 300.)

CONRAN'S HABITAT
A fine selection of bed linens in a range of solids and prints, as well as all-cotton duvet covers, thermal blankets, and Marimekko's boldly patterned linens for cribs and children's bunk beds. (See **Furniture,** p. 267.)

DESCAMPS
723 Madison Avenue, near 64th Street

355-2522
Mon.–Sat.: 10 a.m.–6 p.m.

454 Columbus Avenue, near 82nd Street
769-9260
Mon.–Sat.: 11 a.m.–7 p.m.; Sun.: 12 noon–6 p.m.
AE, MC, V

The setting may be spare and high-tech—commercial gray carpeting and industrial metal shelving—but the linens are pale and romantic. They come in delicate prints and sherbety colors that would look right in a Connecticut or Hamptons country home. But this French company has recently added Bordier's sophisticated designs—malachite patterning, Art Deco inspirations, a graffiti look. In addition to linens for the bed Descamps carries plush toweling; thirsty terry-cloth robes for men, women, and children; along with crib sheets, nightdresses, slippers, bibs, and changing bags for babies.

D. F. SANDERS
Place mats and table napkins geared to a modern sensibility that are simple in design and come in natural fabrics, yet manage to be very elegant—solids, stripes, floral chintzes, textured tweeds, and pristine white piqués. (See **Housewares and Hardware,** p. 337.)

D. PORTHAULT & CO.
18 East 69th Street
688-1660
Mon.–Fri.: 10 a.m.–6 p.m.; Sat.: 10 a.m.–5 p.m.
AE, MC, V

Linens that grace the beds of kings and queens are housed in D. Porthault's elegant town house just off Madison Avenue. On the shop's two floors that are set up like a home—complete with living rooms and bedrooms—you'll find the most exquisite fabrics transformed into flower-strewn sheets, pillowcases, quilted coverlets, terry towels, tablecloths, napkins, and breakfast mats. Since everything is designed, woven, printed, and embroidered by the company's own French design studio, there are endless numbers of patterns to choose from and scores of color combinations, and the weaves are of such density they will last for generations. Spring bouquets adorn cotton nightgowns and terry-cloth robes and Porthault's enchanting baby clothes. The finest-quality cotton is used for the beautifully smocked dresses and rompers and for the tiny pants, shirts, and hooded terry-cloth robes (in sizes newborn to six years old). Although you will find affordable baby bibs and travel cases, just about everything else costs a king's ransom.

E. BRAUN & CO.
717 Madison Avenue, near 63rd Street
838-0650

Mon.–Sat.: 10 a.m.–6 p.m.
AE, MC, V

E. Braun & Co. originated in Vienna in 1892, and this Old World shop is filled with very classic and exquisite Irish linens. Most are embroidered and lace-trimmed and come in white or pastels, and in addition to sheets and pillowcases the store offers sets of linen tablecloths with matching napkins and an irresistible selection of monogrammed blanket covers. E. Braun is also a fine source for unusual bed linens: extra-long or extra-narrow sheets, dust ruffles for higher-than-normal beds, or quilts with an extra-long drop. And hidden among the fine linens are enchanting hand-embroidered and hand-smocked baby things—dresses, rompers, blouses, and beautiful hand-knit sweaters—at surprisingly gentle prices.

FRETTE
799 Madison Avenue, near 68 Street
988-5221
Mon.–Fri.: 10 a.m.–6:00 p.m.; Sat.: 10 a.m.–5:30 p.m.
AE, MC, V

Frette has stocked the linen closets of Italy's aristocracy with classic white Irish linens for more than 125 years yet in the company's elegant outpost on Madison Avenue you'll also find bed linens with a contemporary look. Percale, linen, jacquard, voile, and piqué embellished with scalloped edges or hand embroidery or lace are the company's specialties. Colors tend to be soft and pretty, prints subdued, and sets of coordinated sheets, bedcovers, blankets, and comforters often have matching terry-cloth towels and robes. Frette carries classic damask and white linen tablecloths and napkins as well. Expensive.

THE GAZEBO
The largest selection of handmade patchwork quilts in the country, some old, some new. (See **Early American Quilts**, p. 385.)

HANDBLOCK
Traditional and not-so-traditional Indian motifs have been transformed into bedspreads and duvet covers that come in a full range of sizes, along with appealing cotton tablecloths, place mats, and napkins. (See **Ethnic Items**, p. 211.)

HANDS ALL AROUND, INC.
986 Lexington Avenue, near 71st Street
744-5070
Mon.–Sat.: 10 a.m.–6 p.m.;
closed Sat. in summer
MC, V

The sunny country setting replete with cast-iron beds and antique painted furniture is an appropriate foil for Addie Havemeyer and Tanya

Thomas Smith's collection of patchwork quilts and quilted accessories. The quilts are re-created from old patterns using traditional techniques, and they come in a range of pastels or rich deep shades and in sizes that range from crib to king. The shop carries quilted place mats, runners, tablecloths, pillows, ceramics, and hooked rugs, too, along with a selection of Paper White's pristine white linens and Daniel Mack's wonderful twig furniture.

LAURA ASHLEY HOME FURNISHINGS

Bed linens match the Laura Ashley fabrics, paints, and wall-coverings for a coordinated look, so tiny floral prints appear on sheets and pillowcases, bedspreads, diamond-quilted coverlets, goose-down comforters, and towels. (See **Furniture**, p. 275.)

LAYTNER'S BED AND BATH CENTER

2270 Broadway, near 82nd Street
724-0180
Mon.–Fri.: 10 a.m.–7:30 p.m.; Sat.: 10 a.m.–6:30 p.m.;
Sun.: 12 noon–5 p.m.
AE, MC, V

Laytner's is a favorite with West Siders who come to this friendly store for its wide selection of top-brand and designer-name bed, bath, and table linens in whites and a wide-range of colors and prints. The shop is well stocked with cozy flannel sheets, goosedown and thermal comforters, towels, and a handsome selection of cotton and wool blankets as well.

LERON

745 Fifth Avenue, near 57nd Street
753-6700
Mon.–Fri.: 9:30 a.m.–5:30 p.m.; Sat.: 10 a.m.–5 p.m.
AE, MC, V

Leron is a charmingly old-fashioned linen shop that's best known for its delightful selection of very traditional monogrammed blanket covers in linen, embroidered cotton, and cotton plissé. But Leron is well stocked with very classic embroidered, appliquéd, and lace-trimmed bed linens in whites or pastels, and any size sheet can be custom-made, including linens for private jets, boats, or unusual-size beds. Leron also handles custom orders on damask and linen tablecloths.

MAISON HENRI

42 East 59th Street
355-5463
Mon.–Fri.: 10 a.m.–6 p.m.; Sat.: 10 a.m.–5 p.m.
AE, MC, V

Since 1939 Maison Henri has been offering New Yorkers an irresistible array of coordinated bed linens. The sheets are embroidered with lily of the valley or other delicate flowers—or they're white-on-white appliquéd—and the tiny shop carries matching shams, boudoir cases, and blanket covers. There's a selection of embroidered or custom-monogrammed towels, along with finely worked tablecloths, and Maison Henri is well-stocked with charming children's things: receiving blankets, tiny gowns, and other layette items, as well as sweetly smocked dresses and romper suits in sizes up to toddler four.

POLO/RALPH LAUREN

Expect the unexpected in bed linens at Ralph Lauren—sheets come in oxford cloth, paisley, mattress ticking, and English florals in a range of unlikely colors; blankets in houndstooth and glen plaids; duvet covers in assorted pinstripes; and just about everything can be monogrammed. (See **Clothing,** p. 124.)

PRATESI

829 Madison Avenue, near 69th Street
288-2315
Mon.–Sat.: 10 a.m.–6 p.m.
AE, MC, V

The first Pratesi store opened in Tuscany in 1906, and four generations of the family have been involved in producing the legendary Pratesi linens that have filled the linen closets of Prince Charles, the Vatican, Elizabeth Taylor, and Saudi kings. Sheets, pillowcases, quilts, and blanket covers are all made in the family-run factory and flawlessly crafted from the finest Chinese silks, Belgian linens, and Sudanese cottons in exceptionally high thread counts per square inch that result in their incomparable soft feel. The designs and workmanship are classic, so you'll find a large selection of hemstitched, chain-embroidered, or lace-trimmed sheets in white, soft pastels, and gentle prints, along with a few surprises, such as cherry-red garlands embroidered on stark white sheets, others done in intense blues, jewel-like purples, and honey golds. Jacquard tablecloths, cashmere blankets, satin quilts, and thirsty bath towels are as beautifully crafted as the bed linens, and Pratesi offers a winning array of children's things—crib sheets, infants' stretchy wool-knit leggings with matching sweaters, and lace-trimmed wool-challis dresses, hand-smocked blouses, and charming cotton dresses and blouses for girls up to six years old.

RENÉ

Embroidered and lace-trimmed European bed linens and blanket covers, along with attractive linens for the table. (See **Furniture,** p. 309.)

SCANDIA DOWN SHOPS

1011 Madison Avenue, at 78th Street
734-8787
Mon.–Fri.: 10 a.m.–6 p.m.; Sat.: 10 a.m.–5 p.m.
AE, MC, V

Scandia Down Shops is famous for the high quality of its down comforters and pillows. Mostly white goose down, they're covered in the most tightly woven cotton ticking possible. There's a large selection to choose from in a full range of sizes; cotton duvet covers in prints and solids, along with sheets and pillowcases in fine European cottons or easy-care cotton-and-polyester blends. Old-fashioned feather beds and pillows, too.

S. CHAPELL
An exquisite stock of hand-embroidered bed and table linens. (See **Carpets and Tapestries,** p. 63.)

SEVENTEENTH STREET GALLERY
Along with the antique quilts are new ones in traditional quilting patterns. (See **Linens and Quilts,** p. 386.)

SHERIDAN
595 Madison Avenue, at 57th Street
308-0120
Mon.–Sat.: 10 a.m.–6 p.m.
AE, MC, V

Sheridan is an Australian-based textile company and this sunny duplex store on Madison Avenue is the company's first retail New York outlet. The selection of bed linens is vast and ranges from Laura Ashley look-alikes to stark black-and-white prints to Ken Done's splashy tropical designs. Indeed, sheets and pillowcases come in ten solid colors and twenty patterns. The store also sells duvet covers and fabric-covered boudoir accessories, along with sheeting by the yard.

TIGER'S EYE BED & BATH
A complete selection of brand-name and designer bed linens, along with bedspreads, duvet covers, and comforters. (See **Bath Accessories,** p. 341.)

TRACEY ZABAR FOR REBECCA JONAS
246 West 80th Street
Third floor
874-6123
By appointment only
No credit cards

Tracey Zabar represents Amish, Mennonite, Appalachian, Ozark, and Southern quilters, and she sells their handmade crib quilts from her attractive shop. Although Zabar carries only crib-size quilts, and they're inspired by classic designs and made the traditional way. She has Iowa basket, Baltimore album, Amish diamond, Mennonite log cabin, and Kentucky flower garden among her enchanting stock.

WOLFMAN GOLD & GOOD COMPANY
Some of the prettiest cotton and linen napkins and place mats around, in jacquards, solids, stripes, and floral chintzes, also tablecloths made from quilting fabrics, and a selection of French paper doilies that make frilly yet practical place mats for summer entertaining. (See **China and Glassware,** p. 80.)

Luggage and Briefcases

VINTAGE

DUKE'S
Large and small vintage suitcases in alligator and leather, along with
gladstone bags, and collar boxes. (See **Clothing,** p. 113.)

JULIAN GRAHAM WHITE
Vintage Vuitton steamer trunks and wardrobes as well as crocodile
suitcases. (**Gifts,** p. 295.)

KENTSHIRE GALLERIES
Alligator suitcases in a range of sizes, along with fitted leather traveling cases. (See **Furniture,** p. 243.)

SECOND HAND ROSE
Matched sets of luggage from the twenties, thirties, and forties, including Amelia Earhart and Oshkosh. (See **Furniture,** p. 257.)

CONTEMPORARY

Barneys New York, Bloomingdale's, Macy's, and Saks Fifth Avenue
have very complete luggage departments; Macy's and Saks carry
Vuitton luggage.

ALFRED DUNHILL OF LONDON
Well-made, sedate, and pricey luggage in classic shapes and colors.
(See **Clothing,** p. 115.)

ASPREY LIMITED

On the lower level is Asprey's handsome collection of luggage in calfskin, exotic leathers, and old-fashioned-looking fabrics; sizes include everything from doctor's bags, to overnighters, to steamer trunks. (See **Gifts**, p. 299.)

BALLY OF SWITZERLAND

Classic styling and fine leathers in a well-edited collection of carry-on duffles, garment bags, sports bags, attaché cases, and briefcases. (See **Shoes**, p. 483.)

BOTTEGA VENETA

Sensational Italian luggage in great colors and luxurious leathers in hard and soft styles, and in sizes that range from classic train cases to full-size suitcases; also a splendid array of briefcases. (See **Handbags**, p. 316.)

THE COACH STORE

A fine selection of briefcases that are exceptionally durable and timeless in their simplicity. (See **Handbags**, p. 317.)

CROUCH & FITZGERALD

400 Madison Avenue, at 48th Street
755-5888
Mon.–Sat.: 9 a.m.–6 p.m.
All major

Since 1839 Crouch & Fitzgerald has been selling fine luggage to world travelers, and this venerable company maintains an extraordinary stock of classic goods and a very traditional and personalized approach to selling. On the first floor are handbags, and these include all the better-known brands (Judith Leiber, Ghurka, Dooney & Bourke, Louis Vuitton, Shariff), along with the firm's own private label imports from Italy and West Germany. Here, too, is the city's largest selection of attaché cases and briefcases in a range of styles and sizes and in canvas, leathers, and exotic skins. Wallets and other small leather goods are here as well. Upstairs you'll find the store's spacious and well-stocked luggage department filled with every major line, the entire Vuitton signature collection, along with pieces made expressly for the store. In addition to traditional hard-frame suitcases there's a large assortment of soft carry-ons and garment bags, and prices range from pleasantly affordable to costly.

DAVIDE CENCI

Handsome classic suitcases, mostly in rich browns, with brass fittings. (See **Clothing**, p. 121.)

DINOFFER, INC.

22 West 57th Street

586-2158

Mon.–Sat.: 9:30 a.m.–6 p.m.
AE, DC, MC, V

Dinoffer has been supplying traveling New Yorkers with luggage since 1890, and most of its stock is custom designed, exclusive to the store, and imported from France and Italy. Among the wide choices are tapestry-covered leather-trimmed luggage in every size, from doctor's bag to three-suiter; hard-frame calfskin classics with brass fittings in shapes that range from train cases to steamer trunks; and lightweight canvas carry-ons and garment bags in all the most wanted sizes. Dinoffer carries a full line of briefcases, and its array of small leather goods includes everything from tiny change purses to leather-bound photo albums, and it offers a noteworthy collection of conservatively styled handbags in leathers and exotic skins.

GUCCI
A large inventory of Italian luggage in a variety of leathers and colors: soft carry-on pieces and garment bags, and hard-frame suitcases in sizes from weekender to steamer trunk. (See **Clothing,** p. 154.)

HUNTING WORLD/ANGLER'S WORLD
Battue-cloth duffle bags and soft carry-ons with the distinctive Hunting World leather seal, along with the more fashionable and even more pricey hard-frame white-goatskin suitcases and train cases. (See **Sporting Goods,** p. 460.)

IL BISONTE
Soft-leather luggage in natural colors and in such old-fashioned shapes as satchels, duffels, and carpet bags, along with simply styled briefcases. (See **Handbags,** p. 318.)

J. & F. MARTELL
Handsome briefcases and buttery-soft suitcases and travel bags (discreetly stamped with the J. & F. Martell seal) in textured Indian kid or ecru calfskin. (See **Handbags,** p. 319.)

LA BAGAGERIE
Luxurious leather suitcases along with lightweight and long-wearing nylon garment bags and carry-ons in a variety of colors. (See **Handbags,** p. 320.)

LANCEL
The "Jet Set" collection offers polyurethane carry-ons trimmed in natural leathers that are soft, unconstructed, and incredibly lightweight; Lancel also carries soft vinylized-canvas totes, duffels, and garment bags as well as classic hard-frame suitcases in a range of sizes. (See **Handbags,** p. 320.)

LEDERER DE PARIS, INC.
Handsome unconstructed-nylon and canvas carry-ons and garment

bags (including the city's largest collection of Hartmann luggage), a fine array of attaché cases and portfolios, along with wallets, jotters, and other small-scale leather goods. (See **Handbags,** p. 320.)

LOEWE

A stunning collection of luxurious leather luggage in classic hard-frame styles along with soft carry-on pieces. (See **Clothing,** p. 109.)

LOUIS VUITTON

51 East 51st Street
371-6111
Mon.–Fri.: 10 a.m.–5:30 p.m.; Sat.: 10 a.m.–5 p.m.
All major

The cachet of traveling with matched sets of Vuitton luggage is anything but new. In the nineteenth century Louis Vuitton produced luggage for French royalty, and ever since owning Vuitton has conferred status. In the company's elegant, if somewhat cold and snobby, New York outpost you'll find the complete inventory of laminated-vinyl on Egyptian-cotton-canvas luggage (replete with the world-famous logo) that includes everything from train cases to steamer trunks, golf bags to kitty carriers, wig boxes to attaché cases. The emporium also offers Vuitton's latest collection, "Epi," crafted of real leathers in exciting colors with a mere hint of signature V's. There are handbags in all the classic shapes, along with weekenders and duffels, wallets, and small leathergoods.

MARK CROSS

High-quality leathers, fine Italian workmanship, and excellent design distinguishes the Mark Cross luggage that comes in everything from leather-trimmed nylon flight bags to ostrich two-suiters to leather garment bags with brass fittings. (See **Gifts,** p. 307.)

MCM

717 Madison Avenue, at 63rd Street
688-2133
Mon.–Thurs.: 10 a.m.–6:30 p.m.; Fri. & Sat.: 10 a.m.–6 p.m.
AE, MC, V

The glitzy marble-and-brass neoclassic interior is the fitting setting for the pricey MCM luggage that's stamped all over with the company's logo—numerals for the year 1900, the beginning of the era of mobility—and in the Vuitton-mode, they're covered in resinated canvas. Handmade in West Germany, the luggage and handbags are lined in pigskin and have brass fittings and cowhide trim. Among the vast stock are hard-frame pieces in every size and shape—train case to dog carrier, make-up case to camp trunk—along with a large selection of handbags in all the classic styles.

PETER HERMANN LEATHER GOODS

The elegant and tailored luggage in mostly black leather includes soft satchels, oversized hatboxes, and carry-ons. (See **Handbags,** p. 321.)

PRADA

Beautifully made luggage, handsome briefcases. (See **Handbags,** p. 321.)

T. ANTHONY

480 Park Avenue, at 58th Street
750-9797
Mon.–Fri.: 9:30 a.m.–6 p.m.; Sat.: 10 a.m.–6 p.m.
All major

Society's darlings come to this teak-paneled store when they want luggage that's a bit more discreet than Vuitton. They know that T. Anthony's luggage is luxurious, distinctive, well-made, and wonderfully durable. Classic hard-frame pieces in sizes that go from train cases to steamer trunks are the main attraction, and these often come in delightfully old-fashioned prints or untraditional colors, yet there's a stunning group of leather-trimmed soft canvas carry-ons in vivid reds, greens, blues, and yellows. T. Anthony offers handsome briefcases and portfolios, handbags in leathers and exotic skins, and classic Briggs of London slim-blade silk umbrellas, along with desk sets, wallets, agendas, key cases, sewing kits, photo albums, and all the other small leather goods that make perfect gifts. Service is attentive. Pricey.

Maps

ANTIQUE AND VINTAGE

ARGOSY BOOK STORE

The city's most comprehensive collection of antique and vintage maps includes early ones of Europe and North America, as well as old maps of New York City, every state in the United States, and vintage county maps of the northeastern states. See also **Books, Antiquarian.**

E. FORBES SMILEY III

Place des Antiquaires
125 East 57th Street
371-0054
Mon.–Sat.: 11 a.m.—6 p.m.

16 East 79th Street
861-8358
By appointment
AE

Edward Forbes Smiley III has collected and sold maps, atlases, and globes for years, operating out of a gallery on 79th Street that is filled with an impressive inventory of Early American maps, city views and plans, and globes. Two years ago, Smiley opened a shop in the Place des Antiquaires, and here he offers early and important European and Asian engraved and colored maps, views, library globes, and sailing charts. You'll find everything from late-fifteenth-century woodblocks to nineteenth-century wall maps. Smiley also handles museum-quality matting and framing.

H. P. KRAUS

Extremely rare and early maps. (See **Books,** p. 17.)

NEW YORK BOUND BOOKSHOP
New and old maps of New York City. (See **Books,** p. 39.)

THE OLD PRINT SHOP
A large collection of eighteenth-century maps of America, as well as early New York City and state maps. (See **Engravings, Prints, and Posters,** p. 200.)

PAGEANT BOOK & PRINT SHOP
Maps of the ancient world, along with an extensive array of early county maps for the northeastern states, including Long Island, Connecticut, and New Jersey. (See **Books,** p. 17.)

PHYLLIS LUCAS GALLERY & OLD PRINT CENTER
Early maps of the city. (See **Engravings, Prints, and Posters,** p. 200.)

RICHARD B. ARKWAY, INC.
Rare sixteenth- and seventeenth-century maps and atlases. (See **Books,** p. 18.)

CONTEMPORARY

THE COMPLETE TRAVELLER BOOKSTORE
Travel maps and guides for just about every known country. (See **Books,** p. 48.)

DOWN EAST SERVICE CENTER
Maps for hikers, campers, and skiers, as well as the United States Geodetic Service topographical maps. (See **Sporting Goods,** p. 452.)

HAGSTROM MAP AND TRAVEL CENTER
57 West 43rd Street
398-1222
Mon.–Fri.: 8:45 a.m.–5:45 p.m.
AE, MC, V

Hagstrom has been supplying New Yorkers with maps since 1910, and today the range of maps and charts available in this fascinating and well-organized store boggle the mind. Since Hagstrom is an official government agent for nautical and aeronautical charts, as well as a source for topographical maps for hiking and drilling, the company can offer aeronautical charts of one's hometown, geodetic surveys of neighboring waters, local street maps, and topographical hiking guides. But Hagstrom also carries foreign travel maps, road maps of all kinds, outline maps, political wall maps, astronomy ones, even those for

401

sales and marketing, and it offers a full selection of globes and atlases, too.

NEW YORK BOUND BOOKSHOP
Out-of-print city maps. (See **Books,** p. 39.)

NEW YORK NAUTICAL INSTRUMENT & SERVICE CORP.
World-wide navigational charts and geodetic surveys, along with lake surveys. (See **Sporting Goods,** p. 461.)

RAND MCNALLY MAP AND TRAVEL STORE
150 East 52nd Street
758-7488
Mon.–Fri.: 9:30 a.m.–6 p.m.
AE, MC, V

Rand McNally is the city's oldest map store, and it carries more than 10,000 vacation planning guides, along with an inventory of specialty maps that is equally impressive. Neatly organized on slide-out flat wooden shelves are little-known government maps, topographic and isometric ones, street maps for 500 cities, and zip-code maps. *The United States Military Installation Guide,* campground directories, travel guides, road atlases (including one designed for the business traveler), library globes of every kind, antique map reproductions, and books on travel complete the vast inventory.

SOUTH STREET SEAPORT BOOK & CHART STORE
Navigational charts and geodetic surveys. (See **Museum Gift Shops,** p. 409.)

STAR MAGIC
Maps of the stars and constellations. (See **Gifts,** p. 311.)

TRAVELLER'S BOOKSTORE
A very complete inventory of maps and travel guides to countries near and far. (See **Books,** p. 49.)

URBAN CENTER BOOKS
An excellent selection of New York City maps. (See **Books,** p. 21.)

Museum
Gift Shops

More than 150 institutions in New York City call themselves museums, and almost every one has an area it calls a shop. Although many of these shops are a fine source for books, prints and posters, postcards, T-shirts, jewelry, and such, below are the museum shops whose stock extends beyond the usual items, those which offer a broad range of gifts.

AMERICAN MUSEUM OF NATURAL HISTORY
Central Park West at 79th Street
769-5150
Mon., Tues., Thurs.–Sun.: 10 a.m.–5:45 p.m.; Wed.: 10 a.m.–7:45 p.m.
AE, MC, V

It seems fitting that the American Museum of Natural History, famous for its dinosaurs, should have gift shops that offer wonderful selections of prehistoric animals—along with domestic, wild, and fanciful ones, too—transformed into an astonishing range of gifts. In addition to cuddly stuffed species large and small, there are slimy plastic critters, dinosaur backpacks, baby animal sponges, along with jungle-animal pot holders, fish ties. Since each of the museum's collections is represented in the gift shops, you'll see an impressive stock of traditional Native American pottery and silver-and-turquoise jewelry, as well as a colorful array of minerals. And since the collections touch every continent, there are things from every corner of the world—from straw-skirted African dolls to Peruvian pots.

ASIA SOCIETY
725 Park Avenue, at 70th Street
288-6400
Daily: 10 a.m.–6:30 p.m.
AE, MC, V

Asia Society's small, artfully arranged bookstore holds a surprising range of titles. Pictorial English-Japanese dictionaries and textbooks on colloquial Chinese are here, along with volumes on the religions, history, art, films, and sports of each of the Asian countries; enchanting children's stories; maps; guides; and language tapes. The adjoining gift shop offers a charming selection of antique fabrics, as well as contemporary baskets, pillows, stoneware vases, embroidered shawls, and jewelry. Among the assortment are old Chinese trading beads strung into necklaces; multistrand Naga necklaces fastened with old Indian coins; silver bangle baskets, and an impressive selection of earrings.

THE CATHEDRAL CHURCH OF ST. JOHN THE DIVINE

Amsterdam Avenue at 112th Street
222-7200
Daily: 9 a.m.–5 p.m.
AE, MC, V

Although the mix of gifts in the Cathedral's cavernous and awe-inspiring gift shop may seem startling and random, everything somehow relates to the Bible or the Cathedral itself. There are kits to build one's own Cathedral and St. John the Divine chocolates. The selection of gardening tools, packaged foods, and cookbooks is inspired by the biblical garden in the Cathedral's courtyard; Noah and the Ark appear in many guises, and since they're a part of God's kingdom, there are stuffed animals of every species. One of the shop's strengths is in its reproductions of Cathedral ornamentation, its anorectic baptistry angels, small beasties, and stone grotesques. And the reproduction antique mirrors are splendid. There are striking examples of crosses, extraordinary hand-painted and hand-carved crèches, and delightful Christmas tree ornaments year round.

CHILDREN'S MUSEUM OF MANHATTAN

314 West 54th Street
765-5904
Tues.–Fri.: 1 p.m.-5 p.m.; Sat., Sun.: 10 a.m.–5 p.m.
No credit cards

Toys and games in the museum's tiny gift shop are ever-changing and reflect current exhibitions. For a recent show on the culture of the North American Indian the shop was stocked with tepees, adobes, Indian bracelets, tiny birchbark canoes. But there are always educational games, along with many small and inexpensive gifts that are great party favors—colorful plastic Slinkys, plastic gemstone rings, tiny animal erasers, face-paint sticks.

COOPER-HEWITT MUSEUM

2 East 91st Street
860-6878

Tues.: 10 a.m.–9 p.m.; Wed.–Sat.: 10 a.m.–5 p.m.; Sun: 12 noon–

5 p.m
AE, MC, V

The Cooper-Hewitt Museum's gift shop is unusual because 90 percent of its stock relates to current exhibits, and so the merchandise is always changing. Among the constants are the outstanding selection of books on architecture and the decorative arts, puzzles, stationery items, and wrapping papers. During the holidays this small place shines, transformed by pine garlands and Christmas trees strung with a splendid assortment of ornaments (all for sale). You'll find traditional European Christmas toys—Pinocchios and Nutcrackers large and small, German lead skating figures, glorious Noah's Arks, snow-scene globes—along with mini trees made from wood shavings and Advent calendars. Among the shop's beguiling assortment of stocking stuffers you might find rubber juggling balls, Chinese ribbon toys, and matchbox size puzzles.

JEWISH MUSEUM
Fifth Avenue at 92nd Street
860-1895
Mon.–Wed., Thurs.: 12 noon–5 p.m.; Tues.: 12 noon–8 p.m.;
Sun.: 1 p.m.–6 p.m.
AE, MC, V

The Jewish Museum's sunny gift shop is always well stocked with menorahs. Some, inspired by the mosaics of an ancient temple, have the patina of age; others, crafted of brass, are sleekly modern; still others, made of colorful pottery, have a joyful primitive quality. You'll find mezuzahs (cases for rolled-paper prayers), Elijah's cups, Passover plates, charity boxes, and just about any ceremonial object that relates to the observance of Jewish holidays and the Sabbath. For Hanukkah there's an array of Surprise Boxes for all ages filled with a gift—such as wood dreidels, mini-Torahs, chocolate coins, "tsuris" dolls—for each night of the holiday.

METROPOLITAN MUSEUM OF ART
Fifth Avenue at 82nd Street
879-5500
Tues.: 9:30 a.m.–8:45 p.m.; Wed.–Sun.: 9:30 a.m.–5:15 p.m.
AE, DC, MC, V

The Metropolitan Museum of Art's gift shops are unique in that all of the decorative objects for sale are copies of works of art—the majority from the Met's own collections and created in the Met's own workrooms or under its supervision. The assortment of jewelry is superb—Sumerian, Frankish, Korean, Indian, Scythian—designed as long ago as 2,500 B.C. and as recently as the forties. But you'll find sculptures, wall reliefs, glassware, china, silver serving pieces, glorious shawls, paper goods, ties, and mufflers here as well. Glass counters are filled with Tobacco

405

Leaf, Blue Canton, and Famille Verte china, as well as emerald green glassware and cobalt-blue pitchers. And the Met's selection of books is astounding; art, architecture, fashion, the decorative arts, cooking, and travel are all covered. The second floor, a treasure trove for children, is filled with games of pilgrimages, castle-construction kits, punch-out medieval towns, oil paints, songbooks, and musical instruments. The Metropolitan Museum also has gift shops at several locations around the city—including Macy's—that offer a selection of the Museum's most popular reproductions.

THE MUSEUM OF AMERICAN FOLK ART
62 West 50th Street
247-5611
Mon.–Sat.: 10:30 a.m.–5:30 p.m.

2 Lincoln Square
496-2966
Mon.–Tues., Sat.: 11 a.m.–6 p.m.; Wed.–Fri.: 11 a.m.–7:30 p.m.;
Sun.: 12 noon–6 p.m.
AE, MC, V

Crafts by contemporary artists working in the folk-art tradition are the specialty at the Museum of American Folk Art shops, and they offer an exuberant array of stenciled, jigsawed, whittled, hooked, braided, and quilted things. Utilitarian household objects (knife boxes, candlesticks, salt-glaze jars), and historical items (whirligigs of Abraham Lincoln and George and Martha Washington dolls), coexist with lovable things for children (gingerbread men, wooden Humpty Dumpty rabbits, a menagerie of animal pull toys) and Daniel Hale's enchanting jewelry and animal-shaped tables.

THE MUSEUM OF MODERN ART
The MOMA Design Store
44 West 53rd Street
708-9700
Mon.–Wed., Fri., Sat., Sun.: 10 a.m.–6 p.m.; Thurs.: 10 a.m.–8:45 p.m.
AE, MC, V

As this book went to press the Museum of Modern Art was preparing to open a new retail emporium, the MOMA Design Store, directly across from the Museum itself. This 3,000 square foot space by Hambrecht Terrell International replaces the existing Annex and will sell furniture and accessories directly related to the Museum's collection. In addition to small objects for the home, office, and travel, and an array of toys and tools, the new space will be a mecca for anyone hunting for Retro furniture and lighting since it will stock a greatly expanded selection of authorized versions of tables, chairs, chaise longues, and such by Alvar Aalto, Mario Bellini, Marcel Breuer, Le Corbusier, Charles Eames, Isamu Noguchi, Eileen Gray, Dieter Rams, Ludwig Mies van der Rohe, and Frank Lloyd Wright. It will also carry bold area rugs designed by Sam Francis, Sol Lewitt, Roy Lichtenstein, and Arata Isozaki. The present Museum Store will be renamed the MOMA Book Store and will offer a much larger inventory of books, publications, posters, and slides.

THE MUSEUM OF THE AMERICAN INDIAN
Broadway at 155th Street
283-2420
Tues.–Sat.: 10 a.m.–5 p.m.; Sun.: 12 noon–5 p.m.
AE, MC, V

The handsome and well-organized gift shop of the Museum of the American Indian offers traditional Native American crafts, the work of contemporary Alaskan, Canadian, South American, and American crafts people. It carries a tempting mix of Navaho rugs; Hopi, Santa Clara, and Acoma pottery; traditional sterling-silver-and-turquoise jewelry and concha belts; and clay pueblo house-shaped candle holders. And for youngsters, sterling-silver rattles, tiny buckskin moccasins, arrowheads, bright knotted friendship bracelets, little birchbark canoes, Navaho dolls, and plush buffaloes. In the fine book section are histories of the American Indian, along with titles on Indian lore, arts and crafts, and Indian folk tales for children.

THE MUSEUM OF THE CITY OF NEW YORK
Fifth Avenue at 103rd Street
534-1672
Tues.–Sat.: 10 a.m.–5 p.m.; Sun.: 1 p.m.–5 p.m.
AE, MC, V

Teddy bears in many guises, tin soldiers, cast-iron mechanical banks, and books greet you at the gift shop of the Museum of the City of New York. The shop has a turn-of-the-century flavor and stocks toys and games that evoke earlier times: Humpty Dumpty, Cheshire cats, Campbell Soup kids, puppets, and old-fashioned dolls. Plastic bins hold tiny and inexpensive toys—whistles, pancake dolls, wooden tops, tiny kaleidoscopes—but there are treats for adults, too, including pristine lace-trimmed tea towels and reproduction blue-and-white export china. And the museum carries an impressive assortment of books, everything from illustrated volumes to the *AIA Guide*, to sociological treatises, to novels set in New York. Year round the tiny back room sparkles with old-fashioned Christmas ornaments.

THE NEW-YORK HISTORICAL SOCIETY
170 Central Park West, at 77th Street
873-3400
Tues.–Sat.: 10 a.m.–5 p.m.; Sun.: 10 a.m.–5 p.m.
MC, V

The New-York Historical Society's gift shop is a quiet oasis stocked with pretty things. Audubon prints, silk scarves, trivet tiles made from old-fashioned trade labels, baskets in all sizes, and tiny hand-painted replicas of historic houses share the space with reproductions of eighteenth- and nineteenth-century paperweights and perfume bottles, salt-glaze crocks, and redware platters. There's also an enticing collection of children's toys: Early American dolls, stuffed animals, puzzles, games, and stocking stuffers. The appealing selection of books includes titles on American history, and the fine and decorative arts, along with classics and reissues of old-time favorites.

NEW YORK PUBLIC LIBRARY SHOP

Fifth Avenue and 42nd Street
930-0678
Mon.–Sat.: 10 a.m.–5:45 p.m.
AE, MC, V

With its burnished oak-paneled walls and floor of cork and rose-colored marble, the Library Shop resembles an intimate, Old World study. Its inventory reinforces that image. Among the fine printing and letterpress items are address books and party invitations from the Victoria and Albert Museum, wrapping paper from the National Gallery, note cards from the Tate Galleries, and playing cards reproduced from the Royal Albert Museum. *Faux* marble Library Lion bookends immortalize Patience and Fortitude, the regal pair who guard the library entrance. The selection for children includes Winnie-the-Pooh diaries, colorful folding alphabet books, beautifully illustrated editions of children's classics, stuffed animals, puzzles, and word games.

THE PIERPONT MORGAN LIBRARY

29 East 36th Street
685-0008
Tues.–Fri.: 10:30 a.m.–4:45 p.m.; Sat.: 10:30 a.m.–4:45 p.m.; Sun.:
1 p.m.–4:45 p.m.
No credit cards

The gift shop at the Pierpont Morgan Library is filled with a well-edited array of books and bookish things—exquisite facsimile editions of Books of Hours, for instance, and facsimile editions of manuscript scores by Mozart, Schubert, and Beethoven. The shop also offers items that would look handsome on a desk—address and blank books, clipboards, brass bookends, and picture frames. For library walls there are reproductions of Old Masters drawings and Furber's botanical prints, and for children, Beatrix Potter tea sets and toys.

SEAPORT MUSEUM STORES

South Street Seaport
669-9400
Mon.–Sat.: 10 a.m.–9 p.m. ; Sun.: 11 a.m.–7 p.m.
AE, MC, V

Seaport Museum Shops, like the museum itself, spill out all over South Street Seaport. In the **Book & Chart Store** (209 Water Street) you'll find the official National Ocean Service charts for waters from Cape May to the Canadian border, as well as the largest stock of maritime books and magazines around—from naval histories to boat building to racing to cooking. There's a small but fascinating selection of vintage titles that might include an old treatise on naval engineering or an early Jack London novel. The boat-model kits here are standouts. The **Curiosity Shop** (Canon's Walk) is stocked with the commercial stuff: mugs, coasters, ashtrays, and towels adorned with ships, seashells, and semaphore flags. Across the way at 14 Fulton Street is the **Seaport Museum Shop,** which carries much the same merchandise, along with sweatshirts, T-shirts, and ponchos.

STUDIO MUSEUM IN HARLEM
144 West 125th Street
864-0014
Wed.–Fri.: 10 a.m.–5 p.m.; Sat., Sun.: 1 p.m.–6 p.m.
MC, V

The bright and airy gift shop at the Studio Museum in Harlem is crammed with handicrafts and art from Africa, the Harlem community, black America, and the African diaspora. Baskets and hand-carved Ivory Coast masks mix with richly patterned Kente cloth belts and ceramic pottery in earthy colors. There's dazzling jewelry that ranges from the traditional to the trendy, as well as dolls in nineteenth-century calico dress, animal puppets, games, and toys for children.

THE UKRAINIAN MUSEUM
203 Second Avenue, near 12th Street
228-0110
Wed.–Sun.: 1 p.m.–5 p.m.
No credit cards

This narrow sliver of a gift shop is not much bigger than a closet, yet it offers some fine examples of contemporary Ukrainian crafts that are made in the age-old way. Much of the stock comes from Hutzal, the mountain region that is known for its richly ornamented folk art, and includes incised and colorfully painted earthenware mugs, bowls, and plates, as well as amusing rooster-shaped jugs. There are woodsy things—intricately carved and inlaid photo albums and candelabra—along with elaborately embroidered blouses and table linens.

UNITED NATIONS HEADQUARTERS
833 U.N. Plaza
First Avenue at 46th Street
963-7700
Mon.–Sun.: 9:15 a.m.–5:15 p.m.
AE, MC, V

If you love handcrafted things, you'll love this shop on the lower level of the United Nations Headquarters. There are hundreds of tiny, inexpensive treasures perfect as stocking stuffers or party favors: delicate silk pincushions, hand-carved animals, carved-wood combs, bright leather coin purses, German matchbox fairy-tale puzzles. An entire wall is devoted to bracelets, pins, rings, and necklaces in a range of styles and prices. There are dolls in authentic native dress from each of the member nations, wood Pinocchios and Nutcrackers, antique Russian lacquerware boxes and frames. And for the house, baskets from Ethiopia, handsome Japanese cherrywood storage boxes, and Indonesian batik napkins.

THE WHITNEY MUSEUM
Store Next Door
943 Madison Avenue, near 75th Street
606-0200
Tues.: 10 a.m.–8 p.m.; Wed.–Sat.: 10 a.m.–6 p.m.; Sun.: 12 noon–
6 p.m.
AE, MC, V

The Whitney Museum has only recently opened a gift shop of its own and it seems fitting that it is filled with American designs that are American-made. Household objects, furniture, jewelry, and lighting have all been created by leading American architects, designers, and crafts people, and it's an ever-changing mix. You might find Ron Rezak's zinc lamps, David Kirk's wooden banks, and Tekna flashlights, along with Wendy Stevens's metal handbags, Mary Coltor's "Super Chief" china, and Michael Ellis's "narrative" jewelry.

Music Boxes

DETRICH PIANOS
211 West 58th Street
245-1234
Mon.–Fri.: 10 a.m.–6 p.m.; Sat.: 10 a.m.–4 p.m.
No credit cards

Kalman Detrich deals in antique and new pianos that he sells, rents, tunes, and repairs, but he also has amassed a stock of contemporary music boxes. Almost all of them are in the shape of pianos, but they come in a variety of materials—porcelain, metal, and plastic. Some play classical music, others pop tunes, and they're all pleasantly affordable.

THE LAST WOUND UP
A delightful collection that includes antique, restored, and new boxes of every description. Many of the antique ones are European and heavily encrusted with gold and gemstones or made of crystal, but there are simpler ones and modern versions, as well as all the components for making your own. (See **Toys**, p. 497.)

RITA FORD MUSIC BOXES
19 East 65th Street
535-6717
Mon.–Sat.: 9 a.m.–5 p.m.
MC, V

Walk into Rita Ford's delightful shop and you're greeted by the tinkling of at least a dozen music boxes playing everything from "Annie Laurie" to "Madame Butterfly." Ford began as a collector, and she's now considered the city's expert, and she knows all about music boxes' workings, casings, and scores. Among her array of American and European treasures you'll find Swiss cylinder boxes, bird cages, disk boxes, and early automata (tiny moving figures) that date from 1830 through 1910, and they're all in working order. Ford carries a full complement of contemporary boxes, too, and her prices range from under $15 for a new

Japanese-made example to more than $75,000 for an extremely rare antique one. Rita Ford also stocks musical jewelry boxes.

A VICTORIAN HOLIDAY
A small but irresistible collection of birdhouse-shaped music boxes that look like Victorian confections. (See **Gifts**, p. 313.)

Records

BLEECKER BOB'S GOLDEN OLDIES RECORD SHOP
118 West 3rd Street
475-9677
Daily: 12 noon–1 a.m.
AE, MC, V

Even though Bleecker Bob's Golden Oldies Record Shop isn't on Bleecker Street, there is a Bob, Bob Plotnik, and his store on West Third Street is a Village institution. Rock is Plotnik's specialty, and he carries just about every rock record ever recorded. Out-of-print and rare records share the crowded space with new British imports and independent labels, so in addition to the oldies there's a good selection of current new wave and punk singles.

DAYTON'S RECORDS
48 East 11th Street
254-5084
Mon.–Fri.: 11 a.m.–6:30 p.m.; Sat.: 11 a.m.–6 p.m.; Sun.: 12 noon–5 p.m.
No credit cards

Dayton's has been in the record business for more than thirty-five years, and the shop has more than two million records in stock. Out-of-print, long-playing records are the chief attraction, and it has assembled the largest collection of out-of-print classical albums in the city. But you'll find every possible category in this amazing store—from the spoken word to jazz, from movie sound tracks to original-cast Broadway-show albums, and from Bach to rock (including new D.J. records). In fact, if it has ever been recorded, you're likely to find it at Dayton's.

FOOTLIGHT RECORDS
113 East 12th Street
533-1572

Mon.–Fri.: 11 a.m.–7 p.m.; Sat.: 10 a.m.–6 p.m.; Sun.: 12 noon–5 p.m.
AE, DC, MC, V

Gene Dingenary and Ed McGrath have assembled more than 250,000 records, cassettes, and compact discs, and Footlight Records, their well-organized rare-album shop, is crowded with New York's largest selection of old musicals and film sound tracks. Since they specialize in out-of-print and rare recordings, you're likely to find a copy of *Hello, Dolly!* in Russian, the Mexican cast recording of *Grease*, or hard-to-find early Sinatra singles. But among the prodigious inventory is about every big band record ever made, as well as the vocalists of the forties and fifties, jazz recordings, and early rock 'n' roll.

THE GOLDEN DISC
239 Bleecker Street
255-7899
Mon.–Fri.: 11:30 a.m.–6:30 p.m.; Sat.: 11:30 a.m.–8 p.m.; Sun.: 1 p.m.–5 p.m.
AE, MC, V

The Golden Disc has recently expanded and added to its already vast hoard of used oldies. Although the focus in this friendly shop is on rock, jazz, American root music, blues, rockabilly, and doo-wop, you'll find a large Reggae and African section, along with new esoteric European music, such as Pog. The shop's stock of rare 45s is noteworthy, and there's now a large CD section.

GRYPHON RECORD SHOP
251 West 72nd Street
874-1588
Mon.–Sat.: 10 a.m.–8 p.m.; Sun.: 12 noon–6 p.m.
MC, V

Marc Lewis and Henry Holman have crammed their Gryphon Record Shop with more than 30,000 out-of-print and rare LPs. Classical labels account for 99 percent of the stock, with the remainder jazz recordings. The **Gryphon Bookshop** carries in-print classical and popular records in addition to its inventory of unusual books, and at the **Annex** you'll find a mix of books and in-print and out-of-print records, including original-cast Broadway shows and movie sound tracks.

JAZZ RECORD CENTER
135 West 29th Street
Twelfth floor
594-9880
Tues.–Sat.: 10 a.m.–6 p.m.
AE, MC, V

New York's only jazz specialty shop is a one-man operation, owned and run by jazz expert Frederick Cohen. His vast and splendid stock includes rare, out-of-print, and jazz-related records of all speeds and in all sizes. Besides commercial recordings, Cohen sells one-of-a-kind test pressings, books, magazines, posters, and research materials on jazz, and if you can't find what you're looking for, Cohen offers a search service and will even make house calls.

MUSIC INN
169 West 4th Street
243-5715
Tues.–Fri.: 1 p.m.–7 p.m.; Sat.: 12 noon–7 p.m.
All major

This tiny store is dense with an unusual assortment of offbeat ethnic records and obscure international ones that include African, English, Irish, and Celtic folk music. More mainstream is the shop's fairly extensive offerings of in- and out-of-print jazz and blues recordings.

MUSIC MASTERS
25 West 43rd Street
840-1958
Mon.–Fri.: 10 a.m.–5:30 p.m.; Sat.: 10 a.m.–2:30 p.m.
AE, MC, V

In a comfortable setting that looks more like a library than a record store you'll find rare, hard-to-find, and unique orchestral and operatic recordings, including out-of-print and never-released materials. Owner Nicholas Iovanna has access to 250,000 private-label tapes of operas, concerts, and Broadway musicals not available anywhere else in the world, and Iovanna also produces a line of nostalgic recordings of artists from the twenties, thirties, and forties.

NOSTALGIA . . . AND ALL THAT JAZZ
217 Thompson Street
420-1940
Mon.–Thurs.: 1:30 p.m.–8:30 p.m.; Fri. & Sat.: 1:30 p.m.–10 p.m.; Sun.: 1:30 p.m.–8:30 p.m.
No credit cards

The name tells it all. This small store is filled with nostalgia and jazz records. Sound tracks of old movies, recordings of early radio programs, and out-of-print jazz records are among the expected offerings, but owners Kim Deuel and Mort Alavi have also put together a noteworthy group of posters, movie and jazz stills, and show-biz photographs.

RECORDS REVISITED
34 West 33rd Street
Second floor
695-7155
Mon.–Fri.: 9 a.m.–5 p.m.; Sat.: 9 a.m.–3 p.m.
No credit cards

415

Records Revisited is an old-fashioned music store that looks like a relic from the forties. There are more than 150,000 records in stock, and everything is carefully catalogued. In the shop's two small rooms you'll find records that are as early as 1895 and as recent as 1958, vintage 78s, as well as early LPs and 45s.

VENUS RECORDS, INC.
61 West 8th Street
Second floor
598-4459
Mon.–Sat.: 11 a.m.–7 p.m.; Sun.: 1 p.m.–6 p.m.
MC, V

Venus Records' logo reads "Rock & Roll from around the World." The shop's main focus is on independent and imported labels, and it offers a large inventory of out-of-print, used, and reissued fifties and sixties British rock. But in addition to the rock there's an impressive array of heavy metal, rockabilly, doo-wop, 60s pop, garage psychedelic, new wave, and hardcore punk. There are new CDs, too, the kind that are not available at the popular record stores.

Shoes

CHILDREN'S SHOES

Bloomingdale's, Macy's, and Saks Fifth Avenue have well-stocked children's shoe departments that offer a wide variety of styles, ranging from classic to trendy.

BILLY MARTIN'S WESTERN WEAR
The city's largest selection of children's cowboy boots. (See **Men's Shoes,** p. 421.)

CHOU CHOU
Cutting-edge soft velvet and canvas shoes for tots. (See **Clothing,** p. 94.)

CITYKIDS
A noteworthy group of children's shoes, including imported high-fashion looks and playful sneaker styles. (See **Clothing,** p. 94.)

COLE-HAAN
Soft camp moccasins in pastel hues, canvas sneakers in dozens of fashion shades, along with classic saddles and oxfords. (See **Men's Shoes,** p. 422.)

EAST SIDE KIDS
1298 Madison Avenue, near 92nd Street
360-5000
Mon.–Sat.: 9:30 a.m.–5:45 p.m.

2330 Broadway, near 84th Street
874-4262
Mon.–Sat.: 9:30 a.m.–6:45 p.m.; Sun.: 12 noon–4:45 p.m.
AE, MC, V

417

East Side Kids stores are popular with both children and their parents. They have popcorn machines and grandstands for youngsters to sit on while trying on the latest in sporty-looking shoes, and the stores are roomy enough to accommodate the stroller set. Enrico Coveri, Westies Jr., Keds, Weebok, G. H. Bass, Reebok, Esprit, and OshKosh are some of the popular names you'll find here (in sizes to fit infants through teenagers), and in winter there's a fine assortment of rain and snow boots, and in summer a good selection of sandals and camp shoes.

HARRY'S SHOES

StrideRite, Capezio, Jumping Jacks, Reebok, Timberland, and Bass, along with fashionable European styles. (See **Men's Shoes**, p. 423.)

INDIAN WALK SHOES

956 Madison Avenue, near 75th Street
288-1941
Mon.–Sat.: 9 a.m.–5:45 p.m.
AE, MC, V

Since 1910 Indian Walk has been supplying Upper East Side children with quality shoes. There are party styles from Capezio and Baby Botte; sneakers from Nike, Keds, and Adidas; along with cowboy boots and classic school shoes by all the popular names. In addition to the enormous variety of styles there's a wide range of sizes.

JOAN & DAVID

Pricey party shoes in leathers and metallics for little girls. (See **Women's Shoes**, p.433.)

LITTLE ERIC

1331 Third Avenue, near 76th Street
288-8250
Mon.–Fri.: 11 a.m.–7 p.m.; Sat.: 11 a.m.–6 p.m.; Sun.: 1 p.m.–6 p.m.
AE, MC, V

Little Eric is the children's version of the popular women's shoe stores. It's spacious enough to accommodate strollers, and there's a TV and stacks of "Sesame Street" videos to keep little ones amused. Shelves are crammed with canvas running shoes, animal-puppet slippers, and froggy boots, along with classic Mary Janes, two-tone saddle shoes, and oxfords.

MARAOLO

Among the high-fashion shoes for girls are stylish ballet slippers, woven leathers, two-tone lace-ups, and adorable cowboy boots. (See **Women's Shoes**, p. 434.)

MY SHOES

1712 First Avenue, near 88th Street

410-2129
Mon.–Sat.: 10 a.m.–7 p.m.; Sun.: 11 a.m.–4 p.m.

458 Third Avenue, near 31st Street
779-8535
Mon.–Sat.: 10 a.m.–7 p.m.; Sun.: 11 a.m.–4 p.m.
AE, MC, V

My Shoes carries a full line of all the most wanted children's shoe styles in its spacious, friendly, neighborhood-type stores. Athletic sneakers are a specialty, but there's a complement of dress and school shoes, high-fashion imports, and a first-rate selection for preteen girls at very affordable prices. The fitters here are pros.

SHOOFLY
506 Amsterdam Avenue, near 84th Street
580-4390
Mon.–Sat.: 11 a.m.–7 p.m.; Sun.: 12 noon–6 p.m.
AE, MC, V

The hats in Roz Viemeister's magical children's-shoe-and-accessory store perch on toy corncobs, lobster claws, and other quirky props. The floor is covered with animal footprints and trompe l'oeil mud, the steam pipes are tree trunks, and weary youngsters can sink into a Flintstones foam-rock chair. Viemeister's selection of shoes, suspenders, socks, and gloves is just as whimsical. Silver-and-black-suede infants' shoes, fleece-lined boots appliquéd with mountains, pointy-toed cowboy boots, and silly sneakers of all kinds, coexist with fish sandals, froggy boots, puppet slippers and classic Mary Janes, ballet slippers, and lace-up oxfords. Among the hats are traditional boaters and sailor berets, as well as Jughead and Sherlock Holmes caps.

TRU-TRED
1241 Lexington Avenue, at 84th Street
249-0551
Mon.–Wed., Sat.: 9:30 a.m.–5:45 p.m.;
Thurs.–Fri.: 9:30 a.m.–7:45 p.m.; Sun.: 12 noon–4:45 p.m.
AE, MC, V

The city's most popular shoe store is constantly crammed with strollers, toddlers, and parents, so it's wise to avoid the weekends and shop on weekdays. Parents come to Tru-Tred for its enormous stock of stylish shoes in a full range of sizes at very fair prices. The assortment of rain, snow, and work boots is outstanding; there are dozens of sneakers to choose from, as well as very classic white bucks, two-tone saddles, and Mary Janes. You'll find Topsider, Timberland, StrideRite, Capezio, Sebago, and Nike, as well as all the most-wanted European names, and the salespeople at Tru-Tred not only know how to fit shoes but actually seem to like children.

419

WICKER GARDEN'S CHILDREN

The well-laid-out shoe department boasts expert fitters as well as a top-notch selection of traditional shoes along with updates on the classics—Mary Janes in red, white, or pastels and saddle shoes in pink or red. (See **Clothing,** p. 100.)

MEN'S SHOES

The department stores offer a full range of men's shoe styles; Barneys New York, Bergdorf Goodman's, Bloomingdale's, and Saks Fifth Avenue carry outstanding selections. See **Men's Clothing, Vintage,** for vintage shoes.

ADAMICI

116 Seventh Avenue, at 17th Street
620-0290
Mon.–Wed., Fri., Sat.: 10 a.m.–7 p.m.; Thurs.: 10 a.m.–8 p.m.
All major

At Adamici you'll find a solid inventory of Italian-made shoes to please a range of tastes and footwear needs. Traditional wing tips, perforated oxford lace-ups, and tassel loafers satisfy the pinstripe crowd; casual moccasins, keltie slip-ons, and ankle-high boots are geared to casual weekend wear; and the high-fashion looks are sure to delight style setters.

BALLY OF SWITZERLAND

711 Fifth Avenue, near 56th Street
751-9082
Mon.–Wed., Fri., Sat.: 9 a.m.–6 p.m.; Thurs.: 9:30 a.m.–7 p.m.

645 Madison Avenue, near 59th Street
832-7267
Mon.–Sat.: 9:30 a.m.–6 p.m.

347 Madison Avenue, near 44th Street
986-0872
Mon.–Sat.: 9 a.m.–6 p.m.

553 Seventh Avenue, at 39th Street
279-7259
Mon.–Fri.: 9:30 a.m.–6 p.m.; Sat.: 9:30 a.m.–4:30 p.m.

2 World Financial Center
385-0995

Mon.–Fri.: 10 a.m.–6 p.m.; Sat. & Sun.: 12 noon–5 p.m.
All major

Bally shoes are imported from Switzerland, Italy, and France, and they're made from lightweight, glove-soft leathers, superbly crafted and classically styled. Most are sensible shoes that are geared to the boardroom, but you will find a few surprises, such as boots and loafers in ostrich or crocodile. Briefcases, small leather goods, belts, carry-on duffels, garment bags, and sports bags are equally well-made and traditional.

BELTRAMI
Classic alligator and lizard slip-ons and lace-ups, along with more trendy styles. (See **Women's Shoes**, p. 429.)

BILLY MARTIN'S WESTERN WEAR
812 Madison Avenue, at 68th Street
861-3100
Mon.–Fri.: 10 a.m.–7 p.m.; Sat.: 10:30 a.m.–6 p.m.;
Sun.: 12 noon–5 p.m.
All major

No matter what the vagaries of fashion, cowboy boots always seem to be au courant, and at Billy Martin's you'll find the city's largest selection for men, women, and children. Simple, unadorned calfskin or suede versions share the cluttered space with others that are elaborately tooled and hand-stitched from exotic skins. But Billy Martin's is crammed with a full range of authentic Western wear: Cripple Creek and Stetson hats, fringed buckskin and leather jackets, handsome leather and lizard belts with sterling-silver buckles, great leather gloves, as well as bolo ties, traditional American Indian jewelry and concha belts. Surprisingly, Billy Martin's boot prices are often lower than the competition.

BOTTICELLI
666 Fifth Avenue, at 53rd Street
582-2984
Mon.–Fri.: 10 a.m.–7 p.m.; Sat.: 10 a.m.–6:30 p.m.

Trump Tower
725 Fifth Avenue, at 56th Street
308-6402
Mon.–Sat.: 10 a.m.–6 p.m.

1021 Third Avenue, near 60th Street
838-9060
Mon.–Fri.: 11 a.m.–8 p.m.; Sat.: 10 a.m.–7 p.m.; Sun: 12 noon–6 p.m.
AE, DC, MC, V

The men's shoe store—unlike the Botticelli for women with its playful designs—is filled with classically styled, traditional footwear that's

421

handcrafted in Italy from fine-quality leathers and skins. There are shoes for the boardroom, as well as styles for formal and weekend wear, that are distinguished by interesting color variations and rich detailing. You'll find a tempting selection of leather and suede jackets, briefcases, and luggage, too.

BROOKS BROTHERS

All the classics are here—wing-tip oxfords, plain front bluchers, tassel slip-ons, and hand-sewn moccasins—and they're crafted from top-quality calfskin, and they're known for their excellent fit. Year-round Brooks offers tan-and-white bucks, and Brooks shoe prices range from inexpensive for most styles to costly for hand-stitched, bench-made beauties. (See **Clothing,** p. 116.)

CHARLES JOURDAN

Men's shoes run the gamut from conservative oxfords to refined avant-garde styles. (See **Women's Shoes,** p. 430.)

CHURCH'S ENGLISH SHOES

428 Madison Avenue, at 49th Street
755-4313
Mon.–Sat.: 9 a.m.–6 p.m.
All major

Men have been coming to Church's since 1873, attracted by the clubby atmosphere and the store's 97 versions of wing-tip oxfords. Church's shoes are handcrafted in England of quality leathers, and they're sturdy and meant to last. In addition to the wing tips you'll find all the other boardroom classics, as well as hand-sewn moccasins, tassel and kiltie slip-ons, and soft Italian-made penny loafers. Church's has the city's largest stock of wide and narrow widths and sizes (from triple-A to triple-E, and from size 6 to 14) but for those with problem feet Church's will make up custom shoes. Prices are good.

COLE-HAAN

667 Madison, at 61st Street
421-8440
Mon., Thurs.: 9:30 a.m.–8 p.m.; Tues., Wed., Fri.,
Sat.: 9:30 a.m.–6:30 p.m.; Sun.: 12 noon–5 p.m.
AE, MC, V

Cole-Haan originated in Yarmouth, Maine, and began by manufacturing soft leather camp and boating moccasins. The company now has shops worldwide, yet in its handsome deep-green-and-mahogany New York flagship store its early beginnings are apparent. Hand-sewn penny loafers and canoe moccasins, made of soft, tumbled leather, come in such colors as peanut and chalk; others are made of burnished leathers in deep, rich hues. In addition to its signature styles, Cole-Haan offers two-tone saddle shoes in a range of exciting color combinations, classic business footwear, rugged driving shoes, and sneakers in a rainbow of shades. Women will find tassel loafers and camp moccasins in brights or pastels, along with classic pumps and sling backs, and a full range of soft casuals and saddle shoes. For children there are camp moccasins in pastel hues, canvas sneakers, along with classic sandles and oxfords. The shop also carries nicely executed luggage, handbags, belts, and umbrellas.

DAVIDE CENCI
The small, but well-edited collection of stylish and well-crafted Italian shoes includes lush suede tassel loafers, two-tone deerskin spectators, classic sandals, handsome lizard and crocodile moccasins, and glove-soft leather driving shoes. (See **Clothing**, p. 121.)

DIEGO DELLA VALLE
Classic, handmade, and pricey Gallo footwear, along with J. P. Tod's soft-leather boating and driving shoes, and Hogan walking shoes made of water-resistant Loritech. (See **Women's Shoes**, p. 431.)

F. R. TRIPLER & CO.
A fine selection of classic business shoes. (See **Clothing**, p. 117.)

GIRAUDON
The cutting-edge footwear includes bulbous funky-toed shoes, leather lace-ups with pony-skin plugs, fringed moccasins, lug-soled brogues and boots, and preppy Topsiders in neon-brights. Since a classicism has recently crept into the line, you'll also find conservative but clunky-looking wing tips and oxfords. Prices are low for such hip styles. (See **Women's Shoes**, p. 432.)

GUCCI
The classic Gucci moccasin with its signature gold-plated horsebit, along with woven-tassel moccasins in soft nappa kid, and lightweight driving shoes with embossed linking G's. (See **Clothing**, p. 154.)

HARRY'S SHOES
2299 Broadway, at 83rd Street
874-2035
Mon.–Sat.: 10 a.m.–6 p.m.
AE, MC, V

Harry's is a huge supermarket of a store, yet it has an old-time neighborhood feeling. Active footwear is the store's specialty, so you'll find such names as Avia, New Balance, Reebok, Adidas, and Nike. But there are comfortable walking shoes in a broad range of sizes and widths, as well as such popular brands as Bally, Florsheim, Selby, Bass, and Sebago. There's a complete selection of StrideRite, Capezio, and Jumping Jacks for children, along with more fashion-forward European styles.

JANDREANI
220 East 60th Street
753-4666
Mon.–Sat.: 11 a.m.–8 p.m.; Sun.: 12 noon–5 p.m.
All major

Jandreani's Italian shoes are slim and sleek and crafted from glove-soft leathers. The shop carries lots of lace-ups, moccasins in lizard and alligator, nicely executed ankle boots, woven leather slip-ons, and handsome dress shoes. The footwear is young-looking without being trendy, and prices are good.

J. M. WESTON
42 East 57th Street
308-5655
Mon.–Sat.: 10 a.m.–6 p.m.
All major

Long considered Paris's most elegant and exclusive shoe emporium, J. M. Weston's has been crafting shoes since 1865. It numbers François Mitterrand, Valéry Giscard d'Estaing, and the most plugged-in Parisians as satisfied customers. Now that the company has a branch in New York, nouvelle society need no longer travel to Paris for shoes. For here, in a handsome duplex setting, among polished mahogany shelves, cozy leather sofas, and crystal chandeliers, New Yorkers can buy the same high-quality, bench-made shoes that once made a trip to Paris mandatory. There are brogues, wing tips, and penny loafers of utterly traditional design, along with boots inspired by English equestrian gear. Each shoe style has its own last and comes in five widths, and a record of a customer's size is kept on file for phone orders. Weston's is wonderfully Old World in look and amenities, and although prices are high, considering the quality and service it offers, they're not outrageous.

JOAN & DAVID
Although the selection of men's shoes is limited, there are handsome loafers in calfskin and crocodile, as well as nicely done suede oxfords. (See **Women's Shoes,** p. 433.)

KENNETH COLE
Cole's take on the traditional wing tip, saddles in unlikely leathers, penny loafers with square toes and jagged rubber soles, oxfords with silver-hardware lacings. (See **Women's Shoes,** p. 434.)

MARAOLO
Maraolo's eclectic offerings include everything from work boots, to conservative wing tips, to casual moccasins, to trendy crepe-soled slip-ons. (See **Women's Shoes,** p. 434.)

MAUD FRIZON

Shoes in a rainbow of colors and skins that are as playful, assertive, and expensive as the women's styles. (See **Women's Shoes,** p. 435.)

MCCREEDY & SCHREIBER

213 East 59th Street
759-9241
Mon., Thurs.: 9 a.m.–9 p.m.; Tues., Wed., Fri., Sat.: 9 a.m.–7 p.m.;
Sun.: 12 noon–6 p.m.

37 West 46th Street
719-1554
Mon.–Sat.: 9 a.m.–7 p.m.
AE, D, MC, V

McCreedy & Schreiber is a family-owned and -operated business that has been supplying New Yorkers with shoes since 1922, and today it's a favorite with college preppies, Wall Streeters, visiting Europeans, and mainstream middle-income businessmen. They come for Lucchese, Larry Mahan, Stewart, Tony Lama, and Dan Post cowboy boots; classic English-made ankle boots; soft Italian loafers; and such all-American brands as Bass, Rockport, Cole-Haan, Sebago, Timberland, Sperry Top-Siders, and Weejuns. And they come for the wide range of widths and sizes (from narrow to triple E, and 6 to 16) and for the excellent prices.

NEW REPUBLIC CLOTHIERS

Although the selection is small, it's neatly done and includes soft leather and suede shoes from England with a Retro look, along with pointy-toed two-toned oxfords. (See **Clothing,** p. 123.)

ORVIS

An impressive stock of hunting and fishing boots that include waders, rubber moccasins, Maine hiking boots, along with snow boots and tennis sneakers. (See **Sporting Goods,** p. 456.)

OTTO TOOTSI PLOHOUND

124 Prince Street
925-6641
Mon.–Fri.: 11:30 a.m.–7:30 p.m.; Sat.: 11 a.m.–8 p.m.;
Sun.: 12 noon–7 p.m.
AE, MC, V

A few doors down from Tootsi Plohound is Otto, filled with shoes for men that are equally young and offbeat as the women's styles. Open-toed loafers, lug-soled slip-ons with elastic vamps, faux-fur lace-ups, moccasins with square snub toes, rubber sandals, fringed oxfords, and orthopedic-looking numbers are what you're likely to find, along with dozens of amusing socks. Prices are excellent for such fun looks.

425

PAUL SMITH
Among the sophisticated updates on traditional styling are wing tips, two-toned saddles, white bucks, penny loafers, and moccasins that have a bit more flair and style than the classics. (See **Clothing,** p. 124.)

PAUL STUART
Handsome interpretations of classic styles are often done in unusual leathers, and there are English Balmorals (many specially tanned and crafted of water-repellent leathers), ankle boots, soft casual loafers, and canvas espadrilles in a rainbow of shades. (See **Clothing,** p. 118.)

POLO/RALPH LAUREN
Bench-made shoes in the classic tradition—elegant crocodile loafers, two-tone saddles, white bucks, oxfords, and ghillies—along with a fine selection of boating moccasins and sporty hand-sewn loafers for those trips to Maine. (See **Clothing,** p. 124.)

REMINISCENCE
The hottest looks from England and France: saddle oxfords, pointy or square-toed slip-ons, and lug-soled moccasins. (See **Clothing,** p. 170.)

ROBERT CLERGERIE
Many of the men's shoe styles have square toes, an elongated vamp, and a refined clunkiness. (See **Women's Shoes,** p. 436.)

SACHA LONDON
Everything from rugged multicolored moccasins to black suede lace-ups to sandals. (See **Women's Shoes,** p. 436.)

SALVATORE FERRAGAMO
730 Fifth Avenue, near 56th Street
246-6211
Mon.–Wed., Fri., Sat.: 10 a.m.–6 p.m.; Thurs.: 10 a.m.–7 p.m.
AE, D, MC, V

Ferragamo offers a fine mix of shoe styles that are crafted of top-quality leathers. Along with classic business and formal footwear, there are many casual styles with a European flair. Woven wing-tip lace-ups in terra-cotta calfskin, two-toned nappa-leather saddle shoes, lush suede moccasins, and soft-calfskin tassel slip-ons are a few of the treats. In addition to shoes Ferragamo carries a first-rate stock of sport jackets, slacks, sweaters, shirts, and ties perfect for nouvelle society's leisure hours.

THE SECOND COMING
The large assortment of vintage shoes includes two-tone saddles, wing tips, and white bucks. (See **Furniture,** p. 426.)

STEPHANE KÉLIAN
Gaultier, Montana, and Kelian's own line of soft leather slip-ons, re-

fined takes on offbeat styles, and leather sneakers. (See **Women's Shoes,** p. 437.)

STEWART ROSS
Although there are only a handful of styles, come here for hip work boots. (See **Clothing,** p. 146.)

SUSAN BENNIS/WARREN EDWARDS
Brogues in colorful suedes, penny loafers in rust Tejus lizard, evening lace-ups in crushed velvets, boots in baby crocodile—the designs are exuberant and the prices steep. (See **Women's Shoes,** p. 437.)

TO BOOT
256 Columbus Avenue, near 72nd Street
724-8249
Mon.–Sat.: 12 noon–8 p.m.; Sun.: 12 noon–7 p.m.

520 Madison Avenue, near 53rd Street
644-5661
Mon.–Wed., Fri., Sat.: 10:30 a.m.–6:30 p.m.; Thurs.: 10:30 a.m.–8 p.m.
All major

It was To Boot's extraordinary selection of cowboy boots that first made the original store on Columbus Avenue an Upper West Side landmark. Without abandoning the boots, owners Robin Steakley, Al Martinez, and Adam Derrick soon moved on to carrying business, casual, and formal footwear and opened a second store on the East Side. So now these understated yet elegant shops stock everything from lug-soled, trendy, Japanese inspired boots to classic wing-tip business shoes, to fashion-forward designs in exotic skins by the fine Italian shoemakers A. Testoni and Cesare Paciotti. There are Maine hand-sewn loafers, English bench-made shoes, Andrea Pfister's designs for men, and trend-setting formal styles. The stores offer a dazzling array of ties, scarves, and socks, too, and prices range from moderate to costly. To Boot also has a boutique on Bergdorf Goodman's second floor.

TRASH AND VAUDEVILLE
The hottest looks in shoes from England—chunky lace-ups, boots with monk straps, rubber-tire soles—whatever is most up-to-the-minute. (See **Clothing,** p. 175.)

WOMEN'S SHOES

All the department stores have well-stocked shoe departments with a full range of styles.

ANDREA CARRANO BOUTIQUE
677 Fifth Avenue, near 52nd Street
752-6111
Mon.–Wed., Fri., Sat.: 10:30 a.m.–6:30 p.m.; Thurs.: 10:30 a.m.–8 p.m.

750 Madison Avenue, near 65th Street
570-9020
Mon.–Sat.: 10 a.m.–6 p.m.
All major

Carrano is internationally known for the spare and clean lines of its Italian-made shoes. Styles range from the classic to the trendy, and the glove-soft kidskin and fine suedes are finely detailed and come in enticing colors. There's an outstanding selection of sophisticated pumps, flats, and boots to choose from, as well as a nicely done group of handbags.

ANN TAYLOR
The shoe departments carry Joan & David's nicely executed footwear that's perfect for work or a night on the town. (See **Clothing**, p. 152.)

BALLY OF SWITZERLAND
689 Madison Avenue, at 62nd Street
751-2163
Mon.–Sat.: 9:30 a.m.–6 p.m.
All major

Classic styling and beautiful leathers are Bally's trademark, and the shoe salon for women is as comfortable and understated as the shoes. Although you're not likely to find any surprises here—the stock is strong on traditional pumps, spectators, and sling-backs—you will find well-made shoes that are sensible and timeless.

BELGIAN SHOES
60 East 56th Street
755-7372
Mon.–Fri.: 9:30 a.m.–4:30 p.m.
All major

The shoe styles in this sleepy shop haven't changed in twenty years and they're a longtime favorite with Connecticut matrons. Recently, however, the shop has become the darling of models and fashionable young things who wait for weeks for their custom-ordered classic leather, velvet, or suede flats with tiny bows to be flown in from Belgium. The shop carries traditional pumps and boots, too, but it's the flats (for men, too) that are the hot sellers here. They come in scores of colors, and they're well made, as comfortable as slippers, and nicely priced. The sales staff is delightfully obliging.

BELTRAMI
711 Fifth Avenue, at 55th Street
838-4101
Mon.–Sat.: 10 a.m.–6 p.m.
AE, MC, V

Beltrami, a name associated with high-fashion footwear, has stores in Florence, Rome, and Milan. Its New York branch is a striking neoclassic space with Florentine marble floors and a fountain, and it offers shoes that are designed to dazzle. Silk evening slippers come encrusted with pearls, stiletto-heeled suede pumps are patchworks of color, and knee-high boots sport patent-leather highlights. Although the signature Beltrami look features elaborate styling, decorative appliqués, and the unusual combination and treatment of leathers and skins, there are classic alligator and lizard shoes for men and quiet spectators for women, along with the glitzier styles. Distinctive belts, handbags, luggage, and leather clothing as well. Expensive.

BILLY MARTIN'S WESTERN WEAR
Among the enormous selection of cowboy boots for women—the city's largest—you'll find simple and unadorned versions along with others that are stitched, embellished, and made from exotic skins. (See **Men's Shoes**, p. 421.)

BOTTICELLI
612 Fifth Avenue, at 49th Street
582-6313
Mon.–Fri.: 10 a.m.–7 p.m.; Sat.: 10 a.m.–6:30 p.m.

416 Columbus Avenue, at 80th Street
496-2222
Mon.–Fri.: 11 a.m.–7 p.m.; Sat.: 11 a.m.–7 p.m.; Sun.: 12 noon–6 p.m.
All major

Botticelli caters to women who enjoy wearing shoes that are witty and amusing. Thong sandals are adorned with crocodiles, tigers, and snakes; cowboy boots and penny loafers come in exotic skins dyed a rainbow of unlikely shades; buttoned ankle boots re-create turn-of-the-century looks; and pumps are a combination of unusual leathers and assertive colors. Recently the company's shoes have become more traditional, so now there's a mix of quieter styles.

CAPEZIO IN THE VILLAGE
177 MacDougal Street
477-5634
Mon.–Sat.: 12 noon–8 p.m.; Sun.: 1 p.m.–6 p.m.
AE, MC, V

Classicists who dislike following the fickle finger of fashion turn to Capezio for traditional and timeless ballet slippers, canvas jazz shoes, espadrilles, Keds, and bow-tied pumps—they know they'll always find a stock of these basics in this spacious two-level emporium. The more fashion conscious come for Jan Jansen's forward shoe styles, as well as for the store's tempting assortment of casual sports separates for men and women at very affordable prices. And traditionalists and the fashion crowd alike come to this Greenwich Village store for the complete Capezio line of tights, leotards, leg warmers, and other dance and aerobic paraphernalia.

CHANDLERS
695 Fifth Avenue, near 54th Street
688-2140
Mon.–Wed., Fri., Sat.: 10 a.m.–6 p.m.; Thurs.: 10 a.m.–7 p.m.

4 World Trade Center
938-1449
Mon.–Fri.: 7:30 a.m.–6:30 p.m. Sat.: 10 a.m.–5 p.m.
AE, MC, V

At Chandlers they take high-fashion, pricey shoe styles and translate them into very affordable footwear, so this is a good store to keep in mind when you have a last-minute date and have the right dress, need a shoe, but don't want to spend a fortune. You'll find national brands here as well as Chandlers' own labels, and belts, hosiery, scarves, and jewelry.

CHARLES JOURDAN
Trump Tower
725 Fifth Avenue, at 56th Street
644-3830
Mon.–Fri.: 10 a.m.–7 p.m.; Sat.: 10 a.m.–6 p.m.; Sun.: 12 noon–6 p.m.

769 Madison Avenue, at 66th Street
628-0133
Mon.–Fri.: 10 a.m.–7 p.m.; Sat.: 10 a.m.–6 p.m.
AE, MC, V

Charles Jourdan is known as a fashion pacesetter, and although his designs are fashion-forward, they are never outré. You'll find sexy stiletto-heeled pumps in a range of exotic leathers and a rainbow of colors, along with glitzy evening sandals and nicely done leather flats. There are romantic florals, luxurious silks and brocades, nautical stripes, and interesting takes on the classic espadrille. Men's shoes run the gamut from conservative oxfords to refined avant-garde styles. The selection of handbags, hats, scarves, and separates is as appealing as the shoes, and prices at Charles Jourdan are good, considering these are designer creations.

COLE-HAAN
Leather moccasins in dazzling colors, classic pumps, and sneakers in a rainbow of shades. (See **Men's Shoes,** p. 422.)

DIEGO DELLA VALLE
462 West Broadway
420–8419
Tues.–Sat.: 11 a.m.–7 p.m.; Sun.: 12 noon–6 p.m.
AE, MC, V

Loft-size, with white walls, polished wood floors, kilim scatter rugs, leather sofas, and Art Deco lighting, Diego Della Valle is filled with shoes that echo the refined good taste of the setting. Here, in addition to Diego Della Valle's own line, you'll find the high-fashion footwear that the company designs under the Gianfranco Ferre, Azzedine Alaïa, Zoran, Christian Lacroix, and Romeo Gigli labels, as well as its casual J. P. Tod's shoes. Diego's own creations lean toward smashing flats in the palest of suedes, although you will find high-heeled pumps and Art Deco–inspired evening shoes. There are quilted suede ballerina shoes for Ferre, straw flats with ribbons for Lacroix, ankle-high boots for Alaïa, and faille flats for Gigli. Downstairs is the men's footwear collection, and it includes the classic, handmade, and pricey styles of Gatto, along with J. P. Tod's soft leather boating and driving shoes, and Hogan' walking shoes made of water-resistant Loritech.

ECCO SHOES
111 Thompson Street
925-8010
Mon.–Fri.: 11 a.m.–8 p.m.; Sat.–Sun.: 12 noon–7 p.m.

324 Columbus Avenue, near 75th Street
799-5229
Mon.–Fri.: 11 a.m.–10 p.m.; Sat.–Sun.: 11 a.m.–7 p.m.

94 Seventh Avenue, near 15th Street
675-5180
Mon.–Fri.: 11 a.m.–8 p.m.; Sat.: 11 a.m.–7 p.m.; Sun.: 12 noon–7 p.m.

1024 Third Avenue, at 61st Street
759-2868
Mon.–Wed., Fri., Sat.: 10 a.m.–7 p.m.; Thurs.: 10 a.m.–8 p.m.; Sun.: 12 noon–7 p.m.
AE, MC, V

Fred Marsh and Albert Cruz specialize in shoes that are fun to wear, and they must be doing something right because their relaxed, low-key shops have sprouted up all over the city. You'll find such inventive styles as the recent Robin Hood in Space Collection of metallic washed suede, boots for the urban cowboy, and flats in denim leather. But there are nicely done classic moccasins in candy colors, and lots of low-heeled pumps in basic black. In addition to the cowboy variety, there's a good stock of handsome yet practical rain and snow boots. Prices at Ecco are surprisingly pleasant.

FAUSTO SANTINI
697 Madison Avenue, near 62nd Street
838-1835
Mon.–Fri.: 10:30 a.m.–6:30 p.m.; Sat.: 10:30 a.m.–6 p.m.
AE, MC, V

Fausto Santini's stark black-and-white shop with its tempting window display offers trendy and colorful designs that are young and playful. The shoes are made in Italy, and pumps, flats, and boots come in a range of colorful and boldly patterned leathers and suedes, as well as basic black. Prices are gentle.

FERRAGAMO
717 Fifth Avenue, near 56th Street
759-3822
Mon.–Wed., Fri., Sat.: 10 a.m.–6 p.m.; Thurs: 10 a.m.–7 p.m.
All major

Salvatore Ferragamo was once known as the "shoemaker to the stars" because of his shoe designs for Hollywood actresses and for Cecil B. DeMille's extravaganzas. Although Salvatore died in 1960, the company is now owned and run by his wife and children, who carry on Salvatore's dedication to high quality. The shoes are crafted in Florence from the finest leathers, and they are favorites with the ladies who lunch at Le Cirque, who treasure the footware for its classic elegance and superb fit. Young-looking pumps and pale calfskin and patent-leather flats with golden buckles and grosgrain bows have recently been added to the collection, but for the most part Ferragamo footwear appeals to those who are not slaves to the dictates of fashion. Expensive.

GIRAUDON
339 West Broadway, near Grand Street
334-9867
Mon.–Sat.: 11 a.m.–7:30 p.m.; Sun.: 1 p.m.–6 p.m.

152 Eighth Avenue, near 17th Street
633-0999
Mon.–Sat.: 11:30 a.m.–7:30 p.m.; Sun.: 1 p.m.–6 p.m.

135 West 72nd Street
769-0800
Mon.–Sat.: 11:30 a.m.–7:30 p.m.; Sun.: 1 p.m.–6 p.m.
AE, MC, V

Alain-Guy Giraudon's downtown shoes go well with cutting-edge finds from Charivari or Comme des Garçons. There are square-toed flats, thick platform sandals, and Louis-heeled pumps for women; elasticized slip-ons, bulbous funky-toed lug-soled brogues, leather lace-ups, and fringed moccasin loafers for men. Recently a classicism has crept into the line, so you'll find a smattering of Retro forties pumps and sling-backs, along with round-toed wing tips for the pinstripe crowd.

GUCCI
Traditional pumps, loafers with the company's signature horse's bit or interlocking G's, along with other conventionally classic styles. (See **Clothing**, p. 154.)

HELENE ARPELS
470 Park Avenue, near 57th Street
755-1623
Mon.–Sat.: 10 a.m.–6 p.m.; closed Sat. in summer
AE, D, MC, V

Deep-green walls, wood paneling, and crystal chandeliers are the elegant setting for Helene Arpels's conservative pumps that are favorites of Nancy Reagan and society's darlings. Slim and sensible low-heeled designs, done up in fine-quality leathers, are the specialty, but there are sexy satin evening styles and casual moccasins as well, along with exquisite crocodile and ostrich handbags. Pricey.

IF BOUTIQUE
A tempting stock of the trendy shoe designs of Robert Clergerie and Azzedine Alaïa. (See **Clothing**, p. 173.)

JOAN & DAVID
816 Madison Avenue, near 68th Street
772-3970
Mon.–Sat.: 10 a.m.–6 p.m.
AE, DC, MC, V

Joan Helpern was a psychologist before she began designing shoes, and she's proud of the fact that her designs are so accommodating they can be worn anywhere and at any time of the day. Her shoes are beautifully styled—chic but never trendy. You'll find up-to-the-minute pumps, stylish boots in soft leathers and suedes, and classic moccasins in ostrich, lizard, and crocodile. The men's selection is limited, but there are some handsome loafers, and for little girls, pricey party shoes in leathers and metallics. The shop is comfortable and spacious with a clubby feeling, and in addition to the shoes, there are nicely executed sports separates, umbrellas, belts, scarves, handbags made from antique kilims, and luggage. Prices range from moderate to costly.

KENNETH COLE
353 Columbus Avenue, near 76th Street
873-2062
Mon.–Sat.: 11 a.m.–8 p.m.; Sun.: 12 noon–6 p.m.
AE, MC, V

This advanced designer is known for using quirky materials and creating way-out shoes, but recently his designs have become more mainstream, just a little off-the-edge. Cole does stylish flats, lace-up oxfords with snipped toes, boots with pointy toes, and pumps with feminine heels in bronze metallic or forest, tobacco, and russet suedes. Men will find classic penny loafers with square toes and jagged rubber soles, and oxfords with silver-hardware lacings. Prices are so gentle, you can find shoes here for under $25.

MANOLO BLAHNIK
15 West 55th Street
582-3007
Mon.–Fri.: 10:30 a.m.–6 p.m.; Sat.: 11 a.m.–5 p.m.
AE, MC, V

Manolo Blahnik creates shoes that somehow manage to be cutting-edge, timeless, and old-fashioned at the same time. They're handmade in Italy of exotic leathers, or velvets and satins used in unlikely color combinations—a strong yellow with midnight blue, pale peach with ecru. There are tempting daytime styles, crocodile flats in lots of colors, and exquisite evening shoes inspired by those of the eighteenth and nineteenth centuries. Brides can choose from strikingly beautiful wedding styles, and at Blahnik they'll custom-make a shoe to match a gown. Very expensive.

MARAOLO
782 Lexington Avenue, near 61st Street
832-8182
Mon.–Wed., Fri., Sat.: 10 a.m.–7 p.m.; Thurs.: 10 a.m.–8 p.m.;
Sun.: 12 noon–5 p.m.

1321 Third Avenue, near 75th Street
535-6225
Mon.–Wed., Fri., Sat.: 11 a.m.–7 p.m.; Thurs.: 11 a.m.–8 p.m.;
Sun.: 12 noon–5 p.m.

835 Madison Avenue, near 69th Street
628-5080
Mon.–Wed., Fri., Sat.: 10 a.m.–6:30 p.m.; Thurs.: 10 a.m.–7 p.m.

All major

Come early in the season to Maraolo. Prices are so good the most popular styles go quickly. All the shoes are made in Italy, and the company carries Georgio Armani and Emporio along with its own lines. Last season's big sellers were crocodile loafers for men and women and crocodile pumps. Boots are a specialty, and women will find dozens to choose from—thigh-high suedes, sleek knee-highs, cowboy boots in suedes and exotic skins, and cozy fur-lined versions—as well as faille and grosgrain flats in a rainbow of colors. The selection for men is just as eclectic and includes everything from work boots, to conservative wing tips, to casual loafers, to trendy crepe-soled slip-ons. There are even high-fashion shoes for little girls: stylish ballet slippers, woven leathers, two-tone lace-ups, and adorable cowboy boots.

MAUD FRIZON
49 East 57th Street
980-1460
Mon.–Sat.: 10 a.m.–6 p.m.
AE, MC, V

Maud Frizon's state-of-the-art footwear is a favorite with designers and fashion-forward women. Frizon pioneered the zipless Russian boot, and her cone-shaped stiletto-heeled pumps are world-famous. She does gold-mesh ankle-tie flats, suede pumps that are inventively embellished, and others that are unlikely combinations of exotic leathers or a riot of polka dots. Her men's designs include skins in a score of colors, and they're as playful, assertive, and expensive as the women's styles. Yet there's good news for cost-conscious customers: Frizon recently introduced the less pricey Miss Maud line of shoes.

PERRY ELLIS SHOES
1136 Madison Avenue, at 85th Street
570-9311
Mon.–Sat.: 10 a.m.–7 p.m.; Sun.: 12 noon–6 p.m.

680 Madison Avenue, near 61st Street
980-7012
Mon.–Fri.: 10 a.m.–6:30 p.m.; Sat.: 10 a.m.–6 p.m.
AE, MC, V

Although Perry Ellis shoes come in very basic, classic shapes, they're anything but staid. Styles include demure Victorian-looking pumps, vampy forties-like sandals, shoes with Louis heels, along with flats cut like a man's—two-toned spectators or perforated oxfords—that are perfect for today's pleated pants. There is a winning group of flats in oversized dots or stripes and the company has recently introduced attractive handbags and accessories. Prices are excellent for designer shoes.

PETER FOX

105 Thompson Street
431-6359
Mon.–Sat.: 12 noon–8 p.m.; Sun.: 12 noon–7 p.m.

378 Amsterdam Avenue, near 78th Street
874-6399
Mon.–Sat.: 12 noon–8 p.m.; Sun.: 12 noon–7 p.m.
AE, MC, V

This English designer's original shop on Thompson Street is not much bigger than a closet, his newer West Side Store is large and spacious, and in both Fox offers offbeat shoes with the look of an earlier era. Satin pumps with silver buckles and eighteenth-century Louis heels (perfect for a bride), lace-up ankle shoes (also with Louis heels), English riding boots, and evening slippers with high-buttoned straps are among the exclusive and limited-edition designs that have old-fashioned lasts and long pointy toes. The staff is obliging and attentive to fit, and considering the quality of the kidskin and the custom-made look, prices are good.

POLO/RALPH LAUREN

On the third floor are women's shoes in leathers and exotic skins that are very classic in style and beautifully executed; the boots—inspired by English riding styles—are winners. (See **Clothing,** p. 124.)

REMINISCENCE

Shoes that include the hottest looks from England and France: saddle oxfords, crepe-soled skimmers with pussycat bows, and dozens more with a Retro look.(See **Clothing,** p. 170.)

ROBERT CLERGERIE

41 East 60th Street
207-8600
Mon.–Thurs.: 10 a.m.–6:30 p.m.; Fri. & Sat.: 11 a.m.–6 p.m.
AE, MC, V

In a tiny, spartan, minimalist store Robert Clergerie's fashion-forward shoes are simply spread out on spindly tables, but even in this uninviting setting the French shoes look appealing. Clergerie's creations have the most beautiful lasts and heels, and many of his designs have square toes, an elongated vamp, and are understated and classic, yet cutting-edge. There are simply done stacked-heeled pumps, seamless wedge designs, beautifully executed oxford lace-ups, fisherman's sandals, along with vampy forties high-heel styles. The men's shoes have a refined clunkiness, and many of the men's styles also have square toes.

SACHA LONDON

294 Columbus Avenue, at 74th Street
873-5788

Mon.–Fri.: 11 a.m.–9 p.m.; Fri., Sat.: 12 noon–8 p.m.
AE, MC, V

Sacha's imported English shoes are young, whimsical, and daring. High heels and flats are adorned with everything from buttons to safety pins, and they're patterned in plaids, stripes, and polka dots, and come in neon colors like fuchsia and yellow. There are sexy spiked-heel pumps, pointy flats, and clunky rubber-soled sandals. The men's selection ranges from rugged multicolored moccasins to black suede lace-ups to sandals.

THE SECOND COMING
The large selection of vintage shoes includes two-tone saddles, white bucks, and pointy flats from the fifties. (See **Furniture,** p. 426.)

STEPHANE KÉLIAN
702 Madison Avenue, near 62nd Street
980-1919
Mon.–Fri.: 10 a.m.–6 p.m.; Sat.: 11 a.m.–6 p.m.
AE, D, MC, V

In a spare, marble setting Stephane Kélian offers shoes that range from traditional to funky. Kélian produces his own line of shoes, along with designs for Gaultier and Montana, and sneakers for American Eagle, and all four labels are available in his New York store. Although many of Kélian's own styles have squared-off toes and a clunky look, his shoes for Montana, although still offbeat, are more refined. There are ever-so-soft leather slip-ons, and crepe-soled boots for men. Sneakers, mostly high-tops, come in everything from laces to plaids to florals.

SUSAN BENNIS/WARREN EDWARDS
440 Park Avenue, at 56th Street
755-4197
Mon., Thurs.: 10 a.m.–7 p.m.; Tues., Wed., Fri.: 10 a.m.–6:30 p.m.;
Sat.: 10 a.m.–6 p.m.
AE, MC, V

Even movie stars not easily put off by high prices are shocked at the prices here, but many faithful customers believe that these shoes are an investment and well worth whatever they cost. All the footwear is created by Susan Bennis and Warren Edwards, an award-winning design team, and then made in Italy. The workmanship is superb, the styling advanced, and materials include the finest exotic skins, furs, fabrics, and leathers. There are striped wedgies with patent-leather trim, opera pumps in crushed velvets, sling backs in floral silk crepe de Chine, vivid suedes, Anna Karenina-inspired boots, black high heels draped with pearls and beaded-and-fringed Indian moccasins. Men will find brogues in colorful suedes, penny loafers in emerald-green ostrich, evening lace-ups in crushed velvets, and boots in baby crocodile. Prices here can soar into the thousands.

TOOTSI PLOHOUND

110 Prince Street
925-8931
Mon.–Fri.: 11:30 a.m.–7:30 p.m.; Sat.: 11 a.m.–8 p.m.; Sun.: 12 noon–
7 p.m.
AE, MC, V

On-the-edge styles and fantastic prices account for this store's popularity with the younger set. Recent sightings included men's classics cut for
women—wing tips, two-tone saddles, dirty and white bucks—along
with wedge-heeled sandals with lace inserts, sling backs with a Retro
look, and snub-toed ballet slippers. In addition to the inexpensive Free-
lance line, there are Stephane Kélian, Gaultier, and Pollini's offbeat and
more costly designs. Also dozens of socks with personality.

TRASH & VAUDEVILLE

The hottest looks in shoes from England: pointy toes, rubber-tire soles,
whatever is most up-to-the-minute. (See **Clothing,** p. 175.)

WALTER STEIGER

739 Madison Avenue, near 64th Street
570-1212
Mon.–Sat.: 10 a.m.–6 p.m.
AE, MC, V

In an elegant, maroon-lacquer and mirrored interior with spare black
furnishings, Walter Steiger's lovely updates on classic styles are presented like jewels. The Swiss-born designer has a knack for making the
simplest shoe fresh and arresting, and his sandals, pumps, and boots
are beautifully done without calling attention to themselves. A master
of proportion in connecting the shoe's body to its heel, Steiger's shoes
are distinguished by his unexpected use of fabric, his distinctive and
innovative heel shapes, and décolleté toe cuts. Expensive.

Silver

ANTIQUE

Barneys New York has a well-edited selection of early Georg Jensen sterling-silver flatware.

À LA VIEILLE RUSSIE
Eighteenth- and nineteenth-century Russian silver. (See **Jewelry**, p. 342.)

ALICE KWARTLER
Place des Antiquaires
125 East 57th Street
752-3590
Mon.–Sat.: 11 a.m.–6 p.m.
AE, MC, V

Tiffany silver gleams against the fascinating shapes of cut and engraved nineteenth-century crystal in Alice Kwartler's small and sparkling shop. Although Tiffany silver is the chief attraction, Kwartler's other treasures include a rare Japanese Art Nouveau sterling coffee set blooming with irises, along with more affordable dresser and desk accessories, candlesticks, picture frames, flasks, enameled Austrian stemware, and English fruit sets with tusk handles.

GOREVIC & GOREVIC LTD.
635 Madison Avenue, at 59th Street
753-9319
Mon.–Sat.: 10 a.m.–5:45 p.m.
All major

For three generations the Gorevic family has offered wealthy New Yorkers fine-quality antique and modern silver along with estate and contemporary jewelry. Seventeenth- to nineteenth-century American, English, and continental sterling, as well as old Sheffield and Victorian plate, are handsomely displayed in this spacious, gleaming two-level shop. Among the old pieces you'll find a mix of wonderfully ornate sweetmeat dishes, beautifully worked tea services, enormous and elaborate silver tureens, along with sedate covered meat dishes, trays in all sizes, pitchers, candlesticks, even sterling-silver baby cups. There are new silver pieces of simpler design, fine examples of antique jewelry, and watches by the most coveted names. Expensive.

FORTUNOFF
681 Fifth Avenue, near 54th Street
758-6660
Mon.–Wed., Fri., Sat.: 10 a.m.–6 p.m.; Thurs.: 10 a.m.–8 p.m.
All major

Originally Fortunoff was a small housewares store in Brooklyn, but this family-owned business has outgrown its Brooklyn roots and now operates department-store-size outposts on Long Island and New Jersey, and today it's Fortunoff's enormous inventory of well-priced precious jewelry that has become the store's chief attraction. Yet in the company's Fifth Avenue branch, which is about one-tenth the size of the suburban stores, the antique silver department outshines the jewelry. Vast, and geared to satisfy a wide range of tastes and budgets, it's filled with magnificently ornate Russian and English tea services, old Sheffield and Victorian-plate sweetmeat dishes, wine coasters, biscuit boxes, spoon warmers, candlesticks and candelabra, and covered dishes of all kinds. There's also a fine assortment of Early American, Georgian, nineteenth-century Chinese, and antique Tiffany silver designs. The silver hollowware selection is outstanding, and Fortunoff offers more than 500 contemporary flatware patterns in sterling, stainless, and gold and silver plate.

HOFFMAN GAMPETRO ANTIQUES
Place des Antiquaires
125 East 57th Street
755-1120
Mon.–Sat.: 11 a.m.–6 p.m.
AE, MC, V

Ronald Hoffman and Anthony Gampetro have assembled one of the most extensive collections of silver of the American aesthetic movement in the country, and their tiny shop glistens with the works of Martele and Chassed, along with engraved pieces in revival styles. There's Art Nouveau silver, too, along with English ceramics, overlaid and engraved glass, and antique jewelry.

JAMES ROBINSON
15 East 57th Street
752-6166
Mon.–Fri.: 10 a.m.–5 p.m.; Sat.: 10:30 a.m.–4:30 p.m.
AE, MC, V

Glowing with a subdued opulence, James Robinson is one of the city's best addresses for seventeenth- to nineteenth-century English hallmark silver, antique china, and estate jewelry, and each period—Georgian to Victorian—is represented by only the finest examples. Candlesticks signed by Matthew Cooper, a John L. Hunt coffeepot, a Frances Pages George II footed waiter, and an elaborately etched George III teapot were among the recent sightings. For more than 400 years James Robinson has produced hand-forged sterling-silver flatware, and it still offers eighteen classic patterns to choose from. Rare porcelain dinner sets from Coalport, Spode, Derby, Minton, and Worcester, and exquisite nineteenth-century jewelry are among the shop's other treasures. Brooches, necklaces, bracelets, cuff links, and rings are delicately worked, many are set with precious stones, and they're all quietly breathtaking. Very expensive.

JAMES II GALLERIES

Among the lavish inventory of Victorian sterling and silver-plate items are candlesticks, trays in all sizes, pitchers, sweetmeats, toast racks, letter openers, spoonwarmers, jam pots, covered vegetable dishes, and domed meat servers. The smaller pieces—serving spoons, soup ladles, berry spoons, mother-of-pearl-handled fish sets—are affordable and make fine wedding or Christmas gifts. (See **China and Glassware,** p. 67.)

JEAN'S SILVERSMITHS

16 West 45th Street
575-0723
Mon.–Thurs.: 9 a.m.–4:45 p.m.; Fri.: 9 a.m.–3:30 p.m.
MC, V

Jean's is not your usual silver store with gleaming pitchers and candlesticks lined like soldiers all in a row. In this cluttered and dusty warren silver is stacked helter-skelter in glass cabinets, or stashed in boxes on the floor, or piled high on open counters, or hung from racks overhead. And none of it is polished. But here you'll find silver that you can't find anywhere else. Jean's specialty is discontinued flatware patterns, and she offers more than 900 of them, some of which have not been produced in fifty years. The rest of the stock is equally as mind-boggling: hundreds of candy dishes, pitchers, and candlesticks; dozens of silver goblets and cordial glasses; scores of trays in every size; complete sets of silver flatware; and Early American, Georgian, and Victorian hollowware. There are discontinued china patterns, too, and a cleaning and repair service. Prices are excellent.

J. MAVEC & COMPANY, LTD.

625 Madison Avenue, near 58th Street
Second floor
888-8100

Mon.–Fri.: 10:30 a.m.–5:30 p.m.; Sat. by appointment
AE

Janet Mavec is known for her unique collection of Georgian and Victorian candlesticks and candelabra, yet her smaller pieces—antique tea-caddy spoons, snuff mulls and boxes, frames, castors, serving pieces, and infant mugs and spoons—are equally outstanding. Her old Sheffield plate wine coasters and small trays would make delightful wedding gifts, and her contemporary English silver frames, treen-topped pillboxes, and silver rulers perfect Christmas presents. Papier-mâché trays, tartanware, and fine Victorian and Edwardian brooches, earrings, necklaces, and bracelets round out her fine hoard.

RALPH M. CHAIT GALLERIES
Rare nineteenth-century Chinese export silver. (See **China and Glassware,** p. 70.)

SAMUEL H. MINTZ STRAUS
Manhattan Art & Antiques Center
1050 Second Avenue, at 55th Street
888-3350
By appointment only
No credit cards

Samuel Mintz's tiny shop is an excellent source for American sterling silver from the turn of the century through the forties. Early Georg Jensen and David Anderson flatware are specialties, but there's also a charming group of vintage sterling-silver souvenir spoons of all kinds, including old ones from Atlantic City and Coney Island. Mintz carries sterling-silver jewelry and pillboxes, too, and his prices are good.

S. J. SHRUBSOLE
104 East 57th Street
753-8920
Mon.–Fri.: 9:30 a.m.–5:30 p.m.
AE, MC, V

Experts consider S. J. Shrubsole, an English company that has been on 57th Street for more than fifty years, the most distinguished silver purveyor in the country. Extremely fine and rare items from the sixteenth through the early nineteenth centuries are the chief attractions, including the work of such great silversmiths as Paul de Lamerie, Hester Bateman, Paul Storr, Myer Myers, and Paul Revere. American, English, Irish, and Scotch silver are represented, and you might find such unique pieces as Matthew Boulton's superb George III *epergne*, Michael Boult's rare George I octagonal teapot, and Richard Green's Queen Anne coffeepot. There's old Sheffield plate along with a winning assortment of antique Irish and English Georgian glass, and an equally fine collection of exquisitely crafted Georgian and Victorian jewelry that includes brooches, bracelets, necklaces, rings, and earrings. Very expensive.

S. WYLER, INC.
941 Lexington Avenue, at 69th Street
879-9848
Mon.–Sat.: 10 a.m.–6 p.m.
AE

The country's oldest silver dealer has been in business since 1890, and it's still a family affair, now run by Seymour Wyler and his son Richard. These acknowledged experts carry very fine antique English sterling silver, along with Victorian and old Sheffield plate. Trays in all sizes, covered meat platters, tea and coffee services, sweetmeat dishes, wine coasters, spoon warmers, candlesticks, and candelabra are among the gleaming array. Surprisingly affordable ladles, stuffing spoons, and serving pieces make wonderful gifts, and the Wylers offer a tantalizing selection of antique porcelain that includes Crown Derby, Coalport, Spode, Royal Worcester, and other coveted names.

TUDOR ROSE ANTIQUES
28 East 10th Street
677-5239
Mon.–Sat.: 10:30 a.m.–6:30 p.m.
All major

Antique Victorian silver flatware and hollowware sparkles from every corner of this small and cluttered shop. Candlesticks, frames, and silver-and-crystal boudoir sets are particularly appealing, but there are dozens of candy dishes, trays, wine coasters, and tea services, too. Among the smaller and more affordable items are serving pieces, pill boxes, and baby mugs, along with sterling-silver reproductions from old molds.

CONTEMPORARY

B. Altman & Co., Bergdorf Goodman, Bloomingdale's, Lord & Taylor, and Macy's all have well-stocked silver departments that offer a broad range of sterling-silver, silver-plate, and stainless-steel flatware, as well as hollowware and silver accessories from all the leading manufacturers.

ASPREY LIMITED
Contemporary sterling-silver flatware, along with a small and select group of silver antiques. (See **Gifts**, p. 299.)

BACCARAT INC.

Puiforcat and Christofle silver flatware with a Deco look. (See **China and Glassware,** p. 72.)

BUCCELLATI, INC.

46 East 57th Street
308-2900
Mon.–Sat.: 9:30 a.m.–5:30 p.m.
All major

Everything in this opulent shop was designed by Mario Buccellati, who modeled his designs after antique Florentine silver. The hand-hammered sterling-silver objects are timeless in their appeal, and the shop offers elaborate sterling-silver flatware patterns along with hollowware bowls, tureens, trays, candlesticks, and coffee services that are exquisitely crafted, ornate, beautiful, and wildly expensive. More affordable is the silver-plate flatware.

PAVILLON CHRISTOFLE

680 Madison Avenue, at 62nd Street
308-9390
Mon.–Sat.: 10 a.m.–6 p.m.
AE

Christofle has provided wealthy Parisiens with elegant silver for more than 150 years and in its New York outpost, a mix of ivory marble floors and caramel-color suede walls, it offers New Yorkers silver with a classic, Art Deco, or just plain moneyed look. There's sterling, gold- and silver-plate flatware, along with tea services, ice buckets, bowls, trays, pitchers, and sugars and creamers. Tiny silver rattles, mugs, forks, and spoons are among the gifts for babies, and the shop carries Raynaud Ceralene and Haviland china, as well as crystal from the grand houses of Baccarat and Saint Louis. Christofle has recently introduced a handsome line of jewelry that mixes sterling silver and gold with brilliant gemstones.

PUIFORCAT

811 Madison Avenue, at 68th Street
734-3838
Mon.–Fri.: 10 a.m.–6 p.m.; Sat.: 10 a.m.–5 p.m.
AE, MC, V

The company was founded in 1820 in the heart of Paris's Marais district by Jean Puiforcat, a silversmith who revolutionized silver tableware with his spare geometric creations. Although selected pieces of Puiforcat's have been available over the years in a few New York stores, it is only the Madison Avenue boutique that carries reproductions of all Puiforcat's Art Deco masterpieces. Here vintage patterns translated into silver plate are displayed next to such original Puiforcat designs as a streamlined silver platter with gold handles and a tulip-shaped tea service in rosewood and sterling silver. The collection includes 180 flatware and 10,000 hollowware patterns (including more ornate Louis XIII designs), a variety of Limoges porcelains, and Art Deco–style jewelry.

ROYAL COPENHAGEN PORCELAIN/GEORG JENSEN SILVERSMITHS

The city's most complete selection of Georg Jensen sterling-silver and stainless flatware patterns (many reissues of Jensen's early designs), as well as sleek silver candlesticks, bowls, and trays. (See **China and Glassware,** p. 78.)

TIFFANY & COMPANY

Sterling-silver flatware patterns with an understated, classy look, along with silver trays, tea services, candlesticks, bowls, dishes, and picture frames in a range of prices and styles, from ornate to austere. (See **Jewelry,** p. 358.)

Sporting Goods

GENERAL SPORTING EQUIPMENT

ABERCROMBIE & FITCH
199 Water Street
South Street Seaport
809-9000
Mon.–Sat.: 10 a.m.–7 p.m.; Sun.: 12 noon–6 p.m.

Trump Tower
725 Fifth Avenue, at 56th Street
832-1001
Mon.–Sat.: 10 a.m.–6 p.m.
All major

Since 1892 Abercrombie & Fitch has supplied sports clothing and equipment to the gentleman athlete, and it's still a fine source for traditional and proper sports gear—everything from safari jackets, to regulation croquet sets, to skeet-shooting equipment. Tennis buffs will find a good selection of classic court separates, A & F's own tennis shoes that combine tradition and technology, as well as some of the best names in rackets. Golf, running, skiing, hunting, and swimming enthusiasts can be equally well-outfitted here. And A & F offers a vast assortment of games—everything from croquet, to darts, to cribbage, to horseshoes, to shuffleboard, to board games of every kind—and pool accessories that include pool floats, rafts, and chairs. For the home-fitness crowd there are rowers, stationary bicycles, slant boards, abdominal machines, Roman chairs, cross-country ski simulators, even Getaway massage chairs. Pricey.

AR-BEE MEN'S WEAR
1598 Second Avenue, at 83rd Street
737-4661

Mon.–Fri.: 9 a.m.–6:45 p.m.; Sat.: 9 a.m.–5:45 p.m.
AE, MC, V

Ar-Bee Men's Wear is one of the oldest sporting goods and work-clothes stores in the city and it looks it: time-smoothed oak counters, peeling tin ceilings, cracked linoleum floors, and overloaded shelves and cubby-holes stuffed with clothing. The Rapoport family has run the business for fifty years, and today Ar-Bee consists of two stores just across the street from one another. One specializes in work clothes, the other in sporting gear, and both are favorites with the Upper East Side private school crowd who come for chamois shirts, chino pants, down vests, jean jackets, rubber moccasins, and the trappings for team sports. Since the sports store specializes in school sports, every game from soccer, to hockey, to baseball, to football, to basketball is amply covered, but there's also a full line of exercise, camping, and hunting equipment. The staff is knowledgeable and adept at dealing with youngsters.

EASTERN MOUNTAIN SPORTS, THE OUTDOOR SPECIALISTS
611 Broadway, at Houston Street
505-9860
Mon.–Wed.: 10 a.m.–7 p.m.; Thurs., Fri.: 10 a.m.–8 p.m.; Sat.:
10 a.m.–6 p.m.; Sun.: 12 noon–6 p.m.

20 West 61st Street
397-4860
Mon.–Fri.: 10 a.m.–8 p.m.; Sat.: 10 a.m.–6 p.m.; Sun.: 12 noon–6 p.m.
AE, MC, V

Eastern Mountain Sports carries everything for the outdoors, yet as its name suggests, climbing and backpacking are the stores' specialties. You'll find one of the city's most complete stock of mountaineering paraphernalia—ropes, picks, straps, rock clips, slings, helmets, shoes, and axes—as well as backpacks of all kinds in a full range of prices. Both downhill and cross-country skiing are also well represented in these large, no-frills stores, and there's well-priced ski clothing, too, along with tennis and running gear. The selection of camping equipment is extensive and includes tents, cots, stoves, and all the trappings.

HERMAN'S WORLD OF SPORTING GOODS
135 West 42nd Street
730-7400
Mon.–Fri.: 9:30 a.m.–7 p.m.; Sat.: 9:30 a.m.–6 p.m.

845 Third Avenue, at 51st Street
688-4603
Mon.–Fri.: 9:30 a.m.–7 p.m.; Sat.: 9:30 a.m.–6 p.m.

1185 Sixth Avenue at 47th Street
944-6689
Mon.–Fri.: 9 a.m.–7 p.m.; Sat.: 9 a.m.–6 p.m.

110 Nassau Street
233-0733
Mon.–Fri.: 9 a.m.–6 p.m.; Sat.: 9 a.m.–5 p.m.

39 West 34th Street
279-8900
Mon.–Fri.: 9:30 a.m.–7 p.m.; Sat.: 9:30 a.m.–6:30 p.m.;
Sun.: 12 noon–5 p.m.
All major

Virtual sporting supermarkets, these warehouse-style stores are stocked with a vast selection of name-brand sporting supplies, apparel, and footwear. You'll find rack upon rack crammed with tennis togs, running shorts, and down jackets. Hundreds of tennis and squash rackets line the walls, and the selection of fishing accoutrements, downhill and cross-country skiing paraphernalia, and camping equipment is enormous. There are stationary bicycles, rowers, boxing gloves, and weights, along with all the proper footwear—aerobics, running, basketball, golf, and tennis. A staff of trained professionals provides ski mounting and racket stringing. Prices are good.

PARAGON SPORTING GOODS

867 Broadway, at 18th Street
255-8036
Mon.–Fri.: 10 a.m.–8 p.m.; Sat.: 10 a.m.–7 p.m.; Sun.: 11 a.m.–6 p.m.
All major

Not only does Paragon carry equipment, clothing, and footwear for more than two dozen different sports; its stock is often superior to shops that specialize in these activities. Just about every sport is covered in this huge multilevel warehouse of a store: boxing, lacrosse, golf, tennis, hockey, wrestling, diving, mountain climbing, martial arts, bowling, squash, soccer, hiking, skiing, swimming, basketball, football, gymnastics, and at least a dozen more. Paragon has very complete camping, fishing, and backpacking departments, too, and it carries all the popular exercise and fitness gear—Precor rowers and cross-country skiing simulators, as well as stationary bicycles and treadmills. Salespeople are knowledgeable and obliging, and prices are excellent.

BASEBALL

AR-BEE MEN'S WEAR
Bats, balls, shoes, and clothing. (See **General Sporting Equipment**, p. 446.)

PARAGON SPORTING GOODS
A full line of bats, balls, shoes, and clothing. (See **General Sporting Equipment**, p. 448.)

THE PLAYING FIELD
905 Third Avenue, near 57th Street
421-0003
Mon.–Wed., Fri., Sat.: 10 a.m.–6 p.m.; Thurs.: 10 a.m.–8 p.m.; Sun.:
12 noon–6 p.m.
All major

You won't find baseball bats or gloves at the Playing Field. What you will find are the official caps, jackets, sweats, jerseys, and T-shirts worn by the New York teams, as well as popular out-of-town ones. And almost everything comes in sizes for men, women, and children.

BICYCLES
AND ACCESSORIES

AMERICAN YOUTH HOSTEL EQUIPMENT STORE
75 Spring Street
431-7100
Mon.–Wed., Fri.: 10 a.m.–7 p.m.; Thurs.: 10 a.m.–9 p.m.; Sat.:
10 a.m.–5 p.m.
AE, MC, V

The American Youth Hostel Equipment Store is located in the American Youth Hostel Headquarters, and it carries all the paraphernalia suggested for A.Y.H. trips, and everything is A.Y.H. approved. Although the shop is no-frills and spartan, the range of stock is impressive. There's everything from repair kits to flashlights, biking gloves to canteens, pumps to parkas, and it's all top quality and prices are excellent. The shop also offers backpacking gear and camping outerwear, too. If you're planning a hosteling trip or just biking on your own, it's

worthwhile checking out the supplies offered in this friendly and helpful store.

BICYCLE HABITAT
194 Seventh Avenue, near 21st Street
691-2783
Mon.–Thurs.: 10 a.m.–7 p.m.; Fri.: 10 a.m.–6:30 p.m.; Sat., Sun.:
10 a.m.–6 p.m.

244 Lafayette Street
431-3315
Mon.–Thurs.: 10 a.m.–7 p.m.; Fri.: 10 a.m.–6:30 p.m.; Sat.: 10 a.m.–
6 p.m.
MC, V

Serious bikers are dedicated to the Bicycle Habitat stores. They cite the
personal attention provided by the sales staff and their concern for
safety. Habitat stocks the city's largest selection of Cannondale frames,
but it also carries Trek, Zebra, Centurion, Fisher, and Univega bikes.
There's always a good selection of cycling accessories, and repairs are
excellent.

BICYCLE RENAISSANCE
491 Amsterdam Avenue, near 83rd Street
362-3388
Mon.–Sat.: 10 a.m.–6 p.m.; Sun.: 10 a.m.–5 p.m.
AE, MC, V

Bicycle Renaissance was one of Columbus Avenue's pioneer stores,
and although it recently moved to roomier quarters on Amsterdam Avenue, it's still crammed with wheels, frames, bikes, and riders. All the
popular biking names are here—Centurion, Maruishi, Diamond Back,
Lotus, Peugeot, Campagnolo, and Trek—and the shop builds and repairs BMX bikes. It stocks city bikes, racing and touring ones, and all
speeds, as well as selling clothing and biking accessories, and handling service and repairs.

CONRAD'S BIKE SHOP
25 Tudor City Place, at 41st Street
697-6966
Tues., Thurs., Fri., Sat.: 10:30 a.m.–5:30 p.m.; Wed.: 10:30 a.m.–7 p.m.
AE, MC, V

Conrad's has long been considered the Rolls-Royce of New York bicycle
shops, as well as the city's most civilized and well-organized one. It's
internationally known for carrying only top-of-the-line frames, bicycles, and parts, and for its fine service and knowledgeable staff, so
Conrad's is a favorite with professional and sophisticated cyclists. Besides all the very best in bikes, the accessories are top-notch, and
there's an excellent selection of used bikes, too, at great savings.

LARRY & JEFF'S BICYCLES PLUS
204 East 85th Street
794-2201

1400 Third Avenue, near 79th Street
794-2929
Daily: 10 a.m–8 p.m.
All major

Every type of bicycle—from triathalon to mountain, from fat tire to touring, and from sport to racing—is crammed into Larry & Jeff's well-stocked stores. You'll find both well-known and esoteric names, including Fat Chance, Cannondale, Tesh, Centurion, Cooks Bros., Gios, and Vitus. There's a fine inventory of Aerolite, Campagnolo, and Cinelli components, as well as helmets, clothing, and biking accessories. And at Larry & Jeff's they'll build and repair skateboards, too.

STUYVESANT BICYCLE
349 West 14th Street
254-5200
Mon.–Sat.: 9:30 a.m.–6 p.m.; Sun.: 12 noon–5 p.m.
AE, MC, V

The Stuyvesant Bicycle shop has been around since 1939, and it's a cycling supermarket filled with an enormous selection of all the top brands. Racing and triathalon frames and bikes, sport touring and folding bicycles share the space with fat tire and BMX bikes, tandems, and unicycles. There's racing equipment (seats, stems, rims, tires, and spokes) and touring paraphernalia (shoes, helmets, gloves, bags, and car racks), spare parts, and all manner of accessories along with a fine selection of wheels for children that includes scooters and tricycles. The obliging staff handles repairs, rentals, and storage, too.

TOGA BIKE SHOP
110 West End Avenue, at 64th Street
799-9625
Mon.–Fri.: 10 a.m.–6 p.m.; Sat.: 10 a.m.–5 p.m.; Sun.: 12 noon–5 p.m.
MC, V

Although Toga Bike Shop is in an out-of-the-way location—around the corner from Lincoln Center—it's always crowded with bikers and bikes. It's a spacious and orderly store, with frames and wheels hanging overhead and hundreds of assembled bikes filling racks on the wall. Fat wheel and racing bikes are the specialty, so you'll find Kestrel, Olmo, Vitus, and Colnago, but Toga also carries the top names in touring, sport, city, and triathlon bikes, and the shop is expert at custom-painting. There's a full line of sleek biking clothing, too, along with cycling accessories.

451

BILLIARDS AND BOWLING

BLATT BILLIARDS
809 Broadway, near 11th Street
674-8855
Mon.–Fri.: 9 a.m.–6 p.m.; Sat.: 10 a.m.–4 p.m.
MC, V

Blatt Billiards has been in business since 1923, and this time-worn store with its creaky wood floor, tin ceiling, old-paneled walls, green-glass ceiling lamps, well-used cue racks, and clutter of new and antique billiard tables looks as though it hadn't changed since then. Blatt claims to carry the world's largest collection of antique, custom, and contemporary pool tables, and its stock is vast. It offers custom cues, balls, cloths, and accessories, too, and handles table repairs and restorations. Blatt also has a fine array of regulation dart boards and darts.

V. LORIA & SONS
178 Bowery, near Spring Street
925-0300
Mon.–Fri.: 10:30 a.m.–6 p.m.; Sat.: 10:30 a.m.–4 p.m.
AE, MC, V

V. Loria is the city's oldest name in billiard equipment. The shop opened in 1912, and it's well-stocked with new, used, custom, and antique tables, along with custom cues, cloths, balls, even lighting fixtures. But V. Loria carries more than billiard paraphernalia. In its large cluttered space you'll find bowling gear—balls, shoes, bags, and accessories—Ping Pong and poker tables, and pinball machines.

CAMPING

DOWN EAST SERVICE CENTER
75 Spring Street
925-2632
Mon.–Fri.: 11 a.m.–6 p.m.; Thurs.: 11 a.m.–7 p.m.; Sat.: 11 a.m.–2 p.m.
AE, MC, V

Leon and Harriet Greenman have filled their small store with an unlikely mix of camping equipment, books and periodicals, and a down cleaning and repair service. It's a friendly shop where you'll find tents, knapsacks, Cordura nylon bags, and Iverson snowshoes, alongside bookshelves filled with Department of the Interior and National Park Service Topo maps and travel guides for hikers, campers, cyclists, and adventurers. But best of all, the Greenmans repair and clean sleeping bags, down parkas, and outdoor gear; and they patch tents, restuff sleeping bags, fix zippers, and modify equipment.

EASTERN MOUNTAIN SPORTS, THE OUTDOOR SPECIALISTS
A large stock of tents, backpacks, stoves, sleeping bags, and accessories. (See **General Sporting Equipment**, p. 447.)

HERMAN'S WORLD OF SPORTING GOODS
The large stock of tents includes everything from fieldmaster to alpine to geodesic; also a good selection of sleeping bags, backpacks, and cots. (See **General Sporting Equipment**, p. 447.)

PARAGON SPORTING GOODS
All the top names and an enormous assortment of camping, backpacking, and hiking equipment. (See **General Sporting Equipment**, p. 448.)

TENTS AND TRAILS
21 Park Place
227-1760
Mon.–Wed., Fri., Sat.: 9:30 a.m.–6 p.m.; Thurs.: 9:30 a.m.–7 p.m.;
Sun.: 12 noon–6 p.m.
AE, MC, V

For more than fifty years Tents and Trails has been dedicated to camping, climbing, and mountaineering. Its three floors are crammed with such top names in tents and equipment as Eureka, Moss, Jansport, Kelty, Tent, North Face, Sierra Designs, and Sierra West. In fact, Tents and Trails' inventory covers the alphabet—from Asolo to Marmot to Victorinox—and includes a complete selection of backpacks, stoves, sleeping bags, down jackets, boots, ropes, along with all the accessories, even Boy Scout supplies. And although the stock is vast, the staff is experienced and delightfully helpful. Prices range from inexpensive to pricey, but this is top-of-the-line and state-of-the-art gear.

DARTS

ABERCROMBIE & FITCH
Pub-quality English darts in handsome wooden cases. (See **General Sporting Equipment,** p. 446.)

BLATT BILLIARDS
A fine array of regulation boards and darts. (See **Billiards and Bowling,** p. 452.)

DARTS UNLIMITED
30 East 20th Street
533-8684
Tues.–Fri.: 12 noon–5:30 p.m.; Sat.: 11 a.m.–4 p.m.
MC, V

Darts are a popular English pub sport that is pretty well neglected in this country, and Darts Unlimited is the only store in New York exclusively devoted to English darts and darting equipment. The boards are of tournament quality and the darts top-notch, and you'll find dart racks, scoreboards, and all the other accessories. The salespeople are well informed and very helpful.

EXERCISE EQUIPMENT

ABERCROMBIE & FITCH
The large stock of fitness equipment includes Precor rowers, stationary bicycles, slant boards, and cross-country ski simulators. (See **General Sporting Equipment,** p. 446.)

THE GYM SOURCE AT CUTLER OWENS
45 East 51st Street
688-4222
Mon.–Fri.: 9: a.m.–6 p.m.; Sat.: 10 a.m.–5 p.m.
All major

Top-of-the-line rowers, weight systems, treadmills, stationary bicycles, and free stations fill the Gym Source's sleek, high-tech space. The knowledgeable staff will work with you to devise the proper equipment for your needs, and if you want a sauna or steam room, they have a staff that can design and install one for you. The Gym Source carries a full range of fitness accessories (mats, hand weights, pedometers, even towels), along with tennis and squash rackets, footballs, and basketballs.

HERMAN'S WORLD OF SPORTING GOODS
A large stock of stationary bicycles, rowers, weights, and weight stations. (See **General Sporting Equipment**, p. 447.)

PARAGON SPORTING GOODS
Precor rowers and cross-country skiing simulators, as well as stationary bicycles, weights, weight stations, and treadmills. (See **General Sporting Equipment**, p. 448.)

FENCING

BLADE FENCING
212 West 15th Street
620-0114
Mon.–Fri.: 10 a.m.–7 p.m.; Sat.: 11 a.m.–3 p.m.
MC, V

Blade is known for its fencing instruction, but it also sells everything for the fencer. In its small basement shop you'll find uniforms, weapons, shoes, gloves, and masks in sizes for both men and women. There's an extensive collection of books on fencing, and the staff is helpful and friendly.

FISHING

HUNTING WORLD/ANGLER'S WORLD
A division of Hunting World, Angler's World carries a full range of flies, reels, and rods, including Bob Lee's favorite salmon fly selection and Ernie Schwiebert nymphs. (See **Hunting Sporting Goods**, p. 460.)

CAPITOL FISHING TACKLE CO.
218 West 23rd Street
929-6132

Mon.–Fri.: 8 a.m.–5:30 p.m.; Sat.: 9 a.m.–4 p.m.
MC, V

Capitol Fishing Tackle Co. has been in business since 1897, and al-though its location may seem odd—it occupies a large space in the legendary Chelsea Hotel—this wonderfully old-fashioned shop offers a complete range of fresh, saltwater, big-game, and deep sea rods, reels, lures, lines, and accessories. Capitol prides itself on offering equip-ment for catching everything from giant tuna to tiny pan fish. It stocks inexpensive beginners' outfits, the finest-quality fresh water rods and reels, and big-game ones costing well over two thousand dollars. The staff is knowledgeable about fishing and is very obliging.

GOLDBERG'S MARINE
Big-game fishing tackle. (See **Marine Sporting Goods,** p. 460.)

ORVIS
355 Madison Avenue, at 45th Street
697-3133
Mon.–Fri.: 9 a.m.–6 p.m.; Sat.: 10 a.m.–5 p.m.
AE, MC, V

A Manhattan outpost of a 130-year-old purveyor of fishing and outdoor equipment, Orvis is the oldest surviving rod-building company in Amer-ica, so it carries some of the country's finest fishing gear. There's a complete line of fly-fishing reels, rods, lures, and accessories, as well as the waders, hippers, boots, bags, fishing vests, and jackets to make fishing treks comfortable. Rods are made of graphite, bamboo, and Fiberglas, and the fishing flies are all hand-tied. Orvis also specializes in guns and equipment for upland bird hunting, and it offers safari duds, casual country clothing, and classic and durable Battenkill lug-gage.

URBAN ANGLER LTD.
118 East 25th Street
Third Floor
979-7600
Mon.–Fri.: 10 a.m.–6 p.m.
MC, V

Although Urban Angler is tucked away on the third floor of a nonde-script midtown building miles from the nearest trout stream, owners Steve and Jon Fisher—a father-and-son team—offer all the parapher-nalia a fly fisherman needs for a successful fishing trip. High-quality fly-fishing rods and reels bear the names of Sage, Abel, Simms, Scott, Winston, and Scientific Anglers; and the Fishers stock thousands of American and imported flies neatly set out in bins in a handsome mahogany display case. They carry shirts, vests, nets, and waders, along with fly-tying materials and a complete line of tools for making flies.

GOLF

FOOT-JOY SHOP
7 East 52nd Street
753-8522
Mon.–Fri.: 9:30 a.m.–5:30 p.m.; Sat.: 10 a.m.–4:30 p.m.
All major

Sunny, spacious, and well-organized, with an enormous variety of golf shoes all neatly displayed, Foot-Joy Shop promises the perfect shoe for battle on the links. It carries more than 150 styles—from saddle to wing tip—guaranteed to improve your stance, your game, and certainly your fashion image. Shoes come in a wide range of sizes and widths for both men and women (some with cleats, many without), and the shop carries golf gloves and socks, along with comfortable business and running shoes.

PARAGON SPORTING GOODS
A good stock of pro golf equipment, including clubs, bags, shoes, balls, carts, and clothing. (See **General Sporting Equipment,** p. 448.)

RICHARD METZ GOLF STUDIO
35 East 50th Street
Second floor
759-6940
Mon.–Thurs.: 10 a.m.–8 p.m.; Fri.: 10 a.m.–7 p.m.;
Sat.: 10 a.m.–5 p.m.
MC, V

Walk up the stairs to the Richard Metz Golf Studio and you're greeted by the ping of golf balls. This complete pro shop has practice cages so customers can work on their swing and check the fit of the clubs. Metz, a golf pro himself, carries the top names in clubs and offers state-of-the-art equipment. He has Yamaha clubs with graphite heads and shafts, along with vintage ones from 1900 and putters from the fifties. Costly zebra-skin golf bags share the space with inexpensive lightweight ones. Metz stocks balls, Foot-Joy shoes, clothing and rainwear, and he sells golfing video tapes and books.

THE WORLD OF GOLF
147 East 47th Street
Second floor
242-2895
Mon.–Fri.: 9 a.m.–7 p.m.; Sat.: 9 a.m.–5 p.m.
All major

Hundreds of clubs, all neatly arranged, fill the World of Golf pro shop that is staffed by informed and helpful people. Ping, Lynx, Wilson, Mac-

Gregor, Hogan, Penna, Spalding, and Mizuno are some of the top names you'll find here, along with Callaway Golf Co.'s innovative irons. Row upon row of golf bags, Foot-Joy shoes, Logo balls, clothing, practice aids, and books and videos are here as well, and this shop's selection of clubs and clothing for junior golfers and women is outstanding.

HORSEBACK RIDING

BILLY MARTIN'S WESTERN WEAR
Cowboy boots and hats, belts, deerskin jackets. (See **Shoes,** p. 421.)

CHIPP OF NEW YORK
Custom-made riding garb is a specialty. (See **Clothing,** p. 140.)

HERMÉS
Splendid saddles (which are registered and can be ordered in fashion colors), handsome bridles, sturdy grooming brushes, woolen horse blankets, whips, and elegant equestrian clothing. Scarlet hunt coats, vests, breeches, and riding capes are classically cut from the finest materials. (See **Handbags,** p. 318.)

H. KAUFMAN & SON
139 East 24th Street
684-6060
Mon.–Sat.: 9:30 a.m.–6:30 p.m.
All major

H. Kaufman & Son has been at the same location for years, and it occupies the space where the original Bull's Head horse auctions were once held. Well-stocked with everything for the horse and rider, Kaufman's offers saddles and bridles, grooming and stable supplies, and riding duds. Although it's best known for western saddles, Kaufman's also carries fine English ones, as well as clothing and equipment for dressage, polo, racing, show, and pleasure riding. The selection of boots is outstanding, and includes dress, jodhpur, cowboy, field, and barn boots along with muckers.

MILLER'S
117 East 24th Street
673-1400
Mon.–Sat.: 9 a.m.–5:30 p.m.
All major

Miller's has recently moved to a handsome new store a few doors down from its original location, and whether you want western tack, fox-hunting equipment, or polo gear, you can find it here. Miller's is the official outfitter to the United States Equestrian team, and this company's stock is enormous and first-rate. It carries Hermés, Passier, and Crosly saddles; dressage, equestrian, and polo breeches; grand-prix coats; side-saddle outfits; Kentucky jodhpurs; and western duds. The selection of boots, on the mezzanine, is equally eclectic, and the store has a varied assortment of books, videos, and horsey gift items, too.

M. J. KNOUD
716 Madison Avenue, near 63rd Street
838-1434
Tues.–Sat.: 10 a.m.–5 p.m.; closed Sat. in summer
AE, MC, V

With its time-smoothed wood-paneled walls, well-worn shelves, and smell of old leather, M. J. Knoud is a comforting store. A family-owned horse emporium, it has purveyed fine-quality riding gear in the English tradition since 1913. Now run by David Wright and his daughter Bonnie, Knoud specializes in custom-made clothing—for hunting, racing, polo, pleasure, and show—yet it also offers a good selection of off-the-rack garb. The saddles are outstanding and the custom-made boots top-notch. There's a large and varied assortment of splendid gifts for horse lovers, too: wrought-iron benches, china and glassware personalized with one's own racing-silk colors, car-hood ornaments, vintage jewelry, and handsome leather-encased flasks.

HUNTING

FUNCHIES, BUNKERS, GAKS AND GLEEKS
One of the largest collections of vintage duck and goose decoys in the city. (See **Toys,** p. 491.)

GROVE DECOYS
49 Grove Street
924-4467
Tues.–Fri.: 10 a.m.–6 p.m.; Sat. & Sun.: 12 noon–6 p.m.
All major

New York's only gallery devoted to duck decoys is owned by Bill Bender, a longtime collector. He offers more than 200 rare ducks carved by past masters, as well as contemporary ones for the beginning collector. Bender carries other bird decoys, too—curlews, loons, swans, and oyster catchers—along with vintage fish decoys that were once used for ice fishing. Grove is an appealing shop stocked with some fine examples.

459

HUNTING WORLD/ANGLER'S WORLD
16 East 53rd Street
755-3400
Mon.–Sat.: 10 a.m.–6 p.m.
AE, MC, V

Hunting World's glitzy white-marble and brass store is crowded with tourists snapping up the handbags, luggage, jewelry, and gift items that now occupy the major portion of the store. The statusy garb for the sporting life that made this store so famous now seems relegated to a secondary position. But you can still find everything needed for a safari, except the guns: Bob Lee's safari jackets, slacks, hats, and shooting bags, and his light-weight vinylized-canvas luggage. And the store carries driving shoes and clay-shooter vests, along with a full line of fly fishing gear. There's Bob Lee's angler's vest and his favorite salmon fly selection, superior rods and reels, as well as Ernie Schwiebert nymphs. Expensive.

ORVIS
Shotguns, safari clothing, and upland-hunting gear. (See **Fishing**, p. 456.)

MARINE

GOLDBERG'S MARINE
12 West 37th Street
594-6065
Mon.–Wed., Fri.: 9:30 a.m.–5:45 p.m.; Thurs.: 9:30 a.m.–7:45 p.m.;
Sat.: 9:30 a.m.–3:45 p.m.
AE, MC, V

A nautical supermarket, Goldberg's Marine is stocked with bilge pumps and Explorer compasses, epoxy primers and portable showers, SeaRanger fish finders and Tahiti diving masks. It's a fine source for sailboat fittings, lifesaving gear, marine electronics, inflatable boats, water skis, nonskid china and glassware, and ropes and anchors. And along with all the rest, Goldberg's carries foul-weather gear, big-game fishing tackle, cookware, nautical tables, even compact exercise equipment. In fact, in Goldberg's cavernous space you'll find everything needed for equipping a sail or power boat.

HANS KLEPPER CORPORATION
35 Union Square, near 17th Street
243-3428

Mon.–Fri.: 9:30 a.m.–5:30 p.m.; in summer, Sat.: 9:30 a.m.–5:30 p.m.
MC, V

Johann Klepper built the first practical folding kayak in 1907, and for more than eighty years skilled craftsmen in Rosenheim, West Germany, have been building these masterpieces of design. The Klepper folding boat with its interlocking systems can be stored in a closet, transported in two canvas bags, then assembled by hand (without tools or bolts) anywhere. The company also sells sails, paddles, parkas, high-flotation jackets, cold-weather mittens, helmets, and books on kayaking. It's a beguiling store run by an enthusiastic staff.

ISLAND WINDSURFING
1623 York Avenue, near 85th Street
744-2000
Hours vary
AE, MC, V

Best known for its windsurfing lessons, Island Windsurfing also stocks the city's largest selection of mistral boards and gear. In a large basement store you'll find all the top names, quality hardware, racks, travel bags in Day-Glo colors, slalom and surf seats, and harnesses. There's also a complete array of wetsuits, drysuits, and steamers, as well as gloves and shoes.

NEW YORK NAUTICAL INSTRUMENT & SERVICE CORP.
140 West Broadway
962-4522
Mon.–Fri.: 9 a.m.–5 p.m.; Sat.: 9 a.m.–12 noon
No credit cards

Sober and serious, New York Nautical is filled with oak display cabinets and long wooden drawers that hold official navigational charts, and it looks more like a library than an instrument store. The company has been in business for seventy-five years, and it offers new and antique chronometers housed in handsome mahogany boxes with brass hardware, ship's bell clocks, barographs in elegant glass cases, telescopes, compasses, sextants, nautical flags, and books on navigation.

PAN AQUA DIVING
166 West 75th Street
496-2267
Mon.–Fri., Sun.: 12 noon–7 p.m.; Sat.: 10 a.m.–7 p.m.
AE, MC, V

Tucked away on a side street on the Upper West Side, Pan Aqua Diving is presided over by a friendly dog and a TV that plays videos of the deep to remind customers what diving is all about. A tiny store, it's filled with top-quality diving gear—tanks, depth gauges, air compres-

461

sors, wet suits, dive planners, gloves, and fins. It carries ScubaPro equipment and Tabata masks made of soft silicone for a better fit, along with a nice library of books about diving.

RICHARDS AQUA LUNG AND SPORTING GOODS CENTER
233 West 42nd Street
947-5018
Mon.–Wed., Fri: 9 a.m.–7 p.m.; Thurs. & Sat.: 9 a.m.–8 p.m.
All major

For years Richards was known as a source for army and navy surplus, and although it still carries a large stock of surplus clothing, it has now become the city's largest outlet for diving gear. In this very complete aqua-lung and scuba-diving center you'll find rubber wet suits and equipment by such popular names as Oceanic, Cressi, Dacor, and O'Neil—all at excellent prices. There's a fine assortment of competitive swimwear, too, by Speedo, Ocean Pool, Triathlon, and Olympic.

SAILWAYS MANHATTAN
859 Broadway, near 18th Street
Second floor
727-8850
Mon.–Fri.: 10 a.m.–8 p.m.; Sat. 10 a.m.–7 p.m.; Sun.: 12 noon–6 p.m.
MC, V

The space may be no-frills, but the gear at Sailways Manhattan is state-of-the-art. This New York branch of a Northeastern chain of windsurfing stores offers the very latest in boards and sails. Although the shop specializes in high-tech equipment for advanced lovers of the sport it also carries complete packages for beginners. In addition to boards and sails, there are skegs for every kind of water condition; board covers and totes; wet suits, dry suits, and bathing suits; and all the necessary paraphernalia. It's staffed by windsurfing enthusiasts who are obliging and very knowledgeable.

SCUBA NETWORK
116 East 57th Street
Second floor
750-9160
Mon.–Fri.: 11 a.m.–7 p.m.; Sat.: 11 a.m.–6 p.m.; Sun.: 12 noon–4 p.m.

175 Fifth Avenue, near 28th Street
228-2080
Mon.–Fri.: 11 a.m.–7 p.m.; Sat.: 11 a.m.–6 p.m.

303 Park Avenue South, near 23rd Street
Mon.–Sat.: 11 a.m.–6:30 p.m.
AE, MC, V

Attractively displayed in these clean and orderly stores is the very latest in scuba-diving equipment. All the top names in wet suits, tanks, diving gauges, shoes, gloves, knives, air compressors, and diving gear are represented. There's a good stock of books and travel guides, too. The shop on 57th Street carries the broadest range of gear; the downtown branches offer edited selections.

SCUBA WORLD
167 West 72nd Street
Second floor
496-6983
Mon: 1 p.m.–6 p.m.; Tues.–Sat.: 11 a.m.–7 p.m.
AE, MC, V

At Scuba World the salespeople are divers themselves, so they're knowledgeable about the sport, and the store offers such top manufacturers of scuba and snorkeling equipment as Dacor, Cressi, Mares, Ikelite, Sea Quest, Tekna, and Henderson. You'll find all the standards here—tanks, wet suits, air compressors, depth gauges, knives, gloves, masks, and fins.

RUNNING, AEROBICS, WALKING, AND DANCE

ATHLETIC STYLE
118 East 59th Street
838-2564
Mon.–Sat.: 10 a.m.–6 p.m.
AE, MC, V

You're sure to find the brand and style you want in running and aerobic shoes in this well-stocked store that offers more than 100 styles to choose from. Athletic Style also carries a full line of tennis and basketball shoes. There's a good selection of functional clothing for running and aerobics, along with attractive sports separates—shorts, tops, and pants—in bold colors. Salespeople are attentive, friendly, and knowledgeable about running and proper fit.

CAPEZIO DANCE-THEATER SHOP
755 Seventh Avenue, at 50th Street
Second floor
245-2130
Mon.–Wed., Fri., Sat.: 9:30 a.m.–5:45 p.m.; Thurs.: 9:30 a.m.–7 p.m.

Capezio East
136 East 61st Street

758-8833
Mon.–Fri.: 10 a.m.–6:30 p.m.; Sat.: 11 a.m.–6 p.m.;
Sun.: 12 noon–5 p.m.

Capezio at Steps
2121 Broadway, at 74th Street
Third floor
799-7774
Mon.–Fri.: 11 a.m.–8 p.m.; Sat., Sun.: 12 noon–6 p.m.
AE, MC, V

Capezio has been catering to student and professional dancers since 1887. Ballet, tap, aerobic, and ballroom dancers come here for their shoes, tights, unitards, leotards, leg warmers, dance bags, dance belts, taps, and rosin. The fashionable come because they happen to like the look.

CAPEZIO IN THE VILLAGE

This independent Capezio store carries a very complete stock of leotards, tights, leg warmers, and dance shoes of all kinds. (See **Shoes,** p. 430.)

FREED OF LONDON

922 Seventh Avenue, at 58th Street
489-1055
Mon.–Sat.: 10 a.m.–5:45 p.m.
All major

A New York outpost of the famed London company, Freed carries some of the best in traditional ballet and dance clothing and supplies. Among the British-made dance shoes you'll find satin pointe slippers for professionals, Greek sandals for practice, shoes for gymnastics and tap, jazz, and ballroom dancing, along with period shoes—everything from medieval to Gothic to Victorian—for stage productions. Also tutus, leotards, leg warmers, skirts, and the full line of regulation wear for the Royal Academy of Dance.

GILDA MARX

1416 Third Avenue, near 80th Street
879-4810
Mon.–Fri.: 10:30 a.m.–7 p.m.; Sat.: 11 a.m.–6 p.m.;
Sun.: 12 noon–5 p.m.
All major

Gilda Marx is the doyenne of aerobics teachers, and her spacious store is filled with her famous Flexatards. Marx's designs are functional and fashionable, and her unitards, leotards, cutoffs, and tights come in all the hottest looks, fabrics, and colors, and they're well-made and long-wearing. There's a selection of body wear and tights for children (many of the styles are cut-down versions of the grown-up line), and she carries swimwear, too.

JUMP
353 East 77th Street
879-6470
Mon.–Fri.: 11 a.m.–7:30 p.m.; Sat.: 11 a.m.–6 p.m.;
Sun.: 12 noon–6 p.m.
AE, MC, V

Although no bigger than a closet, Jump is crammed with some of the most sought-after names in dance and exercise wear. Leotards, tights, matching skirts, running garb, socks, and leg warmers are by Dance France, Bonnie August, Danskin, Flexatard, Moving Comfort, Nike, Marika, and Pineapple. Jump also carries exercise wear for men.

NEW YORK BODY SHOP
49 West 57th Street
838-1008
Mon.–Fri.: 9:30 a.m.–7:30 p.m.; Sat: 10 a.m.–7 p.m.; Sun.: 12 noon–
6 p.m.

1195 Third Avenue, near 69th Street
737-6670
Mon.–Fri.: 9:30 a.m.–7:30 p.m.; Sat.: 10 a.m.–7 p.m.; Sun.: 12 noon–
6 p.m.
AE, MC, V

At New York Body Shop's spacious Upper East Side location you'll find a futuristic high-tech setting with graphic displays of bodywear, and separate sections devoted to each of the store's specialties—exercise garb, sportswear, swimsuits, and hosiery. Although the older 57th Street shop is about half the size of the newer one, both stores carry a full stock of exercise wear that includes such names as Dance France, Danskin, Bonnie August, Nike, Reebok, Allita, and Capezio.

SUPER RUNNERS SHOPS
1337 Lexington Avenue, at 89th Street
369-6010
Mon.–Wed., Fri.: 10 a.m.–7 p.m.; Thurs.: 10 a.m.–9 p.m.;
Sat.: 10 a.m.–6 p.m.; Sun.: 12 noon–5 p.m.

360 Amsterdam Avenue, at 77th Street
787-7665
Mon.–Wed., Fri., Sat.: 10 a.m.–7 p.m.; Thurs.: 10 a.m.–9 p.m.;
Sun.: 1 p.m.–6 p.m.

1170 Third Avenue, near 68th Street
249-2133

Mon.–Wed., Fri.: 10 a.m.–7 p.m.; Thurs.: 10 a.m.–9 p.m.;
Sat.: 10 a.m.–6 p.m.; Sun.: 12 noon–6 p.m.

1 Herald Center, at 34th Street
564-9190
Mon.–Sat.: 10 a.m.–6:30 p.m.
AE, MC, V

The staff at each of the Super Runners Shops is well-informed, since they're runners themselves, and the selection of running shoes they offer is broad and covers a wide range of individual preferences and needs. All the top names in aerobic shoes are here as well—Avia, New Balance, Reebok, and Nike. The stores carry basketball, tennis, and hiking shoes, too, along with running shorts, sweats, cycling garb, swimwear, leotards, and tights.

U. S. ATHLETICS
34 East 8th Street
260-0750
Mon.–Sat.: 10 a.m.–8 p.m.

757 Third Avenue, near 47th Street
832-1750
Mon., Thurs., Fri.: 10 a.m.–8 p.m.; Tues.: 10 a.m.–7 p.m.;
Sat.: 10 a.m.–6:30 p.m.; Sun.: 12 noon–6 p.m.

500 Fifth Avenue, near 42nd Street
575-1680
Mon.–Fri.: 10 a.m.–7 p.m.; Sat.: 10 a.m.–6:30 p.m.; Sun.: 12 noon–
8 p.m.

820 Lexington Avenue, near 62nd Street
935-2667
Tues.–Wed.: 10 a.m.–7 p.m.; Mon., Thurs., Fri., 10 a.m.–8 p.m.;
Sat.: 10 a.m.–6:30 p.m.; Sun.: 1 p.m.–6 p.m.

1211 Sixth Avenue, near 48th Street
997-8404
Mon.–Fri.: 10 a.m.–6:45 p.m.; Sat.: 10 a.m.–6:30 p.m.
Additional branches all over town
AE, MC, V

One of the first athletic footwear stores in the city, there are now more than a dozen U. S. Athletics branches and they offer one of the largest selections of top-of-the-line shoes for running, aerobics, tennis, basketball, squash, soccer, and hiking. Yet in the Sixth Avenue outlet owner Matt Zayle has added even more. He's outfitted this store with footwear for just about every sport, from skydiving to curling, bobsledding to volleyball, boxing to parachuting. Zayle carries shoes for infants and children, along with functional sports separates.

WANNA DANCE
230 Columbus Avenue, near 70th Street
595-5512
Mon.–Fri.: 11 a.m.–8 p.m.; Sat.: 11 a.m.–7 p.m.; Sun.: 1 p.m.–6 p.m.
AE, DC, MC, V

Come to Wanna Dance for high-fashion workout garb in all the most wanted styles, colors, and fabrics. It's a small shop, yet it's well stocked with such popular names as Marika, Danskin, Gilbert Gear, Trip, Nike, and Baryshnikov. There are dancewear and ballet shoes, too, and a selection of leotards and tights for children.

WOMEN'S WORKOUT GEAR
121 Seventh Avenue, near 17th Street
627-1117
Mon.–Fri.: 11 a.m.–7 p.m.; Sat.: 11 a.m.–6 p.m.;
Sun.: 1:30 p.m.–5:30 p.m.
AE, MC, V

Paula Shirk, a marathon runner, has assembled athletic shoes and sportswear designed especially for women who are serious about sports, and committed to fit more than fashion. Her running shoes are a bit narrower in the heel, her shorts wider through the hips. She carries Moving Comfort and Hind Winter garb for runners, along with Saucony, New Balance, and Brooks running shoes. For swimmers she offers Speedo suits, Barracuda goggles, and AAI Seahands. And for aerobics lovers, Gilbert Gear, Dance France, and Capezio leotards, unitards, and tights, as well as Avia aerobics shoes. It's a well-organized, attractive store with roomy dressing rooms and attentive salespeople.

SKATING AND SKATEBOARDS

AR-BEE MEN'S WEAR
A good selection of skates, skateboards, and hockey sticks. (See **General Sporting Equipment**, p. 446.)

GERRY COSBY & CO.
3 Penn Plaza
563-6464
Mon.–Fri.: 9:30 a.m.–6:30 p.m.; Sat.: 9:30 a.m.–6 p.m.;
Sun.: 12 noon–5 p.m.
AE, MC, V

For more than fifty years Gerry Cosby has outfitted New Yorkers with fine ice hockey skates, but the shop also carries an excellent selection of figure skates and roller blades. Football, baseball, basketball, soccer, and lacrosse teams come here for authentic gear, and the company offers tennis rackets and shoes, and boxing gloves. The salespeople know skates, and they're friendly and helpful.

LARRY & JEFF'S BICYCLES PLUS
There's a large skateboard department with Powell, Vision, Hosoi, and Cross Bones boards. (See **Bicycles and Accessories,** p. 451.)

PARAGON SPORTING GOODS
A good selection of roller, figure, and hockey skates, as well as skateboards. (See **General Sporting Equipment,** p. 448.)

PECK & GOODIE SKATES
919 Eighth Avenue, near 54th Street
246-6123
Mon.–Fri.: 10 a.m.–6 p.m.; Sat., Sun.: 12 noon–5 p.m.
AE, MC, V

Peck & Goodie is generally acknowledged as the city's finest skate shop, and for more than forty years it has supplied discriminating athletes with figure, roller, and hockey skates. It carries only the best names—S. P. Terri boots and M. K. & Wilson blades. Almost all the boots are leather and custom-made, and the staff is expert at proper fit. Peck & Goodie handles skate sharpening and repairs, too.

SKIING

BOGNER
655 Madison Avenue, at 60th Street
752-2282
Mon.–Sat.: 10 a.m.–6 p.m.
AE, MC, V

Back in the fifties Bogner revolutionized skiwear when it introduced stretch pants to the slopes, and this German company is still making waves with its high-fashion ski looks. Skintight one-piece jumpsuits for both men and women in white or bold colors are a specialty, but there are ski jackets with gold fringed epaulets, others accented with fake fur that might be worn with such striking accessories as a silver coyote hat and gauntlet mittens. Stylish sweaters and hats, along with conservative off-the-slope fashions—classic slacks, jackets, and skirts cut from the finest corduroys, twills, and gabardines—are here as well.

EASTERN MOUNTAIN SPORTS, THE OUTDOOR SPECIALISTS
A large stock of skis, poles, boots, bindings, waxes, and accessories for downhill and cross-country skiing. (See **General Sporting Equipment**, p. 447.)

KINDERSPORT OF ASPEN
Serious skiwear for children, including suits, goggles, gloves, and hats. (See **Clothing**, p. 97.)

MASON'S TENNIS MART
A well-edited collection of skiwear by the major European designers. (See **Tennis**, p. 472.)

PARAGON SPORTING GOODS
An excellent selection of all the top names in skis, boots, poles, skiwear, and accessories. (See **General Sporting Equipment**, p. 448.)

SCANDINAVIAN SKI AND SPORTS SHOP
40 West 57th Street
757-8524
Mon.–Wed., Fri.: 9 a.m.–6:45 p.m.; Thurs.: 9 a.m.–7:45 p.m.; Sat.:
9 a.m.–6 p.m.
All major

The Scandinavian Ski and Sports Shop is one of the best sources in the city for ski equipment. This store has three large floors crammed full of the newest and finest in gear and skiwear. All the top names are here—Colmar, Nordica, Rossignol, Pre, Atomic, Fischer, Strolz, Solomon, Bogner, and HCC. There's an extensive inventory of children's skis, boots, poles, and clothing, too, and a fine assortment of tennis, golf, hiking, and running gear, along with an outstanding selection of competitive swimwear.

SOCCER

AR-BEE MEN'S WEAR
A large stock of soccer equipment. (See **General Sporting Equipment**, p. 446.)

GERRY COSBY & CO.
A complete selection of soccer gear. (See **Skating and Skateboards**, p. 467.)

PARAGON SPORTING GOODS

A good selection of shoes and equipment. (See **General Sporting Equipment,** p. 448.)

SOCCER SPORT SUPPLY COMPANY

1745 First Avenue, near 90th Street
427-6050
Mon.–Fri.: 9:30 a.m.–6 p.m.; Sat.: 9:30 a.m.–3 p.m.
AE, MC, V

This Yorkville institution has been around for more than fifty years, and it carries the most complete stock of soccer and rugby equipment in the country. The company imports equipment from around the world and also develops quality products that are designed by soccer players. You'll find Adidas, Puma, Doss and Patrick, team equipment and uniforms, as well as gear for lacrosse, softball, and basketball. The staff knows the field and is friendly and helpful.

SWIMWEAR

All the major department stores have large swimwear departments. Barneys New York offers an extensive selection for men; Bergdorf Goodman and Henri Bendel carry cutting-edge styles, and Bloomingdale's has the city's largest array and the broadest range of styles.

CAMEO WATER WEAR

1349 Third Avenue, near 77th Street
570-6606
Mon.–Fri.: 11 a.m.–7 p.m.; Sat.: 11 a.m.–6 p.m.

1225 Madison Avenue, at 84th Street
439-7877
Mon.–Sat.: 10 a.m.–6 p.m.
AE, MC, V

Cameo Water Wear offers swimwear year around, but during the peak season these shops carry more than 250 styles. You'll find hundreds of bikinis, as well as maillots, by all the leading names along with styles by less well-known European designers. The stores specialize in suits designed to camouflage and flatter problem figures, many of the suits have matching cover-ups, and they sell tops and bottoms separately for better fit. Attentive service and enormous stock account for these stores' popularity, and they provide a pleasing alternative to bathing suit shopping in crowded department stores.

THE FINALS
487 Broadway, at Broome Street
431-1414
Mon.–Sat.: 10 a.m.–6 p.m.; Sun.: 12 noon–5 p.m.
AE, MC, V

Serious swimmers come to the Finals since only competitive-style bathing suits are stocked in this large and cluttered store. Suits come in nylon or Lycra and in solids and stripes. There's a full complement of goggles, racing caps, kickboards, paddles, buoys, and pace clocks, too. But if swimming is not your sport, the Finals also offers running, cycling, and aerobic wear.

OMO NORMA KAMALI
Her bathing suit designs are among the best around. (See **Clothing**, p. 164.)

RICHARDS AQUA LUNG AND SPORTING GOODS CENTER
A complete line of competitive swimwear. (See **Marine Sporting Goods**, p. 462.)

SCANDINAVIAN SKI SHOP
A large inventory of bathing suits. (See **Skiing**, p. 469.)

SCREAMING MIMI'S
An assortment of suits for men and women from the forties, fifties, and sixties, including skirted suits for women and jams in Day-Glo colors for men. (See **Clothing**, p. 113.)

UNDER WARES
A good selection of swim trunks that ranges from sedate to outrageous. (See **Clothing**, p. 142.)

TENNIS

GRANDSTAND
1149A Second Avenue, near 60th Street
755-5297
Mon.–Sat.: 10 a.m.–7 p.m.; Sun.: 11 a.m.–5 p.m.

588 Columbus Avenue, near 88th Street
874-5297
Mon.–Fri.: 12 noon–8 p.m.; Sat.: 10 a.m.–7 p.m.; Sun.: 11 a.m.–5 p.m.
AE, MC, V

Jay Schweid and his staff have provided such tennis superstars as John McEnroe, Martina Navratilova, Boris Becker, and Jimmy Connors with customized rackets and personalized stringing, and at Grandstand, Schweid offers customers the same expert services he does the pros. The shops feature sky-blue ceilings and floors that are actual court surfaces, and they carry the newest and best in tennis equipment. The selection of rackets (one of the largest in the city) is arranged by categories based on the properties of the frame, rather than by manufacturer, and shoes and accessories are from such top names as Ellesse, Fila, Sergio Tacchini, Head, New Balance, Le Coq Sportif, Nike, and Puma.

MASON'S TENNIS MART
911 Seventh Avenue, near 57th Street
757-5374
Mon.–Sat.: 10 a.m.–6 p.m.
AE, D, MC, V

High-fashion European tennis wear for men, women, and children fills every inch of this well-stocked store. Mason carries Ellesse, Fila, 10-S, and Tacchini, and each year the company adds a new European line not available anywhere else in New York. Many of the styles are updates of the classic, so there are flirty skirts, ruffled pants, and tennis dresses in old-fashioned cotton piqué. But you'll find everything for looking good on the court—shorts, warm-up suits, skirts, sweaters, and shoes. Mason stocks rackets, balls, bags, and ball machines, and offers same-day stringing service. Fall and winter the shop is filled with a well-chosen collection of European skiwear.

PARAGON SPORTING GOODS
A large selection of rackets, balls, and tennis clothing. (See **General Sporting Equipment,** p. 448.)

Stationery

Bergdorf Goodman and Bloomingdale's have well-stocked stationery departments.

BOWNE & CO. STATIONERS
South Street Seaport
211 Water Street
669-9419
Mon.–Sat.: 10 a.m.–5 p.m.; Sun.: 11 a.m.–5 p.m.
AE, MC, V

Bowne & Co. still looks the way it did in 1836. Part of the South Street Seaport Museum, this restored stationers is a working printing shop where you can have personal and business stationery, business cards, wedding announcements, and party invitations letter printed. There's a selection of vintage typefaces, along with antique illustrations to choose from, excellent-quality papers, and a lovely assortment of sedate inks. The staff is exceedingly helpful.

CARTIER
Beautifully executed formal and classic engravings on heavy stock paper for all one's stationery needs, including wedding and birth announcements. (See **Jewelry,** p. 352.)

DEMPSEY & CARROLL
38 East 57th Street
486-7508
Mon.–Fri.: 9:30 a.m.–6 p.m.; Sat.: 10 a.m.–5:30 p.m.

110 East 57th Street
486-7526
Mon.–Fri.: 9:30 a.m.–6 p.m.; Sat.: 10 a.m.–5:30 p.m.
AE, MC, V

For more than 100 years Dempsey & Carroll has handled the stationery needs of elite New Yorkers who come here secure in the knowledge that whatever this venerable company prints will be totally correct. At Dempsey & Carroll they insist that hand engraving is the only way to go, they offer sixty lettering styles and seventy-five monograms, and they use only 100 percent imported heavy cotton stock papers such as French Lalo or Smythson's Bond Street or Crane. The company does party and wedding invitations (ecru is the proper color for these), wedding announcements, engraved calling cards (once again in vogue), business and correspondence cards, letter papers, and birth announcements. And they carry charming notepapers, along with fine desk accessories and a lovely selection of very classic Christmas cards.

FFOLIO 72
33 East 68th Street
879-0675
Mon.–Fri.: 10 a.m.–6 p.m.; Sat.: 11 a.m.–5:30 p.m.
AE

ffolio is the place the knowledgeable come to fill their more casual paper needs. A cluttered warren, this emporium offers top-quality papers in enticing shades, a wide choice of printing type, and delightful ideas for party invitations—and everything is engraved or imprinted by special order. Boxes covered in marbleized papers, chunky bamboo-handled pens, desk accessories, and beautifully bound leather albums and blank books can also be ordered.

IL PAPIRO
1021 Lexington Avenue, near 73rd Street
288-9330
Mon.–Sat.: 10 a.m.–6:30 p.m.; Dec.: Sun.: 12 noon–5 p.m.

Herald Center
1 Herald Square, at 34th Street
288-9330
Mon.–Fri.: 10 a.m.–7 p.m.

World Financial Center
385-1688
Mon.–Fri.: 10 a.m.–6 p.m.; Sat.: 12 noon–5 p.m.
AE, MC, V

These plush little wood-paneled shops are filled with a profusion of Florentine papers made from a centuries-old process—*papier à cuve*. Il Papiro is responsible for launching the revival of marbleized paper, and this Italian company uses it to fashion elegant stationery and to cover a whole range of accessories—picture frames, tissue holders, desk accessories, blank and address books, agendas, photo albums, even obelisks.

KROLL OFFICE PRODUCTS
145 East 54th Street
750-5300
Mon.–Fri.: 8:30 a.m.–5:45 p.m.
All major

Kroll's is primarily your standard office-supply store, but in the back of the shop you'll discover an excellent selection of stationery for both office and personal use. Crane papers come in a range of fashionable shades, and there's a large choice of typefaces. Kroll's prints birth announcements as well as party and wedding invitations; the printing is neatly done, and prices are good.

TIFFANY & COMPANY
Tiffany is *the* fashionable store for engraved wedding invitations and all one's stationery needs. Tiffany offers fine workmanship and traditional paper colors and type choices, and Tiffany is more amenable to printing versus engraving of invitations. There's a charming group of gift enclosure cards reprinted from the store's archives, along with a seductive selection of traditional Christmas cards. (See **Jewelry,** p. 358.)

Tiles

ANTIQUE
AND VINTAGE

COBWEB
An assortment of vintage Spanish decorative tiles. (See **Furniture,**
p. 273.)

COUNTRY FLOORS
Seventeenth-century Spanish decorative tiles, along with antique Dutch
and Portuguese ones. (See **Contemporary Tiles,** p. 477.)

MALVINA L. SOLOMON
Floral and figurative tiles from turn-of-the-century through the thirties.
(See **China and Glassware,** p. 68.)

SOLAR ANTIQUE TILES
971 First Avenue, near 55th Street
755-2403
By appointment only

Solar Antique Tiles is well-known to interior designers who come here
for exceptionally fine antique Portuguese tiles. Owner Pedro Leitao has
collected tiles for more than forty years and he carries an impressive
selection of fifteenth-century Moorish tiles in blue and green geometrics, seventeenth-century murals depicting Portugal's discoveries in
the New World, and thirties Art Deco advertisements done in tiles.
Although most of Leitao's stock is stored in Portugal, he has samples
here in New York, and he offers individual tiles, as well as small four-
tile murals and large-scale ones.

CONTEMPORARY

CHRISTIAN BELFOR DESIGNS
1556 Third Avenue, near 87th Street
722-5410
By appointment only
No credit cards

Christine Belfor uses tiles as a canvas and paints them in grisaille and *faux* finishes, and creates decorative tiles with a fresco look. She does custom-made Ionic and Corinthian columns, putti friezes, and classic pediments that can be assembled from individual tiles, and entire rooms for such as Carolyne Roehm and Henry Kravis. The columns can be used to frame a door, and individual rosettes or putti tiles can border a kitchen or bathroom.

COUNTRY FLOORS
15 East 16th Street
627-8300
Mon.–Wed., Fri.: 9 a.m.–6 p.m.; Thurs.: 9 a.m.–8 p.m.;
Sat.: 9 a.m.–5 p.m.
MC, V

Just about anything you ever wanted—or even dreamed about—in floor or wall tiles is available in Country Floors's winning multilevel showroom. Innovative uses for tiles are displayed in vignette settings, and this store's tile choices—imported from every tile-producing country, large or small—is vast. Country Floors stocks ceramic, hand-molded, hand-painted, terra-cotta, glazed, unglazed, and marble tiles, even giant pavers for patios. Garlands adorn one group of tiles from Portugal; red poppies a group from Italy; and peaches, tulips, revolutionary scenes, and children's games those from Spain, England, France, and Holland. There are antique tiles, too, seventeenth-century Spanish examples as well as early ones from Holland and Portugal. Although most of the tiles have Country Floors's distinctive rustic country look, there's a fine selection of sleek and sophisticated ones as well. And the terra-cotta planters and urns, glazed jungle animals, capitals, and enchanting hand-painted plates, pitchers, and platters from Spain and Italy (many reproductions of fifteenth- and sixteenth-century museum pieces) make this shop worth a visit even if you're not in the market for tiles.

ELIZABETH EAKINS
Hand-painted floor and wall tiles in soft pastels. (See **Carpets and Tapestries,** p. 61.)

HASTINGS
A dazzling variety of bold and bright Italian and Spanish floor and wall   477

tiles for bathrooms and kitchens that include the innovative ceramic designs of Gabbianelli, Bardelli, and Vogue, who turn out polka dots, stripes, reptile-patterns, and Post-Modern looks. (See **Bath Accessories,** p. 11.)

IDEAL TILE
405 East 51st Street
759-2339
Mon.–Fri.: 8:30 a.m.–5:30 p.m.; Sat.: 10:30 a.m.–5 p.m.
AE, MC, V

Ideal Tile imports its tiles directly from Italy, and this small and sunny shop is filled with a distinctive collection of hand-painted beauties. You'll find such names as Co-Em, Monocibec, Cerdisa, Ceramica, and S'Agostino. The tiles are appropriate for use in both a rustic and more formal setting and come in dozens of colors and patterns. The store carries floor and wall tiles from Mexico as well, along with hand-painted Italian pottery, including over-sized decorative platters and vases.

JUDITH STILES
392 Bleecker Street
645-7693
Daily: 12 noon–7 p.m.
AE, MC, V

In her pretty peach-colored store Judith Stiles offers her own decorative tiles as well as the work of other American ceramists. There's a selection of hand-painted animals, flowers, figures, geometric, and abstract designs to choose from, or Stiles will duplicate an antique tile, match a wallpaper sample, even capture the look of a family dog. Stiles also stocks inexpensive American Olean tiles in more than forty colors for customers to mix and match with her custom tiles.

NEMO TILE CO.
48 East 21st Street
505-0009
Mon.–Fri.: 8 a.m.–6 p.m.; Sat.: 11 a.m.–5 p.m.
AE, MC, V

In this showroom tiles are displayed in vignette settings, and Nemo has tiles for every room in the house. The company carries a vast selection of fine domestic and imported ceramic and marble tiles from Villeroy & Boch, Summitville, Inas, Romany, Marazzi, Briare, Impo, and Buchtal, as well as the company's own line. Colorful modern tiles are a specialty, but there's also a charming collection of hand-painted ones from Portugal, France, Italy, and Mexico. There's a complete selection of bathroom vanities and medicine cabinets, along with an attractive array of towel bars and soap dishes in brass and bright colors.

THE QUARRY
114 East 32nd Street
679-2559
Mon.–Fri.: 9 a.m.–6 p.m.; Sat.: 10 a.m.–4 p.m.
MC, V

The Quarry is filled with tiles in bright colors and bold patterns that the company imports from Italy, England, Holland, South America, Spain, Mexico, and Portugal. Many are hand-painted and have an antique look. The Quarry also stocks slate, mosaic, and marble tiles, as well as bathroom fixtures.

TILES
42 West 15th Street
255-4450
Mon.–Wed., Fri.: 9:30 a.m.–6 p.m.; Thurs.: 9:30 a.m.–6 p.m.
and by appointment; Sat.: 10 a.m.–5 p.m.
No credit cards

Tiles's owner Bruce Levitt has two tile showrooms in Boston, and he specializes in hand-painted artists' tiles. In his snappy store in the Flatiron district Levitt offers Jacqueline Karch's creations—she presses real flowers and leaves into ceramic and porcelain tiles; Liette Marcil's wedding bouquets and Picasso-like faces; and Jill Rosenwald's kitcheny scenes. Although much of Levitt's stock is custom-made and exclusive to his stores, he also carries such commercial names as Walker Zanger and DeMuth, along with sculptural embossed tiles, and others of stone, onyx, travertine, marble, and granite.

Timepieces

ANTIQUE

Bonwit Teller, Macy's, and Saks Fifth Avenue have antique watch departments. See also **Jewelry, Antique.**

AARON FABER GALLERY
Among the vast selection of unusual vintage watches you might find an edge-of-wrist driver's watch, a pink-gold Patek Philippe, or a Longines right-angle tank, but you'll also find dozens of more common (and more affordable) Elgins, Bulovas, and Hamiltons, too, along with bejeweled ladies' watches from the twenties and thirties and handsome gold and gold-filled pocket watches from the turn of the century. (See **Jewelry,** p. 349.)

BERNARD & S. DEAN LEVY
Willard banjo and tall-case clocks. (See **Furniture,** p. 228.)

CHIUZAC GALLERY
510 Madison Avenue, near 52nd Street
832-2233
Mon.–Fri.: 10 a.m.–5:30 p.m.; Sat.: 11 a.m.–5:30 p.m.
AE, MC, V

The ChiuZac company was the publisher of the acclaimed book on wristwatches, *A Time to Watch,* and like the book its small gallery is dedicated to watches of outstanding craftsmanship and design. All the top names are represented, but in addition to the rare examples this shop stocks an impressive selection of more affordable vintage watches. Gold and gold-filled pocket watches are another attraction, along with a unique group of metal and leather watchbands from the thirties and forties. Since the shop also handles repairs, everything here is in fine working order.

THE CLOCK HUTT LTD.
Manhattan Art & Antiques Center
1050 Second Avenue, near 55th Street
759-2395
Mon.–Fri.: 10:30 a.m.–5:30 p.m.; Sat.: 10:30 a.m.–6 p.m.;
Sun.: 12 noon–5:30 p.m.
MC, V

Although it occupies a large gallery space, the Clock Hutt is so crammed with timepieces its long-case clocks overflow onto the Manhattan Art & Antiques Center arcade. Eighteenth- and nineteenth-century European and American long-case clocks are the chief attraction, but there are dozens of elaborate marble and gilded figural ones, bracket clocks, carriage clocks in all sizes, and train-station-size wooden wall-hung ones. The Hutts, who have been in business for more than twenty years, carry a selection of vintage wristwatches, too, and they handle repairs.

DALVA BROTHERS
Important eighteenth-century bronze and porcelain bracket and mantel clocks, as well as a few long-case clocks. (See **Furniture,** p. 248.)

DARROW'S FUN ANTIQUES
Gary Darrow claims to have the largest character watch collection in the country, and nostalgia freaks will love his early Mickey Mouse and other Disney character watches, along with his Lone Rangers, Babe Ruths, and Betty Boops; and political buffs will giggle at his Spiro Agnews. (See **Toys,** p. 491.)

FANELLI ANTIQUE TIMEPIECES
1131 Madison Avenue, near 84th Street
517-2300
Mon.–Fri.: 10 a.m.–6 p.m.; Sat.: 11 a.m.–5 p.m.
AE, MC, V

The name Fanelli has been synonymous with carriage clocks for years, and in Joe Fanelli's tranquil shop dozens of splendid French and English examples that date from the 1880s through the twenties are on display. Some are adorned with jewels, others are gilded or enameled, still others have porcelain, hand-painted, cloisonné, or champlevé faces. Recently, however, Fanelli's inventory of long-case, bracket, and wall clocks has challenged the carriage clocks in number, and he now offers American beauties, rare Japanese stick clocks, banjos, early automatons, even Bohemia glass ones. Vintage wristwatches by Patek Philippe, Vacheron & Constantin, and Meylan, along with early Oysters, delicate diamond-encrusted ladies' wristwatches, and antique pocket watches with hand-painted enamel, mother-of-pearl, or gold cases are here as well. And since the owner is a pro at repairing old clocks, everything is in working order.

FOSSNER TIMEPIECES
1059 Second Avenue, near 55th Street
249-2600
Mon.–Fri.: 10 a.m.–6:30 p.m.; Sat.: 11 a.m.–5 p.m.
AE

For four generations the Fossner family has been known for its fine watch repairs, but this small, cluttered store also offers gilded and enameled carriage clocks, pendulum clocks, and a complete selection of vintage wristwatches that date from the teens through the fifties. All the most wanted names are represented, along with dozens of character watches, silver and gold pocket watches, and lovable German and Swiss cuckoo clocks that only look old. Prices are good.

FREDERICK P. VICTORIA AND SON, INC.
A very fine selection of eighteenth-century French clocks including figural bracket ones. (See **Furniture,** p. 249.)

HYMORE HODSON ANTIQUES LTD.
903 Madison Avenue, near 72nd Street
Second floor
517-6235
Mon.–Sat.: 10 a.m.–6 p.m.
No credit cards

In this New York outpost of a London company, gleaming walnut, oak, and mahogany long-case clocks stand like handsome sentinels. Mostly eighteenth- to early nineteenth-century examples (although there are the occasional seventeenth-century pendulum ones), many are inlaid with marquetry, and they've been polished until they glisten. Hymore Hodson provides purchasers with a unique service—they will fly an expert over from England to set up the clocks. In addition to the long-case beauties, the gallery offers skeleton, bracket, and mantel clocks as well as barometers and nautical instruments. Everything at Hymore Hodson is English and very fine and very expensive.

MASSAB BROTHERS
A splendid assortment of Victorian and Edwardian pocket watches in silver and gold. (See **Jewelry,** p. 346.)

MATTHEW SCHUTZ LTD.
Museum quality Louis XVI through Empire figural bracket clocks. (See **Furniture,** p. 251.)

MOOD INDIGO
Kitchen clocks from the thirties and forties along with a large assortment of electric clocks from the same period with Bakelite, peach glass, or chrome cases. (See **Furniture,** p. 256.)

NEIL ISMAN GALLERY
Rolex, Hamilton, and Patik Philippe wristwatches from the twenties and thirties. (See **Jewelry,** p. 357.)

NEW YORK NAUTICAL INSTRUMENT & SERVICE CORP.
Brass ship's bell clocks and barometers. (See **Sporting Goods,** p. 461.)

OLDIES, GOLDIES & MOLDIES
Turn-of-the-century wood and marble mantel clocks, Bakelite clocks from the thirties and forties, along with restored and refurbished neon clocks from the thirties through the fifties. (See **Furniture,** p. 236.)

TIME WILL TELL
962 Madison Avenue, near 75th Street
861-2663
Mon.–Sat.: 10 a.m.–6 p.m.
AE, MC, V

Stuart Unger, owner of Time Will Tell, was one of the leading lights behind the current fascination with vintage wristwatches, and his friendly shop is a gathering spot for collectors, investors, and the fashion-minded. Filled with a thousand-or-so watches dating from the teens through the fifties, the gallery offers everything from the exceptional Patek Philippe, Audemars Piguet, and Vacheron & Constantin, to novel moon phase, skeleton, perpetual calendar, doctor, and early character watches, to more common and affordable vintage timepieces. Since the shop handles repairs, all the watches have their original innards and are in working order.

TOURNEAU
Tucked away on the second floor of the Madison Avenue store is the vast Tourneau vintage timepiece collection. (See **Contemporary Timepieces,** p. 485.)

VERNAY & JUSSEL, INC.
A memorable collection of extremely fine early clocks. (See **Furniture,** p. 246.)

CONTEMPORARY

The major department stores carry a large selection of wristwatches and clocks. See also **Jewelry.**

ASPREY LIMITED
Among the dazzling array are shagreen quartz clocks in mantel and

night-table size, exquisitely constructed travel clocks with wood, brass, or gold-plated cases, and handsome leather desk clocks. (See **Gifts,** p. 299.)

CARTIER
The name Cartier has been associated with fine watches since 1904, when the founder created one of the earliest wristwatches, the Santos, for Brazilian pilot Santos Dumont, and later developed the "tank" watch for the U.S. Army during World War I; these classics are still sold at Cartier, along with the sleek Panther. (See **Jewelry,** p. 352.)

CONTRE-JOUR
A small and select group of cutting-edge watches including a Swiss-made black-leather watch by Hans Koppel for Ole Mathiesen and a high-tech Pictowatch. (See **Gifts,** p. 301.)

D. F. SANDERS
A small group of minimalist, high-tech watches in black or stainless steel. (See **Housewares and Hardware,** p. 337.)

FORTUNOFF
In addition to Fortron, Fortunoff's own brand of affordable watches that comes in all the most wanted styles (including diver's watches and dual-time-zone ones), the store carries a broad assortment of popular name-brand wristwatches, along with hundreds of clocks in every possible style, from classic mantel to long-case, from carriage clocks to wall models, and from trendy Post-Modern examples to lovable ones for children's rooms. (See **Silver,** p. 440.)

FRED JOAILLIER
The large inventory includes Fred's own designs (including quartz watches set in hand-woven bracelets of stainless steel), Audemars Piguet's Meridian collection, Piaget, Baume & Mercier, and Rolex. (See **Jewelry,** p. 353.)

GOREVIC & GOREVIC, LTD.
Among the large stock of costly watches are Rado's 18-karat-gold Anatom, Patek Philippe's diamond-encrusted gold timepieces, and Audemars Piguet's moon phase favorites. (See **Silver,** p. 439.)

ROYAL COPENHAGEN PORCELAIN/GEORG JENSEN SILVERSMITHS
Sleek and simple high-tech looks in stainless-steel or matte-black metal. (See **China and Glassware,** p. 78.)

SOINTU
Distinctive ultramodern timepieces in stainless steel or matte-black created by innovative designers. (See **Gifts,** p. 310.)

TIFFANY & COMPANY

Many of the timepieces, such as the Atlas, are Tiffany's own and exclusive to the store, but there's a broad selection of Concord, Rolex, Baume & Mercier, Patek Philippe, and Audemars Piguet watches, along with handmade Breguets that are true treasures. Styles range from classic to high-tech and include chronographs, dual-time zones, and diamond bracelet watches. There's a handsome assortment of mantel, carriage, desk, night table, and travel clocks, too. (See **Jewelry**, p. 358.)

TOURNEAU

500 Madison Avenue, at 52nd Street
758-3265
Mon.–Fri.: 10 a.m.–5:45 p.m.; Sat.: 10 a.m.–5:30 p.m.

200 West 34th Street
563-6880
Mon.–Fri.: 9 a.m.–6 p.m.; Sat.: 10 a.m.–6 p.m.; Sun.: 12 noon–5 p.m.
AE, MC, V

At any time of day Tourneau is crowded with customers who come here because it's the city's most complete watch store. They come for its enormous stock of more than 3,000 timepieces by every maker of note, and for the world's largest collection of Rolex watches. Almost every Swiss company is represented—Audemars Piguet, Ebel, Omega, Piaget, Baume & Mercier, Longines, Le Coultre—as well as every important Japanese and American manufacturer, along with Tourneau's own brand. There's every possible kind (skeleton, moon phase, dual-time, diving) and every possible style (classic to funky, formal to sporty) at prices to please every pocketbook. Tucked away on the second floor of the Madison Avenue store is the Tourneau vintage watch collection, an archive of the world's most wanted timepieces.

VAN CLEEF & ARPELS

The complete collection of Van Cleef & Arpels watches. (See **Jewelry**, p. 359.)

WEMPE JEWELERS

695 Fifth Avenue, near 54th Street
751-4884
Mon.–Sat.: 10 a.m.–6 p.m.
AE, MC, V

Wempe, an elegant Fifth Avenue shop, offers a stunning collection of important watches and clocks. All the great names are here—Rolex, Piaget, Jaeger-Le Coultre, Ebel, Patek Philippe, Audemars Piguet—and they're represented by their most popular designs. Mixed with the watches is a glittering array of classically designed gold and gemstone jewelry.

Tobacconists

ANTIQUES

Bergdorf Goodman carries antique humidors. See also **Gifts, Antique.**

BOB PRYOR ANTIQUES
Eighteenth-century humidors; tobacco tins of wood, brass, and ceramic; pipe tamps; and brass match strikes and cigar cutters. (See **Gifts,** p. 293.)

JAMES II GALLERIES
Nineteenth-century mahogany and marquetry humidors and tobacco tins. (See **China and Glassware,** p. 67.)

PIPEWORKS & WILKE
Vintage pipes and antique tobacco tins. (See **Contemporary Tobacconists,** p. 488.)

R. BROOKE LTD.
Mahogany and tortoise humidors, pipe tamps, cigar cutters, crocodile cigarette cases, and match strikes. (See **Gifts,** p. 297.)

CONTEMPORARY

Bloomingdale's and Bergdorf Goodman offer a large selection of humidors, pipe stands, tobacco pouches, and other smoking accessories.

ALFRED DUNHILL OF LONDON
Fine-quality and tasteful pipes, humidors, stands, and smoking accoutrements, along with custom-blended tobaccos, an excellent choice of

cigars, and the complete line of Dunhill's legendary lighters. (See **Clothing,** p. 115.)

BARCLAY-REX, INC.
7 Maiden Lane
962-3355
Mon.–Fri.: 8 a.m.–6 p.m.

70 East 42nd Street
692-9680
Mon.–Fri.: 8 a.m.–6:30 p.m.; Sat.: 10 a.m.–5:30 p.m.
AE, DC, MC, V

Pipe smokers come to Barclay-Rex for owner Vincent Nastri's custom-made pipes that are made right in the Maiden Lane store, and for his impressive stock of quality imported ones. Nastri offers more than 10,000 cigars and every type of tobacco (including his own special blend), lighters, and a full stock of smoking accessories. He carries leather wallets and other small leather goods, and Mont-Blanc, Dunhill, and Cartier pens. Nastri has a reputation for prompt and reasonable pipe repairs.

THE CONNOISSEUR PIPE SHOP LTD.
51 West 46th Street
247-6054
Mon.–Fri.: 10 a.m.–6 p.m.; Sat.: 10 a.m.–5 p.m.
AE, MC, V

The pipes Edward Fredrick Burak sells in his small, intimate shop are handmade from his own designs, and they're so special they've been exhibited at the American Craft Museum, and his pipe drawings are in the Museum of Modern Art's design collection. Graceful, with soaring shapes, Burak's pipes are small art objects that are also great smokes, so they're collected by smokers and nonsmokers alike. The pipes are made from ébauchon (brierwood imported from Greece) that's left natural, never lacquered or stained, only buffed and polished with beeswax. In addition to his pipes, Burak offers custom-blended tobaccos, pipe racks and humidors crafted of fine walnut, and tobacco pouches of suede, gazelle, or glove leathers, and the shop handles pipe restorations, repairs, and appraisals.

DAVIDOFF OF GENEVA
535 Madison Avenue, near 54th Street
751-9060
Mon.–Sat.: 9 a.m.–6:30 p.m.; Sat.: 10 a.m.–6 p.m.
AE, DC, MC, V

In its handsome Madison Avenue outpost Davidoff of Geneva stocks only the finest tobacco products, pipes, and smoking accessories. There are hand-rolled cigars from Honduras; exotic-hardwood humidors fitted with special humidity regulators; and pipes, in classic shapes, made from top-quality brier. Silver, mahogany, and porcelain tobacco jars; tobacco pouches of lamb nappa; and attaché cases with removable cigar humidors coexist with fine wood pipe racks, S. T. Dupont lighters, titanium-and-gold Swiss watches, Mont-Blanc and Cartier pens, and silk ties.

NAT SHERMAN CIGARS
711 Fifth Avenue, at 55th Street
751-9100
Mon.–Fri.: 9 a.m.–6:30 p.m.; Sat.: 9 a.m.–6:15 p.m.;
Sun.: 11 a.m.–6 p.m.
AE, DC, MC, V

Nat Sherman is best known for personalized and colored cigarettes, and the store offers dozens of colored papers that can be imprinted with a name or special message. But here you'll also find thirty blends of tobacco, a wide choice of cigars, pipes, and humidors, as well as all manner of smoking accessories.

PIPEWORKS & WILKE
16 West 55th Street
956-4820
Mon.–Fri.: 9:30 a.m.–5:45 p.m.; Sat.: 9:30 a.m.–5 p.m.
AE, MC, V

Pipeworks & Wilke is New York's oldest pipe shop—it dates back to 1872—and it's filled with handsome vintage pipes, Dunhills from the thirties, aged pipes from the sixties, antique tobacco tins, and lots of Old World charm. But there are contemporary pipes as well, and these are designed and hand-cut from start to finish by owner Elliott Nachwalter and Carole Burns, who use only Grecian, Corsican, or Algerian brier. Nachwalter also offers custom-blended tobaccos that are as special as everything else in his beguiling shop.

TOBACCO PRODUCTS
137 Eighth Avenue, near 16th Street
989-3900
Mon.–Fri.: 7 a.m.–6 p.m.; Sat.: 9 a.m.–5 p.m.
AE, MC, V

Dusty and old-fashioned with a creaky wood floor and antique statues and figurines piled everywhere, Tobacco Products is a favorite with the neighborhood smoking crowd. They come for the impressive array of cigars that are handmade right in the store from first-rate tobacco leaves from Mexico, South America, Honduras, and the Dominican Republic. And they come, too, for the selection of Meerschaum pipes, one of the city's largest, and the myriad smoking accessories.

Toys

ANTIQUE
AND VINTAGE

ALEXANDER GALLERY
996 Madison Avenue, near 77th Street
Second floor
472-1636
Tues.–Sat.: 9:30 a.m.–5:30 p.m.
No credit cards

Alexander Acevedo is an art dealer who specializes in paintings of the
Hudson River School, American folk art, Western art, and American
Indian artifacts. But Acevedo is also a lover of antique trains and toys,
and he displays his playthings as if they were rare works of art. The
very best of nineteenth- and early twentieth-century European and
American examples can be found on his shelves: trains, trucks, dolls,
automatons, windup toys, Mickey Mouse memorabilia, and cartoon
figures. Pricey.

BACK PAGES ANTIQUES
125 Greene Street
460-5998
Mon.–Sat.: 9 a.m.–6 p.m.; Sun.: 12 noon–6 p.m.
No credit cards

Although Back Pages is famous for its slot machines, one-eyed bandits,
and Würlitzer jukeboxes, owner Alan Luchnick has recently developed a
passion for early Coca-Cola vending machines, and these have now
joined the general clutter. He's found everything from small picnic-sized
machines to standard commercial ones and examples from just about
every year. To please nostalgia buffs Luchnick always has an occasional
bumper car, old arcade and amusement park Love Testers and Fortune

Tellers, along with fifties airplane-shaped barber chairs, oak swings, old metal porch gliders, and kiddie-sized horse and buggies.

BIZARRE BAZAAR
Place des Antiquaires
125 East 57th Street
688-1830
Mon.–Sat.: 11 a.m.–6 p.m.
AE, MC, V

Bizarre Bazaar recently moved to the Place des Antiquaires, where it occupies a space twice as large as its former tiny nook. Here you'll find antique and vintage toys that are in pristine condition; indeed, many are in their original boxes and look as if they'd never been played with. Vehicular playthings are the chief attraction—windup cars, trains, airplanes, trucks, boats, ships, even submarines—but there are windup animals and early robots, too. It's a well-edited selection of one-of-a-kind pieces for the serious collector.

BURLINGTON ANTIQUE TOYS
1082 Madison Avenue, near 81st Street
Lower level
861-9708
Tues.–Sat.: 12 noon–6 p.m.
AE, MC, V

In the dusty, dark basement of Burlington Books, Steve Balkin sells the kind of toys *he* loved as a child. Antique and vintage racing cars, hand-painted and authentically detailed tin soldiers, wooden boats, airplanes, and trucks are his chief passions, but he has new toys, too, along with stuffed animals that are re-creations of old favorites. It's a warm and friendly shop, and prices are surprisingly affordable.

CHILDREN OF PARADISE
154 Bleecker Street
473-7148
Tues.–Sat.: 11 a.m.–6 p.m.; Sun.: 12 noon–6 p.m.
AE, MC, V

Well-stocked with both vintage and new toys, Children of Paradise appeals to collectors who come to this comfortably cluttered and friendly store for such fifties classics as original Gumby and Pokey, Batman and Superman, friction convertible cars, early robots, tin cars and trucks, and vintage Japanese playthings. Educational toys, Lego, Brio trains, puzzles, and games are among the new offerings.

CLASSIC TOYS
69 Thompson Street
941-9129

Wed.–Sun.: 12 noon–6:30 p.m.
No credit cards

Jay Facciolo, a corporate lawyer, and Jon Rettich, a graphic designer, have turned a passion for toys into a delightful store. Since vehicles and miniature figures are their specialty, Classic Toys is crammed with whole armies and every conceivable type of car or truck. Hundreds of antique and contemporary tin soldiers; diecast and white metal cars; and commercial, farm, and city trucks coexist with Louis Marx Playsets from the fifties and sixties; and all manner of zoo, farm, and prehistoric animals. This shop is a true find for toy lovers.

DARROW'S FUN ANTIQUES
309 East 61st Street
838-0730
Mon.–Fri.: 11 a.m.–7 p.m.; Sat.: 11 a.m.–4 p.m.
AE, MC, V

Chick Darrow opened Darrow's Fun Antiques in 1964, and it was one of the city's first shops devoted to nostalgia. It's now run by his son Gary, and it's crammed with playthings guaranteed to evoke smiles and giggles. Although a few toys (such as cast-iron banks) are as early as Victorian, most are the stuff of childhood memories: Howdy Doody games and dolls, Mickey Mouse watches, cartoon character memorabilia, Charlie McCarthy dummies, just about every television game ever made (many in their original boxes), battery-operated and friction cars and trucks, gumball and slot machines, toy soldiers, and dozens of rare and early robots. For political buffs there are Spiro Agnew watches and every conceivable campaign button. The mix is as early as an 1890s windup toy and as recently nostalgic as an E.T. clock. Gary Darrow's prices are excellent.

FUNCHIES, BUNKERS, GAKS AND GLEEKS
Manhattan Art & Antiques Center
1050 Second Avenue, at 55th Street
980-9418
Mon.–Sat.: 12:30 p.m.–5 p.m.; Sun.: 1:30 p.m.–5:30 p.m.
AE, MC, V

The array of collectibles at Funchies, Bunkers, Gaks and Gleeks is as whimsical as its name, and although the clutter may seem hopeless, the owners can magically retrieve exactly the treasure you're looking for. Photographs of the fine selection of antique appliqué and patchwork quilts are carefully catalogued in albums, and everything in the shop is organized by color or type. A browser's delight, there are dolls that are as early as the 1880s, as recent as the forties, and as eclectic as porcelain-faced Victorian beauties, Dopey and other of the Dwarf bunch, and early American Indian dolls. Stieff animals, old and bedraggled Teddy bears, regiments of lead soldiers, windup toys, tin cars

491

and trucks, a solid selection of vintage trains, not to mention scores of still and mechanical banks, are here as well. And this unique shop offers old scientific, medical, and nautical instruments, cast-iron door-stops, and the largest collection of old duck and goose decoys in the city. The owners are warm and friendly and impressively knowledge-able and their prices are good.

HILLMAN-GEMINI ANTIQUES
743 Madison Avenue, near 64th Street
Second floor
734-3262
Mon.–Sat.: 12 noon–5 p.m.
No credit cards

Hillman-Gemini shares space with Ruth Bigel Antiques, and here you'll discover, attractively displayed in vignette settings, an enchant-ing collection of antique toys dating from 1865 through late 1945. Among these playthings from an earlier age are cast-iron still and mechanical banks, early windup animals, cast-iron and tin cars, trucks, and trolley cars. The dolls are especially winning—in addition to early china and bisque babies, there are nineteenth-century pine dolls, old rag ones, and other comforting and homey kinds that were meant for play, not show.

IRIS BROWN
253 East 57th Street
593-2882
Mon.–Fri.: 11 a.m.–6 p.m.; Sat.: 12:30 p.m.–5:30 p.m.
AE, MC, V

Small, dusty, and cluttered, Iris Brown's shop is where collectors go when they're looking for museum-quality dolls. Iris Brown is a known expert in the field, and her collection includes everything from delicate porcelain and bisque Victorian dolls to mini-French and German bisque ones. She has antique dollhouses and the furniture to fill them with, porcelain tea sets, delightful doll's clothing, and child-size furni-ture. Costly.

JAMES II GALLERIES
Among the assortment of nineteenth-century games are chess sets, checkers, cribbage, dominoes, and alphabet blocks, and the gallery always has a colorful array of Victorian children's tea sets. (See **China and Glassware,** p. 67.)

J. B. KANSAS, INC.
416 West Broadway
Second floor
966-0494
Mon.–Fri.: 10 a.m.–6 p.m.; Sat.: 12 noon–5 p.m.
No credit cards

Mostly J. B. Kansas handles color xeroxing and sells artists' supplies, but wherever you look in this cluttered store you'll see toys both old and new. Tin toys are a specialty, and there are vintage planes, zeppelins, boats, cars and trucks, along with dozens of windups. Even the new playthings lean toward the nostalgic, with reissues of Gumby and Pokey and other TV favorites. Inflatable monsters of all kinds hang overhead, and there are bins filled with small and inexpensive notions—dolphin and monster pencil sharpeners, slimy plastic animals, and all manner of silly erasers—that make perfect party favors.

LE MONDE MAGIQUE
Place des Antiquaires
125 East 57th Street
755-4120
Mon.–Sat.: 11 a.m.–6 p.m.
AE, MC, V

Parisian Christian Bailly, an expert on automata and antique toys, has filled his welcoming gallery with ingeniously mounted displays of nineteenth-century toys, carousel animals, games, automata, and European dolls. Lavishly gowned and coiffed ladies, and dear little babies, are all in attendance, along with appropriately outfitted snake charmers, magicians, and jesters. Antique board games, cribbage, dominoes, alphabet blocks, and puzzles, too. Pricey.

LITTLE RICKIE
A large collection of fifties and sixties games, Jon Gnagy drawing kits, Batman friction cars, Mickey Mouse Club hats, old paper dolls, vintage tin toys, along with reproductions of classic fifties convertibles. (See **Contemporary Toys**, p. 497.)

MYTHOLOGY
The nostalgia selection of vintage toys from the thirties to the fifties includes tin Ferris wheels, boats, and trucks, as well as old metal beach pails. (See **Gifts**, p. 308.)

NEW YORK DOLL HOSPITAL
787 Lexington Avenue, near 61st Street
Second floor
838-7527
Mon.–Sat.: 10 a.m.–6 p.m.
No credit cards

Since 1900 little mothers have been carting their sick and injured baby dolls to the New York Doll Hospital, and here, in addition to making dolls well again, Irving Chais (grandson of the original owner) sells antique and vintage dolls. Look beyond the dozens of torsos, arms, legs, heads, and wigs, and you'll find early-nineteenth or turn-of-the-century French and German babies, original Shirley Temple dolls, early Barbies and Kens, Betsy Wetsies, even W. C. Fields and Charlie

Chaplin dolls. The selection is small and constantly changing, but if you're looking for a hard-to-find doll it's worthwhile checking here.

SECOND CHILDHOOD
283 Bleecker Street
989-6140
Mon.–Sat.: 11 a.m.–6 p.m.
AE, MC, V

As much a toy museum as antiques shop, Second Childhood is filled with mesmerizing displays of rare and hard-to-find toys that are as early as 1850 and as recent as 1950. Tin playthings are the chief attraction, and there's always a supply of windup toys, cars and trucks, and old railroad stations. But there are also scores of cast-iron soldiers, mechanical banks, vintage marbles, and early wooden trains, dollhouses, a few dolls, miniatures of all kinds (including rare metal dollhouse furniture), and robotic toys both old and new. From inexpensive to costly.

THE SOLDIER SHOP
A selection of rare and unusual antique toy soldiers along with reissues of old regiments, so the shop always has hundreds of toy soldiers on hand (See **Books,** p. 37.)

CONTEMPORARY

B. Altman & Co., Bloomingdale's, and Macy's have large toy departments; Lord & Taylor and Saks Fifth Avenue offer a large assortment of stuffed animals. See also **Museum Gift Shops.**

BEN'S FOR KIDS
The front of the store is stocked floor to ceiling with popular learning toys. (See **Furniture,** p. 264.)

BIG CITY KITES
1201 Lexington Avenue, near 81st Street
472-2623
Mon.–Tues., Sat.: 10 a.m.–6 p.m.; Wed., Thurs., Fri.: 10 a.m.–7 p.m.;
Sun.: 12 noon–5 p.m. (in the spring)
AE, MC, V

Kites in every possible color and shape hang from the ceiling and cover entire walls at Big City Kites (formerly called Go Fly a Kite), the city's only store devoted to kites. Silk kites from China, paper ones from Japan, two-string acrobatic stunt varieties, air toys, and playful nylon versions emblazoned with just about every kind of farm, zoo, or wild animal can be purchased in this friendly store. Kite devotees stop by periodically to check out the latest imports.

CHILDREN OF PARADISE
A complete selection of educational toys and popular name-brand playthings. (See **Antique and Vintage Toys,** p. 490.)

THE CHOCOLATE SOUP
Handmade and hand-painted nontoxic wooden animals of all kinds, including dinosaurs; finger puppets, soft and cuddly tiny dolls, old-fashioned-looking tin windup toys. (See **Clothing,** p. 93.)

CITYKIDS
Among the imaginative selection of toys are La Peluche's whimsical plush animals that include penguins, ducks, and rabbits. (See **Clothing,** p. 94.)

CLASSIC TOYS
Hundreds of contemporary tin soldiers, cars and trucks, and all manner of zoo, farm, and prehistoric animals. (See **Antique and Vintage Toys,** p. 490.)

DINOSAUR HILL
The eye-filling jumble of toys offers an amazing variety of hand puppets, stuffed dinosaurs, robots, hand-beaded African dolls, colorful mobiles, books and games, along with a tempting array of inexpensive party favors. (See **Clothing,** p. 94.)

THE DOLL HOUSE
Among the outstanding stock of dolls, one of the largest in the city, are storybook dolls, foreign ones in native dress, every kind of baby doll, even Barbie and Ken. (See **Dollhouses and Furnishings,** p. 500.)

DOLLSANDREAMS
1421 Lexington Avenue, near 92nd Street
876-2434
Mon.–Fri.: 10:30 a.m.–5:45 p.m.; Sat.: 11 a.m.–6 p.m.
All major

Tiny, tidy, and well-organized, this intelligent toy store is stocked with a fine selection of imported and domestic toys that have been hand-picked and chosen for quality and educational value. T. C. Timber wooden trains and play sets, Caran d'Arche art supplies, Ravensburger puzzles, and Playmobile share the white-and-blond-wood space with Kathy Kruse and Gotz dolls, and La New Born from Spain—a soft, lifelike, and anatomically correct baby doll. Learning games, stuffed animals, sturdy wooden dollhouses and accessories, wooden trains, books, party favors, and dozens of safe crib toys are here as well.

495

THE ENCHANTED FOREST

85 Mercer Street
925-6677
Daily: 11 a.m.–7 p.m.
All major

Within this magical forest setting furry stuffed animals and trolls live in tall trees, a waterfall nestles under a wooden bridge that leads from one level to the next, and everywhere you look there are animals that are as enchanting as the shop itself. Almost all the cross-eyed penguins, elaborately plumed birds, cuddly cats, lifelike geese, daffy-looking bears, and silly lions are exclusive to the store and are made by crafts people around the country. And although there's a notable selection of finely made kaleidoscopes, simple wooden musical instruments, books, and such old-time favorites as Yo-Yos and jacks, just about everything else in David Wallace's remarkable gallery is animal related, including the Raku masks and terracotta urns.

F. A. O. SCHWARZ

767 Fifth Avenue, at 58th Street
644-9400
Mon.–Wed., Fri., Sat.: 10 a.m.–6 p.m.; Thurs.: 10 a.m.–8 p.m.; Sun.:
12 noon–5 p.m.
AE, MC, V

At F. A. O. Schwarz it's Christmas year round, for this block-long two-story store is crammed with the stuff that children's wishes are made of. Life-like, life-sized polar bears, gorillas, giraffes, and Shetland ponies occupy the main floor, along with smaller, cuddly creatures and exuberantly dressed clowns. Ride the glass elevator to the second, larger level and you'll find miniature powered racing cars and Mercedes' that youngsters can drive, and robots they can command, along with hundreds of electric trains. There are rocking horses, dragons, and frogs, every conceivable kind of battery-operated car, plane, and truck, and scores of games, books, and records. Here, too, are the telescopes and chemistry sets, Brio's castles and railroads, the huge Lego department, and wooden blocks that can be purchased by the pound. Doll lovers will find the classic Madame Alexander beauties, Traum Kinder from West Germany, Raggedy Ann and Andy, Cinderella and bridal dolls, Barbie and Ken, plus baby carriages, doll clothing, and dollhouses. "Grandma's Corner" offers handmade christening gowns and beautifully classic infant clothing, and "Kidswear" high-fashion designer clothes—leather bomber jackets and rhinestone-studded pants—in sizes 0 through 6X.

FORBIDDEN PLANET

The latest sci-fi toys and games, robots, Popeye cartoon characters, pet monsters, and fright masks and wigs. (See **Books,** p. 46.)

JOHNNY JUPITER
1185 Lexington Avenue, near 80th Street
744-0818
Mon.–Sat.: 10 a.m.–6 p.m.
AE, MC, V

An overwhelming clutter of toys covers every inch of space at Johnny Jupiter. Piñatas and plastic blowups hang from the ceiling, water pistols and party favors overflow baskets on the floor, and the shelves are piled high with Russian stacking dolls, Steiff animals, painted tin cars, trucks, and planes, party supplies, a sprinkling of antique toys, and jokes, magic, and tricks. A sunny back room is filled with assorted antique housewares, curiosities, and collectibles. Christmastime there's a delightful assortment of tree ornaments, and year round there are scores of small and inexpensive kiddie treats.

THE LAST WOUND UP
290 Columbus Avenue, near 73rd Street
787-3388
Mon.–Thurs.: 10 a.m.–6 p.m.; Fri.: 10 a.m.–8 p.m.; Sat.: 10 a.m.–
10 p.m.; Sun.: 11 a.m.–6 p.m.

889 Broadway, at 19th Street
529-4197
Mon.–Sat.: 10 a.m.–6 p.m.

Pier 17
South Street Seaport
393-1128
Sun.–Fri.: 10 a.m.–7 p.m.; Sat.: 10 a.m.–8 p.m.; Sun.: 11 a.m.–7 p.m.
AE, MC, V

If it can be wound up, you'll find it in Nathan Cohen's whimsical stores. The scores of daffy windup toys are sure to delight, but to be doubly sure, there are playpens where children and adults can try out their choices. Most of the windups are plastic and inexpensive—jogging shoes, false teeth, woodpeckers, walking telephones, mini-movie cameras, and the like—but there are more costly tin versions, a selection of antiques, and since these, too, must be wound, music boxes, some of which are new, others gems from the turn of the century.

LITTLE RICKIE
49 1/2 First Avenue, at 3rd Street
505-6467
Mon.–Sat.: 11 a.m.–8 p.m.; Sun.: 11 a.m.–7 p.m.
AE, MC, V

When Philip Retzky first opened Little Rickie on First Street in 1985, it caused a small-scale explosion. Packed to the ceiling with nostalgic baby-boomer treasures—lava lamps, Gumby and Pokey, Howdy Doody stuff, Mr. Potato Head, ray guns, Mickey Mouse club hats, friction cars—it immediately became a favorite with people young and old. Two years ago Retzky moved his novelty cum vintage toy store to larger quarters, and here, joined by partner Mitchell Cantor, he has ample room for even more of his slightly zany treasures. Along with the $1 photo booth and lucky charm machine and all the Elvis stuff, Little Rickie offers vintage Vogue dress patterns, pint-size little girls' plastic pocketbooks, and such religious items as Jesus night lights, holy soil, ceramic angels. There's a newborn department with delicate embroidered-cotton crib linens, antique baby dolls, silver spoons; a magic department; a lighting section filled with chili-pepper and Tiki Cod hanging lights; and an old-fashioned revolving watch display case crammed with Mexican Day of the Dead skeletons.

MARY ARNOLD TOYS
962 Lexington Avenue, near 70th Street
744-8510
Mon.–Fri.: 9 a.m.–6 p.m.; Sat.: 10 a.m.–5 p.m.
AE, MC, V

At Mary Arnold Toys the enormous stock of games, toys, stuffed animals, and dolls leans to the commercial and mass-produced kind, so if there's a "must-have" your child has seen on television you're likely to find it here. But there are educational toys, as well as electronic games, books, and party favors, and a notable selection of matchbox-type cars and trucks, along with larger ones and ride-ons. Youngsters love this store because they can leave a Christmas or birthday "wish" list.

MATT MCGHEE
An enchanting and ever-changing selection of cuddly animals that might include life-size geese, soft lambs, chickens, and other barnyard pets, along with jungle animals and birds. (See **Gifts,** p. 308.)

PENNY WHISTLE TOYS
448 Columbus Avenue, near 81st Street
873-9090
Mon.–Fri.: 10 a.m.–7 p.m.; Sat.: 10 a.m.–6 p.m.; Sun.: 12 noon–6 p.m.

1283 Madison Avenue, near 91st Street
369-3868
Mon.–Sat.: 9 a.m.–6 p.m.; Sun.: 11 a.m.–5 p.m.

132 Spring Street
925-2088
Daily: 11 a.m.–7 p.m.
AE, MC, V

At Penny Whistle Toys children are actually *encouraged* to touch the playthings. Owner Meredith Brokaw, a former teacher, has personally selected the toys and games that encourage creativity and learning, and everything in her tidy stores is unusual, educational, top-quality, and fun. Dolls and stuffed animals, plastic and wooden ride-ons, child-size kitchen sinks and stoves, contemporary dollhouses and furniture, wooden trains, water toys and inflatable pool floats, science kits, games, and sporting equipment fill every inch of floor, wall, and ceiling space. There's always a fine selection of unusual imported baby toys, too, along with scores of tiny, inexpensive items that make ideal party favors.

PLANET EARTH
Vivid kaleidoscopes, refraction glasses, robots, dinosaurs (including a huge brontosaurus blowup), scientific kits, mini solar-energy labs, and a large assortment of globes. (See **Gifts,** p. 309.)

STAR MAGIC
Science kits, scientific-inspired games and toys, telescopes in all sizes. (See **Gifts,** p. 311.)

TOY PARK
112 East 86th Street
427-6611
Mon.: 10 a.m.–6 p.m.; Tues., Wed., Fri., Sat.: 10 a.m.–7 p.m.; Thurs.: 10 a.m.–8 p.m.; Sun.: 12 noon–5 p.m.

626 Columbus Avenue, near 90th Street
769-3880
Mon.: 10 a.m.–6 p.m.; Tues., Wed., Fri., Sat.: 10 a.m.–7 p.m.; Thurs.: 10 a.m.–8 p.m.; Sun.: 12 noon–5 p.m.
MC, V

These two stores are New York's toy supermarkets, and they rival those in the suburbs for their enormous selection of brand-name and TV-advertised toys and games. Whatever is the hot new toy, you'll find it at Toy Park, along with just about every other plaything on the market. Wagons and scooters, dolls of all kinds (including Barbie and Ken), scores of action and board games, puzzles, sporting goods, stuffed animals, cars and trucks in all sizes, and arts and crafts supplies fill these cavernous spaces.

WEST SIDE KIDS
498 Amsterdam Avenue, at 84th Street
496-7282
Mon.–Wed., Fri., Sat.: 10 a.m.–6 p.m.; Thurs.: 10 a.m.–7 p.m.; Sun.: 12:30 p.m.–5:30 p.m.
AE, MC, V

Once a children's clothing resale store, West Side Kids is now a bright and colorful neighborhood toy store that carries good-quality educational toys. Although you might not find the toys advertised on TV, you will find puppet theaters, Corolle dolls, ride-on fire engines, Tonka trucks, T. C. Timber trains, Lego, Ravensburger puzzles, wooden blocks, arts and crafts supplies, and games, along with the classic Fisher Price and Playskool items. Dozens of straw baskets in the front of the store hold such tiny party favors as rubber Sesame Street characters, jacks, whistles, windup toys, dolls, plastic planes, and magnifying glasses.

YOUTH AT PLAY
1120 Madison Avenue, near 84th Street
737-5036
Mon.–Sat.: 10:30 a.m.–6 p.m.
AE, MC, V

Youth at Play has been at the same location since 1950, and every bit of space is filled with a jumble of games and puzzles, roller skates and skateboards, dolls and doll carriages, guns and soldiers, scooters and wagons, and cars and trucks of every size. Amidst the clutter are domestic and imported educational toys and games, musical instruments, arts and crafts supplies and hobby kits, and they share the space with magic sets, radio-control cars and boats, dollhouses and a complete supply of furniture and accessories. Custom-made costumes are a specialty. It's a jam-packed, chaotic store, but the staff is friendly and obliging and can magically put their hands on whatever you're looking for.

DOLLHOUSES AND FURNISHINGS

THE DOLL HOUSE
176 Ninth Avenue, near 20th Street
989-5220
Wed.: 12 noon–5 p.m.; Thurs.: 12 noon–7 p.m.;
Fri. & Sat.: 12 noon–5 p.m.
AE, MC, V

Jenny and Herman Grunewald have been repairing broken dolls and selling dollhouses and furnishings for more than forty-five years, and they've assembled one of the largest collections of dollhouses, accessories, and dolls in the city. They carry pre-assembled houses in just about every style, kits for making your own, along with individual rooms that can be arranged to create the dollhouse of your dreams. The stock of 10,000 accessories includes everything from wing chairs to champagne glasses, chandeliers to wallpapers, Oriental rugs to tea sets, and typewriters to bags of potatoes. And the Grunewalds' offer a profusion of storybook characters, foreign dolls in native dress, dozens of baby dolls, even Barbie and Ken.

DOLL HOUSE ANTICS
1308 Madison Avenue, near 92nd Street
876-2288
Mon.–Fri.: 11 a.m.–5:30 p.m.; Sat.: 11 a.m.–5 p.m.
AE, MC, V

A snug little neighborhood store, Doll House Antics caters to both children and collectors of dollhouse things. The houses and furnishings
range in style from Colonial to Victorian to contemporary, and there are
ready-made houses and kits. But the shop will also handle custom
orders to replicate an ancestral home complete with electricity and
reconstructed furniture. All the accessories, from a Victorian settee to a
Queen Anne chair, are perfectly detailed.

DOLLSANDREAMS
Sturdy contemporary-style dollhouses and furnishings. (See **Contemporary Toys,** p. 495.)

F. A. O. SCHWARZ
Dollhouses in many styles, along with an extensive selection of furnishings. (See **Contemporary Toys,** p. 496.)

GULLIVER'S MINIATURES
50 Grove Street
255-0978
Tues.–Sat.: 11:30 a.m.–6 p.m.
MC, V

Many of Carl Brumer's customers are not classic collectors (although
they come here, too) but adults who are buying a dollhouse for themselves because they're eager to decorate a house of their own. The
dollhouses are exact reproductions of a range of styles—including New
York town houses—and the selection of furnishings is exquisite. Lighting fixtures really work; accessories include rugs, wallpaper, and tapestries; and there's a collection of butlers, downstairs and upstairs
maids, along with beautifully gowned and coiffed ladies to people the
houses. But there's a lot here to delight children, too, at prices they can
afford. Brumer also carries electric trains; radio-controlled cars and
planes, and hobby kits, and you'll find him friendly, enthusiastic, and
helpful.

IRIS BROWN
A small but very select array of antique Victorian dollhouses, dolls,
and furniture. (See **Antique and Vintage Toys,** p. 492.)

PENNY WHISTLE TOYS
Sturdy contemporary-style wooden dollhouses and furnishings. (See
Contemporary Toys, p. 498.)

501

SECOND CHILDHOOD

Antique and vintage dollhouse furniture that includes unusual lead living room and porch sets. (See **Antique and Vintage Toys,** p. 494.)

TINY DOLL HOUSE

231 East 53rd Street
752-3082
Mon.–Sat.: 11 a.m.–5:30 p.m.
AE, MC, V

Almost as Lilliputian as the miniatures owner Ellen Omond sells, this tiny sliver of a store is crammed with treats for everyone, from children to advanced collectors. The range of styles in dollhouses, furnishings, and accessories—from Queen Anne to Victorian, to Art Deco, to rustic, to modern—makes this shop especially appealing. There's an exhaustive inventory, including a full supply of electrical fixtures, lots of handmade items, and every possible price. And Omond will create miniature copies of real furniture and accessories, and will even landscape dollhouse gardens.

YOUTH AT PLAY

Dollhouses and a complete inventory of furnishings and accessories. (See **Contemporary Toys,** p. 500.)

MODELS

AMERICA'S HOBBY CENTER

146 West 22nd Street
675-8922
Mon.–Fri.: 9 a.m.–5 p.m.; Sat.: 9 a.m.–3:30 p.m.
No credit cards

Model building is serious business at America's Hobby Center, and this shop's inventory is enormous. Vehicular models are the chief attraction, so expect to find scores of boats, trains, cars, and planes. Railroads come in HO and N-guage; there's a large inventory of plastic planes, boats, and cars, along with radio-control materials, books, tools, and everything else model builders need.

JAN'S HOBBY SHOP

1431A York Avenue, at 76th Street
861-5075
Mon.–Sat.: 10 a.m.–7 p.m.; Sun.: 11 a.m.–5 p.m.
AE, MC, V

Although Jan's Hobby Shop carries models for all ages and levels of proficiency, much of the stock is geared to the serious adult hobbyist. The selection of planes, ships, tanks, and cars is notable (especially the plastic-scale models, which are the shop's specialty), but you'll find remote-control materials, as well as brushes, paints, and books on model building. At Jan's they'll make custom models and restore antique ones.

POLK'S HOBBY STORE
314 Fifth Avenue, near 31st Street
279-9034
Mon.–Sat.: 9:30 a.m.–5:30 p.m.
AE, MC, V

Nat and Irwin Polk have been promoting model building for more than fifty years, and Polk's Hobby Store is where serious model makers come for the newest in boat, plane, car, and train kits. On five large floors the Polks stock plastic kits from around the world; lead soldiers; radio-control equipment for cars, boats, and planes; racing sets; and all the needed model building supplies.

TRAINS

F. A. O. SCHWARZ
An incredible array of domestic and imported electric trains in standard and miniature sizes. (See **Contemporary Toys,** p. 496.)

RED CABOOSE
16 West 45th Street
Fourth floor
575-0155
Mon.–Fri.: 10 a.m.–7 p.m.; Sat.: 10 a.m.–5 p.m.
AE, MC, V

Allan Spitz, owner of the Red Caboose, caters more to adult model-train fanciers than to children, and although it's a large shop, it's filled to overflowing with an incredible selection of imported brass locomotives, cars of every kind, tracks, HO and N-gauge equipment, and train accessories. Spitz also carries the city's largest inventory of model boats and radio-controlled cars.

THE TRAIN SHOP
23 West 45th Street
Basement
730-0409

Mon.–Fri.: 10 a.m.–6 p.m.; Sat.: 10 a.m.–5 p.m.
MC, V

Crammed-full of models of all kinds, the Train Shop takes special pride in its enormous stock of model railroad equipment. It claims to have the largest selection of handmade, limited-production brass train models in the East, as well as being the biggest dealer in Marklin trains. Its inventory of plastic model kits—military planes, ships, space vehicles, cars, and trucks—is equally impressive, as is its supply of scale-model detail parts. Given its vast inventory, it's nice to know the staff is well-informed and helpful.

PARTY FAVORS

See **Museum Gift Shops;** the **Children's Museum of Manhattan,** the **Museum of the City of New York,** and the **United Nations Gift Shop** have excellent selections.

B. SHACKMAN
85 Fifth Avenue, at 16th Street
989-5162
Mon.–Fri.: 9 a.m.–5 p.m.; Sat.: 10 a.m.–4 p.m.
No credit cards

B. Shackman has been around since 1898, and although it is primarily a wholesale toy and novelty operation, the store sells to retail customers as well. Its neatly organized shelves hold all manner of tiny and inexpensive treasures: tin and plastic windup toys, imported matchbox puzzles, reissues of vintage picture books, little dolls, cutout and coloring books, miniature paint sets, dollhouse accessories, and enchantingly decorated small cardboard boxes to fill with candy. At Christmas the shop is crowded with reproductions of old-fashioned holiday treats.

THE CHOCOLATE SOUP
The wide range of small and inexpensive items that make ideal party favors include tiny dolls, matchbox puzzles, miniature painting sets, and wooden and plastic animals of all kinds. (See **Clothing,** p. 93.)

CITYKIDS
Lots of small and inexpensive toys ideal as party favors. (See **Clothing,** p. 94.)

DINOSAUR HILL
Tiny kaleidoscopes, rubbery dinosaurs, wooden tops, and a range of

inexpensive straw toys perfect for stuffing Christmas stockings. (See **Clothing,** p. 94.)

E.A.T. GIFTS
Almost everything is miniature here and can be used as party favors for children or adults; tiny bear-embellished cardboard boxes filled with gummy bears, Santa Claus and animal candles, tiny English cars and trucks, small pillows filled with potpourri, exquisite little address and blank books. (See **Gifts,** p. 302.)

JEREMY'S PLACE
322 East 81st Street
628-1414
Daily: 12 noon–7 p.m.
No credit cards

Jeremy Sage is the city's most popular children's party entertainer, and his toy store is chockablock with plastic bins filled with party favors. Although most are the kind of slimy creatures and monsters you try to encourage your children *not* to buy, there are rubber balls, jacks, animal erasers, plastic windup toys, assorted rubber stamps, tiny books and puzzles.

JOHNNY JUPITER
Matchbox puzzles and games, plastic windup toys, light-bulb erasers, jacks, tiny Gumbys and Pokeys, magic tricks, rubber balls. (See **Contemporary Toys,** p. 497.)

THE LAST WOUND UP
Most of the stock of plastic windup toys is inexpensive enough to double as party favors for children or adults. (See **Contemporary Toys,** p. 497.)

MYTHOLOGY
Hundreds of rubber stamps, all manner of amusing mini-erasers, tiny robotic toys, sponges that look like bologna sandwiches, tiny ray guns, and water pistols. (See **Gifts,** p. 308.)

PENNY WHISTLE TOYS
Bins hold a large selection of inexpensive small toys that include tiny puzzles and games, water guns, plastic animals, rubber balls, pencils topped with animals, and such. (See **Contemporary Toys,** p. 498.)

WEST SIDE KIDS
Tiny straw baskets offer such treats as rubber Sesame Street favorites, jacks, whistles, windup toys, dolls, plastic planes, and magnifying glasses. (See **Contemporary Toys,** p. 499.)

Vintage
Magazines

See also **Books, Comic.**

A & S BOOK COMPANY
304 West 40th Street
714-2712
Mon.–Fri.: 10 a.m.–6:30 p.m.; Sat.: 10 a.m.–5 p.m.

274 West 43rd Street
695-4897
Mon.–Fri.: 10:15 a.m.–6:30 p.m.; Sat.: 10 a.m.–5 p.m.
No credit cards

A & S Book Company stocks back issues of nearly every periodical published from the thirties through the fifties. It offers early issues of all the most popular titles—*Life, The Saturday Evening Post,* and *Vanity Fair*—but it specializes in old movie, fashion, sports, and "girlie" magazines. Prices are reasonable.

JAY-BEE MAGAZINES
134 West 26th Street
675-1600
Mon.–Fri.: 9:30 a.m.–5 p.m.; Sat.: 10 a.m.–4 p.m.
No credit cards

Jay-Bee Magazines is the largest back-date magazine store in the country, and it carries more than two million issues, all carefully catalogued. There are magazines from 1885, every issue of *Life,* early editions of *The Saturday Evening Post,* and *TV Guides* from 1953, the first year of publication. If Jay-Bee doesn't happen to have what you're looking for, it offers a search service.

JERRY OHLINGER'S MOVIE MATERIAL STORE
A large selection of old movie magazines. (See **Engravings, Prints, and Posters,** p. 204.)

Walking Sticks, Canes, and Umbrellas

ANTIQUE

Bergdorf Goodman offers a fine selection of nineteenth-century silver and ivory canes and walking sticks, along with others made of resin that only look old.

BOB PRYOR ANTIQUES
A handsome array of nineteenth-century hand-carved wooden walking sticks, many with animal heads. (See **Gifts**, p. 293.)

JAMES II GALLERIES
A splendid collection of Victorian and Edwardian canes, walking sticks, and umbrellas, some with ornate silver, horn, and ivory handles, others of intricately carved wood. (See **China and Glassware**, p. 67.)

LINDA HORN ANTIQUES
Rare and ornate antique walking sticks, many embellished with intricately carved animal heads. (See **Furniture**, p. 251.)

MAN-TIQUES LTD.
A large assortment of walking sticks and canes of all ages. Many are from the nineteenth- and early-twentieth centuries and have silver or elaborately carved wooden handles; others are from the twenties and thirties and were originally sold as Atlantic City and Coney Island souvenirs. (See **Gifts**, p. 296.)

R. BROOKE LTD.
Nineteenth-century silver, ivory, and horn-handled walking sticks. (See **Gifts**, p. 297.)

CONTEMPORARY

All the major department stores, and many handbag and leather-goods shops, carry umbrellas.

GLORIA UMBRELLA MANUFACTURING COMPANY
39 Essex Street
475-7388
Sun.–Thurs.: 10 a.m.–5 p.m.; Fri.: 10 a.m.–2 p.m.
No credit cards

The Gloria Umbrella Company has been in the business of making umbrellas for more than fifty years, and the present owner, Tony Margulis, is the third generation of his family to work in the company. There's a full range of styles, sizes, and colors, and in addition to new umbrellas the company carries a group of antique ones. Gloria also repairs umbrellas.

MARK CROSS
Well-made and well-priced standard and folding umbrellas in a range of prints and colors, some with birds or horses' heads, some in plaids or checks. (See **Gifts,** p. 307.)

SULKA & CO.
The store carries its own brand of umbrellas and there's an elegant cherrywood one with a brass-covered pencil hidden in the handle, and a sturdy doorman's umbrella with a thick aluminum shaft and re-inforced frame. (See **Clothing,** p. 118.)

T. ANTHONY
Classic English slim-blade silk umbrellas from Swaine, Adeney, Brigg (the firm that supplies the Royal Family) with handsome wood or staghorn handles. (See **Luggage and Briefcases,** p. 399.)

UMBRELLO
Colorful Indonesian batik umbrellas. (See **Furniture,** p. 278.)

UNCLE SAM
161 West 57th Street
247-7163
Mon.–Fri.: 9:30 a.m.–6 p.m.; Sat.: 10 a.m.–5 p.m.
All major

Uncle Sam is the city's oldest umbrella maker. The company has been making umbrellas since 1866, and it makes them in every size (from small ones for children to the oversized beach kind), and in every style (from parasols, to sturdy doorman types, to classic English silks, to golf umbrellas), and in every color. Many of them are hand-sewn, hand-carved, and hand-assembled. Uncle Sam also stocks Briggs of London umbrellas—considered by many the world's finest—and it carries canes and walking sticks. You'll find such versatile varieties of walking sticks as the folding kind, others that hold a pool cue or a brandy flask. At Uncle Sam they'll repair worn-out or damaged umbrellas, too. Prices range from moderate to expensive.

WORTH & WORTH
A fine stock of English umbrellas. (See **Hats,** p. 332.)

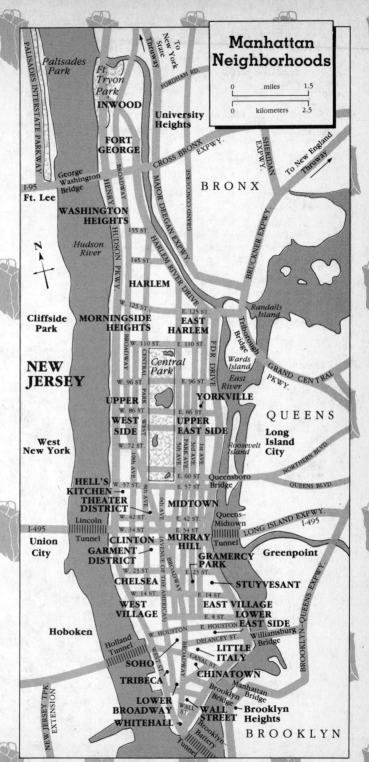

Manhattan Neighborhoods

0   miles   1.5

0   kilometers   2.5

To New York State Thruway

FORDHAM RD.

PALISADES INTERSTATE PARKWAY

Palisades Park

Ft. Tryon Park

INWOOD

University Heights

FORT GEORGE

CROSS BRONX EXPWY.

SHERIDAN EXPWY.

To New England Thruway

George Washington Bridge

I-95

Ft. Lee

WASHINGTON HEIGHTS

HENRY HUDSON PKWY.

BROADWAY

155 ST.

145 ST.

MAJOR DEEGAN EXPWY.

GRAND CONCOURSE

B R O N X

BRUCKNER EXPWY.

Hudson River

HARLEM

HARLEM RIVER DRIVE

Randalls Island

Triborough Bridge

GRAND CENTRAL PKWY.

Cliffside Park

MORNINGSIDE HEIGHTS

W. 125 ST.

E. 125 ST.

EAST HARLEM

Wards Island

W. 110 ST.

E. 110 ST.

BROADWAY

CENTRAL PARK WEST

Central Park

FDR DRIVE

East River

NEW JERSEY

W. 96 ST.

E. 96 ST.

West New York

UPPER WEST SIDE

W. 86 ST.

E. 86 ST.

YORKVILLE

Q U E E N S

WEST END AVE.

UPPER EAST SIDE

W. 72 ST.

Roosevelt Island

Long Island City

1st AVE.
3rd AVE.
PARK AVE.
5th AVE.

10th AVE.

E. 60 ST.

Queensboro Bridge

NORTHERN BLVD.

HELL'S KITCHEN

W. 57 ST.

8th AVE.

E. 57 ST.

QUEENS BLVD.

THEATER DISTRICT

6th AVE.

MIDTOWN

Lincoln Tunnel

W. 42 ST.

E. 42 ST.

Queens-Midtown Tunnel

LONG ISLAND EXPWY.

I-495

I-495

W. 34 ST.

E. 34 ST.

Union City

CLINTON

MURRAY HILL

Greenpoint

GARMENT DISTRICT

GRAMERCY PARK

W. 23 ST.

E. 23 ST.

CHELSEA

BROADWAY

STUYVESANT

W. 14 ST.

E. 14 ST.

WEST VILLAGE

AVENUE OF THE AMERICAS

EAST VILLAGE

LOWER EAST SIDE

E. 4 ST.

Hoboken

W. HOUSTON

E. HOUSTON

Williamsburg Bridge

Holland Tunnel

DELANCEY ST.

WEST ST.

BROADWAY

LITTLE ITALY

SOHO

CANAL ST.

CHINATOWN

TRIBECA

Brooklyn Bridge

Manhattan Bridge

NEW JERSEY TPK. EXTENSION

LOWER BROADWAY

WALL ST.

WALL STREET

Brooklyn Heights

WHITEHALL

Battery

Brooklyn Tunnel

B R O O K L Y N

BROOKLYN-QUEENS EXPWY.

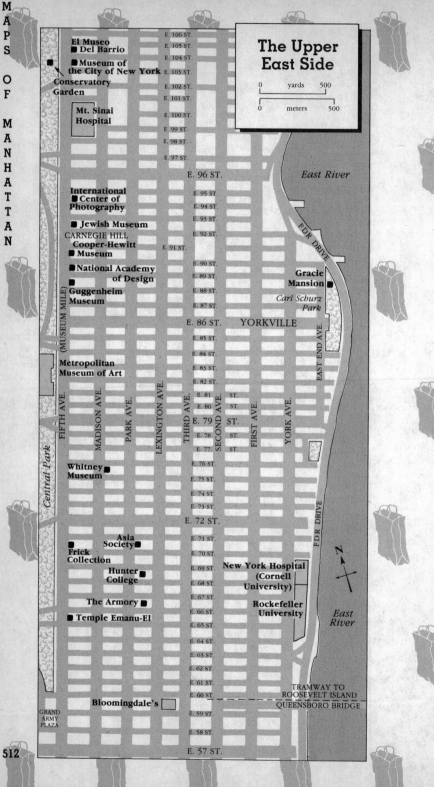

The Upper East Side

0   yards   500

0   meters   500

E. 106 ST.
E. 105 ST.
E. 104 ST.
E. 103 ST.
E. 102 ST.
E. 101 ST.
E. 100 ST.
E. 99 ST.
E. 98 ST.
E. 97 ST.

El Museo Del Barrio
Museum of the City of New York
Conservatory Garden

Mt. Sinai Hospital

East River

E. 96 ST.

International Center of Photography

E. 95 ST.
E. 94 ST.
E. 93 ST.

Jewish Museum

E. 92 ST.

CARNEGIE HILL
Cooper-Hewitt Museum

E. 91 ST.

National Academy of Design

E. 90 ST.
E. 89 ST.
E. 88 ST.
E. 87 ST.

Guggenheim Museum

Gracie Mansion

Carl Schurz Park

(MUSEUM MILE)

FDR DRIVE

E. 86 ST.   YORKVILLE

E. 85 ST.
E. 84 ST.
E. 83 ST.
E. 82 ST.

Metropolitan Museum of Art

EAST END AVE.

E. 81 ST.
E. 80 ST.
E. 79 ST.
E. 78 ST.
E. 77 ST.

FIFTH AVE.
MADISON AVE.
PARK AVE.
LEXINGTON AVE.
THIRD AVE.
SECOND AVE.
FIRST AVE.
YORK AVE.

E. 76 ST.

Whitney Museum

E. 75 ST.
E. 74 ST.
E. 73 ST.

Central Park

E. 72 ST.

E. 71 ST.

Asia Society

E. 70 ST.

Frick Collection

E. 69 ST.

New York Hospital (Cornell University)

Hunter College

E. 68 ST.
E. 67 ST.

The Armory

Rockefeller University

E. 66 ST.

Temple Emanu-El

E. 65 ST.
E. 64 ST.
E. 63 ST.

East River

E. 62 ST.
E. 61 ST.

FDR DRIVE

E. 60 ST.

TRAMWAY TO ROOSEVELT ISLAND
QUEENSBORO BRIDGE

Bloomingdale's

E. 59 ST.

GRAND ARMY PLAZA

E. 58 ST.

N

E. 57 ST.

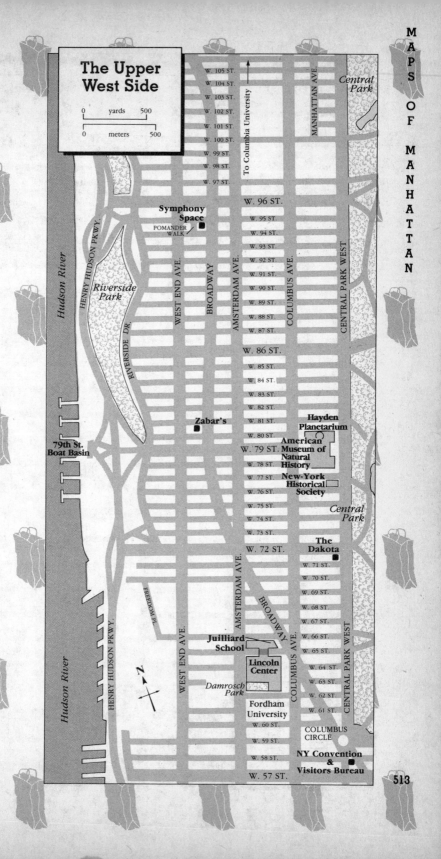

The Upper West Side

0 yards 500

0 meters 500

W. 105 ST.
W. 104 ST.
W. 103 ST.
W. 102 ST.
W. 101 ST.
W. 100 ST.
W. 99 ST.
W. 98 ST.
W. 97 ST.

To Columbia University

Central Park

MANHATTAN AVE.

W. 96 ST.
W. 95 ST.
W. 94 ST.
W. 93 ST.
W. 92 ST.
W. 91 ST.
W. 90 ST.
W. 89 ST.
W. 88 ST.
W. 87 ST.

Symphony Space
POMANDER WALK

WEST END AVE.

BROADWAY

AMSTERDAM AVE.

COLUMBUS AVE.

CENTRAL PARK WEST

Riverside Park

RIVERSIDE DR.

HENRY HUDSON PKWY.

Hudson River

W. 86 ST.
W. 85 ST.
W. 84 ST.
W. 83 ST.
W. 82 ST.
W. 81 ST.
W. 80 ST.

Zabar's

Hayden Planetarium

American Museum of Natural History

W. 79 ST.
W. 78 ST.
W. 77 ST.
W. 76 ST.
W. 75 ST.
W. 74 ST.
W. 73 ST.

79th St. Boat Basin

New-York Historical Society

Central Park

W. 72 ST.

The Dakota

W. 71 ST.
W. 70 ST.
W. 69 ST.
W. 68 ST.
W. 67 ST.
W. 66 ST.
W. 65 ST.
W. 64 ST.
W. 63 ST.
W. 62 ST.
W. 61 ST.

AMSTERDAM AVE.

BROADWAY

COLUMBUS AVE.

FREEDOM PL.

WEST END AVE.

Juilliard School

Lincoln Center

Damrosch Park

Fordham University

W. 60 ST.
W. 59 ST.

COLUMBUS CIRCLE

W. 58 ST.

NY Convention & Visitors Bureau

W. 57 ST.

N

HENRY HUDSON PKWY.

Hudson River

513

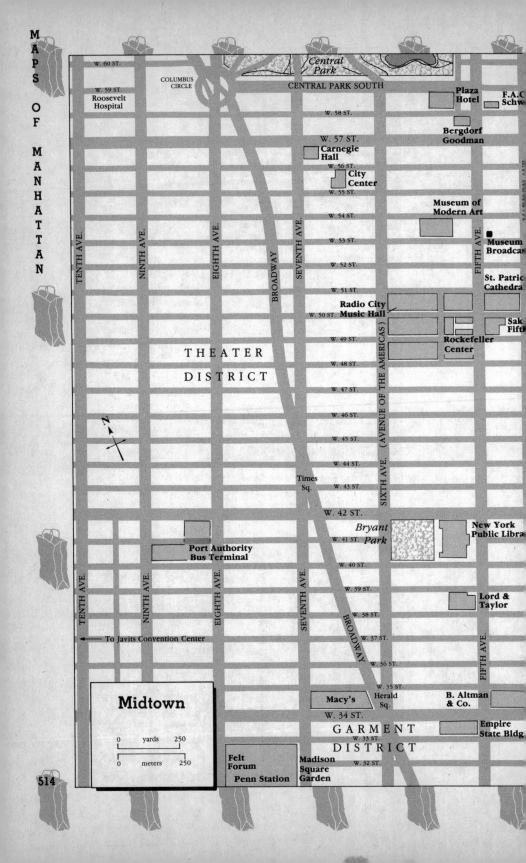

W. 60 ST.

W. 59 ST.
Roosevelt Hospital

COLUMBUS CIRCLE

Central Park

CENTRAL PARK SOUTH

Plaza Hotel

F.A.C Schw

W. 58 ST.

Bergdorf Goodman

W. 57 ST.

Carnegie Hall

W. 56 ST.

City Center

W. 55 ST.

W. 54 ST.

Museum of Modern Art

W. 53 ST.

Museum Broadcas

W. 52 ST.

W. 51 ST.

St. Patric Cathedra

Radio City
W. 50 ST. **Music Hall**

W. 49 ST.

Rockefeller Center

Sak Fift

W. 48 ST.

THEATER

W. 47 ST.

DISTRICT

W. 46 ST.

N

W. 45 ST.

W. 44 ST.

Times Sq.
W. 43 ST.

W. 42 ST.

Bryant Park
W. 41 ST.

New York Public Libra

Port Authority Bus Terminal

W. 40 ST.

W. 39 ST.

Lord & Taylor

W. 38 ST.

← To Javits Convention Center

W. 37 ST.

W. 36 ST.

W. 35 ST.
Herald Sq.

Macy's

B. Altman & Co.

W. 34 ST.

Midtown

0   yards   250

0   meters   250

G A R M E N T
W. 33 ST.

D I S T R I C T

W. 32 ST.

Empire State Bldg

Felt Forum

Penn Station

Madison Square Garden

TENTH AVE.

NINTH AVE.

EIGHTH AVE.

BROADWAY

SEVENTH AVE.

SIXTH AVE. (AVENUE OF THE AMERICAS)

FIFTH AVE.

514

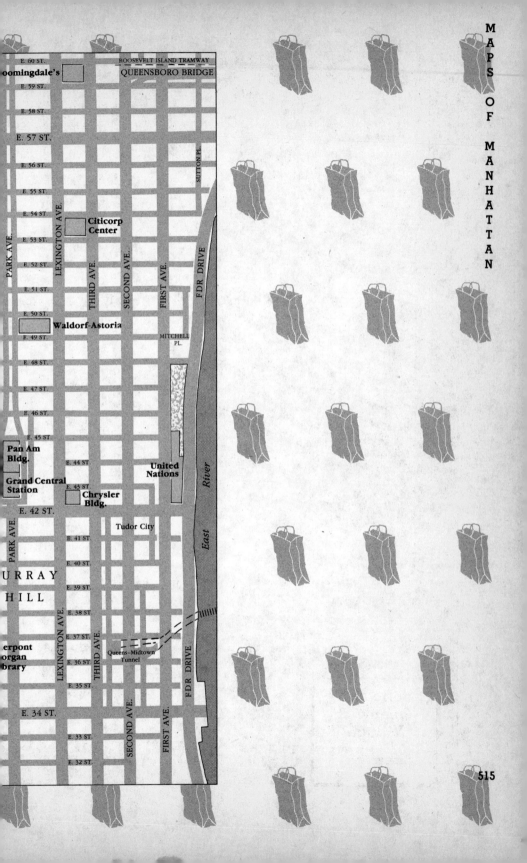

E. 60 ST.

oomingdale's

ROOSEVELT ISLAND TRAMWAY

QUEENSBORO BRIDGE

E. 59 ST.

E. 58 ST.

E. 57 ST.

E. 56 ST.

E. 55 ST.

E. 54 ST.

E. 53 ST.

Citicorp Center

E. 52 ST.

E. 51 ST.

E. 50 ST.

Waldorf-Astoria

E. 49 ST.

MITCHELL PL.

E. 48 ST.

E. 47 ST.

E. 46 ST.

E. 45 ST.

Pan Am Bldg.

E. 44 ST.

Grand Central Station

United Nations

E. 43 ST.

Chrysler Bldg.

E. 42 ST.

Tudor City

E. 41 ST.

E. 40 ST.

URRAY

E. 39 ST.

HILL

E. 38 ST.

erpont
organ
brary

E. 37 ST.

Queens–Midtown
Tunnel

E. 36 ST.

E. 35 ST.

E. 34 ST.

E. 33 ST.

E. 32 ST.

PARK AVE.
LEXINGTON AVE.
THIRD AVE.
SECOND AVE.
FIRST AVE.
FDR DRIVE
SUTTON PL.

East River

515

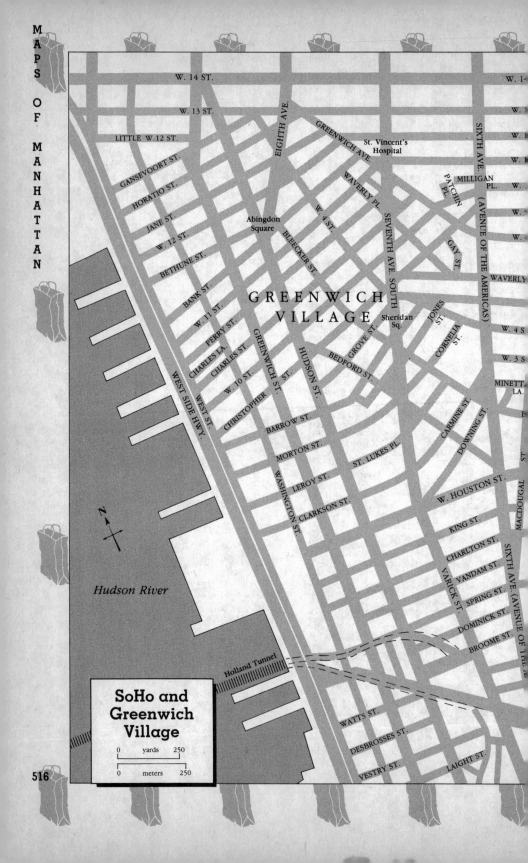

W. 14 ST.

W. 1

W. 13 ST.

W.

LITTLE W.12 ST.

W.

GANSEVOORT ST.

GREENWICH AVE.

St. Vincent's
Hospital

W.

EIGHTH AVE.

SIXTH AVE.

HORATIO ST.

W.

WAVERLY PL.

PATCHIN
PL.

MILLIGAN
PL.

W.

JANE ST.

Abingdon
Square

W.

W. 12 ST.

W. 4 ST.

W.

BETHUNE ST.

BLEECKER ST.

SEVENTH AVE. SOUTH

GAY ST.

WAVERLY

BANK ST.

GREENWICH
VILLAGE

Sheridan
Sq.

JONES
ST.

CORNELIA
ST.

W. 4 S

W. 11 ST.

PERRY ST.

GROVE ST.

W. 3 S

CHARLES LA.

CHARLES ST.

BEDFORD ST.

MINETT.
LA.

GREENWICH ST.

W. 10 ST.

HUDSON ST.

CHRISTOPHER ST.

CARMINE ST.

DOWNING ST.

WEST SIDE HWY.

WEST ST.

BARROW ST.

MORTON ST.

ST. LUKES PL.

W. HOUSTON ST.

MACDOUGAL

LEROY ST.

WASHINGTON ST.

CLARKSON ST.

KING ST.

N

CHARLTON ST.

VARICK ST.

VANDAM ST.

SIXTH AVE. (AVENUE OF THE AMERICAS)

SPRING ST.

Hudson River

DOMINICK ST.

BROOME ST.

Holland Tunnel

WATTS ST.

**SoHo and
Greenwich
Village**

DESBROSSES ST.

VESTRY ST.

LAIGHT ST.

0   yards   250

0   meters   250

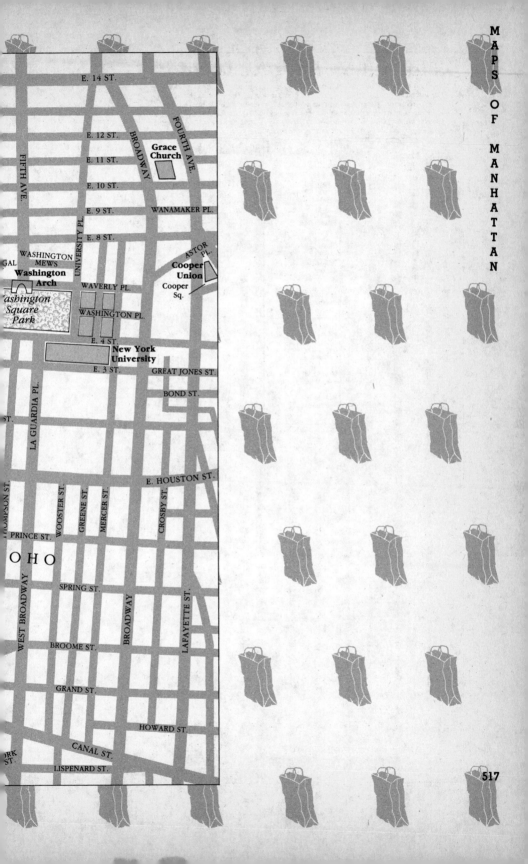

E. 14 ST.

E. 12 ST.

BROADWAY

FOURTH AVE.

E. 11 ST.

Grace
Church

E. 10 ST.

FIFTH AVE.

E. 9 ST.

WANAMAKER PL.

UNIVERSITY PL.

E. 8 ST.

WASHINGTON
MEWS

ASTOR
PL.

Cooper
Union

GAL

Washington
Arch

Cooper
Sq.

WAVERLY PL.

ashington
Square
Park

WASHINGTON PL.

E. 4 ST.

New York
University

E. 3 ST.

GREAT JONES ST.

LA GUARDIA PL.

BOND ST.

ST.

E. HOUSTON ST.

WOOSTER ST.

GREENE ST.

MERCER ST.

CROSBY ST.

PRINCE ST.

O H O

SPRING ST.

WEST BROADWAY

BROADWAY

LAFAYETTE ST.

BROOME ST.

GRAND ST.

HOWARD ST.

RK
ST.

CANAL ST.

LISPENARD ST.

Manhattan Address Locator

To find an avenue address, cancel the last figure in the address number, divide by 2, and add (+) or subtract (−) the key number below. The result is the nearest numbered cross street. Cross-street addresses increase east or west from Fifth Avenue, which runs north to south (see examples on 57th Street below). The cross streets west of Central Park (see West 72nd Street), which increase from Central Park West, are the exception.

Ave. A, B, C, D	+ 3
1st, 2nd Ave.	+ 3
3rd Ave.	+ 10
4th Ave.	+ 8
5th Ave.	
Up to 200	+ 13
Up to 400	+ 16
Up to 600	+ 18
Up to 775	+ 20
775 to 1286	Cancel last figure and .... − 18
To 1500	+ 45
Above 2000	+ 24
6th Ave. (Ave. of the Americas)	− 12
7th Ave.	+ 12
8th Ave.	+ 10
9th Ave.	+ 13
10th Ave.	+ 14
Amsterdam Ave.	+ 60
Broadway (23-192 Sts.)	− 30
Columbus Ave.	+ 60
Central Park West	Divide house no. by 10 and .... + 60
Lexington Ave.	+ 22
Madison Ave.	+ 26
Park Ave.	+ 35
Riverside Dr.	Divide house no. by 10 and add 72 (up to 165th St.)
St. Nicholas Ave.	+ 110
West End Ave.	+ 60
York Ave.	+ 4

W. 96 ST.   E. 96 ST.

W. 86 ST.   E. 86 ST.

W. 79 ST.   E. 79 ST.

W. 72 ST.   E. 72 ST.

CENTRAL PARK SOUTH

W. 57 ST.   E. 57 ST.

W. 42 ST.   E. 42 ST.

W. 34 ST.   E. 34 ST.

W. 23 ST.   E. 23 ST.

W. 14 ST.   E. 14 ST.

RIVERSIDE DR. — WEST END AVE. — BROADWAY — AMSTERDAM AVE. — COLUMBUS AVE. — CENTRAL PARK WEST

FIFTH AVE. — MADISON AVE. — PARK AVE. — LEXINGTON AVE. — THIRD AVE. — SECOND AVE. — FIRST AVE. — YORK AVE.

ELEVENTH AVE. — TENTH AVE. — NINTH AVE. — EIGHTH AVE. — SEVENTH AVE. — SIXTH AVE. (AVENUE OF THE AMERICAS) — BROADWAY — FIFTH AVE. — MADISON AVE. SOUTH — PARK AVE. — LEXINGTON AVE. — THIRD AVE. — SECOND AVE. — FIRST AVE.

PARK AVENUE SOUTH — IRVING PL.

N

Index